# KERLY'S LAW OF TRADE MARKS AND TRADE NAMES

# KERLY'S LAW OF TRADE MARKS AND TRADE NAMES

FIRST SUPPLEMENT TO THE SIXTEENTH EDITION

By

JAMES MELLOR
*One of Her Majesty's Counsel, 8 New Square*

DAVID LLEWELYN
*Professor of Intellectual Property Law, King's College London;*
*Professor (Practice), School of Law, Singapore Management University;*
*Advocate & Solicitor (Singapore), David Llewelyn & Co LLC*

THOMAS MOODY-STUART
*One of Her Majesty's Counsel, 8 New Square*

DAVID KEELING
*Former Member, Boards of Appeal, EUIPO*

IONA BERKELEY
*Barrister, 8 New Square*

ASHTON CHANTRIELLE
*Barrister, 8 New Square*

SWEET & MAXWELL

Published in 2021 by Thomson Reuters, trading as Sweet & Maxwell.
(Registered in England & Wales, Company No 1679046.
Registered Office and address for service:
5 Canada Square, Canary Wharf, London E14 5AQ )

For further information on our products and services, visit
*www.sweetandmaxwell.co.uk*

Printed and bound in Great Britain by CPI Group (UK) Ltd,
Croydon, CR0 4YY

A CIP catalogue record for this book is available from the British Library.

ISBN 9780414079342 (print)

ISBN 9780414079397 (e-book)

# Previous Editions

| | |
|---|---|
| First edition by D.M. Kerly | 1894 |
| Second edition by D.M. Kerly | 1901 |
| Third edition by D.M. Kerly | 1908 |
| Fourth edition by F.G. Underhay | 1913 |
| Fifth edition by F.G. Underhay | 1923 |
| Sixth edition by F.G. Underhay | 1927 |
| Seventh edition by R.G. Loyd and F.E. Bray | 1951 |
| Eighth edition by R.G. Loyd | 1960 |
| Ninth edition by T.A. Blanco White | 1966 |
| Tenth edition by T.A. Blanco White and Robin Jacob | 1972 |
| Eleventh edition by T.A. Blanco White and Robin Jacob | 1983 |
| Twelfth edition by T.A. Blanco White and Robin Jacob | 1986 |
| Thirteenth edition by D. Kitchin, D. Llewelyn, J. Mellor, R. Meade and T. Moody-Stuart | 2001 |
| Fourteenth edition by D. Kitchin, D. Llewelyn, J. Mellor, R. Meade, T. Moody-Stuart and D. Keeling | 2005 |
| Fifteenth edition by J. Mellor, D. Llewelyn, T. Moody-Stuart, D. Keeling and I. Berkeley | 2011 |
| First Supplement to the Fifteenth edition by J. Mellor, D. Llewelyn, T. Moody-Stuart, D. Keeling and I. Berkeley | 2014 |
| Sixteenth edition by J. Mellor, D. Llewelyn, T. Moody-Stuart, D. Keeling, I. Berkeley, A. Chantrielle and W. Duncan | 2018 |

# PREFACE TO FIRST SUPPLEMENT

When we came to work on this Supplement (much of the work occurring during the UK lockdown), there was a surprising amount of updating to cover. Some of the trickiest updating concerned the effects of the large number of EU Exit statutory instruments which have an impact on the topics covered in *Kerly*. Bearing in mind that publication of this Supplement appeared likely roughly to coincide with IP completion day, we concluded that the (hopefully) most useful set of appendices we could put into this Supplement are those presented, but readers should note in particular the following inclusions:

1. Versions of the Trade Marks Act 1994 and the Trade Mark Rules 2008 in force from 14 January 2019 (the date of implementation of the 2015 TM Directive) down to 31 December 2020—see Appendices 1 and 2.
2. Versions of the Trade Marks Act 1994 and the Trade Mark Rules 2008 in force after IP completion day (i.e. from 1 January 2021 onwards)—see Appendices 1A and 2A.
3. The 2015 Trade Mark Directive (Appendix 5).
4. The updated EUTM Implementing and Delegated Regulations (Appendices 7 and 8), along with the amended Community Trade Mark Regulations 2006 (Appendix 9).
5. The text of two important EU Regulations which have been revised and retained as part of UK law as from 1 January 2021, namely:
   a. Regulation 1151/2012 on quality schemes for agricultural products and foodstuffs, i.e. dealing with PDOs and PGIs (Appendix 10); and
   b. Regulation 608/2013 concerning customs enforcement of intellectual property rights (Appendix 19).
6. The Quality Schemes (Agricultural Products and Foodstuffs) Regulations 2018 (Appendix 10A), which fill a lacuna we noted in previous editions regarding specific procedures for the enforcement of PDOs, PGIs and TSGs in the UK (see the updates to Ch.13).
7. The revised Intellectual Property (Enforcement etc) Regulations 2006 (Appendix 13A) and the amended Trade Marks (International Registration) Order 2008 (Appendix 15).

This First Supplement to the 16th edn of *Kerly* has been prepared over a period of time, which in this instance largely coincided with the period of the "lockdown" in the UK, although we have tried to include major developments down to the end of August 2020.

James Mellor QC

8, New Square

October 2020

# HOW TO USE THIS SUPPLEMENT

This is the First Supplement to the Sixteenth edn of *Kerly's Law of Trade Marks and Trade Names* and has been compiled according to the structure of the main volume.

At the beginning of each chapter of this supplement the mini table of contents from each chapter of the main work has been included. Where a heading in this table of contents has been marked with the symbol ■, this indicates that there is relevant information in the Supplement to which the reader should refer.

Within each chapter, updating information is referenced to the relevant paragraph in the main volume.

# TABLE OF CONTENTS

# TABLE OF CASES

# TABLE OF STATUTES

# TABLE OF STATUTORY INSTRUMENTS

# TABLE OF EUROPEAN LEGISLATION

## REGULATIONS

## DIRECTIVES

# TABLE OF TREATIES AND CONVENTIONS

# TABLE OF CIVIL PROCEDURE RULES

Chapter 1

# INTRODUCTION AND FUTURE DEVELOPMENTS

Table of Contents



## 1. Future Developments

*Replace paragraph:*

Although uncertainty will continue as a lasting legacy of the 2016 UK Referendum, during the preparation of this First Supplement to the 16th edn of *Kerly*, we seem to have achieved a measure of certainty as to the immediate effects on the law of registered trade marks of the UK finally ceasing to be subject to EU law on 31 December 2020. Although Brexit was originally scheduled to take place in April 2019, as readers will know, it was on 31 January 2020 ("exit day") that the UK ceased to be a Member State of the EU subject to an implementation period currently expiring on 31 December 2020 ("IP completion day"), at which time all EU law will be converted into domestic law or repealed. So far as registered trade marks and the related rights dealt with in *Kerly* are concerned, there are a number of EU Exit statutory instruments in existence which will take effect on IP completion day. Their effects on registered trade marks and related rights appear to be set whatever the nature of the deal (if any) which the UK might reach with the EU prior to IP completion day. It is for that reason that we considered it versions of the Trade Mark Act and Rules in the form they are expected to take following IP completion day—see Appendices 1A and 2A—all the relevant statutory instruments in this Supplement as it appears they are very unlikely to change over the coming months. We provide an overview of the effects of Brexit in Ch.4 and also in each of the chapters where Brexit has an impact. **1-001**

*Replace paragraph:*

In the meantime, the majority of the equivalent reforms in the 2015 TM Directive are required to be implemented by Member States no later than 14 January 2019. Member States have an extra four years to implement art.45 which requires them to provide for efficient and expeditious administrative procedures for the revocation or invalidity of national trade marks. Since the UK already has such **1-003** procedures in place, we can leave art.45 on one side. The UK implemented the new provisions in the 2015 TM Directive via the Trade Marks Regulations 2018 (SI 2018/825) which came into force on 14 January 2019. These regulations effected a series of important amendments to the Trade Marks Act 1994—see Appendix 1 for the version of the Act in force from 14 January 2019 to 31 December 2020, and Appendix 2 for the Trade Mark Rules in force over the same period. The effects of these reforms are discussed in the relevant chapter. They bring national trade mark systems into line with the new regime for EU trade marks introduced in the EU TM Regulation 2017/1001.

## 11. THIS EDITION OF KERLY

*Add at end of paragraph:*

**1-022** As usual, this First Supplement to the 16th edn of *Kerly* has been prepared over a period of time, which in this instance largely coincided with the period of the "lockdown" in the UK, although we have tried to include major developments down to the end of August 2020.

Chapter 2

# THE FUNCTION(S) AND CHARACTERISTICS OF A "TRADE MARK" IN EU TRADE MARK LAW

Table of Contents



Introduction

1. The Essential and Other Functions of a Trade Mark

## The Origin Function

*Add to end of paragraph:*

In *Municipality of Oslo* (E-5/16), the EFTA Court had to consider attempts by the City of Oslo to obtain trade mark protection for various well-known works of art on display in the City for which copyright protection had expired. In the course of their considerations, the court referred to the essential origin function at [67]–[69] to explain why it was essential for trade mark protection to be, in principle, indefinite provided that the conditions for registration set out in art.3 of the Trade Mark Directive continue to be fulfilled **2-016**

## The Communication, Investment and Advertising Functions

*Replace paragraph:*

In his judgment following the trial of *Interflora v Marks & Spencer*[12] Arnold J attempted to explain the difference between the investment function and the advertising function, in the light of the CJEU ruling[13] in *Interflora* itself. The reasoning may be summarised in the following propositions: **2-019**

(1) The CJEU has ruled unequivocally that keyword advertising does not adversely affect the advertising function but nevertheless ruled that it may affect the investment function.
(2) The fact that a competitor's keyword advertising increases the cost and decreases the prominence of the proprietor's own keyword advertising does not amount to an adverse affect on the advertising function—see *Google France*.
(3) The investment function is adversely affected when the third party's use af-

fects the mark's reputation (i.e. its ability to attract consumers and retain their loyalty). Conversely, the investment function is not adversely affected just because the proprietor has to pay more to preserve the reputation of the mark.

(4) The distinction which the CJEU appears to be making (in [63] and [64] of *Interflora* (CJEU)) is between what may be termed normal competition as regards the price paid for keyword advertising, as opposed to keyword advertising which adversely affects the reputation of the mark, e.g. where the image the trade mark conveys is damaged. Only the latter adversely affects the investment function.

It seems likely that it is only with the passage of time that the CJEU will explain precisely what they mean with the various functions they have discussed. The latest explanation from the CJEU on the various functions was in *Mitsubishi Shoji Kaisha Ltd v Duma Forklifts NV*[13a]:

"34. The Court has held on many occasions that that exclusive right of the proprietor of the mark was conferred in order to enable him to protect his specific interests as proprietor, namely to ensure that the trade mark can fulfil its function, and that the exercise of that right must therefore be reserved to cases in which a third party's use of the sign affects, or is liable to affect, the functions of the trade mark. Amongst those functions is not only the essential function of the mark which is to guarantee to consumers the origin of the product or service, but also the other functions of the mark, such as, in particular, that of guaranteeing the quality of the product or service, or those of communication, investment or advertising (see the judgments of 12 November 2002, *Arsenal Football Club*, C-206/01, EU:C:2002:651, paragraph 51; of 18 June 2009, *L'Oréal and Others*, C-487/07, EU:C:2009:378, paragraph 58; of 23 March 2010, *Google France and Google*, C-236/08 to C-238/08, EU:C:2010:159, paragraphs 77 and 79, and of 22 September 2011, *Interflora and Interflora British Unit*, C-323/09, EU:C:2011:604, paragraphs 37 and 38).

35. As regards those functions, it must be borne in mind that the essential function of a trade mark is to guarantee the identity of the origin of the marked goods or service to the consumer or end user by enabling him to distinguish the goods or service from others which have another origin (judgment of 23 March 2010, *Google France and Google*, C-236/08 to C-238/08, EU:C:2010:159, paragraph 82 and the case-law cited). It serves in particular to guarantee that all the goods or services bearing it have been manufactured or supplied under the control of a single undertaking which is responsible for their quality, which it does in order to fulfil its essential role in the system of undistorted competition (see, to that effect, the judgments of 12 November 2002, *Arsenal Football Club*, C-206/01, EU:C:2002:651, paragraph 48, and of 12 July 2011, *L'Oréal and Others*, C-324/09, EU:C:2011:474, paragraph 80).

36. The function of investment of the mark includes the possibility for the proprietor of a mark to employ it in order to acquire or preserve a reputation capable of attracting customers and retaining their loyalty, by means of various commercial techniques. Thus, when the use by a third party, such as a competitor of the trade mark proprietor, of a sign identical to the trade mark in relation to goods or services identical with those for which the mark is registered substantially interferes with the proprietor's use of its trade mark to acquire or preserve a reputation capable of attracting consumers and retaining their loyalty, the third party's use adversely affects that function of the trade mark. The proprietor is, as a consequence, entitled to prevent such use under Article 5(1)(a) of Directive 2008/95 or, in the case of an EU trade mark, under Article 9(1)(a) of Regulation No 207/2009 (see, to that effect, the judgment of 22 September 2011, *Interflora and Interflora British Unit*, C-323/09, EU:C:2011:604, paragraphs 60 to 62).

37. As to the function of the advertising of the mark, it is that of using a mark for advertising purposes designed to inform and persuade consumers. Accordingly, the proprietor of a trade mark is, in particular, entitled to prohibit a third party from using, without the proprietor's consent, a sign identical with its trade mark in relation to goods or services which are identical with those for which that trade mark is registered, where that use adversely affects the proprietor's use of its mark as a factor in sales promotion or as an instrument of commercial strategy (see, to that effect, the judgment of 23 March 2010, *Google France and Google*, C-236/08 to C-238/08, EU:C:2010:159, paragraphs 91 and 92)."

[12] [2013] EWHC 1291 at [271]–[274]. Notwithstanding the fact that his judgment was overturned on appeal and a new trial ordered, nothing in the appeal judgments affects this reasoning.

[13] (C-323/09) EU:C:2011:604 [2012] E.T.M.R. 1.

[13a] (C-129/17) (EU:C:2018:594) at [34]–[37].

*Add new paragraph:*

Despite the rather bizarre outcome of the *Mitsubishi* ruling (see the update to para.18-139), the CJEU has now got to the stage where it provides consistent explanations for: (a) the essential function of a trade mark (which appears to include the guarantee of quality); (b) the investment function (which is to acquire or preserve a reputation); and (c) the advertising function (using a mark for advertising purposes designed to inform and persuade customers). Despite consistent mention of the "communication function" as one of the "other" functions, its nature has yet to be explained at the CJEU level, but see para.2-021 in the Main Work for the explanation from the General Court in *SIGLA*. **2-019A**

*Add new paragraph:*

The EFTA Court, in *Municipality of Oslo* (E-5/16) at [71], referred also to the other functions of a trade mark, but without any further elucidation of the concepts involved. **2-019B**

## 4. SIGN

*Add new paragraph:*

The mark applied for in *Red Bull GmbH v EUIPO* (C-124/18) was only slightly better in that the mark comprised a square block in two halves, one blue and one silver along with this description: "Protection is claimed for the colours blue (RAL5002) and silver (RAL9006). The ratio of the colours is approximately 50%–50%." The General Court ruled that the graphic representation was insufficiently precise and contrary to art.7(1)(a) since it did not constitute a systematic arrangement associating the colours in a predetermined and uniform way, and the CJEU dismissed the further appeal. **2-044A**

## 5. THE REPRESENTATION OF THE SIGN ON THE REGISTER

*Add new paragraph:*

The issue arose in somewhat unusual circumstances in *Oy Hartwall AB* (C-578/17) where the sign in question was designated as a "colour mark", i.e. a colour combination without contours. The drawing of the mark comprised a label or banner in a specific form coloured blue and grey with the description "The colours of the sign are blue (PMS 2748, PMS CYAN) and grey (PMS 877)". Thus there was an inconsistency between the classification of the mark designated by the applicant and the sign in question. The CJEU ruled that this inconsistency meant that it was impossible to determine exactly the subject matter and scope of the protec- **2-054A** tion sought, and in those circumstances the competent authority must refuse registration of the mark on account of the lack of clarity and precision of the application.

*Ad new paragraph:*

2-060A Glaxo's appeal was dismissed,[44a] and its registration cancelled, so its action proceeded only in passing off and failed.[44b] The CJEU dismissed the appeal in *Red Bull GmbH v EUIPO* (C-124/18).

[44a] See [2017] EWCA 335.

[44b] [2019] EWHC 2545.

## Single Colours

*Add new paragraph:*

2-085A By contrast, the issue in *Fromageries Bel SA v J Sainsbury Plc*[72a] was whether the particular hue of red needed to be specified for the mark to satisfy s.3(1)(a). The mark comprised a pictorial representation of a Mini Baby Bel cheese with dimensions added along with this description: "The mark is limited to the colour red. The mark consists of a three-dimensional shape and is limited to the dimensions shown above." It was held that a specific hue of red was required to satisfy s.3(1)(a). An application to add a specific Pantone reference to the description was rejected for the same reason as a similar attempt in *Nestlé*—it would not merely limit the rights conferred, but would also introduce an additional feature into the mark to make it distinctive—it would affect the description.

[72a] [2019] EWHC 3454 (HHJ Hacon, on appeal from the UK IPO).

Chapter 3

# AVERAGE CONSUMER

Table of Contents



## 1. Introduction

*Add new paragraph:*

A recent attempt to exploit and expand the bounds of the average consumer in the context of a likelihood of confusion test occurred in an appeal to the Appointed Person (Daniel Alexander QC) in *Zohara/Zara* (O-040-20). It appears that the argument was not concerned with different classes of consumers where they form substantial sub-groups of consumers as a whole (although this was the third of a series of points made by the Appointed Person at [21]–[29]. Instead, it appears the tribunal was urged to take into account the range of responses from a diverse population which might occur in possible situations in which the marks might be used: **3-003A**

"24. Fourth, in order to evaluate whether confusion is likely, a tribunal may properly (and in many cases must) consider a range of situations in which the mark is likely to be encountered in use. Equally, a tribunal must consider the different ways in which the respective marks (and particularly the mark under challenge) may be perceived by consumers. In such case, that is often in part an exercise of imagination as much as anything else, since in proceedings before the Registrar evidence of actual consumer responses is often unavailable.

25. However that cannot be taken too far: consideration of the range of responses does not require a microscopic analysis of the assumed characteristics of large numbers of possible individual consumers or possible kinds of situation in which the marks might be used. Moreover, it does it follow from the fact that it is possible to envisage situations in which confusion might arise in such imagined scenarios, that this suffices for a conclusion that confusion on the part of the average consumer is likely. Consideration must be given also to how realistic or likely such situations are as well as how typical of the normal manner in which the marks in question would be encountered. The more remote such scenarios are from a situation in which a mark would normally be perceived or presented, having regard to the nature of the goods and the nature of the trade in them, the greater the caution that must be exercised before taking such into account and concluding that the statutory test is satisfied.

26. A tribunal is also entitled to be alert to the fact that it may be possible to provide evidence to show that notwithstanding that a particular manner in which confusion is said to arise appears prima facie unlikely, in fact, it takes place to a significant extent. In the absence of evidence where such could be obtained in principle a tribunal is entitled to proceed on the basis that such is not realistically likely: a tribunal cannot be criticised for not assuming the worst if the worst remains a speculative rather than proven possibility.

27. Fifth, those considerations affect the extent to which, for example, scenarios involving the use of the mark outside the normal context of purchase or advertisement should be given significant weight in determining whether, taken as a whole, confusion is likely. More generally, in evaluating the likelihood of confusion, a tribunal is entitled to focus more on the typical part of the "spectrum of consumers" (in the words of Birss J in *Thomas Pink v Victoria's Secret* [2014] EWHC 2631) and typical purchasing or advertising situations among the range of all situations in which the marks in question might be presented. If confusion is not likely in that part of the spectrum, the fact that it is possible to imagine not wholly fanciful scenarios in which it may happen elsewhere, does mean that confusion is likely.

28. Sixth, a tribunal must carry out a global assessment and evaluate whether even if one kind of confusion (which in this case has particularly focussed on aural) is possible, that is really likely in the light of the fact that goods of the kind in question are predominantly selected by reference to visual or other criteria. This is well established and summarised by the General Court in *New Look v OHIM* In Joined Cases T-117/03 to T-119/03 and T-171/03) at [49]–[50] as follow to which the hearing officer referred:

> '49. However, it should be noted that in the global assessment of the likelihood of confusion, the visual, aural or conceptual aspects of the opposing signs do not always have the same weight. It is appropriate to examine the objective conditions under which the marks may be present on the market (*BUDMEN*, paragraph 57). The extent of the similarity or difference between the signs may depend, in particular, on the inherent qualities of the signs or the conditions under which the goods or services covered by the opposing signs are marketed. If the goods covered by the mark in question are usually sold in self-service stores where consumer choose the product themselves and must therefore rely primarily on the image of the trade mark applied to the product, the visual similarity between the signs will as a general rule be more important. If on the other hand the product covered is primarily sold orally, greater weight will usually be attributed to any aural similarity between the signs.
>
> 50. The applicant has not mentioned any particular conditions under which the goods are marketed. Generally in clothes shops customers can themselves either choose the clothes they wish to buy or be assisted by the sales staff. Whilst oral communication in respect of the product and the trade mark is not excluded, the choice of the item of clothing is generally made visually. Therefore, the visual perception of the marks in question will generally take place prior to purchase. Accordingly the visual aspect plays a greater role in the global assessment of the likelihood of confusion.'"

## 3. IDENTIFYING THE AVERAGE CONSUMER(S)

*Add new paragraph:*

**3-011A** *Bjornekulla* and *Schütz* were considered by the Court of Appeal in *London Taxi*, where the issue concerned whether the average consumer of taxis comprised not only taxi drivers and other purchasers of taxis but also hirers of taxis (i.e. akin to end users of the goods). Arnold J had decided that the average consumers in that case did not include members of the public who hire taxis. Although it was not necessary for the Court of Appeal to reach a concluded view on this issue, Floyd LJ (Kitchin LJ agreeing) inclined to the view that taxi hirers are not excluded in principle from consideration as a relevant class of consumer. Although the test he applied (at [34]) to reach this view is strictly obiter, it is nonetheless useful:

> "As with all issues in trade mark law, the answer to disputed questions is normally provided by considering the purpose of a trade mark which, broadly speaking, is to operate as a guarantee of origin to those who purchase or use the product. In principle, therefore, and in the absence of any authority cited to us which is directly in point, I would consider that the term average consumer includes any class of consumer to whom the guarantee of origin is directed and who would be likely to rely on it, for example in making a decision to buy or use the goods. Against that background, I would not have thought it mattered whether a user was someone who took complete possession of the goods, or someone who merely hired the goods under the overall control of a third party."

CHAPTER 4

# BREXIT

TABLE OF CONTENTS



This chapter has been renamed: "BREXIT (or UK Withdrawal From the EU)".

## 1. GENERALLY

*Replace paragraph:*

**4-001** The purpose of this chapter is to outline the process for the disentanglement of the UK from the EU and to explain the principal effects on: (a) registered trade marks which have force in the UK; (b) trade mark owners who currently own EU registered trade marks yet use them exclusively or principally in the UK; and (c) other EU rights which cover or relate to the UK or otherwise impact on trade marks here. It will be appreciated that Brexit will affect the subject matter of many chapters in this work. This chapter is intended to provide an overview.

*Replace paragraph:*

**4-002** On 31 January 2020 ("exit day"), the UK ceased to be a Member State of the European Union subject to an implementation period currently expiring on 31 December 2020 ("IP completion day"), at which time all EU law will be converted into domestic law or repealed.

**4-003** *Change title of section and replace paragraph:*

## 2. THE "EUROPEAN UNION (WITHDRAWAL) ACTS"

**4-003** Until IP completion day and notwithstanding the formal withdrawal of the UK from the EU on 31 January 2020, EU law effectively continues to apply in the UK by virtue of the European Union (Withdrawal Agreement) Act 2020 s.1.[a1] All Acts of Parliament passed to implement Directives remain in force, as do EU Regulations with direct effect as at exit day (as EU-derived domestic legislation). Thus, for example, the Trade Marks Act 1994 (as amended) continues in force unaffected, although it will be further amended on IP completion day by the Trade Marks (Amendment etc.) (EU Exit) Regulations 2019/269—for the amended Act, see Appendix 1A; for example to replace references to EUTMs with references to comparable trade marks (EU). From IP completion day the Supreme Court and Court of Appeal are no longer bound to follow retained EU case law.[b1]

[a1] This effectively delays until IP completion day (currently 31 December 2020) the repeal of the European Communities Act 1972 by the European Union (Withdrawal) Act 2018 (the "2018 Withdrawal Act") s.1. European Union (Withdrawal Agreement) Act 2020 Sch.5 Pt 1 changes to "IP completion day" all references to "exit day" made in and by the 2018 Withdrawal Act.

[b1] European Union (Withdrawal) Act 2018 s.6. By s.6(5) the Supreme Court and Court of Appeal "must apply the same test as it would apply in deciding whether to depart from its own case law."

*Replace paragraph:*

At first glance, this way forward seems relatively straightforward. However, there remain significant areas of uncertainty. One of the key policy decisions in this field now the UK has withdrawn from the EU is the extent to which the UK law of trade marks and related rights such as geographical indications continues in step with EU law. That decision will be directly affected by the type of relationship which the UK has with the EU following IP completion day. Furthermore, it may be recalled that the principles applied by the CJEU in interpreting EU law are founded in the four "fundamental freedoms" of the EU, including free movement of goods, persons and services. These principles will no longer apply following IP completion day. How are the UK courts to interpret those parts of EU law which it has chosen to retain in its domestic law when those freedoms no longer apply? We discuss these points later, but first it is necessary to outline the effects of the UK's withdrawal from the EU on the various rights which either apply to the UK or benefit entities based in the UK. **4-004**

## 3. The Effect on UK Registered Trade Marks

*Replace paragraph:*

After IP completion day, the immediate effect on UK registered trade marks will be limited. They will continue in force under the provisions of the Trade Marks Act 1994 (as amended)—see Appendix 1A. EU trade marks will no longer constitute "earlier marks" for the purposes of relative grounds of invalidity. EU trade marks existing at that date[c1] will automatically become "comparable trade marks (EU)" under the TMA (as amended) on 1 January 2021 and be "earlier marks", with effect from the filing date for the EU trade marks on which they are based.[d1] In relation to proof of use under TMA s.6A, the defence in TMA s.11A or revocation on the ground of five years continuous non-use under TMA s.46, use of such a comparable trade mark (EU) anywhere in the EU prior to 1 January 2021 shall be regarded as relevant use but after 1 January 2021 only use of such a mark in the UK is relevant[e1]: the practical effect is that an owner of a EUTM that has become a comparable trade mark (EU) on 1 January 2021 will have five years to use it in the UK provided it has been used somewhere else in the EU prior to IP completion day. **4-005**

[c1] By TMA Sch.2A para.25 (as amended by the Trade Marks (Amendment etc.) (EU Exit) Regulations (SI 2019/269)), a EUTM application pending on IP completion day may be converted to a comparable trade mark (EU) by an application made, together with the appropriate fee, within nine months of IP completion day only.

[d1] TMA Sch.2A para.1(8) (as amended by the Trade Marks (Amendment etc.) (EU Exit) Regulations (SI 2019/269)).

[e1] TMA Sch.2A paras 7 and 8 (as amended by the Trade Marks (Amendment etc.) (EU Exit) Regulations (SI 2019/269)).

*Replace paragraph:*

The provisions of the 2015 TM Directive were implemented in the UK on 14 **4-006**

January 2019.[1] For the text of the Trade Mark Act in force from 14 January 2019 to 31 December 2020, see Appendix 1. It may be noted that the equivalent new provisions in the EUTMR have applied since 1 October 2017.[2]

[1] Directive EU 2015/2436 art.54(1). The UK already has procedures sufficient to satisfy art.45, which other Member States must implement by 14 January 2023.

[2] Regulation 2017/1001 art.212.

## 4. The Effect on EU Registered Trade Marks

*Replace paragraph:*

4-007 When the Community Trade Mark system first came into force in 1994, the CTM Regulation provided that all Community trade marks would have unitary character and have equal effect throughout the Community. These basic characteristics remain in the latest EU Trade Mark Regulation, where "Community" was replaced by "European Union", but they were and are only possible because of the underpinnings of the Treaties and other Regulations, in particular relating to jurisdiction and enforcement of judgments.[3] The EUTM Regulation contains a set of rules on jurisdiction which are a modification of the general rules and the current system for recognition of judgments enables, for example, a judgment of an EU Trade Mark Court in a particular Member State to be enforced throughout the EU. Article 67(1)(b) of the Withdrawal Agreement provides that the jurisdiction provisions of the EUTM Regulation 2017 shall continue to be given effect to in the UK (and in the Member States of the EU insofar as such proceedings involve the UK)[3a] even after the end of the transition period ("IP completion day") insofar as proceedings for infringement of a EUTM were commenced before that date.[3b]

[3] The current position is governed by the Regulation 1215/2012 on Jurisdiction and the Recognition and Enforcement of Judgments in Civil and Commercial Matters ("the Recast Brussels Regulation"), in force since January 2015.

[3a] It is not clear how this will work in practice.

[3b] This provision of the Withdrawal Agreement is given effect to by the Trade Marks (Amendment etc.) (EU Exit) Regulations (SI 2019/269) Sch.5 para.7(2).

*Replace paragraph:*

4-008 Following the end of the implementation period, all EU trade mark registrations will continue to have unitary effect throughout the territory of the European Union, but that territory will shrink, because it will no longer include the UK.

*Replace paragraph:*

4-009 In the main work we expressed a preference for a solution which required a positive decision from the EUTM owner that they want the specific UK right (as this would reduce the number of unused UK(EU) registrations and thus reduce the number of conflicts) but this is not the solution adopted in the Withdrawal Agreement and now implemented in the TMA as amended, of automatic conversion without charge of all existing EUTMs[3c] to comparable trade marks (EU). Proprietors of such comparable trade marks (EU) who are using the equivalent EUTM elsewhere in the EU on IP completion day will have five years in which to start using them in the UK before they become susceptible to an attack on the ground of non-use but at least the addition of another right to their portfolio will make trade mark owners focus on their rights in the UK. Of course, it cannot be ruled out that this will result in the ignition of many conflicts which might otherwise have remained dormant. It is also likely to make harder the task of finding a registrable

UK trade mark, as there will be many comparable trade marks (EU) which have never been used in the UK and never would have been had not a UK right been given, without charge or action on its part, to the proprietor of the equivalent EUTM.

[3c] There were 1.789 million registrations of EUTMs between September 1997 and May 2020 (*www.euipo.europa.eu* [Accessed 1 July 2020]).

### Revocation for non-use

*Replace paragraph:*

Whilst the territory covered by a EUTM will automatically shrink on IP completion day, there will be no instant change in the trading which employs that EUTM. One consequence will be that many EUTMs which are essentially only used in the UK will become vulnerable to revocation for non-use five years after that date and their owners will need to ensure that there is sufficient use within the EU if they wish to maintain their rights. This issue will not be confined to UK businesses. **4-010**

## 6. Other EU Rights in Various Denominations

*Replace paragraph:*

The EU system of protection for PGIs, PDOs and TSGs is provided in Regulation 1151/2012. There are three aspects to consider. First, on IP completion day, existing PGIs, PDOs and TSGs which apply to UK products and businesses will continue in force but will now belong to a third country organisation. Secondly, their effect will be limited after IP completion day to the new territory of the EU but it seems the UK will retain an amended version of Regulation 1151/2012, applicable in the UK only—see amended Appendix 10. The related third point concerns the status and role of the absolute grounds which are designed to protect PGIs, PDOs, TSGs as well as traditional terms for wine (see arts 7(1) (j), (l) and (k) respectively of the EUTMR and arts 4(1)(i), (k) and (j) respectively of the 2015 TM Directive). Similar considerations arise in relation to Community Plant Variety rights, protected by Regulation 2100/94. Although these are said to be akin to patent rights, Community Plant Variety denominations (as well as denominations provided in national laws and international agreements to which the EU is a party) are (or will be) protected by a further absolute ground (see art.7(1)(m) of the EUTMR and art.4(1)(l) of the 2015 TM Directive). With effect from IP completion day, the absolute ground concerning geographical indications, TMA s.3(4A) (as amended), will no longer refer to the EU and therefore EU PDOs and PGIs will no longer form a basis for this ground of refusal; and the words "provision of EU law" will be deleted in TMA s.3(4). **4-015**

*Change title of section and replace paragraph:* **4-016**

## 7. "Hard" vs "Soft" Withdrawal

Notwithstanding the fact that the UK has already withdrawn from the EU, there continues to be talk of a "Hard" Brexit or a "Soft" Brexit, however inaccurate those amorphous terms actually are. A "Hard" Brexit, where the UK reaches the end of the implementation period without any further agreements in place to govern the future relationship with the EU and therefore would apply WTO tariffs, would mean that the decisions as to how to proceed would remain in the hands of the UK, influenced, no doubt, by the type of relationship which the UK wishes to achieve **4-016** with the EU in the future. On 19 May 2020 the UK Government published a draft UK-EU Comprehensive Free Trade Agreement. Although publication of the draft appears to be a negotiating tactic and has been characterised by the EU negotiating team as such, it does give some indication of the position the UK Government will adopt in negotiations on the future relationship and contains provisions on intellectual property rights except GIs where it is notably silent. Overall, trade mark law is a very small cog in the very large and complex post-Brexit world. We will have to see how it fares, as we move closer to and through the end of the implementation period.

CHAPTER 5

# THE UK REGISTER OF TRADE MARKS

TABLE OF CONTENTS



## 1. THE REGISTER

### Rule-making Power

*Replace paragraph:*

Particular instances of the rule-making powers include the making of provisions for filing applications and other documents, for making and filing translations, for service, for rectifying irregularities, and for setting and extending time limits.[3] The current rules are the Trade Marks Rules 2008, as amended.[4] They are referred to herein, in their amended form, as "the 2008 Rules". Note that the Trade Marks Rules 2008 will be substantively amended by the Trade Marks (Amendments etc.) (EU Exit) Regulations (SI 2019/269) and the Designs and International Trade Marks (Amendment etc.) Regulations (SI 2019/638) on the Implementation Period Completion day, or IP Completion day, (23.00 on 31 December 2020) which marks the end of the Transition or Implementation Period as set out within the European Union (Withdrawal Agreement) Act 2020, see s.39(1) and Sch.5 para.1. **5-003**

[3] s.78(2).

[4] SI 2008/1797 as amended by the Trade Marks (Amendment) Rules 2008 (SI 2008/2300), The Tribunals, Courts and Enforcement Act 2007 (Transitional and Consequential Provisions) Order 2008 (SI 2008/2683), Patents, Trade Marks and Designs (Address for Service) Rules 2009 (SI 2009/546), Trade Marks and Patents (Fees) (Amendment) Rules 2009 (SI 2009/2089), Trade Marks and Trade Marks (Fees) (Amendment) Rules 2012 (SI 2012/1003), Trade Marks and Registered Designs (Amendment) Rules 2013 (SI 2013/444), Trade Marks (Fast Track Opposition) (Amendment) Rules 2013 (SI 2013/2235), European Union Trade Mark Regulations (SI 2016/299), and the Trade Marks Regulations (SI 2018/825). Note that the Trade Mark Rules 2008 will be substantively amended by the Trade Marks (Amendment etc.) (EU Exit) Regulations (SI 2019/269) and the Designs and International Trade Marks (Amendment etc.) (EU Exit) Regulations (SI 2019/638) on the Implementation Period Completion day, or IP Completion day, (23.00 on 31 December 2020) which marks the end of the Transition or Implementation Period as set out within the European Union (Withdrawal Agreement) Act 2020, see s.39(1), and Sch.5 para.1. The Trade Marks (Fees) Rules 2008 (SI 2008/1958) are to be construed as one with the 2008 Rules. The Trade Mark (Fees) Rules (SI 2008/1958) has been amended by The Trade Marks and Patents (Fees) (Amendment) Rules 2009 (SI 2009/2089), The Trade Marks and Patents (Fees) (Amendment) Rules 2010 (SI 2010/33), The Trade Marks and Trade Marks (Fees) (Amendment) Rules

2012 (SI 2012/1033), and The Trade Marks (Fees) (Amendment) Rules 2013 (SI 2013/2236). The Rules made under the 1938 Act may be found in previous editions of *Kerly*.

## 2. The Comptroller or Registrar

### Exclusion of Liability of the Registrar

*Add to the end of the paragraph:*

**5-006** Note that liability is explicitly excluded with regard reminders for renewal of registrations. Under r.34(1), subject to r.34(2) at least six months before the expiration of the last registration of a trade mark, the registrar shall send to the registered proprietor notice of the approaching expiration and inform the proprietor at the same time that the registration may be renewed in the manner described in r.35. At r.34(2A), it is stated that "The registrar is not subject to any liability by any reason of any failure to notify the proprietor in accordance with paragraph [34](1) and no proceedings lie against any officer of the registrar in respect of any such failure."

## 4. Entries on the Register

### Details of Registered Marks to be Entered on the Register

*Replace paragraph with:*

**5-011** Details of registered trade marks are required to be entered on the Register by s.63(2)(a) of the 1994 Act, and the matters to be entered in respect of them are stipulated by the 2008 Rules.[13] The matters are:

(1) The effective date of registration (i.e. the date of filing of the application for registration).[14]
(2) The actual date of registration (i.e. the date of entry in the Register).
(3) The priority date (if any).
(4) The name and address of the proprietor.
(5) The address for service (if any).[15]
(6) Any disclaimer or limitation.
(7) Any memorandum or statement of the effect of any memorandum relating to a trade mark of which the Registrar has been informed.
(8) The goods or services in respect of which the mark is registered.
(9) Where the mark is a collective or certification mark, that fact.
(10) Where the mark has been registered pursuant to s.5(5) on the basis of consent of the proprietor of an earlier trade mark or other earlier right, that fact.
(11) Where the mark is registered pursuant to a transformation application, (i) the number of the international registration, and (ii) either: (a) the date accorded to the international registration under art.3(4) of the Madrid Protocol, or (b) the date of recordal of the request for extension to the UK of the international registration under art.3*ter* of the Madrid Protocol, as the case may be.
(12) Where the mark arises from the conversion of a EU trade mark or an application for a EU trade mark, the number of any other registered trade mark from which the EU trade mark or the application for a EU trade mark claimed seniority and the earliest seniority date.
(13) Where the mark is a collective mark and amended regulations have been accepted by the registrar, that fact, including the date of entry.

Please note that the matters as stipulated to be entered on the Register by the 2008 Rules will be significantly amended by the Designs and International Trade Marks (Amendment etc.) (EU Exit) Regulations 2019 (SI 2019/638) and the Trade Marks (Amendment etc) (EU Exit) Regulations 2019 (SI 2019/269) on 31 December 2020 to deal with matters concerning Comparable trade marks (EU) and Comparable trade marks (IR) which will be the UK Trade marks derived from existing EU trade marks and existing IR(EU) trade marks.

[13] r.47.

[14] In accordance with s.40(3).

[15] Under r.11, an address for service is required for many purposes under the Act. In particular, all applicants for registration must provide one. In accordance with r.11(4), an address for service under this rule shall be an address in the UK another EEA state (this is due to be amended to read "an EEA state" on 31 December 2020, see the Trade Marks (Amendment etc) (EU Exit) Regulations 2019 (SI 2019/269) Sch.4 para.6)), or the Channel Islands.

## Procedure for Giving Notice of a Registrable Transaction

### Transactions concerning applications for registration

*Replace paragraph:*

5-023 Section 27(1) of the Act provides that the provisions of ss.22–26, which relate to registered trade marks as objects of property, assignments and registrable transactions and ss.28–31 (which relate to licensing), also apply to applications for registration. However, applications for registration and transactions concerning them are not registered as such. Instead, where an application for registration has been made and is the subject of a transaction which would have been registrable were the mark already registered, notice is given to the Registrar of the details of the transaction.[25]

[25] s.27(3).

## 5. Alteration of Entries on the Register

*Replace paragraph:*

5-027 The powers to amend the Register[28] considered here, which arise under ss.10B 44, and 64 of the 1994 Act, are distinct from the powers to revoke or invalidate a registered trade mark under ss.46, and 47 of the 1994 Act.[29]

[28] Note that, as set out at s.63, the Register concerns registered trade marks and registrable transactions affecting them. Powers to amend trade mark applications which arise under s.39 are dealt with in Ch.7.

[29] As to which, see Ch.12.

## Alteration of a Registered Trade Mark

*After "substantially affect the identity of the mark.", add new footnote 29a:*

5-028 [29a] Note that Trade Marks Act s.44 was considered in *Cadbury UK Ltd v Comptroller General of Patents, Designs and Trade Marks* [2018] EWCA Civ 2715; [2019] F.S.R. 7, in particular see [16]–[17]. It was also referred to by the Court of Appeal in *Caspian Pizza Ltd v Shah* [2017] EWCA Civ 1874; [2018] ETMR 8 at [26].

5-029 *Change title of sub-section:*

## Rectification Relating to Acts of Agents or Representatives carried out without the Trade Mark Proprietor's consent

*Replace paragraph:*

5-029 Under s.10B(2) there are specific powers of rectification relating to acts of agents or representatives in registering trade marks carried out without the Trade Mark Proprietor's consent. Where a trade mark is registered in the name of an agent or representative of a person ("P") who is the proprietor of the trade mark, without P's consent,[35] that person, P, may apply for the rectification of the register so as to substitute P's name as the proprietor of the registered mark.[36] The power does not apply if the agent or representative[37] justifies their action.[38] The 2008 Rules do not provide a specified form or procedure to be used with this specific application for rectification (neither did they with regards the now repealed s.60). Therefore, it is presumed that the procedure set out at r.44 and Form TM26(R) concerning rectifications under s.64 should be used.

[35] See s.10B(1). This is a new section of the Trade Marks Act 1994, inserted by the Trade Marks Regulations (SI 2018/825) Pt 2 reg.11. This was added to the Act as part of the Implementation of Directive (EU) 2015/2436, in particular it implements Directive (EU) 2015/2436 art.13. Section 10B replaces s.60, which has been repealed by the Trade Marks Regulations (SI 2018/825). Section 60 originally implemented art.6*septies* of the Paris Convention for the Protection of Industrial Property (see Appendix 16).

[36] See s.10B(2). Under s.10B(2)(a) the registered proprietor may also, or in the alternative to rectification, prevent the use of the trade mark by the agent or representative (notwithstanding the rights conferred by the Act in relation to a registered trade mark). Note that strict identity of the marks in question was not necessary under the now repealed s.60(1) to apply. Richard Arnold QC (as he then was), sitting as the Appointed Person, in *Sribhan Jacob Company Ltd's Application* (SRIS O/066/08) (Appointed Person) held that if the agent or representative has applied for a mark which differs in elements which do not affect the distinctive character of the principal's mark, then this will fall within the provisions of, the now repealed, s.60(1) (see [46] of the Decision). The Appointed Person left open the question of whether, the now repealed, s.60(1) could apply to marks less similar than this.

[37] The meaning and scope of "agent or representative" in repealed s.60, is considered by the Appointed Person in *Sribhan Jacob Company Ltd's Application* (SRIS O/066/08) (Appointed Person).

[38] s.10B(2). Richard Arnold QC (as he then was), sitting as the Appointed Person, in *Sribhan Jacob Company Ltd's Application* (SRIS O/066/08) (Appointed Person) held the remedy for rectification under the now repealed s.60(3)(b) was not a discretionary remedy. If the applicant for rectification under the repealed s.60 established that the case fell within the s.60(1) of the Act, and the respondent to the application failed to justify its action, then the applicant was entitled to a declaration of invalidity or in the alternative rectification (see [43] of the Decision).

## Errors Affecting Validity

*Replace paragraph:*

5-034 On the other hand, however, if the proviso under s.64(1) is interpreted too broadly, so that an excessively wide range of matters are treated as "affecting the validity" of the mark in question, the effect will be that proprietors are unfairly precluded from making inoffensive corrections. It should be recalled that if s.64 cannot be invoked, the only procedural alternatives are: (i) s.10B as discussed above at para.5-029, and (ii) ss.45, 46 and 47, and under those provisions the only possible results which alter the Register are the complete or partial surrender, revocation or invalidity of the mark.

## 6. INSPECTION OF THE REGISTER AND OBTAINING INFORMATION

## Searches

*After "International Registration designating the UK).", add new footnote 78a:*

5-059 [78a] After the Implementation Period Completion day, or IP completion day (23.00 on 31 December

2020), the UK Register will no longer include EU trade marks or International Registrations designating the EU but will then include Comparable trade marks (EU) and Comparable trade marks (IR) which will be the UK Trade marks derived from existing EU trade marks and existing IR(EU) trade marks.

*Change title of section:* **5-064**

## 8. INTERNATIONAL TRADE MARKS AND EU TRADE MARKS

*At to the end of the paragraph:*

Note after the Implementation Period Completion day, or IP Completion day, (23.00 on 31 December 2020) the UK register will no longer include International Registrations designating the EU but will then include comparable trade marks (IR) which will be the UK Trade marks derived from existing IR(EU) trade marks. **5-064**

*Replace paragraph:*

The EUIPO maintains the EU Trade Mark Register. After the Implementation Period Completion day, or IP Completion day (23.00 on 31 December 2020), the UK Register will no longer include EU trade marks but will then include comparable trade marks (EU) which will be the UK Trade marks derived from existing EU trade marks. For more information on EU Trade Marks see Ch.8. **5-065**

## Chapter 6

# CLASSIFICATION OF GOODS AND SERVICES

Table of Contents



## 2. The Structure of the Nice Classification

*Replace paragraph:*

**6-005** The Nice "home page" contains six tabs: Classes, Alphabetical, Class headings, General remarks, Modifications and Search. If the "Classes" tab is opened, the heading "List of Goods and Services by Class Order" appears. On the left there are two tables of numbers: 1–34 for goods, and 35–45 for services. Clicking on one of these numbers will open a page which shows a "class heading" followed by an "Explanatory Note" and an alphabetical list of goods or services. For example, if one clicks on the number 12, the heading "Vehicles; apparatus for locomotion by land, air or water" appears. That is the class heading for Class 12. Below the class heading there is an Explanatory Note stating that certain items are included in Class 12 and that certain other items are not included. After that comes a long list of goods in alphabetical order, starting with "adhesive rubber patches for repairing inner tubes" and ending with "yachts".

*Replace first sentence of paragraph with:*

**6-007** The supposed purpose of the "Explanatory notes" is to provide some guidance as to what is or is not included in each class.

*Add new paragraph:*

**6-011A** The "Modifications" tab provides information about additions, deletions and changes in classification that have occurred.

*Delete paras 6-009 to 6-011.*

## 3. The Purpose and Relevance of Classification

*Add new paragraph:*

**6-013A** In certain circumstances it may be appropriate, and indeed necessary, to take classification into account for the purpose of defining precisely what goods or services are covered by a registration. Sometimes the words chosen are too vague or capable of referring to goods or services in more than one class. In such cases, the class in which they have been placed "may be used as an aid to interpret what the words mean with the overall objective of legal certainty of the specification of goods and services".[7a] The trade mark manuals of the UKIPO and of the EUIPO both suggest that the class number should be taken into account, together with the ordinary and natural meaning of the words, to determine whether the specification of goods and services is sufficiently clear and precise.[7b]

[7a] *Pathway IP Sarl v Easygroup Ltd* [2018] EWHC 3608 (Ch) at [94] per Carr J; see also the extensive discussion by Mr David Stone, sitting as deputy High Court Judge, in *Multi-Access Ltd v Guanghzhou Wong Lo Kat Great and Health Business Development Co Ltd* [2019] EWHC 3357 (Ch) at [84]–[86].

[7b] *Pathway IP Sarl v Easygroup Ltd* at [103].

## 7. The Legislative Changes Introduced in 2015

*Add new paragraph:*

The provisions contained in art.39 of the 2015 TM Directive were transposed into UK law by SI 2018/825 amending the Trade Mark Rules 2008.[35a] The amendments came into force on 19 January 2019. **6-032A**

[35a] See r.8 of the 2008 Rules.

*Add new section:*

## 9. The Consequences of a Lack of Clarity and Precision

Examiners are under a duty to ensure that goods and services are classified correctly and that the specification complies with the requirements of clarity and precision laid down in the *IP TRANSLATOR* judgment and subsequently enshrined in the legislation. Failure to comply with those requirements should lead to the rejection of the application.[57] **6-047**

It is nonetheless inevitable that some applications containing an insufficiently clear and precise specification of goods and services will slip through the net. Can the resulting registration be declared invalid, in whole or in part, on the ground that the specification lacks clarity or precision? That question arose in the *SkyKick* case. The claimants (Sky Plc and Others) owned four EU trade marks and one UK trade mark containing or consisting of the word "Sky". The specifications of goods and services included items such as "computer software" that appeared to lack the necessary precision. The defendants supplied "cloud migration" IT services under the trade mark "SkyKick". Sky Plc and Others sued the defendants for trade mark infringement. The defendants counterclaimed for a declaration that the claimants' trade marks were invalid on the ground that they had been registered in respect of goods or services that were not specified with sufficient clarity and precision. The High Court sought guidance from the CJEU.[58] **6-048**

One of the questions referred to the CJEU asked whether a registered trade mark could "be declared wholly or partially invalid on the ground that some or all of the terms in the specification of goods and services are lacking in sufficient clarity and precision to enable the competent authorities and third parties to determine on the basis of those terms alone the extent of the protection conferred by the trade mark". The CJEU answered that question in the negative. The court pointed out that the absolute grounds of invalidity laid down exhaustively in art.51 of Regulation 40/94 (corresponding to art.59 of the current EUTM Regulation) and in art.3 of Direc- **6-049** tive 89/104 (corresponding to art.4 of the 2015 TM Directive) did not expressly include lack of clarity and precision of the terms used to designate the goods and services covered by the registration. A lack of clarity and precision in those terms did not therefore constitute a specific ground of invalidity.[59]

**6-050** The court went on to consider whether a lack of clarity and precision in the specification of goods and services could be brought within the scope of any of the absolute grounds of invalidity expressly listed in the legislation. It rejected the possibility of applying the ground of invalidity laid down in art.7(1)(a) in conjunction with art.4 of Regulation 40/94 or in art.3(1)(a) in conjunction with art.2 of Directive 89/104; those provisions required clarity and precision in the representation of the sign constituting the trade mark but it could not be inferred therefrom that such a requirement of clarity and precision should also apply to the specification of goods and services.[60]

**6-051** Nor was it possible to declare a registration invalid on the ground that a lack of clarity and precision in the specification of goods and services was contrary to public policy within the meaning of art.7(1)(f) of Regulation 40/94 and art.3(1)(f) of Directive 89/104. The court stated that the concept of public policy "cannot be construed as relating to characteristics concerning the trade mark application itself, such as the clarity and precision of the terms used to designate the goods or services covered by that registration, regardless of the characteristics of the sign for which the registration as a trade mark is sought".[61] Here the CJEU was following, without citing, the case law of the General Court, which had held that all the absolute grounds for refusal (including the ground relating to public policy and accepted principles of morality) "refer to the intrinsic qualities of the mark claimed".[62] (It is submitted, nonetheless, that there must be circumstances in which a trade mark application can be refused, or a registration declared invalid, on account of the nature of the goods or services. In one case the EUIPO Board Appeal took the view that a trade mark should be refused on grounds of public policy in so far as the specification of services included "assisted suicide", since assisted suicide was illegal in most EU Member States.[63])

**6-052** The *SkyKick* case also raised the issue of bad faith in relation to unduly broad specifications. The CJEU held that the relevant provisions of the Regulation and the Directive must be interpreted as meaning that a trade mark application is tainted with bad faith in so far as it is made without any intention to use the trade mark in relation to the specified goods and services, "if the applicant had the intention either of undermining, in a manner inconsistent with honest practices, the interests of third parties, or of obtaining, without even targeting a specific third party, an exclusive right for purposes other than those falling within the functions of a trade mark".[64] In the light of that ruling, the High Court declared the claimants' registrations partially invalid. In particular, the court found that bad faith had been proved in so far as the claimants applied to register the trade marks for computer software "as part of their strategy without any commercial justification".[65] It did not follow, however, that the registrations were wholly invalid in so far as they concerned computer software; on the contrary, the claimants had clearly intended to use the trade marks in relation to certain types of computer software, as was proved by the evidence of actual use. The court therefore considered it appropriate to cut the specification back in a manner that "reflects the extent of the bad faith proved, but no more".[66]

**6-053** The CJEU also ruled that a provision such as s.32(3) of the 1994 Act is compatible with the Directive.[67]

Although the CJEU's ruling in the *SkyKick* case concerned the interpretation of the original versions of the TM Directive and the Community Trade Mark Regulation, the principles established by that ruling appear to be equally applicable under the current legislation. **6-054**

[57] As regards the position in UK law, see r.9 of the 2008 Rules. The relevant provision in the 2015 TM Directive is art.39(4). As regards EU trade marks, the corresponding provision is art.33(4) of the EUTM Regulation.

[58] *Sky Plc, Sky International AG and Sky UK Ltd v SkyKick UK Ltd and SkyKick Inc* [2018] EWHC 155 (Ch) and [2018] EWHC 943 (Ch), per Arnold J.

[59] *Sky Plc, Sky International AG and Sky UK Ltd v SkyKick UK Ltd and SkyKick Inc* (C-371/18) EU:C:2020:45 at [60].

[60] At [64].

[61] At [66]–[67].

[62] *Duferrit GmbH v OHIM* (T-224/01) [2003] E.C.R. II-1589 at [76] and *Sportwetten GmbH Gera v OHIM* (T-140/02) [2005] E.C.R. II-3247 at [28].

[63] *Verein StHD* (R 1940/2013-4), decision of 5 May 2014 at [14].

[64] At [81].

[65] *Sky Plc, Sky International AG and Sky UK Ltd v SkyKick UK Ltd and SkyKick Inc* [2020] EWHC 990 (Ch) at [28].

[66] At [29].

[67] At [87].

Chapter 7

# UK REGISTRATION PROCEDURE

Table of Contents



## 1. Preliminary

*Replace footnote 1:*

**7-001** [1] Currently the Trade Mark Rules 2008. Note that the Trade Mark Rules 2008 will be substantively amended by the Trade Marks (Amendments etc.) (EU Exit) Regulations (SI 2019/269) and the Designs and International Trade Marks (Amendment etc.) Regulations (SI 2019/638) on the Implementation Completion Day (31 December 2020 at 11pm) which marks the end of the Transition or Implementation Period as set out within the European Union (Withdrawal Agreement) Act 2020, see s.39(1), and Sch.5 para.1.

*Replace footnote 4:*

**7-002** [4] See Section 3 of the Tribunal Section of the IPO Manual of Trade Mark Practice for general procedural matters concerning notices of opposition filed in respect of international registrations regarding which protection is sought in the UK.

## 2. Procedure on National Application to Register

### Essential Particulars of an Application

*Replace list:*

**7-006**
(1) a request for registration of a trade mark;
(2) the name and address of the applicant (note that partnerships applying to register a mark may be recorded as a partnership without naming each individual partner)[7];
(3) a statement of the goods or services in relation to which it is sought to register the trade mark; and
(4) a representation of the mark which is capable of being represented in the register in a manner which enables the registrar and other competent authorities and the public to determine the clear and precise subject matter of the protection afforded to the proprietor.[8]

[7] *Manual of Trade Marks Practice*, New Applications, Section 3.

[8] Regarding national trade marks, under art.3(b) of the 2015 TM Directive (Directive (EU) 2015/2436) which was implemented by the UK on 14 January 2019, a graphical representation is no longer required, merely a representation which is clear and precise, see amended s.1(1)(a) of the 1994 Act, as amended by Trade Marks Regulations (SI 2018/825) Pt 2 reg.3.

## Form of the Application

### General requirements

*Replace list:*

(1) *Marks consisting exclusively of colours*[12]: Such marks may be represented by giving a written description of the colours and/or by identifying the colours using an internationally recognised colour identification system, such as the Pantone number. Other means of graphical representation will only be accepted if they are presented in a way that is "clear precise, self contained, easily accessible, intelligible, durable and objective."[13] Where the mark consists of the colour(s) applied to goods, a description of the goods or a picture or diagram should be provided. The representation should include "a systematic arrangement associating the colours in a predetermined and uniform way".[14] In *Société des Produits Nestlé SA v Cadbury UK Ltd*[15] the Court of Appeal held that a mark consisting of the colour purple defined by reference to a Pantone number and "applied to the whole visible surface, or being the predominant colour applied to the whole visible surface, of the packaging of goods" was not registerable because the reference to being the "predominant" colour introduced uncertainty as to the sign being claimed and the sign "thus lacks the required clarity, precision, self-containment, durability and objectivity" for registration.[16] **7-007**

(2) *Colour in device marks*[17]: If the mark is depicted in colour, the registration will be limited to those colours unless otherwise stated.[18] If a device is shown in black and white, those colours are not generally considered to be a feature of the mark unless otherwise stated in the application, in which case the entry on the Register will contain a statement to that effect.

(3) *Three Dimensional marks*[19]: Applications for 3D marks must be identified on the application form and unless the shape of the mark can be represented completely by a single perspective view, multiple views should be shown. Where a pictorial representation of a shape is put forward as only one example of the shape sought to be registered, it is likely that the application will be rejected as not meeting the requirement for a clear, precise and unambiguous representation of the mark applied for.

[12] *Manual of Trade Marks Practice*, New Applications section, section 2.4.5.

[13] See the decisions of the ECJ in *Libertel* (C-104/01) [2004] F.S.R. 4 and *Sieckmann v Deutsches Patent und Markenamt* (C-273/00) [2003] R.P.C. 38.

[14] See the judgment of the Court of Justice in *Heidelberger Bauchemie GmbH* (C-49/02) [2004] E.T.M.R. 99 at [33]. This judgment is quoted at the *Manual of Trade Marks Practice*, New Applications section, section 2.4.5.

[15] [2014] R.P.C. 7.

[16] Also see *Glaxo Wellcome UK Ltd v Sandoz Ltd* [2016] F.S.R. 36 for a recent case where a combination colour per se EUTM was found to be invalid for lack of certainty under art.7(1)(a) and art.4 of Council Regulation 207/2009. The version of art.4 that was in issue in this case was the version in force at that time, as the new amended version did not apply until 1 October 2017, see art.4 of the Amending Regulation 2015/2424. The decision in *Glaxo Wellcome UK Ltd v Sandoz Ltd* [2016] F.S.R. 36 was appealed to the Court of Appeal and the appeal was dismissed, see *Glaxo Wlelcome Ltd v Sandoz Ltd* [2017] F.S.R. 33. See also *Cadbury UK Ltd v Société des Produits Nestlé SA* (O/198/19); [2019] E.T.M.R. 39 (a decision of the UK IPO) where the description in a UK trade mark application for the colour purple to the "whole visible surface" of the goods' packaging which stated "as shown on the form of application", accompanied by an additional Pantone number, was sufficiently clear and precise to meet the requirements for registrability under s.1(1)(a) of the 1994 Act. However, applications for colour marks referring to colour "applied to the packaging of the goods" or failing to specify how the colour was to be used, were held to be ambiguous.

[17] *Manual of Trade Marks Practice*, New Applications section, section 2.4.2.

[18] However, see the discussion of the genuine use of black and white marks in Ch.12 and the discussion of relative grounds for refusal of a mark in black and white in Ch.11, following the adoption of the Common Communication on the Common Practice of the Scope of Protection of Black and White Marks of 15 April 2014.

[19] *Manual of Trade Marks Practice*, New Applications section, section 2.4.3.

## Application May Relate to More than One Class

*Replace paragraph:*

**7-011** The classification of goods and services is addressed in Ch.6. An application may be made for registration of a trade mark in respect of goods and services in more than one class.[23] Every application must specify the class to which it relates and list the goods or services appropriate to that class, described in such a way as to indicate clearly the nature of those goods and services and allow them to be classified in the classes in the Nice Classification.[24] This aspect of the specification has an important role to play in determining the boundaries of the registration. If the application does not comply with these requirements, a notice will be sent to the applicant specifying a period of not less than one month in which the default must be rectified, failing which the registrar must reject the application. If the application does not comply with these requirements, a notice will be sent to the applicant specifying a period of not less than one month in which the default must be rectified, failing which the application will be treated as abandoned.[25] Where an application covers more than one class then additional fees are payable for each further class.

[23] 2008 Rules r.8 and Form TM3A.

[24] 2008 Rules r.8(2)(a) and (b). See also r.8(2A) which was added by reg.36(3) of the Trade Marks Regulations (SI 2018/825) on 14 January 2019 which states "For the purposes of [r.8] paragraph (2)(b) an application may specify the general indications included in the class headings of the Nice Classification or other general terms provided that they satisfy the requirement that the goods or services be described with sufficient clarity and precision referred to in [r.8] paragraph (2)(b)". Further, see also r.8(2B) which was added by reg.36(3) of the Trade Marks Regulations (SI 2018/825) on 14 January 2019 which states "Where the specification contained in the application describes the goods or services using general terms, including the general indications included in the class headings of the Nice Classification, the application shall be treated as including only the goods or services clearly covered by the literal meaning of the term or indication".

[25] 2008 Rules r.9.

*Replace footnote 27:*

**7-012** [27] *Manual of Trade Marks Practice*, the Classification Guide section, section 3.11.

## Use or Bona Fide Intention to Use

*Replace second sentence of paragraph:*

**7-014** To this end the Form TM3 contains the statement "Trade mark is being used by the applicant, or with his or her consent, in relation to the goods or services shown, or there is a bona fide intention that it will be used in this way".

*Replace the first sentence of the paragraph with:*

**7-016** Secondly, it is not at all clear what is meant by the words "there is a bona fide intention that it will be used in this way".

## Deficiencies in the Application

*Replace footnote 37:*

[37] 2008 Rules r.77 and *Manual of Trade Marks Practice*, New Applications section, section 1.3. 7-019

## Examination of the Application

*Replace footnote 38:*

[38] *Manual of Trade Marks Practice*, Examination Guide, section 5.13 and see the Trade Marks (Relative Grounds) Order 2007 (SI 2007/1976). 7-021

*Replace footnote 41:*

[41] 2008 Rules r.14(2). As of 23.00 on 31 December 2020, references in s.14(2) to the proprietor of a trade mark will also include a person who has applied for registration of a trade mark which, if registered, would be an earlier trade mark by virtue of s.6(1)(a) or (aa) and s.6(1)(ab) of the Trade Marks Act 1994 as a result of Sch.4 para.7 and Sch.7 para.6 (respectively) of the Designs and International Trade Marks (Amendment etc.) (EU Exit) Regulations (SI 2019/638). 7-022

### Is the mark a trade mark?

*Replace paragraph:*

The Registrar must consider whether the mark applied for is a trade mark within the meaning of s.1 of the 1994 Act. Particular consideration is given to shapes, colours, sounds and smells. To satisfy the requirements of s.1, these must be capable of: (a) being represented in a manner which enables the registrar and other competent authorities and the public to determine the clear and precise subject matter of the protection afforded by the proprietor; and (b) of distinguishing goods or services of one undertaking from those of other undertakings.[44] Care should be taken in the case of shapes that they do accurately represent the mark sought to be protected. In the case of colours it must be expected that the Registry will take a conservative line in respect of single colours, and much may depend upon the choice of colours and the way they are used.[45] As to sounds and smells, these pose particular problems when it comes to graphical representation and it must also be expected that the Registry will require convincing evidence that they are capable of distinguishing the goods or services of the applicant (see further Chs 2 and 10). 7-024

[44] Regarding national trade marks, as a result of the implementation of the 2015 TM Directive (Directive (EU) 2015/2436) on 14 January 2019, a graphical representation is no longer required, rather a representation which is clear and precise (via art.3(b) of the 2015 TM Directive), see amended s.1(1)(a) of the 1994 Act, as amended by Trade Mark Regulations (SI 2018/825) Pt 2 reg.3.

[45] See, e.g. *Ty Nant Spring Water Ltd's Application* [2000] R.P.C. 55; [1999] R.P.C. 392.

## Evidence of Use

*Replace footnote 47:*

[47] See further paras 7-105 to 7-120, in particular para.7-116. See also *Manual of Trade Marks Practice* Ch.7, Tribunal section, section 4.8.10, Hearsay. 7-028

## Limitation and Disclaimer

*Replace footnote 60:*

[60] *Manual of Trade Marks Practice*, Examination Guide section, sections 2.8 and 3 (disclaimers). 7-034

## Division

*Add new paragraph after para.7-046:*

By virtue of s.41(1)(aa) of the 1994 Act (added by reg.20 of the Trade Marks 7-046A

Regulations (SI 2018/825)), a registration can also be divided into several registrations. This issue is also dealt with in r.26A of the 2008 Rules (added by reg.39 of the Trade Marks Regulations SI 2018/825). Under r.26A, the proprietor of a trade mark can apply by sending a request on Form TM12R, indicating for each divisional registration the specification of goods or services. Each divisional registration must be treated as a separate registration with the same date of registration as the original registration. No request under para.(1) of Rule 26A may be granted in respect of the registration of a trade mark which is the subject of proceedings for its revocation or invalidation, where the request would introduce a division amongst the goods or services in respect of which the proceedings are directed (See r.26A(3)). Any disclaimers or limitation will also apply, as well as a grant of licence, security interest, right in or under the original registration or any memorandum (see r.26A(4)).

## Earlier Registrations of the Applicant

*Replace footnote 71:*

7-047 [71] Detailed guidelines setting out the approach adopted by the Registrar in relation to such prior registrations can be found in the *Manual of Trade Marks Practice*, Examination Guide section, Section 6 on Prior Rights.

## Applications to Register Collective Marks

*Replace paragraph:*

7-068 An application may be made to register a collective mark under the provisions of s.49 and Sch.1 to the 1994 Act. The substantive topic of collective marks is addressed in Ch.14. Such a mark is used to distinguish the goods or services of members of an association which is the proprietor of the mark from those of other undertakings.[103a] Paragraph 4 of Sch.1 indicates that collective marks shall not be registered if the mark would mislead the public as regards its character or significance, in particular if it is likely to be taken as something other than a collective mark. In practice, this means that an objection will be raised if the mark is likely to be taken as something other than its true designation, i.e. that it is more likely to be taken as an ordinary trade mark as opposed to its true designation.[104]

[103a] Under s.49(1A) of the 1994 Act (which was added by reg.24 of the Trade Marks Regulations SI 2018/825), the following may be registered as the proprietor of a collective mark—(a) an association of manufacturers, producers, suppliers of services or traders which has the capacity in its own name to enter into contracts and to sue or be sued; and (b) a legal person governed by public law.

[104] *Manual of Trade Marks Practice*, Certification and Collective Marks section, section 2.5, and following.

## Applications to Register Certification Trade Marks

*Replace paragraph:*

7-073 As in the case of a collective mark, an application is made for a certification trade mark in the same way as for an ordinary trade mark. The formalities of it are checked as for an ordinary mark and, if they are satisfied, it will be examined. Again, as with a collective mark para.5 of Sch.2 indicates that certification marks shall not be registered if the mark would mislead the public as regards its character or significance, in particular if it is likely to be taken as something other than a certification mark. In practice, this means that an objection will be raised if the mark is likely to be taken as something other than its true designation, i.e. that it is more likely to be taken as an ordinary trade mark as opposed to its true designation.[108]

Paragraph 4 of Sch.2 indicates that a certification mark shall not be registered if the proprietor carries on a business involving the supply of goods of the kind certified. To overcome an objection of this sort it is sufficient for the applicant to make a statement that they do not carry on a business in the goods or services certified. There is no equivalent prohibition in Sch.1 relating to collective marks.[109]

[108] *Manual of Trade Marks Practice*, Certification and Collective Marks section, section 2.5, and following.

[109] *Manual of Trade Marks Practice*, Certification and Collective Marks section, section 2.4.

## 3. OPPOSITION TO REGISTRATION

### Procedure on Opposition

*Replace footnote 114:*

[114] SI 2008/1797 which has been amended by SI 2008/2300, SI 2008/2683, SI 2009/2089, SI 2009/546, SI 2012/1003, SI 2013/444, SI 2013/2235, SI 2016/299, and the Trade Marks Regulations SI 2018/825. Note that the Trade Mark Rules 2008 will be substantively amended by the Trade Marks (Amendment etc.) (EU Exit) Regulations (SI 2019/269) and the Designs and International Trade Marks (Amendment etc.) (EU Exit) Regulations (SI 2019/638) on the Implementation Completion day (23.00 on 31 December 2020) which marks the end of the Transition or Implementation Period as set out within the European Union (Withdrawal Agreement) Act 2020, see s.39(1), and Sch.5 para.1. The 2008 Rules came into force on 1 October 2008. For proceedings commenced before that date, see the transitional provisions at r.83 of the 2008 Rules. **7-078**

*Replace paragraph:*

As set out at r.17(2) of the 2008 Rules, within two months beginning immediately after the date on which the application was published, notice of opposition must be sent to the Registrar in the prescribed form (TM7).[115] However as set out at r.17(3) of the 2008 Rules, before the expiry of this two-month period, by using form TM7A a request for an extension of time can be made for the filing of form TM7.[116] If a TM7A form is so filed the time period for filing a TM7 form is extended to three months beginning immediately after the date on which the application was published for any person (or in the case of a company, any subsidiary or holding company of that company or any other subsidiary of that holding company[117]) having filed a form TM7A. Form TM7A is available to be filed online[118] and is called a "notice of threatened opposition" and there is no fee associated with this form. The time limits in rr.17(2) and 17(3) (whether the periods have expired or not) may only be extended if the irregularity or prospective irregularity is attributable, wholly or in part, to a default, omission or other error by the Registrar, the Intellectual Property Office or the International Bureau; and it appears to the Registrar that the irregularity should be rectified.[119] A copy of the notice will be sent by the Registrar to the applicant and the date upon which the TM7 is sent to the applicant is known as "the notification date".[120] The notice of opposition must include a statement of the grounds of opposition. Where the opposition is based on an earlier registered trade mark, then the notice must include a representation of the earlier trade mark, the details of the authority with which the mark is registered, the registration number of that mark, the goods and services in respect of which it is registered and upon which the opposition is based. Further, where the registration period for the earlier mark was completed more than five years before the date of application for registration or, if any, the date of priority, the statement of grounds must include a declaration detailing whether the earlier mark has been put to genuine use in relation to each of the goods or services on which the opposition is based, and if not, detailing any proper reasons for non-use. This statement is known as "the statement of use".[121] **7-079**

[115] See TPN 1/2013 which sets out the practice of the Registry in determining the date by which the TM7 or TM7A must be filed after the Trade Marks and Registered Designs (Amendment) Rules 2013 (SI 2013/444) came into force. It is now the case that the opponent should ensure that the Notice of Opposition is filed within two months beginning immediately after the date of publication. For example, a trade mark application published in the trade mark journal on 11 April 2013 would have a latest date of 11 June 2013 by which to file an opposition on a TM7 Form or request an extension to the opposition period on a TM7A Form, rather than 10 June 2013 as it was previously.

[116] See fn.115 with regards the time period within which a TM7A must be filed.

[117] The meaning of "subsidiary" and "holding company" in r.17 of the 2008 Rules have the same meaning as in the Companies Act 2006, see r.17(9) of the 2008 Rules.

[118] See r.17(4) of the 2008 Rules which states: "Where a person makes a request for an extension of time under paragraph (3). Form TM7A shall be filed electronically using the filing system provided on the office website or by such other means as the registrar may permit".

[119] See Sch.1 and rr.77(5) and 77(1) of the 2008 Rules.

[120] r.17(8) of the 2008 Rules.

[121] r.17(5) of the 2008 Rules. In Practice the TM7 form contains a specific section of questions concerning the statement of use.

*Replace footnote 126:*

7-081 [126] r.18(7) of the 2008 Rules. It should be noted that the 2008 Rules define the person opposing the registration as the "opposer", see r.20(2) rather than the "opponent". Both terms will be used within this work.

*Replace paragraph:*

7-086 If the preliminary indication is a partial success for the opposition and no Form TM53 is filed by either party, if a straightforward deletion of goods and/or services can overcome the objection, then those goods and/or services will be removed and the application allowed to proceed to registration in this amended form.[140] However, if a TM53 has not been filed by either party and if the objection to registration cannot be resolved by a straightforward deletion of goods and/or services, then the applicant has a further period of one month (after the initial one-month period from the indication date within which a Form TM53 should have been filed) to file a TM21 Form to request that the application's specification be restricted to those goods and services for which it appears that the mark could be registered.[141] Failure to file Form TM21 within the time period specified will result in the application being refused for the entirety of the goods and/or services opposed.[142]

[140] See *Sensornet Trade Mark Application* [2007] R.P.C. 10 (Appointed Person) at [50]–[59]. See further TPN 1/2012 which summarises the guidance provided in the cases of *Sensornet Trade Mark Application* [2007] R.P.C. (Appointed Person) and *Giorgio Armani SpA v Sunrich Clothing* [2011] R.P.C. 15 on this issue. TPN 1/2012 states that amendments to the list of goods/services made by the applicant (via the TM21B Form) after publication will continue to be published and the amendment open to opposition for a period of one month as required by r.25 of the 2008 Rules. However, deletion of particular descriptions of goods/services, whether by "blue pencilling" or through the addition of "save for [the unregistrable goods or services]-type qualifications, will not be regarded as an amendments under s.39 of the Trade Mark Act 1994 and do not require filing of a TM21B form and therefore will not be subjected to the further one month opposition period required under r.25 of the 2008 Rules.

[141] See the *Manual of Trade Marks Practice*, Tribunal Section, section 3.1.9 and see *Sensornet Trade Mark Application* [2007] R.P.C. 10 (Appointed Person) at [50]–[59].

[142] See the *Manual of Trade Marks Practice*, Tribunal Section, section 3.1.9.

*After "Practice Notice 2/2010.", add new footnote 149a:*

7-089 [149a] See also the *Manual of Trade Marks Practice*, Tribunal Section, section 4.8.2.1.

*At the end of the first sentence, add new footnote 153a:*

7-091 [153a] See also the *Manual of Trade Marks Practice*, Tribunal Section, section 4.8.

## Who May Oppose

*Replace paragraph:*

Any person may oppose a trade mark application.[155] However the Registrar shall not refuse to register a trade mark on a ground mentioned in s.5 of the Act (relative grounds for refusal) unless objection on that ground is raised in opposition proceedings by the proprietor of the earlier trade mark or other earlier right.[156] Further, where a notice of opposition is filed on the basis of one or more earlier trade marks or other earlier rights: (a) the rights (if plural) must all belong to the same proprietor, and (b) the notice may be filed on the basis of part, or the totality, of the goods or services in respect of which the earlier right is protected or applied for.[156a] If the opposition or part of it is based on the relative grounds for refusal set out in ss.5(1), (2) or (3) a licensee of the earlier mark on which the opposition is based, or an authorised user of the earlier mark where the opposition is based on an earlier collective or certification mark, may file an application to the Registrar on Form TM27 for leave to intervene. After hearing the parties concerned, if so required, the Registrar may refuse leave or grant leave to intervene upon such terms and conditions (including any undertaking as to costs) as the Registrar thinks fit.[157] Any person granted leave to intervene, subject to any terms and conditions imposed in respect of the intervention, shall be treated as a party to the proceedings for the purposes for the applications of the provisions of rr.19 (Preliminary Indication), 20 (evidence rounds) and 62–73 (Proceedings Before and Decision of Registrar, Evidence and Costs).[158] 7-093

[155] Trade Marks Act 1994 s.38(2).

[156] See Trade Mark (Relative Grounds) Order 2007 (SI 2007/1976) art.2.

[156a] Trade Marks Act 1994 s.38(2A).

[157] rr.21(1) and (3) of the 2008 Rules.

[158] r.21(2) of the 2008 Rules.

## Grounds of Opposition

*Replace list:*

(1) The sign the subject of the application is not a trade mark within the meaning of the 1994 Act because it is not capable of being represented in the register in a manner which enables the registrar and other competent authorities and the public to determine the clear and precise subject matter of the protection afforded to the proprietor[159] or because it is not capable of distinguishing. 7-094

(2) The mark is devoid of any distinctive character such that registration would be contrary to s.3(1)(b).

(3) The mark consists exclusively of descriptive matter prohibited by s.3(1)(c) or (d).

(4) The mark consists exclusively of a shape or another characteristic as prohibited by s.3(2).

(5) The mark is of such a nature as to deceive the public (for example as to nature, quality, or geographical origin of the goods or service) or is contrary to public policy or to accepted principles of morality.

(6) Use of the mark is prohibited in the UK by an enactment or rule of law or by a provision of EU law[159a] other than the law relating to trade marks.

(6A) If the registration is prohibited by or under any enactment of rule of law, any provisions of EU law or any international agreement to which the UK or EU is party[159b] providing for: (a) the protection of designation of origin or geographical indications; or (b) the protection of traditional terms for wine or traditional specialities guaranteed.

(6B) If the registration consists of, or reproduces in its essential elements, an earlier plant variety denomination registered as mention in s.3(4D)[159c] and in respect of plant varieties of the same or closely related species.

(7) The application was made in bad faith (ss.3(6)).

(8) The mark conflicts with an earlier trade mark and registration would be contrary to s.5(1)–(3).

(9) Use of the mark is liable to be prevented by virtue of a rule of law, such as passing off, or by the proprietor of another earlier right such as copyright, design right or a registered design (see ss.5(4), 5(4A) and 5(4B)).[159d]

(10) Registration would be contrary to the provisions of ss.56–59 (relating to the Paris Convention) or s.5(6) which states that where an agent or representative ("R") of the proprietor of a trade mark applies, without the proprietor's consent, for the registration of the trade marks in R's own name, the application is to be refused unless R justifies that action (also relating to the Paris Convention).

(11) The mark consists of a specially protected emblem (ss.3(5) and 4).

[159] Regarding national trade marks, now that the 2015 TM Directive (Directive (EU) 2015/2436) has been implemented and s.1(1) of the 1994 Act has been amended as of 14 January 2019, a graphical representation is no longer required, rather s.1(1) states that: In this Act "trade mark" means any sign which is capable of being represented in the register in a manner which enables the registrar and other competent authorities and the public to determine the clear and precise subject matter of the protection afforded to the proprietor (as derived from art.3(b) of the 2015 TM Directive). See further Ch.10.

[159a] s.3(4) of the 1994 Act is due to be amended on the IP completion day (23.00 on 31 December 2020) so as to remove reference to EU law.

[159b] subs.3(4A) and (4B) of the 1994 Act are due to be amended on the IP completion day (23.00 on 31 December 2020) so as to remove reference to EU law or any international agreement to which the EU is a party.

[159c] subs.3(4D) of the 1994 Act is due to be amended on the IP completion day (23.00 on 31 December 2020) so as to remove reference to EU law or any international agreement to which the EU is a party.

[159d] s.5(4) of the 1994 Act is due to be amended on the IP completion day (23.00 on 31 December 2020) so as to remove reference to EU law.

## Statement of Grounds of Opposition and Counter-statement: Content and Presentation

*Replace footnote 165:*

7-098 [165] TPN 4/2000 sets out the Registry's practice concerning form and content of statements of case and counter statements in oppositions, revocation and invalidity proceedings. Paragraphs 4 and 5 of TPN 4/2000 explains that the Registry will carry out a preliminary examination of statements of case and counter statements and that the Registry may request that a party amends these documents if it believes they have not been adequately particularised. See also "*Wild Child*" [1998] R.P.C. 455 (Appointed Person) at 459. In the event that the party chooses not to amend their statement of case then the Registrar may move to strike out any ground which in the Registrar's view is adequately particularised. TPN 4/2000 is framed in terms of the 2000 Rules, rather than the 2008 Rules. However, the 2008 Rules provide the Registry the same relevant procedural powers to require information (r.62(1)(a) of the 2008 Rules is in the almost identical terms as r.57 of the 2000 Rules) and therefore it appears that the same effective practice should apply with regards Statements of Case and Counter Statements. The Registry has issued a practice direction concerning pleadings in opposition and invalidation proceedings relying on s.5(4)(b) of the Trade Marks Act 1994 in relation to copyright, design right and registered designs and what these specific pleadings should contain, see TPN 1/2010. See also *Manual of Trade Marks Practice*, Tribunal section, section 4.12 on pleadings generally.

*Replace footnote 166:*

[166] TPN 1/2000 paras 20–25, TPN 4/2000 paras 9–21 and see *Manual of Trade Marks Practice*, Tribunal section, section 4.12. **7-099**

*Add new paragraph after para.7-099:*

The Registry has issued TPN 1/2018 providing specific guidance concerning pleadings based on earlier marks. TPN 1/2018 makes clear, amongst other things, that from 1 January 2019, where pleadings in trade mark opposition/invalidation proceedings under s.5(1)–(3) of the Act are not sufficiently clear, the registrar's casework examiners may require further information, particularly if: (i) the number of earlier marks exceeds six, and/or (ii) it is not obvious why goods/services covered by an earlier mark are claimed to be identical or similar to the opposed goods/services. For example, where more that six earlier marks are relied upon, where there is no apparent and justifiable reasons for doing so, and the number of earlier marks therefore appears unnecessary and disproportionate, the registrar may direct that the party filing the form TM7/26(I) nominates its "best case" earlier marks for consideration. Guidance is also provided when the similarity of goods/services are not obvious or explained, such as requiring the provision of further information. TPN 1/2018 provides various possible consequences that may arise if the registry directions concerning these issues are not followed (see para.11), for example there may be cost consequences or where there is a serious risk of unfairness to, or oppression of the other party, directions will be made subject to the condition (per r.62(3)) that failure to comply with them will result in the opposition/application being struck out in whole or in part. **7-099A**

## Amending Grounds of Opposition

*Replace footnote 171:*

[171] *Pharmedica's Application* [2000] R.P.C. 536; cf. *Kirkbi AG's Applications* [1999] R.P.C. 733. See also the Trade Mark Registry, *Manual of Trade Marks Practice*, Tribunal section, section 4.17, substitution of parties, and see *Asia Five Eight LLC's Application* (O-004-11) decision date 4 January 2011 (Appointed Person). **7-102**

## Disclosure

*Replace footnote 175:*

[175] TPN 1/2000. See also *Manual of Trade Marks Practice*, Tribunal section, section 4.7 on disclosure. **7-104**

## Evidence

### General

*Replace footnote 182:*

[182] *Joe Cool (Manchester) Ltd's Application* [2000] R.P.C. 926. See r.62 of the 2008 Rules. See also *Manual of Trade Marks Practice*, Tribunal section, section 4.8.11 on the withdrawal of evidence, which states that a party may apply to withdraw evidence already filed and that any such request will be considered in light of comments from the other party. **7-105**

### Challenging evidence and cross-examination

*Add new sentence to end of paragraph:*

See also *Manual of Trade Mark Practice*, Tribunal Section, section 6.8.3 on cross examination. **7-113**

### Registrar may require evidence

*Replace footnote 205:*

7-115 [205] r.62(1)(a) of the 2008 Rules. In the *Manual of Trade Marks Practice*, Tribunal section, section 4.8, it is stated that the general rule is for the parties to decide on the evidence that they file. However, in practice Hearing Officers are making requests for information. For example, see *Asia Five Eight LLC's Application* (O-004-11) decision date 4 January 2011 (Appointed Person) at [29]. See also para.7-091 which deals with TPN 1/2015. This Practice Notice introduces restrictions on the volume of evidence that may be filed in opposition and cancellation proceedings before the IPO, without seeking permission from the Registrar's hearing officer.

### Hearsay evidence

*Replace footnote 208:*

7-116 [208] See *Manual of Trade Marks Practice*, Tribunal section, section 4.8.10 on hearsay evidence.

*Replace footnote 211:*

7-117 [211] In Tribunal Practice Notice 5/2009 the Registry has given further guidance as to its assessment of hearsay "to whom it may concern" letters. See also *Manual of Trade Marks Practice*, Tribunal section, section 4.8.10 on hearsay evidence.

### Survey and expert evidence

*Replace footnote 212:*

7-118 [212] See TPN 2/2012. This Practice Notice pre-dates the guidance given by the Court of Appeal in *Marks & Spencer v Interflora* [2013] E.T.M.R. 11 on the admissibility of survey evidence and may need to be updated to bring it into line with the principles set out by Lewison LJ. See also *Manual of Trade Marks Practice*, Tribunal section, section 4.8.4.5 on survey evidence. The importance of the case management powers in the Trade Marks Registry concerning survey evidence were emphasised by Arnold LJ in the High Court case of *Glaxo Wellcome UK Ltd v Sandoz Ltd* [2019] EWHC 2545 (Ch) at [207].

### Importance of quality of evidence

*Replace footnote 213:*

7-119 [213] "*Wild Child*" [1998] R.P.C. 455 at 465. The same ought to be the case for any objection which the Registrar cannot assess for themselves, such as an objection under s.5(3) which is supported by a contention that the earlier trade mark is particularly distinctive through use or an objection under s.5(6). See also under "Onus", at para.7-127.

### Evidence not in proper form

*Replace footnote 215:*

7-120 [215] Manual of Trade Mark Practice, Tribunal section, section 4.8.6.

## Case Management and Pre-hearing Reviews and Procedural Hearings

*Replace paragraph:*

7-121 The Registrar may at any stage of any proceedings direct that the parties to the proceedings attend a case management conference, pre-hearing review or procedural hearing.[216] The purpose of this provision is to allow the Registrar to take a more pro-active role in the conduct of the hearing and to consider such matters as the need to clarify the issues, the degree of complexity of the matter, any related actions between the parties, and any wider public interest issues.[217] The general position with regards notice of hearings is that the parties should be given 14 days notice from the date on which the notice of hearing is sent, unless the parties consent to shorter notice.[218]

[216] r.62 of the 2008 Rules. See also TPN 2/2011 concerning case management of inter partes proceed-

ings and paras 4–6 which deal specifically with case management conferences. It is stated in this TPN that case management conferences will normally take place by telephone conference (see para.6). See also *Manual of Trade Marks Practice*, Tribunal section, section 6.6 (including sections 6.6.1–6.6.3) on case management conferences and section 6.7 (including sections 6.7.1–6.7.3) on Procedural Hearings.

217 See TPN 2/2011 concerning case management of inter partes proceedings and paras 4–6 which deal specifically with case management conferences. See also *Manual of Trade Marks Practice*, Tribunal section, section 6.6 on case management conferences and section 6.7 (including sections 6.7.1–6.7.3) on Procedural Hearings.

218 r.63 of the 2008 Rules. See also para.6 of TPN 2/2011. See also TPN 1/2016 on certain points of procedure concerning case management conferences.

## Stay of Proceedings

*Replace footnote 221:*

221 For a detailed statement of the Registry's approach on this issue see TPN 1/2009, TPN 2/2011 para.7 and *Manual of Trade Marks Practice*, Tribunal section, section 4.9.2 on Stay of Proceedings. **7-124**

## The Opposition Hearing

### Presentation

*Replace footnote 221:*

227 TPN 1/2000. Note that all hearings concerning an extension of time request will now be dealt with by video conference or in the alternative by telephone conference or by attendance in Newport, see Law Practice Direction, "Interlocutory Hearings: Extension of time requests". See also TPN 2/2011 para.6 which states that case management conferences will normally take place by telephone conference. See also Manual of Trade Marks Practice, Tribunal section, sections 6.6.1 and 6.7.1 which state that case management conferences and procedural hearings will normally take place via telephone conference. **7-126**

### Presentation of new evidence at the hearing

*Replace paragraph:*

The practice of introducing new evidence at or shortly before hearings is to be discouraged and such evidence will only rarely be allowed. See *Property Renaissance Ltd (T/A Titanic Spa) v Stanley Dock Hotel Ltd (T/A Titanic Hotel)*[230] considered at para.7-145 for the relevant factors to be considered when a party applies to file late additional evidence. Documents may, however, be introduced in cross examination where designed to test the honesty or reliability of a witness.[231] **7-129**

230 [2017] E.T.M.R. 12; [2017] R.P.C. 12.

231 TPN 1/2000 para.46 and see *Manual of Trade Marks Practice*, Tribunal section, section 6.8.3 on cross-examination.

## Costs

### General

*Replace paragraph:*

Under s.68 of the 1994 Act and r.67 of the 2008 Rules the Registrar may, in any proceedings under the Act or the 2008 Rules, by order award to any party such costs as the Registrar may consider reasonable, and direct how and by what parties they are to be paid. In a contested opposition costs usually follow the event. With regards interlocutory or preliminary hearings the Hearing Officer dealing with the proceedings will consider dealing with costs as the cause of them arises, either specifically making no award if the issues were fairly well balanced or making an award to the successful party.[235] By tradition costs were awarded in accordance with **7-133** published scales which were not intended to cover all expenses actually incurred. However, the Registry has the ability to award costs off the scale, approaching full compensation, to deal proportionately with wider breaches of rules, delaying tactics or other unreasonable behaviour. The overriding factor, when deciding whether to depart from the published scale is that the Hearing Officer should act judicially in all the facts of a case.[236] Costs will not be awarded against rights owners or applicants when an opposition, revocation or invalidity action has been brought without prior notice and the action was undefended and the application or rights were immediately withdrawn or surrendered.[237] If one of the parties in dispute before the Registrar has a conditional fee arrangement with their legal representative, any success fee will not be taken into account when assessing costs whether the award is based on the normal scale or on off scale costs.[238] Note that a specific cost cap applies in fast track oppositions which are dealt with at paras 7-147 to 7-150.[239]

[235] TPN 4/2007 para.10. TPN 4/2007 updates and supplements TPN 2/2000. TPN 4/2007 provides the scale of costs which is applicable in proceedings commenced on or after 3 December 2007 until 30 June 2016. TPN 2/2016 updates and supplements TPN 2/2000 and TPN 4/2007 and provides the scale of costs which applies to proceedings commenced on or after 1 July 2016. With regards to an award of costs in favour of a litigant in person, guidance was provided by the Appointed Person in South *Beck Trade Mark Application* (O-160-08), see [30]–[38] of the decision, and see *Manual of Trade Marks Practice*, Tribunal section, section 5.6.2 on costs awards made in favour of unrepresented parties.

[236] TPN 4/2007 paras 5–7, and see *Manual of Trade Marks Practice*, Tribunal section, section 5.6.

[237] TPN 4/2007 para.9. See also TPN 6/2008 which explains that where both a notice of threatened opposition (Form TM7a) and a subsequent notice of opposition (Form TM7) are filed and the opposition is undefended, an award of costs will usually be made against the applicant. See also Manual of *Trade Marks Practice*, Tribunal section, section 5.8.

[238] TPN 4/2007 paras 11–12.

[239] See TPN 2/2015 on the fast track opposition cost cap. The costs cap is £500, excluding official fees.

### Security for costs

*Replace footnote 242:*

7-134 [242] TPN 2/2000. See also Law Practice Direction, "Security for costs under r.61 of the Trade Mark Rules 2000" and *Manual of Trade Marks Practice*, Tribunal section, section 5.7 on security for costs.

## Alteration of Time Limits by the Registrar

*After "r.41(6) (counter-statement for invalidity)," add new footnote 246a:*

7-138 [246a] For an Appointed Person decision upholding the Registry's decision refusing to extend the time limit under r.41(6) see *Chevron Card Ltd Trade Mark Registration* (No. 2650833) 24 June 2019, (O-385/19).

*Replace paragraph:*

7-142 It should be noted that under the old Rules it was specified that where the Registrar did have power to grant an extension, then the party seeking an extension should apply for the extension before the time limit has expired. If the request was not made until after the time had expired, then the Registrar could nevertheless grant an extension only if they were satisfied with the explanation for the delay in requesting the extension and it appeared to them just and equitable so to do.[252] The 2008 Rules do not contain these same provisions and therefore the Registrar's general discretion to extend time limits as provided by r.77(1) is unfettered whether or not the application for an extension is made before or after the period in question expired. However, it seems likely that where a request for an extension of time is made after the period in question has expired, the Registrar may still wish to understand why the request was made after the period had expired, as this is one of the potentially relevant factors to be taken into account when making the determination as to whether the extension requested should be granted at all.[252a] Further, it should be noted that TPN 2/2010 concerning the time periods for the submission of evidence and submissions in trade mark proceedings states that requests for the extension of the time period in which to file evidence or written submissions should be brought to the Registrar's attention as soon as possible and made by filing Form TM9, and that the form must be accompanied by full and detailed reasons.[253]

[252] See r.68(4) and (5) of the 2000 Rules.

[252a] Note that in *Permanent Secretary, Ministry of Energy, Commerce and Tourism, Republic of Cyprus v John & Pascalis Ltd* [2018] EWHC 3226 (Ch) concerning an Appeal of a decision of the Registry refusing an extension of time it was held by Mr Justice Arnold as he then was at [29] that: "it is implicit in rule 77 that the Registrar only has the power to extend time in proceedings which are still extant in the sense that no final decision has yet been taken. Once a final decision has been taken, the Registrar is functus and the only remedy open to a party adversely affected by that decision (other than an application under rule 43) is to appeal pursuant to rule 70(1)."

[253] TPN 2/2010 para.22. See also TPN 2/2011 paras 2 and 3 concerning time periods for filing evidence and submissions. See also *Manual of Trade Marks Practice*, Tribunal section, section 4.9.1 on extensions of time.

*Replace footnote 258:*

[258] See [29]–[33] of the decision [2017] ETMR 12 where the court considered *Lappet Manufacturing Co Ltd v Yosif Abdulrahman Al-Bassam Trading Establishment* (O/467/02) and the *Manual of Trade Marks Practice*, Tribunal section, section 4.8.5. **7-145**

## 5. Appeal From the Registrar

### The Tribunal of Appeal

*Replace footnote 270 with:*

[270] The meaning of "decision" in the context of s.76(1) was considered in *Pavel Maslyukov v Diageo Distilling Ltd* [2010] R.P.C. 21; [2010] E.T.M.R. 37. Arnold J, in this appeal from a decision of the Registrar in the High Court, held that, in the context of opposition proceedings the meaning of "decision" for the purposes of s.76(1) is the Hearing Officer's decision to uphold or reject the opposition, not his conclusion with regard the individual grounds or opposition (see the judgment at [52]–[57]). See also *Consolidated Developments Ltd v Cooper* [2018] EWHC 1727 (Ch); [2019] F.S.R. 2, which considered the findings on the meaning of a "decision" in the context of s.76(1) in the *Pavel Maslyukov* case and applied them at [16] and [17]. **7-151**

### The Nature of the Appeal

*Replace paragraph:*

What constituted an error of principle was further explained by Lindsay J in *esure Insurance Ltd v Direct Line Insurance Plc*[280]: **7-155**

> "An error of principle such as to justify or require departure from the decision below … includes the taking into account of that which should not have been, the omission from the account of that which should have been within it and the case (explicable only as one in which there must have been an error of principle) where it is plain that no tribunal properly instructing itself could, in the circumstances, have reasonably arrived at the conclusion that it reached."

In *"Talk for Learning" Trade Mark Application*,[280a] a decision of Daniel Alexander QC, sitting as the Appointed Person, the Appellate function of the Appointed Person and the relevant case law was considered in detail at [14]–[52]. In particular at [23] it was held "Put simply, there has to be sufficient clarity that there has been error (rather than mere difference in evaluation) not that the error itself has to be a particularly clear one." See also *Consolidated Developments Ltd v Cooper*,[280b] where Henry Carr J hearing a trade mark Appeal from the IPO held: " It should be borne in mind that Appeals from the IPO are not to be regarded as opportunities to run the same arguments for a second time, in the hope of obtaining a better result. Generally, a distinct and material error of law or principle must be identified. No such error was identified in the present case."[280c]

[280] [2008] R.P.C. 6 at [12]. What amounts to an error of principle was further considered in *Digipos Store Solutions Group Ltd v Digi International Inc* [2008] R.P.C. 24 (appeal from the Registrar's decision to the High Court).

[280a] BL O-017-17, [2017] R.P.C. 17.

[280b] [2018] EWHC 1727 (Ch), [2019] F.S.R. 2.

[280c] Also of relevance is *Actavis Group PTC EHF v ICOS Corp* [2019] UKSC 15 at [78]–[81].

## Evidence on Appeal

*Replace paragraph:*

**7-167** On appeal before the court or the Appointed Person new evidence may be admitted only with leave.[307] The onus is on the party applying for leave to admit the evidence to justify the exercise of discretion in their favour. However, there are no express limits placed upon the discretion or criteria set for its exercise, save that the discretion should be exercised in accordance with the overriding objective and the concept of proportionality.[308] Relevant factors (as listed in *Hunt Wesson ("Swiss Miss")*) are likely to include the following[309]:

(1) Whether the evidence could have been filed earlier and, if so, how much earlier.
(2) If it could have been, what explanation for the late filing has been offered to explain the delay.
(3) The nature of the mark.
(4) The nature of the objections to it.
(5) The potential significance of the new evidence.
(6) Whether the other side will be significantly prejudiced by the admission of the evidence in a way which cannot be compensated, for example by an order for costs.
(7) The desirability of avoiding multiplicity of proceedings.
(8) The public interest in not admitting invalkid marks onto the Register.

[307] CPR 52.21, previously RSC Ord.55 r.7(2).

[308] *Du Pont Trade mark* [2004] F.S.R. 15 CA and the judgment of Hale LJ in *Hertfordshire Investments Ltd v Bubb* [2000] 1 W.L.R. 2318 at 2325D–H. See also *Club Europe* [2000] R.P.C. 329; *Julian Higgins' Application* [2000] R.P.C. 321, both decisions of the Vice-Chancellor; *Hunt Wesson ("Swiss Miss")* [1996] R.P.C. 233. In his judgment in *Swiss Miss* Laddie J reviews the earlier authorities; *Dualit v Rowlett Catering Appliances* [1999] F.S.R. 865. For recent applications of the case law concerning an application to adduce further evidence on appeal see *Vibe Technologies Ltd's Application No.2390030* [2009] ETMR 12 (Appointed Person). Richard Arnold QC sitting as the Appointed Person held that in the case of an ordinary appeal from an ex parte decision of the Registrar, the principles governing whether permission should be given to adduce further evidence were the same as those regarding an inter partes decision. See also *Omega Engineering Inc v Omega SA* [2010] F.S.R. 26 Ch D. at [97]–[102] and *Toppy Trademarks Ltd*'s Application No. 2379969 (O-092-11) (Appointed Person) at [19]–[32]. For a recent example of a case where fresh evidence was admitted on Appeal, see *Gerry Weber International AG v Guccio Gucci SPA* [2015] R.P.C. 9 at [12]–[37], (decision of the Appointed Person). See also *Property Renaissance Ltd (T/A Titanic Spa) v Stanley Dock Hotel Ltd (T/A Titanic Hotel)* [2016] EWHC 3103 (Ch) at [43] and [44], where the court commented that the test for admissibilty of late evidence on appeal is more difficult to satisfy than the test of admissibility of late evidence in the first instance proceedings.

[309] per Laddie J, in *("Swiss Miss")* [1996] R.P.C. 233 at 241–242; although these matters will, in most

cases, be the important ones, the Vice-Chancellor has cautioned against any attempt to confine the statutory discretion within a straightjacket: *Club Europe* [2000] R.P.C. 329 at 338. See also "*Wunderkind*" [2002] R.P.C. 45 and "*Mezzacorona*" [2004] R.P.C. 25. See also *Gerry Weber International AG v Guccio Gucci SPA* [2015] R.P.C. 9 at [26] and following (decision of the Appointed Person).

*Add new paragraph after para.7-167:*

The cases concerning the admission of fresh evidence on Appeal were considered by the High Court in *Consolidated Development Ltd v Cooper*,[309a] a trade mark Appeal referred to the High Court by the Appointed Person. After considering the relevant cases, Henry Carr J summarised the principles those cases established in respect of the admissibility of fresh evidence in trade mark appeals, sought to be introduced for the first time on appeal, as follows[309b]: **7-167A**

"(i) the same principles apply in trade mark appeals as in any other appeal under CPR part 52 . However, given the nature of such appeals, additional factors may be relevant;

(ii) the *Ladd v Marshall*[309c] factors are basic to the exercise of the discretion, which are to be applied in the light of the overriding objective;

(iii) it is useful to have regard to the *Hunt-Wesson* factors;

(iv) relevant factors will vary, depending on the circumstances of each case. Neither the *Ladd v Marshall* factors nor the *Hunt-Wesson* factors are to be regarded as a straightjacket;

(v) the admission of fresh evidence on appeal is the exception and not the rule;

(vi) the *Gucci*[309d] decision does not establish that the court or the Appointed Person should exercise a broad remedial discretion to admit fresh evidence on appeal so as to enable the appellant to re-open proceedings in the Registry; and

(vii) where the admission of fresh evidence on appeal would require that the case be remitted for a rehearing at first instance, the interests of the parties and of the public in fostering finality in litigation are particularly significant and may tip the balance against the admission of such evidence."

309a [2018] EWHC 1727 (Ch); [2019] F.S.R. 2.

309b At [33], *Consolidated Development Ltd v Cooper* [2018] EWHC 1727 (Ch); [2019] F.S.R. 2.

309c [1954] 1 W.L.R. 1489 at 1491 Denning LJ set out a three-part test for admission of fresh evidence on appeal. In particular: "(i) it must be shown that the evidence could not have been obtained with reasonable diligence for use at the trial; (ii) the evidence must be such that, if given, it would probably have an important influence on the result of the case, though it need not be decisive; and (iii) the evidence must be such as is presumably to be believed, or in other words, it must be apparently credible, though it need not be incontrovertible."

309d At *Gerry Weber International AG v Guccio Gucci SPA* [2015] R.P.C. 9.

## Modification of the Application on Appeal

*Replace footnote 310:*

310 Practical difficulties are also presented in that where the amendment requested by an applicant pursuant to s.39 affects the representation of the trade mark or the goods or services the subject of the application, the Registrar is required by r.25 of the 2008 Rules to publish the amendment for opposition purposes. On the other hand, where an application is amended under s.13, the Registrar is required by r.31 to publish the amendment, but it is not then open to opposition. Note that deletion of particular descriptions of goods/services, whether by "blue pencilling" or through the addition of "save for [the unregistrable goods or services]"-type qualifications, will not be regarded as an amendments under s.39 of the Trade Mark Act 1994 and therefore do require the filing of a TM21B Form by the applicant and will not be subjected to the further one month opposition period required under r.25 of the 2008 Rules (see TPN 1/2011). Amendments which go beyond that will be subject to the further one month opposition period, and will need to be made by application via a TM 21B Form (as the onus under s.39 of the Trade Marks Act 1994 lies on the applicant). See also *Manual of Trade Marks Practice*, Tribunal section, section 4.14 on publication of amendments. It would be wise for the applicant to put forward any **7-168**

proposals regarding amendment of the specification at an early stage to avoid adverse costs consequences.

7-172 *Replace footnote 319:*

## 6. Judicial Status of Opposition Proceedings

319 For consideration of the issues of estoppel and abuse of process in the context of successive attacks on a registered trade mark see *Hormel Foods Corp v Antilles Landscape Investments NV* [2005] R.P.C. 28 Ch D. and *Evans v Focal Point Fires Plc* [2010] R.P.C. 15 Ch D. For an authoritative and more recent decision concerning res judicata more generally, see *Virgin Atlantic Airways Ltd v Zodiac Seats UK Ltd* [2013] UKSC 46, a decision of the Supreme Court, a case concerning patents. See further Ch.12.

CHAPTER 8

# EU TRADE MARKS

TABLE OF CONTENTS



## 1. THE RELEVANT LEGISLATION

*Replace paragraph:*

Detailed rules governing proceedings in the EUIPO were laid down in Commission Regulation 2868/95 ("the former Implementing Regulation"),[12] which was amended several times. Further procedural rules governing appeals to the EUIPO Boards of Appeal were contained in Commission Regulation 216/96 ("the Appeals Regulation"),[13] as amended by Commission Regulation 2082/ 2004.[14] The fees payable in respect of proceedings before the EUIPO were originally set out in Com- **8-004** mission Regulation 2869/95 ("the Fees Regulation").[15] The former Implementing Regulation was repealed in 2017, as were the Appeals Regulation and the Fees Regulation. Detailed rules governing proceedings in the EUIPO are now to be found in two separate Commission regulations, namely:

- Commission Implementing Regulation 2018/626 of 5 March 2018 laying down detailed rules for implementing certain provisions of Regulation 2017/1001 on the EU trade mark ("the EUTM Implementing Regulation"); and
- Commission Delegated Regulation 2018/625 of 5 March 2018 supplementing Regulation 2017/1001 on the EU trade mark ("the EUTM Delegated Regulation").

Those two regulations replaced Regulations 2017/1431 and 2017/1430, which had briefly replaced the former Implementing Regulation. The content of Regulations 2018/626 and 2018/625 is identical to that of Regulations 2017/1431 and 2017/1430 (apart from the "final provisions" dealing with transitional measures, entry into force and such like).

[12] [1995] OJ L303, p.1.

[13] [1996] OJ L28, p.11.

[14] [2004] OJ L360, p.8.

[15] [1995] OJ L303, p.33.

*Add new paragraphs:*

**8-004A** The fees payable in respect of proceedings before the EUIPO are now set out in Annex 1 to the EUTM Regulation.[16a]

**8-004B** Consolidated versions of the main legislative texts are published on the EUIPO website.[16b]

[16a] Many of the detailed rules that were previously laid down in the former Implementing Regulation are now provided for in the EUTM Regulation.

[16b] *http://www.euipo.europa.eu* [Accessed 30 August 2017].

## 2. The Basic Provisions Governing the Registration of EU Trade Marks

*Replace paragraph:*

**8-009** Bad faith may, on the other hand, be relied on as the basis for a declaration of invalidity of a registered EUTM on application to the EUIPO or by way of a counterclaim in infringement proceedings.[22] The EUIPO does not, however, interpret bad faith as including the practice of registering a trade mark for goods or services in relation to which there is no intention of use. That practice may have to be revised in the light of the ruling of the CJEU in the *SkyKick* case.[22a]

[22] art.59(1)(b). However, bad faith is not a ground of opposition in the EUTM system.

[22a] *Sky Plc, Sky International AG and Sky UK Ltd v SkyKick UK Ltd and SkyKick Inc* (C-371/18) EU:C:2020:45 at [81].

## 8. Time Limits

### The Consequences of Non-compliance with Time Limits

*Add new paragraphs:*

**8-044A** The EUIPO challenged the *FISHBONE* judgment of the General Court in the CJEU, which criticised the General Court for having held that the Regulation contained no provision fixing a time limit for the submission of evidence in relation to an application for a declaration of invalidity based on an absolute ground for refusal. Despite that error of law, the CJEU did not annul the judgment of the General Court since its operative part had been shown to be well founded for other legal reasons. The CJEU observed that the General Court had based the annulment of the Board of Appeal's decision not on the fact that there was no time limit for the submission of evidence, but on the fact that the Board of Appeal had erred in deciding that the evidence produced by the cancellation applicant for the first time before the Board of Appeal did not have to be taken into consideration because of its late submission.[112a] The CJEU went on to enunciate the principle that it is always possible to submit evidence for the first time before the Board of Appeal in order to challenge the reasons given by the Cancellation Division in the contested decision. That evidence may be either evidence supplementary to that submitted in the proceedings before the Cancellation Division or evidence on a new matter which could not be raised during those proceedings. However, the court insisted that the onus is on the party presenting the evidence for the first time before the Board of Appeal to justify why that evidence is being submitted at that stage of the proceedings, and to demonstrate that submission during the proceedings before the Cancellation Division was impossible.

Logically, the judgment of the General Court should have been annulled since it had clearly implied that the Board of Appeal had no power to refuse to admit the supplementary evidence submitted on appeal. The CJEU's failure to annul that judgment led to further problems when the case was subsequently remitted to a differently constituted Board of Appeal. The Board, evidently focusing on the confirmation of the General Court's judgment rather than on the CJEU's reasoning, proceeded on the assumption that it was compelled to admit the supplementary evidence submitted by the cancellation applicant on appeal. In the light of that evidence it had no difficulty concluding that the FITNESS trade mark was descriptive and should be declared invalid. The proprietor of the mark appealed to the General Court, which set aside the Board's decision on the ground that the Board had erred in law by treating the supplementary evidence as automatically admissible. Instead, the Board should have considered whether the cancellation applicant had justified the late submission of the evidence and demonstrated that submission of the evidence during the proceedings before the Cancellation Division was impossible. Accordingly, it was for the Board of Appeal to assess the merits of the reasons put forward by the cancellation applicant in order to exercise its discretion as to whether or not the evidence should be taken into account.[112b] **8-044B**

[112a] *EUIPO v European Food SA* (C-634/16 P) EU:C:2018:30 at [33]–[34].

[112b] *Société des produits Nestlé SA v EUIPO and European Food SA* EU:T:2019:737 (T-536/18) EU:T:2019:737 at [44]. A further appeal to the CJEU, lodged by European Food SA, was not allowed to proceed, pursuant to art.58a of the Statute of the CJEU: *European Food SA v Société des produits Nestlé SA and EUIPO* EU:C:2020:212 (C-908/19 P) EU:C:2020:212.

## 10. DECISIONS

*Add new paragraph:*

The duty to state reasons also applies when a party invokes the EUIPO's previous decision-making practice as a precedent. In *EUIPO v Puma SE* the opponent relied on the reputation of its earlier trade mark. It cited three previous decisions in which the EUIPO had recognised that the mark enjoyed a reputation and was well known to the relevant public. Instead of taking due account of those earlier decisions, the Board of Appeal had merely observed that the EUIPO was not bound by its previous decision-making practice. The General Court cited the well-established **8-067A** case law according to which the EUIPO must, when examining an application for registration of an EU trade mark, take into account the decisions already taken in respect of similar applications and consider with especial care whether it should decide in the same way. The Board of Appeal could not depart from the EUIPO's previous decision-making practice without providing an explanation of the reasons that had led it to consider that the findings of fact about the reputation of the trade mark were no longer relevant.[151a] The CJEU confirmed that the Board of Appeal must state explicit reasons for its decision if it adopts an approach diverging from that taken in previous decisions cited by a party to the proceedings.[151b]

[151a] *Puma SE v EUIPO and Gemma Group Srl* (T-159/15) EU:T:2016:457 at [34].

[151b] *EUIPO v Puma SE* (C-564/16 P) EU:C:2018:509 at [96].

*Add new paragraph:*

**8-071A** The General Court considers that the EUIPO's power to raise points of law of its own motion, by virtue of the principle *iura novit curia*, relates only to the application of EU law. National law, on the other hand, "is an issue of fact, where facts must be adduced and the requirements of the burden of proof apply, and the content of national law must be demonstrated where necessary by the production of evidence". However, where the parties provide the EUIPO with some information on national law, it may be under a duty to undertake further research of its own motion, if it is necessary to do so for the purpose of assessing the conditions for the application of a ground for refusal to register (such as an unregistered right relied on in opposition proceedings under art.8(4)).[155a]

[155a] *Moravia Consulting spol. s r. o. v EUIPO* (T-316/16) EU:T:2017:717 at [72].

## 11. Appeals

## Further Appeals to the General Court and Court of Justice of the EU

### *F. Further Appeal to the Court of Justice of the EU*

*Add new paragraph:*

**8-104A** Since 1 May 2019, it has become even more difficult to challenge a judgment of the General Court in the field of intellectual property. Any appeal lodged after that date against a judgment of the General Court concerning a decision of an EUIPO Board of Appeal "shall not proceed unless the Court of Justice first decides that it should be allowed to do so". The CJEU may only allow the appeal to proceed, wholly or in part, "where it raises an issue that is significant with respect to the unity, consistency or development of Union law". The decision as to whether the appeal should be allowed to proceed or not must be reasoned.[229a] Not surprisingly, the CJEU has interpreted that provision strictly. As of 31 May 2020, it had issued 43 decisions refusing to allow an appeal to proceed on the ground that the appellant had failed to demonstrate that the appeal raised an issue that was significant with respect to the unity, consistency or development of Union law.[229b] At the time of writing there was not a single case in which the court had held that requirement to be met. The court appears to be sending out a message that it is satisfied with the work done by the General Court in the field of trade mark law and does not wish to be involved in fine-tuning the principles established by the existing case law.

[229a] The Protocol on the Statute of the CJEU art.58a. That provision was added by Regulation 2019/629 of the European Parliament and of the Council of 17 April 2019 amending Protocol No.3 on the Statute of the CJEU (OJ 2019 L 111, p.1). Article 58a also applies to various other EU bodies with independent boards of appeal, including the Community Plant Variety Office.

[229b] All the cases except one concerned decisions of an EUIPO Board of Appeal The remaining case concerned a decision of a Board of Appeal of the Community Plant Variety Office. The use of art.58a in relation to decisions of that body (and also in relation EUIPO Board of Appeal decisions concerning the registered Community design) is much more questionable because there is not such a substantial body of case law in those areas.

## 12. CORRECTION OF MISTAKES

*Add new paragraph:*

In the *Repower* case the General Court recognised the existence of a general principle of law, according to which "the retrospective withdrawal of an unlawful administrative act which has created individual rights is permissible, provided that the institution which adopted the act complies with the conditions relating to reasonable time limits and the legitimate expectations of beneficiaries of the act who have been entitled to rely on its lawfulness".[240a] The court held that the EUIPO Boards of Appeal may exercise that general power to withdraw an unlawful act, even where the legislature has laid down a specific procedure for withdrawing unlawful acts.[240b] In the *Repower* case the Board of Appeal revoked its decision in cancellation proceedings after becoming aware, while an action against the decision was pending before the General Court, that it had failed to give adequate reasons for the decision. **8-111A**

[240a] *Repower AG v EUIPO and repowermap.org* (T-727/16) EU:T:2018:88 at [60]. The CJEU held on appeal that the decision in question could have been revoked under the provision now contained in Art 103, thus rendering recourse to the general power to withdraw unlawful decisions unnecessary: *Repower AG v EUIPO and repowermap.org* (C-281/18 P) EU:C:2019:916. The CJEU did not, however, deny the existence of a general power to withdraw unlawful decisions when the conditions governing the exercise of a specific power of revocation do not apply

[240b] At [65].

## 15. THE EU TRADE MARK APPLICATION PROCEDURE: FROM FILING TO PUBLICATION

### Disclaimers

*Add new paragraph:*

It is questionable whether disclaimers have any role to play in EU trade mark law following the judgment of the CJEU in the RoslagPunsch case. A figurative mark dominated by the word element Roslags Punsch had been registered in Sweden for alcoholic beverages. The registration was accompanied by a disclaimer stating that registration did not give an exclusive right over the words Roslags Punsch. The disclaimer was required by the Swedish registrar because the term "Roslags" referred to a region of Sweden and the term "Punsch" described an alcoholic beverage. Notwithstanding the disclaimer, the registrar refused a later application to register ROSLAGSÖL, for non-alcoholic beverages and beers, on the ground that it was likely to be confused with the earlier figurative mark. The applicant challenged the refusal judicially. The Swedish appeal court referred several questions to the CJEU about the effects of a disclaimer on the global assessment of the likelihood of confusion. In reply, the CJEU ruled that art.4(1)(b) of Directive 2008/95 (identical to art.5(1)(b) of the 2015 Trade Mark Directive) "must be interpreted as precluding national legislation making provision for a disclaimer whose effect would be to exclude an element of a complex trade mark, referred to in that disclaimer, from the global analysis of the relevant factors for showing the existence of a likelihood of confusion within the meaning of that provision, or to at- **8-173A** tribute to such an element, in advance and permanently, limited importance in that analysis".[337a] The ruling was no doubt inevitable, given that the CJEU, like the General Court, focuses exclusively on the state of mind of the relevant consumer when assessing likelihood of confusion; the judges are reluctant to admit that some confusion is inevitable if undertakings use descriptive elements in their trade marks and that tolerating some degree of confusion might be preferable to allowing the monopolisation of descriptive elements. It is nonetheless encouraging to note the CJEU's observation that, where the earlier trade mark and the mark applied for coincide in an element that is weakly distinctive or descriptive, the global assessment of the likelihood of confusion will not often lead to a finding that such a likelihood exists. However, the court went on to insist that a finding that a likelihood of confusion exists could not, because of the interdependence of the relevant factors, be ruled out in advance and in any event.[337b]

[337a] *Patent- och registreringsverket v Mats Hansson* (C-705/17) EU:C:2019:481 at [62].

[337b] At [55].

## 25. THE CANCELLATION OF EU TRADE MARKS BY THE EUIPO

### Acquiescence

*Add new paragraph:*

**8-292A** The case law suggests that the burden of proving acquiescence is not easily discharged. The proprietor of the contested EUTM must prove "the actual awareness of the use of that mark by the proprietor of the earlier mark".[521a] It is not sufficient to "prove the potential awareness of the use of the [contested] trade mark by the proprietor of an earlier trade mark or establish consistent evidence giving rise to the presumption of the existence of such awareness".[521b]

[521a] *Asolo Ltd v EUIPO and Red Bull GmbH* (T-150/17) EU:T:2018:641 at [34].

[521b] *Asolo Ltd v EUIPO and Red Bull GmbH* (T-150/17) EU:T:2018:641 at [35]; see also *Tronios Group International BV v EUIPO and SkyTec* (T-77/15) EU:T:2016:226 at [34].

*Add new paragraph:*

**8-293A** If the proprietor of a contested EUTM wishes to plead acquiescence, that plea should be raised before the Cancellation Division "at the very beginning of the cancellation proceedings" and cannot be raised for the first time before the Board of Appeal.[521b] The Board of Appeal is entitled to reject as inadmissible evidence of acquiescence produced for the first time on appeal when the issue had not been raised before the Cancellation Division. A fortiori, evidence of acquiescence adduced for the first time before the General Court is inadmissible.[521c]

[521b] *Erkan Ilhan v Time Gate GmbH* (R 974/2016-5) 13 September 2017 at [22].

[521c] *Ercan Ilhan v EUIPO and Time Gate GmbH* (T-785/17) EU:T:2019:29 at [27].

## 26. ENFORCEMENT OF EU TRADE MARKS

### Jurisdiction Rules

*Replace footnote 568:*

**8-322** [568] art.125(5). Article 125(5) must be interpreted as meaning that a EU trade mark proprietor which considers that its rights have been infringed by the use without its consent, by a third party, of a sign identical to its mark in advertising and offers for sale displayed electronically in relation to products that are identical or similar to the goods for which its mark is registered, may bring an infringement action against the third party before a EU trade mark court of the Member State within which are located the consumers or traders to whom the advertising and offers for sale are directed, notwithstanding that the third party took decisions and steps in another Member State to bring about the electronic display: *AMS Neve Ltd v Heritage Audio SL and Rodriguez Arribas* (C-172/18) EU:C:2019:674.

## Contesting the Validity of the Claimant's EUTM

*Add new paragraph:*

An infringement action brought before an EU trade mark court may not be dismissed on the basis of an absolute ground for invalidity, without that court having upheld the counterclaim for a declaration of invalidity brought by the defendant in the infringement proceedings on the basis of the same ground for invalidity. The EU trade mark court is not precluded from dismissing the infringement action on the basis of an absolute ground for invalidity, even though the decision on the counterclaim for a declaration of invalidity, based on the same ground for invalidity, has not become final.[583a] **8-329A**

[583a] *Raimund v Aigner* (C-425/16) EU:C:2017:776.

## Related Actions

*Replace footnote 585:*

[585] art.132(1). In *CeramTec* the invalidity applicant in proceedings before the EUIPO was allowed to discontinue those proceedings after filing a counterclaim for a declaration of invalidity in infringement proceedings pending against it before a EU trade mark court in France. The EUIPO proceedings had been pending for over two years when the invalidity applicant filed the counterclaim for a declaration of invalidity in the French court. The General Court held that the consent of the proprietor of the contested EU trade mark to the discontinuance of the proceedings before the EUIPO was not required and that the invalidity applicant's conduct did not amount to an abuse of procedure: *CeramTec GmbH v EUIPO and C5 Medical Werks* (T-193/17, T-194/17 and T-195/17) EU:T:2018:248, confirmed by the CJEU in *CeramTec GmbH v EUIPO and C5 Medical Werks* (C-463/18 P) EU:C:2019:18. **8-331**

## Simultaneous and Successive Actions Based on EU Trade Marks and National Trade Marks

*Add new paragraphs:*

The interpretation of the above provisions is far from straightforward, as is shown by the ruling of the CJEU in *Merck KGaA v Merck & Co Inc*.[597a] Merck KGaA (a German company) owned a UK registration for the trade mark MERCK. It also owned a EU registration protecting an identical trade mark. In the USA the MERCK trade mark belonged to Merck & Co Inc (a US corporation) and associated companies. The German and American companies—which were once part of the same concern but had been separate undertakings since 1919—were both using the name MERCK on their respective websites. The German company sued the American company and its associates in the High Court of England and Wales for infringing its UK trade mark. A few days later it commenced proceedings in the Hamburg Regional Court against the same parties for infringing the EU trade mark. It subsequently amended its heads of claim before the German court and stated that it was withdrawing its action in so far as it related to the territory of the UK. The defendants contended that the action before the German court was inadmissible under art.109(1)(a) of Regulation 207/2009 (now art.136(1)(a) EUTMR), at least in so far as it related to the alleged infringement of the claimant's EU trade mark in the entire EU. The German court referred a number of questions to the CJEU concerning the interpretation of the provision that is now contained in art.136(1)(a) EUTMR. **8-338A**

The essential point that emerges from the judgment of the CJEU is that the expression "involving the same cause of action" in art.136(1)(a) considerably reduces the circumstances in which the court other than the court first seised will **8-338B** be required to decline jurisdiction. The CJEU noted that the actions initiated before the High Court and the Hamburg Regional Court concerned claims which only partially overlapped. Even though both the actions concerned the use of the name MERCK on the internet, the content of which was accessible worldwide, the action in the High Court, which was based on a UK trade mark, sought to prohibit the use of the name MERCK in the UK, while the action brought before the Hamburg Regional Court, which was based on a EU trade mark, sought to prohibit the use of that name in the territory of the EU. The CJEU ruled that art.136(1)(a) applied only in so far as the alleged infringements related to the same territory.[597b] A logical consequence of that finding was that the Hamburg court was required to decline jurisdiction only in respect of the part of the dispute relating to the territory of the UK.[597c] The partial withdrawal (with regard to the UK) of the action commenced in Germany on the basis of the EU trade mark meant that the two sets of proceedings no longer concerned the same cause of action, since they no longer related to an alleged infringement of a national trade mark and an identical EU trade mark in the territory of the same Member States.[597d]

**8-338C** The CJEU also ruled that in view of the clear wording of art.136(1)(a), the Hamburg court was required to decline jurisdiction only in so far as the EU and UK trade marks covered identical goods or services.[597e]

**8-338D** The position taken by the CJEU in *Merck* is questionable. It was motivated by the belief that any other interpretation would mean that the proprietor of a EU trade mark who first commenced infringement proceedings on the basis of an identical national trade mark would be unfairly deprived of the possibility of enforcing the EU trade mark in the rest of the EU. Two comments may be made in that respect. First, Merck KGaA decided of its own volition to initiate proceedings in London on the basis of its UK trade mark three days before it launched parallel proceedings in Hamburg alleging infringement of its EU trade mark; it thus found itself in a situation that was entirely of its own making. Secondly, there was an easy way for Merck KGaA to extricate itself from that situation if it wished to enforce its rights in the MERCK trade mark throughout the EU (including the UK in those pre-Brexit times), all that it needed to do was to abandon the proceedings in the High Court, thus freeing the Hamburg Court of its obligation to decline jurisdiction. The position taken by the CJEU leads to the unnecessary multiplication of fora and the possibility of conflicting judgments. It also stacks the odds in favour of the claimant, at least in the kind of factual situation that occurred in the *Merck* case, where success in either forum would probably give full satisfaction to Merck KGaA, regardless of the outcome in the other forum. The ruling facilitates oppressive conduct on the part of claimants and is likely to inflict unfairness on defendants, who may be forced to litigate in more than one jurisdiction. That is hardly compatible with the aim of art.136 or of the EU trade mark system in general.

[597a] *Merck KGaA v Merck & Co Inc, Merck Sharp & Dohme Corp, and MSD Sharp & Dohme GmbH* (C-231/16) EU:C:2017:771.

[597b] At [41]–[44].

[597c] At [53]. As is customary with preliminary rulings, the CJEU expressed this idea in more abstract terms. The effect of the ruling, when applied to the facts of the case, was that the Hamburg court could retain jurisdiction as regards alleged infringements occurring in the whole of the EU minus the territory of the Member State in which the earlier action based on a national registration had been commenced.

[597d] At [57]–[58]. Once again we have stated the effect of the ruling when applied to the facts of the case.

[597e] At [60]–[62].

CHAPTER 9

# THE MADRID SYSTEM

TABLE OF CONTENTS



## 1. THE MADRID AGREEMENT AND PROTOCOL

*Replace footnote 2:*

[2] At the time of writing all the EU members except Malta had acceded to the Protocol. As of 15 September 2020, the Madrid Union had 106 members, all of whom belonged to the Protocol. The members include the USA, Canada, Mexico, Brazil, Russia, India, Japan, China, South Korea, Singapore, Australia, Switzerland, and Turkey. **9-002**

## 4. UK AND EU LEGISLATION IMPLEMENTING THE PROTOCOL

*Add to the end of the paragraph:*

With effect from 14 May 2018, Regulations 2017/1431 and 2017/1430 were replaced by Commission Implementing Regulation 2018/626 and Commission Delegated Regulation 2018/625 of 5 March 2018. The content of Regulations 2018/626 and 2018/625 is identical to that of Regulations 2017/1431 and 2017/1430 (apart from the "final provisions" dealing with transitional measures, entry into force and such like). **9-014**

## 11. THE LINK BETWEEN THE PROTOCOL AND THE EUTM SYSTEM

### (a) International registration designating the EU

*Replace footnote 49:*

[49] EUTM Regulation art.189. International registrations designating the EU, including those designations made during the transition period (scheduled to end on 31 December 2020 unless extended), will continue to have effect in the UK during that period: WIPO Information Notice No 2/2020, Madrid Protocol Concerning the International Registration of Marks, Agreement on the Withdrawal of the United Kingdom from the European Union: Implications for International Applications and Registrations Under the Madrid System. After the end of the transitional period, the trade marks protected by such registra- **9-040**

tions must continue to enjoy protection in the UK under the terms of art.56 of the Agreement on the Withdrawal of the UK from the EU.

## (b) International registration based on a EUTM or a EUTM application

*Replace footnote 65:*

9-050 [65] Protocol art.2(1)(ii). The Protocol does not define nationality. It is for each EU Member State to determine which individuals and corporate bodies possess its nationality. As far as the UK is concerned, it would be logical to apply by analogy the terms of para.1(2) of Sch.3 to the 2008 Order to determine who possesses UK nationality for the purpose of filing an international application through the EUIPO. UK nationals and those who are domiciled or have a real and effective industrial or commercial establishment in the UK, and in whose name stands an application or registration with the EUIPO, may continue to file international applications with the EUIPO, as Office of origin, during the transitional period (that is to say, until 31 December 2020, unless the transitional period is extended): WIPO Information Notice No 2/2020, Madrid Protocol Concerning the International Registration of Marks, Agreement on the Withdrawal of the United Kingdom from the European Union: Implications for International Applications and Registrations Under the Madrid System.

Chapter 10

# ABSOLUTE GROUNDS FOR REFUSAL OF REGISTRATION

Table of Contents



## Introduction

*Replace table with:* **10-002**

### Absolute Grounds—Correspondence Table

| Summary | 1994 Act | 2015 TMD | EUTMR 2017 |
|---|---|---|---|
| Not a "trade mark" | s.3(1)(a) | art.4(1)(a) | art.7(1)(a) |
| Devoid of dis char | s.3(1)(b) | art.4(1)(b) | art.7(1)(b) |
| Descriptive | s.3(1)(c) | art.4(1)(c) | art.7(1)(c) |
| Generic | s.3(1)(d) | art.4(1)(d) | art.7(1)(d) |
| Acquired Distinctiveness | Proviso | arts 4(4) and 4(5)[1] | art.7(3) |
| Nature of goods | s.3(2)(a) shape | art.4(1)(e)(i) | art.7(1)(e)(i) |
| Technical result | s.3(2)(b) shape | art.4(1)(e)(ii) | art.7(1)(e)(ii) |
| Substantial value | s.3(2)(c) shape | art.4(1)(e)(iii) | art.7(1)(e)(iii) |
| Public policy | s.3(3)(a) | art.4(1)(f) | art.7(1)(f) |
| Deceptive | s.3(3)(b) | art.4(1)(g) | art.7(1)(g) |
| Paris Convention art.6*ter* Protected emblems | s.3(5), s.4(3) and s.57 | art.4(1)(h) | art.7(1)(h) |

| | | | |
|---|---|---|---|
| Other public emblems[4] | s.3(5) and s.4 specially protected emblems | art.4(3)(a),(b),(c) | art.7(1)(i) |
| PDOs, PGIs | s.3(4) | art.4(1)(i) | art.7(1)(j) |
| Traditional terms for wine | s.3(4B) | art.4(1)(j) | art.7(1)(k) |
| TSGs | s.3(4B) | art.4(1)(k) | art.7(1)(l) |
| Plant varieties | s.3(4C) | art.4(1)(l) | art.7(1)(m) |
| Grounds only exist in part of the EU | - | - | art.7(2) |
| Bad faith | s.3(6) | art.4(2) | - |

[1] art.7(1)(a) concerns the new forms of representation permitted by EUTMR art.4 and EUTMIR art.3. Likewise for the 2015 TMD art.4(1)(a).

[1] art.4(5) concerns distinctive character acquired before the date of *registration*.

[2] All of the art.7(1)(e) provisions (and their equivalents in the 2015 TMD) apply to a shape *or another characteristic of the goods*.

[4] There are differences in the detail, so these are not necessarily directly equivalent provisions.

## 1. OVERVIEW OF ABSOLUTE GROUNDS

*Add to the end of the paragraph:*

10-003 In *Municipality of Oslo* (E-5/16), the EFTA Court had to consider attempts by the City of Oslo to obtain trade mark protection for various well-known works of art on display in the City for which copyright protection had expired. The ruling contains an interesting overview of the main absolute grounds applicable to the registrability of works of art, namely arts 3(1)(b), (c), (e) and (f).

## 2. DISTINCTIVE CHARACTER

### 2.1 Acquired Distinctive Character—the Proviso to s.3(1), art.3(3), art.7(3)

#### *Is Recognition and "Association" Enough?*

*Replace paragraph:*

10-027 The answer to this question depends on the meaning one gives to "associate", but in general terms the answer is "no". The issue tends to arise in cases where the applicant for the trade mark has enjoyed (due to other intellectual property rights) a period of de facto monopoly in the shape of the product or some part of it. As Patten J put it, "The difficulty lies in establishing during the monopoly period what more is required, beyond association of the product with the actual manufacturer, for it to achieve trade mark status." The latest illustration of this was an attempt to register as a series, various shapes of the Land Rover Defender. The appeal from the UK IPO was dismissed—the survey evidence failed to establish that the mark possessed acquired distinctiveness through the use made of it. The surveys were found to have established a 20–40 per cent degree of recognition—*Jaguar Land Rover Ltd v Ineos Industrial Holdings Ltd.*[42a] Similarly, recognition of the Ferrero Rocher packaging did not establish that a mark comprising a picture of a single Ferrero Rocher chocolate in its packaging had acquired distinctive character in Singapore under the equivalent of the proviso to s.3(1): see *In the Matter of a Trade Mark Application by Ferrero Spa.*[42b]

[42a] [2020] EWHC 2130, HHJ Melissa Clarke.

[42b] [2019] SGIPOS 19 (Mr David Llewellyn, IP Adjudicator).

## 5. SECTION 3(1)(B)/ART.3(1)(B), ART.7(1)(B) EUTMR: NON-DISTINCTIVE MARKS

### Slogans

*Add new paragraph:*

One of the latest attempts concerned a word mark "#darferdas?" (a hashtag meaning "can he do that?") for clothing—*AS v Deutsches Patent- und Markenamt.*[121a] The referring court had found that there were two likely uses of the mark in relation to clothing—both on the exterior of the goods and on labels sewn inside the garment. The CJEU advised the national court that the examining authority had to assess whether the average consumer, on seeing those two types of placement, or at least one of them, would perceive the sign as a trade mark. So it was for the national court to determine whether the average consumer, on seeing the sign on the front of a t-shirt or the label inside would perceive that sign as an indication of commercial origin of the item and not simply as a decorative element or social message. **10-085A**

[121a] (C-541/18).

### Shape Marks—Comprising the Product Itself or its Packaging

*Replace paragraph:*

Although marks comprising the shape of goods or their packaging are usually dealt with under arts 3(1)(b)/7(1)(b), there is nothing which in principle excludes the application of arts 3(1)(c)/7(1)(c) or 3(1)(d)/7(1)(d). The Court of Justice emphasised this point in *Linde.*[122] In *August Stork KG v EUIPO,*[122a] an attempt to register a mark comprising a representation of a shape of a white, grey and blue square-shaped packaging for confectionary was rejected under art.7(1)(b), an entirely predictable outcome. Similarly, an attempt to register in Singapore the appearance of a Ferrero Rocher in its packaging was rejected under the equivalent of s.3(1)(b): see *In the Matter of a Trade Mark Application by Ferrero Spa.*[122b] **10-087**

[122] (C-53/01) [2003] E.C.R. I-3161; [2003] R.P.C. 45; [2003] E.T.M.R. 78, see [63]–[77], especially [69].

[122a] (C-417/16).

[122b] [2019] SGIPOS 19 (Mr David Llewellyn, IP Adjudicator).

## 6. SECTION 3(1)(C)/ART.3(1)(C), ART.7(1)(C) EUTMR: DESCRIPTIVE MARKS

### Commentary

*Add to the end of the paragraph:*

As an illustration, see the decision of the Appointed Person (Prof. Ruth Annand) in *SAKURA SAKURA!* (O-146-19), where Sakura signified cherry blossom tea. The UK IPO Hearing Officer was held to be wrong to find that the repetition of the word took the mark outside s.3(1)(c), but the mark for tea still fell foul of s.3(1)(b). **10-104**

### Geographical Origin

*Add to the end of the paragraph:*

The Bavarian state registered "NEUSCHWANSTEIN" as a EUTM for a wide **10-107** range of goods. An application to invalidate under art.7(1)(b) and (c) failed. Although Neuschwanstein Castle was well known and famous for its unusual architecture, the General Court held it was first and foremost a museum location, the primary function of which is not the manufacture or marketing of souvenir products or the provision of services, but heritage conservation. The CJEU held that the General Court did not err in finding that, as Neuschwanstein Castle is not a place where goods are produced or services rendered, the mark could not be indicative of the geographical origin of the goods and services in question. Although the CJEU's decision was based on its appeal function, overall the decision appears dubious because it is difficult to see why the name of the famous castle would possess inherent distinctive character, even if the reasoning under art.7(1)(c) was correct, which it probably is not.

## 8. Miscellaneous Points

### 8.3 Secondary Meaning

*Replace list item "(3)" with:*

10-144 (3) The extent to which the secondary distinctive meaning must displace the primary descriptive meaning to justify registration as a trade mark is a question of degree, which will depend upon the degree of descriptiveness of the sign. The more descriptive the sign, the greater the extent to which the primary descriptive meaning must be displaced. The more descriptive a sign is, the greater are the negative (descriptive) qualities of the sign which must be displaced and overcome by positive distinctive qualities. Ultimately, when making this judgment the tribunal is likely to be influenced by considerations which were familiar under the old Act. To what extent would registration interfere with the rights of honest traders? To what extent does this sign really operate as a trade mark? To what extent is it thought necessary to keep this sign free for others to use?[191]

[191] Compare the various submissions made in *Windsurfing* (C-108/97) [1999] E.C.R. I-2779; [2000] Ch. 523 and the fact that the Court of Justice sensibly avoided any attempt at evaluating the need to which a sign should be kept free for others.

## 9. Shapes—s.3(2)—or Another Characteristic of the Goods—EUTMR art.7(1)(e)

*Replace paragraph:*

10-167 "s.3(2): A sign shall not be registered as a trade mark if it consists exclusively of—

(a) the shape, or another characteristic, which results from the nature of the goods themselves,

(b) the shape, or another characteristic, of goods which is necessary to obtain a technical result, or

(c) the shape, or another characteristic, which gives substantial value to the goods."

Section 3(2) of the Trade Marks Act 1994 has now been amended into the form shown above to implement the expanded list of absolute grounds in art.4(2) of the 2015 TM Directive to reflect the EUTMR 1001/2017. Much of the discussion below concerns the application of these provisions to shapes. It still remains to be seen how significant these grounds will prove as regards other characteristics.

## Derivation

*Replace paragraph:*

The operative part of s.3(2) as amended is identical to the wording in art.4(2) of the 2015 TM Directive and identical to the equivalent provisions in the EUTMR 1001/2017. **10-168**

## Sign and Shape

*Replace paragraph:*

For the most part, the "shapes" considered against these provisions will be three-dimensional shapes and two-dimensional representations of them, but not exclusively so. It is possible to conceive of two-dimensional shapes (such as silhouettes[232]), and there are certain types of laminar goods which can be argued to be essentially two-dimensional (such as novelty greetings cards), even though they are in fact three-dimensional. The real distinction is between external or exterior features (i.e. three-dimensional shapes and two-dimensional representations of them, including silhouettes) and patterns or designs applied to the surface or interior of goods.[233] Fortunately, it is likely to be evident when a sign comprises the shape of goods or their packaging, as opposed to being a two-dimensional design or pattern.[234] Having said that, it took two Opinions from AG Spunzar for the CJEU to rule in *Louboutin v Van Haren Shoenen BV*[234a] that the mark applied for, which appeared to be an application to protect the famous/infamous Louboutin red sole, was not a shape mark at all. The mark in question comprised a 2D image of a high heeled fashion shoe (shown in broken lines) with the sole of the shoe coloured red, along with the following description "The mark consists of the colour red (Pantone 18-1663TP) applied to the sole of a shoe as shown (the contour of the shoe is not part of the trade mark but is intended to show the positioning of the mark)." Accordingly, the sign applied for was not a specific shape at all. **10-175**

[232] One of the marks sued upon in *Julius Sämaan* [2006] EWHC 529, [2006] E.T.M.R. 75, was essentially a silhouette. Since the alleged infringements were air fresheners made in the shape of the marks, Kitchin J commented (at [95]): "They are graphic marks but, on the claimants' case, they are also representations of the shape of air fresheners". Accordingly the registrations could not escape a challenge under art.3(1)(e)(iii) (substantial value), even though the challenge failed.

[233] Under similar but not identical provisions in Benelux law, the Benelux Court of Justice held that shapes only cover three-dimensional designs and not two-dimensional patterns such as the Burberry check: *Burberrys* 16 December 1991.

[234] Note, however, the debate over the precise characterisation of the sign in *Louboutin* (red sole of a high-heeled shoe). At the time of writing AG Szpunar has concluded that the sign comprises a shape plus colour. (C-163/16) EU:C:2017:495. The new rules as to representation (for the moment, see art.4(b) of the EUTMR and art.3 of the EUTMIR) are designed to eliminate these types of issue, such that it should be clear from the application what sort of mark it is, and its scope should be clearly defined by the representation.

[234a] (C-163/16).

*Add new paragraphs:*

The CJEU also ruled that a sign, such as that in issue, cannot be regarded as consisting "exclusively" of a shape where the main element of the sign is a specific colour designated by an internationally recognised identification code. **10-175A**

In *Textalis Ltd v Svenskt Tenn AB*,[234b] the case concerned a figurative mark comprising an image of a fabric design known as the Manhattan Print. The issue **10-175B** was whether the mark comprised a shape which gave substantial value to the goods under art.7(1)(e)(iii). The CJEU ruled, not surprisingly, that a 2D decorative motif affixed to goods did not "consist exclusively of the shape".

[234b] (C-21/18).

## Philips No.2

*After item "(7)", add:*

**10-185** (8) The 3D mark was of a Lego Man. An action to invalidate the registration under art.7(1)(e)(i) and (ii) failed. The applicant alleged all the essential characteristics of the mark performed a technical function, but this argument was rejected at all levels including the CJEU. On the assumption that the holes under the feet and inside the backs of the legs and the hands "may have a technical function", the General Court nonetheless held that those elements could not be held to constitute the most important elements of the mark, nor an essential characteristic of the shape in question. The CJEU upheld the General Court's decision—*Best-Lock (Europe) Ltd v EU IPO.*[253a]

[253a] (C-451/15).

## Substantial Value

*Add new paragraphs:*

**10-197A** The CJEU ruling in *Gomboc Kft v Szellemi*[261a] provided additional guidance on all three points. The case concerned an application to register the Gömböc, a 3D self-righting object which always comes to rest in the same position since it has a single point of stable equilibrium and a single point of unstable equilibrium, in respect of "decorative items" and "decorative crystalware and chinaware". The referring court found that the substantial value of the product was conferred on it by the fact that the shape has become the tangible symbol of a mathematical discovery.

**10-197B** So far as the scope and purpose of this ground, the CJEU explained, when answering the third question referred:

> "50. ... the objective of the ground for refusal of registration provided for in Article 3(1)(e)(iii) of Directive 2008/95, like that of the ground for refusal of registration provided for in Article 3(1)(e)(ii) of that directive, as referred to in paragraph 27 above, is, indeed, to prevent the exclusive and permanent right that a trade mark confers from serving to extend indefinitely the life of other rights in respect of which the EU legislature has sought to impose time limits (see, by analogy, judgment of 18 September 2014, *Hauck*, C 205/13, EU:C:2014:2233, paragraph 19).
>
> 51. However, such an objective does not mean that EU intellectual property law prevents the coexistence of several forms of legal protection."

so

> "55. Accordingly, the fact that the appearance of a product is protected as a design as a result, inter alia, of that design's individual character, does not mean that a sign which consists of the shape of that product may not be registered as a trade mark because the ground for refusal provided for in Article 3(1)(e)(iii) of Directive 2008/95 is applicable."

and

> "62. ... Article 3(1)(e)(iii) of Directive 2008/95 must be interpreted as meaning that the

ground for refusal of registration provided for in that provision must not be applied systematically to a sign which consists exclusively of the shape of the product where that sign enjoys protection under the law relating to designs or where the sign consists exclusively of the shape of a decorative item."

As to the analysis required, it is explained in the court's answer to the second question:

"40. The application of this ground for refusal is based therefore on an objective analysis, intended to demonstrate that the shape in question, on account of its characteristics, has such a great influence on the attractiveness of the product that restricting the benefit of the shape to a single undertaking would distort the conditions of competition on the market concerned.

41. As a result, in order for the ground for refusal provided for in Article 3(1)(e)(iii) of Directive 2008/95 to apply, it must be apparent from objective and reliable evidence that a consumer's decision to purchase the goods in question is, to a very great extent, determined by one or more features of the shape which alone forms the sign.

42. Characteristics of the product not connected to its shape, such as technical qualities or the reputation of the product are, on the other hand, irrelevant."

"44. ... it must be borne in mind that, although the presumed perception of the sign at issue by the average consumer is not, in itself, a decisive element when applying the ground for refusal set out in Article 3(1)(e)(iii) of Directive 2008/95, it may, nevertheless, be a useful criterion of assessment for the competent authority in identifying the essential characteristics of that sign (see, by analogy, judgment of 18 September 2014, *Hauck*, C 205/13, EU:C:2014:2233, paragraph 34).

45. It follows that, in a situation such as that at issue in the main proceedings, Article 3(1)(e)(iii) of Directive 2008/95 allows the competent authority to find, in the light of the perception of the sign at issue by the relevant public and the knowledge of that public, that the shape which alone forms the sign is the tangible symbol of a mathematic discovery. Since it took the view that that fact makes that shape special and striking, the competent authority was entitled to conclude that it is an essential characteristic, within the meaning of the case-law referred to in paragraph 44 above, and that it was necessary to assess whether, as a result of that fact, the shape which alone forms the sign at issue gives substantial value to the goods.

46. The fact that such a characteristic does not, in itself, concern the aesthetic merits of the shape does not exclude the application of Article 3(1)(e)(iii) of Directive 2008/95. It should be borne in mind, in this regard, that the concept of a 'shape which gives substantial value to the goods' is not limited to the shape of goods having an exclusively artistic or ornamental value. The question as to whether the shape gives substantial value to the goods may be examined on the basis of other relevant factors, including, inter alia, whether the shape is dissimilar from other shapes in common use on the market concerned (see, by analogy, judgment of 18 September 2014, *Hauck*, C 205/13, EU:C:2014:2233, paragraphs 32 and 35).

47. It follows from the foregoing that the answer to the second question is that Article 3(1)(e)(iii) of Directive 2008/95 must be interpreted as meaning that the perception or knowledge of the relevant public as regards the product represented graphically by a sign that consists exclusively of the shape of that product may be taken into consideration in order to identify an essential characteristic of that shape. The ground for refusal set out in that provision may be applied if it is apparent from objective and reliable evidence that the consumer's decision to purchase the product in question is to a large extent determined by that characteristic."

Finally, it is clear from the ruling that the assessment of whether the value is *substantial* is a value judgment for the competent authority and/or the national court.

261a (C-237/19) 23 April 2020.

## 10. Public Policy, Deceptive Marks

### Public Policy, Accepted Principles of Morality

*Add new paragraphs:*

**10-207A** The CJEU has now ruled on the test to be applied under art.7(1)(f) of the EUTMR, a test which will also apply to the equivalent provisions in the TM Directive. In *Fack Ju Göhte*,[279a] the CJEU overturned the judgment of the General Court (upholding the Board of Appeal) which had found that the word mark "*Fack Ju Göhte*" (meaning "Fuck you, Goethe" to German speakers) was contrary to the accepted principles of morality (it declined to rule on the alternative ground—public policy—in art.7(1)(f)). The CJEU explained the correct approach in these paragraphs (by reference to the provision in the CTM Regulation):

"39. As regards that ground for refusal, it should be noted that, since the concept of 'accepted principles of morality' is not defined by Regulation No 207/2009, it must be interpreted in the light of its usual meaning and the context in which it is generally used. However, as the Advocate General observes in essence in point 77 of his Opinion, that concept refers, in its usual sense, to the fundamental moral values and standards to which a society adheres at a given time. Those values and norms, which are likely to change over time and vary in space, should be determined according to the social consensus prevailing in that society at the time of the assessment. In making that determination, due account is to be taken of the social context, including, where appropriate, the cultural, religious or philosophical diversities that characterise it, in order to assess objectively what that society considers to be morally acceptable at that time.

40. Moreover, in the context of the application of Article 7(1)(f) of Regulation No 207/2009, the examination as to whether a sign, in respect of which registration as an EU trade mark is sought, is contrary to accepted principles of morality requires an examination of all the elements specific to the case in order to determine how the relevant public would perceive such a sign if it were used as a trade mark for the goods or services claimed.

41. In that connection, in order to come within the scope of Article 7(1)(f) of Regulation No 207/2009, it is not sufficient for the sign concerned to be regarded as being in bad taste. It must, at the time of the examination, be perceived by the relevant public as contrary to the fundamental moral values and standards of society as they exist at that time.

42. In order to establish whether that is the case, the examination is to be based on the perception of a reasonable person with average thresholds of sensitivity and tolerance, taking into account the context in which the mark may be encountered and, where appropriate, the particular circumstances of the part of the Union concerned. To that end, elements such as legislation and administrative practices, public opinion and, where appropriate, the way in which the relevant public has reacted in the past to that sign or similar signs, as well as any other factor which may make it possible to assess the perception of that public, are relevant.

43. The examination to be carried out cannot be confined to an abstract assessment of the mark applied for, or even of certain components of it, but it must be established, in particular where an applicant has relied on factors that are liable to cast doubt on the fact that that mark is perceived by the relevant public as contrary to accepted principles of morality, that the use of that mark in the concrete and current social context would indeed be perceived by that public as being contrary to the fundamental moral values and standards of society."

On the facts, the CJEU concluded that the mark was not perceived as morally unacceptable by the German-speaking public at large, principally because two comedy films (and a further sequel) under the mark had been very successful in Germany and Austria, the first film "*Fack Ju Göhte*" having been seen by over 7.4 million people, but also because the German-speaking public does not necessarily perceive the English phrase "Fuck You" in the same way as it would perceive the German translation of that phrase.

Contrast two earlier decisions by the General Court. First, in *La Mafia Franchises SL v EUIPO*,[279b] a figurative mark comprising the principal words "La Mafia" with a red rose for clothing, bars and cafes was declared invalid on application by the Italian Government as being contrary to public policy, since the mark refers to a criminal organisation and trivialises the serious harm done by that organisation to the fundamental values of the EU. It would not only shock and offend the victims of that criminal organisation and their families, but also anyone with average sensitivity and tolerance thresholds. **10-207B**

In *Santa Conte v EUIPO*[279c] a figurative mark featuring the words "CANNABIS store Amsterdam" against a background featuring cannabis leaf motifs for a variety of goods and services including baked goods, confectionary, beer and services for providing food and drink was refused registration as being contrary to public policy since the word cannabis would be understood as referring to the narcotic which is illegal in a number of EU countries. The General Court followed *La Mafia* and applied the characterisation of public policy stated by AG Bobek in *Fack Ju Göhte*, namely, that "public policy is a normative vision of values and goals, defined by the relevant public authority, to be pursued now and in the future, that is, prospectively. Public policy thus expresses the public regulator's wishes as to the norms to be respected in society." **10-207C**

In *Municipality of Oslo*,[279d] the EFTA Court had to consider attempts by the City of Oslo to obtain trade mark protection for various well-known works of art on display in the City for which copyright protection had expired. The court ruled that such registrations were not in themselves contrary to public policy or accepted principles of morality within art.3(1)(f) of the TM Directive. The court held that ground would apply only if registration of such a sign would constitute a genuine and sufficiently serious threat to a fundamental interest of society. **10-207D**

[279a] (C-240/18) 27 February 2020.

[279b] (T-1/17) 15 March 2018.

[279c] (T-683/18).

[279d] (E-5/16).

*Add new section:*

## 11A. PDOs, PGIs, TSGs and Plant Varieties

The implementation of the 2015 TM Directive resulted in the introduction of the new s.3(4A). Since the provisions are self-explanatory, we set them out here: **10-226A**

"(4A) A trade mark is not to be registered if its registration is prohibited by or under—
(a) any enactment or rule of law,
(b) any provision of EU law, or
(c) any international agreement to which the United Kingdom or the EU is a party,
providing for the protection of designations of origin or geographical indications.

(4B) A trade mark is not to be registered if its registration is prohibited by or under—
(a) any provision of EU law, or
(b) any international agreement to which the EU is a party,

providing for the protection of traditional terms for wine or traditional specialities guaranteed.

(4C) A trade mark is not to be registered if it—

(a) consists of, or reproduces in its essential elements, an earlier plant variety denomination registered as mentioned in subsection (4D), and

(b) is in respect of plant varieties of the same or closely related species.

(4D) Subsection (4C)(a) refers to registration in accordance with any—

(a) enactment or rule of law,

(b) provision of EU law, or

(c) international agreement to which the United Kingdom or the EU is a party,

providing for the protection of plant variety rights."

**10-226B** The purpose of these provisions is clear, since the nature of the indication provided by a PDO, a PGI, a traditional term for wine, a TSG or a plant variety right is inconsistent with registration as a normal trade mark. The introduction of these provisions reflects the equivalent provisions in the EUTMR 1001/2017 art.7(1)(j)–(m), which are already discussed briefly in the Main Work at para.10-252.

## 14. Bad Faith—s.3(6)

### Derivation

*Replace paragraph:*

**10-254** Section 3(6) derives from art.3(2)(d) of the 1988 TM Directive which was repealed and replaced by the 2008 TM Directive which has in turn been repealed and replaced by the new Trade Mark Directive, Directive (EU) 2015/2436 of the European Parliament and the Council of the European Union (which will be referred to as the "2015 TM Directive").[350]

[350] Codified Directive of the European Parliament and of the Council 2008/95, which following repeated amendment of Directive 89/104, repealed and replaced the original Council Directive 89/104, the 1988 TM Directive. Directive 2008/95 has been repealed with effect from 15 January 2019 (see art.55 of Directive (EU) 2015/2436) and replaced with the recast Directive, Directive (EU) 2015/2436 of the European Parliament and of the Council of 16 December 2015 to approximate the laws of the Member States relating to trade marks. Directive (EU) 2015/2436 of the European Parliament and of the Council came into force on 16 January 2016 and arts 1, 7, 15, 19, 29, 21 and 54–57 shall apply from 15 January 2019 (see art.56).

*Add new paragraph after para.10-254:*

**10-254A** The bad faith ground of invalidity in relation to registered trade marks was an optional provision of the 1988 and 2008 TM Directives.

*Replace paragraph:*

**10-255** The 2015 TM Directive is now in force.[351] Member States had to transpose almost all of this Directive into their national laws by 15 January 2019.[352] Article 4(2) of the 2015 TM Directive states:

> "A trade mark shall be liable to be declared invalid where the application for registration of the trade mark was made in bad faith by the applicant. Any Member State may also provide that such a trade mark is not to be registered".

Therefore, the bad faith ground of invalidity in relation to registered marks is now a mandatory provision. However, this ground of objection will continue to be optional in individual Member States with regards trade mark applications. It should be noted that the wording "… the application for registration of the trade mark was made in bad faith by the applicant" at art.3(2)(d) of 2008 TM Directive is repeated in art.4(2) of the 2015 TM Directive,[353] so it is assumed that the CJEU will continue to interpret bad faith under the 2015 TM Directive as it has done under the 2008 TM Directive.

[351] Directive 2008/95 was repealed with effect from 15 January 2019, see art.55 of Directive (EU) 2015/2436 of the European Parliament and of the Council. Directive (EU) 2015/2436 of the European Parliament and of the Council came into force on 16 January 2016 and arts 1, 7, 15, 19, 29, 21 and 54–57 applied from 15 January 2019 (see art.56).

[352] It should be noted that art.45 of Directive 2015/2436 concerning administrative procedures for applications for revocation and invalidity does not have to be brought into force until 14 January 2023.

[353] However, the wording of the recitals of the 2008 TM Directive and the 2015 TM Directive do differ, see further para.10-297A.

## Equivalent Provision in the EUTM Regulation

*Replace footnote 355:*

[355] EUTM Regulation art.59.1.b. The application can be made to EUIPO or by way of counterclaim in infringement proceedings, i.e. in any of the EU Trade Mark Courts. **10-256**

*Delete sub-section "The Position in Various Member States".*

## General Introduction

*Replace second paragraph with:*

The relevant provisions contemplate bad faith extending to the whole or only part of the application.[358] If the whole of an application is made in bad faith, it indicates (though not exclusively) that the applicant has no entitlement to the mark, i.e. the applicant is not the true proprietor of the mark. It is worth noting that this is the only ground of refusal under which issues of proprietorship can be raised.[359] If the bad faith extends to only part of an application, that indicates (again not exclusively) that the scope of the application is too broad, the prime example being that the specification of goods or services sought is too wide. Those two situations may be the main ones which arise. However, the bad faith provision is of flexible scope. The making of any false statement or representation, even implicit, in connection with an application for a trade mark may form part of the circumstances giving rise to a finding of bad faith.[360] **10-259**

[358] Not as explicitly as the 1988 and 2008 TM Directives art.13—see G. Hobbs QC as the Appointed Person in *DEMON ALE* [2000] R.P.C. 345 at 355.

[359] An Italian judge has observed that the purpose of the bad faith provision is there to provide "advanced protection to any party which, even if it has planned to register a trade mark it uses, has not actually done so yet." and also to those situations where the proprietor is still preparing to use their mark, where they have a "legitimate expectation" of protection. See *Benckiser v Henkel* [1999] E.T.M.R. 614 at 637, Court of Naples.

[360] See Ruling 3 by the CJEU in *Sky Plc v SkyKick UK Ltd* (C-371/18) which makes clear that a false statement under s.32(3) of the Trade Marks Act 1994 does not constitute, in itself, a ground for invalidity of a trade mark already registered. See also *Sky Plc v SkyKick UK Ltd* [2020] EWHC 990 (Ch) which is the judgment of Arnold LJ dated 29 April 2020, given following the CJEU's Judgment in *Sky v SkyKick* (C-371/18). Paragraph 22 of the 29 April 2020 judgment states: "[22] In the case of UK604, there is the additional factor that Sky made a partly false section 32(3) declaration in order to obtain such protection. That is plainly inconsistent with honest practices in industrial and commercial matters, and thus strengthens the conclusion that, to that extent, Sky made that application in bad faith." G. Hobbs QC (as the Appointed Person) explained in *DEMON ALE* [2000] R.P.C. 345 at 356, "I do not think that section 3(6) requires applicants to submit to an open-ended assessment of their commercial morality".

*Replace footnote 361:*

10-260 [361] See para.10-254.

*Replace paragraph:*

10-261 After a considerable wait the Court of Justice[362] provided some guidance about the application of the concept of "bad faith" in *Chocoladefabriken Lindt & Sprüngli AG v Franz Hauswirth GmbH*[363] which we consider in detail below.[364] Further guidance has also been provided in *Malaysia Dairy Industries Pte Ltd v Ankenoevnet For Patenter Og Varemaerker*.[365] More recently the CJEU has provided much awaited guidance in its judgment in *Sky Plc v SkyKick UK Ltd* (C-371/18). Before considering these judgments we will reflect on the development of the case law on bad faith in the UK[366] and at OHIM (now the "EUIPO").[367]

[362] Now the CJEU.

[363] [2009] E.T.M.R. 56.

[364] See paras 10-278 to 10-284. We also consider at paras 10-285 to 10-296 the application of the Court of Justice judgment in *Lindt* in subsequent UK cases.

[365] (C-320/12) [2013] E.T.M.R. 36.

[366] See paras 10-262 to 10-269.

[367] See paras 10-270 to 10-274.

## The Law as it has Developed in the UK

*After "Court of Justice", replace "has now provided some limited" with:*

10-262 and now the CJEU has provided some much needed

## The Focus on the "Mental Element"

*After "In the", at the start of the paragraph, add:*

10-264 past due to the

*After "deciding whether the", replace "applicants" with:*

10-269 applicant's

## Development of the Concept of "Bad Faith" at OHIM (now EUIPO)

*Replace footnote 387:*

10-274 [387] See para.10-268.

## Guidance from the Court of Justice in Lindt

*Replace quotation:*

10-279 "[T]he answer to the questions referred is that, in order to determine whether the applicant is acting in bad faith within the meaning of art.51(1)(b) of Regulation 40/94 [now art.52(1)(b) of Council Regulation 207/2009],[403a] the national court must take into consideration all the relevant factors specific to the particular case which pertained at the time of filing the application for registration of the sign as a Community trade mark, in particular:

- the fact that the applicant knows or must know that a third party is using, in at least one Member State, an identical or similar sign for an identical or similar product capable of being confused with the sign for which registration is sought;
- the applicant's intention to prevent that third party from continuing to use such a sign; and

- the degree of legal protection enjoyed by the third party's sign and by the sign for which registration is sought."

403a now art.59(1)(b) of Regulation (EU) 2017/1001 of the European Parliament and of the Council.

*After "surrounding bad faith", replace "have not been resolved." with:*
were not resolved by it. **10-281**

*Replace paragraph with:*
If these paragraphs quoted above are read as a whole and considered in conjunction with [58] of the AG's opinion, it is possible that the Court of Justice's statement in *Lindt* at [42], quoted above could be interpreted as follows: **10-284**

> "[The applicant's intention [*specifically whether that intention contained an element that amounted to bad faith*] at the relevant time is a subjective factor which must be determined by reference to the objective circumstances of the particular case."

However, the Court of Justice's finding on the issue of the "Applicant's intention" in *Lindt* is somewhat ambiguous. Some further guidance on the "Applicant's intention" was provided in the recent CJEU case of *Koton* (C-104/18P) dated 12 September 2019 which held:

> "47. The intention of an applicant for a trade mark is a subjective factor which must, however, be determined objectively by the competent administrative or judicial authorities. Consequently, any claim of bad faith must be the subject of an overall assessment, taking into account all the factual circumstances relevant to the particular case (see, to that effect, judgment of 11 June 2009, *Chocoladefabriken Lindt & Sprüngli*, C-529/07, EU:C:2009:361, paragraphs 37 and 42). It is only in that manner that a claim of bad faith can be assessed objectively."

*Change title of sub-section:* **10-285**

## Application of the Court of Justice's Guidance on Bad Faith from the Lindt case

*Replace paragraph with:*
The Appointed Person overturned the Hearing Officer's decision and found that the opposition should have succeeded on the s.5(3) ground of unfair advantage but found that the bad faith objection under s.3(6) was not made out.[427] In another decision the Appointed Person summarised the issue of bad faith as follows: "The line which separates legitimate self-interest from bad faith can only be crossed if the Applicant has sought to acquire rights of control over the use of the sign graphically represented in his application for registration in an improper manner or for an improper purpose."[428] The Appointed Person in *Simmons Trademark*[429] further held that the CJEU's approach in *Lindt* (specifically the summary of its conclusions at [53]), which requires the tribunal to make an assessment of the conduct of the applicant for registration, based on all relevant factors, but not to required proof of actual dishonesty, accorded with the approach of the English Court in *Ian Adam*[430] and *Gromax Plasticulture Ltd v Don & Low Nonwovens Ltd*.[431] **10-291**

427 The Appointed Person in *Socks World* [2011] R.P.C. 11 went through the factors specifically identified in *Lindt* (C-529/07) and assessed them and considered the other factors he thought relevant to an assessment of bad faith at [86]–[90] of the judgment. See also *"Talk for Learning" Trade Mark Application* (O-017-17) [2017] R.P.C. 17 where the Appointed Person upheld the Hearing Officer's finding that an objection under s.5(4) of the Act was made out but that in his view the Hearing Officer had been wrong to make a finding of bad faith under s.3(6) of the Act, the Appointed Person commented: "There is a fundamental difference between pursuing an aggressive, self-interested but nonetheless bona fide

trade mark application strategy with a view to seeking maximum protection for one's own business and limiting the freedom of others to use marks known to be theirs or otherwise acting in bad faith."

[428] See *Ian Adam* [2011] F.S.R. 11 at [33] and more generally [32]–[35]. See also [21] of *CKL Holdings NV v Paperstacked Ltd* (O-036-18) 18 December 2017, Appointed Person.

[429] See (O-468-12) 26 November 2012 at [72] and [73].

[430] [2011] F.S.R. 11 at [33].

[431] [1989] R.P.C. 367 at 379.

*Replace paragraph:*

**10-292** In the High Court case of *Red Bull GMBH v Sun Mark Ltd, Sea Air & Land Forwarding Ltd*[432] Arnold J in his judgment (at [130]–[138]) helpfully summarised "a number of general principles concerning bad faith for the purposes of Section 3(6) of the 1994 Act/Article 3(2)(d) of the Directive/Article 52(1)(b) of the Regulation which are now fairly well established." These are set out below:

"131. First, the relevant date for assessing whether an application to register a trade mark was made in bad faith is the application date: see Case C-529/07 *Chocoladenfabriken Lindt & Sprüngli AG v Franz Hauswirth GmbH* [2009] ECR I-4893 at [35].

132. Secondly, although the relevant date is the application date, later evidence is relevant if it casts light backwards on the position as at the application date: see *Hotel Cipriani Srl v Cipriani (Grosvenor Street) Ltd* [2009] EHWC 3032 (Ch), [2009] RPC 9 at [167] and cf. Case C-259/02 *La Mer Technology Inc v Laboratoires Goemar SA* [2004] ECR I-1159 at [31] and Case C-192/03 *Alcon Inc v OHIM* [2004] ECR I-8993 at [41].

133. Thirdly, a person is presumed to have acted in good faith unless the contrary is proved. An allegation of bad faith is a serious allegation which must be distinctly proved. The standard of proof is on the balance of probabilities but cogent evidence is required due to the seriousness of the allegation. It is not enough to prove facts which are also consistent with good faith: see *BRUTT Trade Marks* [2007] RPC 19 at [29], *von Rossum v Heinrich Mack Nachf. GmbH & Co KG* (Case R 336/207962, OHIM Second Board of Appeal, 13 November 2007) at [22] and *Funke Kunststoffe GmbH v Astral Property Pty Ltd* (Case R 1621/2006-4, OHIM Fourth Board of Appeal, 21 December 2009) at [22].

134. Fourthly, bad faith includes not only dishonesty, but also 'some dealings which fall short of the standards of acceptable commercial behaviour observed by reasonable and experienced men in the particular area being examined': see *Gromax Plasticulture Ltd v Don & Low Nonwovens Ltd* [1999] RPC 367 at 379 and *DAAWAT Trade Mark* (Case C000659037/1, OHIM Cancellation Division, 28 June 2004) at [8].

135. Fifthly, section 3(6) of the 1994 Act, Article 3(2)(d) of the Directive and Article 52(1)(b) of the Regulation are intended to prevent abuse of the trade mark system: see *Melly's Trade Mark Application* [2008] RPC 20 at [51] and *CHOOSI Trade Mark* (Case R 633/2007-2, OHIM Second Board of Appeal, 29 February 2008) at [21]. As the case law makes clear, there are two main classes of abuse. The first concerns abuse vis-à-vis the relevant office, for example where the applicant knowingly supplies untrue or misleading information in support of his application; and the second concerns abuse vis-à-vis third parties: see *Cipriani* at [185].

136. Sixthly, in order to determine whether the applicant acted in bad faith, the tribunal must make an overall assessment, taking into account all the factors relevant to the particular case: see *Lindt v Hauswirth* at [37].

137. Seventhly, the tribunal must first ascertain what the defendant knew about the matters in question and then decide whether, in the light of that knowledge, the defendant's conduct is dishonest (or otherwise falls short of the standards of acceptable commercial behaviour) judged by ordinary standards of honest people. The applicant's own standards of honesty (or acceptable commercial behaviour)

are irrelevant to the enquiry: see *AJIT WEEKLY Trade Mark* [2006] RPC 25 at [35]–[41], *GERSON Trade Mark* (Case R 916/2004-1, OHIM First Board of Appeal, 4 June 2009) at [53] and *Campbell v Hughes* [2011] RPC 21 at [36].

138. Eighthly, consideration must be given to the applicant's intention."[433]

The judge then quoted the CJEU judgment in *Lindt v Hauswirth* (at [41]–[45]) referred to at para.10-280.[434] These principles have been further summarised along with a summary of the CJEU's judgment in *Koton* (C-104/18P)[434a] in a decision of the Appointed Person in *Carry On Films Ltd's Trade Mark* (BL O/567/19) 27 September 2019 at [23]-[24].

[432] [2013] E.T.M.R. 53.

[433] For a case where the third point set out in *Red Bull GMBH v Sun Mark Ltd, Sea Air & Land Forwarding Ltd* at [133] was the basis for an overturning of a finding of bad faith on appeal see *Unilever Plc v Technopharma Ltd (also known as "New York Fair and Lovely TM")* (O-532-14) 9 December 2014, decision of the Appointed Person, in particular at [65].

[434] This case along with *Williams v Canaries SeaSchool SLU (CLUB SAIL Trade Marks)* [2010] R.P.C. 32 and *Campbell v Hughes (IAN ADAM Trade Mark)* [2011] R.P.C. 21 were helpfully summarised by Birss J in *Hearst v Avela* [2015] at [57]–[58]. The case of *Lindt v Hauswirth* was also considered in *Jaguar Land Rover Ltd v Bombardier Recreational Products Inc* [2016] EWHC 3266 (Ch), in particular at [44]–[46] of the judgment. Here the judge considered the AG's opinion in *Lindt*, particularly at [57]–[60] and stated that: "That seems very similar to what was said by Lindsay J in *Gromax Plasticulture Ltd v Don & Low Nonwovens Ltd* [1999] RPC 567 at 379, summarised by Arnold J in *Red Bull* at [134]."

[434a] See para.10-284.

*Replace paragraph:*

In the later decision of *Malaysia Dairy Industries Pte Ltd v Ankenævnet For Patenter Og Varemærker*[435] the concept of bad faith was again considered by the CJEU. This reference was made in the context of art.4(4)(g) of the 2008 TM Directive (Directive 2008/95).[436] Article 4(4)(g) was an optional provision of the 2008 TM Directive and reads: **10-293**

> "Any Member State may, in addition, provide that a trade mark shall not be registered or, if registered, shall be liable to be declared invalid where, and to the extent that ... (g) the trade mark is liable to be confused with a mark which was in use abroad on the filing date of the application and which is still in use there, provided that at the date of the application the applicant was acting in bad faith."[437]

See also the CJEU's recent decision in *Koton* (C-104/18P) dated 12 September 2019 quoted at para.10-284 which considers the "Applicant's intention".

[435] (C-320/12) [2013] E.T.M.R. 36.

[436] Which was identical to the corresponding provision of Directive 89/104 art.4(4)(g).

[437] This optional provision has not been specifically implemented into UK law under the Trade Marks Act 1994. It should be noted that there is no express directly equivalent provision to Directive 2008/95/EC art.4(4)(g) in the new Trade Mark Directive 2015/2436.

## Implementation of the 1988/2008 TM Directive: is s.32(3) of the Act Compatible with the 1988/2008 TM Directive (and, for that matter, with TRIPS)?

*Replace footnote 441:*

[441] Almost identical passages are found in the seventh Recital of the original Directive 89/104. **10-297**

*Add new paragraph after para.10-297:*

Almost identical wording to the first passage quoted above is found in the twelfth Recital in the 2015 TM Directive (Directive 2015/2436). Almost identical word- **10-297A** ing to the second passage quoted above is found in the fourteenth Recital in the 2015 TM Directive. However, no similar wording to the third passage quoted above is found in 2015 TM Directive, rather the 2015 TM Directive states at the ninth Recital: "For the purpose of making trade mark registrations throughout the Union easier to obtain and administer, it is essential to approximate not only provisions of substantive law but also procedural rules. Therefore, the principal procedural rules in the area of trade mark registration in the Member States and in the EU trade mark system should be aligned. As regards procedures under national law, it is sufficient to lay down general principles, leaving the Member States free to establish more specific rules." Under the 2015 TM Directive the bad faith ground of invalidity in relation to registered marks is a mandatory provision. The wording "… the application for registration of the trade mark was made in bad faith by the applicant" at art.3(2)(d) of 2008 TM Directive is repeated in art.4(2) of the 2015 TM Directive (albeit the recitals are different as explained above), it is assumed that the CJEU will continue to interpret bad faith under the 2015 TM Directive as it has done under the 2008 TM Directive.

*Replace paragraph:*

**10-300** In the context of s.32(3), the Appointed Person[444] has held that "Insofar as the applicant makes a materially false statement in this regard then I believe the application is made in bad faith.", where the requirement that the false statement be "material" allows all the facts and circumstances to be taken into account.

[444] Mr David Kitchin QC as he then was in *Kinder (Ferrero SpA and Soremartee SA v Soldan Holding & Bonbonspezialitaten GmbH* (0-279-03) [2004] R.P.C. 29 at [23].

*Replace paragraph:*

**10-301** There has long been debate in the UK about whether s.32(3) was compatible with EU law. Two Appointed Persons (Messrs Hobbs and Kitchin (as he then was)) have stated they see no reason to doubt that s.32(3) was compatible with Community law.[445] Whereas, Neuberger J has stated[446] it was arguable that the sub-section was not valid at least if it was interpreted as requiring the applicant to verify their intention to use the mark in relation to the full width of the specification of goods or services set out in the application form. In *Red Bull GMBH v Sun Mark Ltd, Sea Air & Land Forwarding Ltd*,[447] Arnold J helpfully reviewed the main cases concerning the lack of intention to use as a ground of bad faith.[448] After this review he observed that, with regards the Community Trade Mark Regulation (now the EU Trade Mark Regulation):

> "As the law presently stands, it appears that there is no requirement under the Regulation that an applicant for registration of a Community trade mark must intend to use the mark. Accordingly, a lack of intention to use does not, at least without more, constitute bad faith: see *TRILLIUM* and *Psytech*. As Jacob J observed in *LA MER*, however, it is open to question whether this is correct. Indeed, it would seem arguable that the reasoning of the CJEU in *Lindt v Hauswirth* at [44]–[45] is applicable: where the applicant has no intention to use the mark, the mark cannot fulfil its essential function of indicating the origin of the applicant's goods or services."[449]

[445] *DEMON ALE* [2000] R.P.C. 345 (G. Hobbs QC); *KINDER* (O-279/03) [2004] R.P.C. 29 at [20] and [24]) (D. Kitchin QC). In *Total v You View* [2015] F.S.R. 7 Sales J refused to make a reference to the CJEU when deciding that there was no bad faith in relation to the applicant's declaration made pursuant to s.32(3) of the 1994 Act, see [77] of the judgment. For further discussion of this case see para.10-309.

[446] *Knoll AG's Trade Mark* [2003] R.P.C. 10 at [34].

[447] [2013] E.T.M.R. 53.

[448] See [139]–[157] of the judgment.

[449] See *Red Bull GMBH v Sun Mark Ltd, Sea Air & Land Forwarding Ltd* [2013] E.T.M.R. 53 at [158]. In this case s.32(3) of the 1994 Act was not in issue however, the requirement for a declaration of intention to use imposed on applicants for international trade marks by the UK under r.7(2) of the Common Regulation under the Madrid Agreement concerning the International Registration was in issue, whereby a contracting party could make a notification that it required a declaration of intention to use the International Marks registered in the contracting state (the case concerned a registration under (International Registration) Order 1996 (SI 1996/714), see para.10-298, fn.440). It was argued that this requirement was incompatible with the 2008 TM Directive or in the alternative it was argued that even if the requirement for such a declaration was compatible with the TM Directive, the making of a false declaration of intent to use did not amount to bad faith within art.3(2)(d) of the TM Directive. The judge recognised that these arguments raised important and difficult issues of European law and that guidance from the CJEU will be required on these issues at some point. However, he concluded that, due to his factual findings, it was not necessary to make a reference in this case.

*Replace paragraph:*

The case of *Jaguar Land Rover Ltd v Bombardier Recreational Products Inc*[450] **10-302** also expressly considered the issue of lack of intention to use in the context of an application for a declaration of invalidity in relation to a EU trade mark. In this case the judge was concerned with a pleading of bad faith on the basis that there was a lack of intention to use the mark when it was applied for, or, more accurately, the trade mark owner had no intention of using the mark for the entire range of goods covered by the application. The court found (at [42]): "On the basis that the decision in *Psytech* being a decision of the General Court, and hence of the Court of Justice of the European Union, is binding on me, I find that the pleaded allegation in support of the bad faith contention cannot as a matter of law constitute bad faith within the meaning of the Regulation. In those circumstances there is no reasonable prospect of the defendant succeeding in its counterclaim to invalidate the EU trade mark. That is sufficient, it seems to me, to justify summary judgment being given for the claim of infringement of the EU trade mark."[451]

[450] [2016] EWHC 3266 (Ch); [2017] F.S.R. 20.

[451] See *Jaguar Land Rover Ltd v Bombardier Recreational Products Inc* [2016] EWHC 3266 (Ch); [2017] F.S.R. 20 at [42]. However the judge went on at [43] to state: "However, I am conscious that there have been expressions of disquiet, to put it no higher, by much more qualified English judges than me on whether that is really the law and in case I am wrong about that there is to my mind another reason why the proposed defence fails. ..." He went on to find at [43]–[50] that the trade mark owner had not been shown to have behaved in a way that could amount to bad faith as there was no fair narrower specification of goods that should have been applied for. For further discussion of this case, see paras 10-321 and 10-327.

*Delete paras 10-303, 10-304, 10-305.*

*Replace paragraph:*

The CJEU found in the case of *Malaysia Dairy Industries Pte Ltd v Ankenævnet For Patenter Og Varemærker*[456] **10-306** that "the answer to the first question is that art.4(4)(g) of Directive 2008/95 must be interpreted as meaning that the concept of 'bad faith', within the meaning of that provision is an autonomous concept of European Union law which must be given a uniform interpretation in the European Union." Also in this case, the CJEU held that the concept of bad faith within the meaning of art.4(4)(g) of Directive 2008/95 should be interpreted in the same manner as in the context of art.52(1)(b) of Council Regulation (EC) No.207/2009, according to which a EU trade mark is to be declared invalid "where the applicant was acting in bad faith when he filed the application for the trade mark". The court held this was necessary in light of the need for harmonious interaction between the two systems of EU and national marks.[457] As stated by the AG in her Opinion in *Lindt*, given the way the legislation is organised there must be a single EU concept of bad faith for both the EU Trade Mark Regulation and the Trade Mark Directive:

> "Article 51 of the Regulation [now Article 52] provides for both OHIM and the national courts to declare a Community trade mark invalid on the basis of bad faith in filing the application, and the same concept must obviously be used by both. Nor does it seem appropriate, given the need for harmonious interaction between the two systems, that national courts should use one concept for Community trade marks and another for national trade marks."[457a]

The CJEU in *Malaysia Dairy Industries* then went on to apply its own case law concerning art.52(1)(b) of Council Regulation (EC) No.207/2009 (i.e. the *Lindt* case) to determine the meaning of bad faith under art.4(4)(g) of Directive 2008/95.

[456] (C-320/12) [2013] E.T.M.R. 36.

[457] *Malaysia Dairy Industries Pte Ltd v Ankenævnet For Patenter Og Varemærker* (C-320/12) [2013] E.T.M.R. 36, CJEU at [35].

[457a] See the AG's Opinion in *Chocoladefabriken Lindt & Sprüngli AG v Franx Hauswirth GmbH* (C-529/07) [2009] E.T.M.R. 56 at [42].

*Delete para.10-307.*

*Replace paragraph:*

**10-308** The Court of Justice in *Lindt* was not directly concerned with the issue of an "intention to use" requirement. However, the Court of Justice did touch on the issue of intention to use albeit in the specific circumstances it was concerned with (which were at the time when the application for registration was filed, several producers were using, on the market, identical or similar signs for identical or similar products capable of being confused with the sign for which registration was sought). In *Lindt* the Court of Justice made clear that the intention to prevent a third party from marketing a product may, in certain circumstances, amount to bad faith on the part of an applicant and held that this would be so when it became apparent subsequently that the applicant applied for a CTM without intending to use it, his sole objective being to prevent a third party from entering the market. The Court of Justice stated that in such a case the CTM does not fulfil its essential function, namely that the consumer or end user can identify the origin of the product or service from those of different origin, without any confusion and referred to the Court of Justice case of *Henkel v OHIM*.[459] Therefore, in *Lindt* the Court of Justice considered that the lack of intention to use a trade mark when it is applied for is a factor which may be taken into account when assessing bad faith.[460]

[459] (C-456/01P and C-457/01P). See Court of Justice judgment in *Chocoladefabriken Lindt & Sprüngli AG v Franx Hauswirth GmbH* (C-529/07) [2009] E.T.M.R. 56 at [44] and [45] where the Court of Justice referred to Joined Cases *Henkel v OHIM* (C-456/01P and C-457/01P) E.C.R. I-5089, [2005] E.T.M.R. 44 at [48].

[460] See also *Red Bull GMBH v Sun Mark Ltd, Sea Air & Land Forwarding Ltd* [2013] E.T.M.R. 53 at [158], where Arnold J considered the CJEU decision in *Lindt* with regards intention to use and bad faith and see paras 10-292 and 10-327.

**10-309** *Change title of sub-section and delete footnote 461:*

## What Sort of Intention will Satisfy the Requirement of s.3(2)(3) of the Act?

*Add new sub-section:*

## Guidance from the CJEU in Sky v SkyKick

**10-314A** In *Sky Plc v SkyKick UK Ltd*[470a] the case before the High Court was such that a detailed reference to the CJEU concerning the much debated issue of an "intention to use" requirement was made. The case concerned the claimant, Sky, the well known television and broadband supplier. The defendants were SkyKick who were involved in providing Microsoft Office 365 migration goods and services. Sky relied on several EU trade marks and one UK trade mark for the mark "Sky" (both word only and figurative with the word "Sky" in a particular font) and complained of SkyKick's use of the sign "SkyKick" in various forms. For the purposes of Sky's infringement claim under art.9(2)(b) of the Regulation/s.10(2)(b) of the Act, Sky relied upon various different parts of the specifications of its various trade marks. Some of the trade mark specifications were simply for the class headings in the Nice Classification for each of the respective classes. Other of the marks' specifications were for the headings of the Nice Classifications along with a series of increasingly detailed descriptions of the various types of goods and services. The specifications relied on included the term computer software (Class 9) which forms part of the relevant Class heading. SkyKick's main attack on the trade marks in suit was to allege that all the Sky marks in issue were invalid in their entirety or partially invalid on the basis of: (a) bad faith, or that (b) part of the specification were unclear or imprecise. Arnold J (as he then was) considered in detail the legal context and the case law in the UK and the EU concerning these issues in his extremely helpful and detailed judgment. He concluded that the law in relation to these issues was not acte clair and therefore he determined it was necessary to make a reference to the CJEU. The following questions were referred to the CJEU:

(1) Can a EU trade mark or a national trade mark registered in a Member State be declared wholly or partially invalid on the ground that some or all of the terms in the specification of goods and services are lacking in sufficient clarity and precision to enable the competent authorities and third parties to determine on the basis of those terms alone the extent of the protection conferred by the trade mark?
(2) If the answer to question (1) is yes, is a term such as "computer software" too general and covers goods which are too variable to be compatible with the trade mark's function as an indication of origin for that term to be sufficiently clear and precise to enable the competent authorities and third parties to determine on the basis of that term alone the extent of the protection conferred by the trade mark?
(3) Can it constitute bad faith simply to apply to register a trade mark without any intention to use it in relation to the specified goods or services?
(4) If the answer to question (3) is yes, is it possible to conclude that the applicant made the application partly in good faith and partly in bad faith if and to the extent that the applicant had an intention to use the trade mark in relation to some of the specified goods or services, but no intention to use the trade mark in relation to other specified goods or services?
(5) Is the UK Trade Marks Act 1994 s.32(3) compatible with Directive 2015/2436 and its predecessors?[470b]

On 29 January 2020 the CJEU handed down its judgment in *Sky v SkyKick* (C-371/18). The CJEU carefully framed its judgment stating that the request for a preliminary ruling must be examined in light of the provisions of Regulation No.40/94 for the EU marks and with regards the national trade marks at issue, the First Directive 89/104, due to the dates of filing of the relevant marks in issue. However, it seems likely that the CJEU's judgment will also be used to apply to cases concerning the 2008/2015 Directives and the 2009/2017 Regulations. In *SkyKick* the CJEU ruled as follows: **10-314B**

"[1] Articles 7 and 51 of Council Regulation (EC) No 40/94 of 20 December 1993 on the Community trade mark, as amended by Council Regulation (EC) No 1891/2006 of 18 December 2006, and Article 3 of First Council Directive 89/104/EEC of 21 December 1988 to approximate the laws of the Member States relating to trade marks must be interpreted as meaning that a Community trade mark or a national trade mark cannot be declared wholly or partially invalid on the ground that terms used to designate the goods and services in respect of which that trade mark was registered lack clarity and precision.[470c]

[2] Article 51(1)(b) of Regulation No 40/94, as amended by Regulation No 1891/2006, and Article 3(2)(d) of First Directive 89/104 must be interpreted as meaning that a trade mark application made without any intention to use the trade mark in relation to the goods and services covered by the registration constitutes bad faith, within the meaning of those provisions, if the applicant for registration of that mark had the intention either of undermining, in a manner inconsistent with honest practices, the interests of third parties, or of obtaining, without even targeting a specific third party, an exclusive right for purposes other than those falling within the functions of a trade mark. When the absence of the intention to use the trade mark in accordance with the essential functions of a trade mark concerns only certain goods or services referred to in the application for registration, that application constitutes bad faith only in so far as it relates to those goods or services.

[3] First Directive 89/104 must be interpreted as not precluding a provision of national law under which an applicant for registration of a trade mark must state that the trade mark is being used in relation to the goods and services in relation to which it is sought to register the trade mark, or that he or she has a bona fide intention that it should be so used, in so far as the infringement of such an obligation does not constitute, in itself, a ground for invalidity of a trade mark already registered."

The CJEU judgment is *SkyKick* is important as it provides clear guidance on some significant issues in the area of bad faith, in particular with its rulings 2 and 3.

**10-314C** In Ruling 2 the CJEU has made clear that a finding of bad faith can result in partial invalidity, if the finding of bad faith only relates to limited goods and services within the specification. The UK courts had been working on this basis already, however the EUIPO had previously provided guidance on a contrary basis stating that "when bad faith of the EUTM owner is established, the whole EUTM is declared invalid, even for goods and services unrelated to those protected by the invalidity applicant's mark."[470d] This guidance was provided following the General Court's judgment in *SA.PAR Srl v OHIM (GRUPPO SALINI)* (T-213/10) EU:T:2013:372 which held at [48] "As OHIM rightly states, the existence of bad faith at the time of the application for registration is filed entails the nullity in its entirety of the mark in issue". Following the CJEU's judgment in *SkyKick*, and in particular Ruling 2, it is clear that the General Court's approach on this issue was incorrect.

**10-314D** Ruling 2 of the CJEU's judgment in *SkyKick* also deals with the issue of an "intention to use" requirement. The CJEU has now ruled that a lack of intention to use the trade mark applied for only constitutes bad faith if it is coupled with the "intention either of undermining, in a manner inconsistent with honest practices, the interests of third parties, or of obtaining, without even targeting a specific third party, an exclusive right for purposes other than those falling within the functions of a trade mark." Some further guidance on this additional intention element is found with the CJEU's *SkyKick* judgment at [74]–[78], and in particular [77] and [78], which state:

"[77] However, as the Advocate General observed in point 109 of his Opinion, the registration of a trade mark by an applicant without any intention to use it in relation to the goods and services covered by that registration may constitute bad faith, where there is no rationale for the application for registration in the light of the aims referred to in Regulation No 40/94 and First Directive 89/104. Such bad faith may, however, be established only if there is objective, relevant and consistent indicia tending to show that, when the application for a trade mark was filed, the trade mark applicant had the intention either of undermining, in a manner inconsistent with honest practices, the interests of third parties, or of obtaining, without even targeting a specific third party, an exclusive right for purposes other than those falling within the functions of a trade mark.

[78] The bad faith of the trade mark applicant cannot, therefore, be presumed on the basis of the mere finding that, at the time of filing his or her application, that applicant had no economic activity corresponding to the goods and services referred to in that application."

The CJEU therefore makes clear that where there is no intention to use the trade mark (at the application date[470e]) "in relation to the goods and services covered by that registration may constitute bad faith where there is no rationale for the application for registration in light of the aims referred to in Regulation No 40/94 and First Directive 89/104". Further the CJEU has made clear that bad faith may, however, only be established if there is "objective, relevant and consistent indicia tending to show" that, when the application for a trade mark was filed the applicant had the additional intention as set out in Ruling 2 and quoted above. This reflects the principle that a person is presumed to have acted in good faith unless the contrary is proved. An allegation of bad faith is a serious allegation which must be distinctly proved (see *BRUTT Trade Marks* [2007] R.P.C. 19 at [29], *von Rossum v Heinrich Mack Nachf. GmbH & Co KG* (Case R 336/207962, OHIM Second Board of Appeal, 13 November 2007) at [22] and *Funke Kunststoffe GmbH v Astral Property Pty Ltd* (Case R 1621/2006-4, OHIM Fourth Board of Appeal, 21 December 2009) at [22]). The CJEU in *SkyKick* also made clear at [78] that bad faith cannot be presumed on the basis of the mere finding that at the time of filing of the application, that the applicant had no economic activity corresponding to the goods and services to in that application, i.e. a genuine future intention to trade in those goods and services may suffice.

Ruling 3 is important because it finally answers the much debated question as to **10-314E**
whether s.32(3) of the Act is compatible with the 1988 TM Directive. Ruling 3 in *SkyKick* finds that the 1988 Directive (89/104) must be interpreted as not precluding a provision of national law under which an applicant for registration of a trade mark must state that the trade mark is being used in relation to the goods and services for which it is sought to register the trade mark, or that they have a bona fide intention that it should be so used. Therefore, s.32(3) of the Act is not prima facie incompatible with EU law. However, the CJEU made clear that such a provision can only be compatible with EU law in so far as the infringement of such an obligation does not constitute, in itself, a ground for invalidity of a trade mark already registered. This means that a finding that a declaration under s.32(3) of the Act is false cannot of itself in isolation give rise to a finding of bad faith so as to invalidate a trade mark. The CJEU set out its reasoning behind Ruling 3 at [82]–[88] of the judgment. In particular the CJEU held:

"[85] It follows that while Member States may fix the provisions of procedure which appear to them to be appropriate, such provisions cannot, in practice, have the effect of introducing grounds of refusal of registration or invalidity not provided for by First Directive 89/104.

[86] Consequently, a provision of national law under which an applicant for registration of a national trade mark must, pursuant to a mere procedural requirement relating to the registration of that mark, state that the trade mark is being used in relation to the goods and services in relation to which it is sought to register the trade mark, or that he or she has a bona fide intention that it should be so used, cannot be considered incompatible with the provisions of First Directive 89/104. While the infringement of such an obligation to make such a statement may constitute evidence for the purposes of establishing possible bad faith on the part of the trade mark applicant when he or she filed the trade mark application, such an infringement cannot, however, constitute a ground for invalidity of the trade mark concerned."

The CJEU's judgment in this regard is somewhat of a fudge. Section 32(3) of the Act does go further than a "mere procedural requirement", however the CJEU's judgment is not surprising. The key point that should be taken from the judgment is that a finding that a declaration under s.32(3) of the Act is false cannot of itself lead to a finding of invalidity on the basis of bad faith, more is required. This finding also fits well with the CJEU's judgment in *Lindt* which states when considering bad faith "the national court must take into consideration all the relevant factors specific to the particular case which pertained at the time of filing the application for registration of the sign as a Community trade mark".[470f] The CJEU's guidance in *SkyKick* on this issue is also in line with the judgment of Mr David Kitchin QC as he then was, sitting as an Appointed Person in *Kinder (Ferrero SpA and Soremartee SA v Soldan Holding & Bonbonspezialitaten GmbH*.[470g] Here he expressed the view that "Insofar as the applicant makes a materially false statement in this regard then I believe the application is made in bad faith." The requirement that the false statement be "material" allows all the facts and circumstances to be taken into account.

**10-314F** On 29 April 2020 Arnold LJ handed down his judgment in *Sky Plc v SkyKick UK Ltd*,[470h] following the CJEU's Ruling. The court found that, following the guidance provided by the CJEU, certain parts of Sky's trade marks had been applied for in bad faith. In particular the judgment held as follows:

"[19] The key findings of fact in the Main Judgment[470i] were as follows:

'250. The conclusion I draw from Mr Tansey's evidence is that, at the dates of applying for the Trade Marks, Sky did not intend to use the Trade Marks in relation to all of the goods and services covered by the specifications. Sky were already using the Trade Marks in relation to some of the goods and services; Sky had concrete plans for using the Trade Marks in relation to some other goods and services; and Sky had a reasonable basis for supposing that they might wish to use the Trade Marks in the future in relation to some further goods. But the specifications include goods and services in respect of which Sky had no reasonable commercial rationale for seeking registration. I am forced to conclude that the reason for including such goods and services was that Sky had a strategy of seeking very broad protection of the Trade Marks regardless of whether it was commercially justified.

251. It is important to note that the specifications included goods and services in relation to which I find that Sky had no intention to use the Trade Marks in three different ways. First, the specifications included specific goods in relation to which I find that Sky no intention to use the Trade Marks at all. Examples of this are "bleaching preparations" (Class 3, EU992 and UK604), "insulation materials" (Class 17, EU992 and UK604) and "whips" (Class 18, EU352, EU619, EU992 and UK604).

> Secondly, the specification included categories of goods and services that were so broad that Sky could not, and did not, intend to use the Trade Marks across the breadth of the category. The paradigm example of this is "computer software" in EU112, EU992 and UK604, but there are others … . Thirdly, the specifications were intended to cover all of the goods and services in relevant classes. For example, the Class 9 specifications, including the Class 9 specifications in EU352 and EU619, were intended to cover not just any computer software, but a great deal more besides. …'

[20] In addition, in the case of UK604, I found that Sky plc's section 32(3) declaration was partly false: see the Main Judgment at [254].

[21] In my judgment Sky applied for the Trade Marks partly in bad faith in each of the three ways referred to in the Main Judgment at [251]. Not merely did they not intend to use the Trade Marks in relation to some goods and services covered by the specifications at the application dates, but there was no foreseeable prospect that they would ever intend to use the Trade Marks in relation to such goods and services. Moreover, Sky made the applications pursuant to a deliberate strategy of seeking very broad protection of the Trade Marks regardless of whether it was commercially justified. Sky thus applied for the Trade Marks with the intention of obtaining an exclusive right for purposes other than those falling within the functions of a trade mark, namely purely as a legal weapon against third parties, whether in threats of infringement claims or actual infringement claims or oppositions to third party applications for registration (as to which, see also the Main Judgment at [69]–[72]).

[22] In the case of UK604, there is the additional factor that Sky made a partly false section 32(3) declaration in order to obtain such protection. That is plainly inconsistent with honest practices in industrial and commercial matters, and thus strengthens the conclusion that, to that extent, Sky made that application in bad faith."

The court then went on to consider how the specifications of the goods and services for the trade marks should be cut down following this finding of bad faith. Of particular importance are [24] and [25] of the judgment which state:

"[24] It is convenient once again to start with 'computer software' in Class 9. SkyKick's primary contention is that, given that I have concluded that Sky acted in bad faith in the second way identified in the Main Judgment at [251], it follows that the Trade Marks should be declared invalid in so far as they are registered for 'computer software'. In my judgment, this does not follow. The fact that Sky did not intend to use the Trade Marks across the breadth of this category of goods does not mean that they did not intend to use the Trade Marks in relation to any computer software. On the contrary, I made findings in the Main Judgment that Sky had actually used the Trade Marks in relation to some kinds of software.

[25] In the alternative, SkyKick contend that the Court should adopt a similar approach to that adopted in the context of revocation for non-use (as to which, see *Merck KGaA v Merck Sharp Dohme Corp* [2017] EWCA Civ 1834, [2018] ETMR 10 at [242]–[249]). In my judgment, however, there is a significant difference between the Court's tasks in the two contexts. In the non-use context the Court's task is to devise a fair specification having regard to the use of the trade mark during the relevant period which has been established by the proprietor (on whom the burden of proving use rests). In this context the Court's task is to determine the extent to which it is necessary to cut down the specification having regard to the bad faith of the trade mark proprietor which has been established by the opposing party (on whom the burden of proving bad faith rests). To the extent that bad faith is not proved, then the specification must be left alone. Subject to that, I accept that there is a similarity between the two tasks, in that the

Court must consider in both cases the extent to which a broad category of goods or services embraces subcategories which are, as Kitchin LJ put it in *Merck*, 'capable of being viewed independently', and thus fall to be separately considered."

In this case SkyKick put forward a proposed new, more limited specification to replace "computer software", Sky did not put forward a proposed new specification. The judge found that the SkyKick's proposed new specification was based upon the judge's findings as to the use Sky Plc had actually made of the trade marks in issue. However, this was problematic because as stated by the judge "it does not follow that Sky had no commercial justification for seeking protection wider than their actual use. On the contrary, it is well established that trade mark proprietors have a legitimate interest in seeking protection in respect of goods or services in relation to which they may wish to use the trade mark in question in future. Furthermore, as the non-use cases show, even in that context proprietors also have a legitimate interest in seeking a modest penumbra of protection extending beyond the specific goods and services in relation to which use had been proved (but not to distinct categories or subcategories of goods and services)."[470j]

**10-314G** Therefore, the judge concluded:

"[29] In the absence of any alternative proposal from Sky, I must do the best I can to devise a specification which reflects the extent of the bad faith proved, but no more. The conclusion I have reached is that the Trade Marks should be declared invalid in relation to 'computer software' except for the following: 'computer software supplied as part of or in connection with any television, video recording or home entertainment apparatus or service; computer software supplied as part of or in connection with any telecommunications apparatus or service; electronic calendar software; application software for accessing audio, visual and/or audio-visual content via mobile telephones and/or tablet computers; games software'

[30] I am conscious of the fact that the first two parts of this wording could be said to be somewhat imprecise, but I have not been able to devise more precise wording which gives Sky fair protection. I should explain that I consider that telephony, broadband, wifi, email and instant messaging are all embraced by 'telecommunications'. Although it might be argued that 'electronic calendar software' and 'application software for accessing audio, visual and/or audio-visual content via mobile telephones and/or tablet computers' would be covered by 'computer software supplied … in connection with … any telecommunications … service', I have included them separately in order to make sure that they are covered. Although it does not appear to me that Sky have supplied, or intended to supply, games software as a good, rather than as a service, I consider that they cannot be accused of bad faith in seeking protection for it as a good as well."

The judge went on to consider other parts of the specifications which he held had been applied for in bad faith and produced alternative specifications for these parts.[470k]

470a [2018] EWHC 155 (Ch); [2018] R.P.C. 5.

470b See [47] of *Sky Plc v SkyKick UK Ltd* (CJEU) (C-371/18) dated 29 January 2020.

470c For the reasoning behind this ruling see [54]–[71] of the CJEU's judgment in *SkyKick* (C-371/18). It should be noted that at [64] of the judgment the CJEU made reference to the *Sieckmann* case (C-273/00) [2003] R.P.C. 38 (ECJ) which was concerned with the requirement of graphic representability under art.2 of the 1988 Directive (89/104), which means that operators must, with clarity and precision, be able to find out about registrations or applications made by third parties. However, the CJEU in *SkyKick* made clear that these considerations only apply in order to identify the signs of which a trade mark may consist of, i.e. not its specifications. The fact that the CJEU in *SkyKick* expressly referred to the *Sieckmann* case implies that if the same point concerning whether a specification lacking clarity or precision, but registered under art.3 of the 2015 TM Directive or art.4 of the 2017 Regulation, could be declared invalid, the same ruling would be given by the CJEU as that given in Ruling 1 of *SkyKick*. The CJEU's Ruling 1 in *SkyKick* accords with the view put forward by Arnold J as he then was in *Stichting BDO v BDO Unibank Inc* [2013] F.S.R. 35. Due to the response given in Ruling 1 the CJEU determined that there was no reason to answer the second question referred. This means the problems created by imprecise and unclear registered trade mark specifications as identified by Laddie J in *Mercury Communications Ltd v Mercury Interactive Ltd* [1995] F.S.R. 850 at 864-865 where he stated: "In my view it is thoroughly undesirable that a trader who is interested in one limited area of computer software should, by registration, obtain a statutory monopoly of indefinite duration covering all types of software, including those which are far removed from his own area of trading interest.", other than by revocation after the designated five-year period on non-use is still to be resolved. The CJEU in *Sky v SkyKick* (C-371/18) at [68]–[70] considered the issue of revocation on the basis of non-use in relation to registered specifications that lack clarity and precision. Note that in *Sky Plc v SkyKick UK Ltd* [2020] EWHC 990 (Ch), which is the High Court's judgment following the CJEU's ruling, Arnold LJ held that: "[12] It is clear from the CJEU's first ruling that the Trade Marks cannot be declared wholly or partly invalid on the ground that their specifications are lacking in clarity or precision. It follows that that part of SkyKick's counterclaim must be dismissed."

[470d] See *EUIPO Guidelines for Examination of European Trade Marks*, Part D Cancellation (1 October 2017 ed), para.3.3.5.

[470e] See *Chocoladefabriken Lindt & Sprüngli AG v Franz Hauswirth GmbH* [2009] ETMR 56 (C-529/07) EU:C:2009:361; [2009] E.T.M.R. 56 at [35].

[470f] See *Chocoladefabriken Lindt & Sprüngli AG v Franz Hauswirth GmbH* (C-529/07) EU:C:2009:361; [2009] E.T.M.R. 56 at [38] and [53].

[470g] (O-279-03); [2004] R.P.C. 29 at [23].

[470h] [2020] EWHC 990 (Ch).

[470i] The main judgment is found at *Sky Plc v SkyKick UK Ltd* [2018] EWHC 155 (Ch); [2018] R.P.C. 5.

[470j] See *Sky Plc v SkyKick UK Ltd* [2020] EWHC 990 (Ch) at [28].

[470k] See *Sky Plc v SkyKick UK Ltd* [2020] EWHC 990 (Ch) at [31]–[33].

## When May the Issue of Bad Faith Arise?

*Replace footnote 471:*

[471] Trade Mark Rules 2008 (SI 2008/1797) r.8(2)(b) states: "Where the specification contained in the application describes the goods or services using general terms, including the general indications included in the class headings of the Nice Classification, the application shall be treated as including only the goods or services clearly covered by the literal meaning of the term or indication" and r.8(2)(a) states: " For the purposes of paragraph 2(b) an application may specify the general indications included in the class headings of the Nice Classification or other general terms provided that they satisfy the requirement that the goods or services be described with sufficient clarity and precision referred to in paragraph (2)(b)." **10-315**

*Replace paragraph:*

Under ss.47 and 48, the allegation that an application was made in bad faith can **10-317** be raised in relation to any registered trade mark, whether the application for it was examined under the 1994 Act or under previous legislation. Although not necessarily determinative, the statements made by the applicant to the Registry at the time of application and during the application stage are likely to be relevant to the issue of bad faith. Hence it may be necessary to examine what statements and representations were actually made at the time of application, even under previous Acts. It should also be noted that the Appointed Person in *CKL Holdings NV v Paperstacked Ltd* (O-036-18) 18 December 2017 held:

> "[19] At this point I must emphasise that s.3(6) proceeds upon the premise that the right to apply for registration of a trade mark cannot validly be exercised in bad faith. The invalidity of the application is not conditional upon the trade mark itself being either registrable or unregistrable in relation to any goods or services of the kind specified. The objection is absolute in the sense that it is intended to prevent

abusive use of the system for acquiring title to a trade mark by registration. Any natural or legal person with the capacity to sue and be sued may pursue an objection on this ground: see the judgment of the CJEU in Case C-408/08P *Lancome parfums et beaute & Cie SNC v OHIM* EU:C:2010:92 at paragraph [39] and the Opinion of Advocate General Ruiz-Jarabo Colomer in that case EU:C:2009:634 at paragraphs [63] and [64]. Since there is no requirement for the objector to be personally aggrieved by the filing of the application in question, it is possible for an objection to be upheld upon the basis of improper behaviour by the applicant towards persons who are not parties to the proceedings provided that their position is established with enough clarity to show that the objection is well-founded."

## Pleading and Practice

*Replace footnote 477:*

**10-319** [477] [2007] R.P.C. 19. See also *Sky Plc v SkyKick UK Ltd* [2020] EWHC 990 (Ch), where the defendants in this case sought a very late amendment (post-trial and post-reference to the CJEU) to allege that a further part of the claimants' trade mark specification was applied for in bad faith, Arnold LJ held at [15]: "In my judgment it is far too late for SkyKick to seek to raise this allegation now. As Sky point out, bad faith is a serious allegation which must be distinctly pleaded and proved. Sky cannot be deprived of the opportunity of adducing evidence to answer such an allegation, which is the effect of what SkyKick are proposing. The only alternative would be to have a second trial on these issues, but SkyKick do not suggest taking that course and in any event to do so would in my view amount to an abuse of process."

*Add new paragraph after para.10-320:*

**10-320A** For a case where a finding of bad faith was made where the Trade Mark applicant led no positive evidence as to their intention see *CKL Holdings NV v Paperstacked Ltd "Alexander TM"* (O-443-17), the finding of bad faith was upheld on Appeal by the Appointed Peron in the decision at (O-036-18) 18 December 2017. In this decision the Appointed Person proposed that the tribunal should determine the following:

> "[8] The key questions for determination by the Hearing Officer were: (1) what in concrete terms, was the objective that CKL [the trade mark Applicant] had been accused of pursuing? (2) was that objective for the purposes of which the contested application could not properly be filed? (3) was it established that the contested application was filed in pursuit of that objective?"

Another case where a finding of bad faith was made where the Trade Mark applicant led no positive evidence as to their intention was *Trump International Ltd v DTTM Operations LLC* (O-409-18), where the applicant applied for the mark "TRUMP TV" but was unconnected to Mr Donald Trump. This decision was appealed to the High Court and the Appeal was dismissed by the court in *Trump International Ltd v DTTM Operations LLC*.[480a] The Comptroller General of Patents, Designs and Trade Marks intervened in the Appeal to seek guidance over some general issues of concern. The High Court provided the following guidance for the Registry at [85]:

> "(i) Where an application is made for a well-known trade mark with which the applicant has no apparent connection, this requires explanation and justification by the applicant;
>
> (ii) other instances of such applications by the applicant (or persons or companies connected to the applicant) may be admissible as similar fact evidence and may refute the explanation and justification provided by the applicant;
>
> (iii) it is necessary to distinguish between unsubstantiated allegations and established facts of direct relevance to the case before the IPO. In the present case the similar fact evidence was potentially probative and it was just to consider it;

(iv) the *Alexander* questions [taken from the case of *CKL Holdings NV v Paper-stacked Limited* and quoted above] provide a useful structure for considering allegations of bad faith, as shown by the Decision of the hearing officer in the present case. However, like the *Pozzoli* questions, which provide a structured approach to the issue of inventive step in relation to patents, they are not a substitute for the statute and do not have to be used in every case. Bad faith has numerous manifestations and cannot be classified comprehensively;

(v) the Registrar may strike out proceedings brought for an ulterior and improper purpose as an abuse of process; and

(vi) the power to strike out must be exercised with caution. However, where a prima facie case of bad faith is established, and no evidence in answer is filed on behalf of the applicant, it may well be appropriate to exercise that power."

[480a] [2019] EWHC 769 (Ch); [2019] F.S.R. 28.

*Replace footnote 482:*

[482] See in particular *Jaguar Land Rover Ltd v Bombardier Recreational Products Inc* [2016] EWHC 3266 (Ch); [2017] F.S.R. 20 at [47]–[52]. **10-321**

*Replace footnote 485:*

[485] See for example *TWG Tea Co v Mariage Fréres, SA* (O-131-16) 7 January 2016; [2016] R.P.C. 7. **10-322** In this case the Appointed Person held at [22] that in circumstances where the applicant had provided a signed witness statement which denied any copying of the mark applied for from material of the opponent that, although the hearing officer was not obliged to accept the applicant's witness evidence on every point, in the case of a serious accusation of bad faith, the tribunal should be slow to disbelieve evidence of the accused party which was not challenged in cross-examination, unless there are very cogent and persuasive reasons for doing so. Also see, in general, paras 7-105 to 7-114 concerning registry practice concerning challenging evidence and cross-examination.

## Examples

### Ownership of the mark

*Replace list item "(6)" with:* **10-324**

*Bad faith established—examples*

(6) The proprietor of the registered trade marks in issue (which included inter alia the marks "BRUTT HELICAL", "BRUTT" and "BRUTT BOND") had been involved in a joint venture with the founder of the applicant companies. The applicant companies applied for the declaration of invalidity of the trade marks in issue on the basis of inter alia bad faith. The joint venture was to manufacture and market products in line with those found in the specification of the trade marks in issue and was carried out using a jointly owned company and these joint venture products were marketed under trade marks which included the trade marks in issue. Also the trade marks in issue derived from the applicant companies' founder's family name "Brütt". Further the proprietor of the registered trade marks in issue was one of a number of distributors of products supplied by the joint venture company and the other distributors understood that the marks belonged to the applicant companies. Neither the joint venture company nor the Brütt family had consented to the trade mark applications in issue. No explanation was provided as to the timing of the applications, which were made at a time where the joint venture relationship was in difficulties. It was held that the inference was irresistible that the trade mark proprietor anticipated that the relationship was likely to come to an end soon. The Appointed Person considered this to be "a case of a party seeking to lay its hands on

the trade marks of another with whom it had contractual or quasi contractual relations" and held that the s.3(6) ground had been made out and allowed the appeal.[492]

[492] *BRUTT Trade Marks* [2007] R.P.C. 19 (Appointed Person), see particuarly [96]–[100]. The original Hearing Officer had dismissed the s.3(6) objection on the basis that the applicant for the declaration of invalidity had not discharged the burden of proof.

## No bona fide intention to use the mark

**10-325** *Replace list item "(1)" with:*

*Bad faith not established—examples*

(1) The claimant, Jaguar Land Rover Ltd, was a manufacturer of vehicles, and until early 2016 sold a range of vehicles under the name "Defender". These vehicles were very well known. The claimant was the registered proprietor of a EU trade mark filed in October 2014 for various goods and service including in class 12 "Land vehicles; motor vehicles; motor land vehicles". The defendant was a Canadian company who also made vehicles, including a vehicle which was referred to as a "side by side" vehicle and was described as a fun recreational off roader but was not road legal nor designed for road use. This vehicle was marketed under the name "Defender". The claimant alleged inter alia that the defendant's use of the sign Defender infringed its EU trade mark for the mark "Defender". The defendant counterclaimed inter alia for a declaration that the EU trade mark was invalid on the ground that the applicant/claimant was acting in bad faith when it filed the application for the trade mark application. The pleaded basis for the bad faith allegation was that at the time of filing the applicant/claimant had no intention to use the term "DEFENDER" in relation to any other land vehicle, motor vehicle or motor land vehicle, save for the ones it had used it on which was alleged to have been a single car whose essential features had remained the same since 1948. The judge explained that in his view the allegation should be more accurately described as one where the claimant had no intention of using the mark for the entire range of goods covered by the application. The judge held that in relation to EU trade marks that the pleaded allegation in support of bad faith could not as a matter of law constitute bad faith within the meaning of the EUTM Regulation.[501] Further, the judge went on to find[502] that the trade mark owner had not been shown to have behaved in a way that could amount to bad faith. In particular the judge held that before the applicant could be found to have acted in bad faith on the basis that he applied for too wide a specification of goods, elementary principles of pleading required that the person making such a charge had to say in what respect it was too wide. Unless the defendant could point to some narrower specification which could be characterised as a fair specification, the judge held that the defendant could not establish that the claimant in applying for a wider specification acted in bad faith, as the whole premise of the allegation was that he was acting in a way that fell short of standards of acceptable commercial behaviour observed by reasonable experienced men in the trade, which relied on an alternative fair narrower specification being pleaded and demonstrated. In oral argument the defendant submitted that a fair narrower specification would be "motor cars, automobiles and cars". However, the claimant was able to show the court

that "cars" was too narrow due to the different styles of Defender vehicles that had been made available by the claimant. The judge therefore rejected as unarguable the suggestion that a fair specification for the claimant's vehicles would have been cars and ultimately found that the defendant had no real prospect of success in its counterclaim for a declaration of invalidity of the EU trade mark on the grounds of bad faith.[502a]

[501] See *Jaguar Land Rover Ltd v Bombardier Recreational Products Inc* [2016] EWHC 3266 (Ch) at [41]–[42], where the judge particularly relied on *Psytech* [2011] E.T.M.R. 46 (a decision of the General Court, referred to above at para.10-302).

[502] See [43]–[52] of *Jaguar Land Rover Ltd v Bombardier Recreational Products Inc* [2016] EWHC 3266 (Ch); [2017] F.S.R. 20.

[502a] See *Jaguar Land Rover Ltd v Bombardier Recreational Products Inc* [2016] EWHC 3266 (Ch); [2017] F.S.R. 20, in particular [43]–[52].

## Width of specification

*After item "(3)", add:* **10-328**

*Bad faith established—examples*

(4) The claimant, Sky Plc, was found by the High Court to have applied for certain Trade Marks partly in bad faith because, in relation specifications such as "computer software" in Class 9, ... "[21] ... Not merely did they not intend to use the Trade Marks in relation to some goods and services covered by the specifications at the application dates, but there was no foreseeable prospect that they would ever intend to use the Trade Marks in relation to such goods and services. Moreover, Sky made the applications pursuant to a deliberate strategy of seeking very broad protection of the Trade Marks regardless of whether it was commercially justified. Sky thus applied for the Trade Marks with the intention of obtaining an exclusive right for purposes other than those falling within the functions of a trade mark, namely purely as a legal weapon against third parties, whether in threats of infringement claims or actual infringement claims or oppositions to third party applications for registration" and further at [22]: "In the case of UK604, there is the additional factor that Sky made a partly false s.32(3) declaration in order to obtain such protection. That is plainly inconsistent with honest practices in industrial and commercial matters, and thus strengthens the conclusion that, to that extent, Sky made that application in bad faith."[526a]

[526a] See *Sky Plc v SkyKick UK Ltd* [2020] EWHC 990 (Ch) which is considered above at para.10-314F.

## Other situations

*Replace paragraph:*

*The specification of goods or services is too broad—examples*

Some discussion of these examples is required. Where there is a clear discrepancy between actual use/intended use and the specification applied for, bad faith can be found with relative ease. Often the discrepancy will not be so obvious.[537] The difficulty is in deciding the appropriate level of generality and scope of a specification which gives adequate protection to the trader concerned. Often, the appropriate scope can only be decided with knowledge of the trade concerned, **10-335** but this type of enquiry is not compatible with bad faith. Consideration of the case of *Total v You View*[538] is important in this regard. In particular this case is considered at paras 10-309 and 10-327. Reference should also be made to *Jaguar Land Rover Ltd v Bombardier Recreational Products Inc*[539] which is considered at paras 10-302, 10-321 and 10-327. Reference should also be made to *Sky Plc v SkyKick UK Ltd*[539a] which is considered at paras 10-314F and 10–328. The CJEU's guidance in its Ruling 2 in *SkyKick* is a critical importance here which states: "a trade mark application made without any intention to use the trade mark in relation to the goods and services covered by the registration constitutes bad faith, within the meaning of those provisions, if the applicant for registration of that mark had the intention either of undermining, in a manner inconsistent with honest practices, the interests of third parties, or of obtaining, without even targeting a specific third party, an exclusive right for purposes other than those falling within the functions of a trade mark."[539b]

537 See *TESCO WE SELL FOR LESS* (O-256-04) [2005] R.P.C. 17, Appointed Person. Ruth Annand, where a "wide-claiming" allegation of bad faith failed: see [17]–[27] especially [24].

538 [2015] F.S.R. 7. See in particular [74]–[76] of the judgment.

539 [2016] EWHC 3266 (Ch); [2017] F.S.R. 20.

539a [2020] EWHC 990 (Ch).

539b See the discussion of Ruling 2 at para.10–314D.

## Marks Incorporating the Name or Image of a Well-known Person, Without their Agreement

*Add to the end of the paragraph:*

**10-341** For a recent case where a famous person succeeded in opposing a trade mark application for their name, by an unconnected business, see *Vera Lynn* (O-766-19) dated 12 December 2019. In this case the trade mark applicant applied for the trade mark "VERA LYNN" for goods in class 33 "Alcoholic beverages (except beer); spirits" they also had a fallback position of a registration just for "gin" in class 33. The Hearing Officer found that the opposition by Dame Vera Lynn succeeded on both the main and fallback position on the basis of an objection under s.5(4)(a) and under s.3(6). In relation to the s.3(6) objection, the Hearing Officer held as follows:

> "[68] The relevant date is 14 June 2018, by which point the applicant must have known of the existence of Vera Lynn for the entertainment and charity services for which it accepts she has goodwill. Having found that the mark applied for and the earlier right are identical and that there is a likelihood of deception amongst a significant proportion (majority) of the public, I have accepted that, viewed objectively, there is a prima facie case of bad faith. The case law is clear that an allegation of bad faith is a serious one which must be proven. For the purposes of a bad faith claim which relies entirely on the applicant's intention, it is not possible for the opponent to file evidence which will show it. The applicant, on the other hand had ample opportunity to file such evidence and has not done so… . There are no witness statements and there is no evidence which illustrates the rational for the applicant filing the trade mark.
>
> [69] The applicant may well believe it has acted legitimately in pursuit of its business. However, as per point seven of the decision in *Red Bull* the applicant's own standards of honesty, or what the applicant considers to be acceptable commercial behaviour, is irrelevant. What matters is whether the applicant's actions are such as would be judged by other honest people in business to be bad faith. Having considered all of the material before me, I find that on the balance of probabilities, they would be.

[70] I find that the opposition in respect of section 3(6) succeeds."

Chapter 11

# RELATIVE GROUNDS FOR REFUSAL OF REGISTRATION

Table of Contents



## 1. Introduction

*Add to end of the paragraph:*

**11-006** During the implementation period 1 February to 31 December 2020 ("IP completion day") the meanings of the terms "earlier trade marks" and "earlier rights" remain unchanged. Following IP completion day and the entry into force of the amendments brought by the Trade Marks (Amendment etc.) (EU Exit) Regulations 2019/269 (the "TM Exit Regulations"),[2a] EU rights and marks are excluded from the scope of these terms (subject to subsisting claims to seniority in the UK), and in consequence relative grounds for the purposes of the 1994 Act are to be limited to national rights (including "comparable trade marks (EU)", constituting EUTMs registered as at IP completion day). Conversely, with its departure from the EU, the UK is no longer a Member State and (subject to the continuation of the status quo during the implementation period) provisions of the EUTM Regulation no longer apply to the UK or to UK-founded earlier trade marks or earlier rights.

[2a] Trade Marks (Amendment etc.) (EU Exit) Regulations 2019/269 Sch.3 para.3. Note that the term "Exit Day" (31 January 2020) has been globally replaced by "IP completion day" (31 December 2020) by European Union (Withdrawal Agreement) Act 2020 Sch.5 para.1.

*Replace paragraph:*

**11-009** Secondly, on 1 May 2004 the European Community (now Union) was enlarged by the accession of 10 new Member States. As from the date of accession what was then called a Community trade mark registered or applied for before the date of accession was automatically extended to the territory of those new Member States in order to have equal effect throughout the EU.[3] With effect from IP completion day (presently 31 December 2020), the UK will cease to be a part of the EU trade mark system. Section 52A and Sch.2A of the 1994 Act[3a] provide for all EU trade marks existing immediately before then to be treated as UK trade marks in respect of the same goods and/or services as registered for at the EUIPO. Such trade marks are categorised as "comparable trade marks (EU)").[3b]

[3] art.209 of the EUTM Regulation. For the purposes of relative grounds, an exceptional opposition right was established. Where an application for what was then called a Community trade mark was filed in the six months prior to the date of accession then earlier trade marks or earlier rights in the new Member States could be relied upon in opposition proceedings, provided they were acquired in good faith, art.209(3) of the EUTM Regulation.

[3a] As amended by the Trade Marks (Amendment etc.) (EU Exit) Regulations (SI 2019/269) Cl.2 and Sch.1.

[3b] Sch.2A cl.2 provides for the proprietor of a EU Trade Mark to opt out of conversion to a comparable trade mark (EU).

## 2. Conflict With Earlier Trade Marks

## A. Meaning of an Earlier Trade Mark

### Position under the 1994 Act

*Add to the end of the paragraph:*

Following IP completion day, the definition of earlier trade mark under s.6(1) of the 1994 Act excludes EU trade marks (save for comparable trade marks (EU) with a valid claim to seniority in the UK) and only extends to Madrid Protocol marks ("International Registrations") which are protected in the UK. However, in that all International Registrations designating the EU will give rise to an equivalent UK mark registered in respect of the same specification, the position of proprietors of such International marks remains essentially the same. Further, the proprietor of any EU-protected International Registration will remain entitled to rely on the seniority claimed for that registration under the EUTM Regulation. **11-011**

### Registered Trade Marks, the Madrid Protocol and EU Trade Marks

*Add to the end of the paragraph:*

Where a UK trade mark or International Registration has been surrendered or allowed to lapse but a valid claim for seniority of the equivalent EU trade mark has been made, the equivalent EU trade mark or International Registration remains a relevant earlier trade mark in the UK and the proprietor remains entitled to claim seniority even after IP completion day.[11a] **11-017**

[11a] s.6 (as amended after IP completion day).

### Applications for Registration

*Replace footnote 12:*

[12] s.6(2). Following IP completion day applications for registration under the EU trade mark system and applications for Madrid Protocol marks which designate the EU are no longer earlier marks for the purposes of s.6 as to be amended. However, for a period of nine months following IP completion day, applicants for such marks are entitled to file equivalent UK applications in respect of which the priority date is that of the EU trade mark application or Madrid Protocol application as appropriate (para.24-025, Sch.2A and Sch.2B para.28 of the Act respectively). **11-018**

### Position under the EU Trade Mark Regulation

*Replace list item "(1)" with:*

(1) EU trade marks, national trade marks registered in any Member State, or, in the case of Belgium, the Netherlands or Luxembourg, at the Benelux Trade Mark Office and any trade marks registered under international arrangements which have effect in a Member State or in what is now the EU (previously, the Community)[16] (i.e. under the Madrid system). Under the terms of the Withdrawal Agreement the UK is to be treated as a Member **11-021**

State (despite leaving the EU) until 31 December 2020, IP completion day;

[16] Added by Council Regulation 992/2003 to Regulation 40/94. This amendment came into force on the date on which the Madrid Protocol entered into force with respect to the European Community, namely 1 October 2004. and now forms part of the EUTM Regulation.

## B. Use Provisions

### The 1994 Act

*Replace paragraph:*

**11-025** Use includes use in a form differing in elements which do not alter the distinctive character of the mark in the form in which it was registered,[25] referred to as a variant form, regardless of whether such variant form is also registered in the name of the proprietor. Use in the UK includes affixing the trade mark to goods or to the packaging of goods in the UK solely for export purposes.[26] Where the earlier trade mark is a EU trade mark then the genuine use must have taken place in the EU.[27] Following IP completion day EU trade marks are no longer earlier trade marks for the purposes of the 1994 Act, however each such mark is to be treated as if it had been applied for and registered as a UK trade mark (a "comparable trade mark (EU)") unless and until the proprietor gives notice to the IPO that it wishes to opt out.[27a] For the purposes of the proof of use provisions, such marks are treated as UK trade marks and genuine use in the UK must be shown.

[25] 1994 Act s.6A(4) and under arts 18(2)(a) and 49(2) and (3) of the EUTM Regulation: see *Laboratorios RTB v OHIM* (T-162/01) ECLI:EU:T:2003:199 at [44].

[26] 1994 Act s.6(A)(4); s.47(2C). See also the discussion in Ch.16, paras 16-021 to 16-023.

[27] Trade Marks Act 1994 s.6(A)(5); s.47(2D).

[27a] Sch.2A para.1 of the 1994 Act.

## D. Section 5(1) of the 1994 Act/EUTM Regulation art.8(1)(a): Where the Marks and the Goods or Services are Identical

### The goods or services must be identical

*Add to the end of the paragraph:*

**11-035** Where grounds for refusal exist in respect of only some of the goods or services for which the application is made, the application will be refused in relation to those goods and services only.[43a]

[43a] 1994 Act s.5A, TM Directive art.13.

## E. Section 5(2) of the 1994 Act/ EUTM Regulation art.8(1)(b): Where the Marks and the Goods or Services are Identical or Similar and There is a Likelihood of Confusion

### General

*Add to the end of the paragrpah:*

**11-041** Where the conditions of s.5(2) are satisfied in respect of only some of the goods or services for which the application is made, the application will be refused in relation to those goods and services only.[50a]

[50a] 1994 Act s.5A, TM Directive art.13.

## Assessment of the likelihood of confusion

*(i) Introduction*

*Replace paragraph:*

The words of art.4 of the TM Directive and s.5(2) of the 1994 Act require that the likelihood of confusion is caused by the identity or similarity of the marks and the goods or services.[60] It is "an indispensable requirement" that the marks are at least similar[61] and: **11-046**

> "[W]here there is no similarity between the earlier mark and the challenged mark, the reputation or recognition enjoyed by the earlier mark and the fact that the goods or services are identical or similar are not sufficient for it to be found that there is a likelihood of confusion between the marks".[62]

Similarly, it is not enough that the likelihood of confusion is caused by some other factors external to the marks, such as associated advertising materials or packaging.[63] In addition, these provisions require a likelihood of confusion as to origin, a matter discussed further below.

[60] So also in the case of EUTM Regulation art.8(1). In *MIP Metro Group Intellectual Property GmbH & Co KG v Metro International SA* (T-193/12) ECLI:EU:T:2015:44; [2015] E.T.M.R. 17, the Irish Controller summarised the CJEU's guidance to decision makers on the assessment of likelihood of confusion as follows: "Imagine a typical purchasing scenario involving the average consumer who already knows the product sold under the earlier trade mark and ask yourself whether it is likely that he will select and purchase a product bearing the mark put forward for registration in the mistaken belief that it is the product that he knows by the earlier mark (direct confusion) or that it is related to that product (indirect confusion by association). It is not necessary to find that every consumer would be confused and nor [sic] is it sufficient to find that some consumers might be confused in order to refuse registration of a trade mark under the section. The question is whether it is likely or unlikely that the average consumer would be confused in the course of the typical purchasing scenario." At [39].

[61] *Stradivarius Espana v OHIM* (T-340/06) [2009] E.T.M.R. 11 at [61]. In *Westlake Chemical Corp's Application for Invalidity* (BL 0-067-19) the Appointed Person (G. Hobbs QC) reviewed the EU authorities and concluded, at [14] "there is no rule that 'complementarity' always or necessarily equals 'similarity' for the purposes of s.5(2)(b) of the 1994 Act. It is necessary to assess the greater or lesser likelihood that a single economic undertaking would naturally be regarded as responsible for providing goods or services of the kind that are said to be 'similar', taking account of the degree to which they can realistically be regarded as 'complementary'."

[62] *Ferrero SpA v OHIM* (C-552/09 P) ECLI:EU:C:2011:177; [2011] E.T.M.R. 30 CJEU at [65], in relation to the mark "Kinder" and the challenged figurative mark including the words "TiMiKinderjoghurt" (the latter meaning children's yoghurt in German). In *Westlake Chemical Corp's Application for Invalidity* (BL 0-067-19) the Appointed Person (G. Hobbs QC) explained, at [10]: "Both as between marks and as between goods and services, the evaluation of 'similarity' is a means to an end. It serves as a way of enabling the decision taker to gauge whether there is 'similarity' of a kind and to a degree which is liable to give rise to perceptions of relatedness in the mind of the average consumer of the goods or services concerned. This calls for a realistic appraisal of the net effect of the similarities and differences between the marks and the goods or services in issue, giving the similarities and differences as much or as little significance as the relevant average consumer (who is taken to be reasonably well-informed and reasonably observant and circumspect) would have attached to them at the relevant point in time."

[63] This is obvious in relation to the assessment under the relative grounds, where the comparison is between earlier mark and mark applied for, but in relation to infringement: [existing text]. See generally, Ch.16, particularly para.16-089A. "[C]ircumstances prior to, simultaneous with or subsequent to the use of the sign may be relevant to a claim for passing off ... but they are not generally relevant to a claim for infringement under Art.9(1)(b)" [of what was then the CTM Regulation]: per Arnold J in *Och-Ziff v OCH Capital* [2011] E.T.M.R. 1 at [78].

*(ii) General principles*

## (b) The relevant public

*Replace paragraph:*

11-050 The matter must be considered through the eyes of the average consumer of the goods or services in issue.[69] For the purposes of the global appreciation, the average consumer of the category of products concerned is deemed to be reasonably well informed and reasonably observant and circumspect.[70] On the other hand, it is clear that the average consumer can differ in their level of attention: for example, specialist IT equipment is likely "to be selected with considerable care by knowledgeable and discriminating consumers"[71]; and end users of pharmaceutical products show "a high degree of attentiveness"[72] even in relation to prescription medicines where the healthcare professional will make the final purchasing decision.

[69] *Sabel v Puma* [1997] E.C.R. 1-6191; [1998] R.P.C. 199 at [22]–[24]. See generally the treatment of the "average consumer" in Ch.3. The position of the trade is also likely to be relevant. If the trade is confused then it is likely the average consumer will be too. However, on the use of evidence from branding "experts" in relation to the question of "likelihood of confusion", see the scathing comments of all three members of the Court of Appeal (Arden, Jacob and Maurice Kay LJJ) in *eSure Insurance Ltd v Direct Line Insurance Plc* [2008] E.T.M.R. 77.

[70] *Lloyd Schuhfabrik Meyer* [1999] E.T.M.R. 690 at [26]–[27]; *Gut Springenheide and Tusky* [1998] E.C.R. 1-4657 at [31].

[71] per D. Alexander QC, sitting as a Deputy High Court judge, in *Digipos Store Solutions v Digi International* [2007] E.W.H.C. 3371 (Ch) at [97]. The judge continued: "The warning in *Reed* [[2004] R.P.C. 40 CA] against an overly "nanny" approach to comparison of marks has particular force ... in the context of specialist products which are not selected in the hurly burly of the high street." See also, *Elena Grebenshikova v OHIM* (T-394/10) ECLI:EU:T:2013:627; [2014] E.T.M.R. 22, in which the General Court drew attention to the fact that the software covered by the mark applied for (a figurative mark including the word "solvo") was aimed at a specialist, commercial market, at [21], when overturning the Board of Appeal's decision that there was a likelihood of confusion with "Volvo", registered also for computer software. In *Cambridge Neurotech's Application* (BL 0-03-20), the Appointed Person (A. Michaels) found that "the specialist knowledge of the average consumer, and the specialist nature of the [neurotechnology] goods at issue, militate against a likelihood of confusion", at [34].

[72] *Alcon v OHIM* (C-412/05 P) [2007] E.T.M.R. 68 CJEU at [61]. In *Cadila Healthcare Ltd v OHIM* (T-288/08) ECLI:EU:T:2012:124; [2012] E.T.M.R. 60, it was noted, at [36], that this "applies even where pharmaceutical preparations are available to consumers over the counter, since those goods relate to their health. Likewise, the relevant public displays a relatively high level of attention with regard to vetinary preparations insofar as they affect the state of health of animals." A "particularly high" level of attentiveness was also attributed to consumers of incontinence products in *Paul Hartmann AG v OHIM* (T-504/11) ECLI:EU:T:2013:57; [2013] E.T.M.R. 26 at [32].

*At the end of the paragraph, add new footnote 73a:*

11-051 [73a] In *Application to register Zohara* (BL O-040-20), the Appointed Person (D.Alexander QC) cautioned, at [25], that a consideration of the different ways in which the marks may be used and perceived by consumers "cannot be taken too far: consideration of the range of responses does not require a microscopic analysis of the assumed characteristics of large numbers of possible individual consumers or possible kinds of situation in which the marks might be used." Also, he noted, at [27], that "in evaluating the likelihood of confusion, a tribunal is entitled to focus more on the typical part of the "spectrum of consumers" (in the words of Birss J in *Thomas Pink v Victoria's Secret* [2014] EWHC 2631) and typical purchasing or advertising situations among the range of all situations in which the marks in question might be presented. If confusion is not likely in that part of the spectrum, the fact that it is possible to imagine not wholly fanciful scenarios in which it may happen elsewhere, does [*sic*: not] mean that confusion is likely."

### (c) The degree of similarity between the marks

*Replace footnote 76:*

11-052 [76] *Dainichiseika Colour & Chemicals Mfg Co Ltd v OHIM* (T-389/03) ECLI:EU:T:2008:114; [2008] E.T.M.R. 45 at [107]. In *Longevity Health Products Inc v OHIM* (C-81/11 P) [2012] E.T.M.R. 61, the General Court rejected the argument that differences in typeface between the earlier mark as used and the mark applied for should be taken into account, noting that the protection that arises from registration of a word mark relates to the word indicated in the application and not to its particular graphic or stylistic aspects, at [35]. In *Dirmode SA's Application* (BL O-566-19) the applicant to register PINKIES for a range of goods in Class 14 including rings contended that it intended to use the mark on rings to be put on the little finger (pinkie rings) and therefore there was no likelihood of confusion with the opponent's mark PIMKIE: the Appointed Person (G. Hobbs QC) emphasised that the test requires consideration of the two marks in relation to all the goods/services for which registration is sought, not just those the applicant says it intends to use it for.

## (d) Overall impression of the marks is to be considered

*Replace paragraph:*

The global appreciation of the likelihood of confusion must, as regards the visual, aural or conceptual similarity of the marks in question, be based upon the overall impression created by them, bearing in mind, in particular, their distinctive and dominant components.[79] The perception of marks in the mind of the average consumer of the category of goods or services in question plays a decisive role in the global appreciation of the likelihood of confusion.[80] The average consumer normally perceives a mark as a whole and does not proceed to analyse its various details.[81] However, it should be noted that it is not open to the owner of an earlier word mark to rely upon use of figurative elements which form no part of the mark as registered[82]: the comparison is between the earlier registered mark and the mark being applied for.[83] **11-053**

[79] In *Seven for all Mankind LLC v OHIM* [2013] E.T.M.R. 24, the CJEU emphasised that "the determination of distinctive character, or lack of distinctive character, of the various elements of a sign, their importance in the overall impression given by the sign as well as the finding of conceptual similarity in relation to another sign involves a weighing up of those criteria which entails a factual analysis", at [85], and therefore presumably is not susceptible to an appeal available only on a question of law.

[80] In *Annco v OHIM* (T-385/09) [2011] E.T.M.R. 37 the General Court found that the mark applied for, "Ann Taylor Loft", did not give rise to a likelihood of confusion with the earlier mark "Loft", particularly as the target public would view "Ann Taylor" as the mark's most distinctive element and that was not the same as the sole element of the earlier mark, at [43]–[50]. The court noted in this connection that "it is common for a single clothing manufacturer to use sub-brands ... in order to distinguish its various clothing lines from one another", at [45]; cf. *L'Oréal v OHIM* (T-21/07) [2009] E.T.M.R. 48 in which the General Court made the same observation in relation to cosmetics but with the opposite consequence, finding that it could lead consumers to believe that use of the earlier mark "Spa" in the mark applied for, "Spa Therapy", meant that the latter was a line extension of the earlier mark, at [32]. In *PIA HALLSTROM* [2018] F.S.R. 5 the Appointed Person (D. Alexander QC) commented, at [33], "if a trader chooses a forename as a trade mark, the average consumer is not particularly likely to think that another trader who uses a full name incorporating that forename is thereby denoting goods or services from the first undertaking rather than those connected with someone else who happens to share that forename. That is a problem which arises as a result of a choice of mark which, precisely because it is a name which others either do or could reasonably wish to use to denote themselves, does not start high on the distinctiveness scale. Large-scale use of such a mark does not, as such, enhance its distinctiveness in a relevant way, namely so as to increase the likelihood of confusion."

[81] *Sabel v Puma* [1997] E.C.R. 1-6191; [1998] R.P.C. 199 at [23] and [25]. And see generally, paras 11-084 to 11-100. In *Drillisch Alphatel TM Application* [2009] E.T.M.R. 27, which concerned an opposition by the owner of the "Alcatel" mark to the registration of "DrillischAlphatel", the German Supreme Court rejected the opponent's argument that the exception to the general rule laid down by the Court of Justice in *Medion AG v Thomson Multimedia Sales Germany & Austria GmbH* [2005] E.C.R. 1-8551, that individual elements of a composite mark may be independently distinctive and therefore likely to confuse, could be extended to situations where the later mark incorporated only a similar element together with the company name of the owner, at [11]. In *Aveda Corp v Dabur India Ltd* [2013] E.T.M.R. 33, Arnold J reviewed the authorities which had referred to *Medion*, at [23]–[38], and concluded at [45] that "[a]lthough the decision ... does not in terms extend to cases in which the composite sign incorporates a sign which is similar to, rather than identical with, the trade mark and some of the Court of Justice's reasoning would not apply to such a case, I consider that the underlying logic is equally applicable." The judgment of the CJEU in *Medion* does not provide authority for the proposition that the mere fact two marks share a common element means that they will be treated as confusingly similar. The common element in composite marks may have no or very limited independent distinctive role in the whole. *PIA HALLSTROM* [2018] F.S.R. 5 Appointed Person, at [15].

[82] *Kraft Foods Schweiz Holding GmbH v OHIM* (T-357/10) ECLI:EU:T:2012:312; [2012] E.T.M.R. 51 at [37]–[38].

[83] In *L'Oréal SA v EUIPO* (T-144/15) [2016] E.T.M.R. 35, the General Court considered irrelevant the argument that "the proprietor of an earlier mark cannot require operators seeking to register a mark to keep greater distance from the earlier mark than that which the proprietor kept in relation to [marks earlier than its own]", at [33].

### (e) The distinctive character of the earlier mark

*Replace footnote 86:*

11-054 [86] *Sabel v Puma* [1997] E.C.R. 1-6191, [1998] R.P.C. 199 at [22]–[24]; *Lloyd Schuhfabrik Meyer* [1999] E.T.M.R. 690 at [22]–[23]. And see generally, paras 11-085 to 11-086. On collective marks, see *Foundation for the Protection of the Traditional Cheese of Cyprus named Halloumi v EUIPO* (C-766/18 P). AG Kokott noted in her Opinion (17 October 2019), at [77] that "there are no grounds to assume that a collective mark necessarily—even by virtue of its registration—enjoys particular distinctive character". The CJEU judgment of 5 March 2020 remitted the case to the GC to apply the standard global appreciation test for likelihood of confusion to the application mark "BBQLOUMI", having made it clear that the test for likelihood of confusion in relation to a collective mark is no different to that for any other registered trade mark.

### (g) Similarity of the goods or services

*Replace paragraph with:*

11-056 Appreciation of the likelihood of confusion also depends on the degree of similarity between the goods or services identified.[90] It is the goods or services covered by the specifications of the marks at issue that must be considered when making this assessment, and not the goods or services actually marketed under those marks.[91] In addition, it should be noted that the classification of goods or services serves almost exclusively an administrative purpose and goods or services may not be regarded as similar merely on the ground that they appear in the same class under the Nice Classification. Conversely goods or services may not be regarded as dissimilar merely because they appear in different classes.[92] When considering general terms (such as class headings) of potentially broad scope, Arnold LJ (sitting in the High Court) provided the following guidance having considered the relevant UK and EU authorities[92a]:

> "(1) General terms are to be interpreted as covering the goods or services clearly covered by the literal meaning of the terms, and not other goods or services. (2) In the case of services, the terms used should not be interpreted widely, but confined to the core of the possible meanings attributable to the terms. (3) An unclear or imprecise term should be narrowly interpreted as extending only to such goods or services as it clearly covers. (4) A term which cannot be interpreted is to be disregarded."

[90] *Sabel v Puma* [1997] E.C.R. 1-6191; [1998] R.P.C. 199 at [22]–[24]. See the discussion in paras 11-062 to 11-075 as to whether there is a threshold requirement that the goods or services be similar; and in paras 11-074 to 11-075 as to the factors to be considered. In *Omega Engineering Inc v Omega SA* [2012] EWHC 3440, Arnold J reviewed the authorities on the proper construction of the specification of goods or services, at [21]–[33]: "[i]n short, the words used in the specification should be given their natural and usual meaning. They should neither be given such a broad interpretation that the limits of the specification become fuzzy, nor strained to produce a narrow meaning", per the same judge in *Aveda Corp v Dabur India Ltd* [2013] E.T.M.R. 33 at [56].

[91] *Present–Service Ullrich GmbH & Co KG v OHIM* (T-66/11) ECLI:EU:T:2013:48; [2013] E.T.M.R. 29 at [45]. In that context, how to treat the use of class headings for EUTM applications is now governed by EUIPO Communication No.2/2012, following the CJEU judgment in *Chartered Institute of Patent Attorneys v Registrar of Trade Marks* (C-307/10) [2012] E.T.M.R. 42. See further Ch.5.

[92] In relation to the EUTM, see Rule 2(4) of the EUTM Implementing Regulation 2868/95, referred to in its then form as CTM Implementing Regulation and applied in *P.P.TV v OHIM* (T-118/07) ECLI:EU:T:2011:58; [2011] E.T.M.R. 38 at [35]: the same should apply to national marks.

[92a] *Sky Plc v Skykick UK Ltd* [2020] EWHC 990 (Ch) at [56]. Guidance given in the context of the interpretation of "telecommunication services" on the resumed hearing following the reference to the CJEU of questions concerning bad faith and invalidity on grounds of lack of clarity.

#### *(iii) Confusion as to origin*

*Replace footnote 104:*

11-061 [104] *LA Sugar v Back Beat* BL O-360-09, decision of Iain Purvis QC sitting as the Appointed Person. It should be noted that the Appointed Person (J. Mellor QC) in *Duebros* (BL O-547-17), at [81], cautioned against relying on [16] and [17] of the *LA Sugar* decision in a fashion akin to applying a statutory test to conduct an overly detailed analysis of what should be, in his view of the CJEU authorities, "an emulation of an instinctive reaction in the mind of the average consumer when encountering the later mark with an imperfect recollection of the earlier mark in mind." To the same effect, see *Miss Dope* (BL O-601-19) (A. Michaels) at [29] and *Kingsley Beverages Application* (BL O-024-20) (P. Johnson) at [22].

### *(v) Similar goods or services—the objective factors to be considered*

*Replace list:*

**Similar goods or services** **11-077**

- "Organic fertilisers" are similar goods to "chemicals used in horticulture and forestry" since they have a similar function and are likely to be sold in the same shops.[131]
- "Insecticides for killing dust mites" are similar goods to pharmaceutical preparations taken by persons suffering from respiratory problems, as the products would be more effective if used in a complementary way.[132]
- "Wines" are similar to "whisky" and "bar services", since people would think that the supplier of one was engaged in the supply of the other.[133]
- "Vodka" is similar to "cigarettes", as they display sufficient similarity in terms of their respective uses "as to be above the level of de minimis".[134]
- "Coffee, tea and cocoa" are similar to "coffee substitutes" as they are intended for the same use.[135]
- "Skin care, sun care and hair care preparations; perfumery, essential oils, soaps" are similar to "perfumes; cosmetics; non-medicated toilet preparations; soaps; shampoos; preparations for the hair; dentifrices; anti-perspirants; deodorants for personal use".[136]
- "Leather goods, leather bags, other leather goods not specifically made for the things they contain, containers and purses" are similar to "clothing".[137]
- "Services offered by beauty salons; solarium services" are similar to "business assistance with beauty preparations, sales" and "beauty preparations, perfumery, cosmetics dietetic substances" since the goods and services of the conflicting marks could be offered together and be intended for the same public.[138]
- "Consultancy on the organisation and management of commercial and industrial businesses" is similar to "assistance to industrial and commercial businesses; consultancy information, research, inquiries or business management" in that they both have the same objective of the provision of specific industrial and commercial knowledge to commercial entities in the determination of their choice of business.[139]
- "Buttons, press studs, buckles (clothing accessories), buckles for footwear and garments, eyelets and buttonholes for footwear and garments, patches and rivets for garments" in Class 26 are similar to "outer and inner wear, knitwear including boots, shoes and slippers; clothing articles including boots, shoes and slippers; outer and inner garments of fabric and knitwear, including boots shoes and slippers; clothing articles, shoes and hats".[140]
- Milk and cheese are similar since, in the eyes of the relevant public, they belong to a single product family and may easily be regarded as components of a general range of milk products capable of having a common commercial origin.[141]
- Footwear is similar to clothing since they are both worn, have the function of

covering and protecting and are often sold in the same outlets.[142] However, in *Sergio Rossi v OHIM*,[143] the GC stated:

> "… [T]he fact that consumers regard a [fashion and clothing] product as a complement of or accessory to another is not sufficient for them to believe that those products have the same commercial origin. For that to be the case, consumers would also have to consider it usual for those products to be sold under the same trade mark."

[131] *Humic* [1999] E.T.M.R. 26 EUIPO.

[132] *Astex Therapeutics Ltd v OHIM* (T-48/06) [2009] E.T.M.R. 3 at [40]–[44]. In *Westlake Chemical Corp's Application for Invalidity* (BL 0-067-19) the Appointed Person (G. Hobbs QC) upheld, at [22], the Hearing Officer's decision that "chemicals (styrene) for insertion into vehicle tyres to protect them and chemical preparations (styrene) for repairing tyres were 'similar' to tyres, inner tubes and casings by reason of 'complementarity' in the sense that the former were indispensable or important for the use of the latter in such a way that consumers may think that the same undertaking is responsible for those goods."

[133] "*Balmoral*" [1999] R.P.C. 297. See the review by the Appointed Person (E. Himsworth QC) of the various authorities on whether "whisky" and "beer" are similar goods in *Mont Blanc TM Application* (BL-0-693-19), at [61]–[63], before she concluded that in the UK "whisky" and "beer" are similar but only to a low degree, at [72], while acknowledging that different jurisdictions around the EU have expressed different views on the question, at [73]. In *Tiny Rebel Brewing Co Ltd's Application* (BL O-482-19) the Appointed Person (Prof R. Annand) upheld, at [27] and [28], the hearing officer's decision that there was a medium degree of similarity between "beers" and "non-alcoholic drinks, namely, fruit drinks, fruit juices and fruit-based drinks", having noted the evidence on the market presence of low- and non-alcoholic beers and fruit beers.

[134] *Belvedere's Application (Jan III Sobieski)* [2007] E.T.M.R. 18 Pat. Off. Ireland at [35].

[135] *Lutz Quasdorf v Les Sirenes* [1999] E.T.M.R. 152 OHIM but not similar to sweets and confectionery: *ZakladyPrzemysluCukierniczegoMiesko v Leaf UK* [2009] E.T.M.R. 31 Pat. Off. Ireland at [17].

[136] "*Naturelle*" [1999] R.P.C. 326.

[137] "*QSby S. Oliver*" [1999] R.P.C. 520.

[138] *Beauty Free Shop* [1999] E.T.M.R. 20 EUIPO.

[139] *Mars* [1999] E.T.M.R. 402 EUIPO.

[140] *Zanella SNC's Application* [2000] E.T.M.R. 69 EUIPO.

[141] *Pedro Diaz v OHIM (Granjas Castello intervening)* (T-85/02) EU:T:2003:288; [2004] E.T.M.R. 42 at 575.

[142] *O'Neill Inc's Application* [2004] E.T.M.R. 50 EUIPO.

[143] [2005] E.C.R. II-685 at [63], upheld by the CJEU, [2006] E.C.R. I-7057.

*Replace list:*

**Goods or services which are not similar**

11-078
- "Bags, cases and pocket wallets made of leather; umbrellas and parasols" not similar to "cigarette lighters and lighter fuel".[144]
- "Sports bags, shopping bags, toilet bags, key bags" not similar to "clothing".[145]
- "Electronic devices for attracting and killing insects" not similar to "aromatherapy diffusing apparatus".[146]
- Alcoholic beverages other than beer not similar to coffee.[147]
- Financial services to dentists not similar to dental services.[148]
- Milk products (Class 29), flour and preparations made from cereals (Class 30) not similar to foodstuff for animals, including non-medicated food additives and food supplements for animals (Class 31).[149]
- Pharmaceutical products not similar to medical devices.[150] Beverages and tobacco products are dissimilar.[150a]

[144] "*Zippo*" [1999] R.P.C. 173.

[145] *"QS by S.Oliver"* [1999] R.P.C. 520.

[146] *"Lifesystems"* [2000] R.P.C. 851.

[147] *Casa Girelli's Application* [2002] E.T.M.R. 66 at 748.

[148] *Harding v Smilecare* [2002] F.S.R. 37 at 589.

[149] *LidlStiftung v Heinz Iberica* [2003] E.T.M.R. 25 EUIPO BoA at 312.

[150] *Innodis Plc's Application* [2004] E.T.M.R. 36 Cour d'Appel de Paris at 502.

[150a] *Gogo Marin's Application* (BL 0-024-19), Appointed Person (G. Hobbs QC).

## Examples

*After "In making that assessment, account should be taken, in particular, of the inherent characteristics of the mark.", add new footnote 162a:*

[162a] In *Cambridge Neurotech's Application* (BL 0-03-20), the Appointed Person (A. Michaels) commented of the opponent's registered mark "CAMBRIDGE": "Cambridge is a well-known city, of a substantial size, with a world-renowned university. The average consumer of all of parties' goods and services would be aware of that and in my view would also be likely to know that there are industries and trades of various kinds and around based in the city. CAMBRIDGE is unlikely to be a very distinctive term for many goods and services." At [26]. **11-085**

*After "Use of a mark does not prove it is distinctive.", add new footnote 164a:*

[164a] In *Pia Hallstrom Ltd's Application* [2018] F.S.R. 5 the Appointed Person (D. Alexander QC) emphasised, at [27], that "it is well established that mere volume of use does not, of itself, increase the propensity of marks to cause confusion. Extensive use may increase the distinctiveness in the sense that it may make the mark more well-known but it does not follow that it will therefore be afforded a greater scope of protection under section 5(2)(b)." **11-086**

*Distinctive character of the later mark*

*Replace paragraph:*

If the reputation attaching to the earlier mark is relevant in determining the likelihood of confusion, in particular as a factor likely to increase the likelihood of confusion, then it may be anticipated that an applicant for registration will contend that the reputation attaching to their mark is a factor likely to reduce any risk of confusion.[168] It is clear that s.5(2)(b) requires a consideration of the scope of protection of the earlier mark rather than that of the mark applied for, and therefore any evidence of enhanced distinctiveness of the later mark through use should be ignored when deciding the likelihood of confusion under the global appreciation test.[169] It should be borne in mind that post-registration there is no obligation on the applicant to continue using the mark applied for as it has been used prior to registration, even where it has possibly acquired distinctiveness as a result of that use. The global appreciation should take into account all possible uses by the applicant of the mark for which it is applying. **11-087**

[168] It may be argued such an approach is consistent with the TM Directive art.3(3), which makes special provision with regard to the absolute grounds for refusal of art.3(1)(b), (c) or (d) where the mark has acquired a distinctive character, cf. *Leroy Merlin v K2* [2003] E.T.M.R. CN3 EUIPO BoA.

[169] *Wanda Films, SL and Wanda Vision, SA v EUIPO* (T-533/18) EU:T:2019:727 at [54]–[55].

*Similarity of marks*

*Replace paragraph:*

For most cases it is sufficient to follow the guidance given in *Sabel v Puma* that account should be taken of the visual, aural and conceptual similarity of the marks in question,[172] including the overall impression given by the marks, and bearing in mind, in particular, their respective distinctive and dominant components.[173] It is not appropriate, however, either to concentrate on the similarities to the exclusion of **11-089** the differences between the marks[174] or, where there is a composite mark comprised of both graphic and word elements, to systematically regard the word elements as dominant.[175] Also, one cannot assume that because an element of the marks is identical that the marks are similar unless the identical part constitutes the dominant element in the overall impression created by each mark, such that all the other components are insignificant.[176] Where the concept of a word mark is so closely associated with an image that the words will be perceived spontaneously and inevitably by the average consumer on exposure to an image, it is possible that a word mark may be confusingly similar to an image mark or vice versa. It is a question of fact in each case: an example is *Hearst Holdings Inc v AVELA Inc*,[177] in which images of the character Betty Boop were held to infringe the word mark "BETTY BOOP".

[172] It is not necessary that the marks be similar in each of these respects: *Mystery Drinks v OHIM, KarlsbergBrauerei intervening (MYSTERY)* (T-99/01) [2004] E.T.M.R. 18. There is no special test to be applied to a comparison of "short" marks: *Bosco/Bosch* (BL O-301-20), Appointed Person (J. Mellor QC), at [44].

[173] See [22]–[24] of the judgment, cited in para.11-047 of the text. In *Harman International v OHIM* (C-51/09 P) [2009] E.T.M.R. 38 at [22]–[43], the General Court made the global assessment in all its aspects before holding that there was a likelihood of confusion between the earlier mark "Becker" and the later "Barbara Becker": but the Court of Justice, [2010] E.T.M.R. 53, set aside the General Court's judgment, noting that account must be taken of the fact that the person seeking registration of the first name and surname was well known as that "may obviously influence the perception of the mark by the relevant public", at [37]. In *El Corte Inglés SA v OHIM* [2013] E.T.M.R. 3 the General Court emphasised that although consumers may attribute greater distinctiveness to the surname than the forename in a particular case, "that rule, drawn from experience, cannot be applied automatically without taking account of the specific features of the case", at [55] and held that the BoA was correct in its finding that in the mark "Emidio Tucci" the forename Emidio had a distinctive character at least as significant as the surname Tucci and therefore was different visually and phonetically to "Pucci", at [65]. *Giovanni Cosmetics Inc v OHIM, Vasconcelos & Goncalves SA* (T-559/13), GC, and *Whyte and Mackay Ltd v Origin Wine UK Ltd & Dolce Co Invest Inc* [2015] EWHC 1271 (Ch) both suggest that this should not be a general rule.

[174] See, e.g. *Croom's Trade Mark Application* [2005] R.P.C. 2; and *Rousselon Frères et Cie v Horwood Homewares Ltd* [2008] R.P.C. 30. Also, in *Medion* [2006] E.T.M.R. 13 CJEU, the court found that it was not necessary for the overall impression produced by a composite mark to be dominated by the part which is represented by the earlier mark in order to find a likelihood of confusion, at [211]–[31]; applied by Warren J in *Rousselon* at [90], et seq.

[175] *L&D v OHIM* [2008] E.T.M.R. 62 CJEU at [55]. Indeed, in *Shaker v OHIM* the CJEU held that the General Court had erred in not considering the phonetic or conceptual aspects of the other elements of a composite mark after it had found the graphic element to be dominant in the overall impression: "it is only if all the other elements of the mark are negligible that the assessment of the similarity can be carried out solely on the basis of the dominant element." At [42]. In *Tictrac Ltd's Application* (BL 0-223-18) the Appointed Person commented, at [16]: "it is a dangerous short-cut to approach the assessment of marks on the basis that some types of element [eg, word versus device] are 'in principle' more distinctive than others. Many factors go into the question of distinctiveness of individual elements of a mark (e.g. degrees of descriptiveness, common use by other traders, extent of acquired distinctiveness through use, prominence of the elements in the mark as a whole) and each case must therefore be assessed on its merits. That is the message the CJEU were conveying in *L&D*, and it is plainly correct."

[176] *Matratzen Concord v OHIM* [2003] E.T.M.R. 31 GC at [33]; *Calvin Klein Trademark Trust v OHIM* (C-254/09P) [2011] E.T.M.R. 5 CJEU at [56].

[177] [2014] EWHC 439; [2014] E.T.M.R. 34.

*Replace footnote 180:*

**11-090** [180] *Ferrero v OHIM* (C-552/09) [2011] E.T.M.R. 30 CJEU ("Kinder"/figurative mark including the words "TiMiKinderjoghurt"); *Gateway Inc v OHIM* (C-57/08 P) [2009] E.T.M.R. 32 CJEU ("GATEWAY"/"ACTIVY Media Gateway"). The fact that a common element of a composite mark is found to play an independent distinctive role within the later mark does not inexorably lead to a finding of likelihood of confusion: it remains necessary to carry out the global assessment taking into account all relevant factors: *Viomichania mpiskoton kai eidon diatrofis EI Papadopoulos SA v EUIPO* (T-628/18) EU:T:2019:750 at [33]–[35].

*Replace paragraph:*

The public will not generally consider a descriptive element forming part of a complex (or composite) mark as the dominant element of the overall impression created by the mark;[181] it is the dominant elements of the marks that are critical in the overall evaluation,[182] although it is only if all the other components are negligible that the assessment can be carried out solely on the basis of the dominant elements.[183] **11-091**

[181] *Alejandro v OHIM (BUDMEN)* [2004] E.T.M.R. 15 GC; *GFK AG v OHIM* (T-135/04) [2006] E.T.M.R. 58 at [70]. Weak distinctiveness does not necessarily prevent an element being regarded as dominant in a composite mark (see, e.g. *Patent- och registreringsverket v Mats Hansson* (C-705/17) EU:C:2019:481 at [41]–[55]).

[182] *Mulhens v OHIM* [2006] E.C.R. 1-2717 at [18]–[19]. A recent example of such an overall evaluation of a composite mark, where reasonable people might disagree, can be found in *Brewdog Plc's Applications* (BL O-048-18) where the Appointed Person (P. Johnson) upheld the Hearing Officer's findings that, with regard to identical goods namely beer, there was a likelihood of confusion between the earlier mark ELVIS and the applied-for mark ELVIS JUICE (as "coming from the same stable", at [32]) but not between ELVIS and the other applied-for mark BREWDOG ELVIS JUICE, at [46].

[183] *Société des Produits Nestlé v OHIM* [2007] E.C.R. 1-114 at [42]–[43]; *United States Polo Association v OHIM* [2013] E.T.M.R. 12 CJEU. In *Virgin Enterprises Ltd v Casey* [2011] E.T.M.R. 35, the judge refused to interfere with the hearing officer's finding that there was a low level of conceptual similarity between the opponent's mark "VIRGIN" and the mark being applied for, "CARBON VIRGIN". In *Pia Hallstrom Ltd's Application* [2018] F.S.R. 5 the Appointed Person upheld the dismissal of the opposition to registration of "PIA HALLSTROM" relying on the earlier mark "PIA", observing that "... if a trader chooses a forename as a trade mark, the average consumer is not particularly likely to think another trader who uses a full name incorporating that forename is thereby denoting goods or services form the first undertaking ...".

*Replace paragraph:*

In the global assessment of the likelihood of confusion, the visual, aural or conceptual aspects of the opposing marks do not always have the same weight. It is appropriate to examine the objective conditions under which the goods may be present on the market.[187] So, for example, it is possible that a mere phonetic similarity between trade marks may create a likelihood of confusion.[188] On the other hand, the degree of phonetic similarity will be of less importance if the goods are marketed in such a way that the relevant public will usually see the trade mark[189]; or if one of the marks has a clear conceptual meaning.[190] All will depend upon the global assessment. With EU trade marks it may be relevant how a particular mark is pronounced in one of the Member States but not in others.[191] Also, in *Loutfi SARL v AMJ Meatproducts NV, Halalsupply NV*,[192] the Court of Justice held that, where the average consumer was a Muslim consumer of Arab origin who consumes "halal" food products in the EU and who has at least a basic knowledge of Arabic, there must be taken into account in deciding whether there is a likelihood of confusion the substantially different meaning and pronunciation of words that may be visually similar. **11-093**

[187] *New Look v OHIM (NLSPORT)* (T-117/03) [2005] E.T.M.R. 35; *Astex Therapeutics Ltd v OHIM* (T-48/06) [2009] E.T.M.R. 3 at [74]: "[Pharmaceuticals] are very rarely visible from the counter, unlike the non-pharmaceutical (though health-related) goods ... protected by the earlier mark-which are sold on get-ups that are directly visible and accessible to the customers." In *Pia Hallstrom Ltd's Application* [2018] F.S.R. 5, when considering a mark applied for in relation to fashion articles, the Appointed Person (D. Alexander QC) noted, at [14], that "For such articles, there is a well established practice, of which in my view any tribunal is entitled to take judicial notice, of the use of two-word brands comprising the full names (forename and surname) of the designer of the products in question. Although in some cases such designers may also have brands which comprise one or other, but not both, of first name or surname, the average consumer of the goods in question is likely to be well accustomed to treating such two-word marks as names, comprising a first name and a surname."

[188] *Lloyd Schuhfabrik Meyer*, at [28]; *Mystery Drinks* [2004] E.T.M.R. 18 at [4]; *Phillips-Van Heusen v OHIM (BASS)* [2004] E.T.M.R. 60.

[189] See, e.g. *Mulhens v OHIM (ZIRH)* [2006] E.C.R. 1-2717 CJEU at [21]–[22], and *Mederer GmbH v OHIM* (T-210/14) ECLI:EU:T:2016:105; [2016] E.T.M.R. 26 at [89]–[91] as regards confectionery.

[190] See, e.g. *El Corte Inglés v OHIM (MUNICOR/MUNDICOLOR)* (T-183/02) [2004] E.T.M.R. 103 and *Les Éditions Albert René v OHIM (MOBILIX/OBELIX)* [2009] E.T.M.R. 21 CJEU.

[191] *Honda Motor Europe Ltd v OHIM* [2009] E.T.M.R. 34 GC in which it was held that as the mark "Seat" was highly distinctive in Spain as a trade mark for cars and would be pronounced in Spanish as "se-at", rather than the common English word "seat", and as it could not be ruled out that the applicant's "Magic Seat" mark would be pronounced in Spain as "magic se-at", there was a likelihood of confusion.

[192] [2015] E.T.M.R. 35 CJEU at [26].

*Use of a family of marks*

*Add to the end of the paragraph:*

**11-094** Not all of the family of marks relied upon must be registered, but they must be in use.[195a]

[195a] *W3 v easyGroup* [2018] EWHC 7; [2018] E.T.M.R. 40 at [235].

*(vii) The standard to be applied*

*Replace paragraph:*

**11-097** In *Comic Enterprises Ltd v Twentieth Century Fox Film Corp*[200] Kitchin LJ (as he then was) set out guidance on what level of confusion must be likely: "a significant proportion of the relevant public is likely to be confused such as to warrant the intervention of the court"[201]: although this guidance was given in an infringement case under section 10 it applies equally to section 5.[202] It has also been said that the likelihood of confusion must be "genuine and properly substantiated",[203] although this is perhaps a choice of words appropriate more for an infringement action than an opposition (in which the assessment is primarily hypothetical). Also, there may be a likelihood of confusion within the meaning of the TM Directive (and the EUTM Regulation) even though the purchaser is not, in the end, confused.[203a] This is clearly the case with regard to an advertisement giving rise to a likelihood of confusion, regardless of whether the advertisement leads to a sale and whether the consumer remains confused at the time of the sale.[203b] However, this is highly unlikely to be relevant in the registration context where the comparison is between the mark applied for and an earlier mark stripped of context, except where the earlier mark has heightened distinctiveness. Confusion can either be direct, in which the marks in question are mistaken for each other by the average consumer, or indirect, in which the similarities lead that consumer to form the mistaken view that they originate from the same or linked undertakings.[203c]

[200] [2016] EWCA Civ 41; [2016] F.S.R. 30.

[201] [2016] EWCA Civ 41 at [34(v)].

[202] *Application to register Zohara* (BL O-040-20), Appointed Person (D. Alexander QC), at [24].

[203] See Opinions of AG Jacobs in *Sabel v Puma* [1997] E.C.R. 1-6191, [1998] R.P.C. 199 at [52] and [55], and in *Marca Mode v Adidas* [2000] E.T.M.R. 561 at [47]. In *Marca Mode* the CJEU concluded (at [42]) that it was not enough that the possibility of confusion "cannot be ruled out". See also *10 Royal Berkshire Polo Club Trade Mark* [2001] R.P.C. 32; *Raleigh International Trade Mark* [2001] R.P.C. 11.

[203a] See the analysis of this issue in the context of infringement by Arnold J in *Och-Ziff v OCH Capital* [2011] E.T.M.R. 1 at [79]–[101].

[203b] *Die BergSpechte Outdoor* [2010] E.T.M.R. 33 at [35], in relation to internet users using Google and being shown, on the basis of a keyword similar to a mark, a third-party advertisement.

[203c] *LA Sugar v Back Beat* BL O-360-09, decision of Iain Purvis QC sitting as the Appointed Person.

## F. Section 5(3) of the 1994 Act/EUTM Regulation art.8(5): Where the Use of the Mark Without Due Cause Would Take Unfair Advantage of or be Detrimental to the Distinctive Character or Repute of the Earlier Mark

### General

*Add to the end of the paragraph:*

From IP completion day, the words "(or in the case of a European Union trade mark or international trade mark (EC) in the European Union)" will be deleted. Section 5(3A) further provides: "Subsection (3) applies irrespective of whether the goods and services for which the trade mark is to be registered are identical with, similar to or not similar to those for which the earlier trade mark is protected".[209a] **11-101**

[209a] 1994 Act s.5(3A) added as of 14 January 2019 by Trade Marks Regulations (SI 2018/825) Pt 2 reg.5(2).

### (I) The Earlier Trade Mark Must Have a Reputation

*Replace paragraph:*

The earlier mark must have a reputation in the UK (in the case of a national registration) or the EU (in the case of a EUTM).[222] There is no requirement that the reputation must extend over the whole of the relevant territory but it must exist in a significant part of it.[223] In the context of a EU trade mark, reputation within one Member State may suffice in some circumstances.[224] There is no express requirement as to the extent of the reputation necessary, although the degree of required recognition must be considered to be reached when the mark is known by "a significant part" of the public concerned by the products or service covered by the trade mark.[225] The relevant public is that concerned by the earlier trade mark, that is to say, depending on the product or service marketed, either the public at large or a more specialised public, for example traders in a specific sector.[225a] Where a mark satisfies the requirement of reputation in part but not all of the EU, registration of a national mark may still be prevented even in a territory where the mark does not have a reputation if a "commercially significant part" (as opposed to a "a substantial part") of the public in that state is aware of the mark in issue.[226] In considering whether a reputation has been demonstrated, the court must take into account "all the relevant facts of the case" including in particular the market share held by the trade mark, the intensity, geographical extent and duration of its use and the size of the investment made by the undertaking promoting it,[227] in each case (it is suggested) in respect of the goods and services relied upon.[227a] **11-112**

[222] Or, in the case of a EU trade mark, a reputation in the Union: TM Directive art.4(3).

[223] *General Motors v Yplon* [1999] All E.R. (EC) 865, [1999] E.T.M.R. 950 CJEU at [28]. See also *PAGO* (C-301/07) [2009] E.C.R. 1-9429, [2010] E.T.M.R. 5. What constitutes a "significant part" of the general public as required by General Motors was discussed by Hacon HHJ in *Burgerista Operations GmbH v Burgista Bros Ltd* [2018] EWHC 35 (IPEC) in reference to the *PAGO* case: "73. It can be concluded that if the market for the goods or services for which a trade mark is registered is similarly broad and the mark is known throughout a Member State the size of Austria, this will constitute knowledge of the mark among a significant part of the public of the EU. The mark will qualify for the status of having a reputation in the Union. 74. That said, it is very hard to be sure about where the knowledge threshold lies in such a case (or any case). One clue is that the Court and the Advocate General [in *PAGO*] did not imply that knowledge throughout Austria was so self-evidently sufficient that the adequacy of the mark's reputation barely merited discussion. My impression is that if knowledge had been confined to limited parts of Austria, that might not have been enough."

[224] *PAGO* (C-301/07) [2009] E.C.R. 1-9429, [2010] E.T.M.R. 5 at [30]; *Iron & Smith Kft v Unilever NV* [2015] E.T.M.R. 45.

[225] *General Motors* [1999] All E.R. (EC) 865; [1999] E.T.M.R. 950 CJEU at [26]; *PAGO* [2010] E.T.M.R. 5; *Iron & Smith Kft v Unilever NV* [2015] E.T.M.R. 45. In *TMR Restaurant Ltd's Application* [2013] E.T.M.R. 37, the Controller of the Irish Patents Office stated "[i]t is well established that the reputation which s.10(3) [equivalent to s.5(3) of the 1994 Act] seeks to protect is that of an extremely well–known trade mark that would be defined as such under the Paris Convention. Such reputation is expected to extend beyond the limited class of consumers of the Opponent's goods and to penetrate the consciousness of the wider public such that a substantial number of people would know and recognise the mark even if they had never used the Opponent's goods", at [56]. It is respectfully agreed that this is a correct statement of what the law should be but the proposition that "reputation" for the purposes of s.5(3) (and s.10(3)) requires a mark to be extremely well-known is not in line with the prevailing CJEU authorities. There are a significant number of cases in which the threshold has been set much lower, e.g. it is difficult to see how the packaging marks at issue in the *L'Oréal v Bellure* case would have satisfied the Irish Controller's test.

[225a] In *Applications to register Spirit Energy marks* (BL 0-034-20), the Appointed Person (P. Johnson), after referring to the statement by AG Wahl in *Iron & Smith* (C-125/14) EU:C:2015:195 at [17], that the size of the relevant market for the particular goods or services "ought to assume a paramount role in the analysis", commented: "Clearly, if the relevant public comprises a few hundred people then knowledge need only be proved in a very small group, but where it comprises the general public then the knowledge requirement is much higher. While I am not suggesting a bright-line threshold, it is apparent that a million people with knowledge of a mark would be enough to establish reputation (using the comparative population size of Austria to the EU scaled to the United Kingdom). I should add, following Hacon HHJ's comments [in *Burgerista Operations GmbH v Burgista Bros Ltd* [2018] EWHC 35 (IPEC)], one million people would be well-over the line and not the line itself", at [18].

[226] *Iron & Smith Kft v Unilever NV* [2015] E.T.M.R at [34].

[227] *PAGO* (C-301/07) [2009] E.C.R. 1-9429; [2010] E.T.M.R. 5 at [25].

[227a] See [17] of the Opinion of AG Wahl in *Iron & Smith* (referring to the "paramount role" of the significance of the relevant market for the given goods and services in assessing reputation) and the helpful synthesis of principles from the CJEU authorities given by HHJ Hacon in *Burgerista v Burgista Bros* [2018] E.T.M.R 16: "(1) An EU trade mark has a reputation within the meaning of art.9(2)(c) if it was known to a significant part of the relevant public at the relevant date. (2) The relevant public are those concerned by the products or services covered by the trade mark. (3) The relevant date is the date on which the defendant first started to use the accused sign. (4) From a geographical perspective, the trade mark must have been known in a substantial part of the EU at the relevant date. (5) There is no fixed percentage threshold which can be used to assess what constitutes a significant part of the public; it is proportion rather than absolute numbers that matters. (6) Reputation constitutes a knowledge threshold, to be assessed according to a combination of geographical and economic criteria. (7) All relevant facts are to be taken into consideration when making the assessment, in particular the market share held by the trade mark, the intensity, geographical extent and duration of its use, and the size of the investment made by undertaking in promoting it. (8) The market for the goods or services in question, and from this the identity of the relevant public, ought to assume a paramount role in the assessment. (9) The territory of a single Member State (large or small) may constitute a substantial part of the EU, but the assessment must be conducted without consideration of geographical borders."

## (III) Link

*After "Such a link may be merely the 'calling to mind'", add new footnote 232a:*

11-116 [232a] Where the taking of unfair advantage (or detriment) depends on comparison of mark for sign in the mind of the average consumer, it is "obvious" that the necessary link cannot be established without the use of the sign bringing the mark to mind. *Argos Ltd v Argos Systems Inc* [2018] EWCA Civ 2211; [2019] F.S.R. 3 per Floyd LJ.

## (IV) Unfair Advantage/Detriment

### Unfair advantage

*Replace paragraph:*

11-134 The more difficult case is where the earlier trade mark is likely to be brought to mind by the use of the mark that is the subject of the application, where members of the public are unlikely to believe there is any economic connection between the suppliers (non-origin association). Simply being reminded of a similar trade mark with a reputation for dissimilar goods does not amount to taking unfair advantage of the repute of the mark.[273] So the use of dictionary words which allude to the nature of the goods and cause non-origin association is unlikely to be regarded as sufficient in itself to result in the application of the prohibition.[274] It is suggested that the position would be different if the applicant has adopted a highly distinctive earlier trade mark and the use of the mark will inevitably result in an advantage accruing to the applicant and where there is no justification for that use.[275] It will cover cases where there is clear exploitation and free-riding on the coattails of a famous mark[276] or an attempt to trade upon its reputation.[277]

[273] See para.11-119.

[274] See, e.g. *Oasis Stores* [1998] R.P.C. 631.

[275] See *Dimple* [1985] G.R.U.R. 550 and the discussion in *Premier Brands v Typhoon* [2000] E.T.M.R. 1071; [2000] F.S.R. 767. In *Helena Rubenstein SNC v OHIM* [2012] E.T.M.R. 40 CJEU, the argument that the determination of parasitic intent by the General Court was unsupported by evidence was rejected by the Court of Justice, which noted that the owners of the marks "BOTOLIST" and "BOTOCYL" had conceded at the hearing that, even though their products did not contain any, they intended to take advantage of the reputation of "botulinum toxin" from which the "BOTOX" trade mark was derived.

[276] See, e.g. *Pat Walsh v British Sky Broadcasting Group* [2013] E.T.M.R. 27 at [86] finding that the applicant was taking unfair advantage, although was found not to be seeking to pass off contrary to s.10(4)(a) of the Irish Trade Marks Act 1996 (the equivalent of s.5(4) of the 1994 Act, see para.11-149, et seq). Also, *Versatile Solutions (Hong Kong) Ltd's Application* O/071/17 where the Hearing Officer (A. James) rejected the opposition under s.5(4) but allowed it under s.5(3) on the ground that the applicant to register KRüG for fitness equipment was "taking unfair advantage of the communication and quality functions of the [opponent's] KRUG trade mark [for champagne]", at [50].

[277] See [39] of the Opinion of the AG in *Adidas v Fitnessworld* [2004] E.T.M.R. 10. He suggests, by way of example, that Rolls Royce would be entitled to prevent a manufacturer of whisky from exploiting the reputation of the Rolls Royce mark in order to promote his brand. See also *Intima's Application* [2000] R.P.C. 661: use of the applicant's mark would be "parasitic", unjustly drawing upon the recollection of the opponent's trade mark. It was noted by the Appointed Person (P. Johnson) in *Applications to register Spirit Energy marks* (BL 0-034-20), at [23], that "When considering the relevant public and thereby defining the market, it does not require the great precision applied in competition law, but enough clarity is needed to provide context so that the evidence led to establish reputation can be assessed adequately. For instance, a trader selling 1,000 units a year might be sufficient to establish reputation if a total of 5,000 units are sold each year in the United Kingdom, but wholly inadequate if sales total 50million units. Likewise, a turnover of £100,000 might be enough in a very small market but insignificant in a larger one. Context is everything."

*Replace paragraph:*

An advantage may be unfair even if it causes no harm to the distinctive character **11-135**
or repute of the mark or more generally to the interests of the trade mark proprietor.[278] From this it seems clear that the CJEU considers that the mere fact of taking advantage without paying is enough to render the advantage unfair. However, the Court of Appeal in *Whirlpool*[279] rejected the submission that mere advantage was enough to give rise to infringement, holding that either an intention to imitate the mark or some other factor was necessary to render a commercial advantage unfair. Subsequent to the decision of the Court of Appeal in *Whirlpool*, the CJEU re-iterated in *Interflora* that an advantage is unfair for the purposes of the provision in cases:

> "[W]here, by reason of a transfer of the image of the mark or of the characteristics which it projects to the goods identified by the identical or similar sign, there is clear exploitation on the coat-tails of the mark with a reputation,"[280]

but, in apparent recognition that the breadth of this definition might lead to competition being hindered, the Court went on to state that where the alleged infringement did not dilute or tarnish the mark and did not otherwise affect the functions of the earlier mark, its use would not be "without due cause".[281] Thus although the requirement imposed by the Court of Appeal in *Whirlpool* that mere advantage is not of itself unfair is not consistent with the approach required by the CJEU and must be viewed as incorrect, in many cases a similar result will be reached by following the CJEU's guidance on the interpretation of "due cause". Nevertheless, the Court of Appeal in *Argos v Argos Systems*[281a] has subsequently re-iterated the position that mere economic advantage and no more is not sufficient to establish "unfair" advantage.

[278] *L'Oréal v Bellure* (C-487/07) [2009] E.C.R. 1-5185, [2010] R.P.C. 1 at [43].

[279] *Whirlpool v Kenwood* [2010] R.P.C. 2 at [136].

[280] *Interflora v Marks & Spencer* (C-323/09) at [75].

[281] *Interflora* at [91].

[281a] *Argos Ltd v Argos Systems Inc* [2018] EWCA Civ 2211; [2019] F.S.R. 3 at [108].

## G. Acts of Agents or Representatives

*Replace paragraph:*

**11-144** The Act provides special protection against the unauthorised acts of agents or representatives in seeking to register marks. If an application for registration of a trade mark is made by a person who is an agent or representative of a person who is the proprietor of the mark in a Paris Convention or WTO Agreement[303] country then, if the proprietor opposes the application, registration shall be refused unless the agent or representative justifies their action.[304] The terms "agent" or "representative" must be interpreted broadly: according to EUIPO in relation to the corresponding provision in the EUTM Regulation art.8(3), it is sufficient:

> "[T]hat there is some kind of agreement of commercial cooperation ... that gives rise to a fiduciary relationship by imposing on the applicant, whether expressly or implicitly, a general duty of trust and loyalty as regards the interests of the TM owner".[305]

Thus it may also extend to licensees or authorised distributors. In addition, the provision gives protection against registration of a mark that differs in elements that do not affect the distinctive character of the principal's mark.[306] Section 60 provides both a ground of opposition and the right to apply for a declaration of invalidity or rectification of the register, subject to a three-year limitation period. Section 60 of the Act was repealed as of 14 January 2019[306a] and replaced by a further relative ground under s.5(6), which provides;

> "Where an agent or representative ('R') of the proprietor of a trade mark applies, without the proprietor's consent, for the registration of the trade mark in R's own name, the application is to be refused unless R justifies that action."

This is both less clear and potentially more broad in scope than s.60. It is not on its face limited to marks "owned" in any particular country but in the absence of any mention of Convention countries (as in s.60) there is no reason on its face to extend its scope to marks owned outside the UK. The wording of art.3(c) of the 2015 Directive (from which s.5(6) derives) provides no further guidance. Following the repeal of s.60, s.47(2ZA) allows this ground to be relied on in invalidity proceedings but the three-year limitation period has now been removed.

[303] The WTO was added by the Intellectual Property (Enforcement, etc) Regulations 2006 (SI 2006/1028).

[304] 1994 Act (s.60(l), (2) and (5), implementing art.6*septies* of the Paris Convention. Section 60(4) also provides that the proprietor may apply for an injunction to restrain the use of the trade mark in the UK.

[305] *Promat Ltd v Pasture BV* Decision 164C/00054844/1, Cancellation Division. 19 December 2002: in *Sriblian Jacob Co Ltd's Application for Rectification* (0-066-08) 3 March 2008, the Appointed Person

(R. Arnold QC) held that the words in s.60 should be interpreted in the same way as the same words in art.8(3) of the CTM (now EUTM) Regulation and referred to the OHIM (now EUIPO) decisions at fn.307. See also *Safariland LLC v OHIM* (T-262/09) ECLI:EU:T:2011:171; [2011] E.T.M.R. 47 at [64]–[65].

[306] *Sribhan Jacob Co Ltd's Application for Rectification* (0-066-08) 3 March 2008 at [46]. The Appointed Person was of the view also that it was at least arguable that it would protect principals who own rights in unregistered marks, at [49].

[306a] Trade Marks Regulations (SI 2018/825) Pt 2 reg.28.

## 3. Conflict With Earlier Rights

### General

*Replace paragraph:*

11-146 Section 5 of the 1994 Act also prohibits registration where or to the extent that the use of the mark in the UK is liable to be prevented by what the Act describes as "earlier rights". These are defined under s.5(4)[308a] by reference to three categories, namely, where the use of the trade mark is liable to be prevented:

(1) by virtue of any rule of law (in particular, the law of passing off) protecting an unregistered trade mark or other sign used in the course of trade (where the rights to the unregistered mark or sign were acquired prior to the date of application for the registration or the priority date claimed[308b]);
(2) by virtue of any provision any provision of EU law, or any enactment or rule of law, providing for protection of designations of origin or geographical indications (where the application for such designation of origin was submitted prior to the date of application for the registration or the priority date claimed, it is subsequently granted)[308c]; or
(3) by virtue of an earlier right other than those referred to in s.5(1)–(3) (earlier trade marks) or para.(1) or (2) above, in particular by virtue of the law of copyright or the law relating to industrial property rights.[309]

[308a] As amended from 14 January 2019.

[308b] 1994 Act ss.5(4)(a) and (4A).

[308c] 1994 Act ss.5(4)(aa) and (4B), implementing art.3(c) of the 2015 Directive.

[309] 1994 Act s.5(4)(b).

*Replace paragraph:*

11-147 This provision implements the optional provisions of art.4(4) of the TM Directive. Depending upon the circumstances it may apply in respect of all or only some of the goods or services that are the subject of the application. Although not in terms so limited, for practical purposes the objections likely to be considered are those based upon the identified rights in passing off, copyright, design rights and registered designs and designations of origin or geographical indications.[310]

[310] The latter are expressly identified by the mandatory provisions of art.3(c) of the 2015 Directive as giving rise to a right of opposition, required to be implemented into national law by 14 January 2019 and as expressly provided for by s.5A of the 1994 Act.

### The Protection of an Unregistered Trade Mark—Passing Off and Related Rights

*Replace paragraph:*

11-149 This limb of the prohibition protects a goodwill established in a business conducted under an unregistered mark and imports into the relative grounds of objection a consideration of the requirements of the cause of action in passing off.[312]

These are considered in detail in Ch.18.[313] The Registry accordingly looks for evidence of use sufficient to attract a relevant goodwill.[314] The goodwill must be more than nominal: as Lord Neuberger stated in *Starbucks (HK) Ltd v British Sky Broadcasting Group Plc*,[314a] a claimant in a passing off claim "must show that it has a significant goodwill, in the form of customers, in the jurisdiction".[314b]

312 For some of the problems, see *Last Minute Network v OHIM* [2010] E.T.M.R. 35 GC.

313 The basic principles were explained by the House of Lords in terms of the "classical trinity" in *Reckitt v Coleman v Borden ("Jif")* [1990] R.P.C. 341. See, particularly, Lord Oliver at 406 and Lord Jauncey at 416.

314 "*Wackers*" [1999] R.P.C. 453.

314a [2015] F.S.R. 29. In *TWG Tea Co Pte Ltd v Mariage Frères SA*, BL O/358/17, the Appointed Person (P. Johnson) summarised the position, at [32]: "whether a particular trader has developed sufficient goodwill to be protectable is a matter of "fact and degree" and passing off can protect large or small businesses (and by extension, product lines with smaller turnovers), but there is a point where protecting the goodwill developed is inappropriate as it is "trivial"."

314b [2015] F.S.R. 29 at [52]. In *Applications to register Recup* (BL O-304-20), the Appointed Person (T. Mitcheson QC) reviewed the authorities and summarised the position as follows: "A successful claimant in a passing-off action needs to demonstrate significant or substantial goodwill and at the very least sufficient goodwill to be able to conclude that there would be substantial damage on the basis of the misrepresentation relied upon", at [34]. On the evidence, the AP found that it was not established that a substantial goodwill existed at the relevant date, noting at [41] that "[t]he element of descriptiveness in the [Recup] sign sought to be used means that it will take longer to carry out sufficient trade with customers to establish sufficient goodwill in that sign so as to make it distinctive of [the opponent's] goods."

*Add to the end of the paragraph:*

**11-151** However, where the geographical extent of the senior user's goodwill was too limited to entitle it to restrain use by a subsequent user in a different area, the later user could rely on its own later goodwill to oppose the senior user's application, unless the application was subject to a geographical limitation to disclaim the territory within which the later user had established goodwill through its own activities.[318a]

318a *Caspian Pizza v Shah* [2017] EWCA Civ 1874; [2018] E.T.M.R. 8.

## Copyright, Design Right and Registered Designs, Designations of Origin or Geographical Indications

*Add to the end of the paragraph:*

**11-153** Section 60 was repealed as of 14 January 2019[322a] and replaced by s.10B which no longer expressly extends the right to proprietors of trade marks in territories outside the UK.

322a Repealed by Trade Marks Regulations (SI 2018/825) Pt 2 reg.28.

## Position Under the EUTM Regulation

*Add to the end of the paragraph:*

**11-157** Article 8(6) of the EUTM Regulation now provides a right of opposition based on protected designations of origin and geographical indications.

## 5. ACQUIESCENCE

*Replace paragraph:*

**11-166** Acquiescence for the purposes of the section does not equate to the common law meaning of the term.[343] In *Budweiser*,[344] the Court of Justice acknowledged that the notion of "acquiescence" (contained in both the TM Directive art.9(1), and the EUTM Regulation art.61(1)) is a concept of EU law that should be interpreted in a uniform fashion.[345] In the view of the court, the word implies that the person who acquiesces remains inactive when faced with a situation which he would be in a position to oppose. Thus, it must:

> "[b]e interpreted as meaning that the proprietor of an earlier trade mark cannot be held to have acquiesced in the long and well-established honest use, of which he has long been aware, by a third party of a later trade mark which is identical with that of the proprietor if that proprietor was not in any position to oppose that use."[346]

The question of whether the sending of letters threatening infringement proceedings without such proceedings being commenced was sufficient to avoid "acquiescence" in the use of a registered mark was considered (obiter) in *W3 Ltd v easyGroup*.[346a] The court expressed the view that the sending of draft proceedings and letter before claim were sufficient to "stop the clock" for the purposes of acquiescence, but stated that had the issue been central to the case, a reference to the CJEU would have been necessary. However, even in the absence of statutory acquiescence, *Budweiser* establishes that, in exceptional cases, a long period of honest concurrent use may defeat a TM Directive art.4/ EUTM Regulation art.8 objection.

[343] *Budějovický Budvar, národní podnik v Anheuser-Busch Inc* [2010] R.P.C. 7.

[344] *Budějovický Budvar, národní podnik v Anheuser-Busch Inc* (C-482/09) ECLI:EU:C:2011:605; [2012] E.T.M.R. 2.

[345] *Budějovický Budvar, národní podnik v Anheuser-Busch Ine* (C-482/09) ECLI:EU:C:2011:605; [2012] E.T.M.R. 2 at [37].

[346] *Budějovický Budvar, národní podnik v Anheuser-Busch Ine* (C-482/09) ECLI:EU:C:2011:605; [2012] E.T.M.R. 2 at [44]–[45].

[346a] [2018] EWHC 7; [2018] E.T.M.R. 40 at [252].

Chapter 12

# VALIDITY AND REMOVAL OF TRADE MARKS FROM THE REGISTER

Table of Contents



## 1. Preliminary Matters

### Firecraft

*Add new paragraphs:*

**12-027A** The effect of *Firecraft* was considered by Mr Allan James in the UK IPO in *Boyer v Stockbridge*[24a] in circumstances where the earlier invalidation proceedings (brought by S involving s.3(6)(bad faith), s.5(4)(a) (earlier unregistered mark) and s.5(4)(b) (earlier copyright) grounds) had succeeded due to the proprietor's (B) failure to file a counterstatement. In later opposition and invalidation proceedings between the same parties, B applied to add further grounds of opposition to S's applications and to his application to invalidate her existing trade mark. This was opposed on the basis that the additional grounds should be struck out as res judicata or summarily dismissed.

**12-027B** Mr James found that the decision in the earlier invalidation proceedings was akin to a default judgment and, by applying guidance from *Kok Hoong v Leong Cheong Kweng Mines Ltd*,[24b] the bare essence of what was necessarily decided was that the earlier trade mark was invalidly registered pursuant to ss.3(6), 5(4)(a) and 5(4)(b). By contrast, the factual assumptions the Registrar was required to make in order to dispose of that earlier invalidation action should not be treated as final determinations of those facts. Consequently, he concluded there was no scope for a claim of issue estoppel. He added that differences between (i) the trade marks, (ii) the goods/services, and (iii) the different filing dates may have prevented an issue estoppel arising in whole or in part, but it was not necessary to investigate those points. Hence, S's cross-applications to strike out and for summary judgment were dismissed.

**12-027C** Issue estoppel was also argued in *Bentley 1962 Ltd v Bentley Motors Ltd.*[24c] In the infringement action before the judge, one issue was whether the so-called Combination Sign used by the car company, Bentley Motors, comprising a winged "B" logo above the word "BENTLEY", comprised the use of one sign or two. The claimant (Bentley Clothing) argued that the question of whether the Combination

Sign was one sign or two had already been decided in earlier proceedings in the UK IPO, creating an issue estoppel in its favour. This argument was rejected on the basis that the Hearing Officer made no finding which created an issue estoppel. On a fair reading of the Hearing Officer's decision, he took use of the Combination Sign to be use of the word "BENTLEY" alone, when he made a clear finding that Bentley Motors owned goodwill in a clothing business under the sign "BENTLEY". However, it was clear that the Hearing Officer did not consider whether the average consumer would have perceived the Combination Sign to be one or two signs, since there was no need to do so.

[24a] [2019] F.S.R. 20, BL O-796-18.

[24b] [1964] A.C. 933 PC.

[24c] [2019] EWHC 2925, [2020] F.S.R. 15, HHJ Hacon.

## 2. Invalidity

*Replace paragraph with:*

Subject to one exception, if the trade mark is found to have been registered in breach of any of the absolute or relative grounds for refusal, then the registration is declared invalid. Attention is therefore directed primarily at the position at the date of application for the mark. In *BDO*[26] Arnold J held that it was clear that "lack of clarity and precision in the specification of goods and services is not a ground of invalidity". The judge was dealing with an argument to that effect, founded on *IP Translator*,[27] which was run but withdrawn prior to judgment being given. So, despite the fact this passage was strictly obiter, it does provide the answer to any attempt to found an invalidity attack based on *IP Translator*. A similar argument was run and also withdrawn in *Mattel v Zynga*.[28] The CJEU has now confirmed in *Sky v Skykick*[28a] that neither a EU trade mark nor a national trade mark can be declared wholly or partially invalid on the basis that terms in the specification of goods or services for which the mark is registered lack clarity or precision. One consequence of this point is that litigants, tribunals and courts have to bring an appropriate degree of clarity and precision through the often difficult process of interpreting terms in a specification which may lack clarity or precision. On this, see Ch.6 and para.12-072, and the updates to that chapter and paragraph. **12-030**

[26] [2013] EWHC 418 at [44].

[27] *Chartered Institute of Patent Attorneys v Registrar of Trade Marks* (C-307/10) [2012] E.T.M.R. 42.

[28] [2013] EWHC 3348.

[28a] (C-371/18) at [71].

## 3. Revocation for Lack of Genuine Use

*Replace paragraph:*

The latest summary of the applicable principles is from *Walton International Ltd v Verweij Fashion BV*,[40] Arnold J: **12-050**

> "114. *The law with respect to genuine use.* The CJEU has considered what amounts to "genuine use" of a trade mark in a series of cases: Case C-40/01 *Ansul BV v Ajax Brandbeveiliging BV* [2003] ECR I-2439,*La Mer* (cited above), Case C 416/04 P *Sunrider Corp v Office for Harmonisation in the Internal Market (Trade Marks and Designs)* [2006] ECR I 4237, Case C-442/07 *Verein Radetsky-Order v Bundervsvereinigung Kamaradschaft 'Feldmarschall Radetsky'* [2008] ECR I-9223, Case C-495/07 *Silberquelle GmbH v Maselli-Strickmode GmbH* [2009]

ECR I-2759, Case C-149/11 *Leno Merken BV v Hagelkruis Beheer BV* EU:C:2012:816, [2013] ETMR 16, Case C-609/11 P *Centrotherm Systemtechnik GmbH v Centrotherm Clean Solutions GmbH & Co KG* EU:C:2013:592, [2014] ETMR, Case C-141/13 P *Reber Holding & Co KG v Office for Harmonisation in the Internal Market (Trade Marks and Designs)* EU:C:2014:2089 and Case C-689/15 *W.F. Gozze Frottierweberei GmbH v Verein Bremer Baumwollborse* EU:C:2017:434, [2017] Bus LR 1795.

115. The principles established by these cases may be summarised as follows:

(1) Genuine use means actual use of the trade mark by the proprietor or by a third party with authority to use the mark: *Ansul* at [35] and [37].

(2) The use must be more than merely token, that is to say, serving solely to preserve the rights conferred by the registration of the mark: *Ansul* at [36]; *Sunrider* at [70]; *Verein* at [13]; *Leno* at [29]; *Centrotherm* at [71]; *Reber* at [29].

(3) The use must be consistent with the essential function of a trade mark, which is to guarantee the identity of the origin of the goods or services to the consumer or end user by enabling him to distinguish the goods or services from others which have another origin: *Ansul* at [36]; *Sunrider* at [70]; *Verein* at [13]; *Silberquelle* at [17]; *Leno* at [29]; *Centrotherm* at [71]. Accordingly, affixing of a trade mark on goods as a label of quality is not genuine use unless it guarantees, additionally and simultaneously, to consumers that those goods come from a single undertaking under the control of which the goods are manufactured and which is responsible for their quality: *Gözze* at [43]–[51].

(4) Use of the mark must relate to goods or services which are already marketed or which are about to be marketed and for which preparations to secure customers are under way, particularly in the form of advertising campaigns: Ansul at [37]. Internal use by the proprietor does not suffice: *Ansul* at [37]; *Verein* at [14] and [22]. Nor does the distribution of promotional items as a reward for the purchase of other goods and to encourage the sale of the latter: *Silberquelle* at [20]–[21]. But use by a non-profit making association can constitute genuine use: *Verein* at [16]–[23].

(5) The use must be by way of real commercial exploitation of the mark on the market for the relevant goods or services, that is to say, use in accordance with the commercial raison d'être of the mark, which is to create or preserve an outlet for the goods or services that bear the mark: *Ansul* at [37]–[38]; *Verein* at [14]; *Silberquelle* at [18]; *Centrotherm* at [71]; *Reber* at [29].

(6) All the relevant facts and circumstances must be taken into account in determining whether there is real commercial exploitation of the mark, including: (a) whether such use is viewed as warranted in the economic sector concerned to maintain or create a share in the market for the goods and services in question; (b) the nature of the goods or services; (c) the characteristics of the market concerned; (d) the scale and frequency of use of the mark; (e) whether the mark is used for the purpose of marketing all the goods and services covered by the mark or just some of them; (f) the evidence that the proprietor is able to provide; and (g) the territorial extent of the use: *Ansul* at [38] and [39]; *La Mer* at [22]–[23]; *Sunrider* at [70]–[71], [76]; *Leno* at [29]–[30], [56]; *Centrotherm* at [72]–[76]; *Reber* at [29], [32]–[34].

(7) Use of the mark need not always be quantitatively significant for it to be deemed genuine. Even minimal use may qualify as genuine use if it is deemed to be justified in the economic sector concerned for the purpose of creating or preserving market share for the relevant goods or services. For example, use of the mark by a single client which imports the relevant goods can be sufficient to demonstrate that such use is genuine, if it appears that the import operation has a genuine commercial justification for the proprietor. Thus there

is no de minimis rule: *Ansul* at [39]; *La Mer* at [21], [24] and [25]; *Sunrider* at [72] and [76]–[77]; *Leno* at [55].

(8) It is not the case that every proven commercial use of the mark may automatically be deemed to constitute genuine use: *Reber* at [32].

117. Counsel for the Claimants suggested that there was a difference between the assessment of what amounted to genuine use of a trade mark, and in particular the quantitative extent of the use required, depending on whether the trade mark was a national trade mark or an EU trade mark. As counsel for the Defendant pointed out, however, the Court of Justice has expressly held that the same principles are applicable to the interpretation of the relevant provisions of both the Directive and the Regulation: see *Leno* at [31]."

In *BDO*[47] Arnold J adapted the propositions set out in *SANT AMBROEUS* by adding references to *Sunrider v OHIM*.[48] The *BDO* formulation has since been applied by Asplin J in *TOMMY NUTTER*.[49]

[40] [2018] EWHC 1608.

[47] [2013] EWHC 418 at [51].

[48] *Sunrider v OHIM* (C-416/04) EU:C:2006:310.

[49] [2013] EWHC 3459.

## Small Scale Use

*Add new paragraph:*

In cases involving small scale use at the UK IPO, it is frequently the case that the evidence from the proprietor designed to establish genuine use could have been much better. There are numerous decisions from various Appointed Persons and the court warning litigants that they must adduce their best evidence first time around in view of the difficulty in satisfying the requirements for the admission of fresh evidence on appeal—see, most recently, in particular *Consolidated Developments Ltd v Cooper*,[53a] and *Silver Spectre* O-265-19 (Mr James Mellor QC) at [44]. **12-053A**

[53a] [2018] EWHC 1727, Henry Carr J.

## The Use Required to Sustain a EUTM

*Replace paragraph:*

It confirmed, nevertheless, that the territorial extent of the use was one of the relevant factors in that assessment (at [56]): **12-071**

"That assessment must have regard to all the facts and circumstances relevant to the main proceedings, including the characteristics of the market concerned, the nature of the goods or services protected by the trade mark and the territorial extent and scale of the use as well as its frequency and regularity."

See also Arnold J in *BDO*.[70] Accordingly, to the eight principles from *Walton International*, set out at para.12-050, Arnold J added the following further three principles applicable when assessing genuine use in the Union:

"118. *The law with respect to genuine use in the Union.* Whereas a national mark needs only to have been used in the Member State in question, in the case of a EU trade mark there must be genuine use of the mark 'in the Union'. In this regard, the Court of Justice has laid down additional principles to those summarised above which I would summarise as follows:

(9) The territorial borders of the Member States should be disregarded in the assessment of whether a trade mark has been put to genuine use in the Union: *Leno* at [44], [57].

(10) While it is reasonable to expect that a EU trade mark should be used in a larger area than a national trade mark, it is not necessary that the mark should be used in an extensive geographical area for the use to be deemed genuine, since this depends on the characteristics of the goods or services and the market for them: *Leno* at [50], [54]–[55].

(11) It cannot be ruled out that, in certain circumstances, the market for the goods or services in question is in fact restricted to the territory of a single Member State, and in such a case use of the EU trade mark in that territory might satisfy the conditions for genuine use of a EU trade mark: *Leno* at [50]."

[70] [2013] EWHC 418 at [52].

## Relevant Goods or Services

*Replace paragraph with:*

**12-072** The use must be in relation to goods or services within the specification.[71] Use on any other goods or services is irrelevant. If an issue arises as to whether particular goods or services do or do not fall within the specification, it may be necessary to construe what the words used in the specification actually mean. The general approach to construction has been described thus:

> "When it comes to construing a word used in a trade mark specification, one is concerned with how the product is, as a practical matter, regarded for the purposes of trade. After all, a trade mark specification is concerned with use in trade."[72]

The words in the specification must be construed as at the date of application for the mark in question. On the issue of how to interpret words used in a specification, in *Sky v Skykick*,[72a] following the CJEU ruling, Arnold LJ had to decide how to interpret the term "telecommunications services". He summarised the applicable principles of interpretation in the following four propositions:

(1) General terms are to be interpreted as covering the goods or services clearly covered by the literal meaning of the terms, and not other goods or services.
(2) In the case of services, the terms used should not be interpreted widely, but confined to the core of the possible meanings attributable to the terms.
(3) An unclear or imprecise term should be narrowly interpreted as extending only to such goods or services as it clearly covers.
(4) A term which cannot be interpreted is to be disregarded.

The other problem which can arise is whether a particular use was or was not in relation to goods or services within the specification. For a recent illustration, see *Guanghzou Wong Lo Kat v Multi-Access*,[72b] applying *Pathway IP Sarl v Easygroup Ltd*,[72c] and deciding that "canned (liquid) herbal tea" was not a beverage in class 32, but would have been classified as a tea in class 30.

[71] Under the 1938 Act, the proprietor could rely on use on goods of the same description, under s.26(1). The only use which can be taken into account under the 1994 Act is use on goods or services for which the mark is registered.

[72] Jacob J in *British Sugar Pic v James Robertson & Sons Ltd* [1996] R.P.C. 281 at 288.

[72a] [2020] EWHC 990.

[72b] [2019] EWHC 3357; [2020] F.S.R. 16 (David Stone sitting as a Deputy Judge) at [66]–[103],

[72c] [2018] EWHC 3608, [2019] F.S.R. 8, Henry Carr J.

*Add new sub-section:*

## Use in relation to second-hand goods

The claimed use in *Ansul* (see para.12-054 in the Main Work) was "after-sales" use. On occasion, proprietors seek to rely on use of their mark when their used or second-hand goods are traded. If the proprietor is involved in the trading, and possibly engaged in refurbishment, such that the use preserves a market for the goods under the mark, there is little problem that such use constitutes or may contribute to genuine use. Two recent decisions exemplify the other end of the scale. First, in *London Taxi* at first instance, Arnold J took the approach that sales of second-hand goods could in principle contribute to a finding of genuine use. On the facts, the claimant relied on its sale of some 264 used Fairway taxis at an average price of £585 and some 314 disposals for scrap. Production of the Fairway had long since ceased and even sales of used vehicles had dried up, and this limited use could not save the registration of the appearance of the Fairway taxi because it was not use to create or preserve a market for the goods in question. Upheld on appeal—see *The London Taxi Corp Ltd v Fraser-Nash Research Ltd.*[78a] **12-079A**

Secondly, in *Aiwa Co Ltd v Aiwa Corp,*[78b] there had been no retail sales of new goods under the marks since 2008. The issue was whether second-hand sales (not involving the proprietor) and some repair or support services were sufficient to found genuine use. The second-hand sales were relied upon as being subject to an implied consent from the proprietor provided when the original sale took place. Not surprisingly, this argument failed because the proprietor's rights were exhausted on the original sale. As in *London Taxi*, the use was not to create or preserve a market for the goods. The other activity was described as "the most basic after-sales service" and "sparse and unparticularised" and not sufficient to amount to "real commercial exploitation of the mark in the relevant period". **12-079B**

[78a] [2017] EWCA 1729 at [81].

[78b] [2019] EWHC 3468, [2020] F.S.R. 17.

## Use of Variants of the Registered Mark

*Replace paragraph:*

Under this heading, there are two types of "variant" to be considered. The first is the normal type where the sign which has been used is different in certain respects to the mark on the register. The second type of "variant" is more subtle and, in some cases, may not amount to a variant at all. This second type is concerned with signs which are presented to the consumer in combination but the elements of the combination are registered separately. Then the question can arise: if the separately registered elements are not used separately but are always presented in the combination, has there been genuine use of each separate element or can the use of the combination constitute genuine use of the separate element(s)? The same objective underlies whatever type of variant is under consideration. As Arnold J stated in *Walton International Ltd v Verweij Fashion BV*[84a] at [119]: **12-091**

> "The CJEU stated in Case C-252/12 *Specsavers International Healthcare Ltd v Asda Stores Ltd* [EU:C:2013:497], [2013] ETMR 46 ('*Specsavers (CJEU)*') at [29] that the objective of what is now Article 18(1)(a) of the Regulation was:
>
> > 'by avoiding imposing a requirement for strict conformity between the form used in trade and the form in which the trade mark was registered, ... to allow the proprietor of the mark, in the commercial exploitation of the sign, to make variations in the sign, which, without altering its distinctive character, enable it to be better adapted to the marketing and promotion requirements of the goods or services concerned.'"

[84a] [2018] EWHC 1608.

*Replace paragraph:*

12-095 In *NIRVANA*,[89] the Appointed Person (Richard Arnold QC) reviewed the UK and General Court case law and OHIM guidance and concluded (subject to one or two comments) that "the normal approach to the assessment of distinctive character applies in this context". Confirmed by Arnold J in *Walton International Ltd v Verweij Fashion BV*[89a] at [120], by reference to the decision of the CJEU in *EUIPO v Cactus SA*[89b] at [68]–[71].

89 O/262/06. See in particular, [9]–[21], especially [15].

89a [2018] EWHC 1608.

89b (C-501/15) EU:C:2017:750

*Add new paragraph:*

12-095A For a useful summary of the applicable principles, see *Walton International* at [119]–[123] per Arnold J.

## 6. PROCEDURE

### Applications to the Court Where There are Existing Proceedings

*Replace paragraph:*

12-174 If the applicant is a party to existing proceedings in court concerning the trade mark, then common sense and the overriding objective say that an application for a declaration of invalidity or revocation or rectification must be brought by way of counterclaim or other CPR Pt 20 claim. Often such claims are made in response to a claim for infringement. If, however, the applicant is not a party to existing proceedings concerning the trade mark, they must still bring their application before the court.[183] It is then open to the court or any of the parties to the proceedings to consider whether all matters relating to the trade mark should be determined at the same time. Whatever the method of initiating the application in court, under the general CPR rules, the claimant is obliged to plead the objections to the validity of the registration or of any grounds of revocation or rectification on which they rely. A copy of any claim (whether Pt 20 claim or originating claim) together with "accompanying documents" must be served on the Registrar.[184] The Registrar is entitled to take such part in the proceedings as they may think fit, but need not serve a defence or other statement of case unless ordered to do so by the court.[185] Where there is a counterclaim for revocation or invalidity of a EUTM, the party filing it must inform the EUTM court that the court itself must inform the EUIPO.[186] Thereafter, the application for invalidity or revocation is dealt with as part and parcel of the action. If the case involves non-use, the registered proprietor is not generally required to submit their evidence of use until the normal exchange of witness statements, and this is one of the principal differences between proceeding in the Registry and court in such cases. Where any Order of the court affects the validity of an entry in the register of trade marks, the court and the party in whose favour the Order was made must serve a copy on the Registrar within 14 days.[187] Similarly, where a EUTM court has given a judgment which has become final on a counterclaim for revocation or a declaration of invalidity of a EUTM, the court must send a copy of the judgment to the EUIPO in accordance with EUTMR art.128(6). The party in whose favour the judgment has been given is obliged to inform the court of this procedure.[188] We should draw attention to a jurisdictional issue regarding a counterclaim to revoke or invalidate a EUTM. In *Adobe Systems Inc v Netcom*

*Distributors*,[188a] Mann J decided that the High Court, as a Community Trade Mark Court, only had jurisdiction under art.96(d) of the CTM Regulation (now art.124(d) of the EUTM Regulation 1001/2017) to entertain a counterclaim, in so far as it was capable of providing a defence to infringement. In that case, the defendant counterclaimed to revoke the claimant's EUTM for lack of genuine use in classes which did not feature in the infringement claim. Mann J decided that the court did not have jurisdiction to determine that revocation claim which had to be pursued at the EU IPO. Somewhat controversially, Mann J also decided that the issue was clear and did not need to be made the subject of a reference to the CJEU. Similar claims levelled against UK national marks were allowed to proceed.

[183] The old Practice Direction. Patents, etc. used to specify such a claim had to be brought under CPR Pt 8, a procedure which was not always appropriate. Now there is no such provision in the Practice Direction to CPR Pt 63, so the applicant can use an ordinary claim form or the Pt 8 route, as appropriate.

[184] CPR Pt 63.14(3).

[185] CPR pt 63.15. Frequently, the Registrar plays no part in the proceedings, simply requesting to be kept informed of the outcome.

[186] CPR PD 63 paras 21.2 and 21.3. see also Ch.22, para.22-063, fn.133.

[187] CPR PD 63 para.20.1.

[188] CPR PD 63 paras 21.4 and 21.5. see also Ch.22, para.22-063, fn.133.

[188a] [2012] EWHC 1087.

## CHAPTER 13

# GEOGRAPHICAL INDICATIONS AND APPELLATIONS OF ORIGIN

TABLE OF CONTENTS



## 1. OVERVIEW OF PROTECTION OUTSIDE THE EU REGULATION

*Replace footnote 8:*

13-003 [8] [1970] R.P.C. 489. In the EU, see Reg.110/2008. For an example of how broad the protection accorded by the EU GI legislation can be, see the application to the facts by the Landgericht Hamburg (6 February 2019) of the CJEU's guidance on the interpretation of Reg.11/2008 in *Scotch Whisky Association v Michael Klotz* (C-2018-415 of 7 June 2018), where the German court held that the use of the word "Glen" on a whisky distilled near Stuttgart in Germany (and therefore not "Scotch Whisky") is a misleading indication liable to convey a false impression as to origin contrary to art.16(3) of the Regulation and additional information on the label that may dispel that false impression should not be taken into account. This can usefully be compared with the judgment in the Singapore HC in *Scotch Whisky Association v Isetan Mitsukoshi Ltd* [2019] SGHC 200 concerning the SWA's opposition to an application to register the trade mark "Isetan Tartan". The judge (Lee Seiu Kin J) held, at [39], after referring to the CJEU judgment in *Klotz*: "it is apparent that the scope of protection offered by the EU legislation is significantly wider than that which is offered under Singapore's equivalent legislation. Reading s.7(5) of the TMA [the equivalent of s.3(4) of the UK Act] with s 2 of the [Geographical Indications Act], it is clear that only 'use of a geographical indicator' is proscribed. I am therefore guided by the plain and ordinary meaning of the word 'use'. Wider forms of 'use' such as 'indirect commercial use' and 'evocation' do not fall within the definition of 'use' under the GIA." The judge also rejected SWA's submission "that the respondent had used 'Scotch Whisky'. It is manifestly obvious that what is being 'used' by the respondent is the trade mark 'Isetan Tartan'. After all, this is the subject of its application for registration of a trade mark. There is no evidence whatsoever that the respondent is attempting to register the trade mark 'Scotch Whisky, or is using the words 'Scotch Whisky' in any other manner." At [40].

*Replace paragraph:*

13-004 The Trade Marks Act 1994 provides in s.3(1)(c)[14] that trade marks which consist exclusively of signs or designations which serve to indicate geographical origin should not be registered[15] and the *Windsurfing Chiemsee* judgment of the Court of Justice[16] interpreted that provision to mean that "geographical names which are liable to be used by undertakings must remain available to such undertakings as indications of the geographical origin of the category of goods concerned".[17] Also, the 1994 Act provides in ss.49 and 50 for the registration of geographical names as certification and collective marks.[18]

[14] Based on TM Directive art.3(1)(c). For EU trade marks, see art.7(1)(j) for PDOs and PGIs (see below at para.13-005), (k) for traditional terms for wine, and (l) for traditional specialities guaranteed (see fn.19) EUTM Regulation (Regulation 2017/1001).

[15] See Ch.10, para.10-097.

[16] [1999] E.T.M.R. 585.

[17] [1999] E.T.M.R. 585 at [30]. In *Nordic Saunas Ltd's Trade Mark* [2002] E.T.M.R. 18 the Appointed Person (S. Thorley QC) rejected a contention that it was only in rare cases that a mark indicating

geographical origin could be registered without evidence of use: "Each geographical name must be considered in relation to the goods in question and where there is no current association of that geographical name with the goods in question, all relevant factors must be taken into account in assessing whether the name is capable of designating the geographical origin of that category of goods to the average consumer", at [17].

[18] See Ch.14. In *Foundation for the Protection of the Traditional Cheese of Cyprus named Halloumi v EUIPO* (C-766/18 P) AG Kokott observed at the outset of her Opinion (17 October 2019) that the procedure to register "Halloumi" as a PGI had started in 2014 but had not yet been completed. In the meantime, the Foundation had been attempting to prevent third party use, or registration of marks including the word, through reliance on its registered collective mark: having considered the Foundation's grounds of appeal and, without coming to a final view, casting some doubt as to whether "Halloumi" could perform the function of a registered trade mark, she noted that "the EUIPO rightly asserts that it would be contradictory if producers' associations could obtain equivalent or even stronger protection for geographical designations on the basis of trade mark law than in the protected designation of origin system." At [86].

*Add new heading and paragraph:*

## Impact of Brexit

In February 2019 the Government announced its intention to introduce UK schemes for the protection of GIs with effect from the end of the transition period, 1 January 2021.[18a] The proposed schemes will mirror the existing EU schemes. For agricultural products and foodstuffs, these are currently set out in EU Regulation 1151/2012, which provides for registration of designations of origin ("PDOs") and geographical indications ("PGIs") (see below at para.13-005 and following).[18b] Following the transition period, all EU and UK PDOs and PGIs registered, respectively, under the EU Regulation and the proposed UK regulations will be protected in the UK and EU on a reciprocal basis, pending the future treaty on the relationship between the UK and the EU.[18c] As at 7 August 2019, there were 88 UK food names protected under the EU schemes[18d] and approximately 5 per cent of the around 1,500 PDOs/PGIs registered under EU Regulation 1151/2012 came from the UK. **13-004A**

[18a] See the DEFRA publication at *https://www.gov.uk/guidance/protecting-food-and-drink-of names-if-theres-no-brexit-deal* [Accessed 2 May 2020]. This was unaffected by the October 2019 amendments to the 2018 Draft Withdrawal Agreement. The Withdrawal Agreement signed on 12 November 2019 (2019/C 384I/01 of 12 November 2019) was subsequently ratified by the UK following passage of the European Union (Withdrawal Agreement) Act 2020 and the UK ceased to be a Member State of the EU on 31 January 2020. At that time, the EU GI Regulation 1151/2012, as amended by The Food and Drink, Veterinary Medicines and Residues (Amendment etc.) (EU Exit) Regulations 2019 (SI 2019/865) r.7 and The Agricultural Products, Food and Drink (Amendment) (EU Exit) Regulations 2019 (SI 2019/1366), to replace terms no longer relevant to the UK as a non-Member State, e.g. replacing "Commission" with "Secretary of State", became part of "EU retained law" pursuant to the EU Withdrawal Act.

[18b] Regulation 1151/2012 also provides for a register of traditional speciality guaranteed ("TSG") products, which relate to specific features that distinguish agricultural products or foodstuffs but not where, inter alia, they are due to geographical origin (this was previously governed by Regulation 509/2006 (that, in turn, replaced Regulation 2082/92). The only two TSGs registered by the UK as at 6 February 2017 were Traditional Farmfresh Turkey and Traditionally Farmed Gloucestershire Old Spots Pork. These are beyond the scope of this work: see generally, A. Tosato, "The Protection of Traditional Foods in the EU: Traditional Specialities Guaranteed" (2013) 19 E.L.J. 545. However, it should be noted here that the latter TSG (at the time only applied for but not registered) was used to oppose registration as a trade mark of "Bramley Old Spot Pork" under s.5(4) of the 1994 Act; as the TSG was not registered, the Hearing Officer rejected that ground of opposition but refused the application under s.3(3)(b): *Axle Associates Ltd v Gloucestershire Old Spots Pig Breeders' Club* [2010] E.T.M.R. 12.

[18c] Withdrawal Agreement, 2019/C 384I/01 of 12 November 2019, art.54(2). Such reciprocal protection will continue until a treaty is agreed on the future relationship between the UK and EU. On 19 May 2020 the UK Government published a draft UK-EU Comprehensive Free Trade Agreement. Although publication of the draft appears to be a negotiating tactic, it does give some indication of the position the UK Government will adopt in negotiations on the future relationship. While setting out in Ch.24 various detailed provisions on intellectual property rights and their enforcement, the draft states baldly on

GIs: "The provisions of this sub-section shall supersede Article 54(2) of the Withdrawal Agreement. [Further text on the provisions of this sub-section to be proposed]", art.24.25. It can be surmised that this coyness is the UK Government's response to the US' recently-voiced objections to the EU GI system (see n.21a below).

[18d] See *https://www.gov.uk/government/collections/protected-food-name-scheme-uk-registered-products* [Accessed 2 May 2020].

*Add new heading and paragraph:*

### Proposed UK schemes

**13-004B** In addition to the scheme to protect geographical names of agricultural products and foodstuffs (including beer, cider and perry) through registration as geographical indications or designations of origin, the new arrangements to take effect from 1 January 2021 will introduce schemes providing for protection under domestic law for the geographical names of spirit drinks, wines, aromatised wines (such as vermouth), as well as what DEFRA describes as "traditional terms for wine names". At the date of writing (May 2020), details of the new UK schemes were still to be published, but with effect from the date of the UK's exit from the EU (31 January 2020), EU Regulation 1151/2012, as amended by The Food and Drink, Veterinary Medicines and Residues (Amendment etc.) (EU Exit) Regulations (SI 2019/788) r.7 to replace terms no longer relevant to the UK as a non-Member State, e.g. replacing "Commission" with "Secretary of State", had become part of "EU retained law" pursuant to the European Union (Withdrawal) Act 2018. For the text of retained but amended version of Regulation 1151/2012, see Appendix 10.

## 2. REGULATION 1151/2012 ON QUALITY SCHEMES FOR AGRICULTURAL PRODUCTS AND FOODSTUFFS (REPLACING REGULATION 510/2006 ON THE PROTECTION OF GEOGRAPHICAL INDICATIONS AND DESIGNATIONS OF ORIGIN FOR AGRICULTURAL PRODUCTS AND FOODSTUFFS)

### Introduction

*Replace paragraph:*

**13-005** Under Regulation 1151/2012 (the Regulation),[20] which replaced both Regulation 510/2006 on the Protection of Geographical Indications and Designations of Origin for Agricultural Products and Foodstuffs and Regulation 509/2006 on traditional speciality guaranteed products,[21] protection can be obtained for designations of origin ("PDOs") and for geographical indications ("PGIs") for agricultural products and foodstuffs.[21a] Wine products or spirit drinks are covered by other legislation.[22] Protection can be obtained by following the application procedure either in the Member State or in any other third country[23] in which the geographical area is located. Once registered, the protection can be used to prevent commercial use of the particular designation or indication on products "comparable" to those for which it is registered. Also, the right may be used by any producer who complies with the conditions of production laid down in the specification; it is not limited to those who made the application in the first place.

[20] [2012] OJ L343/1. This Regulation, which came into force on 3 January 2013, was passed "in the interests of clarity and transparency" (Recital 14) and makes certain amendments to the scheme for the protection of PGIs and PDOs previously contained in Regulation 510/2006 and, prior to that, Regulation 2081/92 ("the original Regulation"). The original Regulation setting up the register came into force on 25 July 1993. For a detailed analysis of the draft Regulation, see G.E. Evans, "The Simplification

of European Legislation for the Protection of Geographical Indications: The Proposed Regulation on Agricultural Product Quality Schemes" [2012] E.I.P.R. 770.

[21] As noted in fn.19, the TSG system is beyond the scope of this work, although its close relationship to that of PGIs and PDOs (at least in the view of the European Commission) is made clear by the fact that all three forms of protection are now governed by Regulation 1151/2012, Recital 10 of which states that they "have certain common objectives and provisions". Notwithstanding this, the TSG designation cannot, in any meaningful sense, be viewed as an intellectual property right, whereas "indications of source" and "appellations of origin" were included in the scope of "industrial property rights" in art.1 of the Paris Convention 1883 and "geographical indications" are defined in art.22 of the 1994 Agreement on Trade-Related Aspects of Intellectual Property Rights ("TRIPs"). Indeed, Recital 22 of Regulation 1151/2012 acknowledges the need to adapt the earlier definitions of the PDO and PGI to take into account the definition in TRIPs art.22. Article 4 of the Regulation includes, as one of the objectives of the PDO/PGI scheme, ensuring "uniform protection of the names as an intellectual property right" in the Union (the objective of the TSG set out in art.17 is notably silent on this subject and it must remain moot whether the UK will adopt such a right in domestic law post-Brexit).

[21a] In its 2020 Special 301 Report, the Office of the U.S. Trade Representative made sweeping criticisms of the EU's GI system: highlighting "the negative market access effects of the approach of the European Union (EU) to the protection of geographical indications ("GIs") in the EU and third-country markets on US producers and traders, particularly those with prior trademark rights or who rely on the use of common name", see [19]–[22]. It is likely that these criticisms will need to be taken into account by the British team negotiating a post-Brexit free trade agreement with the USA.

[22] See, for example, Reg.1308/2013 which provides PDOs and PGIs for certain wines: this Regulation was relied on by the proprietor of the PDO "Prosecco", Consorzio di Tutella della Denominazione di Origine Controllata Prosecco, in its successful opposition to the application to register a label including the word "Nosecco" for "Non-alcoholic wines; non-alcoholic sparkling wines" under TMA s.3(3)(b) and 3(4), O/691/19.

[23] See Recital 24 and arts 11(2) and 49(5) of Regulation 1151/2012.

## Designations for Which Protection is Available

*Replace footnote 36:*

[36] Regulation 1151/2012 art.6(1). Article 3(6) defines "generic terms" as "the names of products which, although relating to the place, region or country where the product was originally produced or marketed, have become the common name of a product in the Union". On this issue under Reg.510/2006, see the discussion of "feta", at para.13-024. **13-009**

## The Application Process

### Names from third countries

*Add to the end of the paragraph:*

Although it is not possible to state with certainty that this will be the case, it **13-019** seems likely that after the transition period the UK will be treated in the same way as all other non-Member States.

## Protection Granted

*Add new paragraph:*

In the "*Manchego Cheese*" case,[85a] the CJEU held that the name of a PDO could **13-027A** be "evoked" by figurative signs as much as it could by a name. The PDO "*queso manchego*" covers cheeses made in the region of La Mancha (in Spain) from sheep's milk in accordance with traditional production, preparation and ageing requirements set out in the specification.[85b] The defendant in the Spanish proceedings that gave rise to the reference to the CJEU was selling cheeses bearing illustrations and names associated with Don Quixote de La Mancha, the fictional character created by Cervantes, including images of windmills like those tilted at by Don

Quixote in La Mancha and of a "bony" horse and the use of "Rocinante", the name of Don Quixote's horse. The CJEU's judgment leaves to the Spanish Supreme Court the decision as to whether there is sufficiently clear and direct conceptual proximity between the PDO and the figurative signs and names used by the defendant so that "queso manchego" is triggered directly.[85c]

[85a] *Fundacion Consejo Regulador de la Denominacion de Origen Protegida Queso Manchego v Industrial Quesera Cuquerella SL* (C-614/17) of 2 May 2017.

[85b] *Fundacion Consejo Regulador de la Denominacion de Origen Protegida Queso Manchego v Industrial Quesera Cuquerella SL* (C-614/17) of 2 May 2017, at [12].

[85c] *Fundacion Consejo Regulador de la Denominacion de Origen Protegida Queso Manchego v Industrial Quesera Cuquerella SL* (C-614/17) of 2 May 2017, at [39]–[41].

## Enforcement

*After "Once names are registered, they are enforced in the UK by the Trading Standards (Environmental Health) Department of the various local authorities.", add:*

**13-031** Until the end of the transition period following the UK's 31 January 2020 exit from the EU, PDOs and PGIs may be enforced as normal in the UK, generally by the relevant food authority designated under the Food Safety Act 1990. Filling a lacuna mentioned in previous editions of this work, specific procedures for the enforcement of PDOs, PGIs and TSGs under EU Regulation came into force in the UK on 1 January 2019, following passage of The Quality Schemes (Agricultural Products and Foodstuffs) Regulations 2018.[88a] The Regulations provide for inter alia a maximum penalty of £40,000 for non-compliance with an enforcement notice (which may be enforced as a civil debt). The Regulations also specify that appeals against a decision by the Secretary of State to refuse an application for registration of a PGI or PDO may be made to the First-Tier Tribunal.

[88a] SI 1275/2018.

*Add new paragraph:*

**13-031A** Under the UK-EU Withdrawal Agreement art.52(2)(1)[88b] the UK agrees that "without re-examination" the owner of a PDO, PGI and TSG registered under the EU legislation as at the end of the transition period "shall be granted at least the same level of protection under the law of the United Kingdom".[88c]

[88b] 2019/C 384I/01 of 12 November 2019.

[88c] art.52(2)(3) specifies that this does not apply to any PDOs or PGIs registered in the EU pursuant to international agreements to which the EU is party (as the UK is not a party to those agreements).

*At the start of the paragraph, replace "Despite this, in" with:*

**13-032** In

*Replace paragraph:*

**13-033** In an attempt to close this lacuna, Regulation 1151/2012 art.13(3) now requires that Member States "take appropriate administrative and judicial steps to prevent or stop the unlawful use of [PDOs and PGIs] ... that are produced or marketed in that Member State." In addition, art.38 requires Member States to carry out checks to ensure compliance with the requirements of the Regulation and to take all measures necessary to deal with breaches. Rather belatedly, the UK has complied with these provisions by introducing the Quality Schemes (Agricultural Products and Foodstuffs) Regulations 2018.[92a]

[92a] SI 1275/2018.

## Conflict with Trade Marks

*Replace paragraph:*

Article 14(1) of Regulation 1151/2012 sets out the consequence of a PDO or PGI on a subsequent trade mark application relating to a "product of the same type"[97a]: it is submitted that this should not be assessed in the same way as "similar goods" under s.5(2) of the 1994 Act but more narrowly. If the application for a trade mark was made after the date of submission to the Commission of the registration application for the PDO or PGI,[98] the trade mark application should be refused and any trade mark registered in breach of this provision should be invalidated.[99] If registered despite the existence of an earlier PDO or PGI, the trade mark shall be declared invalid.[100] Presumably, s.3(4) of the 1994 Act would be relied upon for such refusal or invalidity, although it is not clear by whom it should be declared invalid as there is no mechanism in the Act for ex officio removal. Section 4A of the TMA (as amended by the Trade Marks Regulations 2018) provides an absolute ground of refusal on the basis of an earlier GI, although from IP completion day (presently 31 December 2020) the reference to "any provision of EU law" will be deleted and thus earlier PDOs and PGIs will not be included; the same applies to s.4B on TSGs. **13-038**

[97a] In the equivalent Regulation dealing inter alia with wines, Reg.1308/2013, the comparable provision on trade marks, art.102(1), refers to the categories of products that are relevant and art.103 sets out the protection accorded to PGIs and PDOs in the sector. In *Les Grands Chais De France SA v Consorzio di Tutela della Denominazione di Origine Controllata Prosecco* [2020] EWHC 1633 (Ch), Nugee J upheld the hearing officer's decision to reject the application mark "Nosecco" on the basis of an opposition by the consortium owning the PGI "Prosecco" under TMA s.3(3(b) and 3(4).

[98] This date can be ascertained from the European Commission's Database of Origin Registration ("DOOR") accessible via: *http://www.defra.gov.uk/food-farm/food/protected-names/* [Accessed 20 September 2017]. In the case of PDOs and PGIs registered under the art.17 simplified procedure in Reg.2081/92, the relevant date is the entry into force of the registration: *Bayerischer Brauerbund eV v Bavaria NV* [2011] E.T.M.R. 209 CJEU, concerning the trade mark "Bavaria" (registered in 1995 for beer) and the PGI "*Bayerisches Bier*" (meaning, in English, Bavarian beer) which was registered in 2001 by virtue of Regulation 1347/2001, although applied for in January 1994. In the earlier *Bavaria NV and Bavaria Italia Srl v Bayerischer Brauerbund eV* [2009] E.T.M.R. 61 case, the CJEU rejected a challenge to the validity of the registration of "Bayerisches Bier" as a PGI on the ground that "beer" is not a foodstuff and therefore falls outside Regulation 2081/92.

[99] The *UKIPO Trade Marks Manual* at pp.186-188 deals with an objection under TMA s.3 on the basis of a PDO or PGI. For a recent example, see the decision by the Hearing Officer (Ms C. Boucher) in *SA Vina Santa Rita's Application* O/079/20 concerning an unsuccessful opposition under s.3(3)(b) and 3(4) by the Instituto Nacional de Defensa de la Competencia y de la Protección de la Propriedad Intelectual, a Peruvian government agency tasked with the defence of Peruvian PGIs including "Pisco". The Hearing Officer held, at [15], that the opponent had no standing to bring a claim under s.5(4)(a) as it owned no goodwill. The Guidelines for the Examination of EU Trade Marks issued by EUIPO in February 2017 set out in detail in Ch.10 of Section 4 the procedure for refusing a trade mark application under EUTM Regulation art.7(1)(j) on the basis of a PDO or PGI.

[100] art.14(1). In Regulation 2081/92 art.14(1) it was stated specifically that this applied to trade marks applied for before publication (in the Official Journal) but registered after the publication. However, this is omitted from the new provision. Article 8(6) of the EUTM Regulation deals with opposition to a EUTM by the owner of a PDO or PGI.

## The Gorgonzola Case

*Replace paragraph:*

The court found that use of the mark "Cambozola" "evoked" the term "Gorgonzola" since "Cambozola" "ends in the same two syllables and contains the same number of syllables, with the result that the phonetic and visual similarity **13-043** between the two terms is obvious".[111] It further found that:

> "'evocation', as referred to in article 13(1)(b) of Regulation No. 2081/92, covers a situation where the term used to designate a product incorporates part of a protected designation, so that when the consumer is confronted with the name of the product, the image triggered in his mind is that of the product whose designation is protected ...
>
> [It] is possible, ... for a protected designation to be evoked where there is no likelihood of confusion between the products concerned and even where no Community [now Union] protection extends to the parts of that designation which are echoed in the term or terms at issue."[112]

[111] [1999] E.T.M.R. 454 at [27]. For a recent case involving the equivalent regulation on inter alia wines (art.93 and following), see *Les Grands Chais De France SA v Consorzio di Tutela della Denominazione di Origine Controllata Prosecco* [2020] EWHC 1633 (Ch).

[112] [1999] E.T.M.R. 454 at [25] and [26]. See *Viniiverla Oy v Sosiaali-ja terveysalan lupa-ja valvontavirasto* (75-15) CJEU, where the Court of Justice held in relation to the same question under art.16(b) of Reg.110/2008 concerning PDOs and PGIs for spirit drinks: "the national court must essentially rely on the presumed reaction of consumers in the light of the term used to designate the product at issue, it being essential that those consumers establish a link between that term and the protected name", at [22]. In response to the fact that the defendant's sign (VERLADOS), to which the owners of the PGI CALVADOS was objecting, used the name of the Finnish town in which it was manufactured and this was known to Finnish consumers, the court stated, at [27]: "the concept of 'consumer' ... covers European consumers and not merely consumers of the Member State in which the product giving rise to the evocation of the protected geographical indication is manufactured" and, at [48], "in order to assess whether the name 'Verlados' constitutes an 'evocation' within the meaning of [art.16(b)] of the protected geographical indication 'Calvados' with respect to similar products, the referring court must take into consideration the phonetic and visual relationship between those names and any evidence that may show that such a relationship is not fortuitous, so as to ascertain whether, when the average European consumer, reasonably well informed and reasonably observant and circumspect, is confronted with the name of a product, the image triggered in his mind is that of the product whose geographical indication is protected."

## Chapter 14

# COLLECTIVE AND CERTIFICATION MARKS

Table of Contents



## 1. Generally

*Replace footnote 1:*

[1] See *UK IPO Work Manual of trade marks practice*, Ch.4 (available at *http://www.gov.uk* [Accessed 8 February 2017]). Chapter 4 was amended in January 2019 to incorporate various amendments made to Sch.1 by the Trade Marks Regulations 2018 (SI 2018/825) that came into force on 14 January 2019. **14-001**

## 3. Collective Marks

### Who May Own a Collective Mark?

*After "The position is even clearer where the application is for a EU Trade Mark as art.74(1) of the EUTM Regulation makes it clear that legal personality is a pre-requisite for ownership.", add new footnote 11a:*

[11a] For example, the unsuccessful opponent in BL 0/152/20 (Hearing Officer Ms C Boucher) was the owner of the EU collective mark "HALLOUMI": the Foundation for the Protection of the Traditional Cheese of Cyprus named Halloumi. **14-007**

### Indications of Geographic Origin

*Replace footnote 17:*

[17] See Ch.13. It is not clear why an indication which could be registered as a PGI should also be proper subject matter for a collective mark as the two systems, that for the protection of PDOs and PGIs and that for registered trade marks, have different and potentially conflicting scopes of protection. For an example of the problems that can arise, see *Alberto Severi v Regione Emilia- Romagna* [2009] E.T.M.R. 64 CJEU, concerning the designation "Salame Falino", which was registered in Italy as a collective mark and subsequently an application had been made to register it also as a Protected Geographical Indication (PGI) (see Ch.13). For a description of the difficulties that may arise, see [71]–[86] of the Opinion of AG Kokott in *Foundation for the Protection of the Traditional Cheese of Cyprus named Halloumi v EUIPO* (C-766/18 P). **14-009**

### Regulations

*Replace footnote 27:*

[27] 1994 Act Sch.1 para.5(2). Paragraph 3 of Sch.2 to the TMA (added, along with consequential amendments, by the Trade Marks Regulations 2018 (SI 2018/825) regs 1(1), 33(2)(c) (with Pt 5)) provides that the regulations "must authorise any person whose goods or services originate in the geographical area concerned to become a member of the association which is the proprietor of the mark, provided that the person fulfils all the other conditions of the regulations". **14-011**

*Add new paragraph:*

**14-011A** By Sch.2A para.4 TMA (as amended by the Trade Marks (Amendments etc) (EU Exit) Regulations 2019) where a comparable trade mark (EU) is entered on the UK Register derived from a EU collective mark and the proprietor is so notified, the proprietor must file a copy of the regulations governing the use of the EU collective mark as at IP completion day, and where these are not in English a translation of the same.

## Other Respects

*At the end of the paragraph, add new footnote 32a:*

**14-016** [32a] See, for example, in the UK "*Hajdu Halloumi*" BL/0/152/20 (Hearing Officer Ms C Boucher) and in the *EU Foundation for the Protection of the Traditional Cheese of Cyprus named Halloumi v EUIPO* (C-766/18 P). In the latter, AG Kokott noted in her Opinion (17 October 2019), at [77] that "there are no grounds to assume that a collective mark necessarily—even by virtue of its registration—enjoys particular distinctive character". Indeed, the AG cast some doubt on the ability of the 'Halloumi' geographical collective mark to perform the function of a registered trade mark as envisaged by art.66 of the EUTM Regulation, at [71]–[86], concluding "the EUIPO rightly asserts that it would be contradictory if producers' associations could obtain equivalent or even stronger protection for geographical designations on the basis of trade mark law than in the protected designation of origin system." At [86]. The CJEU judgment of 5 March 2020 remitted the case to the GC to apply the standard global appreciation test for likelihood of confusion to the application mark "BBQLOUMI", having made it clear that the test for likelihood of confusion in relation to a collective mark is no different to that for any other registered trade mark.

## 4. Certification Marks

## The Regime

*At end of paragraph, add new footnote 36a:*

**14-021** [36a] Thus, for example, John & Pascalis Ltd successfully applied under s.47 to invalidate the certification mark "Halloumi" registered for "Cheese made from sheep's and/or goat's milk; cheese made from blends of cow's milk; all included in Class 29" and owned by the Ministry of Energy, Commerce and Tourism of the Republic of Cyprus: see further the judgment of Arnold J (as he then was), [2018] EWHC 3226 (Ch), dismissing an appeal by the Ministry for permission to adduce evidence after the applicable deadline.

## Regulations

*Add new paragraph:*

**14-026A** By Sch.2A para.4 of the TMA (as amended by the Trade Marks (Amendments etc) (EU Exit) Regulations 2019) where a comparable trade mark (EU) is entered on the UK Register derived from a EU certification mark and the proprietor is so notified, the proprietor must file a copy of the regulations governing the use of the EU certification mark as at IP completion day and where these are not in English a translation of the same.

## Chapter 15

# DEALINGS WITH TRADE MARKS

Table of Contents



## 1. The Scope of This Chapter

*Change title of sub-section:* **15-003**

### Influence of the 2008 Directive and the EUTMR 2017

*Replace footnote 5:*

[5] This was replaced by art.20 of the 2015 Directive as of 14 January 2019 by way of the Trade Marks Regulations (SI 2018/825). **15-003**

*Replace paragraph with:*

**15-004** Readers will be aware of the 2015 TM Directive, which was implemented on 14 January 2019 by way of the Trade Marks Regulations (SI 2018/825), and which replaces the 2008 Directive, contains equivalent provisions in this area as are contained in the EUTMR 2017. Notably, art.25 of the 2015 Directive adds further provisions (to those existing in art.8 of the 2008 Directive): art.25(3) provides that a licensee may bring proceedings for infringement of a trade mark only with the proprietor's consent, and an exclusive licensee may bring proceedings if after formal notice the proprietor has not brought proceedings himself; art.25(4) that a licensee is entitled to intervene in proceedings brought by the proprietor; and art.25(5) requires Member States to have procedures in place to allow for the recordal of licenses in their registers. This latter provision does not require recordal of licenses, merely that the ability to record must exist.

## 3. Trade Marks as Property

*After "in circumstances which assume that national marks have the same", replace "status." with:*

**15-012** status, now confirmed in art.26 of the 2015 Directive.

## 4. ASSIGNMENTS

### The Law of Assignment or Transfer

*Add to end of the paragraph:*

15-013 It should be noted that s.24(1A) (added by reg.14 of the Trade Marks Regulations (SI 2018/825)) provides that a contractual obligation to transfer a business is to be taken to include an obligation to transfer any registered trade mark, except where there is agreement to the contrary or it is clear in all the circumstances that this presumption should not apply

## 5. REGISTRATION OF ASSIGNMENTS AND OTHER TRANSACTIONS IN THE UK

### Registration of Assignments

*Replace paragraph:*

15-021 By s.25 of the 1994 Act, assignments and licences of registered trade marks are registrable transactions, and details of them shall be entered in the Register on application by the proprietor, any other person claiming to have an interest in the mark, or anyone affected by the transaction concerned.[29]

[29] See s.25(1) and (2). Full details of the procedure for registering such a transaction and the matters to be registered are given in Ch.5.

### Effect of Non-registration on Right to Costs

*Replace footnote 36:*

15-033 [36] *Cosmetic Warriors, Lush Ltd v Amazon.co.UK Ltd* [2014] EWHC 1316 (Ch) where Mr Baldwin QC (sitting as Deputy Judge in the Chancery Division), having heard no argument on this point, assumed for those purposes that s.25(4) of the 1994 Act was similar to s.68 of the Patents Act 1977. The effect of s.68 of the Patents Act 1977 was considered in *L'Oréal Société Anonyme & L'Oréal (UK) Ltd v RN Ventures Ltd* [2018] EWHC 391 where the defendant was infringing the claimants' patent for about four years after the licence was granted but prior to it being recorded. The dispute concerned the practical effect of the section on costs, where both patentee (licensor) and exclusive licensee were claimants. The judge held at [17] "In *Schütz*, the Supreme Court rejected an interpretation of s.68 which would 'leave the section with very little bite, as an unregistered licensee could avoid its consequences simply by registering and then starting the proceedings.' In my judgment, the same consequence would follow if I allowed the parent to recover costs which could not be recovered by the subsidiary as a result of failure to register the licence. I consider that the exercise of a discretionary power to award costs should be informed by, and should reflect, the statutory policy. In the present case, I consider that as a matter of discretion, I should deprive both Claimants of a proportion of their costs; the question is what proportion."

### Applications as Objects of Property

*Replace "ss.22–26" with:*

15-035 ss.22–26 and ss.28–31

## 6. REGISTRATION OF TRANSFERS AND LICENCES AT OHIM

*Add new footnote 36a at the end of the paragraph:*

15-036 [36a] Note that art.20 of EUTMR 2017 will be repealed by Sch.5 para.6 of the Trade Marks (Amendment etc.) (EU Exit) Regulations (SI 2019/269) on the Implementation Completion day (31 December 2020 at 23.00) which marks the end of the Transition or Implementation Period as set out within the European Union (Withdrawal Agreement) Act 2020, see s.39(1), and Sch.5 para.1.

*Add new footnote 36b at the end of the paragraph:*

[36b] 36B Note that art.25 of EUTMR 2017 will be repealed by Sch.5 para.6 of the Trade Marks (Amendment etc.) (EU Exit) Regulations (SI 2019/269) on the Implementation Completion day (31 December 2020 at 23.00) which marks the end of the Transition or Implementation Period as set out within the European Union (Withdrawal Agreement) Act 2020, see s.39(1), and Sch.5 para.1. **15-037**

*Add new footnote 36c at the end of the paragraph:*

[36c] 36C Note that arts. 22 and 27 of EUTMR 2017 will be repealed by Sch.5 para.6 of the Trade Marks (Amendment etc.) (EU Exit) Regulations (SI 2019/269) on the Implementation Completion day (31 December 2020 at 23.00) which marks the end of the Transition or Implementation Period as set out within the European Union (Withdrawal Agreement) Act 2020, see s.39(1), and Sch.5 para.1. **15-038**

## 10. Licensing of Registered Trade Marks

### Outline of the Law

*Replace paragraph:*

The equivalent provision to art. 8(2) of the 2008 Directive (which has as of 14 January 2019 been replaced by art.25(s) of the 2015 TM Directive) can be found in s.28(5) of the 1994 Act which was added by reg.16 of the Trade Marks Regulations 2018/825. It enables the registered proprietor to sue for infringement a licensee who contravenes provisions of their licence as to duration, form in which the mark is used, the goods or services licensed, territory or quality. Further, the application of the *Marleasing* doctrine means that the concept of "consent" in ss.9(1) and 12(1) must be interpreted taking into account art.8(2). In *Copad*, the CJEU ruled that a licence agreement does not constitute absolute and unconditional consent of the proprietor to the licensee putting goods bearing the trade mark onto the market. Contravention of a provision listed in art.8(2) precludes exhaustion of the rights conferred on the proprietor.[75] **15-076**

[75] [2009] E.T.M.R. 40 at [47]–[51].

*Replace paragraph:*

As noted above, the additional provisions in art.25(3)–(5) of the 2015 Directive have been implemented as of 14 January 2019. As for the entitlement of a registered proprietor to intervene provided for by art.25(4), this has been implemented in s.30(6) of the 1994 Act which provides "Where the proprietor of a registered trade mark brings infringement proceedings, a licensee who has suffered loss is entitled to intervene in the proceedings for the purpose of obtaining compensation for that loss". **15-077**

### Rights of Licensees as to Infringement Proceedings

*Replace second paragraph:*

By s.31, an exclusive licensee may, by contract with the proprietor of the mark, be given the same rights and remedies as if the licence had been an assignment, including the right to bring proceedings in their own name.[85] Such a right of action, if granted, is concurrent with that of the proprietor.[86] However, it is in no way compulsory for an exclusive licensee to be given such a right, as is clear from the permissive words of s.31(1). Indeed, it is fairly clear from the wording of the section that if the agreement granting the licence is silent, then the exclusive licensee will not have their own right of action. In *Holland and Barrett International Ltd, Health and Diet Centres Ltd v General Nutrition Investment Co*[86a] the Court of Ap- **15-091** peal considered the effect of ss.29–31 of the 1994 Act and stated at [39] "An exclusive licensee of an intellectual property right may have the right to bring infringement proceedings against third parties. The precise nature and scope of those rights varies for different intellectual property rights. For a registered trade mark, an exclusive licensee can bring such proceedings in certain circumstances and depending on the construction of the licence … . In such proceedings the exclusive licensee could bring a claim against a sign which was not identical to the registered trade mark but was confusingly similar to the mark. However, the licensee's rights as against the licensor are and can only be contractual in nature. That is because even if an exclusive licensee of intellectual property has a right to sue a third party for infringement, an act committed by the licensor is necessarily not an infringing act for the simple reason that it has the benefit of the consent of the owner of the intellectual property right—i.e. the very same licensor".

[85] s.31(1).

[86] s.31(2).

[86a] [2018] EWCA Civ 1586.

*Replace paragraph:*

**15-093** The general rule under s.30, and in particular s.30(1A), is that a licensee may only, except so far as the licence provides otherwise, bring proceedings for infringement of the registered trade mark with the consent of the proprietor. It used to be the case that a licensee could also call on the proprietor to bring infringement proceedings in relation to "any matter which affects his interests". However, by virtue of ss.30(2) and 30(3), which have been amended by reg.17(3) of the Trade Marks Regulations (SI 2018/825), this right now only extends to an exclusive licensee. If the proprietor refuses to bring proceedings, or fails to do so within two months, then the licensee may sue as if they were the proprietor/exclusive licensee.[87] It should be noted that under s.30(7), s.30 also applies to an exclusive licensee who has their own right of action obtained by virtue of s.31(1). In contrast with s.31(1), the rights given under s.30(1) and 30(1A) arise automatically unless the licence agreement(s) through which the licensee derives their rights excludes them.[88] If the proprietor refuses to bring proceedings, or fails to do so within two months, then the licensee may sue as if they were the proprietor/exclusive licensee.[89] In contrast with s.31(1), the rights given under s.30 arise automatically unless the licence agreement(s) through which the licensee derives their rights excludes them.

[87] Presumably, if the licensee has unsuccessfully requested the proprietor to apply for interim injunctive relief and itself does so after the two-month period has expired, the court would not penalise the licensee for undue delay in applying for interim relief.

[88] s.30(2).

[89] Presumably, if the licensee has unsuccessfully requested the proprietor to apply for interim injunctive relief and itself does so after the two-month period has expired, the court would not penalise the licensee for undue delay in applying for interim relief.

## Chapter 16

# INFRINGEMENT

Table of Contents



## 1. Preliminary

*Replace footnote 3 with:*

[3] *Marleasing* [1990] E.C.R. I-4135. As a consequence of the Withdrawal Agreement this remains the case over the period from the UK's withdrawal from the EU to the end of the Implementation Period (at least 31 December 2020), after which future decisions of the CJEU will in all likelihood be no more than persuasive, and although the words of the TM Directive (including the recitals) should remain an important guide to interpretation of the 1994 Act, the CJEU's later interpretation of the TM Directive will not be binding. **16-001**

*Add new paragraph:*

Despite the UK's withdrawal from the EU on 31 January 2020, in accordance with the Withdrawal Agreement the UK effectively remains a Member State until the end of the Implementation Period (presently 31 December 2020, referred to in the relevant UK legislation as "IP completion day"). In consequence, until IP completion day the UK's EU Trade Mark Courts have the same jurisdiction to hear infringement proceedings and counterclaims seeking invalidity or revocation of EU trade marks as during the UK's membership of the EU. On IP Completion Day, EU trade marks will no longer be capable of being infringed by acts carried out in the UK because the UK is no longer a Member State. However, all EU trade marks on the register immediately before IP completion day are to be treated as if an equivalent UK trade mark had been granted for the same goods and services (referred to in Sch.2A of the 1994 Act as a "comparable trade mark (EU)"[6a]) and such marks are to be entered on the UK register as soon as practicable after IP completion day. It is intended that existing proceedings before the UK's EU Trade Mark Courts will continue following IP completion day and that the UK court will be able to grant financial and injunctive relief in respect thereof. This is intended to be achieved by two mechanisms. In respect of EU trade marks (which will no longer cover the UK) the 1994 Act[6b] provides that the provisions "contained or referred to in Chapter 10 of the European Trade Mark Regulation" (the provisions concerning jurisdiction and procedure in legal proceedings) will continue to apply to the pending proceedings as if the UK were still a Member State. In respect of the comparable trade mark (EU) (which will then cover the territory of the UK) the **16-003A**

1994 Act provides[6c] that the EU Trade Mark Court hearing the claim will have jurisdiction to grant injunctive and financial relief and to revoke or declare invalid the comparable trade mark (EU) when the proceedings involve a counterclaim for such relief in respect of the EU trade mark.

[6a] 1994 Act Sch.2A para.1.

[6b] 1994 Act Sch.2A para.20(2).

[6c] 1994 Act Sch.2A paras 20(3) and (4).

*Replace paragraph:*

**16-004** The provisions of arts 9(4) and 10 of the EUTM Regulation introduce new (express) rights on the part of the proprietor to prevent goods bearing a trade mark identical to a EUTM being brought into the EU in transit to a final destination outside the EU in which the EUTM proprietor has rights, and to prohibit "preparatory acts" in relation to dealings in packaging bearing marks in respect of which there is a risk of infringement when the packaging is used. Equivalent provisions implementing arts 10(4) and 11 of the 2015 Directive are found in ss.10(3B) and 10A of the 1994 Act.[6d]

[6d] Following IP completion day, s.10A is to be amended to extend to goods from outside the customs territory of the UK rather than that of the EU.

## 2. INFRINGEMENT OF TRADE MARKS

## General

### Introduction

*Replace paragraph:*

**16-008** In addition to these three principal categories of infringement, the 1994 Act introduces a fourth category of infringement in s.10(6) and the EUTM Regulation provides for further catagories of infringement under art.9(4) and art.10 (concerning transhipped goods and dealings in packaging, respectively).[9a] Section 10(6) is a curious provision which has no clear foundation in the TM Directive and had no counterpart in the CTM Regulation.[9b] The EUTM regulation[10] now expressly identifies use of a sign in comparative advertising in a manner that is contrary to the EU Comparative Advertising Directive[11] as a form of use which may be prohibited.[12] Although, even this is not coterminous with the provisions of s.10(6). That section contains, first of all, a saving in respect of the use by a person of a trade mark for the purpose of identifying goods or services as those of the proprietor or a licensee. But then it continues to create a further category of infringement by providing that any such use, other than in accordance with honest practices in industrial or commercial matters, shall be treated as infringing the registered trade mark if the use, without due cause, takes unfair advantage of, or is detrimental to, the distinctive character or repute of the trade mark. This provision was initially treated by the courts as providing a home grown exception to infringement in the case of some, but not all, comparative advertising. In the light of the CJEU's decisions which exclude lawful comparative advertising from the scope of trade mark infringement (addressed in depth in Ch.15), it is now generally accepted that s.10(6) either adds nothing to the three principal categories of infringement or is ultra vires. In the words of Jacob LJ[13]: "It is a pointless provision… . It should be repealed as an unnecessary distraction in an already complicated branch of the law." The identification of use in unlawful comparative advertising as a particular form of infringing use does not detract from this analysis.[14] Section 10(6) was repealed as of 14 January 2019 in parallel with the introduction of s.10(4)(e) which expressly identifies unlawful comparative advertising as a form of infringing use.

[9a] Following the amendment of the 1994 Act to implement the 2015 Directive as of 14 January 2019 (by The Trade Marks Regulations 2018) the categories of infringement under arts 9(4) and 10 of the EUTM Regulation are replicated in a UK context by s.10A and s.10(3B) respectively. Section 10A introduces a right akin to infringement under s.10(1) which entitles the proprietor to prevent goods entering the UK from outside the customs area of the EU without being released for free circulation. After IP completion day the scope of s.10A will be extended to goods entering the UK from outside the customs area of the UK, rather than the EU.

[9b] s.10(6) was repealed on 14 January 2019.

[10] See also the 2015 Directive.

[11] Directive 2006/114/EC of the European Parliament and the Council as amended ("the CAD").

[12] EUTM Regulation art.9(3)(f), 2015 Directive art.10(3)(f), 1994 Act s.10(4)(e) (as of 14 January 2019).

[13] *O2 Holdings Ltd (formerly O2 Ltd) v Hutchison 3G Ltd* [2006] EWCA Civ 1656, [2007] R.P.C. 19 at [58].

[14] EUTM Regulation art.9(3)(f), TM Directive art.10(3)(f), 1994 Act s.10(4)(e) (as of 14 January 2019).

## 3. THE GENERAL CONDITIONS FOR INFRINGEMENT

## (1) Use of a Sign

### Specific activities which constitute use of a sign

*Replace paragraph with:*

It has never been the law that the allegedly infringing mark should be actually affixed to the goods, provided it was so used in relation to them as to be calculated to lead to the belief that the goods were designated by the mark. This position is maintained under the 1994 Act which, in s.10(4) and (5), follows the permissive provisions of art.5(3) of the TM Directive in identifying the various activities which constitute use of a sign for the purposes of the infringement provisions. Section 10(4) specifies that a person uses a sign if, in particular, they: **16-015**

(1) affix it to goods or the packaging thereof;
(2) offer or expose goods for sale, put them on the market or stock them for those purposes under the sign, or offer or supply services under the sign;
(3) import or export goods under the sign; or
(4) use the sign on business papers or in advertising.

Article 9(3)(d) and (f) of the EUTM Regulations further identify use of the sign "as a trade or company name or part of a trade or company name" and "use of the sign in comparative advertising in a manner that is contrary to Directive 2006/114/EC[27]" as particular uses which may be prohibited as infringements.[27a] These additional examples of potentially infringing use do not represent a significant change in the law, but rather render express the position arrived at in the light of the CJEU and national authorities on use of signs. The list of potentially infringing uses is not exhaustive, and the CJEU has held[27b] that the removal of a sign by rebranding a product held in a customs warehouse in the geographical territory of a Member State but before the product was released on the EEA market amounted to "use" of the sign removed. Use of a sign in relation to goods by removal of that sign and replacing it with another is perhaps difficult to reconcile with the normal meaning of the term. However, the CJEU considered that the removal of the mark deprived the trade mark proprietor of the right to control the initial marketing of the goods bearing that mark within the EEA, and the replacement of the mark by a different sign adversely affected the functions of the mark. This appears to be a significant extension of the scope of potentially infringing "use" of a sign, although it is important to note that the acts of removal and replacement took place within the territory of a Member State, albeit under the customs warehousing procedure. It remains to be seen whether the rebranding of goods outside the EU can amount to infringing use within the EU of the sign that was removed.

[27] The CAD.

[27a] These particular forms of potentially infringing "use" are now also identified in the 1994 Act at ss.10(4)(ca) and (e), introduced with effect from 14 January 2019 by The Trade Marks Regulations 2018 (SI 2018/825).

[27b] *Mitsubishi Shoji Kaisha Ltd v Duma Forklifts NV* (C-129/17) [2019] F.S.R. 4.

### Mere possession

*Replace paragraph:*

**16-016** It would appear that mere possession of goods bearing an offending sign is not an infringement under s.10 or art.9(2) unless there is an intention to deal in them within the jurisdiction.[28] This mirrors the historical position as it was under the 1938 Act. The position may now be different in respect of infringement under art.9(4) of the EUTM Regulation and s.10(3B) of the 1994 Act, though even those provisions concern the bringing of goods (and packaging) into the EU[28a] without being released for free circulation, rather than mere possession of such goods.

[28] See *Waterford Wedgwood v David Nagli* [1998] F.S.R. 92 at 105.

[28a] After IP completion day, the UK in the case of s.10(3B) of the 1994 Act.

### Affixes the sign to goods or the packaging

*Replace paragraph:*

**16-019** As to packaging, this provision must be reconciled with s.10(5) which deals with the application of a registered trade mark to material intended to be used for labelling or packaging. This is simply done if this provision is limited to packaging actually enclosing the goods rather than intended to be used in that way in the future.[35] Section 10(5) of the 1994 Act was repealed on 14 January 2019,[35a] in parallel with the commencement of s.10(3B) which enacted the right to prohibit preparatory acts concerning packaging addressed in para.16-020.

[35] *Beautimatic v Mitchell* [2000] F.S.R. 267. See also paras 16-025 to 16-027.

[35a] Trade Marks Regulations 2018 (SI 2018/825).

### Right to prohibit preparatory acts concerning packaging

*Replace paragraph:*

**16-020** Article 10 of the EUTM Regulation (and the equivalent provision under the 2015 Directive, which had to be implemented in national law by 14 January 2019)[35b] introduces the right to prohibit the application of signs identical with or similar to a registered trade mark on "packaging, labels, tags, security or authenticity features or devices"[36] and to prohibit dealings in such materials to which the mark is affixed,[37] namely offering or placing on the market, stocking for those purposes, importing or exporting the materials in issue. The right only arises in respect of acts carried out in the course of trade where a "risk" exists that such materials could be used in relation to goods and services where such use would constitute an infringement under arts 9(2) and (3) of the EUTM Regulation.[37a] Thus there can be no infringement of the art.10 right unless there are circumstances in which goods or services bearing the packaging or security materials in question would actually infringe. But if so, the risk that the materials would be used in such a way appears to give rise to a right to prohibit affixing the sign to materials or dealing in such materials at all, rather than being limited to use which would give rise to infringement. The commentary in respect of art.10 of the EUTM Regulation now applies mutatis mutandis to s.10(3B) of the 1994 Act as amended.

[35b] Now implemented in the UK by s.10(3B) of the 1994 Act.

[36] EUTM Regulation art.10(a).

[37] EUTM Regulation art.10(b).

[37a] In the equivalent provision under s.10(3B) of the 1994 Act, the "risk" is that the materials "could be used in relation to goods or services and that use would constitute an infringement of the rights of the proprietor of the trade mark".

### Offers or exposes goods for sale or offers or supplies services under the sign

*Replace paragraph:*

A person uses a sign if they offer or expose goods for sale, put them on the market or stock them for those purposes under the sign, or offer or supply services under the sign.[38] It is expressly provided that the stocking of goods for sale under a sign is an infringement. This could include the case of a trader using the trade mark as the name of a business dealing in the goods, for example as the name of a shop through which the goods are sold, but only if the sign is used in such a way that a link is established between the sign which constitutes the name of the shop and the goods provided.[39] Note that mere use of a sign as a trading name or business name which does not identify goods or services provided by the entity bearing that name without such a link is not use "in relation to goods or services".[40] This is addressed further under "in relation to" below. Although s.10(4)(ca) expressly identifies use of a sign as (or as part of) a trade or company name as a potentially infringing use, the requirement that such use must be "in relation to" goods or services still stands. **16-021**

[38] 1994 Act s.10(4)(b). At least one of these acts must take place within the jurisdiction: *Waterford Wedgwood v David Nagli* [1998] F.S.R. 92.

[39] *Céline SARL v Céline* [2007] E.T.M.R. 80 CJEU.

[40] *Robelco NV v Robeco Groep NV* [2003] E.T.M.R. 52 CJEU. In *BMW AG v Technosport London Ltd* [2017] EWCA 797, it was noted by Floyd LJ, at [30]: "whilst there are well-known questions about whether, in the case of a trade mark registered for goods, the name of a business is being used in relation to the goods sold by that business, there is normally no such problem in the case of a service mark. The name of the business as the provider of the services is much more readily, if not invariably, taken to be use in relation to the services offered." In *Merck KGaA v Merck Sharp & Dohme* [2017] EWCA Civ 1834; [2018] E.T.M.R. 10 at [275], Kitchin LJ (as he then was) identified the following matters as relevant when determining whether use of a sign on a website was use as a business name or use in relation to particular goods and services provided by that business; "Thirdly, in applying these principles, the judge said that he did not proceed on the basis that every use of the designation 'Merck' on each website constituted use in relation to each and everything characterisable as a product or service appearing anywhere on that site. He was rightly of the view that any suggestion to that effect went too far. The question must always be whether the activity complained of constituted use of the offending sign in the UK and in such a way that consumers were liable to interpret it as designating the origin of the goods or services in question. Moreover, he directed himself, again correctly, that he should ignore use of the word 'Merck' in a context which consumers would understand to be a description of an entity engaged in an activity other than the provision of goods and services, such as 'Merck is active in deal making' or 'At Merck, corporate responsibility is a cornerstone…'."

*Replace paragraph:*

Where goods are offered for sale with the necessary result (if the offer were ac- **16-022** cepted) that the goods would be sold in the EU, then even if the goods themselves remain in bond and have not cleared customs formality and so have not been imported, regardless of where the offer is made or where the purchaser is situated, the goods have been offered for sale or put on the market in the EU.[41] It is not sufficient for the proprietor to show that there is a risk that goods will be put on the market in the EU; there is only infringement if the dealings in the goods necessarily entail the goods being put on the market in the EU.[42] However, with effect from 23 March 2016, under the EUTM Regulation, art.9(4) provides that the proprietor of a EU trade mark is entitled

> "to prevent all third parties from bringing goods, in the course of trade, into the Union without being released for free circulation there, where such goods, including packaging, come from third countries and bear without authorisation a trade mark which is identical with the EU trade mark registered in respect of such goods, or which cannot be distinguished in its essential aspects from that trade mark."[42a]

The 2015 Directive,[43] which must be implemented by Member States by February 2019, contains an identical provision in art.10(4) and thus presumably the UK Government will introduce legislation to give effect to this prior to the implementation date.[43a] On 14 January 2019, s.10A of the 1994 Act came into force implementing art.10(4) of the 2015 Directive, overturning the result of the CJEU judgment in *Montex v Diesel*[44] as far as it relates to infringement by signs which are identical or indistinguishable from national marks and which are applied to goods identical to those for which the marks are registered. The principles in *Montex v Diesel* essentially remain in effect in respect of UK infringement other than under s.10(1) of the 1994 Act.

[41] *Class International v Colgate Palmolive* [2005] E.C.R. I-8735.

[42] *Montex v Diesel* [2007] E.T.M.R. 13 CJEU.

[42a] The same now applies to the UK under s.10A of the 1994 Act. After the Implementation Period, amendments to s.10A will come into force extending it to goods from outside the UK rather than the EU.

[43] EU Council Directive 2015/2436.

[43a] The Trade Marks Regulations (SI 2018/825).

[44] [2007] E.T.M.R. 13 CJEU.

### Materials intended to be used for labelling, packaging, as business papers or for advertising

*Add new paragraph beneath heading, ahead of para.16-028:*

**16-027A** Section 10(5) of the 1994 Act was repealed (as of 14 January 2019) by the Trade Marks Regulations (SI 2018/825). The "analogous" right to prohibit preparatory rights in respect of packaging has now been implemented in the 1994 Act by virtue of s.10(3B). See para.16-020. Paragraphs 16-028 to 16-031 no longer reflect the law and will be deleted from the next edition of *Kerly*.

## (3) In the Course of Trade

*Add new footnote 61a at the end of the paragraph:*

**16-033** [61a] The issue of whether the phrase "and not as a private matter" imposes a separate additional requirement as opposed to providing a contrast to the words "in the context of economic activity with a view to economic advantage" was considered by Arnold J (as he then was) in *Och-Ziff Management v Och Capital LLP* [2010] EWHC 2599 (Ch) at [56]–[66]. Although he identified that one possible explanation for the CJEU's decision in *Google v Louis Vuitton* [2010] R.P.C. 19 that Google did not infringe was that Google had made use that was "private" even though commercial, he expressed the view that the better interpretation of the CJEU's reasoning was that Google avoided infringement because it was not making "use" of the mark at all. Rather it was providing the medium for the use by the advertiser. The matter was considered further by HHJ Melissa Clarke in *APT Training v Birmingham and Solihull Mental Health NHS Trust* [2019] E.T.M.R. 22 in a carefully reasoned passage at [27]–[39], but the issue did not in the end require resolution for the purposes of her decision.

## (4) "In Relation to" Goods or Services

*Replace final sentence of the paragraph:*

It seems unlikely that use purely as a company or trade name will be established to be infringement in many cases concerning trade marks registered for goods, but for trade marks registered for services use in the name of a business "is much more readily, if not invariably, taken to be use in relation to the services offered."[68a] Use as a trade name has now been expressly identified as potentially infringing by s.10(4)(ca) of the 1994 Act and art 9(3)(d) of the EUTM Regulation. **16-038**

[68a] *BMW AG v Technosport London Ltd* [2017] EWCA 797 CA, per Floyd LJ at [30]. Earlier in his judgment, at [28], Floyd LJ said of the defendant's use of "BMW" in its trading style: "... there is nothing in the sign TECHNOSPORT-BMW to indicate that the sign is being used informatively. Whilst phrases such as 'BMW repair specialist' clearly alert the average consumer to the nature of the business, the simple incorporation of BMW into the trading style does nothing of that kind."

*After item "(7)", add:*

(8) In the context of use of the sign MERCK as a trading name and the domain name of websites directed at the UK from which sales were not made but which promoted the business activities of the defendant Merck, the Court of Appeal identified the following matters as relevant when determining whether the use complained of was "in relation to" particular goods and services: **16-039**

> "Thirdly, in applying these principles, the judge said that he did not proceed on the basis that every use of the designation 'Merck' on each website constituted use in relation to each and everything characterisable as a product or service appearing anywhere on that site. He was rightly of the view that any suggestion to that effect went too far. The question must always be whether the activity complained of constituted use of the offending sign in the UK and in such a way that consumers were liable to interpret it as designating the origin of the goods or services in question. Moreover, he directed himself, again correctly, that he should ignore use of the word 'Merck' in a context which consumers would understand to be a description of an entity engaged in an activity other than the provision of goods and services, such as 'Merck is active in deal making' or 'At Merck, corporate responsibility is a cornerstone...'."[76a]

[76a] *Merck KGaA v Merck Sharp & Dohme* [2017] EWCA Civ 1834; [2018] E.T.M.R. 10 at [275] and [275] per Kitchin LJ (as he then was).

*Replace paragraph:*

The important question is how the average consumer understands the sign to be used. No doubt if it is plain that the intention of the defendant is that the sign should be understood to denote the origin of the goods or services in the manner suggested by the claimant, then this will be likely to determine the issue.[76a] Although often the defendant may reasonably contend that the use of the sign is not intended to be so understood and here the defendant's intention cannot be determinative.[77] **16-040**

[76a] In *Beauty Bay Ltd v Benefit Cosmetics Ltd* [2019] EWHC 1140 (Ch), the judge (Roger Wyand QC, sitting as a deputy HC judge) rejected the defendant's argument that its use of "Beauty & the Bay" on cosmetic products was descriptive or decorative because it also used its trade name "Benefit" on the products, noting that "it is very common to have a house brand together with a sub-brand", at [35].

[77] See *Merck KGaA v Merck Sharp & Dohme Corp* [2017] EWCA Civ 1834; [2018] E.T.M.R. 10, per Kitchin LJ (as he then was) at [165]: "One of the issues which arose for consideration in *Argos* was the relevance of the subjective intention of an operator of a website in one territory in assessing whether its internet activity is targeted at the consumers in another territory, in particular the UK. The deputy judge held and I agree that if, viewed objectively from the perspective of the average consumer, a foreign trader's internet activity is targeted at consumers in the UK, the fact that, viewed subjectively, the trader did not intend this result will not prevent the impugned use from occurring in the UK. But that is not to say that the actual intention of the website operator is irrelevant. If the foreign trader does intend to target its internet activity at consumers in the UK then it seems to me that this is a matter which the court may properly take into account." Also, *Beauty Bay Ltd v Benefit Cosmetics Ltd* [2019] EWHC 1140 (Ch) at [30].

## 4. THE CATEGORIES OF INFRINGEMENT

### The scope of the registration

*Replace paragraph:*

**16-066** In the case of services it has been said that:

> "specifications of services should be scrutinised carefully and they should not be given a wide construction covering a vast range of activities. They should be confined to the substance, as it were, the core of the possible meanings attributable to the rather general phrase."[116]

The following general principles of interpretation were identified by Arnold J (as he then was) in *Sky v Skykick*[116a]:

(1) General terms (including the general indications of class heading of the Nice Classification) are to be interpreted as covering the goods or services clearly covered by the literal meaning of the terms, and not other goods or services.
(2) In the case of services, the terms used should not be interpreted widely, but confined to the core of the possible meanings attributable to the terms.
(3) An unclear or imprecise term should be narrowly interpreted as extending only to such goods or services as it clearly covers.
(4) A term which cannot be interpreted is to be disregarded.

[116] per Jacob J in *Avnet* [1998] F.S.R. 16; cited with approval by the Court of Appeal in *Reed* [2004] EWCA Civ 159; [2004] R.P.C. 40 at [43].

[116a] *Sky Plc v Skykick UK Ltd* [2020] EWHC 990 (Ch) at [56], judgment following the further hearing after judgment on reference to the CJEU (C-371/18) which held inter alia that lack of clarity of the specification was not a ground of invalidity.

### (1) Section 10(1)/art.9(2)(a): Where the Marks and the Goods or Services are Identical

#### *General*

*Replace footnote 119 with:*

**16-069** [119] *Interflora Inc v Marks & Spencer* [2015] E.T.M.R. 5 at [67], per Kitchin LJ. See also *Brearly v Nomination de Antonio E Paolo Gensini SRL* [2020] EWCA Civ 103 at [18].

### (2) Section 10(2)/art.9(2)(b): Where the Marks and the Goods or Services are Identical or Similar

#### *Comparison is Mark for Sign*

*Replace paragraph:*

**16-083** As in the case of identity (above), the subsection requires identification of the sign used by the defendant and a determination of the goods or services (if any) in relation to which they are using it.[139] This must be compared to a notional and fair use of the registered mark in relation to all of the goods and services covered by the registration.[140] If the registered mark has been used, then the way it has been used can be said, at the very least prima facie, to be a paradigm case of the use of the mark in a normal and fair manner.[141] In *Specsavers*[142] it was suggested by Kitchin LJ that "where a logo registered in black and white has acquired through use a particular and distinctive character ... that would seem to me to be a matter which ought to be taken into account in the global appreciation analysis",[143] although he found that the law was not clear and needed a reference to the CJEU. He was unimpressed by the argument that third parties should be able to look at the register and work out whether their use infringes the registered mark: "[they] must consider whether a mark has acquired distinctiveness through use in any event."[144] The CJEU's ruling[145] was consistent with the approach preferred by Kitchin LJ, holding that the acquisition of particular distinctive character through use in a particular colour was a relevant factor in the global appreciation of infringement under arts 9(2)(b) and (c) (then arts 9(2)(b) and (c)). The CJEU further held that any particular association in the mind of the public between the defendant and the colour used in the alleged infringement was a relevant factor that militated against infringement. The latter holding is difficult to reconcile with the exclusive rights accorded by art.9 to the owner of a registered trade mark: it is surely counter-intuitive to suggest that in order to avoid a finding of infringement it is sufficient for a defendant to use the claimant's mark in a particular colour, different to that or those used by the claimant, to such an extent that the colour becomes associated with it. We would suggest that use of a particular colour may enhance the distinctiveness of the claimant's mark but the converse, use of a particular colour by the defendant, cannot reduce the likelihood of confusion with it: whilst, to paraphrase Kitchin LJ in *Specsavers*, "context is all", it is also necessary to keep in mind the need to protect registered trade marks against illegitimate use by third parties.[146] A failure so to do could lead to success of the type of defence run by the defendant that failed in *Comic Enterprises Ltd v Twentieth Century Fox Film Corp*[147] and permit swamping of the registered trade mark rights of small enterprises by those able to invest large sums in marketing and promotional activities.[147a]

[139] See paras 16-062 to 16-066 for a discussion of how these matters are determined.

[140] See, for example, *Compass Publishing v Compass Logistics* [2004] R.P.C. 41; in *Rousselon Frères et Cie v Horwood Homewares Ltd* [2008] R.P.C. 30, Warren J rejected (at [99]) the argument that this was no longer correct in view of *02 Holdings Ltd v Hutchison 3G Ltd* [2007] R.P.C. 16 CJEU.

[141] *Premier Brands v Typhoon Europe* [2000] F.S.R. 767. Conversely, it is important to remember that a trade mark proprietor need not make any use at all of their mark (subject to the non-use provisions of the Act and Directive, and those do not have effect until five years after registration) and yet still establish a likelihood of confusion with a sign under s.10(2): *Bentley (1962) Ltd v Bentley Motors Ltd* [2019] EWHC 2925 (Ch) at [66], per HHJ Hacon (sitting as a deputy).

[142] [2012] E.T.M.R. 17 CA.

[143] [2012] E.T.M.R. 17 CA at [96].

[144] [2012] E.T.M.R. 17 CA at [96].

[145] *Specsavers International Healthcare Ltd v Asda Stores Ltd* [2013] E.T.M.R. 46 CJEU.

[146] To this effect, see the comments of Sales J in *Total Ltd v YouView TV Ltd* [2015] F.S.R. 7 at [102].

[147] [2016] EWCA Civ 41.

[147a] See also para.16-098A.

## *Identical or Similar Marks*

*Replace paragraph:*

**16-086** The registered mark and the sign alleged to infringe must be identical or similar; if they are not, the distinctiveness of the mark and the fact that the goods or services are identical are irrelevant.[155] Identity of marks is discussed in paras 16-073 to 16-075. Similarity of marks is a subject discussed in relation to s.5 of the 1994 Act.[156] In short, the condition of similarity requires the existence, in particular, of elements of visual, aural or conceptual similarity.[157]

[155] *Ferrero SpA v OHIM* [2011] E.T.M.R. 30 CJEU at [65] (in relation to relative grounds for invalidity but equally applicable to s.10(2)).

[156] See Ch.11, paras 11-079 to 11-096.

[157] *Sabel v Puma* [1997] E.C.R. I-6191, [1998] R.P.C. 199; *Lloyd Schuhfabrik Meyer v Klijsen Handel* [1999] E.T.M.R. 690 CJEU; *Adidas-Salomon v Fitnessworld* [2004] E.T.M.R. 10 CJEU at [28]. See the analysis of the similarities between the claimant's registered composite device mark and the defendant's sign that was also a composite device in *Red Bull GmbH v Big Horn UK Ltd* [2020] EWHC 124 (Ch): the judge (Richard Bacon QC, sitting as a deputy HC judge) noted, at [31], the visual and conceptual similarity between the claimant's double bull device and the defendant's double ram device, as well as the fact that both animals were depicted as charging with a circle in the background (although the registered mark included a white circle, the judge observed at [30] that the claimant's product advertising frequently featured a yellow-coloured circle, like that featured in the defendant's sign). Although finding that the mark and sign were similar, he considered (at [41]) that the level of similarity was not such as to cause the average consumer to believe that the defendant's products are economically linked to the claimant's products, and therefore there was no infringement under art.9(2)(b).

## *There Exists a Likelihood of Confusion*

*After "It must be borne in mind that the above is only a convenient summary,", add new footnote 162a:*

**16-089** [162a] More recently, the summary set out by Arnold J (as he then was) in *Sky Plc v SkyKick Ltd* [2018] EWHC 155 (Ch) at 287 has been used as an alternative: see, for example, by David Stone, sitting as an Enterprise Judge, in *Nature's Instinct Ltd v Natures Menu Ltd* [2020] EWHC 617 (IPEC) at [60].

*Replace paragraph:*

**16-090** In *Specsavers International Healthcare Ltd v Asda Stores Ltd*,[165] after reviewing the CJEU authorities, Kitchin LJ summed up:

> "the general position is now clear. In assessing the likelihood of confusion arising from the use of the sign the court must consider the matter from the perspective of the average consumer of the goods or services in question and must take into account all the circumstances of the case that are likely to operate in that average consumer's mind in considering the sign and the impression it is likely to make on him. The sign is not to be considered stripped of its context."

More recently, in *Comic Enterprises Ltd v Twentieth Century Fox Film Corp*[166] he explained:

> "the question in every case remains the same, namely whether, having regard to a notional and fair use of the mark in relation to all of the goods or services for which it is registered and the actual use of the sign, there is a risk that the average consumer might think that the goods or services come from the same undertaking or economically linked undertakings, and that is all."[166a]

[165] [2012] E.T.M.R. 17 at [87].

[166] [2016] F.S.R. 31; [2016] EWCA Civ 41 at [79].

[166a] For recent examples, see *Beauty Bay Ltd v Benefit Cosmetics Ltd* [2019] EWHC 1140 (Ch) at [60]; *Red Bull GmbH v Big Horn UK Ltd* [2020] EWHC 124 (Ch) at [41].

### Confusion as to origin

*Replace footnote 170:*

[170] *Comic Enterprises Ltd v Twentieth Century Fox Film* [2016] EWCA Civ 41; [2016] F.S.R. 31. **16-091**

## Distinctive nature of the registered mark

*Replace paragraph:*

If the registered mark has not been used then its inherent distinctiveness must be considered. If it has been used on a substantial scale then that may be taken into account in assessing its distinctiveness;[187] although if the mark has been used extensively on some of the goods for which it is registered but not on others, the relevant average consumer must be the person who buys the goods in respect of which there is enhanced distinctiveness.[188] The time at which that distinctive character is to be assessed is the date that the defendant's sign was first used.[189] In *Interflora v M&S*[189a] Kitchin LJ considered the relationship between distinctiveness and likelihood of confusion: **16-094**

> "It is also important to have in mind that the issue of a trade mark's distinctiveness is intimately tied to the scope of protection to which it is entitled. For example, it is well established that, in assessing an allegation of infringement under Article 5(1)(b) of the Directive (or Article 9(1)(b) of the Regulation) arising from the use of a similar sign, the court must take into account the distinctive character of the trade mark, and there will be a greater likelihood of confusion where the trade mark has a highly distinctive character either per se or as a result of the use which has been made of it. It necessarily follows that the court must therefore have regard to the impact of the accused sign on the proportion of consumers to whom the trade mark is particularly distinctive."

[187] *Reed Executive Plc v Reed Business Information Ltd* [2004] R.P.C. 40 CA at [79]–[81] and [83]–[86]. The consequences of an increase in distinctiveness will vary from case to case for it must ultimately be a question of fact as to whether there is a likelihood of confusion between two marks (or a mark and a sign); see the discussion in Ch.11, paras 11-063 to 11-073.

[188] *Jack Wills Ltd v House of Fraser (Stores) Ltd* [2014] F.S.R. 39 at [61], in which the registered mark had been used extensively in relation to clothing but not to footwear. It is perhaps not easy to distinguish between the characteristics of the average consumer of clothing and of footwear. Arnold J also found, at [62], that the likelihood of confusion must be assessed from the perspective of those to whom the mark has enhanced distinctiveness even though the remainder may have a different perspective (relying on the Court of Justice judgment in *Specsavers* at [36]–[38]).

[189] *Levi Strauss & Co v Casucci SpA* [2006] E.T.M.R. 71 CJEU.

[189a] [2015] F.S.R. 10 at [123].

## Distinguishing material is to be disregarded

*Add new paragraph:*

The importance of context when considering use that is allegedly infringing has given rise to arguments that the defendant's attempts to avoid confusion through the use of distinguishing material may be taken into account. However, it is clear that "the context and circumstances are limited to the actual context and circumstances of the use of the sign itself"[209a]: this highlights again the importance of identifying at the outset what is the defendant's sign and then considering the use in that context.[209b] **16-098A**

[209a] *Och-Ziff Management Europe Ltd v Och Capital LLP* [2010] EWHC 2599 (Ch), [2011] F.S.R. 11, per Arnold J (as he then was), at [78].

[209b] In *Planetart LLC v Photobox Ltd* [2020] EWHC 713 (Ch), Daniel Alexander QC (sitting as a deputy HC judge) characterised this as the "local" context of the sign's use, at [25]. The judge cited and explained [77] and [78] of Arnold J's judgment in *Och-Ziff Management Europe Ltd v Och Capital LLP* [2010] EWHC 2599 (Ch), [2011] F.S.R. 11, as meaning: "it was not appropriate to look so broadly at the context that use which was prima facie infringing was nonetheless to be regarded as non-infringing

because other, separate, acts of the defendant had countered actual deception. An extreme example is where a defendant uses a well-known brand for counterfeit goods but nonetheless makes it very clear that the goods are in fact counterfeit so that no actual purchaser is confused. There may be no actual confusion as a result of the use of the sign but there is nonetheless trade mark infringement because the court must focus on the use of the sign in question not the other statements by the defendant as to the trade origin of the goods." At [24].

## The average consumer

*Replace footnote 212:*

16-099 [212] *Lloyd Schuhfabrik Meyer v Klijsen Handel* [1999] E.T.M.R. 690 at [26]; *Gut Springenheide and Tusky* [1968] E.C.R. I-4657 at [31]. See *Red Bull GmbH v Big Horn UK Ltd* [2020] EWHC 124 (Ch) at [43], where the judge agreed that there would be a low degree of attention given to trade marks by the average consumer of energy drinks; nevertheless, he considered there was no likelihood of confusion between the claimant's and defendant's marks that he had earlier found to be similar (although he found infringement under art.9(2)(c)).

*At the end of the quotation, add new footnote 216a:*

16-100 [216a] See also *Gap (ITM) Inc v Gap 360 Ltd* [2019] E.T.M.R. 42 where, it being alleged that the term "gap travel" would be understood to refer descriptively to travel in a "gap year" the judge held that although there was no significant proportion of the relevant public who would not understand the term "gap year", a significant proportion of consumers would have no or no uniform understanding of the term "gap" when used in the context of travel or the term "gap travel". The average consumer therefore would not regard the term "gap" in "gap travel" as descriptive.

## The date of assessment

*Replace paragraph:*

16-102 As explained, it is now clear that the degree of distinctiveness of the registered mark, including that acquired through use, is likely to increase the risk of confusion. The Court of Justice held in *Levi Strauss & Co v Casucci SpA*[218] that the mark's distinctiveness should be assessed at the date the defendant started using its sign, on the basis that "[if] the likelihood of confusion were assessed at a time after the sign in question began to be used, the user of that sign might take undue advantage of his own unlawful behaviour by alleging that the product had become less renowned, a matter for which he himself was responsible or to which he himself contributed."[219] Where there is a material change in the defendant's use, a fresh assessment of infringement taking into account the circumstances at that date is appropriate. See the analysis of infringement at different dates in *W3 Ltd v easyGroup*.[219a]

[218] [2006] E.T.M.R. 71 CJEU at [17].

[219] [2006] E.T.M.R. 71 CJEU at [18]. In *Interflora I* [2012] EWCA 1501 at [34], Lewison LJ disagreed: "What I find difficult to accept is that they come to the same thing. If most consumers are not confused, how can it be said that the average consumer is? ... In some cases the result will no doubt be the same however, [sic] the question is approached; but I do not think that it is inevitable." When the case came back before Arnold J, [2013] EWHC 1291, he reviewed the authorities and noted inter alia that "the average consumer test is not a statistical test in the sense that, if the issue is likelihood of confusion, the court is not trying to decide whether a statistical majority of the relevant class of persons is likely to be confused" (at [211]) and "it should be sufficient for a finding of infringement of a trade mark that a significant proportion of the relevant class of persons is likely to be confused. That is both damaging to the trade mark proprietor and contrary to the public interest" (at [216]). See further Ch.2.

[219a] [2018] EWHC 7; [2018] E.T.M.R. 40.

## (3) Section 10(3)/art.9(2)(c): Where the Use of the Sign Without Due Cause Takes Unfair Advantage of, or is Detrimental to, the Distinctive Character or the Repute of the Trade Mark

### *The Specific Conditions for Infringement*

#### (i) The registered mark must have a reputation

*Replace paragraph:*

The registered trade mark must have a reputation in the UK (in the case of a national registration)[228] or the EU (in the case of a EUTM). The reputation must exist at the date of the alleged infringement. There is no requirement that the reputation must extend over the whole of the relevant territory but it must exist in a significant part of it.[229] In the context of a EU mark, reputation within one Member State may suffice.[230] There is no express requirement as to the extent of the reputation necessary, although the degree of required recognition must be considered to be reached when the mark is known by a significant part of the public concerned by the products or services covered by the trade mark.[231] The relevant public comprises those concerned by the trade mark, such as those depending on the product or service marketed, either the public at large or a more specialised public. For example, traders in a specific sector. Where a mark satisfies the requirement of reputation in part but not all of the EU, infringement may still follow even in territory where the mark does not have a reputation if a "commercially significant part" (as opposed to a "a substantial part") of the public in that state are aware of the mark in issue.[232] In considering whether a reputation has been demonstrated, the court must take into account "all the relevant facts of the case". In particular, this includes the market share held by the trade mark, the intensity, geographical extent and duration of its use, and the size of the investment made by the undertaking promoting it,[233] in each case (it is suggested) in respect of the goods and services relied upon. See [17] of the Opinion of AG Wahl in *Iron & Smith*[233a] (referring to the "paramount role" of the significance of the relevant market for the given goods and services in assessing reputation) and the helpful synthesis of principles from the CJEU authorities given by HHJ Hacon in *Burgerista v Burgista Bros*[233b]: 16-111

> "(1) An EU trade mark has a reputation within the meaning of art.9(2)(c) if it was known to a significant part of the relevant public at the relevant date. (2) The relevant public are those concerned by the products or services covered by the trade mark. (3) The relevant date is the date on which the defendant first started to use the accused sign. (4) From a geographical perspective, the trade mark must have been known in a substantial part of the EU at the relevant date. (5) There is no fixed percentage threshold which can be used to assess what constitutes a significant part of the public; it is proportion rather than absolute numbers that matters. (6) Reputation constitutes a knowledge threshold, to be assessed according to a combination of geographical and economic criteria. (7) All relevant facts are to be taken into consideration when making the assessment, in particular the market share held by the trade mark, the intensity, geographical extent and duration of its use, and the size of the investment made by undertaking in promoting it. (8) The market for the goods or services in question, and from this the identity of the relevant public, ought to assume a paramount role in the assessment. (9) The territory of a single Member State (large or small) may constitute a substantial part of the EU, but the assessment must be conducted without consideration of geographical borders."

Once reputation in the relevant territory (EU or UK) has been established, the claimant is entitled to rely on the mark as a mark with a reputation throughout the territory. However, it may be that if the mark is not known to the average consumer within a particular geographical area that the defendant may be able to establish that there is no link and no infringement in that particular territory, by analogy with the approach under art.9(2)(b) where a defendant can avoid a EU-wide infringement by establishing that there is no likelihood of confusion in a particular territory. This has been recognised by the CJEU in the context of relative grounds opposition.[233c]

[228] "This is not a particularly onerous requirement", per Arnold J in *Och-Ziff Management Europe Ltd v OCH Capital LLP* [2011] E.T.M.R. 1 at [125]. Certainly this is a reflection of the attitude of English courts but it can be questioned whether it is correct, see, for example, *Nigel Kelly v NGRID Intellectual Property Ltd* [2014] E.T.M.R. 21, Controller of the Irish Patents Office, at [41].

[229] *General Motors v Yplon* [1999] All E.R. (E.C.) 865; [1999] E.T.M.R. 950 CJEU at [28]. See also *PAGO* [2009] E.C.R. I-9429, [2010] E.T.M.R. 5; *Iron & Smith Kft v Unilever NV* [2015] E.T.M.R. 45. Note that in the latter case the CJEU distinguished between the tests and criteria established by the case law concerning "genuine use" of a mark and the requirements of establishing reputation. Proof of use is a miniumum statutory requirement to avoid revocation, whereas a mark with a reputation is entitled to extended protection.

[230] *PAGO* [2009] E.C.R. I-9429, [2010] E.T.M.R. 5 at [30].

[231] *General Motors* [1999] All E.R. (E.C.) 865; [1999] E.T.M.R. 950 CJEU at [26]; *PAGO* [2010] E.T.M.R. 5; *Iron & Smith Kft v Unilever NV* [2015] E.T.M.R.

[232] *Iron & Smith Kft v Unilever NV* [2015] E.T.M.R at [34].

[233] *PAGO* (C-301/07) [2009] E.C.R. 1-9429; [2010] E.T.M.R. 5 at [25].

[233a] (C-125/14) [2015] E.T.M.R 45.

[233b] [2018] E.T.M.R 16.

[233c] *Iron v Smith kft v Unilever NV* (C-125/14) [2015] E.T.M.R 45 at 34.

### (iii) Link

*After "as expressly held by the CJEU in Intel[241] (at [30]).", add new footnote 241a:*

16-115 [241a] Where the taking of unfair advantage (or detriment) depends on comparison of mark for sign in the mind of the average consumer, then it is "obvious" that the necessary link cannot be established without the use of the sign bringing the mark to mind. *Argos Ltd v Argos Systems Inc* [2018] EWCA Civ 2211; [2019] F.S.R. 3 per Floyd LJ.

### (iv) Unfair advantage/detriment

*Replace list:*

16-116 (1) *Detriment to distinctive character*: This concerns harm to the mark's ability to distinguish the goods or services of the proprietor from those of others. In the words of the CJEU in *Intel* (at [29]):

> "As regards, in particular, detriment to the distinctive character of the earlier mark, also referred to as 'dilution', 'whittling away' or 'blurring', such detriment is caused when that mark's ability to identify the goods or services for which it is registered and used as coming from the proprietor of that mark is weakened, since use of the later mark leads to dispersion of the identity and hold upon the public mind of the earlier mark. That is notably the case when the earlier mark, which used to arouse immediate association with the goods and services for which it is registered, is no longer capable of doing so."[245]

The proprietor is entitled to prevent all use which reduces the distinctive character of a mark, without having to wait for the process of dilution to be complete, resulting in the loss of all distinctive character. Use which contributes to turning a mark into a generic term but which does not itself render the mark generic is detrimental to the distinctive character for the purposes of the provision.[245a]

(2) *Detriment to repute*: This concerns harm to the reputation of the mark in question, generally through an injurious association with the sign or the goods to which it is applied. An oft cited example is that of *Lucas Bols* where the mark "Claeryn" for gin was held to be infringed by the use of the sign "Klarein" for detergent (both marks are pronounced identically in Dutch) and the court explained:[246]

> "It is ... possible ... that the goods to which [the use of] a similar mark relates, appealed to the sensations of the public in such a way that the attraction and the 'capacity of the mark to stimulate the desire to buy' the kind of goods for which it is registered, are impaired."

In considering authorities on detriment to repute it is important to bear in mind a potential difference between infringement and invalidity on relative grounds. Assessment of detriment for the purposes of invalidity on relative grounds under s.5(3) requires consideration of the specification of each trade mark, rather than an assessment of the evidence of the inferior quality of the particular goods of the applicant or negative connotations arising from the more general nature of the applicant's business.[247] This is a distinction between the approach under relative grounds and that to be adopted with regard to infringement, where particular negative attributes of the defendant may also be very relevant.

(3) *Unfair advantage*: The judgments of the CJEU in respect of unfair advantage make it difficult to ascertain what, if anything, is necessary to render an advantage unfair for the purposes of infringement. The court in *L'Oréal v Bellure*[248] summarised unfair advantage in the following terms (at [30]):

> "In that regard, where a third party attempts, through the use of a sign similar to a mark with a reputation, to ride on the coat-tails of that mark in order to benefit from its power of attraction, its reputation and its prestige, and to exploit, without paying any financial compensation and without being required to make efforts of his own in that regard, the marketing effort expended by the proprietor of that mark in order to create and maintain the image of that mark, the advantage resulting from such use must be considered to be an advantage that has been unfairly taken of the distinctive character or the repute of that mark."

An advantage may be unfair even if it causes no harm to the distinctive character or repute of the mark or more generally to the interests of the trade mark proprietor.[249] From this it seems clear that the CJEU considers that the mere fact of taking advantage without paying is enough to render the advantage unfair. However, the Court of Appeal in *Whirlpool*[250] rejected the submission that mere advantage was enough to give rise to infringement, holding that either an intention to imitate the mark or some other factor was necessary to render a commercial advantage unfair. This is inconsistent with the CJEU's approach in *L'Oréal v Bellure* as reiterated in *Interflora*[251] but in the light of the CJEU's approach to the meaning of "without due cause" in the latter it may well lead to the correct result in terms of infringement.[252]

[245] *Interflora v Marks & Spencer* [2012] E.T.M.R. 1 at [77] and [94].

[245a] For a successful claim under s.10(3) that the judge himself characterised as marginal, see *Planetart LLC v Photobox Ltd* [2020] EWHC 713 Ch D., Alexander QC, at [177]–[182].

246 (1976) 7 I.I.C. 420, see also [38] of the Opinion of the AG in *Adidas v Fitnessworld* [2003] E.C.R. I-12537.

247 *Unite Group Plc v Unite the Union* [2014] R.P.C. 14.

248 [2009] E.C.R. I-5185, [2010] R.P.C. 1.

249 *L'Oréal v Bellure* [2009] E.C.R. I-5185, [2010] R.P.C. 1 at [43].

250 *Whirlpool v Kenwood* [2010] R.P.C. 2 at [136].

251 *Interflora v Marks & Spencer* (C-323/09) at [89].

252 See paras 16-121 to 16-127.

*At the end of the paragraph, add new footnote 260a:*

**16-118** 260a The correct approach is summarised in the judgment of the Court of Appeal in *Comic Enterprises Ltd v Twentieth Century Fox* [2016] E.T.M.R. 22 at [116]–[118].

*Replace footnote 263:*

**16-119** 263 [2016] E.T.M.R. 22 at [112]–[118]. In *Claridge's Hotel Ltd v Claridge Candles Ltd* [2019] EWHC 2003 (IPEC), that involved the claimant's "CLARIDGE'S" trade mark used for hotel services, which the judge (D. Campbell QC) found clearly had a very substantial reputation, and the defendant's use of the sign "CLARIDGE" on candles, the court applied the *Comic Enterprises* list of matters to be established to establish infringement under s.10(3). In relation to the question whether there was a change in the economic behaviour of customers, the judge found (at [54]): "Transfer of image I consider that notwithstanding the Defendants' own intentions and views, the effect of their use of the CLARIDGE mark will have been to cause a transfer of image from the Claimant's mark to the Defendants' sign in the mind of the average consumer. In particular the Defendants' sign does not merely take advantage of the fact that the Claimants' mark is so well known in relation to hotel services, but also takes advantage of its reputation for luxury, glamour, elegance, and exclusivity. I have no doubt that the Defendants' use of this sign does in fact enable them to charge higher prices for their products, and/or enables them to sell more of their products to consumers. As such it has an effect on the economic behaviour of their customers. This is not merely a commercial advantage but an unfair one." In *Planetart LLC v Photobox Ltd* [2020] EWHC 713 (Ch), D. Alexander QC (sitting as a deputy High Court judge) cautioned against applying too strictly the requirement for proof of change in economic behaviour: "Actual evidence of a change in the economic behaviour of consumers is often difficult to obtain. Moreover, where the distinctiveness of a mark is whittled away, the detrimental impact can, in some circumstances, be reflected just as much in the evasive action that a proprietor needs to take to re-establish distinctiveness. Where a rival creeps up on a brand, a proprietor is sometimes forced to edge away from the new-comer at some cost or devote resources to amplifying its brand message to avoid its original distinctiveness being drowned out by the alleged infringer. In my judgment where the evidence, taken as a whole, shows that damage of that kind is sufficiently likely, it is a corollary of the statement of principle of the Court of Appeal [in *Comic Enterprises*] that it is not invariably necessary for there to be actual evidence that consumers have changed their behaviour as a result of the adoption of the rival mark." At [32].

## (v) Use without due cause

*Replace paragraph:*

**16-121** It falls to a defendant to establish that its use has been with due cause if the other elements of infringement are made out. The requirement that use be without due cause has only recently been the subject of significant judicial analysis by the CJEU or the UK courts.[268] In the light of the broad definition of unfair advantage adopted by the CJEU in *L'Oréal v Bellure* and the broadening of the scope of the functions of the trade mark which are relevant to infringement from that of a badge of origin to including the communication, investment and advertising functions, it seems likely that the issue of whether use of a sign is with due cause will become increasingly important in finding a limit to the broad scope of infringement under s.10(3)/art.9(2)(c).[268a]

268 *Intel* [2009] E.T.M.R. 13 CJEU at [39]; *Argos Ltd v Argos Systems Inc* [2018] EWCA Civ 2211 at [120].

268a See for example *Planetart LLC v Photobox Ltd* [2020] EWHC 713 (Ch) at [42]–[45]; D. Alexander QC (sitting as a deputy High Court judge) noted that the difficulties in this area are not so much conceptual but those that "arise in the practical application of the test [laid down by the EU and CA] to a range of cases", at [41]: as examples of the possible fineness of the distinctions, cf. [177]–[182] and [183]–[186].

*Replace paragraph:*

The use by a competitor of a mark with a reputation as an advertising keyword plainly takes "unfair advantage" of that reputation in the broad sense of that term required by the CJEU in *L'Oréal*[274] and subsequent cases. However, such use may not be "unfair" in the sense of harming the interests of the proprietor or affecting any of the functions of the trade mark. In such circumstances the use is apparently not without due cause for the purposes of infringement. To put it another way, in *Interflora* at [91] the CJEU equates use which is not "without due cause" to use which falls within the ambit of fair competition in the sector for the goods and services concerned. This criterion effectively reinstates the requirement that the advantage taken by the later mark be "unfair" which was removed by *L'Oréal v Bellure*. The approach of the Court of Appeal in *Whirlpool*,[275] which must be regarded as incorrect insofar as it requires some element beyond mere commercial advantage on the part of the defendant to render an advantage "unfair" for the purposes of infringement, is to some extent rehabilitated by importing the same considerations into the requirement that use be "without due cause" in order to infringe. Nevertheless, the Court of Appeal in *Argos v Argos Systems*[275a] has subsequently re-iterated the position that mere economic advantage and no more is not sufficient to establish "unfair" advantage. **16-125**

[274] *L'Oréal v Bellure* (C-487/07) [2009] E.C.R. I-5185, [2010] R.P.C. 1.

[275] *Whirlpool v Kenwood* [2010] R.P.C. 2 at [136]. [2012] F.S.R. 3.

[275a] [2018] EWCA Civ 2211; [2019] F.S.R. 3 at [108].

## 5. ANCILLARY MATTERS

### Joint liability

*Add new footnote 281a at the end of the first sentence:*

[281a] s.10(5) was repealed on 14 January 2019. **16-129**

*Replace paragraph:*

As in the case of national trade marks, a person who becomes involved in counterfeiting or other infringement may nevertheless be liable for directing, procuring or combining with others to infringe.[284] **16-131**

[284] For an exposition of the relevant principles, see *CBS v Amstrad Consumer Electronics* [1988] 1 A.C. 1013.

### Locality of infringement

*Replace paragraph:*

Trade mark rights are territorial. An infringing act committed outside the UK or EU (as appropriate) cannot be sued upon as an infringement of a UK or EU registered trade mark.[290] This may be a point of particular relevance in relation to magazines circulating in the UK and websites. The mere fact that websites can be accessed anywhere in the world does not mean that, for trade mark purposes, the law should regard them as being used everywhere in the world. It all depends upon the circumstances, particularly the intention of the website owner and what the reader will understand if they access the site.[291] **16-134**

[290] *Easygroup Ltd v Empresa Aerea de Servicios y Facilitation Logistica Integral SA-Easyfly SA* [2020]

EWHC 40 (Ch) at [37]. But as for bringing proceedings here in respect of infringements of foreign trade marks and vice versa, see Ch.22.

[291] *1-800 FLOWERS v Phonenames* [2000] E.T.M.R. 369; *Euromarket Designs Inc v Peters* [2001] F.S.R. 20 at 288; *Bonnier Media v Greg Lloyd Smith and Kestrel Trading Corp* [2002] E.T.M.R. 86. See further, Ch.28. See also discussion of jurisdiction and infringement in the context of Internet websites in Ch.28.

*Add new paragraphs:*

### Goods in customs clearance system

**16-135A** Article 9(4) of the EUTM Regulation and s.10A of the 1994 Act each provides the proprietor with a right analogous to those under art.9(2)(a) and s.10(1) that applies to goods originating from outside the EU which are in the customs clearance system whether or not they destined for a customer in the EEA. Use of a mark in relation to such goods would not infringe under art.9(2)(a) or s.10(1) unless they were the subject of an offer for sale within the EU or UK respectively.[294a] Article 9(4) provides that the proprietor shall be entitled "to prevent all third parties from bringing goods, in the course of trade, into the Union without being released for free circulation there, where such goods, including packaging, come from third countries and bear without authorisation a trade mark which is identical with the EU trade mark registered in respect of such goods, or which cannot be distinguished in its essential aspects from that trade mark."

**16-135B** The right extends to goods (or packaging for such goods) identical to those for which a mark is registered which bear a mark identical with or indistinguishable from the essential aspects of the registered mark, whether or not they are destined for the EEA. However, the second paragraph of art.9(4) provides that the right lapses if it is shown (presumably by the defendant) that the trade mark proprietor was not able to prohibit the placing of the goods on the market in the country of final destination. This goes considerably further than *Montex v Diesel*[294b] in that the goods will infringe unless they are destined for a market in which the proprietor has no rights. The equivalent provisions under s.10A of the 1994 Act apply to goods originating from outside the customs territory of the EU but amendments to the 1994 Act which come into force after IP completion day apply s.10A to goods originating from outside the customs territory of the UK.

[294a] See para.16-022 and *Montex v Diesel* [2007] E.T.M.R. 13 CJEU.

[294b] [2007] E.T.M.R. 13 CJEU.

**16-136** *Replace title of paragraph:*

### Reproduction of trade marks in dictionaries

**16-136** *Delete footnote 296.*

*Add new paragraph:*

**16-136A** An equivalent provision for national trade marks was introduced by article 12 of the 2015 Directive. Since 14 January 2019 section 99A of the 1994 Act has provided proprietors of UK trade marks with a right of action against publishers in the UK. Section 99A(4) expressly provides that the right is enforceable by injunction and order for erasure of offending reproductions of the trade mark or destruction of copies in the publisher's control.

### Prohibition on the use of a EU trade mark registered in the name of an agent or representative

*Replace paragraph:*

Articles 13 and 21 of the EUTM Regulation make provision for the protection of a proprietor where an agent or representative registers and uses the mark without their authorisation.[297] In such a case the proprietor is entitled to oppose the use of the mark and to demand an assignment in their favour of the registration, unless the agent or representative justifies their action. It would therefore seem that a number of requirements must be satisfied for the remedies (presumably by injunction) to be available. First, the mark must have been registered by the agent or representative. Secondly, the claimant must be the true proprietor of that registration.[298] Thirdly, the proprietor must show that the registration was secured and that the agent or representative is using the mark or threatening to use it without authorisation. An equivalent UK provision is found in s.10B of the 1994 Act, introduced by amendment as of 14 January 2019. **16-137**

[297] Discussion of the equivalent provisions under the 1994 Act is at paras 16-159 and 16-159A.

[298] And here satisfy the conditions of art.5.

## 8. FURTHER RIGHTS CONFERRED BY THE 1994 ACT

### Acts of an Agent or Representative

*Add to the start of the paragraph:*

The provisions of the 1994 Act concerning unlawful acts of agents or representatives of a trade mark proprietor who apply for or use the proprietor's mark in their own name were originally found in s.60. They have now been repealed and replaced with separate provisions concerning the invalidity of such marks (s.5(6) of the 1994 Act as amended) and the restraint of such use (s.10B of the 1994 Act as amended). This paragraph addresses the now repealed provisions of s.60; s.10B is addressed in para.16-159A. **16-159**

*Add new paragraph:*

Section 10B of the 1994 Act provides that where a trade mark is registered in the name of an agent or representative of "a person ('P') who is the proprietor of the trade mark" without consent, then unless the agent or representative "justifies" the registration of the trade mark, P may: "a) prevent the use of the trade mark by the agent or representative (notwithstanding the rights conferred by this Act in relation to a registered trade mark);" and "(b) apply for the rectification of the register so as to substitute P's name as the proprietor of the registered trade mark." This is similar but not identical to the scope of the infringement limb of the repealed s.60. Differences which may be significant are that s.10B does not on its face extend to proprietors of "marks" outside the UK (whereas s.60 extends to proprietors of marks in all Convention countries) and the right of action under s.10B is not subject to a specific statutory limitation by reason of acquiescence. The nature of "justification" for the purposes of the section remains undefined, and the issue of whether the "mark" owned by the proprietor must be registered is still unclear, though it is suggested that authorities in respect of s.60 may be persuasive on these aspects of s.10B. **16-159A**

# Chapter 17

## DEFENCES TO TRADE MARK INFRINGEMENT CLAIMS

Table of Contents



### 1. Introduction

*Replace footnote 1:*

**17-001** [1] Directive 2008/95 to approximate the laws of Member States relating to trade marks, replacing Directive 89/104 as amended. A further Directive, 2015/2436 ("the 2015 Directive") has been enacted to "recast" the TM Directive, amending substantive provisions and renumbering several articles. The TM Directive remains in force (in parallel with the 2015 Directive) until repealed with effect from 15 January 2019. On 14 January 2019 the 1994 Act was amended by the Trade Marks Regulations (SI 2018/825) to implement the changes effected by the 2015 Directive, including (of particular relevance to this chapter) amendments to s.11(1) and (2) and the introduction of new ss.11(1A), 11(2A) and 11A. Section 11(1A) and 11(1B) will be further amended when the transition period following the UK's departure from the EU comes to an end on 31 December 2020 ("IP Completion Day") and defences concerning use EU trade marks are repealed.

### 2. Exclusions From Infringement Addressed in This Chapter

*Replace list:*

**17-003** (1) The use is use of the defendant's own name or address (s.11(2)(a) of the 1994 Act, art.14(a) of the EUTM Regulation).[4]

(2) The use constitutes use of indications which are not distinctive and/or which

concern the characteristics of goods or services (s.11(2)(b) of the 1994 Act and art.14(b) of the EUTM Regulation).

(3) The use is necessary to indicate the intended purpose of a product or service (s.11(2)(c) of the 1994 Act). On 14 January 2019 s.11(2)(c) was amended to implement the 2015 Directive, bringing it into line with art.14(c) of the EUTM Regulation (sub-para.(4) below). This defence is now a particular instance of a more general defence of use of a mark for the purposes of identifying or referring to goods or services as those of the proprietor of the trade mark.

(4) The use is for the purpose of identifying or referring to goods or services as those of the proprietor (art.14(c) of the EUTM Regulation).

(5) The use is of an earlier right which applies in a particular locality (s.11(3) of the 1994 Act, art.138 of the EUTM Regulation).

(6) The use is of the defendant's own later registered mark in relation to the goods and services for which it is registered, on condition that the later mark is not liable to be declared invalid over the claimant's earlier mark (s.11(1) of the 1994 Act)/art.16 of the EUTM Regulation 4). Prior to amendment on 14 January 2019, s.11(1) of the 1994 Act extended to use of the defendant's own mark whenever registered.

(7) The right to complain of the use is excluded by the statutory acquiescence provisions (s.48 of the 1994 Act, art.61 of the EUTM Regulation).

(8) The use falls within a limitation or disclaimer to which the registered mark is subject (s.13 of the 1994 Act). Disclaimers are no longer available under art.42 the EUTM Regulation,[5] and limitations have never been allowed under the EUTM system. There is no express provision as to the impact of a disclaimer on infringement but disclaimed material should be treated as non-distinctive in the assessment of infringement of EUTMs.

(9) The use is in comparative advertising which complies with the requirements of the CAD. This important defence is not to be found in the trade mark legislation.

(10) The use is not liable to affect the functions of the trade mark. This exclusion (which is not to be found in the trade mark legislation) is addressed in the context of infringement in Ch.16.

(11) Honest concurrent use; although this is properly to be categorised as a specific instance of use not liable to affect the functions of a trade mark, it is properly to be characterised as a defence and is addressed below.

(12) The use is in relation to goods in respect of which the proprietor's rights have been exhausted pursuant to s.12 of the 1994 Act or art.15 of the EUTM Regulation. See further Ch.18.

(13) The use is of a mark which is invalid or liable to be revoked. Invalidity and revocation of trade marks is addressed in Ch.12. However, under the EUTM Regulation a defence that the mark is liable to be revoked for non-use can be run without counterclaiming revocation. This aspect is addressed below. An equivalent defence to infringement of a UK trade mark was introduced from 14 January 2019 by s.11A of the 1994 Act.

(14) The use is in relation to genuine goods or services of the proprietor. Until the amendment of s.11(2)(c) on 14 January 2019 there was no specific defence under UK law which in terms excludes such use from infringement. Regardless, such use was plainly not intended by the legislation to infringe and was generally excluded under one or more of (1), (3), (9), (10) or (11), though

subject to the requirements of those particular defences/exclusions. Under UK law there is no specific defence which excludes such use from infringement in terms. Regardless, such use is plainly not intended by the legislation to infringe and is generally excluded under one or more of (1), (3), (9), (10) or (11), though subject to the requirements of those particular defences/exclusions.

(15) Estoppel and acquiescence as a matter of English law, insofar as available.

[4] On 14 January, s.11(2)(a) of 1994 Act was amended to limit the availability of the defence to individuals.

[5] art.37 of Regulation 207/2009 before amendment.

## 3. USE IN ACCORDANCE WITH HONEST PRACTICES

*At the end of the paragraph, add new footnote 30a:*

**17-013** [30a] See also the summary of the relevant legal principles in *Sky Plc v Skykick UK Ltd* [2018] EWHC 155 (Ch); [2018] E.T.M.R. 23 at [327]–[332].

*Replace paragraph:*

**17-015** Whether use is in accordance with honest practices in industrial or commercial matters may well change over time. Use made in the absence of knowledge of confusion may be within the proviso, but excluded once the confusion is drawn to the attention of the defendant. Similarly, if a defendant had a good justification for the use of a particular sign (a licence from a third party, for example) but that licence was subsequently terminated, the defendant's use complained of may be rendered otherwise than in accordance with honest practices.[32] Mere notification of the existence of confusion is not enough to render previously honest use outwith the scope of the defence. The defendant must be able to make a bona fide assessment of the real likelihood of confusion, having taken appropriate steps to minimise any harm to the earlier mark owner's business.[33] Where parties have coexisted without confusion for some time and the defendant has not taken any steps to increase the likelihood of actual confusion occurring (a "real" as opposed to "hypothetical clash" between the mark and sign) the defendant's use may still be in accordance with honest practices.[34]

[32] See, for example, the use of a regimental badge with, then without, the permission of the MOD in *Samuel Smith Old Brewery (Tadcaster) v Lee (t/a Cropton Brewery)* [2011] EWHC 1879; [2012] F.S.R. 7. The former benefitted from the defence, the latter did not.

[33] *Maier v ASOS Plc* [2013] EWHC 2831 at [157]. The availability of another, non-infringing way of conveying a descriptive message may also be relevant to whether use is in accordance with honest practices. See *London Taxi v Frazer Nash* [2017] EWCA Civ 1729; [2018] E.T.M.R. 7 at [96] in which Floyd LJ observed (obiter) "I do not see why the rights of the registered proprietor of trade marks which, on this hypothesis, convey a clear message about origin, should be trumped because the marks also convey the message that the vehicle is a licensed London taxi. If there are other ways of conveying that second message, which there plainly are, then those ways should be used so as to avoid confusion and detriment to the distinctive character of the mark."

[34] See the list of particular factors in the "rather unusual" circumstances of *Maier v ASOS Plc* [2015] EWCA Civ 220; [2015] E.T.M.R. 26 enumerated by Kitchin LJ at [159]–[160]. See also the consideration of the *Samuel Smith* factors in *Frank Industries Pty Ltd v Nike Retail BV* [2018] EWHC 1893 (Ch); [2019] E.T.M.R. 4 at [130].

## 4. USE OF OWN NAME OR ADDRESS

### "Name" of the Defendant

*Replace paragraph:*

**17-018** As originally formulated, the defence applied both to natural persons and to companies or other legal entities.[38] The CJEU held that a party may, in principle, rely on the exception in relation to the use of a trade name[39] and the Court of Appeal in *Cipriani*[40] expressed the view that it may apply:

> "[I]n respect of a trading name, as well as the corporate name of a company, but it will depend on (a) what the trading name is that has been adopted, (b) in what circumstances it has been adopted and (c), depending on the relevant circumstances, whether the use is in accordance with honest practices."

However, with entry into force of art.14(1)(a) of the EUTM Regulation the defence is limited to natural persons. Otherwise infringing acts carried out prior to the amendment to the EUTM Regulation may still benefit from the defence.[41] On 14 January 2019, s.11(2)(a) of the 1994 Act was amended to implement art.14(1)(a) of the 2015 Directive and the defence now applies only to "the use by an individual of his own name or address". The commentary in respect of the availability of the defence to company names in paras 17-020 to 17-021 is now of relevance only to historical acts of infringement carried out prior to 14 January 2019.

[38] *Anheuser-Busch* (C-245/02) [2005] E.T.M.R. 286 at [77]–[80].

[39] *Anheuser-Busch* (C-245/02) [2005] E.T.M.R. 286 at [81].

[40] *Cipriani v Cipriani (Grosvenor Street)* [2010] R.P.C. 16 at [72].

[41] *Argos Ltd v Argos Systems Inc* [2017] F.S.R. 26 at [312].

*Replace footnote 46:*

[46] *Cipriani v Cipriani (Grosvenor Street)* [2010] R.P.C. 16 at [66]. The use by an individual party of his stage name WARRIOR as a trade mark might in principle have benefitted from the own name defence had the requirement of honest practices been satisfied—*KBF Enterprises Ltd v Gladiator Nutrition 3.0 Ltd* [2019] E.T.M.R. 11, Recorder Amanda Michaels. **17-020**

## 5. USE OF DESCRIPTIVE INDICATIONS

*Replace paragraph:*

Section 11(2)(b) of the 1994 Act and art.14(1)(b) of the EUTM Regulation **17-022** provide that a registered mark is not infringed by the use of "signs and indications which are not distinctive or which concern the kind, quality, quantity, intended purpose, value, geographical origin, the time of production of goods or rendering of services, or other characteristics of goods or services." The reference to use of "signs and indications which are not distinctive" was introduced into the EUTM Regulation and the 1994 Act by amendment.[54] It was intended to close a potential lacuna in the defence as previously formulated, in that a sign or an indication which did not relate to some characteristic of the goods or services in issue but which was nonetheless not distinctive could yet infringe. A mark which is devoid of distinctive character would be precluded from registration, but the defence seems likely to extend to the use in a sign of only non-distinctive parts of a registered mark.

[54] s.11(2)(b) was amended as of 14 January 2019 by the Trade Marks Regulations (SI 2018/825) to implement art.14(1)(b) of the 2015 Directive.

*Replace paragraph:*

The provision requires the consideration of two issues. First, it must be **17-023** considered whether the use complained about is of a non-distinctive sign or indication or an indication concerning one of the specified or other characteristics of the goods or services, and secondly, whether the use is in accordance with honest practices in industrial or commercial matters. The latter is addressed under para.17-005. It is to be noted that the word "necessary" does not appear as a requirement in the provision.[55] The question of whether or not a particular use is an indication concerning a "characteristic" of the goods or services in issue is not always straightforward. The interpretation of the similar provision under the absolute grounds for refusal of registration[56] has been considered on numerous occasions by the CJEU and is addressed within Ch.10. However, the defence concerns indications which in fact concern a characteristic of the goods and services in issue, rather than which "may serve in trade to designate" such characteristics. The hypothetical aspects of the discussion in Ch.10 as to the exclusion from registrability of signs which are not actually in use but which could potentially be used are therefore not relevant to the application of this aspect of the defence. The defence is not limited to aspects which "may serve in trade to designate" a characteristic of goods or services but also extends to signs or indications which are not distinctive. The list of characteristics is not exhaustive, but characteristics in question must be easily recognisable by the relevant class of persons.[57] The use of a purely decorative feature on an article of clothing is not an indication of any characteristic of goods or services.[58] Images of a character or of the crest of a sports club which are not purely decorative may denote a characteristic of the goods, in particular if applied to a T-shirt or poster. This depends in each case on the facts and the message conveyed by the sign. Contrast the decision of the Appointed Person in *Linkin Park's TM Application*[59] (use held to be descriptive of a connection with a rock band) with that in *Hearst Holdings Inc v AVELA Inc*[60] (images of a character on merchandise denoting officially licensed goods rather than a characteristic of the goods).

[55] *Philips v Remington* [1999] R.P.C. 809 CA at 824.

[56] EUTM Regulation art.7(1)(c), 1994 Act s.3(1)(c).

[57] *Technopol v OHIM* (C-51/10P) [2011] E.T.M.R. 34.

[58] *Adidas AG v Marca Mode CV* (C-102/07) [2008] F.S.R. 38 at [48].

[59] [2006] E.T.M.R. 74.

[60] [2014] E.T.M.R. 34.

## Use in a Trade Mark Sense Allowed

*At the end of the first sentence, add footnote 61a:*

**17-025** [61a] Since 14 January 2019, s.11(2)(c) (use of the trade mark for the purposes of identifying or referring to the goods or services as those of the proprietor of that trade mark) has provided an express defence for such use. See also art.14(1)(c) of the EUTM Regulation.

*At the end of the paragraph, add:*

**17-027** The requirement of necessity under art.14(1)(c) and s.11(2)(c) is on the face of the legislation now only a particular instance of the more general defence of use of a mark for the purposes of identifying or referring to goods or services of the proprietor. It is clear that where the use complained of is to indicate the intended purpose of a product or service, it must still be "necessary" for the defence to apply. The extent to which necessity is also a requirement of the more general defence is not certain. If that had been the legislative intent, it would have been easy as a matter of drafting to ensure that the word "necessary" qualified the entire provision. It is suggested that the extent to which use is necessary is relevant to whether the more general defence is in accordance with honest practices.[66a]

[66a] See para.17-029.

## 6. Use Necessary to Indicate Intended Purpose of a Product or Service

*Replace paragraph:*

The changes to the law introduced by the amendments to the EUTM Regulation led to a divergence between the national and EUTM position, until implementation of national law giving effect to the 2015 Directive and the amendment of s.11(2)(c) on 14 January 2019.[66b] Prior to amendment, s.11(2)(c) of the 1994 Act provided that a registered trade mark is not infringed by the use of the trade mark only where it is necessary to indicate the intended purpose of a product or service (in particular, as accessories or spare parts), provided the use is in accordance with honest practices in industrial or commercial matters.[67] The provision is concerned with all products and services, not just accessories and spare parts, and provides protection similar to that afforded by s.4(3)(b) of the Trade Marks Act 1938. Here, and in contrast to the other provisions of s.11(2) of the 1994 Act, the provision expressly permits the use of the trade mark of the proprietor, provided the other specified conditions are satisfied. **17-028**

[66b] Amended by the Trade Marks Regulations (SI 2018/825) Pt 2 reg.12(5).

[67] 1994 Act s.11(2)(c), implementing TM Directive art.6(1)(c), and CTM Regulation art.12(c), prior to amendment.

*Replace paragraph:*

Article14(1)(c) of the EUTM Regulation affords a defence to use of the EU trade mark "for the purpose of identifying or referring to goods or services as those of the proprietor of that trade mark in particular where the use of that trade mark is necessary to indicate the intended purpose of a product or service, in particular as accessories or spare parts." In consequence, it seems that necessity of use to indicate the intended purpose is sufficient to establish the defence, but is no longer a requirement. Further, the scope of the defence has been widened to cover any use of a mark for the purpose of identifying or referring to genuine goods or services, as long as such use is in accordance with honest practices. If the defence is not to undermine the exhaustion provisions of art.15, the "duty to act fairly with regard to the interests of the trade mark proprietor" for the purposes of honest practices will presumably be interpreted to exclude use where there exist legitimate reasons for the proprietor to oppose further commercialisation of genuine goods pursuant to art.15(2). Further, although the defence (on a literal reading) extends to the use of a mark to refer to goods of the proprietor whether or not they have been placed on the market in the EU, it is overwhelmingly likely that use relating to such goods will be considered contrary to honest practices in that such use would not recognise the right of the proprietor to control the first sale of goods under the mark. Otherwise art.14(1)(c) would have the effect of introducing international exhaustion by the back door. There is no indication in the recitals to the EUTM Regulation or 2015 Directive that this is the intent of the provision. Recital (21) of the EUTM Regulation, insofar as it concerns this issue, provides "Use of a trade mark by third parties to draw the consumer's attention to the resale of genuine goods that were originally sold by or with the consent of the proprietor of the EU trade mark in the Union should be considered as being fair as long as it is at the same time in accordance with honest practices in industrial and commercial matters.". This suggests that the provision is intended to allow the advertisement of goods in respect of which the proprietor's rights have been exhausted, not to circumvent the exhaustion regime. **17-029**

## Use is Necessary

17-031 *Replace list item "(4)" with:*

*Examples*

(4) BMW complained of the use of the mark BMW and the BMW roundel in conjunction with the name of a car repair company, "TECHNOSPORT". Finding infringement and overturning the trial judge, the Court of Appeal held that in considering whether the defendant's use was entitled to the defence under art.12(c) of the EUTM Regulation (prior to amendment) the Court had to consider whether the message conveyed by the use of the BMW marks was "informative" (telling the consumer that the business provides genuine parts for and repairs BMW cars) or "misleading" (falsely stating that the repair service was closely connected with BMW).[74]

[74] *BMW v Technosport London Ltd* [2017] EWCA Civ 779; [2017] E.T.M.R. 32.

### 7. USE AND PROTECTION OF AN EARLIER RIGHT IN A PARTICULAR LOCALITY

## Earlier Rights

*Replace paragraph:*

17-034 Earlier rights are concerned with unregistered trade marks and signs. To qualify for protection, the use of the defendant's trade mark or sign must first have been continuous in relation to the relevant goods or services. Secondly, it must have been by a person or a predecessor in title. Each of these requirements is discussed below. Thirdly, the defendant's trade mark or sign must have been used in relation to goods or services from a date prior to whichever is the earlier of the use of the claimant's trade mark in relation to those goods or services or the registration of that trade mark in respect of those goods or services, in each case by the proprietor or a predecessor in title of theirs. This aspect of the provision is all very well if the goods or services of the defendant are the same as those that are the subject of the registration or the use by the claimant or their predecessor. Under the old law this was necessarily the case. However, the new law has extended the rights of proprietors over similar and even dissimilar goods and services to those the subject of the registration. In such cases it is very difficult to see how the provision can sensibly be applied, as shown by the following illustration:

> "X is proprietor of the mark "Revue" registered in respect of sunglasses as of 1994 and has used the mark on a limited scale in respect of sunglasses since 1996. Y began to use the mark "Revue" for spectacle frames in 1996 and rapidly acquired a reputation and goodwill in the locality of his business. The similarity between the goods and the identity of the marks is such that there is a likelihood of confusion. X commences proceedings and Y claims to have a defence under s.11(3) of the 1994 Act. Y has used the mark in relation to spectacle frames from a date prior to the use by X of the mark in relation to spectacle frames or the registration by X of the mark in respect of spectacle frames. It is certainly arguable Y could sue a third party to prevent them from commencing business in his locality and trading off his reputation and goodwill."

The requirement under s.11(3)(a) that the defendant's mark be used from a date prior to the use of the claimant's trade mark concerns the use of the claimant's mark in the particular locality in issue, not its use elsewhere in the UK.[76a] However, a claimant's mark can be put to "use" in a particular locality if its goodwill extends to that area.[76b]

[76a] *Caspian Pizza v Shah* [2015] EWHC 3657 (IPEC); [2016] F.S.R. 23 in a passage expressly approved by the Court of Appeal, albeit obiter. *Caspian Pizza v Shah* [2017] EWCA Civ 1874; [2018] F.S.R. 12 at [14].

[76b] *Student Union Letting Ltd v Essex Student Lets Ltd* [2018] EWHC 419 (IPEC); [2018] E.T.M.R. 21 at [37].

## Applying in a Particular Locality

*Replace paragraph:*

An earlier right applies in a locality if, or to the extent that, its use in that locality is protected by virtue of any rule of law (in particular the law of passing off). So the use by the defendant must be protected. But use is not something which can be protected of itself. Goodwill is required. Accordingly it seems that the court will require that at least some goodwill has been generated in the locality in issue.[77] This is consistent with the approach taken by the CJEU in *Anheuser Busch*[78] in the context of considering whether an earlier right relied on for the purposes of opposition was "of more than merely local significance", which would appear to be the converse of an earlier right in a particular locality. The CJEU held that "significance" had to be assessed both in terms of geographical scope and the use to which a mark had been put. The question then arises as to the date by which that goodwill must have been established. Although no date is specified, it seems from the provision as a whole that the goodwill must have been established at the earlier of the registration or the first use by the proprietor or a predecessor in title of theirs in the location in question, or so as to give rise to protectable goodwill in that location.[78a] It has been held that goodwill which is not sufficient in scope to entitle a defendant to invalidate a mark under s.5(4) of the 1994 Act nonetheless gave rise to a defence under s.11(3) as a right applicable only in a particular locality.[79] **17-036**

[77] See *Antoni Fields v Klaus Kobuk* [2006] EWHC 350 (Ch) at [86].

[78] (C-96/09P) [2011] E.T.M.R. 31.

[78a] See *Student Union Letting Ltd v Essex Student Lets Ltd* [2018] EWHC 419 (IPEC); [2018] E.T.M.R. 21 at [37].

[79] *Redd Solicitors LLP v Red Legal Ltd* [2013] E.T.M.R. 13.

## Continuously Used

### The position under the EUTM Regulation

*Replace footnote 86:*

[86] EUTM Regulation art.138(2). As to the meaning of acquiescence, see para.17-055. See also the analysis in *W3 Ltd v easyGroup Ltd* [2018] EWHC 7 (Ch); [2018] F.S.R. 16 at [339]–[352]. **17-042**

## 8. Use of Own Registration

*Replace paragraph:*

Prior to its amendment on 14 January 2019, s.11(1) of the 1994 Act provided "A registered trade mark is not infringed by the use of another registered trade mark in relation to goods or services for which the latter is registered".[89] This defence was introduced at the Report stage of the Bill and provides equivalent protection to that previously afforded by s.4(4) of the Trade Marks Act 1938. The defence was not derived from the TM Directive and originally had no parallel under the EUTM **17-045** regime. The use of a proprietor's own later registered trade mark has been held by the CJEU not to be excluded from infringement under art.9 of the CTM Regulation as unamended.[90] Under art.16 of the EUTM Regulation a defence was introduced which provides that use of a later registered EUTM or national trade mark does not infringe if the later mark would either not be declared invalid on relative grounds[91] or that invalidity under those grounds is precluded on procedural grounds,[92] because the proprietor of the earlier mark consented,[93] for reasons of statutory acquiescence[94] or because the proprietor of the earlier mark is unable to meet the proof of use provisions.[95] On 14 January 2019, the 1994 Act was amended to implement art.18 of the 2015 Directive by amending s.11(1) and introducing new s.11(1A) and (1B) with the effect that the position under the 1994 Act and the EUTM Regulation is essentially the same. Paragraphs 17-046 to 17-053 below address s.11(1) in unamended form. The amendments to the 1994 Act are considered together with the equivalent defences under art.16 of the EUTM Regulation below at paras 17-054 to 17-056B.

[89] Amended by the Trade Marks Regulations (SI 2018/825).

[90] *Fédération Cynologique Internationale v Federación Canina Internacional de Perros de Pura Raza* (C–561/11) [2013] E.T.M.R. 23.

[91] Pursuant to art.60(1) of the EUTM Regulation or art.8 of the 2015 Directive, rendering infringement unlikely, though not impossible.

[92] Pursuant to art.60(3) of the EUTM Regulation.

[93] Pursuant to art.60(4) of the EUTM Regulation.

[94] Pursuant to art.61 of the EUTM Regulation or art.9 of the 2015 Directive.

[95] EUTM Regulation art.64(2) and 2015 Directive art.46(3).

**17-046** *Replace heading:*

## Section 11(1) Prior to Amendment

**17-054** *Replace heading:*

## Use of Valid Later Registered Mark

*Add new paragraphs:*

**17-056A** Section 11(1) of the 1994 Act as amended provides that a UK mark is not infringed by the use of a later UK registered trade mark where that "would not be declared invalid pursuant to section 47(2A) or (2G) or section 48(1)" of the 1994 Act.[110a] Section 47(2A) concerns the refusal of an application for a declaration of invalidity on the ground that that the earlier mark had been registered for more than five years before the date of application for a declaration for invalidity and did not satisfy the use provisions. Section 47(2G) concerns the refusal of an application for a declaration of invalidity because as at the filing or priority date of the later mark, the earlier mark was liable to be declared invalid under s.3(1)(b), (c) or (d) and had not acquired distinctive character to overcome those grounds, had not acquired sufficient enhanced distinctive character to support a challenge under s.5(2) or had not acquired a reputation for the purposes of s.5(3). Section 48(1) concerns statutory acquiescence by the proprietor of the earlier mark. The defence afforded by s.11(1) is narrower than that under art.16 of the EUTM Regulation, which is afforded to later marks not liable to be declared invalid due to consent by the proprietor of the earlier mark[110b] or on procedural grounds. Otherwise, the analysis in respect of art.16 of the EUTM Regulation applies equally to s.11(1) as amended.

Section 11A of the 1994 Act introduces a defence of use of a later registered EUTM that would not be declared invalid as a result of arts 60(1), (3), (4), 61(1), (2) or 64(2) of the EUTM Regulation. This is in the same terms and has the same scope as the defence under art.16 of the EUTM Regulation itself. Section 11A remains in force during the Implementation Period but will be repealed on IP Completion Day. Where s.11(1) or (1A) applies, the later trade mark cannot be infringed through use of the earlier trade registration.[110c] **17-056B**

[110a] Implementing art.18 of the 2015 Directive, which extends the defence to later marks that would not be declared invalid pursuant to arts 8, 9(1) or (2) or 46(3).

[110b] art.60(4) of the EUTM Regulation.

[110c] s.11(1B) 1994 Act.

## 9. STATUTORY ACQUIESCENCE

*Replace paragraph:*

On the issue of time limits, the CJEU held that the five-year time period for the purposes of statutory acquiescence only begins to run when four conditions have been satisfied; first, the later mark must have been registered; secondly, the application for the later mark must have been made in good faith; thirdly, the later mark must have been used in the relevant territory; and finally, the proprietor of the earlier mark must be aware of both the registration and use of the later mark.[118] The question of whether it is necessary for the proprietor of the earlier right to commence proceedings of some kind to bring a period of acquiescence to an end was considered in *W3 Ltd v easyGroup Ltd*. The court expressed the view that "serious, detailed and credible" threats of infringement proceedings were sufficient to stop the clock on acquiescence without issuing proceedings but considered that the issue was so finely balanced that reference would have been appropriate had the issue been of central importance.[118a] **17-063**

[118] At [62].

[118a] *W3 Ltd v easyGroup Ltd* [2018] F.S.R. 16 at [350]–[352] per Arnold J (as he then was).

*Replace paragraph:*

Both art.61(1) and s.48 limit the scope of acquiescence to the particular goods and services for which the later mark has been used. This is consistent with the requirement that the proprietor must be "fully aware" of the use to which it is said to have acquiesced. It would be logical to suppose that a suitably material change in the nature of the use in issue would have the effect of re-setting the clock for acquiescence, though the matter has not yet been decided by the courts.[118b] A proprietor might be content to stand by when a mark is used in one particular form on certain goods, but not in another which is closer in appearance to a device mark, for example.[118c] **17-064**

[118b] But see *W3 Ltd v easyGroup Ltd* [2018] F.S.R. 16 at [353].

[118c] *W3 Ltd v easyGroup Ltd* [2018] F.S.R. 16 at [353].

## 11. COMPARATIVE ADVERTISING

*Replace paragraph:*

Although the 1994 Act as originally passed had a provision specifically drawn **17-070** to address the issue of comparative advertising, s.10(6), it had no foundation in the TM Directive and had no counterpart in the EUTM Regulation. It has been rendered otiose by the CJEU's decisions which exclude lawful comparative advertising from the scope of trade mark infringement. It is now generally accepted that s.10(6) adds nothing to trade mark law and if it did so, would be ultra vires. In the words of Jacob LJ[125]: "It is a pointless provision … . It should be repealed as an unnecessary distraction in an already complicated branch of the law." Section 10(6) was repealed on 14 January 2019.

[125] *02 Holdings Ltd (formerly 02 Ltd) v Hutchison 3G Ltd* [2006] EWCA Civ 1656, [2007] R.P.C. 19 at [58].

*Replace footnote 130:*

17-072 [130] And art.9 of the 2015 Directive now implemented as s.10(4)(e), which provides that it is use for the purposes of infringement to use "the sign in comparative advertising in a manner that is contrary to the Business Protection from Misleading Marketing Regulations 2008".

## Not Misleading

*Replace paragraph:*

17-082 In summary, if a comparative advertisement misleads through express or implied statement or through act or omission (even if the statement is factually true, but incomplete), then so long as the misleading statement has or is likely to have the effect either that the consumer would change their economic behaviour or enter a transactional decision they would not otherwise have taken or has otherwise caused injury to the competitor, then the advertisement falls outside the scope of permitted comparative advertising. The omission of a fact which would deter a significant number of consumers from making a purchase is sufficient to render an advertisement misleading.[140,140a]

[140] *Lidl v Colruyt* (C-356/04) [2007] E.T.M.R. 28 at [80]. In *Aldi Stores Ireland v Dunnes Stores* [2019] E.T.M.R. 48, the Supreme Court of Ireland considered whether omitting information as to the nature of otherwise comparable products which might be material to the consumer was misleading. At [98] the Supreme Court held that although information as to *Bord Bia* (Irish food board) approval of food products might affect a decision to purchase, the omission of such information from the comparison was not enough to render the comparison misleading. Although such comparisons are a matter of degree, and a different court might draw the line in a different place, the test applied by the Supreme Court was at heart correct. The test of whether a comparison is misleading under the CAD is whether the communication is *likely* to cause a transactional decision that would not otherwise have been taken. Where the information only *might* be material, it follows that the threshold of misleading conduct has not been passed.

[140a] In *Aldi Stores Ireland v Dunnes Stores* [2019] E.T.M.R. 48 at [91], the Supreme Court of Ireland took a broad view as to the requirement that groceries be comparable, holding that price comparisons between face creams with different sun protection factors and between foods which were not both approved by the *Bord Bia* (Irish food board) were nonetheless of products that met the same needs and purposes.

## 14. INVALIDITY AS A DEFENCE

*Add new paragraph:*

17-100A On 14 January 2019, s.11A was introduced into the 1994 Act by amendment,[161a] implementing art.17 of the 2015 Directive. Section 11A provides that the proprietor of a UK trade mark is entitled to prohibit use of a sign only to the extent that their registration is not liable to be revoked for non-use pursuant to s.46(1)(a) or (b) of the 1994 Act. There is no need for the defendant to seek to revoke the mark to take advantage of the defence. If a mark has been registered for more than five years before infringement proceedings are brought (and so potentially vulnerable to attack for non-use), s.11A(3) provides that at the request of the defendant, a trade mark proportion must furnish proof that the mark has been put to genuine use in the UK which are relied on for the purposes of proceedings or establish that there are proper reasons for non-use.

[161a] The Trade Marks Regulations (SI 2018/825).

## 15. Use in Relation to Genuine Goods

*At the end of the first sentence, add new footnote 164a:*

[164a] Section 10(6) was repealed on 14 January 2019 by the Trade Marks Regulations (SI 2018/825). **17-102**

*Replace paragraph:*

On 14 January 2019 s.10(6) was repealed and s.11(2)(c) amended,[166] to provide **17-103** a defence for the use of a trade mark "for the propose of identifying or referring to goods or services as those of the proprietor".[166a] The issue of whether the use of a proprietor's own mark in relation to genuine goods or services constitutes an infringement now primarily falls to be considered under s.11(2)(c) and the exhaustion provisions. In the straightforward case where the trader is doing no more than using the trade mark in relation to the genuine goods in which they are dealing, then there will plainly be no difficulty. A defence will be provided by ss.11(2) or 12 implementing arts 6(1) and 7 of the TM Directive[167] But in other cases the matter will not be so clear. So, for example, the goods may have deteriorated or been altered or adulterated so as to affect their quality. In other cases bulk goods may simply have been broken down. In such cases, it is suggested, the principles of exhaustion should be equally applicable.[168] The CJEU applied this approach in considering whether a trade mark proprietor could legitimately object to the sale of second hand goods in *Portakabin.*[169] Similarly, sale of products in breach of a distribution agreement in a manner which was liable to affect the "aura of luxury" which would otherwise attach to goods under a mark was held to provide legitimate reason for objecting to such sales in *Copad SA v Christian Dior.*[170]

[166] The Trade Marks Regulations (SI 2018/825), implementing art.14(1)(c) of the 2015 Directive.

[166a] See paras 17-027 to 17-029.

[167] Provided they are goods which the trade mark owner has actually adopted as his own: *Primark Stores v Lollypop Clothing* [2001] F.S.R. 37 at 637.

[168] TM Directive art.7. In short, there must be legitimate reasons for opposing the use of the mark: *BMW v Deenik* [1999] E.T.M.R. 339 CJEU.

[169] *Portakabin Ltd v Primakabin BV* (C-558/08) [2010] E.T.M.R.

[170] (C-59/08) [2009] E.T.M.R. 40 CJEU.

## 16. Estoppel and Acquiescence (Non-statutory)

### Availability of Defences not in the EU Legislation

*At the end of the penultimate sentence, add new footnote 174a:*

[174a] 1The UK courts are generally following the approach in Marussia. See, e.g. *Coreix Ltd v Coretx Holdings Plc* [2018] F.S.R. 6. **17-110**

## Acquiescence and Laches

*At the end of the paragraph, add new footnote 176a:*

17-112 [176a] For a useful analysis of some general principles in the context of a trade mark case, see *Coreix Ltd v Coretx Holdings Plc* [2018] F.S.R. 6.

Chapter 18

# EXHAUSTION

Table of Contents



## 7. Article 7(2): Legitimate Reasons

### (2) Repackaging, Relabelling and Rebranding

#### *Introduction*

*Add new paragraphs:*

Hitherto, it seems to have been assumed that any interference with the presentation of a product bearing a trade mark required the parallel importer/reseller to satisfy the five *BMS* conditions in order to avoid infringement. However, in *Junek Europ-Vertrieb GmbH v Lohmann & Rauscher International GmbH & Co KG* (C-642/16), the CJEU identified a route for resellers to bypass the BMS conditions. In *Junek*, the parallel importer had merely affixed an additional label to the unprinted part of the original packaging of the medical device, but the product remained as originally packaged and unopened. The label itself was small and only included information regarding the name, address and telephone number of the parallel importer, along with a barcode and a central pharmacological number. In those circumstances, the CJEU ruled that the *BMS* conditions did not apply. **18-114A**

The CJEU clarified that the previous cases involving the *BMS* conditions all involved the opening of the original packaging in order to insert an information leaflet in a different language from that of the country of origin and/or repackaging in boxes designed by the parallel importer on which the proprietor's mark had (in some cases) been reproduced. In *Junek*, the CJEU ruled that the original presentation of the product had not been affected other than by the attachment of the small additional label, and its content, function, size, presentation and placement did not affect the function of the trade mark to guarantee the origin of the medical device. It appears, therefore, that each case must be assessed on its own facts to ascertain if there is no risk to the guarantee of origin of the goods. If there is such a risk, then the *BMS* conditions apply. If not, then it is a *Junek*-type case. **18-114B**

In *Dansac A/S & Hollister Inc v Salts Healthcare Ltd*,[140a] the defendants applied **18-114C** to strike out the claim against them. Birss J explained *Junek* at [32]. As a result, he examined closely whether there was any arguable risk of harm to the guarantee of origin. Certain allegations were struck out and certain others were permitted to go to trial. The question of whether there was a test for the seriousness of any damage to the reputation of the trade marks in question was a point of law unsuitable for summary determination. In short, the pleas which were struck out were those where there was no risk of harm to the guarantee of origin.

[140a] [2019] EWHC 104.

## *De-branding—Partial or Total*

*Add to the end of the paragraph:*

**18-139** The ruling of the CJEU in *Mitsubishi v Duma Forklifts NV* (C-129/17) is very difficult to understand and is almost certainly wrong. To explain why, it is necessary to examine the reasoning of the CJEU in some detail. The facts were as follows. Duma and an associate company GSI, purchased forklift trucks from an undertaking in the Mitsubishi group and placed them under a customs warehousing procedure. Whilst there, Duma and GSI removed all Mitsubishi marks from the machines, modified them to comply with EU rules and affixed their own trade marks, identification plates and serial numbers. After those works had been completed, the machines were imported into the EEA and sold.

*Add new paragraphs:*

**18-139A** The AG (ECLI:EU:C:2018:292) advised the CJEU (correctly, in our view) that these activities did not result in any use of any Mitsubishi trade marks in the EEA. He referred at [88] to the legal fiction that goods in a customs warehouse procedure are not on the market in the EEA which he said "places those goods on the same footing as goods directly imported from third countries which have also undergone debranding and rebranding: in those circumstances the trade mark proprietor cannot have recourse to trade mark proceedings in order to seize those goods...". It should be noted that this "legal fiction" is well established in CJEU case law—see *Philips and Nokia* (C-446/09 and C-495/09) EU:C:2011:796, at [55] and [56].

**18-139B** However, the CJEU disagreed (ECLI:EU:C:2018:594) holding that a proprietor of a mark is entitled to oppose at third party, without its consent, removing all signs identical to that mark and affixing other signs on products placed in the customs warehouse, as in the main proceedings, with a view to importing them or trading them in the EEA where they have never yet been marketed.

**18-139C** The CJEU gave four reasons for its conclusion, none of which is either convincing or valid.

**18-139D** First, it said that the removal of signs identical to the mark prevents the goods for which that mark is registered from bearing the mark the first time they are placed on the market in the EEA, and hence it deprives the proprietor of the mark of the benefit of the essential right to control the initial marketing in the EEA of goods bearing that mark.

**18-139E** Secondly, it said the removal of the signs identical to the mark and the affixing of new signs "with a view to their first placing on the market in the EEA adversely affects the functions of the mark". Under this head, the CJEU referred to *TOP Logistics*[182a] for the proposition that "any act by a third party preventing the proprietor of a registered trade mark in one or more Member States from exercising this right to control the first placing of goods bearing that mark on the market in the

EEA, by its very nature undermines that essential function of the trade mark". The CJEU also referred to the point raised by the referring court that the relevant average consumer could still identify the machines as originating from the trade mark proprietor even with the marks removed. The CJEU said that, whilst the essential function of the mark may be harmed irrespective of that fact, it is likely to accentuate the effects of such harm. The CJEU also reasoned that these activities affected the investment and advertising functions of the mark.

Thirdly, it said, in effect, that these activities were "contrary to the objective of ensuring undistorted competition". **18-139F**

Fourthly, it said "it must be held that an operation consisting, on the part of the third party, of removing signs identical to the trade mark in order to affix its own signs, involves active conduct on the part of that third party, which, since it is done with a view to importing those goods into the EEA and marketing them there and is therefore carried out in the exercise of a commercial activity for economic advantage ... may be regarded as a use in the course of trade." **18-139G**

The third and fourth reasons are, with respect, just unsupported assertions. In respect of the fourth reason, the CJEU did not explain how its reasoning in *Philips and Nokia* could or should be distinguished. It is very difficult to understand how the removal of a mark in private involves a use of that mark in the course of trade. The first and second reasons both suffer from a fundamental flaw: there was no use by Duma/GSI of any sign identical (or even similar) to any registered mark. The CJEU seems to have elevated certain of the consequences of the right conferred by a registered trade mark (e.g. the right of the proprietor to first place goods under that mark on the market in the EEA, the essential and other functions of a registered trade mark) above the essential precondition for the assertion of those rights against a third party—in this case, the use of a sign identical to the trade mark in relation to identical goods (and in the course of trade). **18-139H**

It is not clear how the CJEU would have ruled if the debranding had occurred outside the EEA, with the rebranded goods then being imported into the EEA (cf. the reasoning of the AG). Overall, this case seems to confirm that the CJEU takes a very broad view indeed of the concept of use in the course of trade (cf. its ruling in *Blomqvist v Rolex SA* (C-198/13)—see para.16-023 in the Main Work). **18-139I**

[182a] (C-379/14) EU:C:2015:497) at [48].

## (3) Luxury Goods and Selective Distribution Networks

*Add new paragraphs:*

In *Nomination De Antonio E Paolo Gensini SNC v Brearley*,[186a] HHJ Hacon applied the two *Dior* cases to a case involving charm link bracelets where the individual links could be detached and re-linked in any order and charms could be added. The defendants (JSC) sold Nomination base links and their own "Daisy Charm" links. In respect of Nomination's own base links, the judge held that the elegant packaging of Nomination's bracelets conveyed an image of luxury to purchasers and this increased the reputation of the marks. Receipt of its products from (JSC) in a small blister pack or polythene bag was likely to damage that reputation. Hence, there were legitimate reasons to oppose JSC's further commercialisation of the goods, and JSC infringed. So far as JSC's sale of its own "Daisy Charm" links, some of them were bundled with Nomination links and that had led to confusion in the mind of some of the public, constituting a misrepresentation amounting to passing off. **18-141A**

**18-141B** Despite dismissing the appeal, Arnold LJ in the Court of Appeal made some criticism of the parties and the judge for having argued and analysed the case involving JSC's own links under art.9(1)(a), where it was said the only issue was whether the "NOMINATION" sign had been used "in relation to" the JSC products. He indicated that Nomination's case involved a reversal of the normal logic, which is that use of the identical sign "in relation to" non-genuine identical goods implies a likelihood of confusion. By contrast, Nomination argued that there was a likelihood of confusion (indeed, actual confusion) and that, therefore, there was use of the sign "in relation to" the goods. Arnold LJ indicated that the case would have been better analysed under art.9(1)(b) and could not be treated as raising the same issue as in the passing off claim. However, since the Court of Appeal concluded the judge was entitled to find passing off, it was not necessary to untangle the knot created by the application of this reverse logic.

[186a] [2019] EWHC 599 IPEC, [2019] F.S.R. 23 (upheld on appeal at [2020] EWCA 103).

CHAPTER 19

# COMPETITION LAW AND TRADE MARKS

TABLE OF CONTENTS



## 1. INTRODUCTION

## Competition Laws of the EU and the UK

*Replace paragraph:*

The competition laws of the EU[1] and UK impose important limitations on the exploitation and enforcement of trade marks. Despite the UK's departure from the EU on 31 January 2020, in accordance with the Withdrawal Agreement (as amended in 2019), the UK effectively remains a Member State until the end of the Implementation Period ("IP completion day" or "exit day", presently 31 December 2020): therefore the competition laws of the EU[1a] continue to apply to the exploitation and enforcement of trade marks in and relating to the UK until exit day. Thereafter, their impact in the UK will be indirect only and it will no longer be possible to raise an alleged breach of EU competition law as a defence to infringement (see below, paras 19-005 to 19-013) or to bring a claim on the basis of an alleged breach (see para.19-014). Put simply, after exit day a UK business will need to give such attention to EU competition law issues as would any other business located in a country that is not a Member State of the EU. For example, where an agreement concerning the exploitation of trade marks entered into by a UK business may have an impact on trade between Member States, it will continue to be necessary to consider arts 101 and 102 TFEU. **19-001**

1 From 1 January 1994 these were extended by the European Economic Area Agreement ("the EEA Agreement)" to Iceland, Norway and Liechtenstein, Member States of the European Free Trade Area ("EFTA"). Switzerland, although a member of EFTA, did not accede to the EEA Agreement. The EEA Agreement arts 53 and 54 reproduce arts 101 and 102 of the Treaty on the Functioning of the European Union, see fn.3.

1a With effect from exit day, the Competition (Amendment etc.) (EU Exit) Regulations 2019 (SI 2019/93) disapplies (by Reg.62) arts 101 and 102 TFEU and amends legislation to remove references to the EU; inter alia, each EU Block Exemption (see para.19-024) becomes a "retained block exemption regulation" (with requisite amendment to remove references to EU issues including, for example, Euro amounts) and functions as an exemption from domestic competition law prohibitions for as long as it remains in force. On 28 January 2020 the Competition & Markets Authority issued its explanatory "UK Exit from the EU: Guidance on the Functions of the CMU under the Withdrawal Agreement" (CM113, available at *http://www.gov.uk/cma* [Accessed 30 September 2020]) setting out the details as they stood on that date.

*Replace paragraph:*

The Competition Act 1998[2] introduced a domestic competition regime for the UK which is modelled on the relevant provisions of the Treaty on the Functioning of **19-002** the European Union ("TFEU"),[3] and as a result the exploitation and enforcement of trade marks within the UK are subject to more potential limitations than was previously the case (or at any rate competition law issues are now raised more frequently both in negotiation and in legal proceedings). With effect from exit day, the UK's domestic legislation will be the only competition law applicable in the UK and the Competition & Markets Authority ("CMA"), the body charged with its enforcement, is likely to increase the level of its activities.

[2] The Act came into force on 1 March 2000. Section 60 of the Act mandates that the UK competition rules be interpreted in a manner consistent with the competition case law of the CJEU: with effect from exit day, Reg.23 of the Competition (Amendment etc.) (EU Exit) Regulations 2019 (SI 2019/93), repeals this section and replaces it with a new s.60A that requires in s.60A(2) that the CMA, courts and tribunals avoid inconsistency between their decisions and EU law and the decisions of the CJEU as at exit day. However, this is subject to the important proviso in s.60A(7) that the CMA, court or tribunal may decline to do so "if it thinks it is appropriate to act otherwise in the light of one or more of the following—(a) differences between the provisions of this Part [of the CA] under consideration and the corresponding provisions of EU law as those provisions of EU law had effect immediately before exit day; (b) differences between markets in the United Kingdom and markets in the European Union; (c) developments in forms of economic activity since the time when the principle or decision referred to in subsection (2)(b) was laid down or made; (d) generally accepted principles of competition analysis or the generally accepted application of such principles; (e) a principle laid down, or decision made, by the European Court on or after exit day; (f) the particular circumstances under consideration."

[3] The 2009 Treaty of Lisbon (which came into force on 1 December 2009) amended the Treaty of the European Union ("TEU") and the Treaty on the Functioning of the European Union ("TFEU"), which was previously known as the Treaty of Rome which set up the European Economic Community in 1957. Consolidated versions of the TEU and TFEU were published in the *Official Journal* on 30 March 2010 [2010] OJ C83.

## 2. ARTICLES 101 AND 102 TFEU

### Procedural Questions

*Add to the end of the paragraph:*

19-037 This will no longer be possible after exit day.

### Effect of EU Law on Registrability or Validity as Such

*After "In principle there seems no reason why", replace "not." with:*

19-039 not, although obviously not after exit day.

## 3. COMPETITION ACT 1998

*Replace footnote 107:*

19-040 [107] s.60. With effect from exit day (presently 31 December 2020), Reg.23 of the Competition (Amendment etc.) (EU Exit) Regulations 2019 (SI 2019/93), repeals this section and replaces it with a new s.60A that, on the one hand, requires (in s.(2)) that the CMA, courts and tribunals avoid inconsistency between their decisions and EU law and the decisions of the CJEU as it stood at the end of the transition period (or IP completion day), while, on the other, leaves open (in s.(7)) the possibility of not doing so in the light of either subsequent developments or different factors applying to the particular circumstances.

*Replace paragraph:*

19-042 Agreements which do not have an "appreciable effect on competition" will not be caught by the Ch.I prohibition.[109] On this question, the CMA may continue to pay some regard to the European Commission's approach in its Notice of Agreements of Minor Importance,[110] even after exit day. So-called "small agreements" which are not price-fixing agreements are given limited immunity if the aggregate market share of the parties, where they are actual or potential competitors, on the relevant market(s) does not exceed 10 per cent. Where the parties are not actual or potential competitors, the market share of each of the parties must not exceed 15 per cent.

[109] s.39. Agreements and concerted practices, OFT Guideline 401, para.2.15, et seq. The limited immunity does not go to substance, may be withdrawn and does not affect third parties.

[110] [2001] OJ C368/13.

*Replace paragraph:*

An agreement which falls within the Ch.I prohibition may be exempted in three ways: (1) by satisfying the exemption conditions for an individual exemption[111]; (2) by falling within a UK block exemption[112]; or (3) by benefiting from a parallel exemption where it is covered by an EU block exemption,[113] or would be so covered if it had an effect on trade between EU Member States. If an agreement falls within the scope of a block exemption, it is automatically exempted so long as all the conditions of the block exemption are met. The individual exemption conditions[114] are very similar to TFEU art.101(3). It is no longer possible to notify agreements to the CMA for individual clearance; instead the parties must self-assess whether the agreement satisfies the individual exemption conditions. **19-043**

[111] ss.4 and 5. See Agreements and concerted practices, OFT Guideline 401, Ch.5.

[112] ss.6–8. (There is only one UK block exemption, which covers public transport ticketing schemes.)

[113] s.10(1). With effect from exit day, the Competition (Amendment etc.) (EU Exit) Regulations 2019 (SI 2019 No/93) Reg.3 amends s.10 to convert each parallel (EU) exemption to a "retained block exemption regulation" and introduces s.10A to give the Secretary of State power to vary or revoke such retained block exemptions.

[114] s.9. They include, in s.9(a)(ii), "promoting technical or economic progress", which may be relevant for intellectual property licences: cf. *Campari* (1978) 22 C.M.L.R. 397.

*Replace footnote 116:*

[116] Commission Regulation 330/2010 of 20 April 2010 on the application of art.101(3) to categories of vertical agreements and concerted practices, [2010] OJ L102/1. With effect from exit day, the Competition (Amendment etc.) (EU Exit) Regulations 2019 (SI 2019/93) Reg.3 amends s.10 to convert this block exemption into a "retained block exemption regulation" and introduces s.10A which gives the Secretary of State power to vary or revoke it. Schedule 3 para 5 of the Regulations makes various amendments to the wording of the exemption to make it applicable to the UK only. **19-044**

CHAPTER 20

# THE ACTION FOR PASSING OFF

TABLE OF CONTENTS



## 2. FOUNDATION AND NATURE OF THE ACTION

### The Extended Form

*Add to the end of the paragraph:*

20-010 An attempt to rely on the mark "mutual" in the context of financial services as denoting a class of entities owned by their customers failed on the facts. The term was not understood to have that meaning by the relevant public and the claim failed.[20a]

[20a] *The Military Mutual Ltd v Police Mutual Assurance Society Ltd* [2018] EWHC 1575 (IPEC); [2018] F.S.R. 32

### A Question of Fact

*Replace footnote 31:*

20-017 [31] cf. *Jif* where all the arguments raised by the defendants on appeal were defeated by the findings of fact. The evidence demonstrated that the lemon shaped container acted as an indicator of origin. Conversely, where a party claimed passing off based on the use by a competitor of the colour purple on an inhaler, the absence of evidence as to the colour playing a distinctive role in the minds of the relevant public was fatal to the claim: *Glaxo Wellcome UK Ltd v Sandoz Ltd* [2019] EWHC 2545 (Ch).

### Reputation

20-021 *After item "(7)", add:*

*Examples*

(8) Although consumers were aware that the claimant supplied inhalers in the colour purple and some consumers used the colour of their inhalers to distinguish between different inhalers having different functions, there was no evidence that the colour purple acted or was relied on as a badge of origin to consumers or medical professionals. Recognition of the colour as being

associated with the claimant was not enough. The claim in respect of the use of purple on a competing inhaler failed: *Glaxo Wellcome UK Ltd v Sandoz Ltd*.[45a]

[45a] [2019] EWHC 2545 (Ch).

## Misrepresentation

*Replace footnote 61:*

[61] (1915) 32 R.P.C. 273 at 284, cited at para.20-016. **20-027**

## Proof of Fraudulent Intention is not Essential

*Replace paragraph:*

**20-029** Passing off cases are often cases of deliberate and intentional misrepresentation, but it is well settled that fraud is not a necessary element of the right of action,[64] and the absence of an intention to deceive is not a defence.[65] Moreover, literal truth is not necessarily innocent of misrepresentation.

> "If a man makes a statement which is true, but which carried with it a false representation and induces the belief that his goods are the plaintiff's goods, he will be restrained by injunction. He cannot rely on the fact that his statement is literally and accurately true if, notwithstanding the truth, it carries with it a false representation."[66]

Proof of fraudulent intention may, however, materially assist a claimant in establishing probability of deception.[67]

[64] *Reddaway v Bentham* [1892] 2 Q.B. 639; 9 R.P.C. 503 CA at 507; Halsbury LC in *Cellular Clothing v Maxton* [1899] A.C. 326 at 334; 16 R.P.C. 397 at 404. But cf. the cases on enabling others to pass off, at para.20-217.

[65] *Bourne v Moore* [1958] R.P.C. 226 at 228.

[66] per Buckley LJ in *Brinsmead v Brinsmead* (1913) 30 R.P.C. 493 at 506.

[67] See para.20-215, and *OT v Cumming* (1915) 32 R.P.C. 69. For if the defendant set out to deceive, the court will readily infer that he succeeded. Fraudulent intent may be implied where the defendant continues to use deceptive marks after complaints have been made to him: *Johnston v Orr Ewing* (1882) 7 App. Cas. 219 at 229; *Weingarten v Bayer* (1906) 22 R.P.C. 341 HL at 357.

*Replace paragraph:*

**20-030** It should be remembered that deliberate imitation of another's goods, get-up, method of trading or trading style does not necessarily involve fraud; a trader is entitled to sail close to the wind, so long as they steer clear of actual misrepresentation.[68] It is, in particular, lawful for a trader to suggest to purchasers that their goods are equivalent to, or a substitute for, those of another,[69] and to choose marks and styles appropriate to that. Furthermore, there are some older cases which would seem to imply that it is lawful to adopt a mark so close to another's that customers (whilst aware that there are two marks) will not bother to distinguish between them[70]; something that can cause very great damage as well as great resentment. On the other hand, a conscious decision on the part of a defendant "is not something which the court is bound to disregard".[71] The person who starts with another's mark or get-up, recognises that it would be deceptive to duplicate it but attempts to design a similar logo which is "safe" from challenge may be held to acknowledge the potential for misrepresentation and deception, even though there was no intent to cause such a result, so providing some evidence for potential deception, albeit of limited weight.[72] However, evidence that the defendant was aware of the risk of deception but thought that sufficient steps had been taken to avoid it, tends to suggest that there is less likelihood of deception, on the basis of the defendant's familiarity with the market.[72a] Further, an awareness of the risk of proceedings being brought is not the same as an awareness of a likelihood of deception.

[68] So Roxburgh J frequently observed, arguendo. He appears never to have put the observation into a judgment, but *Day v Kennedy* (1952) 70 R.P.C. 19 at 21, 22 comes close to it; cf. per Greene MR in *Wright Layman & Umney v Wright* (1949) 66 R.P.C. 149 at 152: "Honest men do not sail near to the wind." But that referred to a man who had passed off. However, there is a fundamental difference between a defendant's intention to copy a claimant's business and a defendant's intention to represent falsely that it is or is connected with the claimant, as Daniel Alexander QC (sitting as a deputy) observed in *PlanetArt LLC v Photobox Ltd* [2020] E.T.M.R. 35 at [80]. The latter may be probative of passing off, the former is not.

[69] cf. para.20-108 and *King v Gillard* (1905) 22 R.P.C. 327 CA (a "get up" case).

[70] cf. *Goya v Gala* (1952) 69 R.P.C. 188; there are similar cases, but the point seems never to have been expressly decided.

[71] *United Biscuits v Asda Stores* [1997] R.P.C. 513 at 531. The defendant had aimed to avoid passing off but deliberately sailed close to the wind in selecting the packaging and name for its "Puffin" biscuits, an intended own-brand equivalent to the claimant's "Penguin".

[72] *Specsavers International Helathcare v Asda Stores* [2010] EWHC 3035 (Ch); [2011] F.S.R. 1, Mann J at [95]–[96]. The approach of the trial judge was expressly endorsed on appeal [2012] EWCA Civ 24; [2012] F.S.R. 19 at [115] and [116].

[72a] *Glaxo Wellcome UK Ltd v Sandoz Ltd* [2019] EWHC 2545 (Ch) at [188], and the helpful analysis of the authorities on the defendant's state of mind at [182]–[189].

## Where Trade Mark Action Fails, Passing Off Action May Succeed on the Same Evidence

*Add to the end of the paragraph:*

**20-035** In passing off, the defendant's acts are considered in a broader context than the comparison for the purpose of trade mark infringement, and so matters external to the sign complained of may give rise to an actionable misrepresentation or negate it.[87a]

[87a] In *PlanetArt LLC v Photobox Ltd* [2020] E.T.M.R. 35 the claimant established trade mark infringement under s.10(2) but failed to establish passing off, in part as a result of distinguishing material surrounding the defendant's sign.

### 3. GOODWILL

## Ownership of Goodwill

*Replace footnote 132:*

**20-049** [132] See, e.g. *Scandecor Development v Scandecor Marketing* [1999] F.S.R. 26 CA. See also *Shua Ltd v Camp and Furnace Ltd* [2020] EWHC 687 (Ch) for the court's consideration of the relevant factual issues in a dispute regarding ownership of goodwill as between a performer and the company organising the events at which he entertained.

## Shared Reputation

*Replace paragraph:*

**20-062** The product names concerned in such cases as "Spanish Champagne" (example (2), above) and "Advocaat" are, of course, not trade marks in the ordinary sense at all; they are terms that describe a type of product, by whomever it is supplied, and action may be taken to protect that goodwill by any member of the class defined as the traders who supply that product. There is no need for the product in issue to have a particular cachet or be a superior or luxury brand.[192a] But where passing off is concerned, there is no real dividing line between such cases and cases such as "*Dent*" (illustration (1), above) where an ordinary trade mark is shared. Note that where two or more parties share reputation in a mark, one may be restrained from damaging the goodwill owned by the others.[193]

[192a] 192a. *Diageo North America Inc v ICB Ltd* [2010] E.T.M.R. 57 CA, "Vodkat" held to pass off in respect of vodka. See also *Fage UK Ltd v Chobani UK Ltd* [2014] F.S.R. 29 CA, goodwill held to subsist in "Greek yoghurt". In each case the goodwill could be relied on by individual traders who dealt in the products.

[193] *Sir Robert McAlpine Ltd v Alfred McAlpine Plc* [2004] R.P.C. 36.

## The Claimant May be Unknown to Customers

*After item "(3)", add:* **20-064**

*Examples*

(4) The claimant sold their medicinal inhalation products in a purple inhaler. Although the evidence established that healthcare professionals and patient consumers might recognise a purple inhaler as coming from the claimant, it did not establish that purple was distinctive of the claimant or was in fact relied upon to denote origin. The sale by the defendant of a competing product in a differently shaped purple inhaler did not amount to passing off. The trial judge distinguished *Hoffmann-La Roche v DDSA*[200a] on the facts but also observed that the branded and generic prescription markets "have changed out of all recognition since 1969, as has the organisation of the NHS": *Glaxo Wellcome UK Ltd v Sandoz Ltd.*[200b]

[200a] [1969] F.S.R. 410.

[200b] [2019] EWHC 2545 at [164]–[169] per Arnold LJ.

## Marks More-or-Less Descriptive

*Replace footnote 239:*

[239] See here the lists in App.31 in previous editions of this work, noting that there is here a distinction to be drawn between passing off and trade mark infringement; and see *McCain v Country Fair* [1981] R.P.C. 69 CA (only the descriptive part of the claimants' mark taken, no passing off); *Fisons v Godwin* [1976] R.P.C. 653 is similar; but cf. *Carlsberg v Tennent* [1972] R.P.C. 847 (OH, Scotland), where an interim interdict was granted to protect the mark "Special brew" for beer; there was some similarity of get-up and the goods were intended to be directly competitive. See also the analysis of Daniel Alexander QC (sitting as a deputy) in *PlanetArt LLC v Photobox Ltd* [2020] E.T.M.R. 35 at [59]–[77]. Even where a descriptive term has acquired a secondary meaning, its use in conjunction with the defendant's own brand may serve to "descriptivise" the term. It all depends on the facts of the particular case. By contrast, the addition of the term "British" to the mark "Asian Achievers Awards" did not serve to distinguish the defendant's services: *Asian Business Publications Ltd v British Asian Achievers Awards Ltd* [2019] EWHC 1094 (IPEC). **20-074**

## Geographical Names

*Replace list with:* **20-088**

*Examples*

(1) The claimant, being owner of all the collieries in Radstock, except a very small one, traded as the "Radstock Coal Co", and the defendants began to sell coal under the same name, and also as "The Radstock Colliery Proprietors". An injunction was granted "to restrain the defendants, unless

and until they shall acquire a colliery or coal mine within the parish of Radstock, from trading under, or using the name or style of 'The Radstock Colliery Proprietors', or any other name or style signifying that the defendants or either of them are proprietors of any colliery or collieries at Radstock": *Braham v Beachim.*[286] Subsequently, the defendants acquired a colliery, but not in Radstock, and began to trade as "The Radstock Coal and Waggon Co, Colliery Proprietors, Radstock, Somerset", and a motion to commit for breach of the injunction was refused on the ground that the terms used by them did no more than imply that they were proprietors of collieries, and that their place of business was at Radstock, and this was true.[287]

(2) On a finding that the name "Whitstable Native Oysters" meant the claimants' oysters, and could not be fairly used of French oysters relaid and brought to maturity at Whitstable, the court granted an interlocutory injunction to restrain the use of "Native"; no order as to "Whitstable": *Free Fishers of Whitstable v Elliott.*[288] In the later case of *Whitstable Oyster Fisheries v Hayling,*[289] it was decided that "Whitstable", as applied to oysters, was descriptive of the place where the oysters reach maturity.

(3) The claimant owned the only quarry in Brereton (in Chester) producing foundry sand. The defendant sold foundry sand as "Brereton sand". There was another Brereton in Staffordshire. An interlocutory injunction was granted restraining the defendant from selling foundry sand as "Brereton", "except sand quarried in the parish of Brereton in the county of Chester or any other parish bearing the name of Brereton"—with a general prohibition of passing off also: *Smith v Fieldhouse.*[290]

(4) In the "*Spanish Champagne*" case, where a number of champagne producers sued in respect of the sale of Spanish sparkling wine as "Spanish Champagne", an injunction was granted restraining the defendants from passing off "as and for wine produced in the district of France known as the Champagne District wine not so produced by advertising, offering for sale or selling the same as Spanish Champagne or under any other name or description that includes the name Champagne": *J Bollinger v The Costa Brava Wine Co Ltd.*[291] Any one of them, with substantial English goodwill in the name "Champagne", could have sued: see "*Advocaat*"[292]; *Bulmer v Bollinger*[293] (where, however, the description "Champagne perry" for perry made sparkling otherwise than by the champagne process and sold in bottles very different from champagne bottles, was held not deceptive).

(5) The injunction granted in the "*Sherry*" case restrained the claimants (who had been sued on a counterclaim) "from using in the course of trade the word 'sherry' in connection with any wine not being wine coming from the Jerez district of Spain otherwise than as part of one or more of the phrases 'British Sherry', 'English Sherry', 'South African Sherry', 'Cyprus Sherry', 'Australian Sherry' and 'Empire Sherry'". The excepted phrases would not have been permitted if there had not been acquiescence: *Vine Products Ltd v Mackenzie & Co Ltd.*[294] Both the "*Champagne*" and "*Sherry*" cases were followed in the "*Whisky*" case, *John Walker v Ost.*[295]

(6) The defendants were marketing a non-alcoholic drink under the name "Elderflower Champagne" in a bottle made up to look like a champagne bottle. In a representative capacity, the champagne house Taittinger sued for passing off. The Court of Appeal found there to have been a misrepresentation that the product was champagne or in some way associated with it and

many members of the public would be deceived: *Taittinger v Allbev*.[296] The court also granted an injunction restraining the use under EC Regulation 823/87 protecting the term "Champagne", at 673.

(7) Where the name "Banbury" was distinctive of the claimants, the following qualification was added to the defendant's undertaking not to trade under that name, "Provided that nothing in the aforementioned undertaking shall prevent the defendant from making bona fide use of the word 'Banbury' as part of the address on any business for the time being bona fide carried on by it in the Borough of Banbury": *Banbury Buildings v Sectional Concrete*.[297] An injunction restraining the use of "Banbury" simpliciter would have prevented the defendant from carrying on its trade in Banbury altogether, since it could not have used its address.

(8) The use of the term "Greek Yoghurt" to describe thick and creamy yoghurt manufactured outside Greece in the manner of traditional Greek yoghurt amounted to passing off in the light of evidence that consumers in the UK regarded the term as denoting not only a style of yoghurt but also its geographical origin.[297a]

[286] (1878) 7 Ch D. 848.

[287] (1878) Seb. Dig. at 633, Fry J.

[288] 4 T.L.R. 273; [1888] W.N. 27.

[289] (1900) 17 R.P.C. 461; 18 R.P.C. 434.

[290] [1961] R.P.C. 110.

[291] [1961] R.P.C. 116 at 127; [1960] R.P.C. 16 at 17.

[292] [1980] R.P.C. 31 HL.

[293] [1978] R.P.C. 79 CA.

[294] [1969] R.P.C. 1 at 32.

[295] [1970] R.P.C. 489.

[296] [1993] F.S.R. 641 CA.

[297] [1970] R.P.C. 463.

[297a] *Fage UK Ltd v Chobani UK Ltd* [2014] F.S.R. 29 CA.

## 4. THE LIMITS OF PASSING OFF

### Passing Off is not a General Tort of Unfair Competition

*Replace footnote 305:*

[305] *L'Oréal v Bellure* [2007] EWCA Civ 968; [2008] E.T.M.R. 1. The Court of Appeal has cautioned that the extended form of passing off "should not by dint of extensions upon extensions trespass beyond the legitimate area of protection of goodwill into an illegitimate area of anti-competitiveness": *Diageo North America Inc v ICB Ltd* [2010] E.T.M.R. 57 at [76] per Rix LJ. **20-093**

## 5. DIRECT MISREPRESENTATION AS TO BUSINESS OR GOODS

### Representation as to Nature of Goods or Services

*Replace paragraph:*

In general, no action lies for passing off goods as "similar to",[388] better than[389] **20-108**
or a substitute for[390] those of another, even though that "other" offers to show that the statements are untrue and are injurious to them.[391] However, as noted by Aldous J in *Ciba-Geigy v Parke Davis*,[392] "care must be taken in applying in 1993 general

statements of the law made in 1898". Goodwill may lie in a reputation for selling particular goods, and if so a false representation by another that their goods are those goods will be actionable.[393] On the other hand, it is not sufficient that the defendant makes a false representation, it must be a false representation related to the claimant's product or goodwill.[394] It is necessary to consider with care what goodwill the claimant owns and whether any misrepresentation was made by the indicia complained of, which was likely to damage that goodwill.[394a]

[388] *Magnolia Metal v Tandem Smelting Syndicate* (1900) 15 R.P.C. 701, 17 R.P.C. 477 HL; *Broad v Graham Building Supplies (No. 1)* [1969] R.P.C. 285 ("as"); *Broad v Cast Iron Drainage* [1970] F.S.R. 363 ("similar to").

[389] *White v Mellin* [1895] A.C. 154.

[390] "*Yeast-Vite*"(1934) 51 R.P.C. 110 HL.

[391] *Hubbuck v Wilkinson* [1899] 1 Q.B. 86; and see cases last cited. This is a matter of public policy, which has developed over the years, so that the courts may well now intervene where a century ago they would not have: see per Lord Diplock in "*Advocaat*" [1980] R.P.C. 31, especially at 94. For example, in *Ciba-Geigy v Parke Davis* [1994] F.S.R. 8, the judge noted that "the common law could apply different standards to statements about pharmaceuticals to those made about flour", at 21. But see the analysis of Arnold J in *Glaxo Wellcome UK Ltd v Sandoz Ltd* [2019] EWHC 2545 (Ch) in refusing to grant relief.

[392] [1994] F.S.R. 8 at 20.

[393] "*Angostura Bitters*" (1878) 7 Ch D. 801; "*Yorkshire Relish*" [1897] A.C. 710, 14 R.P.C. 720 HL; *Masson, Seeley v Embossotype* (1924) 41 R.P.C. 160, illustration para.20-134; *Combe v Scholl* [1980] R.P.C. 1; and the "*Champagne*" line of cases cited below.

[394] *Schulke & Mayr UK v Alkapharm UK* [1999] F.S.R. 161. In *Dr Martens v Figgins* (1999) 44 I.P.R. 281, it was held that use of the words "The Original" on the defendant's look-alike footwear was sufficient to find passing off, even though the product bore the words "Made in Australia" on the instep: "a potential purchaser or consumer cannot be expected to undertake a reasoned analytical exercise when confronted with [the defendant's product]", per Goldberg J at 389 (although passing off was not found in relation to another defendant who used a distinctive mark on "look-alike" products, at 329).

[394a] *Glaxo Wellcome UK Ltd v Sandoz Ltd* [2019] EWHC 2545 (Ch) at [181].

**20-108** *Replace "Example":*

*Examples*

(1) The defendant carried on a business of designing and building exhibition stands under the name "Tabasco Design", on the basis that one of the designers used by the defendant was "hot". The makers of the well-known "Tabasco" sauce failed in its application for interim relief: *McIlhenny v Blue Yonder*.[395a]

> "I accept—it is not in controversy—that [the defendant], in adopting the name Tabasco, sought to take advantage of a well-known characteristic of the [claimant's] product. But there is an appropriation only if some property or right is taken and the appropriation, if there is one, is wrongful only if a rule or principle of law forbids it .... Authority binding on this court requires me to hold that there is no passing off in the absence of a representation of connection between the [defendant] or its services on the one hand and the [claimant] or its product on the other" (per Lehane J at 201).

(2) The claimant alleged that the use by the defendant of the colour purple on medicinal inhalers in competition with the claimant's products amounted to a misrepresentation that the defendant's product originated from the claimant or was equivalent to that of the claimant. Although such misrepresentation might be actionable, on the facts the claimant failed to establish that the colour purple was distinctive of the claimant's product or that the use of purple by the defendant constituted a misrepresentation as to equivalence.

The claim failed.[395a]

[395a] (1998) 39 I.P.R. 187.

[395a] *Glaxo Wellcome UK Ltd v Sandoz Ltd* [2019] EWHC 2545 (Ch) at [181].

## Passing Off One Quality of Goods for Another

*After item "(6)", add:* **20-127**

*Examples*

(7) For a case in which the "outer limits" referred to by Jacob J were exceeded, see *Glaxo Wellcome UK Ltd v Sandoz Ltd.*[486a] Having considered the authorities (including *Hodge Clemco v Airblast*) Arnold J considered the claim that the use by the defendant of the colour purple on medicinal inhalers in competition with the claimant's products amounted to a misrepresentation that the defendant's medicinal product was "equivalent" to that of the claimant. Although in principle a misrepresentation as to equivalence could be actionable as passing off, it was necessary to consider with care what goodwill the claimant owned and where any misrepresentation was made by the indicia complained of which was likely to damage such goodwill. The claimant failed to establish that the colour purple was distinctive of the claimant's product or that the use of purple by the defendant constituted a misrepresentation as to equivalence and the claim was dismissed.

[486a] [2019] EWHC 2545 (Ch) at [170]–[181].

### 7. TRADING NAMES

## Descriptive Names

*After "means that relief will now be granted in many more instances than the old precedents might suggest.", add:*

However, even where the claimant has established a "secondary meaning" of the descriptive words in issue, the full context of the defendant's use must be considered. Use in conjunction with the defendant's own brand may serve to "descriptivise" the term. It all depends on the facts of the particular case.[528a] **20-136**

[528a] See the helpful analysis of the principles by Daniel Alexander QC (sitting as a deputy) in *PlanetArt LLC v Photobox Ltd* [2020] E.T.M.R. 35 at [59]–[77].

*Replace item "(6)":* **20-136**

*Examples*

(6) Further instances: "Music Corporation" was held not descriptive in the above sense: *Music Corp of America v Music Corp (Great Britain)*[532]; "Computervision" for electronic equipment: *Computervision v Computer Vision*[533]; and "Midland Dairies" for an ice-cream business: *Midland Counties v Midland.*[534] "Cool Foods" was held too close to "Chill Foods", although one was wholesale and the other retail: *Chill Foods (Scotland) Ltd v Cool Foods Ltd.*[535] But injunctions have been refused on "Self Drive" (*Drive Yourself v Parish*[536]); "*Credit Management*"[537] and "Tape Recorder Centre" (*Sylpha v Tape Recorders,*[538] one wholesale and the other retail). Injunctions were refused in *Salaried Persons Post Loans v Postal and*

*Salaried Loans of Glasgow*[539] and in *Premier Motor Co v Premier Driving School*[540]). In *Technical Productions v Contemporary Exhibitions*[541] the court refused an interlocutory injunction to restrain the defendants holding an exhibition with a title including "refrigeration" at about the same time as and at a nearby hall to the plaintiffs'. An interlocutory injunction was refused in *Coral Index v Regent Index*[542] because the only similarity between the parties' names was the word "Index" which was descriptive of their businesses of accepting wagers on the Financial Times Share Index; a final injunction was refused in *Industrial Furnaces v Reaves*[543] (addition of "Reaves" to the descriptive words "Industrial Furnaces" a "sufficient difference to avert confusion"); an interlocutory injunction was refused in *Pet Library v Ellson*[544] ("Ellson's Pet Library", a "plain case"); an interlocutory injunction was refused in *Park Court Hotel v Trans-World*[545] ("Hotel International" and "London International Hotel"); and an interlocutory injunction was refused in *County Sound v Ocean Sound*[546] ("The Gold A.M."—too descriptive, not long enough use), referring to *McCain International v Country Fair*[547] ("Oven Chips"). It is of course helpful to a defendant if there are differences in field of activity and if the customers are businesses likely to be clear who they are dealing with, as in "*Credit Management*", above. The addition of the term "British" to the mark "Asian Achievers Awards" did not serve to distinguish the defendant's services: *Asian Business Publications Ltd v British Asian Achievers Awards Ltd.*[547a]

[532] (1947) 64 R.P.C. 41.

[533] [1975] R.P.C. 171.

[534] (1948) 65 R.P.C. 429.

[535] : [1977] R.P.C. 522, (O.H., Scotland).

[536] [1957] R.P.C. 307.

[537] [1961] R.P.C. 157.

[538] [1961]) R.P.C. 27.

[539] [1966] R.P.C. 24 (Scotland).

[540] [1962] R.P.C. 222.

[541] [1961] R.P.C. 242.

[542] [1970] R.P.C. 147.

[543] [1970] R.P.C. 605 at 625.

[544] [1968] F.S.R. 359.

[545] [1970] F.S.R. 89.

[546] [1991] F.S.R. 367.

[547] [1981] R.P.C. 69.

[547a] [2019] EWHC 1094 (IPEC).

## Author's or Artist's Name or Nom-de-Plume

*Replace paragraph:*

**20-155** A cartoonist may sue upon the use by a rival cartoonist of a confusingly similar signature,[600] or an actor to protect their stage name.[601] A nom-de-plume or stage name prima facie belongs to the author or performer and is considered to be their stock-in-trade.[602] Disputes as to the ownership of a nom-de-plume or stage name, however, normally arise as between author and publisher or performer and promoter; and such disputes have in practice been treated as pure questions of contractual right as between the parties, without regard to the considerations peculiar to disputes over a trade mark.[603] Further, it has been held that the writer of a work can maintain an action against the owner of the copyright for the damage occasioned to their reputation by the publication of a new edition of the book, purporting to be prepared by them, but in fact not so prepared.[604]

600 *Marengo v Daily Sketch* (1948) 65 R.P.C. 242 HL ("Kern" and "Kim").

601 *Hines v Winnick* [1947] Ch. 708; 64 R.P.C. 113 ("*Dr. Crock and his Crackpots*"). Although pleaded as a case of passing off one musical sketch for another, the case was decided as one in which to the public the claimant himself was "Dr. Crock".

602 *Landa v Greenberg* (1908) 24 T.L.R. 441 ("*Aunt Naomi*"); referred to in *Modern Fiction v Fawsett* (1949) 66 R.P.C. 230 at 248 ("*Ben Sarto*"); *Forbes v Kemsley Newspapers* (1951) 68 R.P.C. 183 ("*Mary Delane*"); and *Shua Ltd v Camp & Furnace Ltd* [2020] EWHC 687 (Ch) ("Bongo's Bingo").

603 There is always a tendency for disputes as to the ownership of a mark or of goodwill to be decided purely in terms of rights inter partes: see, e.g. *Manus v Fullwood & Bland* (1949) 66 R.P.C. 71 CA (dispute between manufacturer and agent); *"Oranje" v Kuys* [1973] 1 W.L.R. 1126 (PC, New Zealand: Ownership of newspaper title). But the decisions on noms-de-plume seem to show no recognition that the subject of the dispute is of the nature of a trade mark at all.

604 *Archbold v Sweet* (1832) 1 M. & R. 162; 5 C. & P. 219. In *Lee v Gibbings* (1892) 66 L.T. 263, the question was one of libel; interim injunction refused.

## 8. IMITATION OF GET-UP

*Add to the end of the paragraph:*

The distinction between recognition of a feature such as colour or shape as being a characteristic of a particular product or even that feature bringing to mind the brand with from which such products have in the past originated, and requirement that the feature function as a badge of origin is as applicable in the field of passing off as it is in respect of registered trade marks.[673a] **20-164**

673a *Glaxo Wellcome UK Ltd v Sandoz Ltd* [2019] EWHC 2545 (Ch) at [170]–[173], referring to the dicta of Kitchin LJ in *Société des Produits Nestlé SA v Cadbury UK Ltd* [2017] F.S.R. 34 at [77] and [78].

*After item "(4)", add:* **20-165**

*Examples*

(5) The claimant alleged that the use by the defendant of the colour purple on medicinal inhalers in competition with the claimant's products amounted to a misrepresentation, both as to the trade origin of the defendant's product and that the product was equivalent to that of the claimant. The claimant failed to establish that medical professionals or consumers relied on the colour purple as indicating origin or that the use of purple by the defendant constituted a misrepresentation as to equivalence. The claim failed.[683a]

683a *Glaxo Wellcome UK Ltd v Sandoz Ltd* [2019] EWHC 2545 (Ch).

### Claimant Must Prove Reputation

*Add to the end of the paragraph:*

The claimant must establish that the relevant public rely on the get-up in issue as denoting origin. It is not enough to show that the public recognise the goods of that get-up as originating from the claimant or even that the get-up calls the claimant's brand to mind.[698a] **20-170**

698a *Glaxo Wellcome UK Ltd v Sandoz Ltd* [2019] EWHC 2545 (Ch) at [173].

## 9. Assessment and Proof of Likelihood of Deception

### Colour

*Add to the end of the paragraph:*

**20-210** However, where a claimant relies on the use of colour alone as amounting to a misrepresentation they must demonstrate that the colour serves as a badge of origin rather than merely being recognised as being a feature of the claimant's get-up. Recognition and association with the claimant is not enough.[819a]

[819a] *Glaxo Wellcome UK Ltd v Sandoz Ltd* [2019] EWHC 2545 (Ch); see analysis at [165]–[173].

### Fraudulent Intention

*Replace paragraph:*

**20-216** The existence of unexpected and unexplained similarities[836] between the goods of the defendant and those of the claimant, or of similarities which have been modified by colourable differences[837] or by differences and distinctions so arranged as to escape notice[838]; the use by the defendant of descriptions, which, as applied to themselves or their own trade, are inaccurate, and by reason of their inaccuracy approach more nearly to the proper description of the claimant,[839] and the gradual approximation of the defendant's names, get-up or description to those of the claimant,[840] are all obvious badges of fraudulent intention frequently recurring in the cases which come before the court. Although a deliberate intention to deceive may be to support the contention that deception is likely to occur, evidence that a defendant was aware of a risk of deception without intending it may support either claimant or defendant, depending on the surrounding circumstances. Proof that a defendant proceeded recklessly without taking care to avoid such risk may to support the contention that deception was likely even if not intended. Conversely, proof that the defendant was aware of a risk of deception but took what they considered were sufficient steps to avoid it may support the conclusion that deception was not likely.[840a] Further, awareness on the part of the defendant that the claimant may bring proceedings is not the same as awareness of risk of deception. Care must also be taken to distinguish between a legitimate desire to copy the claimant's business model or products, and an illegitimate intent to falsely represent a connection with the claimant.[840b]

[836] per Earl Loreburn in *Claudius Ash v Invicta* (1912) 29 R.P.C. 465 at 475; neither fraud nor probability of deception was proved.

[837] *Slazenger v Feltham* (1889) 6 R.P.C. 531 CA ("Demon", "Demotic").

[838] e.g. "late of", etc. in small letters, para.20-122.

[839] *Holloway v Holloway* (1850) 13 Beav 209. And see *Middlemas v Molivar* (1921) 38 R.P.C. 97 (mark used by defendant not quite his original name, let alone the name he usually used); also see paras 20-113 to 20-115, and cases there cited.

[840] *Boulnois v Peake* (1868) 13 Ch D. 521 n., "Carriage Repository" changed to "New Carriage Bazaar"; *Apollinaris v Herrfeldt* (1887) 4 R.P.C. 478 CA ("*Apollinis*"); *Sanitas v Condy* (1886) 4 R.P.C. 195 and 530, 56 L.T. 621 ("*Condi-Sanitas*"). Lord Macnaghten in the "*Camel Hair Belting* " case (1896) 13 R.P.C. 218 at 233. See also *Colman v Farrow* (1898) 15 R.P.C. 198.

[840a] *Glaxo Wellcome UK Ltd v Sandoz Ltd* [2019] EWHC 2545 (Ch) at [188]–[189].

[840b] *PlanetArt LLC v Photobox Ltd* [2020] E.T.M.R. 35 at [79].

## Enabling Passing Off by Others

*Replace paragraph:*

It used to be thought[845] that the tort of passing off is complete only when decep- **20-218**
tive goods are sold to a middleman. However, it was held in *BT v One in a Million* that the tort is committed where a defendant has equipped themselves or intends to equip another with an instrument of fraud, even though such cases are probably mere quia timet actions.[846] The defendants were so-called cybersquatters who registered Internet domain names such as marksandspencer.com, comprising the names of well-known companies. The Internet domain names themselves were held by the Court of Appeal to be instruments of fraud: *BT v One in a Million.*[847] Cybersquatting is not of itself a comprehensive basis for an allegation of passing off, however. The claimant must establish the relevant reputation and goodwill in the mark relied upon.[847a] The goods in question must be inherently deceptive however. An "instrument of deception" or "instrument of fraud" is an article or product which is so inherently deceptive that its existence on the marketplace constitutes an actionable passing off. In effect an instrument of deception is a misrepresentation waiting to happen, which only needs to be exposed to the ultimate consumer for the tort of passing of to be complete. Jacob LJ summarised the position with admirable succinctness as follows in *L'Oréal v Bellure*[848]:

> "If what is complained of does not inherently tell a lie, it is not an instrument of deception in itself. If it does tell a lie, it is no answer to say, as in effect the defendants in [*BT v One in a Million* and other authorities] were arguing 'but there may be circumstances where the lie will not in fact be understood as such'."

[845] Based on *My Kinda Town v Soil* [1983] R.P.C. 15 at 49, where the judge cited a number of cases, in particular *Edelsten v Edelsten* (1863) 1 De G, J. & S. 185. (*My Kinda Town*, the "Chicago Pizza" case, was overruled by the Court of Appeal, but on another point: [1983] R.P.C. 407).

[846] *BT v One in a Million* [1999] 1 W.L.R. 903 CA at 920, per Aldous LJ. See also at 915–920 for his analysis of the cases.

[847] [1999] 1 W.L.R. 903. "Whether any name is an instrument of fraud will depend upon all the circumstances. A name which will, by reason of its similarity to the name of another, inherently lead to passing off, is such an instrument. If a name would not inherently lead to passing off, it does not follow that it is hot an instrument of fraud. The court should consider the similarity of the names, the intention of the; defendant, the type of trade and all the surrounding circumstances. If it be the intention of the defendant to appropriate the goodwill of another or enable others to do so, I can see no reason why the court should not infer that it will happen, even if there is a possibility that such an appropriation would not take place": Aldous LJ at 920.

[847a] *Media Agency Group Ltd v Space Media Agency Ltd* [2019] EWCA Civ 712; [2019] F.S.R. 27.

[848] [2007] E.T.M.R. EWCA Civ 968; [2008] E.T.M.R 1 at [132].

CHAPTER 21

# TRADE LIBEL AND THREATS

TABLE OF CONTENTS



8. THREATS

## Background to the Provisions

*Replace paragraph:*

**21-099** It has been recognised for many years that threats of proceedings for infringement of intellectual property rights may be extremely pernicious. Some of the reasons for this are considered above.[106] As a result, a statutory cause of action for threats of patent infringement was introduced: now found in the Patents Act 1977 s.70. There were parallel provisions in respect of registered and unregistered designs: the Registered Designs Act 1949 s.26 and the Copyright, Designs and Patents Act 1988 s.253. The 1994 Act introduced a provision making threats of trade mark infringement proceedings actionable. All of these threats provisions have now been amended into a common format by the Intellectual Property (Unjustified Threats) Act 2017, an Act which replaced the original Trade Marks Act 1994 s.21 with ss.21–21F. In *W3 Ltd v Easygroup Ltd*,[106a] Arnold J explained the broad rationale behind the old s.21 which seems to apply equally to the new provisions:

> "The rationale behind s.21(1), which creates a right of action which is not dependent upon proof of malice, is to strike a balance between the legitimate interests of the trade mark proprietor in warning infringers and the rights of others not to be vexed by threats which the proprietor is unwilling to translate into actual proceedings. Hence, in broad terms, threats to persons who are the source of infringing goods and services are allowed, but threats to customers are not."

[106] See paras 21-017 to 21-020.

[106a] [2018] EWHC 7, [2019] F.S.R. 16 at [412].

## Construing the Alleged Threat

*Replace paragraph:*

**21-107** Since an alleged threat falls within the genus of "unilateral statements", the Court of Appeal has held that the normal rules as to the interpretation of such statements in contracts, patents and the like apply equally to threats.[110] Previous dicta are consistent: construing an alleged threat is a practical matter, to be decided on the basis of the effect it would have on an ordinary reader, and should not be an exercise in unrealistic forensic analysis.[111] It is a jury-type question to be decided against the appropriate matrix of fact. In *W3 Ltd v Easygroup Ltd*,[111a] the three letters threatened proceedings in respect of the supply of services, exempt under the old s.21(1). Nonetheless, it was alleged that actionable threats had been made because the letters enclosed undertakings or draft Particulars of Claim which went wider in terms of the undertakings or injunctive relief sought—in the usual way. Arnold J held, in each instance, that a reasonable person in the position of the recipient, W3, with knowledge of the relevant circumstances, would not have understood the letters as containing a threat of proceedings for trade mark infringement other than by the supply of services under the sign "EasyRoommate" and variants thereof.

[110] *Best Buy v Worldwide* [2011] EWCA Civ 618 at [18]. The Master of the Rolls indicated that the meaning of any particular passage or unilateral statement was to be determined by reference to what a reasonable person, in the position of the recipient, with knowledge of all relevant circumstances at the time, would have understood the maker of the statement to have intended, when considered in the context of the whole, drawing on *Mannai Investment Co Ltd v Eagle Star Assurance* [1997] UKHL 19, [1997] A.C. 749 at 775–780; *Investors Compensation Scheme v West Bromwich Building Society* [1997] UKHL 28, [1998] 1 W.L.R. 896 at 912–913; *Kirin-Amgen Ltd v Hoechst Marion Roussel Ltd* [2004] UKHL 46, [2005] 1 All E.R. 667 at [27]–[34]; and *Chartbrook Ltd v Persimmon Homes Ltd* [2009] UKHL 38, [2009] 1 A.C. 1100 at [14].

[111] *Brain v Ingledew Brown Bennison & Garrett (No.3)* [1997] F.S.R. 511; *L'Oréal v Johnson & Johnson* [2000] F.S.R. 686.

[111a] [2018] EWHC 7, [2019] F.S.R. 16 at [414]–[421].

## Effect of Issuing Proceedings Before Making Threat

*Replace paragraph:*

As before, it is not actionable as a threat to report the mere existence of proceedings, subject to the comments above about the risk of malicious falsehood and contempt of court.[155] However, it appears that the mere fact that proceedings are in existence may not avoid liability for the making of a threat. In *Lifestyle Equities CV v Royal County of Berkshire Polo Club*,[155a] the claimant applied for summary judgment dismissing the counterclaim for threats on the basis that when the letters containing the threats were sent, the proceedings had already been issued. Morgan J declined to award summary judgment since it was held and accepted that the letters in question contained a "threat of infringement proceedings" but also because nothing in s.21 (as amended in 2017) took the letters out of that definition if, as a matter of fact, there were in existence proceedings which had been issued. The judge discussed (at [100]) some arguments addressed to the "hypothetical" situation where the recipient knew that proceedings had already been issued, and concluded that it might be arguable that a threat of future proceedings in the communication might be disregarded by such a recipient. **21-140**

[155] See, e.g. *Carl Zeiss Stiftung v Rayner & Keeler* [1961] R.P.C. 1; *Easipower v Gordon Moore* [1963] R.P.C. 8.

[155a] [2018] EWHC 3552, [2019] F.S.R. 14.

*Add new paragraph:*

Although this issue may raise a difficult question of interpretation of the legislation, its significance may be more theoretical than practical. For example, if the communication in question is circulated to third parties (especially customers or potential customers of the alleged infringer) and causes real damage to the business of the alleged infringer, and if the threat is shown to be unjustified, it seems **21-140A** unlikely that the fact that proceedings had already been issued when the communication was sent should save the sender from liability for unjustified threats.

Chapter 22

# CIVIL PROCEEDINGS FOR TRADE MARK INFRINGEMENT AND PASSING OFF

Table of Contents



## 2. Statutory Action for Trade Mark Infringement

### Effects of s.2(2)

*Replace footnote 3:*

[3] *Inter Lotto v Camelot Group* [2004] R.P.C. 9 CA. See also *Lumos Skincare Ltd v Sweet Squared Ltd* [2013] EWCA Civ 671 at [4]. See also *Pinterest Inc v Premium Interest Ltd* [2015] F.S.R. 27 at [32]–[38] where it was held in relation to a registered EUTM that the registration of a EUTM does not provide a defence to a claim for passing off. These cases were also referred to and applied by the Court of Appeal in *R. (on the application of British American Tobacco UK Ltd) v Secretary of State for Health* [2016] EWCA Civ 1182 at [47]–[48]. **22-005**

## 3. The Claimant's Title—Infringement of Registered Trade Marks

### Licensees Without Their Own Right of Action

*Replace paragraph:*

Unless the right is excluded by the agreement(s) from which they derive their **22-022** licence, an exclusive licensee may, under s.30(2) call upon the proprietor to take infringement proceedings in respect of any matter "which affects his interests".[25] If the proprietor refuses to bring proceedings, or fails to do so within two months after being called upon, then the exclusive licensee may bring proceedings in their own name as if they were the proprietor.[26] As with s.31(4) and (5), s.30(4) and (5) provide that the proprietor must be joined as a party unless the court permits otherwise, but that that requirement is not to affect the granting of interim relief, and that the proprietor is not liable for costs if they do not take part in the proceedings. Non-exclusive licences may only bring proceedings for infringement of the registered trade mark with the consent of the proprietor, except so far as the licence provides otherwise.[26a] Further, where the proprietor of a registered trade mark brings infringement proceedings, a licensee who has suffered loss is entitled to intervene in the proceedings for the purpose of obtaining compensation for that loss.[26b]

[25] The scope of this term is considered in Ch.15.

[26] s.30(3).

[26a] Trade Marks Act 1994 s.30(1A), as amended by the Trade Marks Regulations (SI 2018/825) as part of the implementation of 2015 Directive, specifically reg.17(2).

[26b] Trade Marks Act 1994 s.30(6A), as amended by the Trade Marks Regulations (SI 2018/825) as part of the implementation of 2015 Directive, specifically reg.17(6).

*After "Section 30 is unclear as to the remedies which a licensee may obtain if successful in an action brought under s.30, and a particular question appears to arise over their right to recover damages. On the one hand, the section provides for the", add:*

**22-023** exclusive

*Replace paragraph:*

**22-024** Since it is plainly envisaged that damages may be recovered by the proprietor to reflect loss to a licensee (as a result of s.30(6)), and since it is envisaged that sums recovered as a result should be held for and pass to the licensee, it is clear that there is no intention in s.30 to exclude such persons from recovering financial relief altogether. Hence the better view probably is that a licensee can recover damages under s.30. It is unsatisfactory, however, that this does not explain the differences between ss.30 and 31 referred to above. A further possibility is that a licensee may recover damages as a result of s.30, but only through the medium of the proprietor (who will usually also be a party under s.30(4)).

## 6. Service Out of the Jurisdiction

### Service Out of the Jurisdiction Without Permission

*Replace footnote 67:*

**22-039** [67] Council Regulation 1215/2012 replaces Council Regulation 44/2001 and became applicable from 1 January 2015 to any proceedings instituted in an EU court on or before 10 January 2015 (see art.66). It should be noted that for a period Council Regulation 44/2001 applied to all EU Member States apart from Denmark but following an agreement between the EU and Denmark in 2005 the relevant Regulation does now apply to Denmark. Council Regulation 44/2001 superseded the Brussels Convention which was entered into by Member States of the EU and was enacted into UK law by the Civil Jurisdiction and Judgments Act 1982 "the 1982 Act". The 1988 and 2007 Lugano Conventions (which are closely modelled on the Brussels Convention and Council Regulation 44/2001) apply to all states belonging to the European Free Trade Association which includes EU Member States and Norway, Switzerland

and Iceland. The 2007 Lugano Convention came into force in the EU and Norway on 1 January 2010. The Lugano Conventions are enacted into UK law by the Civil Jurisdiction and Judgments Act 1991 and the Civil Jurisdiction and Judgment Regulations 2009 (SI 2009/3131), which came into force on 1 January 2010 and which, amongst other things makes the necessary amendments the 1982 Act. The 2007 Lugano Convention is not affected by Council Regulation 1215/2012 (see art.73(1)). As of 31 December 2020 at 23.00, the Implementation Period completion day, or IP completion day, Regulation 1215/2012 will be repealed by virtue of reg.89 of the Civil Jurisdiction and Judgments (Amendment) (EU Exit) Regulations (SI 2019/479). See also s.39(1) and Sch.5, para.1 of the European Union (Withdrawal Agreement) Act 2020. Regulations 92–94 of Regulations 2019/479 provide some transitional provisions with regard to ongoing litigation which had not been concluded before the IP completion day and to which Regulation 1215/2012 applies.

*Replace paragraph:*

The basic rule of Regulation 1215/2012 is that defendants should be sued in the courts where they are domiciled.[69] However, in cases concerning tort, a defendant may also be sued, if desired, in the courts of the state where the harmful act occurred.[70] Hence in the case of infringements committed in this jurisdiction, proceedings may be served without leave on a defendant domiciled in a state to which r.6.33(2)[71] applies. Where a claimant intends to serve a claim form under rr.6.32 and 6.33 of the CPR, the claimant must file a notice containing a statement of the grounds on which the claimant is entitled to serve the claim form out of the jurisdiction and serve a copy of that notice with the claim form.[72] **22-041**

[69] Regulation 1215/2012 art.4. Also see art.2 of Regulation 44/2001, and art.2 of the Brussels Convention. As of 31 December 2020 at 23.00, the Implementation Period completion Day, or IP completion day, Regulation 1215/2012 and Regulation 44/2001 will be repealed by virtue of reg.89 and reg.84 respectively of the Civil Jurisdiction and Judgments (Amendment) (EU Exit) Regulations (SI 2019/479). See also s.39 (1) and Sch.5, para.1 of the European Union (Withdrawal Agreement) Act 2020. Regulations 92–94 of Regulation 2019/479 provide some transitional provisions with regard to ongoing litigation which had not been concluded before the IP Completion day and to which Regulation 1215/2012 applies.

[70] Regulation 1215/2012 art 7(2). Also see art.5(3) of Regulation 44/2001 and art.5(3) of the Brussels Convention. This has been interpreted by the ECJ to allow a defendant to be sued either where the tortious act was committed or where the damage which it caused was suffered: *Handelskwerkerij v Mines de Potasses d'Alsace* [1976] E.C.R. 1735. As of 31 December 2020 at 23.00, the Implementation Period completion day, or IP completion day, Regulation 1215/2012 and Regulation 44/2001 will be repealed by virtue of reg.89 and reg.84 respectively of the Civil Jurisdiction and Judgments (Amendment) (EU Exit) Regulations (SI 2019/479). See also s.39 (1) and Sch.5, para.1 of the European Union (Withdrawal Agreement) Act 2020. Regulations 92–94 of Regulation 2019/479 provide some transitional provisions with regard to ongoing litigation which had not been concluded before the IP completion day and to which Regulation 1215/2012 applies.

[71] See fn.68 for CPR rules concerning service out of the jurisdiction without leave concerning enactments other than Regulation 1215/2012.

[72] See r.6.34 of the CPR. The current form for this notice is Civil Procedure Form N510.

*Add new paragraph:*

It should be noted that as of 31 December 2020 at 23.00, the Implementation Period completion day, or IP completion day, Regulation 1215/2012 and Regulation 44/2001 will be repealed by virtue of r.89 and r.84 respectively of the Civil Jurisdiction and Judgments (Amendment) (EU Exit) Regulations 2019/479. The Civil Procedure Rules 1998 (Amendment) (EU Exit) Regulations 2019 (SI 2019/521) ("CPR Regulations"), which are dated 7 March 2019, will make extensive amendments to a number of Parts within the Civil Procedure Rules ("CPR"). The effect of the CPR Regulations, which will come into force at the end of the transition period (31 December 2020),[72a] is to remove the various provisions in the CPR which relate to the courts' powers and processes under the EU instruments which will no longer be available or applicable if no further agreement is reached between **22-041A** the EU and the UK. For example, the CPR Regulations will amend CPR r.6 extensively, including extensive changes to the parts concerning service out of the jurisdiction. These amendments can be found at r.4 of the CPR Regulations, "Amendment to Part 6". For example, there are omitted provisions relating to litigants providing as an address for service the address of a European lawyer in a EEA state (which fall away on Exit).

[72a] See s.39(1) and Sch.5 para.1 of the European Union (Withdrawal Agreement) Act 2020.

## Service Out With the Permission of the Court

*Add new paragraph:*

22-042A As of 31 December 2020, at 23.00, the Implementation Period Completion Day, or IP Completion Day, Regulation 1215/2012 will be repealed by virtue of r.89 of the Civil Jurisdiction and Judgments (Amendment) (EU Exit) Regulations (SI 2019/479).[74a] Regulations 92–94 of (SI 2019/479) provide some transitional provisions with regard to ongoing litigation which had not been concluded before the IP completion date and to which Regulation 1215/2012 applies. The Civil Jurisdiction and Judgments (Amendment) (EU Exit) Regulations 2019/479 will also make extensive amendments to the Civil Jurisdiction and Judgments Act 1982. It is unclear what, if any, agreements will be reached between the EU and the UK with regards cross border litigation and recognition and enforcement of foreign judgments. These issues will be resolved during the ongoing negotiation process. On the basis of the current legislation, certain EU Regulations concerning the laws applicable to certain disputes which have been retained in UK law by virtue of the European Union Withdrawal Act 2018 and the European Union (Withdrawal Agreement) Act 2020 will be further amended on the IP Completion Day. For example, this will occur in relation to the Rome I Regulation (Regulation (EC) 593/2008 on the law applicable to contractual obligations) and the Rome II Regulation (Regulation (EC) 864/2007 on the law applicable to non-contractual obligations) which are retained UK law but will also be amended by Pt 4 of the Law Applicable to Contractual Obligations and Non-Contractual Obligations (Amendment etc.) (EU Exit) Regulations 2019 (SI 2019/834), which will take effect upon the expiry of the transition period, namely 31 December 2020 at 23.00 the IP Completion Day. For further information on this topic the reader is invited to consult the appropriate specialist text. The following paragraphs in Section 7 are concerned with the current state of the law as exists before the IP Completion Day. For the transitional provisions concerning pending proceedings in the UK concerning EUTMs (where the UK court was acting as an EU Trade Mark Court) as at the IP Completion Day, see paras 22-90A and 22-90B.

[74a] See also s.39(1) and Sch.5 para.1 of the European Union (Withdrawal Agreement) Act 2020.

### 7. JURISDICTION OVER FOREIGN TRADE MARKS

## Courts Trying Infringement of Foreign Trade Marks

*At the end of the first sentence, add new footnote 74b:*

22-043 [74b] As of 31 December 2020, at 23.00, the Implementation Period Completion Day, or IP Completion Day, Regulation 1215/2012 will be repealed by virtue of the Civil Jurisdiction and Judgments (Amendment) (EU Exit) Regulations (SI 2019/479) r.89. See also s.39 (1) and Sch.5 para.1 of the European Union (Withdrawal Agreement) Act 2020. Regulations 92–94 of (SI 2019/479) provide some transitional provisions with regard to ongoing litigation which had not been concluded before the IP completion day and to which Regulation 1215/2012 applies.

*After "regardless of domicile and overriding the provisions of art.7.", add new footnote 81a:*

[81a] As of 31 December 2020 at 23.00, the Implementation Period completion day, or IP completion day, Regulation 1215/2012 and Regulation 44/2001 will be repealed by virtue of r.89 and r.84 respectively of the Civil Jurisdiction and Judgments (Amendment) (EU Exit) Regulations 2019/479. See also s.39 (1) and Sch.5 para.1 of the European Union (Withdrawal Agreement) Act 2020. Regulations 92–94 of (SI 2019/479) provide some transitional provisions with regard to ongoing litigation which had not been concluded before the IP completion day and to which Regulation 1215/2012 applies. **22-045**

*Replace paragraph:*

A separate issue arises in relation to jurisdiction over EU trade marks which is governed by arts 123-126 of the codified 2017 EUTMR, Regulation 2017/1001.[91] The general rule under art.125(1)[92] of the 2017 EUTMR is that actions should be heard in the EU Member State in which the defendant is domiciled. A relevant exception is provided for at art.125(5)[93] which states that proceedings in respect of actions listed in art.124,[94] (including actions for infringement and invalidity, with the exception of actions for a declaration of non-infringement of an EU trade mark), may also be brought in the courts of the Member State "in which the act of infringement has been committed or threatened". The CJEU in *Coty Germany GmbH v First Note Perfumes NV*[95] held that the concept referred to in that provision of "the Member State in which the act of infringement has been committed or threatened", must be interpreted independently of the concept of "the place where the harmful event occurred or may occur" referred to in art.5(3) of Regulation No.44/2001 (currently art.7(3) of Regulation 1215/2015)[95a] The CJEU went on to state that the wording of art.97(5)[96] implies that that "linking factor relates to active conduct on the part of the person causing that infringement. ... Consequently, jurisdiction ... may be established solely in favour of Community trade mark courts in the Member State in which the defendant committed the alleged unlawful act."[97]*Coty* was considered further and applied in *AMS Neve Ltd v Heritage Audio SL.*[98] This was an IPEC case where the claimant, AMS Neve, a manufacturer of audio equipment whose products include the well-known "1073" microphone pre-amplifier brought proceedings in the IPEC for, inter alia, trade mark infringement of its EU trade mark against a Spanish company Heritage, who had started producing a similar product under the brand "1073" and advertised it on its website. Heritage challenged the English courts' jurisdiction to hear inter alia the EUTM claim, on the basis that Heritage was established in Spain and that all of the alleged acts of infringement had occurred in Spain The court held that the place where the act of putting the sign on the website, and not the place where the event of display of the sign on the website occurred, would have jurisdiction over the EUTM claim which, in that case, was Spain.[99] AMS Neve appealed the judgment to the Court of Appeal which in turn stayed the proceedings and referred questions to the CJEU on the proper interpretation of art.97(5) of Regulation 207/2009 (art.125(1) of the 2017 EUTMR).[99a] The Court of Appeal indicated in its judgment, given when making the reference to the CJEU, that the first instance judgment did not necessarily follow from the CJEU decision in *Coty* and the Court of Appeal expressed doubts as to whether the first instance decision was correct. The Court of Appeal referred various questions to the CJEU in particular: "in circumstances where an undertaking is established and domiciled in member state A and has taken steps in that territory to advertise and offer for sale goods under a sign identical to an EU trade mark on a website targeted **22-049** at traders and consumers in member state B, (i) does the EU trade mark court in member state B have jurisdiction to hear a claim for infringement of the EU trade mark in respect of the advertisement and offer for sale of the goods in that territory [i.e. member state B]". The CJEU in its judgment[99b] inter alia held that:

> "Article 97(5) of Council Regulation (EC) 207/2009 of 26 February 2009 on the [European Union] trade mark must be interpreted as meaning that the proprietor of a European Union trade mark who considers that his rights have been infringed by the use without his consent, by a third party, of a sign identical to that mark in advertising and offers for sale displayed electronically in relation to products that are identical or similar to the goods for which that mark is registered, may bring an infringement action against that third party before a European Union trade mark court of the Member State within which the consumers or traders to whom that advertising and those offers for sale are directed are located, notwithstanding that that third party took decisions and steps in another Member State to bring about that electronic display."

Therefore, the first instance judgment in this case does appear to have been wrongly made. For the transitional provisions concerning pending proceedings in the UK concerning EUTMs (where the UK court was acting as a EU Trade Mark court) as at the IP completion day, see paras 22-90A and 22-90B.

[91] The 2009 EUTMR, following its substantive amendment has been repealed and replaced by the codified Regulation 2017/1001 of the European Parliament and of the Council of 14 June 2017 on the EU Trade Mark ("the 2017 EUTMR"), which applies from 1 October 2017 (see art.212 of the 2017 EUTMR). The Article numbering in the 2017 EUTMR is somewhat different to that used in the 2009 EUTMR and in this chapter we identify both Article numbers in these two different EUTMRs where appropriate. Articles 123–126 of the 2017 EUTMR were Articles 95–98 of the 2009 EUTMR. Note that at 31 December 2020 at 23.00, the Implementation Period completion day, or IP completion day, all EUTMs will no longer cover the UK but a comparable trade mark (EU) for all existing EUTMs will come into existence for the UK. The 2017 EUTMR will be repealed by the Trade Marks (Amendment etc.) (EU Exit) Regulation 2019/269 on the IP Completion day as set out within the European Union (Withdrawal Agreement) Act 2020, see Sch.5 para.1. For the transitional provisions concerning pending proceedings in the UK concerning EUTMs (where the UK court was acting as a EU Trade Mark court) as at the IP Completion Day, see paras 22-90A and 22-90B.

[92] art.125(1) of the 2017 EUTMR.

[93] art.125(5) of the 2017 EUTMR.

[94] art.124 of the 2017 EUTMR.

[95] (C-360/12) [2014] E.T.M.R. 49

[95a] As of 31 December 2020, at 23.00, the Implementation Period completion day, or IP completion day, Regulation 1215/2012 and Regulation 44/2001 will be repealed by virtue of r.89 and r.84 respectively of the Civil Jurisdiction and Judgments (Amendment) (EU Exit) Regulations (SI 2019/479). See also s.39(1) and Sch.5 para.1 of the European Union (Withdrawal Agreement) Act 2020. Regulations 92–94 of (SI 2019/479) provide some transitional provisions with regard to ongoing litigation which had not been concluded before the IP completion day and to which Regulation 1215/2012 applies.

[96] art.125(5) of the 2017 EUTMR.

[97] See *Coty Germany GmbH v First Note Perfumes NV* (C-360/12) [2014] E.T.M.R. 49 at [35]–[37].

[98] [2016] EWHC 2563 (IPEC).

[99] See in particular *AMS Neve Ltd v Heritage Audio SL* [2016] EWHC 2563 (IPEC) at [65]–[69].

[99a] *AMS Neve Ltd v Heritage Audio SL* [2018] EWCA Civ 86; F.S.R. [2018] 23.

[99b] *AMS Neve Ltd v Heritage Audio SL* (C-172/18) [2019] F.S.R. 40.

## Passing Off Abroad

*Replace paragraph:*

Passing off is a tort, and passing off which has taken place abroad may be sued for in England, subject to the defendant being a person over whom the English court can and will exercise jurisdiction. Formerly, it was necessary to satisfy the double actionability rule,[100] but that was changed by ss.10–12 of the Private International Law (Miscellaneous Provisions) Act 1995.[101] Since 11 January 2009, the Rome II Regulation[102] has been in force and, from this time if the English court has jurisdiction over the dispute, the applicable law relating to passing off which has taken place abroad will fall to be determined under the Rome II Regulation.[103] **22-050**

[100] i.e. that the acts complained of would be passing off if committed in the UK and would be actionable in the country where they were committed. See, e.g. *Walker v Ost* [1970] R.P.C. 489 at 509. See also para.22-044 and notes therein.

[101] Since 11 January 2009, Pt III of the 1995 Act (which includes ss.10–12) has been disapplied in cases where rules in the Rome II Regulation apply.

[102] Regulation 864/2007 of the European Parliament and of the Council of 11 July 2007 on the law applicable to non-contractual obligations (Rome II), which applies to claims in relation to which damage occurred after 11 January 2009, (see art.32) and see fn.89. On the basis of the current legislation, certain EU Regulations concerning the laws applicable to certain disputes which have been retain in UK law by virtue of the European Union Withdrawal Act 2018 and the European Union (Withdrawal Agreement) Act 2020 will be further amended on the IP Completion day. For example, this will occur in relation to the Rome I Regulation (Regulation (EC) 593/2008 on the law applicable to contractual obligations) and the Rome II Regulation (Regulation (EC) 864/2007 on the law applicable to non-contractual obligations) which are retained UK law but will also be amended by Pt 4 of the Law Applicable to Contractual Obligations and Non-Contractual Obligations (Amendment etc.) (EU Exit) Regulations 2019 (SI 2019/834), which will take effect upon the expiry of the transition period, namely 31 December 2020 at 23.00 the IP completion day. See also s.39(1) and Sch.5 para.1 of the European Union (Withdrawal Agreement) Act 2020. For further information on this topic the reader is invited to consult the appropriate specialist text.

[103] art.6. On the basis of the current legislation, certain EU Regulations concerning the laws applicable to certain disputes which have been retained in UK law by virtue of the European Union Withdrawal Act 2018 and the European Union (Withdrawal Agreement) Act 2020 will be further amended on the IP completion day. For example, this will occur in relation to the Rome I Regulation (Regulation (EC) 593/2008 on the law applicable to contractual obligations) and the Rome II Regulation (Regulation (EC) 864/2007 on the law applicable to non-contractual obligations) which are retained UK law but will also be amended by Pt 4 of the Law Applicable to Contractual Obligations and Non-Contractual Obligations (Amendment etc.) (EU Exit) Regulations 2019 (SI 2019/834), which will take effect upon the expiry of the transition period, namely 31 December 2020 at 23.00 the IP Completion Day. See also s.39(1) and Sch.5 para.1 of the European Union (Withdrawal Agreement) Act 2020. For further information on this topic, the reader is invited to consult the appropriate specialist text.

*Replace footnote 105:*

[105] The different status of the tort of passing off was commented on in passing by Jacob LJ in the Court of Appeal in *Lucasfilm v Ainsworth* [2010] F.S.R. 10 when he was reviewing the relevant authorities concerning the court's ability to deal with foreign intellectual property claims. At [158], Jacob LJ referred to the fact that passing off was based on a misrepresentation and referred to a judgment of Tipping J in the New Zealand case *Atkinson Footwear v Hodkinson International Services* (1994) 31 I.P.R. 186. At 190, Tipping J distinguished the New Zealand court's ability to deal with foreign passing off claims from foreign copyright claims on the basis that the tort of passing off was based on a misrepresentation and that the wrong is not so territorially circumscribed as copyright. In any event the Court of Appeal's decision in *Lucasfilm v Ainsworth* [2010] F.S.R. 10 on the issue of justiciability of foreign copyrights in the English courts was overturned by the Supreme Court, see 105–110 of the Supreme Court decision, *Lucasfilm v Ainsworth* [2011] 3 W.L.R. 487 and para.22-044. As of 31 December 2020 at 23.00, the Implementation Period completion day, or IP completion day, Regulation 1215/2012 will be repealed by virtue of r.89 of the Civil Jurisdiction and Judgments (Amendment) (EU Exit) Regulations (SI 2019/479). See also s.39(1) and Sch.5 para.1 of the European Union (Withdrawal Agreement) Act 2020. Regulations 92–94 of (SI 2019/479) provide some transitional provisions with regard to ongoing litigation which had not been concluded before the IP completion day and to which Regulation 1215/2012 applies. **22-051**

## Lis Alibi Pendens: arts 29 and 30 and Forum Conveniens

*Replace paragraph:*

**22-052** Because more than one court may have jurisdiction over the same claim under Regulation 1215/2012 (most commonly, for example, the court of the defendant's domicile under art.4 and the court of the place of the tort under art.7.[105a] The damage may be sustained in yet another state), it is necessary that there should be rules to determine which court should proceed if the same or related claims are sought to be brought in more than one court. Article 29 provides that where the same claim between the same parties is brought in more than one court, the court second seised must decline jurisdiction.[106] Article 30 provides that if related claims are brought in different courts ("related" does not mean that the actions need be identical as to parties or claims. As set out in art.30(3) "related" means that the actions are so closely connected that it is expedient to hear and determine them together to avoid the risk of giving rise to irreconcilable decisions), the court second seised may decline jurisdiction; it has a discretion whether or not to do so. The meaning and scope of art.28 of Regulation 44/2001 (now art.30 of Regulation 1215/2012) was considered by the Court of Appeal in *Research in Motion UK Ltd v Visto Corp*,[107] a case concerned with patent actions in different jurisdictions. Here the Court of Appeal held that under art.28 of Regulation 44/2001 it was open for the court to acknowledge a connection or a risk of inconsistent judgments, but to say that the connection was not sufficiently close or the risk sufficiently great to make the actions related for the purposes of art.28. For another application of the principles applied under arts 29 and 30 (arts 27 and 28 of Regulation 44/2001/arts 21 and 22 of the Brussels Convention), see *Mecklermedia v DC Congress*.[108] Article 30 of Regulation 1215/2012 was considered n the context of an action for passing off and an application for joinder of two German entities in *Glaxo Wellcome UK Ltd v Sandoz Ltd*.[109]

[105a] As of 31 December 2020 at 23.00, the Implementation Period completion day, or IP completion day, Regulation 1215/2012 will be repealed by virtue of r.89 of the Civil Jurisdiction and Judgments (Amendment) (EU Exit) Regulations 2019/479. See also s.39(1) and Sch.5 para.1 of the European Union (Withdrawal Agreement) Act 2020. Regulations 92–94 of (SI 2019/479) provide some transitional provisions with regard to ongoing litigation which had not been concluded before the IP completion day and to which Regulation 1215/2012 applies.

[106] This does not preclude an application for interim relief, however, under art.35. As of 31 December 2020 at 23.00, the Implementation Period completion day, or IP completion day, Regulation 1215/2012 will be repealed by virtue of r.89 of the Civil Jurisdiction and Judgments (Amendment) (EU Exit) Regulations 2019/479. See also s.39(1) and Sch.5 para.1 of the European Union (Withdrawal Agreement) Act 2020. Regulations 92–94 of (SI 2019/479) provide some transitional provisions with regard to ongoing litigation which had not been concluded before the IP completion day and to which Regulation 1215/2012 applies.

[107] [2008] F.S.R. 20. As of 31 December 2020 at 23.00, the Implementation Period completion day, or IP completion day, Regulation 1215/2012 will be repealed by virtue of r.89 of the Civil Jurisdiction and Judgments (Amendment) (EU Exit) Regulations 2019/479. See also s.39(1) and Sch.5 para.1 of the European Union (Withdrawal Agreement) Act 2020. Regulations 92–94 of (SI 2019/479) provide some transitional provisions with regard to ongoing litigation which had not been concluded before the IP completion day and to which Regulation 1215/2012 applies.

[108] [1997] F.S.R. 627. As of 31 December 2020 at 23.00, the Implementation Period completion day, or IP completion day, Regulation 1215/2012 will be repealed by virtue of r.89 of the Civil Jurisdiction and Judgments (Amendment) (EU Exit) Regulations 2019/479. See also s.39 (1) and Sch.5 para.1 of the European Union (Withdrawal Agreement) Act 2020. Regulations 92–94 of (SI 2019/479) provide some transitional provisions with regard to ongoing litigation which had not been concluded before the IP completion day and to which Regulation 1215/2012 applies.

[109] [2016] EWHC 2743 (Ch) at [75]–[82]. This decision has been appealed but not in relation to the art.30 of Regulation 1215/2012 issue. As of 31 December 2020 at 23.00, the Implementation Period completion day, or IP completion day, Regulation 1215/2012 will be repealed by virtue of r.89 of the Civil Jurisdiction and Judgments (Amendment) (EU Exit) Regulations 2019/479. See also s.39(1) and Sch.5 para.1 of the European Union (Withdrawal Agreement) Act 2020. Regulations 92–94 of (SI 2019/479) provide some transitional provisions with regard to ongoing litigation which had not been concluded before the IP completion day and to which Regulation 1215/2012 applies.

## 8. Vicarious and Joint Liability

*Replace footnote 113:*

[113] [2009] E.T.M.R. 53. For other recent intellectual property cases on joint liability, see also *Football Dataco Ltd v Sportradar GmbH, Football Dataco Ltd v Stan James (Abingdon) Ltd* [2013] F.S.R. 30 CA at [89]–[100] (a case concerning database right) and *Twentieth Century Fox Film Corp v Newzbin Ltd* [2010] F.S.R. 21 at [103]–[111] (a case concerning copyright infringement), *Cosmetic Warriors v Amazon.co.uk Ltd* [2014] F.S.R. 31, *Vertical Leisure Ltd v Poleplus Ltd* [2015] EWHC (IPEC), and *Glaxo Wellcome UK Ltd v Sandoz Ltd* [2017] F.S.R. 32 CA. See also *Glaxo Wellcome UK Ltd v Sandoz Ltd* [2019] EWHC 2545 (Ch) at [308]–[315], *Red Bull GmbH v Big Horn UK Ltd* [2020] EWHC 124 (Ch) at [45]–[50], and *Lifestyle Equities CV v Santa Monica Polo Club* [2020] EWHC 688 (Ch). **22-054**

### Directors and Promoters

*Replace footnote 124:*

[124] [2002] F.S.R. 26, and see also the useful summary in the judgment at first instance: [2000] E.M.L.R. 743. For an application of the relevant principles concerning whether a director of a company should be found to be liable for the infringing acts of their company, see the decision of Arnold J in *Boegli-Gravures SA v Darsail-ASP Ltd* [2009] EWHC 2690 (Pat), a patent case, where it was found that the director in question was jointly liable with his company, as he had gone beyond performing his constitutional role. For an application of the relevant principles in a trade mark case see *Geolabs Ltd v Geolaboratories Testing Services Ltd and Vaughan Edwards* [2012] EWPCC 45, where a director of a company was found to be liable both as a joint tortfeasor with the defendant company and also found to be personally liable for authorising the acts of trade mark infringement. See also *Lifestyle Equities CV v Santa Monica Polo Club* [2020] EWHC 688 (Ch) at [24]–[27], [41]–[44] and [45]–[51] and see *Red Bull GmbH v Big Horn UK Ltd* [2020] EWHC 124 (Ch) at [45]–[50]. **22-057**

### Parent and Group Companies

*Replace footnote 127:*

[127] *Crédit Lyonnais* [1998] 1 Lloyd's Rep. 19; *Unilever v Chefaro* [1994] F.S.R. 135. A list of most of the numerous authorities on this topic may be found in *Sepracor v Hoechst Marion Roussel* [1999] F.S.R. 746. For an application of these principles see *Fine & Country Ltd v Okotoks Ltd* [2012] EWHC 2230 at [275]–[284], where it was held that the parent company was jointly liable for the acts of trade mark infringement and passing off with their subsidiary. This point was not reviewed on appeal (see *Fine & Country Ltd v Okotoks Ltd* [2014] F.S.R. 11). See also *Glaxo Wellcome UK Ltd v Sandoz Ltd* [2019] EWHC 2545 (Ch) at [308]–[315] where there was an obiter finding on the facts of that case that, if the claimants' passing off case had succeeded (which the court dismissed in any event), two of the defendant companies were not jointly liable with the other two defendant companies, as there was no evidence of common design. In particular, there was no evidence of involvement with the decision to launch the alleged infringing product in the UK. **22-058**

## 9. Overview of Relief Granted

### Outline of the Types of Relief Available

*Replace paragraph:*

By s.14 of the 1994 Act, all relief is available in an action for infringement of a registered trade mark as is available in respect of any other property right, and the same rule applies to EUTMs but only until 31 December 2020 at 23.00, the Implementation Period completion day, or IP completion day, which marks the end of the Transition or Implementation Period as set out within s.39(1), and Sch.5 para.1 of the European Union (Withdrawal Agreement) Act 2020.[129] The section **22-060** does not appear to suggest that the statutory remedies provided by ss.15–19 replace the remedies available at common law and in equity for invasions of property rights, so it appears that they are concurrent. This is unlikely to be of great practical significance unless there is some formal or procedural difficulty with proceeding by the statutory route, in which case a claimant may wish to rely on their common law and equitable rights.[130]

[129] On 31 December 2020 at 23.00, the Implementation Period completion day, or IP completion day, all EUTMs will no longer cover the UK but a comparable trade mark (EU) derived from all existing EUTMs will come into existence for the UK (see The Trade Marks (Amendment etc.) (EU Exit) Regulations 2019 (SI 2019/269) Sch.1 para.2, insertion of new s.52A into the Trade Marks Act 1994 and Sch.1 para.3, the insertion of new Sch.2A of the Trade Marks Act 1994. With regard to the date of the IP Completion day see s.39(1) and Sch.5 para.1 of the European Union (Withdrawal Agreement) Act 2020. Where there are pending proceedings as at the IP completion day concerning a EUTM, transitional provisions will apply from the IP Completion Day which are found at paras 20 and 21 of new Sch.2A of the 1994 Act, as will be added by the Trade Marks (Amendment etc.) (EU Exit) Regulations 2019 (SI 2019/269) Sch.1 para.3. The current position with regards EUTMs is as follows: Community Trade Mark Regulations 2006 (SI 2006/1027) reg.5(1), i.e. all relief is available in an action for infringement of a European Union Trade Mark as is available in respect of any other property right. Regulation 5(3) provides that ss.15–19 of the Trade Marks Act 1994 apply in relation to EUTMs as they apply to a registered mark. Article 102(1) of the 2009 EUTMR (art.130(1) of the 2017 EUTMR) provides obligations on the EU Trade Mark Court, unless there are special reasons for not doing so, to issue an order prohibiting the defendant from proceeding with the acts which infringed or would infringe the EU Trade Mark. Further, the EU Trade Mark Court shall also take such measures in accordance with its national law as are aimed at ensuring that this prohibition is complied with. Article 102(2) of the 2009 EUTMR (art.130(1) of the 2017 EUTMR) states that EU Trade Mark Court may also apply measures or orders available under the applicable law which it deems appropriate in the circumstances of the case.

[130] 1994 Act s.2(1), states that "...the proprietor of a registered trade mark has the rights and remedies provided by this Act", and it has been suggested that this means that the only remedies available to a proprietor are, as a result, those given by the Act. However, it seems that this cannot be right, if for no other reason than that there is no statutory provision for the grant of an injunction. Moreover, the words of s.2(1) do not suggest that the proprietor has no other rights or remedies.

## Submission of Order to Registrar

*Replace footnote 133:*

**22-063** [133] CPR 63PD paras 21.1–21.5 specifies the obligations placed upon the EU Trade Mark Court and a party counterclaiming for revocation or for a declaration of invalidity of an EU Trade Mark in court proceedings with regards giving notice to the EUIPO of the proceedings. However, at the time of writing these provisions had not been updated to take into account the amendments of Council Regulation 207/2009 on the European Union Trade Mark by Regulation 2015/2424 of the European Parliament and of the Council of 16 December 2015. Therefore reference is made directly to art.100(4) and 100(6) of the 2009 EUTMR (arts 128(4) and 128(6) of the 2017 EUTMR). The relevant part of art.100(4) of the 2009 EUTMR (art.128(4) of the 2017 EUTMR) states that "The EU trade mark court with which a counterclaim for revocation or for a declaration of invalidity of the EU trade mark has been filed shall not proceed with the examination of the counterclaim, until either the interested party or the court has informed the Office of the date on which the counterclaim was filed. The Office shall record that information in the Register...". Article 100(6) of the 2009 EUTMR (art.128(6) of the 2017 EUTMR) states: "Where an EU trade mark court has given a judgment which has become final on a counterclaim for revocation or for a declaration of invalidity of an EU trade mark, a copy of the judgment shall be sent to the Office without delay, either by the court or by any of the parties to the national proceedings. The Office or any other interested party may request information about such transmission. The Office shall mention the judgment in the Register and shall take the necessary measures to comply with its operative part". Regarding pending proceedings as at IP Completion Day, para.20(2) of new Sch.2A of the 1994 Act (as will be inserted by Sch.1 para.3 of the Trade Marks (Amendment etc.) (EU Exit) Regulations 2019 (SI 2019/269) states as follows: "Subject to sub-paragraphs (3) and (4), the provisions contained or referred to in Chapter 10 of the European Union Trade Mark Regulation (with the exception of Articles 128 (2), (4), (6) and (7) and 132) continue to apply to the pending proceedings as if the United Kingdom were still a Member State with effect from [IP Completion Day]". Therefore arts 128(4) and 128(6) of the EUTMR 2017 as previously mentioned in this footnote no longer apply to pending proceedings after 23.00 on 31 December 2020.

## 11. Enforcing Agreed Terms

*Section 11 should be renamed:* 22-067

"FORM OF INJUNCTION".

*Change title of paragraph:* 22-068

**Enforcing Agreed Terms**

### Form of Injunction—Infringement of a Registered Trade Mark

*Replace footnote 154:*

154 The Court of Appeal did so in *Parker-Knoll v Knoll International* [1961] R.P.C. 346, a case decided under the 1938 Act, where s.8 was the relevant provision; see the order, printed at 373. The House of Lords showed no disapproval ([1962] R.P.C. 265 at 278, 283, 287, 288, 292); but Harman LJ disapproved strongly, describing the order as made as a contradiction in terms: [1962] R.P.C. 243 at 256. Section 11(2)(a) of the 1994 Act has now been amended such that the defence to infringement only applies to individual. Section 11(2)(a) now reads as follows "A registered trade mark is not infringed by (a) the use by an individual of his own name and address", this amendment was made by The Trade Marks Regulations SI 2018/825 as part of the implementation of 2015 Directive, specifically art.14(1)(a) of the 2015 Directive which reads: "A trade mark shall not entitle the proprietor to prohibit a third party from using, in the course of trade (a) the name or address of the third party, where that third party is a natural person." 22-073

### Form of Injunction—Passing Off Action

*Replace list item "(2)" with:*

(2) In a dispute between a British company and its former German parent, as to the right to use the mark "Adrema" which formed the main part of each party's name, it was held that the goodwill connected with that mark in the UK belonged to the British company, the plaintiff, exclusively. An injunction was granted restraining the defendant from selling, advertising or offering for sale in the UK any addressing or costing machines or equipment therefore under any name or mark comprising the name or mark "Adrema" or any other name or mark so closely resembling the name or mark "Adrema" as to be calculated to pass-off or enable others to pass-off such machines or equipment as and for the plaintiffs' machines or equipment: *Adrema v Adrema-Werke*,[162] following *Sturtevant Engineering v Sturtevant Mill*.[163] But Upjohn LJ has said: "Perhaps that can be justified on the facts of that case but the general practice is to grant an injunction in the qualified form where the defendant is only using his own name": *Parker-Knoll v Knoll International*.[164] 22-075

162 [1958] R.P.C. 323 at 332.

163 (1936) 53 R.P.C. 430.

164 [1961] R.P.C. 346 at 362. Section 11(2)(a) of the 1994 Act has now been amended such that the defence to infringement only applies to individual. Section 11(2)(a) now reads as follows "A registered trade mark is not infringed by (a) the use by an individual of his own name and address", this amendment was made by the Trade Marks Regulations (SI 2018/825) as part of the implementation of 2015 Directive, specifically art.14(1)(a) of the 2015 Directive which reads: "A trade mark shall not entitle the proprietor to prohibit a third party from using, in the course of trade (a) the name or address of the third party, where that third party is a natural person."

## Mandatory Injunctions; Orders to Change Name

*Replace footnote 195:*

22-082 [195] *Nottingham Building Society v Eurodynamics* [1993] F.S.R. 468, [1995] F.S.R. 605 CA. See also *Frank Industries Pty Ltd v Nike Retail BV* [2018] F.S.R. 24 at [22]–[40] where the Court of Appeal considered an appeal concerning a mandatory interim injunction and as part of that consideration, considered the differences between prohibitory and mandatory interim injunctions. In this case the Court of Appeal admitted fresh evidence on the Appeal. This fresh evidence was concerned with the mandatory part of the injunction originally granted by the court in *Frank Industries UK v Nike Retail UK* [2018] EWHC 424 (IPEC). This evidence had not been filed by the defendant in response to the original injunction application as the defendant was not fully aware that a mandatory injunction was sought by the Claimant at first instance. In light of this fresh evidence the Court of Appeal varied the mandatory part of the injunction originally granted.

*Replace footnote 196:*

22-083 [196] *Sony v Saray* [1983] F.S.R. 302, where it was held that undertakings from the defendants were worthless, and they were ordered to put disclaiming stickers on goods of the claimants sold by them pending trial. It should be noted that Lawton LJ commented at 308 in his judgment as follows: "It was said that if we made an order in those terms we would be issuing a mandatory injunction, which is something this court has jurisdiction to order but which is very seldom ordered. In my judgment, we would not be making a mandatory injunction at all. What we would be doing would be saying that the defendants were not to deal in Sony goods unless they complied with the terms of our order. In other words, it would be a prohibitory order with an 'unless' clause attached to it. I see nothing wrong in any such form of order." See also *British Telecommunications Plc v Planet Telecom Plc* [2002] EWHC 553 (Ch) where the defendants were ordered, as part of an interim injunction concerning the passing off proceedings, to put a disclaimer on certain documents explaining that they had nothing to do with the claimant. In his judgment Patten J, as he then was, when dealing with an argument put to him that granting a mandatory interim injunction was inappropriate referred to the reasoning given by Lawton LJ quoted above and went on to find: "The defendants are merely required to make apparent the true nature of their business. If that requires the imposition of a mandatory injunction, then so be it." See also *Frank Industries Pty Ltd v Nike Retail BV* [2018] F.S.R. 24 at [22]–[40] where the Court of Appeal considered an appeal concerning a mandatory interim injunction and as part of that consideration, considered the differences between prohibitory and mandatory interim injunctions. In this case the Court of Appeal admitted fresh evidence on the Appeal. This fresh evidence was concerned with the mandatory part of the injunction originally granted by the court in *Frank Industries UK v Nike Retail UK* [2018] EWHC 424 (IPEC). This evidence had not been filed by the defendant in response to the original injunction application as the defendant was not fully aware that a mandatory injunction was sought by the claimant at first instance. In light of this fresh evidence the Court of Appeal varied the mandatory part of the injunction originally granted.

## Injunctions Against Intermediaries

*Replace footnote 206:*

22-087 [206] The Court of Appeal confirmed that certain threshold conditions had to be met before an ISP could be made subject to a blocking injunction (see [80]–[99] of the Court of Appeal's judgment). The threshold conditions were: First, the ISPs must be intermediaries within the meaning of the third sentence of art.11. Secondly, either the users or the operators of the website must be infringing the claimant's trade marks. Thirdly, the users or the operators of the website must use the services of the ISPs. Fourthly, the ISPs must have actual knowledge of this. Further, whether or not the blocking injunction/relief should be imposed by the court had to be determined by the application of certain specified principles. These principles were that the relief must: (i) be necessary; (ii) be effective; (iii) be dissuasive; (iv) not be unnecessarily complicated or costly; (v) avoid barriers to legitimate trade; (vi) be fair and equitable and strike a "fair balance" between the applicable fundamental rights; and (vii) be proportionate. It was also necessary to consider two other matters: first, the substitutability of other websites for the target websites; and secondly, the requirement in art.3(2) of the Enforcement Directive that remedies should be applied in such as manner as to provide safeguards against their abuse, (see [100]–[101] and further [103]–[131] of the judgment). The Court of Appeal originally found that the costs of implementation of the relief ordered were to be met by the ISPs, see [132]–[150] and [214] of the Court of Appeal judgment, Lord Justice Briggs dissenting, see [197]–[212] of the Court of Appeal's judgment. However, the Supreme Court in *Cartier International AG v British Sky Broadcasting Ltd* [2018] UKSC 28; [2018] R.P.C. 11 (which only concerned the costs orders in the case) held that as a matter of English law the ordinary principle was that, unless there were good reasons for a different order, an innocent intermediary was entitled to be indemnified by the rights holder against the costs of complying with a website blocking order. The position in the present case was no different in principle from the established position in domestic law in the case of *Norwich Pharmacal* orders, freezing orders and other injunctions granted to require an innocent party to assist the claimant in the assertion of its rights against a wrong doer. The Supreme Court found that, in principle, the rights holders should indemnify the ISPs against their compliance costs, that indemnity had to be limited to reasonable compliance costs. However, the Supreme Court also found that that it was critical to its conclusions that the intermediary in question was legally innocent. In this case they were innocent because they were "mere conduits" under art.12 of the E-Commerce Directive (2000/31/EC) and that different considerations might apply to intermediaries engaged in caching or hosting governed by arts 13 and 14 of the E-Commerce Directive (2000/31/EC) but that would depend on the precise facts and on the relevant provisions of national law, (see [36] and [37] of the Supreme Court judgment).

## The Territorial Effect of Prohibitions Issued by an EU Trade Mark Court

*Replace paragraph:*

Article 130 of the 2017 EUTMR (previously art.102 of the 2009 EUTMR)[207] **22-088** states as follows:

"Sanctions

(1) Where an EU trade mark court finds that the defendant has infringed or threatened to infringe an EU trade mark, it shall, unless there are special reasons for not doing so, issue an order prohibiting the defendant from proceeding with the acts which infringed or would infringe the EU trade mark. It shall also take such measures in accordance with its national law as are aimed at ensuring that this prohibition is complied with.

(2) The EU trade mark court may also apply measures or orders available under the applicable law which it deems appropriate in the circumstances of the case."

Article 98 of Council Regulation 40/94 (the equivalent to art.102 under the 2009 EUTMR (and art.130 of the 2017 EUTMR))[208] was the subject of a reference to the CJEU in *DHL Express France SAS v Chronopost SA*.[209] This case concerned a French National and a Community Trade Mark for "WEBSHIPPING". At first instance before the Regional Court in Paris, France the claimant trade mark proprietor was successful in establishing that its French trade mark had been infringed, although it did not adjudicate upon the infringement of the equivalent Community Trade Mark. On Appeal the Court of Appeal in Paris found that the CTM had also been infringed but the prohibition (or injunction) granted, which was also subject to a periodic penalty payment, was only limited to the French Territory and did not extend to the entire area of the EU. The Community Trade Mark proprietor objected to this territorial limitation on the prohibition granted and appealed. As part of this appeal a reference was then made by the Court of Cassation concerning the interpretation of art.98. The CJEU held that art.98(1) of Council Regulation 40/94 "must be interpreted as meaning that the scope of the prohibition against further infringement or threatened infringement of a EU trade mark, issued by a Community trade mark court ... extends, as a rule, to the entire area of the European Union". The default position is therefore that the prohibition granted should be EU-wide, however the CJEU in its decision did recognise that there were situations where the territorial scope of a prohibition should be restricted and determining this issue would be a matter for the Community trade mark court hearing the infringement action to determine.[210] As stated by the CJEU[211]:

"Accordingly, if a Community trade mark court hearing a case ... finds that the acts of infringement of a Community trade mark are limited to a single Member State or to part of the territory of the European Union, in particular because the applicant for a prohibition order has restricted the territorial scope of its action in exercising its freedom to determine the extent of that action or because the defendant proves that the use of the sign at issue does not affect or it not liable to affect the functions of the trade mark, for example on linguistic grounds, that court must limit the territorial scope of the prohibition which it issues."[212]

[207] This article is the same as art.98 under Council Regulation 40/94/EEC which was repealed and replaced by the codified Council Regulation 207/2009/EC. Council Regulation 207/2009/EC was itself extensively amended by Regulation 2015/2436 of the European Parliament and of the Council of 16 December 2015 and has now been repealed and replaced by the codified 2017 EUTMR, Regulation 2017/1001, as of 1 October 2017.

[208] Council Regulation 40/94/EEC has now been repealed and replaced by the codified Council Regulation 207/2009/EC which itself will be be repealed and replaced by the codified 2017 EUTMR, Regulation 2017/1001, as of 1 October 2017). Council Regulation 40/94/EEC was repealed and replaced by the codified Council Regulation 207/2009/EC which itself has now been repealed and replaced by the codified 2017 EUTMR, Regulation 2017/1001, as of 1 October 2017.

[209] (C-235/09) [2011] E.T.M.R. 33.

[210] See [46]–[48] of the CJEU decision, (C-235/09) [2011] E.T.M.R. 33.

[211] See [48] of the CJEU decision, (C-235/09) [2011] E.T.M.R. 33. See also the decision of the CJEU in *Combit Software GmbH v Commit Business Solutions Ltd* (C-223/15) [2016] Bus L.R., in particular [31]–[32], [34] and [36].

[212] Also see the decision of the CJEU in *Combit Software GmbH v Commit Business Solutions Ltd* (C-223/15) [2016] Bus L.R., in particular at [31]–[32], [34] and [36] on when it is appropriate to grant a territorially limited injunction.

*Add new paragraphs:*

**22-090A** On 31 December 2020 at 23.00, the Implementation Period completion day, or IP completion day, all EUTMs will no longer cover the UK. A comparable trade mark (EU) for all existing EUTMs will come into existence for the UK.[216a] Where there are pending proceedings as at the IP completion day concerning a EUTM, transitional provisions will apply from the IP completion day. These transitional provisions are found at paras 20–21 of new Sch.2A to the 1994 Act which comes into force on the IP completion day.[216b] In particular, paras 20(3) and 20(4) concern the UK EU trade mark court's jurisdiction to grant relief in respect of infringement and invalidity counterclaims concerning the comparable trade mark (EU). Paragraph 20(3) of new Sch.2A states that: "Where the pending proceedings involve a claim for infringement of an existing EUTM, without prejudice to any other relief by way of damages, accounts or otherwise available to the proprietor of the existing EUTM, the EU trade mark court may grant an injunction to prohibit unauthorised use of the comparable trade mark (EU) which derives from the existing EUTM". The territorial scope of the injunction in relation to the comparable trade mark (EU) will only be UK wide as the comparable trade mark (EU) is a trade mark registered under the 1994 Act, see para.1(1) and (2) of new Sch.2A.[216c] It should be noted that para.20(2) of new Sch.2A states that: "Subject to sub-paragraphs (3) and (4), the provisions contained or referred to in Chapter 10 of the European Union Trade Mark Regulation (with the exception of Articles 128(2),(4),(6) and (7) and 132) continue to apply to the pending proceedings as if the United Kingdom were still a Member State with effect from exit day". Articles 126 and 130 of the 2017 EUTMR, which are concerned with the EU Trade Mark Court's jurisdiction and the sanctions that should be granted by the EU trade mark court on a finding of infringement of the EUTM, therefore continue to apply to the pending proceedings involving a EUTM in the UK in so far as the EUTM (which post the IP Completion Day, will no longer include the territory of the UK) is concerned. It therefore appears that it is intended that the UK court can grant an injunction relating to the EUTM concerning the territory of the EU excluding the UK in pending proceedings.[216d] The position of pending actions in non-UK EU trade mark courts which concern infringements within the territory of the UK will be a matter of EU law.

Regarding the currently in force injunctions prohibiting performance of acts in the UK which infringe or would infringe an existing EUTM (a "relevant injunction"),[216e] para.21(2) of new Sch.2A states as follows: "(2) Subject to any order of the court to the contrary, a relevant injunction will have effect and be enforceable to prohibit the performance of acts which infringe or would infringe a comparable trade mark (EU) to the same extent as in relation to the EU trade mark from which the comparable trade mark (EU) derives as if it were an injunction granted by the court." Thus the lacuna in the scope of existing injunctions caused by UK territory no being longer covered by existing EUTMs is to be filled. It is unclear whether the term "relevant injunction" includes injunctions granted by non-UK EU trade mark courts which may no longer be directly enforceable in the UK. **22-090B**

[216a] See the Trade Marks (Amendment etc.) (EU Exit) Regulations 2019 (SI 2019/269) Sch.1 para.2, which inserts a new s.52A into the Trade Marks Act 1994 and Sch.1 para.3 which adds a new Sch.2A to the Trade Marks Act 1994. With regard to the date of IP completion day, see s.39 (1) and Sch.5 para.1 of the European Union (Withdrawal Agreement) Act 2020).

[216b] New Sch.2A of the Trade Marks Act 1994 is added to the 1994 Act by The Trade Marks (Amendment etc.) (EU Exit) Regulations 2019 (SI 2019/269) Sch.1 para.3.

[216c] See the Trade Marks (Amendment etc.) (EU Exit) Regulations 2019 SI 2019/269 Sch.1 para.2, insertion of new s.52A into the Trade Marks Act 1994 and Sch.1 para.3 the insertion of new Sch.2A into the Trade Marks Act 1994.

[216d] In this regard it is important to note that para.20(3) or new Sch.2A of the 1994 Act expressly states that it is "without prejudice to any other relief by way of damages, accounts or otherwise available to the proprietor of the existing EUTM", therefore para.20(3) is only concerned that the relief that may be granted in relation to the comparable trade mark (EU) is relevant to the pending proceedings and does not effect the relief that may be granted in relation to the EUTM that is in issue in those pending proceedings.

[216e] See para.21(1) of new Sch.2A of the 1994 Act. New Sch.2A will be added to the 1994 Act by Sch.1 para.3 of the Trade Marks (Amendment etc.) (EU Exit) Regulations 2019 SI 2019/269.

## 12. INTERIM INJUNCTIONS

### Application of American Cyanamid Principles to Trade Mark Cases

*Replace footnote 239:*

[239] See *NWL Ltd v Woods* [1979] 1 W.L.R. 1294 and *Cayne v Global Natural Resources* [1984] 1 All E.R. 225 generally in relation to the principle of assessing the merits where an interim decision is likely to decide the dispute finally. For authorities in the field of passing off and trade mark infringement specifically, see *Boots v Approved Prescription Services* [1988] F.S.R. 45; *Post Office v Interlink* [1989] F.S.R. 369; *Stacey v 2020 Communications* [1991] F.S.R. 49; *Gala of London v Chandler* [1991] F.S.R. 294; *Management Publications v Blenheim Exhibitions* [1991] F.S.R. 348 and 550 CA; *Blazer v Yardley* [1992] F.S.R. 501; *BBC v Talbot* [1980] F.S.R. 228; *Parnass/Pelly v Hodges* [1982] F.S.R. 329; *Elan Digital v Elan Computers* [1984] F.S.R. 373 CA at 386; *BBC v Talksport Ltd* [2001] F.S.R. 6; *Quad International Inc v Goldstar Publications Ltd* [2003] EWHC 2081 (Ch); *Blinkx UK Ltd v Blinkbox Entertainment Ltd* [2010] EWHC 1624 (Ch); *Cowshed Products Ltd v Island Origins* [2011] E.T.M.R. 42. In *Entec v Abacus* [1992] F.S.R. 332 CA, a copyright case, the defendant successfully defeated an application for an interim injunction by arguing that the grant of one would cause its bankruptcy and hence there would never be a trial. The argument succeeded on the basis of the *Cayne* principle. See *NWL Ltd v Woods* [1979] 1 W.L.R. 1294 and *Cayne v Global Natural Resources* [1984] 1 All E.R. 225 generally in relation to the principle of assessing the merits where an interim decision is likely to decide the dispute finally. For authorities in the field of passing off and trade mark infringement specifically, see *Boots v Approved Prescription Services* [1988] F.S.R. 45; *Post Office v Interlink* [1989] F.S.R. 369; **22-100**

*Stacey v 2020 Communications* [1991] F.S.R. 49; *Gala of London v Chandler* [1991] F.S.R. 294; *Management Publications v Blenheim Exhibitions* [1991] F.S.R. 348 C and 550; *Blazer v Yardley* [1992] F.S.R. 501; *BBC v Talbot* [1980] F.S.R. 228; *Parnass/Pelly v Hodges* [1982] F.S.R. 329; *Elan Digital v Elan Computers* [1984] F.S.R. 373 CA at 386; *BBC v Talksport Ltd* [2001] F.S.R. 6; *Quad International Inc v Goldstar Publications Ltd* [2003] EWHC 2081 (Ch); *Blinkx UK Ltd v Blinkbox Entertainment Ltd* [2010] EWHC 1624 (Ch); *Cowshed Products Ltd v Island Origins* [2011] E.T.M.R. 42; and see *Memoria Ltd v Funeral Zone Ltd* [2017] EWHC 2497 (IPEC) and *Planet Art LLC v Photobox Ltd* [2019] EWHC 1688 (Ch). The *Planet Art LLC* case is interesting in that is an example of a case where the interim injunction was not granted, and yet the claimant succeeded at trial, see *Planet Art LLC v Photobox Ltd* [2020] EWHC 713 (Ch). In *Entec v Abacus* [1992] F.S.R. 332 CA, a copyright case, the defendant successfully defeated an application for an interim injunction by arguing that the grant of one would cause its bankruptcy and hence there would never be a trial. The argument succeeded on the basis of the *Cayne* principle.

## Status Quo

*Replace footnote 248:*

**22-102** [248] [1984] A.C. 130. For a recent consideration by the Court of Appeal of the appropriate status quo in an interim injunction application see *Frank Industries Pty Ltd v Nike Retail BV* [2018] F.S.R. 24 at [18]–[21].

*Replace footnote 251:*

**22-103** [251] [1987] F.S.R. 228. For a more recent case where the issue of whether a defendant had embarked on a course of business with full knowledge that it would attract litigation, see *Memoria Ltd v Funeral Zone Ltd* [2017] EWHC 2497 (IPEC). In this case the court held that the extent of the claimant's objection and the defendant's knowledge of that objection were unclear and disputed and therefore this awareness of risk argument could not be determined until trial. No interim injunction was granted because the balance of harm came down in favour of the defendant who was in a middle of an investment round which would be likely to collapse leading to redundancy of staff if the injunction was granted, and the injunction would also require the defendant to rebrand.

## Other Factors Relevant to the Balance of Convenience

*Add new paragraph:*

**22-106A** As the decision concerning whether to grant the interim injunction or not is a discretionary one, it is a difficult decision to Appeal, as held by the Court of Appeal in *Frank Industries Pty Ltd v Nike Retail BV*[259a]:

> "[17] We are not hearing an application for an interim injunction but an appeal. The question is not whether we would have made the same order as the judge, but whether the judge was wrong to make the order that he did. I do not consider that these alleged failings and the judge's treatment of the evidence are such as would entitle an appeal court to intervene. Even where a trial judge evaluates evidence given in writing without the benefit of live evidence an appeal court should generally respect his evaluation, (see *DB v The Chief Constable of Police Service of Northern Ireland* [2017] UKSC 7; [2017] N.I. 301 at [80]). This applies all the more strongly where the remedy that the judge has granted is a discretionary remedy."

In this case, the prohibitory part of the Injunction granted by the first instance court in *Frank Industries UK v Nike Retail UK*[259b] was left undisturbed by the Court of Appeal. However, the Court of Appeal admitted fresh evidence on the Appeal which was concerned with the mandatory part of the injunction originally granted. This evidence had not been filed by the defendant in response to the original injunction application, as the defendant was not fully aware that a mandatory injunction was sought by the claimant at first instance. In light of this fresh evidence, the Court of Appeal varied the mandatory part of the injunction originally granted.

[259a] [2018] F.S.R. 24.

[259b] [2018] EWHC 424 (IPEC).

## 14. Erasure, Destruction, Delivery Up

### To What Articles the Statutory Remedies Apply

*Replace footnote 288:*

[288] 1994 Act s.17(3). Section 17(3) of the 1994 Act is due to be amended on 31 December 2020, the IP completion day, to read: " (3) Nothing in subsection (2) shall be construed as affecting the importation of goods which may lawfully be imported into the United Kingdom by virtue of anything which forms part of retained EU law as a result of section 3 or 4 of the European Union Withdrawal Act 2018". **22-120**

### Statutory Order for Erasure, Removal or Obliteration

*At the end of the paragraph, add new footnote 289a:*

[289a] For a case where relief under s.15 of the 1994 Act was considered, see *Lifestyle Equities CV v Santa Monica Polo Club Ltd* [2017] EWHC 3578 (Ch). **22-124**

### Statutory Order for Delivery Up

*Replace footnote 292:*

[292] For a cogent criticism of the decision and an explanation as to why the proper view is that the goods must be shown actually to be infringing, see C. May QC, L. Lane QC, J. Whyte, D. Alexander QC, M. Tappin QC, I. Berkeley, A. Speck QC, I. Jamal, Q. Cregan, J. Riordan, M. Keay and T. Jones, *Laddie, Prescott & Vitoria: The Modern Law of Copyright and Designs*, 5th edn (London: Butterworths, 2018), paras 26.47 and 26.75. **22-129**

### Costs of Compliance With an Order for Delivery Up or Destruction

*Replace footnote 302:*

[302] CPR 63PD para.26.1. This rule implements art.10(2) of Directive 2004/48/EC on the Enforcement of Intellectual Property Rights. In *Miller Brewing Co v Mersey Docks and Harbour Co* [2003] EWHC 1606 (Ch); [2004] F.S.R. 5 an order for delivery up of goods bearing an infringing mark was made under the Trade Marks Act 1994 ss.16 and 19. The goods in issue were in the physical custody of the dock authority, which had no responsibility for the infringement. It was agreed between the parties that the dock authority should be indemnified against the costs of compliance with the order, and the court ordered that the claimant should also pay the Dock Authority's costs of the litigation. This case was referred to by the Supreme Court in support of its judgment at [14] of *Cartier International AG v British Sky Broadcasting Ltd* [2018] R.P.C. 11 (see para.22-087, n.206). **22-138**

## 16. Financial Remedies—Damages and Accounts of Profits

### Basic Principles for Assessing Damages

*Replace paragraph:*

The basic principles for the assessment of damages in a patent case were considered by Jacob J in *Gerber v Lectra*.[318] The following principles are applicable to trade mark infringement: **22-150**

(1) Damages are compensatory only, to put the claimant in the same position they would have been in had the wrong not been sustained.[319]
(2) The burden of proof lies on the claimant, but damages are to be assessed liberally.[320]
(3) Where the claimant has licensed their right, the damages are the lost royalty.[321]
(4) It is irrelevant that the defendant could have competed lawfully.[322]
(5) Where the claimant has exploited their right by their own sales, they can

claim lost profit on sales by the defendant they would have made otherwise, and lost profit on their own sales to the extent that they were forced by the infringement to reduce their own price.

[318] [1995] R.P.C. 383; Jacob J's (as he then was) decision was reversed in part by the Court of Appeal in *Gerber Garment Technology Inc v Lectra Systems Ltd* [1997] R.P.C. 443 CA, however the general principles set out above were not disputed by the Court of Appeal. A more recent summary of the law relating to the general principles relating to an inquiry as to damages is found at [31] of *SDL Hair Ltd v Next Row Ltd* [2014] EWHC 2084 (IPEC).

[319] *General Tire v Firestone* [1976] R.P.C. 197.

[320] *General Tire v Firestone* [1976] R.P.C. 197. For an example of a case where the court had to assess damages in the face of incomplete, deeply flawed and unreliable evidence from the defendants see *Link Up Mitaka Ltd t/a The Big Word v Language Empire Ltd* [2018] EWHC 2633 (IPEC).

[321] *General Tire v Firestone* [1976] R.P.C. 197. Jacob J held in *Gerber* that this follows from the first proposition. It is less likely to be of application in trade mark cases than in patent cases because the prevalence of exploitation by licensing is less.

[322] *United Horse-Shoe v Stewart* (1888) 5 R.P.C. 260. See also *MVF3 APS (Formerly Vestergaard Fransden A/S) v Bestnet Europe Ltd* [2017] F.S.R. 5 at [81] and [82] (a breach of confidence case).

## Assessment of Damages Where the Defendant had Knowledge of, or Reasonable Grounds to Know of, the Infringing Activity

*Replace footnote 341:*

**22-161** [341] [2015] EWHC 2608 (IPEC). See also *Henderson v All Around the World Recordings* [2014] EWHC 3087 (IPEC) at [80].

## Basic Principles Applicable to an Account

*Replace list with:*

**22-165**
(1) An account is confined to profits actually made, its purpose being to deprive the defendant of unjust enrichment rather than to punish them.[348]
(2) An account is addressed to identifying profits caused, in the legal sense, by the infringement.[349]
(3) The fact that the defendant's profits could have been made in a non-infringing fashion is irrelevant.[350]
(4) The claimant must take the defendant as they find them, and may not argue that the defendant could have made greater profits by trading in a different fashion.[351]
(5) Overheads should be dealt with so as to arrive as closely as possible at the true profit.[352]
(6) With regards to determining the true profit, it is not permissible for a defendant simply to allocate a proportion of its general overheads to the infringing activity. The defendant must show that the relevant overheads are properly attributable to that activity. All will depend on the facts and circumstances of the case.[353]
(7) The defendant cannot generally deduct opportunity cost.[354]
(8) General overheads may be apportioned to the infringing activity, subject to the above principles.[355]
(9) In a recent case, *Lifestyle Equities CV v Santa Monica Polo Club Ltd*[355a] it was held that, in contrast with joint liability as tortfeasors for damages, an account of profits for trade mark infringement operated against each defendant separately, requiring a defendant to disgorge such profits as were shown to have been derived by that defendant from the relevant infringements.

[348] *My Kinda Town v Soll* [1982] F.S.R. 147; *Celanese v BP* [1999] R.P.C. 203.

[349] *Celanese v BP* [1999] R.P.C. 203. See also *Jack Wills Ltd v House of Fraser (Stores) Ltd* [2016] EWHC 626 (Ch) at [61]–[63]. In particular see [62] where the court held: "[62] As it seems to me the position is now that unless the middlemen line of cases applies (as to which see *Woolley* (ante)) or there is a finding that the infringement drove the sale, there must be an apportionment to take account of the fact that the profits to be disgorged are those properly attributable to infringing use of the mark not all the profits derived from sale of the item". See also *Hotel Cipriani Srl v Cipriani (Grosvenor Street) Ltd* [2010] EWHC 628 at [7] and [8] and *OOO Abbott v Design & Display* [2016] F.S.R. 27 at [36]. A different approach was taken in *Woolley v UP Global Sourcing UK Ltd* [2014] F.S.R. 37 due to the facts of the case. The taking of an account of profits was ordered after the claimants had been successful in their claim for passing off in relation to the use of the mark "Henleys" on watches by the defendants. The sales in this case had all been to "middlemen" not the ultimate consumer. The court dealing with the account held that where the court concerned with liability had ordered an account of profits with no form of qualification (i.e. unlike the account ordered by Slade J at first instance in *My Kinda Town Ltd v Soll* [1982] F.S.R. 147, where it was ordered that the Master should "take an account of the profits made by the business of the second defendants carried on under the name L.S. Grunts Chicago Pizza Co … which are properly attributable to the use by the Defendants of such name in the said business"), and where the case concerned "middlemen", the assessment of profits should be made on the basis that the profit in issue related to all products sold under the infringing mark. The court held in *Woolley* that: "[*Celanese v BP* [1999] R.P.C. 203] was a patent infringement action concerning a refinement to a particular method of manufacturing acetic acid. It was not a passing off action. The point that emerges from that case is not that when taking an account in a passing off case it is necessary to identify the portion of the profits attributable to the relevant misrepresentation being operative but the less controversial points that (a) where a defendant has two businesses, one infringing and one not, the claimant can recover on an account only the profits made by the infringing business, and (b) where only part of a product or process infringes then apportionment will be appropriate."

[350] *Celanese v BP* [1999] R.P.C. 203.

[351] *Celanese v BP* [1999] R.P.C. 203; *Dart v Decor* [1994] F.S.R. 567.

[352] *Dart v Decor* [1994] F.S.R. 567. In *OOO Abbott v Design & Display Ltd* [2016] F.S.R. 27 at [39] (a patent case) the Court of Appeal held that the correct question to consider was: "if the defendant had not infringed the patent would he have carried on a non-infringing business which would have been sustained by the overheads in fact used to sustain the infringement?" and at [42]: "It seems to me to be clear that if the infringer would have manufactured or sold non-infringing products had he not infringed and would have incurred overheads in supporting that manufacture or sale, then he ought to be allowed a proportion of his general overheads. The question is not dependent on whether the infringer is or is not working to capacity. The bottom line is whether (a) the overheads would have been incurred anyway even if the infringement had not occurred and (b) the sale of infringing products would not have been replaced by sale of non-infringing products. It is in those circumstances that an allowance for overheads will not be permitted." See generally [38]–[52] of *OOO Abbott v Design & Display Ltd* [2016] F.S.R. 27. For recent applications of these principles in a copyright case, see *Blizzard Entertainment SAS v Bossland GmbH* [2019] EWHC 1665 (Ch) and in a trade mark case, see *Lifestyle Equities CV Santa Monica Polo Club Ltd* [2020] EWHC 688 (Ch).

[353] See *Hollister Inc v Medik Ostomy Supplies Ltd* [2013] F.S.R. 24 at [85] and [87]. See also the Court of Appeal in *OOO Abbott v Design & Display Ltd* [2016] F.S.R. 27 at [39]–[52] and see n.352. Note in particular, Lewison LJ's finding at [42] of *OOO Abbott v Design & Display Ltd* [2016] F.S.R. 27 in relation to Kitchin LJ's obiter observations in *Hollister Inc v Medik Ostomy Supplies Ltd* [2013] F.S.R. 24 at [86]. For recent applications of these principles in a copyright case, see *Blizzard Entertainment SAS v Bossland GmbH* [2019] EWHC 1665 (Ch) and in a trade mark case see *Lifestyle Equities CV Santa Monica Polo Club Ltd* [2020] EWHC 688 (Ch).

[354] *Dart v Decor* [1994] F.S.R. 567 and see the Court of Appeal in *OOO Abbott v Design & Display Ltd* [2016] F.S.R. 27 at [38]–[52]. For an application of these principles see *Jack Wills Ltd v House of Fraser (Stores) Ltd* [2016] EWHC 626 (Ch).

[355] *Dart v Decor* [1994] F.S.R. 567 and see the Court of Appeal in *OOO Abbott v Design & Display Ltd* [2016] F.S.R. 27 at [38]–[52]. For an application of these principles see *Jack Wills Ltd v House of Fraser (Stores) Ltd* [2016] EWHC 626 (Ch).

[355a] [2020] EWHC 688 (Ch). See *Lifestyle Equities CV v Santa Monica Polo Club Ltd* [2020] EWHC 688 (Ch) at [28]–[40], where the court relied on and applied *Hotel Cipriani v Cipriani Grosvenor Street* [2010] EWHC 628 (Ch) and Ultraframe (UK) Ltd v Fielding [2005] EHWC 1638 (Ch).

## 17. COSTS

### Costs in the Discretion of the Judge

#### *New Costs Regime*

*Replace paragraph:*

A new costs regime has applied since 1 April 2013. The overriding Objective of **22-173** the CPR has been amended. In particular CPR 1.1(1) now states that "these rules are a new procedural code with the overriding objective of enabling the court to deal with cases justly *and at a proportionate cost*." With regards to multi-track claims, parties now have to file and exchange cost budgets (usually with the directions questionnaire or 21 days before the first case management conference)[373] except as set out in CPR 3.12. CPR 3.12(1) provides that costs budgets must be filed and exchanged in relation to all Pt 7 multi-track cases except: (a) where the claim is commenced on or after 22 April 2014 and the amount of money claimed as stated on the claim form is £10 million or more; (b) where the claim is commenced on or after 22 April 2014 and is for a monetary claim which is not quantified or not fully quantified, or is for a non-monetary claim and in any such case the claim form contains a statement that the claim is valued at £10 million or more; (c) where in proceedings commenced on or after 6th April 2016 a claim is made by on behalf of a person under the age of 18 (a child) (and on a child reaching majority this exception will continue to apply unless the court otherwise orders); (d) where the proceedings are the subject of fixed costs or scale costs; or (e) where the court otherwise orders. The transitional provisions to Civil Procedure (Amendment No. 4) Rules 2014 (SI 2014/867) provide that the previous version of CPR 3.12 continues to apply to claims started after 1 April 2013 but before 22 April 2014 (see also the CPR 3.12 note of clarification issued on 4 April 2014). The sanction for failing to file a budget within the time prescribed despite being required to do so are severe. As set out at CPR 3.14, "unless the court otherwise orders, any party which fails to file a budget despite being required to do so will be treated as having filed a budget comprising only the applicable court fees."[374] These costs budgets may then be used by the court to make costs management orders.[375] Where costs budgets have been filed and exchanged the court will make a costs management order unless it is satisfied that the litigation can be conducted justly and at proportionate cost in accordance with the overriding objective without such an order being made.[376] When assessing costs on a standard basis where a costs management order has been made, the court will have regard to the receiving party's last approved or agreed budget for each phase of the proceedings and not depart from such approved or agreed budget unless satisfied that there is a good reason to do so, and take into account any comments made pursuant to CPR 3.15(4)[376a] or para.7.4 of Practice Direction 3E and recorded on the face of the order.[377]

[373] See CPR 3.13–3.18 and CPR 26.3(1) and 26.3(6).

[374] CPR r.3.14 was considered in detail in *Andrew Mitchell MP v News Group Newspapers Ltd* [2014] 1 W.L.R. 795.

[375] See CPR 3.15–3.18.

[376] See CPR 3.15(2) (as amended by Civil Procedure (Amendment No. 4) Rules 2014 (SI 2014/867) r.5.

[376a] CPR 3.15(4) states that: "Whether or not the court make a costs management order, it may record on the face of any costs management order any comment it has about the incurred costs which are to be taken into account in any subsequent assessment proceedings."

[377] Paragraph 7.4 of Practice Direction 3E states that: "As part of the costs management process the court may not approve costs incurred up to and including the date of the costs management hearing. The court may, however, record its comments on those costs and will take those costs into account when considering the reasonableness and proportionality of all subsequent budgeted costs." See generally, CPR 3.18(a)–(c). CPR 3.18 also states that attention is drawn to rrr.44.3(2)(a) and 44.3(5), which concern proportionality of costs.

*Add to the end of the paragraph:*

**22-174** which awards costs on a fixed scale.[378a]

[378a] See CPR 45.30 and 45.31 and Tables A and B to Practice Direction to CPR 45, for the scale costs awarded in the IPEC. For an example of a case where the costs of an inquiry to damages in IPEC were awarded off the scale, under CPR 40.30(2)(a), see *Link Up Mitaka Ltd (t/a TheBigWord) v Language Empire Ltd (no. 2)* [2018] EWHC 2728 (IPEC); [2019] F.S.R. 9.

## Offer by Defendant or by Claimant

*Replace footnote 386:*

[386] In *AB v CD* [2011] EWHC 602 (Ch) (a trade mark infringement case) it was held (at [22]) that an offer to settle as referred to in CPR 36 and in particular CPR 36.2 must contain some genuine element of concession on the part of the claimant and cannot simply amount to a request to a defendant to submit to judgment for the entirety of the relief sought by the claimant. Such an offer could not be an "offer to settle" which could give rise to the favourable consequences as found in CPR 36.14. In the circumstances of this case the judge carefully considered the claimant's supposed Pt 36 offer and concluded that the claimant's offer contained no real concession of significant value. It was therefore not an offer of settlement within the meaning of Pt 36, which meant that the claimant was not entitled to the favourable treatment afforded by CPR 36.14 (now CPR 36.17), although the offer remained a relevant consideration for the court to take into account in the exercise of its general discretion on costs. The judge in this case also considered the defendant's Pt 36 offer and whether enough information had been provided by the defendant to allow the claimant to assess the offer. In the circumstances of this case, the judge held that it was far from self-evident that the claimant lacked sufficient information to allow it to assess the offer and in any event the claimant could have made an application under CPR 36.8 which it chose not to do so. Therefore the defendant's offer was a valid Pt 36 offer (see [40]–[50]). This case also considered Pt 36 offers in the context of split trials with liability and quantum being decided at different stages. **22-179**

## Notice of Action is Unnecessary

*Replace paragraph:*

For claims in the Intellectual Property Enterprise Court it should be noted that CPR 63.20(2) states that the particulars of claim must state whether the claimant has complied with para.6 of the Practice Direction (Pre-Action Conduct) which concerns the exchange of information between the parties before proceedings are commenced.[407] If the Particulars of Claim do not contain such a confirmation the defendant has longer within which to file its defence.[4] On the issue of threats, the IPEC guide states: "Potential claimants should be aware that while they should notify the intended defendant of their proposed claim, this should not take the form of an unjustified threat of infringement proceedings. In relation to some intellectual property rights a party making such a threat can be sued. It is beyond the scope of this Guide to explain the (sometimes fine) distinction between informing another party of your intellectual property right and threatening to bring proceedings for its infringement. It is wise to seek professional advice."[409] **22-184**

[407] See also para.4.1 of the IPEC Guide.

[4] See CPR 63.22(2) and (3). See para.4.5 of the IPEC Guide.

[409] See para.4.1 of the IPEC Guide.

### 19. PRACTICE AND EVIDENCE

## Pleading

*Replace footnote 459:*

[459] It is no longer required that the particulars of invalidity, revocation or rectification be set out in a separate document. However at CPR 16.5 concerning the contents of any defence, CPR 16.5(2) specifies that where a defendant denies an allegation they must state their reasons for doing so. Further, in *Mei Fields Designs Ltd v Saffron Cards and Gifts Ltd* [2018] EWHC 1332 (IPEC) the judge reiterated the need to plead fraud properly and that it is not sufficient to allege in a defence that it is up to the claimant to prove that it has not been fraudulent (see [31]). **22-204**

## Disclosure of Documents

*Add new paragraphs:*

22-211A Under the CPR there is a new practice direction PD 51U which sets out the new rules for a mandatory pilot scheme for disclosure in the Business and Property Courts, made under CPR 51.2, which has been in place since 1 January 2019. The disclosure pilot scheme applies from the commencement date, 1 January 2019, for two years to existing and new proceedings in the Business and Property Courts of England and Wales and the Business and Property Courts in Birmingham, Bristol, Cardiff, Leeds, Liverpool, Manchester and Newcastle. It does not apply in the County Court, although this may be reviewed in the course of the pilot. The pilot shall not disturb an order for disclosure made before the commencement date or before the transfer of proceedings into a Business and Property Court, unless that order is varied or set aside. If proceedings are transferred out of one of the Business and Property Courts into a court that is not one of the Business and Property Courts, any order for disclosure made under the disclosure pilot scheme will stand unless and until any other order is made by the transferee court.[482a]

22-211B The disclosure pilot scheme was set up to test a new set of disclosure rules aimed at creating a more flexible, efficient and proportionate disclosure process tailored to each case. A key difference is that the disclosure pilot scheme has codified a number of disclosure duties on both parties and their lawyers which reflect existing duties and best practices under the current regime. These are[482b]:

(a) Preserve documents that may be relevant to issues in the proceedings.
(b) Disclose known adverse documents, unless they are privileged.
(c) Comply with any court order for disclosure.
(d) Undertake a search in a responsible and conscientious manner.
(e) Act honestly in both giving disclosure and reviewing documents disclosed by the other party.
(f) Use reasonable efforts to avoid providing documents that are not relevant to the other party.

22-211C A further key difference is that it has moved away from the standard disclosure regime which is currently in place. Under the pilot scheme the court will be concerned to ensure that disclosure is directed to the issues in the proceedings and that the scope of disclosure is not wider than is reasonable and proportionate in order fairly to resolve those issues.[482c] The process of giving disclosure under the disclosure pilot scheme is separated into two stages; "Initial Disclosure" and "Extended disclosure". Initial Disclosure takes place at the same time that a party files and serves its statements of case. A party must provide the key documents that it has relied upon in support of the claims in its statement of case, and the key documents necessary to enable the other party to understand the case they have to meet. There is no requirement to do a search.[482d] A party wishing to seek disclosure of documents in addition to, or as an alternative to, Initial Disclosure must request Extended Disclosure.[482e] Extended Disclosure will usually take the form of one of the "Disclosure Models" which relates to the "Issues for Disclosure", full details of which can be found at Sections 8 and 9 of PD51U. The objective of relating Disclosure Models to the Issues for Disclosure is to limit the searches required and the volume of documents to be disclosed. The court will determine whether to order Extended Disclosure at the first case management conference or, if directed by the court, at another hearing convened for that purpose or without a hearing.[482f] The court expects the parties (and their representatives) to co-operate with each other and to assist the court so that the scope of disclosure, if any, that is required in proceedings can be agreed or determined by the court in the most efficient way possible.[482g]

[482a] See paras 1.1–1.3 of CPR PD51U.

[482b] See Section 3 of CPR PD51U.

[482c] See para.2.4 of CPR PD51U. In the recent case of *McParland and Partners Ltd v Whitehead* [2020] EWHC 298 (Ch), Sir Geoffrey Vos, Chancellor of the High Court gave some much needed guidance on disclosure given under the disclosure pilot scheme. The hearing related to a request from the parties to seek guidance, by way of a discussion, from the court concerning the scope of Extended Disclosure which was available to them under para.11(1) of PD51U. However, the judge took the opportunity to clarify some aspects of the way in which the disclosure pilot scheme is intended to work.

[482d] See Section 4 of CPR PD51U.

[482e] See Section 6 of CPR PD51U.

[482f] See para.6.2 of CPR PD51U.

[482g] See para.2.3 of CPR PD51U.

## Disclosure of Sales

*Replace paragraph:*

Disclosure in regard to the sales effected by the defendant under the disputed mark is not, in general, where the infringement is denied, material, until the fact that the mark is an infringement of the claimant's rights has been decided.[483] Before a party elects whether to seek an inquiry as to damage or an account of profits, they may seek disclosure before making their election under *Island Records v Tring*.[483a] Disclosure given in such circumstances should be limited to that which is necessary for the claimant to make an informed decision within a reasonable time; they are not entitled to all the disclosure which would be given in the inquiry, and in appropriate circumstances an audited schedule of infringing dealings may be a substitute for documentary disclosure.[483b] **22-212**

[483] See, e.g. *Benbow v Low* (1880) 16 Ch D. 93.

[483a] [1995] F.S.R. 560.

[483b] For further discussion see n.362.

## Shorter and Flexible Trial Procedure

*Replace paragraph:*

Since 1 October 2018, the "Shorter Trial" procedure and the "Flexible Trial" procedure became permanent procedures (both previously pilots under CPR PD 51N). The aim of the schemes is to achieve shorter and earlier trials for business related litigation at a reasonable and proportionate cost. Both schemes apply to cases brought in the Rolls Building courts which include the Chancery Division.[488] Under the Shorter Trial scheme cases are to be case managed by docketed judges with the aim of reaching trial within approximately 10 months of the issue of proceedings and judgment six weeks after that. The Shorter Trial procedure is intended for cases which can be fairly tried on the basis of limited disclosure and oral evidence. The maximum length of trial would be four days including reading time.[489] Cases that are not normally suitable for the Shorter Trial scheme include: (a) cases including an allegation of fraud or dishonesty; (b) cases which are likely to require extensive disclosure and/or reliance upon extensive witness or expert evidence; (c) cases involving multiple issues and multiple parties, save for Pt 20 counterclaims for revocation of an intellectual property right; (d) cases in IPEC; and **22-214**

(e) public procurement cases.[490] The Flexible Trial procedure involves the adoption of flexible case management on the agreement of the parties whereby a more simplified and expedited procedure is used than the full trial procedure normally provided for by the CPR. Costs management does not apply to cases in the Shorter Trial Scheme unless the parties otherwise agree.[491] The rules of procedure applying to the Shorter and Flexible Trial pilot schemes are dealt with in CPR PD 57AB.

[488] See CPR PD57AB para.1.2(b). Paragraph 1.2(c) states that the schemes apply to claims issued on or after 1 October 2015. The Chancery Division of the High Court, which includes the Patents Court and the IPEC, now fall under the "Business and Property Courts of England and Wales" umbrella which was launched on 4 July 2017 and became operational on 2 October 2017. For further information see *https://www.judiciary.gov.uk/announcements/the-business-and-property-courts-of-england-and-wales/* [Accessed 18 May 2020].

[489] CPR PD57AB para.2.56. See paras 2.57–2.59 of PD57AB for other provisions relating to costs.

[490] See CPR PD57AB para.2.2.

[491] See PD 51N para.2.56. See paras 2.57–2.59 of PD 51N for other provisions relating to costs.

## Stay of Other Proceedings

*Replace footnote 509:*

**22-222** [509] [1993] R.P.C. 385 (where the Registry had refused a stay). This decision was upheld by an unreported decision of the Court of Appeal which does not significantly add to or qualify Lindsay J's decision (see *Chorion Plc v Lane decision date* 24 February 1999 at [28], Laddie J). Further, see *Jules Rimet Cup Ltd v The Football Association Ltd* [2006] EWHC 2415 (Ch) for a more recent decision of the High Court staying Registry opposition proceedings while related High Court proceedings were on going, and see generally Ch.7, for the circumstances in which the Registry will itself order a stay. See *Pinterest, Inc v Premium Interest Ltd* [2015] F.S.R. 27 for a decision where the High Court refused to stay proceedings for passing off in circumstances where the High Court passing off proceedings had been commenced two years after OHIM Opposition proceedings had been started which concerned very similar factual issues. See in particular [40]–[60] of the judgment. See also *Grund & Mobil Vertwaltungs v Marks & Spencer Plc* [2017] EWHC 2078 (IPEC) which involved a claim for trade mark infringement and passing off. Here, after receipt of a letter before action from the claimant's trade mark agents, the defendant applied to the EUIPO for a declaration of invalidity of the claimant's EUTM on a number of grounds. It was agreed between the parties that the EU Trade mark infringement part of the subsequently issued claim in the English High Court should be stayed pursuant to art.104 of the 2009 EUTMR. However, the defendant also applied for a stay of the passing off element of claim under CPR 3.1(2)(f) and the inherent jurisdiction of the court. The stay of the passing off part of the claim was refused by the court on the basis of several factors including the point that the claimant was entitled to achieve commercial certainty about its passing off claim as soon as reasonably possible, and the EUIPO proceedings could be subject to several appeals which could delay the resolution of the EUIPO proceedings for several years.

## Stay of Existing Proceedings

*Add new paragraph:*

**22-226A** It should be noted that para.20(2) of new Sch.2A of the Trade Marks Act 1994 which will be added to the 1994 Act at 23.00 on 31 December 2020 (Implementation Period completion day, or IP completion day) by virtue of amendments due to be made by the Trade Marks (Amendment etc) EU Exit Regulations 2019 (SI 2019/269) (para.20 being concerning with existing EUTM pending proceedings as at IP Completion Day) states that: "Subject to sub-paragraphs (3) and (4), the provisions contained or referred to in Chapter 10 of the European Union Trade Mark Regulation (with the exception of Article 128(2),(4),(6) and (7) and 132) continue to apply to the pending proceedings as if the United Kingdom were still a Member State with effect from [IP Completion day]." Therefore, art.132 of the EUTMR 2017 no longer continues to apply after 23.00 31 December 2020 to existing EUTM proceedings. After 23.00 on 31 December 2020, EUTMs will no longer cover the UK territory[528a] and therefore new EUTM infringement proceedings cannot be started in the UK after this date.

[528a] The UK territory for existing EUTMs, will then be covered by a new comparable trade mark (EU), a UK trade mark registered under the 1994 Act derived from the existing EUTM, see new s.52A and para.1 of new Sch.2A of The Trade Marks Act 1994, which will be inserted into the 1994 Act by paras 2 and 3 of Sch.1 of the Trade Mark (Amendment etc) EU Exit Regulations 2019 (SI 2019/269).

## 20. REFERENCES TO THE CJEU

*Add new paragraph:*

From 23.00 on 31 December 2020, IP completion day, there will be no power to make references to the CJEU from the courts in the UK.[531a] **22-228A**

[531a] See European Union (Withdrawal Act) 2018 s.1A(5) which repeals s.1A(1)–(4) on IP completion day ("Implementation Period Completion Day"), which is 23.00 on 31 December 2020. Section 1A(1)–(4) of the European Union (Withdrawal Act) 2018 state in summary that the European Communities Act 1972 and the Treaties continue to have effect in domestic law after Exit Day until IP completion day.

CHAPTER 23

# EVIDENCE

TABLE OF CONTENTS



## 3. SURVEYS AND QUESTIONNAIRES: EVIDENCE FROM CONSUMERS

## Introduction

### *Surveys—the Rules*

*Replace paragraph:*

**23-033** The net effect of these rules, necessary as they are, is that it is very difficult to design a survey which will pass muster in court and their design has become a very specialised art. One technique which improves the chances of useful evidence being obtained is to begin with a very open question, such as "What can you tell me about this product?", and to move on to ones which are gradually more specific, such as "Can you tell me who makes this product?" The evidence of respondents who give useful answers to the very broad question is then untainted, while leaving an opportunity still to get evidence from persons who misunderstand what the interest of the interviewer is[58]: very broad questions are apt to receive an answer quite unrelated to the get-up or mark of interest. For example, it is not uncommon for respondents to say "it looks expensive" or something of that kind, which may be of tangential relevance, and does not mean that the respondent has nothing to say about the principal question. When they are directed a little more, for example by asking about the origin of the goods, they may then give relevant evidence, although there is of course the risk of an accusation of leading. In *Glaxo Wellcome UK Ltd v Sandoz Ltd*,[58a] the claimants relied on four surveys to support claims that a particular shade of purple (Pantone 2587C) had acquired distinctive character through use in the UK amongst GPs and pharmacists. By the time of trial, the claimants no longer contended that health care professionals were deceived as to trade origin by the use of purple on the defendant's inhalers, but relied on the surveys in support of their case that patients would be deceived (despite having conducted no surveys of patients and none in support of the actual case advanced, of equivalence). A number of the guidelines were not complied with, perhaps the most serious default relating to the first. It appears that although an experienced German survey expert designed the surveys, she was not (at least initially) made aware of the specific UK requirements. The result was that the full methodology was only revealed through a series of experts reports. The trial judge, Arnold J was faced with 16 experts reports from six expert witnesses, involving considerable repetition. The judge directed that one expert from each side should be cross-examined. He observed at [207] that two lessons should be learnt from the "unfortunate history":

"First, parties who commission surveys should ensure that the methodology of the survey is fully described in a single document at the outset, and that the conduct of the survey is fully documented thereafter. Secondly, duplicative evidence from survey experts must be avoided. These points apply just as much to proceedings in the Registry as they do to High Court proceedings, and the Registry should not hesitate to use its case management powers to ensure that they are complied with."

[58] This approach was endorsed by Lindsay J in *Weight Watchers (UK) v Tesco's Stores* [2003] EWHC 1109 at [24].

[58a] [2019] EWHC 2545.

## Case Management of Survey Evidence

### *(1) Prior Court Approval*

### Post-Interflora decisions

*Add new paragraph after list:*

*Enterprise Holdings Inc v Europcar Group UK Ltd*[108a]—the claimant was granted permission to rely on three existing surveys and to conduct a fourth for the purpose of establishing that the trade marks relied upon (various representations of its "e" logo) had an enhanced distinctive character, reputation and goodwill. The judge, Morgan J concluded that the evidence would be of real value at the planned four-day trial (plus one day reading). On the cost/benefit test, he considered that the test must be primarily for the purpose of saving costs for the party which opposes the admission of survey evidence. In that case, however, that party (the defendant) had spent £109,000 on the application, seeking to protect itself against the possibility that it would incur estimated costs of £99,000 at trial. The judge observed the costs expended on the application cast doubt on the extent of the defendant's concern as to the cost of survey evidence. **23-051**

[108a] [2014] EWHC 2498.

*Add new paragraphs:*

At trial,[108b] and despite all the criticisms made of the survey evidence, Arnold J held that it was confirmatory of the view he was minded to reach in the light of all the other evidence in the case. He also observed that the result of the procedure prescribed in *Interflora (CA I)* and *Interflora (CA II)* was to put the parties to the cost (amounting to some £215,000) of a two-day hearing in advance of trial which did not save any costs at trial and to require the court to consider Europcar's criticisms of the surveys twice. **23-051A**

In *Glaxo Wellcome UK Ltd v Sandoz Ltd*,[108c] Birss J allowed the claimants' application to rely on survey evidence. The first two surveys had been conducted under the supervision of an experienced German survey expert for use in UK IPO Opposition proceedings, where they had been admitted after consideration of objections. The first survey was conducted using the standard three-step methodology often used in some continental European courts. The second survey used a method which closely followed the method designed for and approved by the Court in *Enterprise Holdings v Europcar* (see above). With the opposition stayed, the claimants applied to use those surveys in the action for passing off. For the most part, the judgment of Birss J was based on the existing UK authorities. Three points to note: first, at [49], the judge observed: "A further reason to permit the three step 2015 surveys to go to trial would be that I would be reluctant at an interim stage to **25-051B** rule out the possibility that a survey of a kind commonly used in other European Union Trade Mark courts is so flawed as to not be permitted at all."; secondly, the estimated substantial costs of the surveys (about £500,000) would not be disproportionate in the context of overall costs of both parties, which was estimated to amount to £6m; and thirdly, the judge's final suggestions at [56] as to how the survey evidence should be case-managed going forward do not seem to have been implemented (save for his suggestion for a joint statement), judging by comments by the trial judge, Arnold J in his judgment at trial.[108d] This is yet another indication if the courts are serious about reducing the cost and time devoted to survey evidence, and will only be achieved if these cases are docketed to and retained by one of the IP judges so that the case can be properly managed throughout.

[108b] [2015] EWHC 17.

[108c] [2017] EWHC 3196.

[108d] [2019] EWHC 2545 at [205].

CHAPTER 25

# CUSTOMS POWERS AND PROCEDURES

TABLE OF CONTENTS



## 2. LEGISLATION MAKING UP THE DOMESTIC REGIME

*Add new paragraphs:*

The Customs (Enforcement of Intellectual Property Rights) (Amendment) (EU Exit) Regulations 2019 (SI 2019/514) make amendments to Regulation (EU) 608/2013. The Explanatory Note to the 2019 Regulations promises that Regulation 608/2013 becomes part of domestic law on exit day by virtue of the European Union (Withdrawal) Act 2018 s.3. The 2019 Regulations are designed to ensure that Regulation 608/2013 "continues to operate effectively without deficiency as part of UK law in the event that the UK leaves the EU without a withdrawal agreement." For the text of the retained but amended Regulation 608/2013, see amended Appendix 19. **25-006A**

Although the 2019 Regulations make a significant number of amendments to Regulation 608/2013 in order to bring it into domestic law, the basic regime seems to be unaltered in the sense that it is only intellectual property rights which have effect in the UK which can be invoked. However, it is a regime which will operate under the auspices and control of Her Majesty's Revenue and Customs ("HMRC"). **25-006B**

It appears therefore that in the UK the two separate regimes will continue—what in the Main Work we termed the "Domestic Regime" and the recast "European Regime" which we will now call the "UK European Regime". **25-006C**

### 3. Legislation Making Up the European Regime

*Replace paragraph:*

**25-007** With effect from 1 January 2014, Council Regulation 1383/2003 has been repealed and replaced by Regulation 608/2013. The text of the 2013 Regulation is found in Appendix 19 of the Main Work, but for the retained but amended Regulation 608/2013, see the amended Appendix 19 in this Supplement. See also the Commission Implementing Regulation 1352/2013 (see Appendix 20) establishing the forms provided for in the 2013 Regulation, which include the Application for Action ("AFA"). The new UK European Regime does not refer to or rely upon the Commission Implementing Regulation 1352/2013 or a transposed version of it. Instead, the UK version of Regulation 608/2013 refers, for example, to the Commissioners for Her Majesty's Revenuc and Customers establishing an application form. It seems likely that (subject to any copyright concerns) HMRC will adopt the same form of "Application for Action" as is contained in the Commission Implementing Regulation.

### 7. Procedure Under the European Regime

*Add new paragraph:*

**25-022A** The European Regime established under the 2013 Regulation will continue to apply in all Member States. Accordingly, if intelligence reveals that infringing goods are about to be imported into Ireland, an AFA can be filed with the Irish Customs Authorities. Similarly, an AFA can continue to be filed with HMRC until IP completion day (currently set to be 31 December 2020) under the European Regime (see HMRC's updated Notice 34 dated 24 June 2020, available at *https://www.gov.uk/government/publications/notice-34-intellectual-property-rights* [Accessed 21 September 2020]).

**25-022B** Following IP completion day, the UK implementation of the 2013 Regulation will take effect (see para.25-026). The UK version of Regulation 608/2013 refers (at art.6(1)) to HMRC establishing an application form which, subject to any copyright concerns being resolved, is likely to mirror the existing AFA and require the input of the same information.

### 11. Exchange of Information

*Replace paragraph:*

**25-033** By art.32, the 2013 Regulation requires the Commission to establish a new central database by January 2015 and indeed, such a database is being developed, currently known as COPIS. It is designed to be an EU-wide system for registering and disseminating applications for action amongst customs authorities. Article 31 obliges customs authorities to notify the Commission of decisions on applications for action, extensions of their duration and suspensions of a decision on an application, as well as information about seized goods (which must exclude personal data). It is planned that part of the database will be accessible to right-holders who will be able to submit information into the respective file by uploading to assist customs officers to identify counterfeit goods. The UK implementation of Regulation 608/2013 (see para.25-026) omits art.32, so from IP completion day (currently set to be 31 December 2020), there will be no formal mechanism for any data from the UK to be added to COPIS.

## 12. Scale of Use of the European Regime

*Add to the end of the paragraph:*

In 2019, a joint report from the EUIPO and EUROPOL entitled "Intellectual Property Crime Threat Assessment 2019" (available on the EUIPO website) published the latest data to 2017. Over the four years to 2017, the number of seizures decreased markedly, although the number of articles seized grew to over 41 million in 2016 before dropping to 31 million in 2017. The value per seizure increased from around €6,500 in 2014 to over €10,000 in 2017. For further details and the key product sectors involved, see the 2019 Report. **25-034**

*Add new paragraph:*

There is also a more detailed "Report on the EU Enforcement of Intellectual Property Rights: Results at EU Borders and in Member States 2013–2017" dated September 2019, also available on the EUIPO website. **25-034A**

CHAPTER 27

# COMPANY AND BUSINESS NAMES

TABLE OF CONTENTS



## 1. COMPANY NAMES

*Replace paragraph:*

**27-003** Once a company has registered its name, the Secretary of State may direct it to change its name if it is the same as or in the opinion of the Secretary of State, "too like" another name on the Registrar's index of companies names or a name that should have appeared in that index at that time.[9] Note that any such direction must be given within 12 months of the company's registration by the name in question and must specify the period within which the company is to change its name.[10] If a company fails to comply with the direction, an offence[11] is committed by the company and every officer of the company[12] who is in default. The ways in which a company may change its name are set out at s.77 of the Companies Act 2006.

[9] Companies Act 2006 ss.67–68 (see s.68(1)–(2)).

[10] See the Companies Act 2006 s.68(1)–(2). The Secretary of State may by a further direction extend that period. Any such direction must be given before the end of the period for the time specified (see the Companies Act 2006 s.68(3)).

[11] A person guilty of an offence under s.68 is liable on summary conviction to a fine not exceeding level 3 on the standard scale and, for continued contravention, a daily default fine not exceeding one-tenth of level 3 on the standard scale (see the Companies Act 2006 s.68(6)).

[12] For this purpose a shadow director is treated as an officer of the company (see the Companies Act 2006 s.68(5)).

## 6. OVERSEAS COMPANIES

*Replace footnote 66:*

**27-019** [66] Companies Act 2006 s.1047. Section 1047(3) of the Companies Act 2006 which states "Subject only to subsection (5), an EEA company may always register its corporate name" as well as s.1047(5) will be repealed by the Companies, Limited Liability Partnerships and Partnerships (Amendment etc.) (EU Exit) Regulations (SI 2019/348) Sch.1 para.14 (a) and (c) which will come into force on IP completion day on 31 December 2020.

Chapter 28

# THE INTERNET

Table of Contents



Introduction

## 2. Aspects of Use Peculiar to the Internet

### Advertising Keywords

*Replace paragraph:*

In *Google v Louis Vuitton*[9] it was held by the Court of Justice that although the selection by an advertiser of a particular keyword constituted use in the course of trade and the provision by a search engine service provider (Google) of the opportunity to select that keyword was undertaken in the course of trade, the service provider had not itself used the sign in the course of trade. As a technical matter the sign was plainly used by the service provider in some sense in the process of displaying the customer's advertisement. The position may be different where the sign complained of is used in the advertisement itself or indeed where by controlling the advertisements selected for display a party selects advertisements that are targeted at a particular jurisdiction, leading to infringement.[9a] However, the sign was not used in the service provider's own commercial communications. These matters are addressed in detail at paras 28-087 to 28-094. **28-030**

[9] (C-236/08), (C-237/08) and (C-238/08) [2010] R.P.C. 19.

[9a] *Argos Ltd v Argos Systems Inc* [2018] EWCA Civ 2211; [2019] F.S.R. 3.

## 3. Disputes Over Domain Name Registrations

*Replace footnote 13:*

### One in a Million[13]

[13] *British Telecommunications Plc v One in a Million Ltd* [1999] 1 W.L.R. 903; [1999] F.S.R. 1 CA. **28-033**

*Replace paragraph:*

Whether a registration constitutes an instrument of fraud depends on all the circumstances. Cybersquatting does not itself provide a comprehensive basis for a claim. The claimant must establish relevant reputation and goodwill in the name taken.[15a] There are essentially two types of case. Some names are so distinctive, denoting one trader and nobody else, that the conclusion may be drawn from the **28-035** domain name itself. Thus:

> "I also believe that domain names comprising the name "Marks & Spencer" are instruments of fraud. Any realistic use of them as domain names would result in passing off...".'[16]

[15a] *Media Agency Group Ltd v Space Media Agency Ltd* [2019] F.S.R. 27.

[16] [1999] 1 W.L.R. 903 at 925A; [1999] F.S.R. 1 at 23. Cf. *Phones 4U Ltd v Phone 4U.co.uk Internet Ltd* [2005] EWHC 334 (Ch) in which insufficient goodwill in the mark "Phones4U" had been generated for the defendants use to constitute a misrepresentation.

## Application of the Decision in One in a Million

*Add to the end of the paragraph:*

**28-037** However, an allegation of cybersquatting or hijacking of some other registered name does not dispense with the need to prove the elements of the tort relied upon, whether threatened infringement of a trade mark or goodwill and reputation in the case of passing off.[19a]

[19a] *Media Agency Group Ltd v Space Media Agency Ltd* [2019] F.S.R. 27.

## Jurisdiction

*Add to the end of the paragraph:*

**28-039** However, where the use complained of amounts to an offer for sale within a particular country or a use otherwise "targeted" to consumers, there then the courts of that state have jurisdiction on the basis that the act of infringing use is carried out within the state so targeted, even where the defendant is domiciled elsewhere and the servers of the electronic network used to display the mark are in a different jurisdiction.[24a]

[24a] *AMS Neve v Heritage Audio* (C-172/18) [2019] F.S.R. 40.

### 4. JURISDICTION AND INFRINGEMENT

*Replace paragraph:*

**28-071** A key question is whether use is "aimed and directed" at a consumer in the UK. In *Dearlove v Combs*[52] the issue of whether the contents of certain web pages constituted use of the sign "Diddy" in the UK was considered by Kitchin J (as he then was). After referring to *1-800 FLOWERS* and *Euromarket v Peters*, he said:

> "I believe it is clear from these authorities that placing a mark on the Internet from a location outside the UK can constitute use of that mark in the UK. The Internet is now a powerful means of advertising and promoting goods and services within the UK even though the provider himself is based abroad. The fundamental question is whether or not the average consumer of the goods or services in issue within the UK would regard the advertisement and site as being aimed and directed at him. All material circumstances must be considered and these will include the nature of the goods or services, the appearance of the website, whether it is possible to buy goods or services from the website, whether or not the advertiser has in fact sold goods or services in the UK through the website or otherwise, and any other evidence of the advertiser's intention."

Kitchen LJ returned to the question in *Merck KgaA v Merck Sharp & Dohme Corp*,[52a] holding in the context of an advertisement offering goods for sale on a website that the mere fact of accessibility from the UK is not sufficient to establish targeting. The issue of targeting must be considered objectively from the perspective of average consumers in the UK taking into account all relevant circumstances. While the issue of subjective intention on the part of the defendant may be relevant, it is not necessarily determinative. Such subjective intention "cannot, however, make a website or page (or part of a page which is plainly, when objectively considered, not intended for the UK, into a page which is so intended." An intention to target the UK cannot "make a page which is objectively not intended for the Uk into a page which is so intended."[52b] The issue of targeting must be considered in respect of each infringing act complained of.

[52] [2008] E.M.L.R. 2

[52a] 2017] EWCA Civ 1834; [2018] E.T.M.R. 10 at [167]–[170].

[52b] *Argos Ltd v Argos Systems Inc* [2018] EWCA Civ 2211; [2019] F.S.R. 3 at [51].

*After item "(4)", add:*

(5) The test is objective based on the reaction of the relevant average consumer. The subjective intention of the defendant may be relevant, but is not necessarily determinative. **28-073**

*Add to the end of the paragraph:*

The outcome may differ depending on the content of a website from time to time. **28-074** Where the domain name at which a webpage was accessible was identical to the claimant's mark but the content of the webpage itself was not directed to consumers in the UK, the issue of targeting was determined by the nature of the advertisements displayed on an advertising section of the webpage. When the advertisements were relevant to UK consumers, the use of the domain in relation to the advertising part of the webpage was targeted at the UK. Otherwise, there was no targeting.[56a]

[56a] *Argos Ltd v Argos Systems Inc* [2018] EWCA Civ 2211; [2019] F.S.R. 3 at [58]–[60].

## Liability of Internet Service Providers

*Replace paragraph:*

Although the allocation of jurisdiction between Member States under art.5(3) of **28-075** the Brussels Regulation was considered in the context of internet use of trade marks in *Wintersteiger v Products 4U*[57] (see para.28-039), it is important to bear in mind that the substantive question of whether use of a sign on a particular website constitutes infringing use within a particular Member State is a matter which "falls within the scope of the examination of the substance of the action that the court having jurisdiction will undertake in the light of the applicable substantive law".[58] Where goods bearing a sign are sold from a website situated outside the territory of the EU but are delivered to a customer within a Member State, the sign is used within the Member State even if the goods have not been the subject, prior to the sale, of an offer for sale or advertising targeting consumers of that state (see *Blomqvist v Rolex SA*[59]). Although such use has been held to constitute infringement where there has been no offer for sale or advertising targeting consumers within the jurisdiction, the scope of injunctive relief is presumably limited to an order preventing the fulfilment of orders from customers within the jurisdiction. The issue of jurisdiction in respect of Internet trade mark use is otherwise decided by reference to the doctrine of targeting, discussed in the previous section. Where the issue of targeting depends on the nature of advertisements displayed on the webpage in issue, the party who controls the advertisements displayed (such as Google, for example) may have liability in respect of the act of targeting.[59a]

[57] (C-523/10) [2012] E.T.M.R. 31 and *AMS Neve v Heritage Audio* (C-172/18) [2019] F.S.R. 40.

[58] *Wintersteiger* [2012] E.T.M.R. 31 at [26]. See also *Argos Ltd v Argos Systems Inc* [2018] EWCA Civ 2211; [2019] F.S.R. 3 at [48].

[59] (C-98/13) [2014] E.T.M.R. 25.

[59a] *Argos Ltd v Argos Systems Inc* [2018] EWCA Civ 2211; [2019] F.S.R. 3 at [64].

*Replace footnote 65:*

**28-077** [65] (C-324/09) [2011] E.T.M.R. 52.

*Replace footnote 67:*

**28-079** [67] [2016] EWCA Civ 658; [2016] E.T.M.R. 43, upholding the decision of Arnold J at first instance. The decision of the Court of Appeal was subsequently upheld on appeal to the Supreme Court other than in respect of who should bear the cost of implementation of blocking measures. *Cartier International AG v British Telecommunications Plc* [2018] UKSC 28; [2018] 1 W.L.R. 3259; [2018] E.T.M.R. 32.

*After "In Cartier, Court of Appeal", in the first sentence, add new footnote 71a:*

**28-080** [71a] The decision of the Court of Appeal was subsequently upheld on appeal to the Supreme Court other than in respect of who should bear the cost of implementation of blocking measures. *Cartier International AG v British Telecommunications Plc* [2018] UKSC 28; [2018] 1 W.L.R. 3259; [2018] E.T.M.R. 32.

## 5. Metatags, Advertising Keywords and "Invisible Use"

### Google v Louis Vuitton

*Replace paragraph:*

**28-092** The issue of jurisdiction in respect of an infringement claim arising from the use of advertising keywords on a search engine using the top level domain of a different Member State to that in which a national trade mark was registered was considered in *Wintersteiger v Products 4U*.[91] Such infringement is actionable either in the place where the trade mark relied on is registered or in the place where the advertiser is located. Where use is targeted at consumers in a particular state, the infringement is also actionable in that state irrespective of whether the defendant is domiciled elsewhere or the servers from which the advertisement or website in issue are controlled are in yet another jurisdiction.[91a]

[91] (C-523/10) [2012] E.T.M.R. 31, see also *AMS Neve v Heritage Audio* (C-172/18) [2019] F.S.R. 40.

[91a] *AMS Neve v Heritage Audio* (C-172/18) [2019] F.S.R. 40.

Chapter 29

# HUMAN RIGHTS AND TRADE MARKS

Table of Contents



## 2. Article 10—Freedom of Expression

*Add new paragraph:*

In *Constantin Film Produktion GmbH v EUIPO*[28a] the CJEU addressed directly the question whether the art.10 right to freedom of expression is of relevance to the trade mark field in the same way it is in the fields of art, culture and literature. The General Court had found that freedom of expression concerns do not exist in the field of trade marks[28b] but the CJEU rejected this in forthright terms: "freedom of expression, enshrined in Article 11 of the Charter of Fundamental Rights of the European Union, must . . . be taken into account when applying Article 7(1)(f) of Regulation No 207/2009."[28c] In other words, freedom of expression is one of the factors to be taken into account when applying the provisions of the EU Trade Mark Regulation but does not override all others.[28d] The *Constantin Film* case arose from the refusal by the EUIPO to register the mark "*Fack Ju Göhte*" by reason of its being contrary to the accepted principles of morality because the words "*fack ju*" were likely to be perceived as shocking and vulgar by the German public (under the general ground for refusal in art.7(1)(f) of the old EU Trade Mark Regulation, No. 207/2009 (now art.7(1)(f) of Regulation 2017/1001)). The German phonetic transcription of the English expression "fuck you" was used along with a misspelling of Goethe as the title of a very successful comedy film series *Fack Ju Göhte* seen by more than 7.4 million people in Germany. In annulling the decision of the GC and EUIPO, the CJEU held that "no concrete evidence has been put forward plausibly to explain why the German-speaking public at large will perceive the word sign '*Fack Ju Göhte*' as going against the fundamental moral values and standards of society when it is used as a trade mark, even though that same public does not appear to have considered the title of the eponymous comedies to be contrary to accepted principles of morality".[28e] Indeed, "the success of the eponymous comedies with the relevant public and, in particular, the absence of controversy as regards their title must be taken into account in order to determine whether the relevant public perceives the mark applied for as contrary to accepted principles of morality and, therefore, to establish whether that absolute ground for refusal precludes its registration."[28f] 29-007A

[28a] (C-240/18 P) 27 February 2020.

[28b] *Constantin Film Produktion v EUIPO (Fack Ju Göhte)* EU:T:2018:27 (T-69/17), not published, EU:T:2018:27, GC, at [29]. In his Opinion in the CJEU case, AG Bobek suggested, at [56] that the GC had perhaps meant "not that there is no role whatsoever for freedom of expression in trade mark law, but rather that, in contrast to the fields of arts, culture, and literature, the weight to be given to freedom

of expression in the area of trade mark law may be somewhat different, perhaps slightly lighter, in the overall balancing of the rights and interests present."

[28c] *Constantin Film Produktion GmbH v EUIPO* (C-240/18 P) CJEU, at [56].

[28d] In his Opinion in *Constantin Film Produktion GmbH v EUIPO* (C-240/18 P), AG Bobek noted (at n.27): "freedom of expression can be also invoked by those wishing to make unauthorised use of a trade mark, for reasons that they consider socially important. See, for example, Geiger, C., and Izyumenko, E. (eds.), 'Intellectual property before the European Court of Human Rights', in Geiger, C., Nard, C.A., and Seuba, X., *Intellectual Property and the Judiciary*, Edward Elgar Publishing, Cheltenham, 2018, pp. 9 to 90, especially pp. 50 to 54, and Senftleben, M., 'Free signs and free use: How to offer room for freedom of expression within the trademark system', in Geiger, C., Research Handbook on Human Rights and Intellectual Property, Edward Elgar Publishing, Cheltenham, 2015, pp. 354 to 376. See also the Opinion of Advocate General Poiares Maduro in Joined Cases *Google France and Google* (C-236/08 to C-238/08, EU:C:2009:569, point 102)."

[28e] *Constantin Film Produktion GmbH v EUIPO* (C-240/18 P) CJEU, at [69]. It was also noted by the CJEU that "the perception of that English phrase by the German-speaking public is not necessarily the same as the perception thereof by the English-speaking public, even if it is well known to the German-speaking public and the latter knows its meaning, since sensitivity in the mother tongue may be greater than in a foreign language. For the same reason, the German-speaking public also does not necessarily perceive the English phrase in the same way as it would perceive the German translation of it. Furthermore, the title of the comedies at issue, and therefore the mark applied for, does not consist of that English phrase as such but of its phonetic transcription in German, accompanied by the element '*Göhte*'." At [68].

[28f] *Constantin Film Produktion GmbH v EUIPO* (C-240/18 P), CJEU, at [70].

*Replace footnote 31:*

29-008 [31] [2002] R.P.C. 628 at [21]. In *Csibi v Romania*, EuCtHR no. 16632/12, 4 June 2019, the European Court of Human Rights rejected a claim by a Romanian trade mark applicant that the refusal by the Romanian Trade Marks Office to register the mark "Szekely Land is not Romania!" by reason of its being contrary to ordre public was an unjustified restriction of his freedom of expression. According to the Office, to suggest that Szekely Land (an unofficial name for three Romanian counties) was not part of Romania could encourage territorial separatists and therefore registration was refused. The EuCtHR found that "such an interference pursued the legitimate aims of protecting Romania's territorial integrity, national security, and public order" (at [41], "the applicant has not proved that the refusal to register the trademark in question had any impact on his possible commercial activities" (at [45]) and therefore "the refusal of registration was . . . proportionate in the circumstances of the present case, which disclose no appearance of a violation of Article 10 of the Convention" (at [46]).

# AMENDED APPENDICES

APPENDIX 1

## TRADE MARKS ACT 1994

*Replace with:*

A1-001 (1994 CHAPTER 26)

An Act to make new provision for registered trade marks, implementing Council Directive No. 89/104/EEC of 21st December 1988 to approximate the laws of the Member States relating to trade marks; to make provision in connection with Council Regulation (EC) No. 40/94 of 20th December 1993 on the Community trade mark; to give effect to the Madrid Protocol Relating to the International Registration of Marks of 27th June 1989, and to certain provisions of the Paris Convention for the Protection of Industrial Property of 20th March 1883, as revised and amended; and for connected purposes.

[21st July 1994]

BE IT ENACTED by the Queen's most Excellent Majesty, by and with the advice and consent of the Lords Spiritual and Temporal, and Commons, in this present Parliament assembled, and by the authority of the same, as follows:—

ARRANGEMENT OF SECTIONS

PART I

REGISTERED TRADE MARKS

*Introductory*

*Section*

## PART I – REGISTERED TRADE MARKS

*Introductory*

### Trade marks.

A1-002 **1.**—[(1) In this Act a "trade mark" meansany sign which is capable—
- (a) of being represented in the register in a manner which enables the registrar and other competent authoritics and the public to determine the clear and precise subject matter of the protection afforded to the proprietor, and
- (b) of distinguishing goods or services of one undertaking from those of other undertakings.

A trade mark may, in particular, consist of words (including personal names), designs, letters, numerals, colours, sounds or the shape of goods or their packaging.]

(2) References in this Act to a trade mark include, unless the context otherwise requires, references to a collective mark (see section 49) or certification mark (see section 50).

### Registered trade marks.

A1-003 **2.**—(1) A registered trade mark is a property right obtained by the registration of the trade mark under this Act and the proprietor of a registered trade mark has the rights and remedies provided by this Act.

(2) No proceedings lie to prevent or recover damages for the infringement of an unregistered trade mark as such; but nothing in this Act affects the law relating to passing off.

*Grounds for refusal of registration*

### Absolute grounds for refusal of registration.

A1-004 **3.**—(1) The following shall not be registered—
- (a) signs which do not satisfy the requirements of section 1(1).
- (b) trade marks which are devoid of any distinctive character.
- (c) trade marks which consist exclusively of signs or indications which may serve, in trade, to designate the kind, quality, quantity, intended purpose, value, geographical origin, the time of production of goods or of rendering of services, or other characteristics of goods or services,
- (d) trade marks which consist exclusively of signs or indications which have become customary in the current language or in the bona fide and established practices of the trade:

  Provided that, a trade mark shall not be refused registration by virtue of paragraph (b), (c) or (d) above if, before the date of application for registration, it has in fact acquired a distinctive character as a result of the use made of it.

(2) A sign shall not be registered as a trade mark if it consists exclusively of—
- (a) the shape [, or another characteristic,] which results from the nature of the goods themselves,

(b) (b) the shape [, or another characteristic,] of goods which is necessary to obtain a technical result, or
(c) (c) the shape [, or another characteristic,] which gives substantial value to the goods.

(3) A trade mark shall not be registered if it is—
(a) contrary to public policy or to accepted principles of morality, or
(b) of such a nature as to deceive the public (for instance as to the nature, quality or geographical origin of the goods or service).

(4) A trade mark shall not be registered if or to the extent that its use is prohibited in the United Kingdom by any enactment or rule of law or by any provision of [EU] law [other than law relating to trade marks].

[(4A) A trade mark is not to be registered if its registration is prohibited by or under—
(a) any enactment or rule of law,
(b) any provision of EU law, or
(c) any international agreement to which the United Kingdom or the EU is a party,

providing for the protection of designations of origin or geographical indications.

(4B) A trade mark is not to be registered if its registration is prohibited by or under—
(a) any provision of EU law, or
(b) any international agreement to which the EU is a party,

providing for the protection of traditional terms for wine or traditional specialities guaranteed.

(4C) A trade mark is not to be registered if it—
(a) consists of, or reproduces in its essential elements, an earlier plant variety denomination registered as mentioned in subsection (4D), and
(b) is in respect of plant varieties of the same or closely related species.

(4D) Subsection (4C)(a) refers to registration in accordance with any—
(a) enactment or rule of law,
(b) provision of EU law, or
(c) international agreement to which the United Kingdom or the EU is a party,

providing for the protection of plant variety rights.]

(5) A trade mark shall not be registered in the cases specified, or referred to, in section 4 (specially protected emblems).

(6) A trade mark shall not be registered if or to the extent that the application is made in bad faith.

**Specially protected emblems.**

**4.**—(1) A trade mark which consists of or contains— **A1-005**
(a) the Royal arms, or any of the principal armorial bearings of the Royal arms, or any insignia or device so nearly resembling the Royal arms or any such armorial bearing as to be likely to be mistaken for them or it,
(b) a representation of the Royal crown or any of the Royal flags,
(c) a representation of Her Majesty or any member of the Royal family, or any colourable imitation thereof, or
(d) words, letters or devices likely to lead persons to think that the applicant either has or recently has had Royal patronage or authorisation,

shall not be registered unless it appears to the registrar that consent has been given by or on behalf of Her Majesty or, as the case may be, the relevant member of the Royal family.

(2) A trade mark which consists of or contains a representation of—

(a) the national flag of the United Kingdom (commonly known as the Union Jack), or

(b) the flag of England, Wales, Scotland, Northern Ireland or the Isle of Man,

shall not be registered if it appears to the registrar that the use of the trade mark would be misleading or grossly offensive.

Provision may be made by rules identifying the flags to which paragraph (b) applies.

(3) A trade mark shall not be registered in the cases specified in—

section 57 (national emblems, &c. of Convention countries), or section 58 (emblems, &c. of certain international organisations)

(4) Provision may be made by rules prohibiting in such cases as may be prescribed the registration of a trade mark which consists of or contains—

(a) arms to which a person is entitled by virtue of a grant of arms by the Crown, or

(b) insignia so nearly resembling such arms as to be likely to be mistaken for them,

unless it appears to the registrar that consent has been given by or on behalf of that person. Where such a mark is registered, nothing in this Act shall be construed as authorising its use in any way contrary to the laws of arms.

(5) A trade mark which consists of or contains a controlled representation within the meaning of the Olympic Symbol etc. (Protection) Act 1995 shall not be registered unless it appears to the registrar—

(a) that the application is made by the person for the time being appointed under section 1(2) of the Olympic Symbol etc (Protection) Act 1995 (power of Secretary of State to appoint a person as the proprietor of the Olympics association right), or

(b) that consent has been given by or on behalf of the person mentioned in paragraph (a) above.

**Relative grounds for refusal of registration.**

A1-006 **5.**—(1) A trade mark shall not be registered if it is identical with an earlier trade mark and the goods or services for which the trade mark is applied for are identical with the goods or services for which the earlier trade mark is protected.

(2) A trade mark shall not be registered if because—

(a) it is identical with an earlier trade mark and is to be registered for goods or services similar to those for which the earlier trade mark is protected, or

(b) it is similar to an earlier trade mark and is to be registered for goods or services identical with or similar to those for which the earlier trade mark is protected,

there exists a likelihood of confusion of the part of the public, which includes the likelihood of association with the earlier trade mark.

(3) A trade mark which—

(a) is identical with or similar to an earlier trade mark, […]

(b) […]

shall not be registered if, or to the extent that, the earlier trade mark has a reputation in the United Kingdom (or, in the case of a [European Union] trade mark [or international trade mark (EC)], in [the European Union]) and the use of the later mark without due cause would take unfair advantage of, or be detrimental to, the distinctive character or the repute of the earlier trade mark.

[(3A) Subsection (3) applies irrespective of whether the goods and services for which the trade mark is to be registered are identical with, similar to or not similar to those for which the earlier trade mark is protected.]

(4) A trade mark shall not be registered if, or to the extent that, its use in the United Kingdom is liable to be prevented—

(a) by virtue of any rule of law (in particular, the law of passing off) protecting an unregistered trade mark or other sign used in the course of trade, [where the condition in subsection (4A) is met,]

[(aa) by virtue of any provision of EU law, or any enactment or rule of law, providing for protection of designations of origin or geographical indications, where the condition in subsection (4B) is met,] or

(b) by virtue of an earlier right other than those referred to in subsections (1) to (3) or paragraph (a) [or (aa)] above, in particular by virtue of the law of copyright [or the law relating to industrial property rights].

A person thus entitled to prevent the use of a trade mark is referred to in this Act as the proprietor of an "earlier right" in relation to the trade mark.

[(4A) The condition mentioned in subsection (4)(a) is that the rights to the unregistered trade mark or other sign were acquired prior to the date of application for registration of the trade mark or date of the priority claimed for that application.

(4B) The condition mentioned in subsection 4(aa) is that—

(a) an application for a designation of origin or a geographical indication has been submitted prior to the date of application for registration of the trade mark or the date of the priority claimed for that application, and

(b) the designation of origin or (as the case may be) geographical indication is subsequently registered.]

(5) Nothing in this section prevents the registration of a trade mark where the proprietor of the earlier trade mark or other earlier right consents to the registration.

[(6) Where an agent or representative ("R") of the proprietor of a trade mark applies, without the proprietor's consent, for the registration of the trade mark in R's own name, the application is to be refused unless R justifies that action.]

**Grounds for refusal relating to only some of the goods or services.**

**[5A.**(1) Where grounds for refusal of an application for registration of a trade mark exist in respect of only some of the goods or services in respect of which the trade mark is applied for, the application is to be refused in relation to those goods and services only.] **A1-006.1**

**Meaning of "earlier trade mark".**

**6.**—(1) In this Act an "earlier trade mark" means — **A1-007**

(a) a registered trade mark, international trade mark (UK), [[European Union] trade mark or international trade mark (EC)] which has a date of application for registration earlier than that of the trade mark in question, taking account (where appropriate) of the priorities claimed in respect of the trade marks, [(b) a [European Union] trade mark or international trade mark (EC) which has a valid claim to seniority from an earlier registered trade mark or international trade mark (UK) [even where the earlier trade mark has been surrendered or its registration has expired],]

(ba) a registered trade mark or international trade mark (UK) which–

(i) has been converted from a [European Union] trade mark or international trade mark (EC) which itself had a valid claim to seniority within paragraph (b) from an earlier trade mark, and

(ii) accordingly has the same claim to seniority, or

(c) a trade mark which, at the date of application for registration of the trade mark in question or (where appropriate) of the priority claimed in respect of the application, was entitled to protection under the Parts Convention [or the WTO agreement] as a well known trade mark.

(2) References in this Act to an earlier trade mark include a trade mark in respect of which an application for registration has been made and which, if registered, would be an earlier trade mark by virtue of subsection (1)(a) or (b), subject to its being so registered.

(3) […]

**[Raising of relative grounds in opposition proceedings in case of non-use.**

A1-008 **6A.**—(1) This section applies where–

(a) an application for registration of a trade mark has been published,

(b) there is an earlier trade mark [of a kind falling within section 6(1)(a), (b) or (ba)] in relation to which the conditions set out in section 5(1), (2) or (3) obtain, and

(c) the registration procedure for the earlier trade mark was completed before the start of the [relevant period].

[(1A) In this section "the relevant period" means the period of 5 years ending with the date of the application for registration mentioned in subsection (1)(a) or (where applicable) the date of the priority claimed for that application.]

(2) In opposition proceedings, the registrar shall not refuse to register the trade mark by reason of the earlier trade mark unless the use conditions are met.

(3) The use conditions are met if–

(a) within the [relevant period] of the application the earlier trade mark has been put to genuine use in the United Kingdom by the proprietor or with his consent in relation to the goods or services for which it is registered, or

(b) the earlier trade mark has not been so used, but there are proper reasons for non-use.

(4) For these purposes–

(a) use of a trade mark includes use in a form [(the "variant form")] differing in elements which do not alter the distinctive character of the mark in the form in which it was registered [(regardless of whether or not the trade mark in the variant form is also registered in the name of the proprietor)], and

(b) use in the United Kingdom includes affixing the trade mark to goods or to the packaging of goods in the United Kingdom solely for export purposes.

(5) In relation to a [European Union] trade mark [or international trade mark (EC)], any reference in subsection (3) or (4) to the United Kingdom shall be construed as a reference to the [European Union].

[(5A) In relation to an international trade mark (EC) the reference in subsection (1)(c) to the completion of the registration procedure is to be construed as a reference to the publication by the European Union Intellectual Property Office of the matters referred to in Article 190(2) of the European Union Trade Mark Regulation.]

(6) Where an earlier trade mark satisfies the use conditions in respect of some only of the goods or services for which it is registered, it shall be treated for the purposes of this section as if it were registered only in respect of those goods or services.

(7) Nothing in this section affects–

(a) the refusal of registration on the grounds mentioned in section 3 (absolute grounds for refusal) or section 5(4)(relative grounds of refusal on the basis of an earlier right), or

(b) the making of an application for a declaration of invalidity under section 47(2) (application on relative grounds where no consent to registration).]

**Raising of relative grounds in case of honest concurrent use.**

**7.**—(1) This section applies where on an application for the registration of a trade mark it appears to the registrar— **A1-009**

(a) that there is an earlier trade mark in relation to which the conditions set out in section 5(1), (2) or (3) obtain, or

(b) that there is an earlier right in relation to which the condition set out in section 5(4) is satisfied,

but the applicant shows to the satisfaction of the registrar that there has been honest concurrent use of the trade mark for which registration is sought.

(2) In that case the registrar shall not refuse the application by reason of the earlier trade mark or other earlier right unless objection on that ground is raised in opposition proceedings by the proprietor of that earlier trade mark or other earlier right.

(3) For the purposes of this section "honest concurrent use" means such use in the United Kingdom, by the applicant or with his consent, as would formerly have amounted to honest concurrent use for the purposes of section 12(2) of the Trade Marks Act 1938.

(4) Nothing in this section affects—

(a) the refusal of registration on the grounds mentioned in section 3 (absolute grounds for refusal), or

(b) the making of an application for a declaration of invalidity under section 47(2) (application on relative grounds where no consent to registration).

(5) This section does not apply when there is an order in force under section 8 below.

**Power to require that relative grounds be raised in opposition proceedings.**

**8.**—(1) The Secretary of State may by order provide that in any case a trade mark shall not be refused registration on a ground mentioned in section 5 (relative grounds for refusal) unless objection on that ground is raised in opposition proceedings by the proprietor of the earlier trade mark or other earlier right. **A1-010**

(2) The order may make such consequential provision as appears to the Secretary of State appropriate—

(a) with respect to the carrying out by the registrar of searches of earlier trade marks, and

(b) as to the persons by whom an application for a declaration of invalidity may be made on the grounds specified in section 47(2) (relative grounds).

(3) An order making such provision as is mentioned in subsection (2)(a) may direct that so much of section 37 (examination of application) as requires a search to be carried out shall cease to have effect.

(4) An order making such provision as is mentioned in subsection (2)(b) may provide that so much of section 47(3) as provides that any person may make an application for a declaration of invalidity shall have effect subject to the provisions of the order.

(5) An order under this section shall be made by statutory instrument, and no order shall be made unless a draft of it has been laid before and approved by a resolution of each House of Parliament. No such draft of an order making such provision as is mentioned in subsection (1) shall be laid before Parliament until after the end of the period of ten years beginning with the day on which applications for Community trade marks may first be filed in pursuance of [Council Regulation (EC) No 40/94 of 20th December 1993 on the Community trade mark].

(6) An order under this section may contain such transitional provisions as appear to the Secretary of State to be appropriate.

*Effects of registered trade mark*

**Rights conferred by registered trade mark.**

A1-011 **9.**—(1) The proprietor of a registered trade mark has exclusive rights in the trade mark which are infringed by use of the trade mark in the United Kingdom without his consent.

The acts amounting to infringement, if done without the consent of the proprietor, are specified in [subsections (1) to (3) of]section 10.

[(1A) See subsection (3B) of section 10 for provision about certain other acts amounting to infringement of a registered trade mark.

(1B) Subsection (1) is without prejudice to the rights of proprietors acquired before the date of filing of the application for registration or (where applicable) the date of the priority claimed in respect of that application.]

(2) References in this Act to the infringement of a registered trade mark are to any [...] infringement of the rights of the proprietor [such as is mentioned in subsection (1) or (1A)].

(3) The rights of the proprietor have effect from the date of registration (which in accordance with section 40(3) is the date of filing of the application for registration):

Provided that—

(a) no infringement proceedings may be begun before the date on which the trade mark is in fact registered; and

(b) no offence under section 92 (unauthorised use of trade mark, &c. in relation to goods) is committed by anything done before the date of publication of the registration.

**Infringement of registered trade mark.**

**10.**—(1) A person infringes a registered trade mark if he uses in the course of trade a sign which is identical with the trade mark in relation to goods or services which are identical with those for which it is registered. **A1-012**

(2) A person infringes a registered trade mark if he uses in the course of trade a sign where because—

- (a) the sign is identical with the trade mark and is used in relation to goods or services similar to those for which the trade mark is registered, or
- (b) the sign is similar to the trade mark and is used in relation to goods or services identical with or similar to those for which the trade mark is registered,

there exists a likelihood of confusion on the part of the public, which includes the likelihood of association with the trade mark.

(3) A person infringes a registered trade mark if he uses in the course of trade [, in relation to goods or services,] a sign which—

- (a) is identical with or similar to the trade mark, [...]
- (b) [...]

where the trade mark has a reputation in the United Kingdom and the use of the sign, being without due cause, takes unfair advantage of, or is detrimental to, the distinctive character or the repute of the trade mark.

[(3A) Subsection (3) applies irrespective of whether the goods and services in relation to which the sign is used are identical with, similar to or not similar to those for which the trade mark is registered.

(3B) Where the risk exists that the packaging, labels, tags, security or authenticity features or devices, or any other means to which the trade mark is affixed could be used in relation to goods or services and that use would constitute an infringement of the rights of the proprietor of the trade mark, a person infringes a registered trade mark if the person carries out in the course of trade any of the following acts—

- (a) affixing a sign identical with, or similar to, the trade mark on packaging, labels, tags, security or authenticity features or devices, or any other means to which the mark may be affixed; or
- (b) offering or placing on the market, or stocking for those purposes, or importing or exporting, packaging, labels, tags, security or authenticity features or devices, or any other means to which the mark is affixed.]

(4) For the purposes of this section a person uses a sign if, in particular, he—

- (a) affixes it to goods or the packaging thereof;
- (b) offers or exposes goods for sale, puts them on the market or stocks them for those purposes under the sign, or offers or supplies services under the sign;
- (c) imports or exports goods under the sign; [...]
- [(ca) uses the sign as a trade or company name or part of a trade or company name;]
- (d) uses the sign on business papers or in advertising[; [and]]
- (e) uses the sign in comparative advertising in a manner that is contrary to the Business Protection from Misleading Marketing Regulations 2008.

(5) [...]

(6) [...]

**Right to prevent goods entering the UK without being released for free circulation**

A1-012.1 **[10A.**—(1) The proprietor of a registered trade mark is entitled to prevent third parties from bringing goods into the United Kingdom in the course of trade without being released for free circulation if they are goods for which the trade mark is registered which—

(a) come from outside the customs territory of the EU; and

(b) bear without authorisation a sign which is identical with the trade mark or cannot be distinguished in its essential aspects from the trade mark.

(2) In subsection (1) the reference to goods for which the trade mark is registered includes a reference to the packaging of goods for which the trade mark is registered.

(3) Subsection (1) is without prejudice to the rights of proprietors acquired before the date of application for registration of the trade mark, or (where applicable) the date of the priority claimed in respect of that application.

(4) The entitlement of the proprietor under subsection (1) is to lapse if—

(a) proceedings are initiated in accordance with the European Customs Enforcement Regulation to determine whether the trade mark has been infringed; and

(b) during those proceedings evidence is provided by the declarant or the holder of the goods that the proprietor of the trade mark is not entitled to prohibit the placing of the goods on the market in the country of final destination.

(5) References in this Act to the "European Customs Enforcement Regulation" are references to Regulation (EU) No 608/2013 of the European Parliament and of the Council of 12 June 2013 concerning customs enforcement of intellectual property rights.]

**Prohibition on the use of a trade mark registered in the name of an agent or representative**

A1-012.2 **[10B.**—(1) Subsection (2) applies where a trade mark is registered in the name of an agent or representative of a person ("P") who is the proprietor of the trade mark, without P's consent.

(2) Unless the agent or representative justifies the action mentioned in subsection (1), P may do either or both of the following—

(a) prevent the use of the trade mark by the agent or representative (notwithstanding the rights conferred by this Act in relation to a registered trade mark);

(b) apply for the rectification of the register so as to substitute P's name as the proprietor of the registered trade mark.]

**Limits on effect of registered trade mark.**

**A1-013** **11.**—(1) A registered trade mark is not infringed by the use of [a later registered trade mark where that later registered trade mark would not be declared invalid pursuant to section 47(2A) or (2G) or section 48(1).]

[(1A) A registered trade mark is not infringed by the use of a later registered European Union trade mark where that later European Union trade mark would not be declared invalid as a result of Article 60(1), (3), (4), 61(1), (2) or 64(2) of the European Union Trade Mark Regulation.

(1B) Where subsection (1) or (1A) applies, the later registered trade mark is not infringed by the use of the earlier trade mark even though the earlier trade mark may no longer be invoked against the later registered trade mark.]

(2) A registered trade mark is not infringed by—

(a) the use by [an individual] of his own name or address,

(b) the use of [signs or indications which are not distinctive or which concern] the kind, quality, quantity, intended purpose, value, geographical origin, the time of production of goods or of rendering of services, or other characteristics of goods or services, or

(c) the use of the trade mark [for the purpose of identifying or referring to goods or services as those of the proprietor of that trade mark, in particular where that use] is necessary to indicate the intended purpose of a product or service (in particular, as accessories or spare parts),

provided the use is in accordance with honest practices in industrial or commercial matters.

(3) A registered trade mark is not infringed by the use in the course of trade in a particular locality of an earlier right which applies only in that locality.

For this purpose an "earlier right" means an unregistered trade mark or other sign continuously used in relation to goods or services by a person or a predecessor in title of his from a date prior to whichever is the earlier of—

(a) the use of the first-mentioned trade mark in relation to those goods or services by the proprietor or a predecessor in title of his, or

(b) the registration of the first-mentioned trade mark in respect of those goods or services in the name of the proprietor or a predecessor in title of his;

and an earlier right shall be regarded as applying in a locality if, or to the extent that, its use in that locality is protected by virtue of any rule of law (in particular, the law of passing off).

**Non-use as defence in infringement proceedings**

**[11A.**—(1) The proprietor of a trade mark is entitled to prohibit the use of a sign only to the extent that the registration of the trade mark is not liable to be revoked pursuant to section 46(1)(a) or (b) (revocation on basis of non-use) at the date the action for infringement is brought. **A1-013.1**

(2) Subsection (3) applies in relation to an action for infringement of a registered trade mark where the registration procedure for the trade mark was completed before the start of the period of five years ending with the date the action is brought.

(3) If the defendant so requests, the proprietor of the trade mark must furnish proof—

(a) that during the five-year period preceding the date the action for infringement is brought, the trade mark has been put to genuine use in the United Kingdom by or with the consent of the proprietor in relation to the goods and services for which it is registered and which are cited as justification for the action, or

(b) that there are proper reasons for non-use.

(4) Nothing in subsections (2) and (3) overrides any provision of section 46, as applied by subsection (1) (including the words from "Provided that" to the end of subsection (3)).]

**Exhaustion of rights conferred by registered trade mark.**

A1-014 **12.**—(1) A registered trade mark is not infringed by the use of the trade mark in relation to goods which have been put on the market in the European Economic Area under that trade mark by the proprietor or with his consent.

(2) Subsection (1) does not apply where there exist legitimate reasons for the proprietor to oppose further dealings in the goods (in particular, where the condition of the goods has been changed or impaired after they have been put on the market).

**Registration subject to disclaimer or limitation.**

A1-015 **13.**—(1) An applicant for registration of a trade mark, or the proprietor of a registered trade mark, may—

(a) disclaim any right to the exclusive use of any specified element of the trade mark, or

(b) agree that the rights conferred by the registration shall be subject to a specified territorial or other limitation;

and where the registration of a trade mark is subject to a disclaimer or limitation, the rights conferred by section 9 (rights conferred by registered trade mark) are restricted accordingly.

(2) Provision shall be made by rules as to the publication and entry in the register of a disclaimer or limitation.

*Infringement proceedings*

**Action for infringement.**

A1-016 **14.**—(1) An infringement of a registered trade mark is actionable by the proprietor of the trade mark.

(2) In an action for infringement all such relief by way of damages, injunctions, accounts or otherwise is available to him as is available in respect of the infringement of any other property right.

**Order for erasure &c. of offending sign.**

A1-017 **15.**—(1) Where a person is found to have infringed a registered trade mark, the court may make an order requiring him—

(a) to cause the offending sign to be erased, removed or obliterated from any infringing goods, material or articles in his possession, custody or control, or

(b) if it is not reasonably practicable for the offending sign to be erased, removed or obliterated, to secure the destruction of the infringing goods, material or articles in question.

(2) If an order under subsection (1) is not complied with, or it appears to the court likely that such an order would not be complied with, the court may order that the infringing goods, material or articles be delivered to such person as the court may direct for erasure, removal or obliteration of the sign, or for destruction, as the case may be.

**Order for delivery up of infringing goods, material or articles.**

A1-018 **16.**—(1) The proprietor of a registered trade mark may apply to the court for an order for the delivery up to him, or such other person as the court may direct, of any infringing goods, material or articles which a person has in his possession, custody or control in the course of a business.

(2) An application shall not be made after the end of the period specified in section 18 (period after which remedy of delivery up not available), and no order shall be made unless the court also makes, or it appears to the court that there are grounds for making, an order under section 19 (order as to disposal of infringing goods, &c.).

(3) A person to whom any infringing goods, material or articles are delivered up in pursuance of an order under this section shall, if an order under section 19 is not made, retain them pending the making of an order, or the decision not to make an order, under that section.

(4) Nothing in this section affects any other power of the court.

**Meaning of "infringing goods, material or articles".**

**17.**—(1) In this Act the expressions "infringing goods", "infringing material" and "infringing articles" shall be construed as follows **A1-019**

(2) Goods are "infringing goods", in relation to a registered trade mark, if they or their packaging bear a sign identical or similar to that mark and—

(a) the application of the sign to the goods or their packaging was an infringement of the registered trade mark, or

(b) the goods are proposed to be imported into the United Kingdom and the application of the sign in the United Kingdom to them or their packaging would be an infringement of the registered trade mark, or

(c) the sign has otherwise been used in relation to the goods in such a way as to infringe the registered trade mark.

(3) Nothing in subsection (2) shall be construed as affecting the importation of goods which may lawfully be imported into the United Kingdom by virtue of an enforceable [EU] right.

(4) Material is "infringing material", in relation to a registered trade mark if it bears a sign identical or similar to that mark and either—

(a) it is used for labelling or packaging goods, as a business paper, or for advertising goods or services, in such a way as to infringe the registered trade mark, or

(b) it is intended to be so used and such use would infringe the registered trade mark.

(5) "Infringing articles", in relation to a registered trade mark, means articles—

(a) which are specifically designed or adapted for making copies of a sign identical or similar to that mark, and

(b) which a person has in his possession, custody or control, knowing or having reason to believe that they have been or are to be used to produce infringing goods or material.

**Period after which remedy of delivery up not available.**

**18.**—(1) An application for an order under section 16 (order for delivery up of infringing goods, material or articles) may not be made after the end of the period of six years from— **A1-020**

(a) in the case of infringing goods, the date on which the trade mark was applied to the goods or their packaging,

(b) in the case of infringing material, the date on which the trade mark was applied to the material, or

(c) in the case of infringing articles, the date on which they were made,

except as mentioned in the following provisions.

(2) If during the whole or part of that period the proprietor of the registered trade mark—

(a) is under a disability, or

(b) is prevented by fraud or concealment from discovering the facts entitling him to apply for an order.

an application may be made at any time before the end of the period of six years from the date on which he ceased to be under a disability or, as the case may be, could with reasonable diligence have discovered those facts.

(3) In subsection (2) "disability"—

(a) in England and Wales, has the same meaning as in the Limitation Act 1980;

(b) in Scotland, means legal disability within the meaning of the Prescription and Limitation (Scotland) Act 1973,

(c) in Northern Ireland, has the same meaning as in the Limitation (Northern Ireland) Order 1989.

**Order as to disposal of infringing goods, material or articles.**

A1-021 **19.**—(1) Where infringing goods, material or articles have been delivered up in pursuance of an order under section 16, an application may be made to the court—

(a) for an order that they be destroyed or forfeited to such person as the court may think fit, or

(b) for a decision that no such order should be made.

(2) In considering what order (if any) should be made, the court shall consider whether other remedies available in an action for infringement of the registered trade mark would be adequate to compensate the proprietor and any licensee and protect their interests.

(3) Provision shall be made by rules of court as to the service of notice on persons having an interest in the goods, material or articles, and any such person is entitled—

(a) to appear in proceedings for an order under this section, whether or not he was served with notice, and

(b) to appeal against any order made, whether or not he appeared;

and an order shall not take effect until the end of the period within which notice of an appeal may be given or, if before the end of that period notice of appeal is duly given, until the final determination or abandonment of the proceedings on the appeal.

(4) Where there is more than one person interested in the goods, material or articles, the court shall make such order as it thinks just.

(5) If the court decides that no order should be made under this section, the person in whose possession, custody or control the goods, material or articles were before being delivered up is entitled to their return.

(6) References in this section to a person having an interest in goods, material or articles include any person in whose favour an order could be made […]

[(a) under this section (including that section as applied by regulation 4 of the Community Trade Mark Regulations 2006 (SI 2006/1027));

(b) under section 24D of the Registered Designs Act 1949;

(c) under section 114, 204 or 231 of the Copyright, Designs and Patents Act 1988; or

(d) under regulation 1C of the Community Design Regulations 2005 (SI 2005/2339).]

**Jurisdiction of sheriff court or county court in Northern Ireland.**

**20.—** Proceedings for an order under section 16 (order for delivery up of infringing goods, material or articles) or section 19 (order as to disposal of infringing goods, &c.) may be brought— **A1-022**

(a) in the sheriff court in Scotland, or

(b) in a county court in Northern Ireland.

This does not affect the jurisdiction of the Court of Session or the High Court in Northern Ireland.

*Unjustified threats*

[**Threats of infringement proceedings.**

**21.—**(1) A communication contains a "threat of infringement proceedings" if a reasonable person in the position of a recipient would understand fom the communication that— **A1-023**

(a) a registered trade mark exists, and

(b) a person intends to bring proceedings (whether in a court in the United Kingdom or elsewhere) against another person for infringement of the registered trade mark by—

(i) an act done in the United Kingdom, or

(ii) an act which, if done, would be done in the United Kingdom.

(2) References in this section and in section 21C to a "recipient" include, in the case of a communication directed to the public or a section of the public, references to a person to whom the communication is directed.

(a) a declaration that the threats are unjustifiable,

(b) an injunction against the continuance of the threats,

(c) damages in respect of any loss he has sustained by the threats;

and the plaintiff is entitled to such relief unless the defendant shows that the acts in respect of which proceedings were threatened constitute (or if done would constitute) an infringement of the registered trade mark concerned.

(3) If that is shown by the defendant, the plaintiff is nevertheless entitled to relief if he shows that the registration of the trade mark is invalid or liable to be revoked in a relevant respect.

(4) The mere notification that a trade mark is registered, or that an application for registration has been made, does not constitute a threat of proceedings for the purposes of this section

**Actionable threats.**

**21A.—**(1) Subject to subsections (2) to (6), a threat of infringement proceedings made by any person is actionable by any person aggrieved by the threat. **A1-024**

(2) A threat of infringement proceedings is not actionable if the infringement is alleged to consist of—

(a) applying, or causing another person to apply, a sign to goods or their packaging,

(b) importing, for disposal, goods to which, or to the packaging of which, a sign has been applied, or

(c) supplying services under a sign.

(3) A threat of infringement proceedings is not actionable if the infringement is alleged to consist of an act which, if done, would constitute an infringement of a kind mentioned in subsection (2)(a), (b) or (c).

(4) A threat of infringement proceedings is not actionable if the threat—

(a) is made to a person who has done, or intends to do, an act mentioned in subsection (2)(a) or (b) in relation to goods or their packaging, and

(b) is a threat of proceedings for an infringement alleged to consist of doing anything else in relation to those goods or their packaging.

(5) A threat of infringement proceedings is not actionable if the threat—

(a) is made to a person who has done, or intends to do, an act mentioned in subsection (2)(c) in relation to services, and

(b) is a threat of proceedings for an infringement alleged to consist of doing anything else in relation to those services.

(6) A threat of infringement proceedings which is not an express threat is not actionable if it is contained in a permitted communication.

(7) In sections 21C and 21D "an actionable threat" means a threat of infringement proceedings that is actionable in accordance withi this section.

**Permitted communications.**

A1-025 **21B.**—(1) For the purposes of section 21A(6), a communication containing a threat of infringement proceedings is a "permitted communication" if—

(a) the communication, so far as it contains information that relates to the threat, is made for a permitted purpose;

(b) all of the information that relates to the threat is information that—

(i) is necessary for that purpose (see subsection (5)(a) to (c) for some examples of necessary information), and

(ii) the person making the communication reasonably believes is true.

(2) Each of the following is a "permitted purpose"—

(a) giving notice that a registered trade mark exists;

(b) discovering whether, or by whom, a registered trade mark has been infringed by an act mentioned in section 21A(2)(a), (b) or (c);

(c) giving notice that a person has a right in or under a registered trade mark, where another person's awareness of the right is relevant to any proceedings that may be brought in respect of the registered trade mark.

(3) The court may, having regard to the nature of the purposes listed in subsection (2)(a) to (c), treat any other purpose as a "permitted purpose" if it considers that it is in the interests of justice to do so.

(4) But the following may not be treated as a "permitted purpose"—

(a) requesting a person to cease using, in the course of trade, a sign in relation to goods goods or services,

(b) requesting a person to deliver up or destroy goods, or

(c) requesting a person to give an undertaking relating to the use of a sign in relation to goods or services.

(5) If any of the following information is included in a communication made for a permitted purpose, it is information that is "necessary for that purpose" (see subsection (1)(b)(i))—

(a) a statement that a registered trade mark exists and is in force or that an application for the registration of a trade mark has been made;

(b) details of the registered trade mark, or of a right in or under the registered trade mark, which—

(i) are accurate in all material respects, and
(ii) are not misleading in any material respect; and
(c) information enabling the identification of the goods or their packaging, or the services, in relation to which it is alleged that the use of a sign constitutes an infringement of the registered trade mark.

**Remedies and defences.**

**21C.**—(1) Proceedings in respect of an actionable threat may be brought against the person who made th threat for— **A1-026**
(a) a declaration that the threat is unjustified;
(b) an injunction against the continuance of the threat;
(c) damages in respect of any loss sustained by the aggrieved person by reason of the threat.

(2) It is a defence for the person who made the threat to show that the act in respect of which proceedings were threatened constitutes (or if done would constitute) an infringement of the registered trade mark.

(3) It is a defence for the person who made the threat to show—
(a) that, despite having taken reasonable steps, the person has not identified anyone who has done an act mentioned in section 21A(2)(a), (b) or (c) in relation to the goods or their packaging or the services which are the subject of the threat, and
(b) that the person notified the recipient, before or at the time of making the threat, of the steps taken.

**Professional advisers.**

**21D.**—(1) Proceedings in respect of an actionable threat may not be brought against a professional adviser (or any person vicariously liable for the actions of that professional adviser) if the conditions in subsection (3) are met. **A1-027**

(2) In this section "professional adviser" means a person who, in relation to the making of the communication containing the threat—
(a) is acting in a professional capacity in providing legal services or the services of a trade mark attorney or a patent attorney, and
(b) is regulated in the provision of legal services, or the services of a trade mark attorney or a patent attorney, by one or more regulatory bodies (whether through membership of a regulatory body, the issue of a licence to practise or any other means).

(3) The conditions are that—
(a) in making the communication the professional adviser is acting on the instructions of another person, and
(b) when the communication is made the professional adviser identifies the person on whose instructions the adviser is acting.

(4) This section does not affect any liability of the person on whose instructions the professional adviser is acting.

(5) It is for a person asserting that subsection (1) applies to prove (if required) that at the material time—
(a) the person concerned was acting as a professional adviser, and
(b) the conditions in subsection (3) were met.

**Supplementary: pending registration.**

A1-028 **21E.**—(1) In sections 21 and 21B references to a registered trade mark include references to a trade mark in respect of which an application for registration has been published under section 38.

(2) Where the threat of infringement proceedings is made after an application for registration has been published (but before registration) the reference in section 21C(2) to "the registered trade mark" is to be treated as a reference to the trade mark registered in pursuance of that application.

**Supplementary: proceedings for delivery up etc.**

A1-029 **21F.**— In section 21(1)(b) the reference to proceedings for infringement of a registered trade mark includes a reference to—

(a) proceedings for an order under section 16 (order for delivery up of infringing goods, material or articles), and

(b) proceedings for an order under section 19 (order as to disposal of infringing goods, material or articles).]

*Registered trade mark as object of property*

**Nature of registered trade mark.**

A1-030 **22.**— A registered trade mark is personal property (in Scotland, incorporeal moveable property).

**Co-ownership of registered trade mark.**

A1-031 **23.**—(1) Where a registered trade mark is granted to two or more persons jointly, each of them is entitled, subject to an agreement to the contrary, to an equal undivided share in the registered trade mark.

(2) The following provisions apply where two or more persons are co-proprietors of a registered trade mark, by virtue of subsection (1) or otherwise.

(3) Subject to any agreement to the contrary, each co-proprietor is entitled, by himself or his agents, to do for his own benefit and without the consent of or the need to account to the other or others, any act which would otherwise amount to an infringement of the registered trade mark

(4) One co-proprietor may not without the consent of the other or others—

(a) grant a licence to use the registered trade mark, or

(b) assign or charge his share in the registered trade mark (or, in Scotland, cause or permit security to be granted over it).

(5) Infringement proceedings may be brought by any co-proprietor, but he may not, without the leave of the court, proceed with the action unless the other, or each of the others, is either joined as a plaintiff or added as a defendant.

A co-proprietor who is thus added as a defendant shall not be made liable for any costs in the action unless he takes part in the proceedings.

Nothing in this subsection affects the granting of interlocutory relief on the application of a single co-proprietor.

(6) Nothing in this section affects the mutual rights and obligations of trustees or personal representatives, or their rights and obligations as such.

**Assignment, &c. of registered trade mark.**

**24.**—(1) A registered trade mark is transmissible by assignment, testamentary disposition or operation of law in the same way as other personal or moveable property. **A1-032**

It is so transmissible either in connection with the goodwill of a business or independently.

[(1A) A contractual obligation to transfer a business is to be taken to include an obligation to transfer any registered trade mark, except where there is agreement to the contrary or it is clear in all the circumstances that this presumption should not apply.]

(2) An assignment or other transmission of a registered trade mark may be partial, that is, limited so as to apply—

- (a) in relation to some but not all of the goods or services for which the trade mark is registered, or
- (b) in relation to use of the trade mark in a particular manner or a particular locality.

(3) An assignment of a registered trade mark, or an assent relating to a registered trade mark, is not effective unless it is in writing signed by or on behalf of the assignor or, as the case may be, a personal representative.

Except in Scotland, this requirement may be satisfied in a case where the assignor or personal representative is a body corporate by the affixing of its seal.

(4) The above provisions apply to assignment by way of security as in relation to any other assignment.

(5) A registered trade mark may be the subject of a charge (in Scotland, security) in the same way as other personal or moveable property.

(6) Nothing in this Act shall be construed as affecting the assignment or other transmission of an unregistered trade mark as part of the goodwill of a business.

**Registration of transactions affecting registered trade mark.**

**25.**—(1) On application being made to the registrar by— **A1-033**

- (a) a person claiming to be entitled to an interest in or under a registered trade mark by virtue of a registrable transaction, or
- (b) any other person claiming to be affected by such a transaction,

the prescribed particulars of the transaction shall be entered in the register.

(2) The following are registrable transactions—

- (a) an assignment of a registered trade mark or any right in it;
- (b) the grant of a licence under a registered trade mark;
- (c) the granting of any security interest (whether fixed or floating) over a registered trade mark or any right in or under it;
- (d) the making by personal representatives of an assent in relation to a registered trade mark or any right in or under it;
- (e) an order of a court or other competent authority transferring a registered trade mark or any right in or under it.

(3) Until an application has been made for registration of the prescribed particulars of a registrable transaction—

- (a) the transaction is ineffective as against a person acquiring a conflicting interest in or under the registered trade mark in ignorance of it, and
- (b) a person claiming to be a licensee by virtue of the transaction does not have the protection of section 30 or 31 (rights and remedies of licensee in relation to infringement).

(4) Where a person becomes the proprietor or a licensee of a registered trade mark by virtue of a registrable transaction [and the mark is infringed before the prescribed particulars of the transaction are registered, in proceedings for such an infringement, the court shall not award him costs unless—

(a) an application for registration of the prescribed particulars of the transaction is made before the end of the period of six months beginning with its date, or

(b) the court is satisfied that it was not practicable for such an application to be made before the end of that period and that an application was made as soon as practicable thereafter.]

(5) Provision may be made by rules as to—

(a) the amendment of registered particulars relating to a licence so as to reflect any alteration of the terms of the licence, and

(b) the removal of such particulars from the register—

(i) where it appears from the registered particulars that the licence was granted for a fixed period and that period has expired, or

(ii) where no such period is indicated and, after such period as may be prescribed, the registrar has notified the parties of his intention to remove the particulars from the register.

(6) Provision may also be made by rules as to the amendment or removal from the register of particulars relating to a security interest on the application of, or with the consent of, the person entitled to the benefit of that interest.

**Trusts and equities.**

A1-034 **26.**—(1) No notice of any trust (express, implied or constructive) shall be entered in the register; and the registrar shall not be affected by any such notice.

(2) Subject to the provisions of this Act, equities (in Scotland, rights) in respect of a registered trade mark may be enforced in like manner as in respect of other personal or moveable property.

**Application for registration of trade mark as an object of property.**

A1-035 **27.**—(1) The provisions of sections 22 to 26 (which relate to a registered trade mark as an object of property) [and sections 28 to 31 (which relate to licensing)] apply, with the necessary modifications, in relation to an application for the registration of a trade mark as in relation to a registered trade mark.

(2) In section 23 (co-ownership of registered trade mark) as it applies in relation to an application for registration the reference in subsection (1) to the granting of the registration shall be construed as a reference to the making of the application.

(3) In section 25 (registration of transactions affecting registered trade marks) as it applies in relation to a transaction affecting an application for the registration of a trade mark, the references to the entry of particulars in the register, and to the making of an application to register particulars, shall be construed as references to the giving of notice to the registrar of those particulars.

*Licensing*

**Licensing of registered trade mark.**

A1-036 **28.**—(1) A licence to use a registered trade mark may be general or limited. A limited licence may, in particular, apply—

(a) in relation to some but not all of the goods or services for which the trade mark is registered, or
(b) in relation to use of the trade mark in a particular manner or a particular locality.

(2) A licence is not effective unless it is in writing signed by or on behalf of the grantor. Except in Scotland, this requirement may be satisfied in a case where the grantor is a body corporate by the affixing of its seal.

(3) Unless the licence provides otherwise, it is binding on a successor in title to the grantor's interest. References in this Act to doing anything with, or without, the consent of the proprietor of a registered trade mark shall be construed accordingly.

(4) Where the licence so provides, a sub-licence may be granted by the licensee; and references in this Act to a licence or licensee include a sub-licence or sub-licensee.

(5) The proprietor of a registered trade mark may invoke the rights conferred by that trade mark against a licensee who contravenes any provision in the licence with regard to—
(a) its duration,
(b) the form covered by the registration in which the trade mark may be used,
(c) the scope of the goods or services for which the licence is granted,
(d) the territory in which the trade mark may be affixed, or
(e) the quality of the goods manufactured or of the services provided by the licensee.

**Exclusive licences.**

**29.**—(1) In this Act an "exclusive licence" means a licence (whether general or limited) authorising the licensee to the exclusion of all other persons, including the person granting the licence, to use a registered trade mark in the manner authorised by the licence. **A1-037**

The expression "exclusive licensee"shall be construed accordingly

(2) An exclusive licensee has the same rights against a successor in title who is bound by the licence as he has against the person granting the licence.

**General provisions as to rights of licensees in case of infringement.**

**30.**—(1) This section has effect with respect to the rights of a licensee in relation to infringement of a registered trade mark. **A1-038**

The provisions of this section do not apply where or to the extent that, by virtue of section 31(1) below (exclusive licensee having rights and remedies of assignee), the licensee has a right to bring proceedings in his own name.

[(1A) Except so far as the licence provides otherwise a licensee may only bring proceedings for infringement of the registered trade mark with the consent of the proprietor (but see subsections (2) and (3)).]

(2) [An exclusive licensee may] call on the proprietor of the registered trade mark to take infringement proceedings in respect of any matter which affects his interests.

(3) If the proprietor [mentioned in subsection (2)]—
(a) refuses to do so, or
(b) fails to do so within two months after being called upon.

the [exclusive] licensee may bring the proceedings in his own name as if he were the proprietor.

(4) Where infringement proceedings are brought by a licensee by virtue of this section [or with the consent of the proprietor or pursuant to the licence] the licensee may not, without the leave of the court, proceed with the action unless the proprietor is either joined as a plaintiff or added as a defendant.

This does not affect the granting of interlocutory relief on an application by a licensee alone.

(5) A proprietor who is added as a defendant as mentioned in subsection (4) shall not be made liable for any costs in the action unless he takes part in the proceedings.

(6) In infringement proceedings brought by the proprietor of a registered trade mark any loss suffered or likely to be suffered by licensees shall be taken into account; and the court may give such directions as it thinks fit as to the extent to which the plaintiff is to hold the proceeds of any pecuniary remedy on behalf of licensees.

[(6A) Where the proprietor of a registered trade mark brings infringement proceedings, a licensee who has suffered loss is entitled to intervene in the proceedings for the purpose of obtaining compensation for that loss.]

(7) The provisions of this section apply in relation to an exclusive licensee if or to the extent that he has, by virtue of section 31(1), the rights and remedies of an assignee as if he were the proprietor of the registered trade mark.

**Exclusive licensee having rights and remedies of assignee.**

**A1-039** **31.**—(1) An exclusive licence may provide that the licensee shall have, to such extent as may be provided by the licence, the same rights and remedies in respect of matters occurring after the grant of the licence as if the licence had been an assignment.

Where or to the extent that such provision is made, the licensee is entitled, subject to the provisions of the licence and to the following provisions of this section, to bring infringement proceedings, against any person other than the proprietor, in his own name.

(2) Any such rights and remedies of an exclusive licensee are concurrent with those of the proprietor of the registered trade mark, and references to the proprietor of a registered trade mark in the provisions of this Act relating to infringement shall be construed accordingly.

(3) In an action brought by an exclusive licensee by virtue of this section a defendant may avail himself of any defence which would have been available to him if the action had been brought by the proprietor of the registered trade mark.

(4) Where proceedings for infringement of a registered trade mark brought by the proprietor or an exclusive licensee relate wholly or partly to an infringement in respect of which they have concurrent rights of action, the proprietor or, as the case may be, the exclusive licensee may not, without the leave of the court, proceed with the action unless the other is either joined as a plaintiff or added as a defendant.

This does not affect the granting of interlocutory relief on an application by a proprietor or exclusive licensee alone.

(5) A person who is added as a defendant as mentioned in subsection (4) shall not be made liable for any costs in the action unless he takes part in the proceedings.

(6) Where an action for infringement of a registered trade mark is brought which relates wholly or partly to an infringement in respect of which the proprietor and an exclusive licensee have or had concurrent rights of action—

(a) the court shall in assessing damages take into account—

(i) the terms of the licence, and
(ii) any pecuniary remedy already awarded or available to either of them in respect of the infringement;

(b) no account of profits shall be directed if an award of damages has been made, or an account of profits has been directed, in favour of the other of them in respect of the infringement; and
(c) the court shall if an account of profits is directed apportion the profits between them as the court considers just, subject to any agreement between them.

The provisions of this subsection apply whether or not the proprietor and the exclusive licensee are both parties to the action, and if they are not both parties the court may give such directions as it thinks fit as to the extent to which the party to the proceedings is to hold the proceeds of any pecuniary remedy on behalf of the other.

(7) The proprietor of a registered trade mark shall notify any exclusive licensee who has a concurrent right of action before applying for an order under section 16 (order for delivery up), and the court may on the application of the licensee make such order under that section as it thinks fit having regard to the terms of the licence.

(8) The provisions of subsections (4) to (7) above have effect subject to any agreement to the contrary between the exclusive licensee and the proprietor.

*Application for registered trade mark*

**Application for registration.**

**32.**—(1) An application for registration of a trade mark shall be made to the registrar. **A1-040**

(2) The application shall contain—

(a) a request for registration of a trade mark,
(b) the name and address of the applicant,
(c) a statement of the goods or services in relation to which it is sought to register the trade mark, and
(d) a representation of the trade mark[, which is capable of being represented in the register in a manner which enables the registrar and other competent authorities and the public to determine the clear and precise subject matter of the protection afforded to the proprietor].

(3) The application shall state that the trade mark is being used, by the applicant or with his consent, in relation to those goods or services, or that he has a bona fide intention that it should be so used.

(4) The application shall be subject to the payment of the application fee and such class fees as may be appropriate

**Date of filing.**

**33.**—(1) The date of filing of an application for registration of a trade mark is the date on which documents containing everything required by section 32(2) are furnished to the registrar by the applicant. **A1-041**

If the documents are furnished on different days, the date of filing is the last of those days.

(2) References in this Act to the date of application for registration are to the date of filing of the application.

**Classification of trade marks.**

A1-042 **34.**—(1) Goods and services shall be classified for the purposes of the registration of trade marks according to a prescribed system of classification.

(2) Any question arising as to the class within which any goods or services fall shall be determined by the registrar, whose decision shall be final.

*Priority*

**Claim to priority of Convention application.**

A1-043 **35.**—(1) A person who has duly filed an application for protection of a trade mark in a Convention country (a "Convention application"), or his successor in title, has a right to priority, for the purposes of registering the same trade mark under this Act for some or all of the same goods or services, for a period of six months from the date of filing of the first such application.

(2) If the application for registration under this Act is made within that six-month period—

(a) the relevant date for the purposes of establishing which rights take precedence shall be the date of filing of the first Convention application, and

(b) the registrability of the trade mark shall not be affected by any use of the mark in the United Kingdom in the period between that date and the date of the application under this Act.

(3) Any filing which in a Convention country is equivalent to a regular national filing, under its domestic legislation or an international agreement, shall be treated as giving rise to the right of priority.

A "regular national filing" means a filing which is adequate to establish the date on which the application was filed in that country, whatever may be the subsequent fate of the application.

(4) A subsequent application concerning the same subject as the first Convention application, filed in the same Convention country, shall be considered the first Convention application (of which the filing date is the starting date of the period of priority), if at the time of the subsequent application—

(a) the previous application has been withdrawn, abandoned or refused, without having been laid open to public inspection and without leaving any rights outstanding, and

(b) it has not yet served as a basis for claiming a right of priority.

The previous application may not thereafter serve as a basis for claiming a right of priority.

(5) Provision may be made by rules as to the manner of claiming a right to priority on the basis of a Convention application.

(6) A right to priority arising as a result of a Convention application may be assigned or otherwise transmitted, either with the application or independently.

The reference in subsection (1) to the applicant's "successor in title" shall be construed accordingly.

**Claim to priority from other relevant overseas application.**

A1-044 **36.**—(1) Her Majesty may by Order in Council make provision for conferring on a person who has duly filed an application for protection of a trade mark in—

(a) any of the Channel Islands or a colony, or

(b) a country or territory in relation to which Her Majesty's Government in the United Kingdom have entered into a treaty, convention, arrangement or engagement for the reciprocal protection of trade marks,

a right to priority, for the purpose of registering the same trade mark under this Act for some or all of the same goods or services, for a specified period from the date of filing of that application.

(2) An Order in Council under this section may make provision corresponding to that made by section 35 in relation to Convention countries or such other provision as appears to Her Majesty to be appropriate.

(3) A statutory instrument containing an Order in Council under this section shall be subject to annulment in pursuance of a resolution of either House of Parliament.

*Registration procedure*

**Examination of application.**

**37.**—(1) The registrar shall examine whether an application for registration of a trade mark satisfies the requirements of this Act (including any requirements imposed by rules) **A1-045**

(2) [...]

(3) If it appears to the registrar that the requirements for registration are not met, he shall inform the applicant and give him an opportunity, within such period as the registrar may specify, to make representations or to amend the application.

(4) If the applicant fails to satisfy the registrar that those requirements are met, or to amend the application so as to meet them, or fails to respond before the end of the specified period, the registrar shall refuse to accept the application.

(5) If it appears to the registrar that the requirements for registration are met, he shall accept the application.

**Publication, opposition proceedings and observations.**

**38.**—(1) When an application for registration has been accepted, the registrar shall cause the application to be published in the prescribed manner **A1-046**

(2) Any person may, within the prescribed time from the date of the publication of the application, give notice to the registrar of opposition to the registration.

The notice shall be given in writing in the prescribed manner, and shall include a statement of the grounds of opposition.

[(2A) Where a notice of opposition is filed on the basis of one or more earlier trade marks or other earlier rights—

(a) the rights (if plural) must all belong to the same proprietor;

(b) the notice may be filed on the basis of part, or the totality, of the goods or services in respect of which the earlier right is protected or applied for.

(2B) A notice of opposition may be directed against part or the totality of the goods or services in respect of which the contested mark is applied for.]

(3) Where an application has been published, any person may, at any time before the registration of the trade mark, make observations in writing to the registrar as to whether the trade mark should be registered; and the registrar shall inform the applicant of any such observations.

A person who makes observations does not thereby become a party to the proceedings on the application.

**Withdrawal, restriction or amendment of application.**

A1-047 **39.**—(1) The applicant may at any time withdraw his application or restrict the goods or services covered by the application.

If the application has been published, the withdrawal or restriction shall also be published.

(2) In other respects, an application may be amended, at the request of the applicant, only by correcting—

(a) the name or address of the applicant,
(b) errors of wording or of copying, or
(c) obvious mistakes,

and then only where the correction does not substantially affect the identity of the trade mark or extend the goods or services covered by the application

(3) Provision shall be made by rules for the publication of any amendment which affects the representation of the trade mark, or the goods or services covered by the application, and for the making of objections by any person claiming to be affected by it.

**Registration.**

A1-048 **40.**—(1) Where an application has been accepted and—

(a) no notice of opposition is given within the period referred to in section 38(2), or
(b) all opposition proceedings are withdrawn or decided in favour of the applicant,

the registrar shall register the trade mark, unless it appears to him having regard to matters coming to his notice [since the application was accepted that the registration requirements (other than those mentioned in section 5(1), (2) or (3)) were not met at that time.]

(2) A trade mark shall not be registered unless any fee prescribed for the registration is paid within the prescribed period.

If the fee is not paid within that period, the application shall be deemed to be withdrawn.

(3) A trade mark when registered shall be registered as of the date of filing of the application for registration, and that date shall be deemed for the purposes of this Act to be the date of registration.

(4) On the registration of a trade mark the registrar shall publish the registration in the prescribed manner and issue to the applicant a certificate of registration.

**Registration: supplementary provisions.**

A1-049 **41.**—(1) Provision may be made by rules as to—

(a) the division of an application for the registration of a trade mark into several applications;
(aa) the division of a registration of a trade mark into several registrations;
(b) the merging of separate applications or registrations;
(c) the registration of a series of trade marks.

(2) A series of trade marks means a number of trade marks which resemble each other as to their material particulars and differ only as to matters of a non-distinctive character not substantially affecting the identity of the trade mark.

(3) Rules under this section may include provision as to—

(a) the circumstances in which, and conditions subject to which, division, merger or registration of a series is permitted, and

(b) the purposes for which an application [or registration] to which the rules apply is to be treated as a single application [or registration] and those for which it is to be treated as a number of separate applications [or registrations].

*Duration, renewal and alteration of registered trade mark*

**Duration of registration.**

**42.**—(1) A trade mark shall be registered for a period of ten years from the date of registration. **A1-050**

(2) Registration may be renewed in accordance with section 43 for further periods of ten years.

**Renewal of registration.**

**43.**—(1) The registration of a trade mark may be renewed at the request of the proprietor, subject to payment of a renewal fee. **A1-051**

(2) Provision shall be made by rules for the registrar to inform the proprietor of a registered trade mark, before the expiry of the registration, of the date of expiry and the manner in which the registration may be renewed.

(3) A request for renewal must be made, and the renewal fee paid, before the expiry of the registration.

Failing this, the request may be made and the fee paid within such further period (of not less than six months) as may be prescribed, in which case an additional renewal fee must also be paid within that period.

[(3A) If a request for renewal is made or the renewal fee is paid in respect of only some of the goods or services for which the trade mark is registered, the registration is to be renewed for those goods or services only.]

(4) Renewal shall take effect from the expiry of the previous registration.

(5) If the registration is not renewed in accordance with the above provisions, the registrar shall remove the trade mark from the register.

Provision may be made by rules for the restoration of the registration of a trade mark which has been removed from the register, subject to such condition (if any) as may be prescribed.

(6) The renewal or restoration of the registration of a trade mark shall be published in the prescribed manner.

**Alteration of registered trade mark.**

**44.**—(1) A registered trade mark shall not be altered in the register, during the period of registration or on renewal. **A1-052**

(2) Nevertheless, the registrar may, at the request of the proprietor, allow the alteration of a registered trade mark where the mark includes the proprietor's name or address and the alteration is limited to alteration of that name or address and does not substantially affect the identity of the mark.

(3) Provision shall be made by rules for the publication of any such alteration and the making of objections by any person claiming to be affected by it.

*Surrender, revocation and invalidity*

**Surrender of registered trade mark.**

A1-053 **45.**—(1) A registered trade mark may be surrendered by the proprietor in respect of some or all of the goods or services for which it is registered.

(2) Provision may be made by rules—

(a) as to the manner and effect of a surrender, and

(b) for protecting the interests of other persons having a right in the registered trade mark.

**Revocation of registration.**

A1-054 **46.**—(1) The registration of a trade mark may be revoked on any of the following grounds—

(a) that within the period of five years following the date of completion of the registration procedure it has not been put to genuine use in the United Kingdom, by the proprietor or with his consent, in relation to the goods or services for which it is registered, and there are no proper reasons for non-use;

(b) that such use has been suspended for an uninterrupted period of five years, and there are no proper reasons for non-use;

(c) that, in consequence of acts or inactivity of the proprietor, it has become the common name in the trade for a product or service for which it is registered;

(d) that in consequence of the use made of it by the proprietor or with his consent in relation to the goods or services for which it is registered, it is liable to mislead the public, particularly as to the nature, quality or geographical origin of those goods or services.

(2) For the purposes of subsection (1) use of a trade mark includes use in a form [(the "variant form")] differing in elements which do not alter the distinctive character of the mark in the form in which it was registered [(regardless of whether or not the trade mark in the variant form is also registered in the name of the proprietor)], and use in the United Kingdom includes affixing the trade mark to goods or to the packaging of goods in the United Kingdom solely for export purposes.

(3) The registration of a trade mark shall not be revoked on the ground mentioned in subsection (1)(a) or (b) if such use as is referred to in that paragraph is commenced or resumed after the expiry of the five year period and before the application for revocation is made:
Provided that, any such commencement or resumption of use after the expiry of the five year period but within the period of three months before the making of the application shall be disregarded unless preparation for the commencement or resumption began before the proprietor became aware that the application might be made.

(4) An application for revocation may be made by any person, and may be made either to the registrar or to the court, except that—

(a) if proceedings concerning the trade mark in question are pending in the court, the application must be made to the court; and

(b) if in any other case the application is made to the registrar, he may at any stage of the proceedings refer the application to the court.

(5) Where grounds for revocation exist in respect of only some of the goods or services for which the trade mark is registered, revocation shall relate to those goods or services only.

(6) Where the registration of a trade mark is revoked to any extent, the rights of the proprietor shall be deemed to have ceased to that extent as from—

(a) the date of the application for revocation, or
(b) if the registrar or court is satisfied that the grounds for revocation existed at an earlier date, that date.

**Grounds for invalidity of registration.**

**47.**—(1) The registration of a trade mark may be declared invalid on the ground that the trade mark was registered in breach of section 3 or any of the provisions referred to in that section (absolute grounds for refusal of registration). **A1-055**

Where the trade mark was registered in breach of subsection (1)(b), (c) or (d) of that section, it shall not be declared invalid if, in consequence of the use which has been made of it, it has after registration acquired a distinctive character in relation to the goods or services for which it is registered.

(2) [Subject to subsections (2A) and (2G), the] registration of a trade mark may be declared invalid on the ground—

(a) that there is an earlier trade mark in relation to which the conditions set out in section 5(1), (2) or (3) obtain, or
(b) that there is an earlier right in relation to which the condition set out in section 5(4) is satisfied,

unless the proprietor of that earlier trade mark or other earlier right has consented to the registration.

[(2ZA) The registration of a trade mark may be declared invalid on the ground that the trade mark was registered in breach of section 5(6).]

[(2A) [The] registration of a trade mark may not be declared invalid on the ground that there is an earlier trade mark unless–

(a) the registration procedure for the earlier trade mark was completed within the period of five years ending with the date of the application for the declaration,
(b) the registration procedure for the earlier trade mark was not completed before that date, or
(c) the use conditions are met.

(2B) The use conditions are met if–

[(a) the earlier trade mark has been put to genuine use in the United Kingdom by the proprietor or with their consent in relation to the goods or services for which it is registered—
   (i) within the period of 5 years ending with the date of application for the declaration, and
   (ii) within the period of 5 years ending with the date of filing of the application for registration of the later trade mark or (where applicable) the date of the priority claimed in respect of that application where, at that date, the five year period within which the earlier trade mark should have been put to genuine use as provided in section 46(1)(a) has expired, or]
(b) it has not been so used, but there are proper reasons for non-use.

(2C) For these purposes–

(a) use of a trade mark includes use in a form [(the "variant form")] differing in elements which do not alter the distinctive character of the mark in the form in which it was registered [(regardless of whether or not the trade mark in the variant form is also registered in the name of the proprietor)], and

(b) use in the United Kingdom includes affixing the trade mark to goods or to the packaging of goods in the United Kingdom solely for export purposes.

(2D) In relation to a [European Union] trade mark [or international trade mark (EC)], any reference in subsection (2B) or (2C) to the United Kingdom shall be construed as a reference to the [European Union].

[(2DA) In relation to an international trade mark (EC), the reference in subsection (2A)(a) to the completion of the registration procedure is to be construed as a reference to the publication by the European Union Intellectual Property Office of the matters referred to in Article 190(2) of the European Union Trade Mark Regulation.]

(2E) Where an earlier trade mark satisfies the use conditions in respect of some only of the goods or services for which it is registered, it shall be treated for the purposes of this section as if it were registered only in respect of those goods or services.]

[(2F) Subsection (2A) does not apply where the earlier trade mark is a trade mark within section 6(1)(c).]

[(2G) An application for a declaration of invalidity on the basis of an earlier trade mark must be refused if it would have been refused, for any of the reasons set out in subsection (2H), had the application for the declaration been made on the date of filing of the application for registration of the later trade mark or (where applicable) the date of the priority claimed in respect of that application.

(2H) The reasons referred to in subsection (2G) are—

(a) that on the date in question the earlier trade mark was liable to be declared invalid by virtue of section 3(1)(b), (c) or (d), (and had not yet acquired a distinctive character as mentioned in the words after paragraph (d) in section 3(1));

(b) that the application for a declaration of invalidity is based on section 5(2) and the earlier trade mark had not yet become sufficiently distinctive to support a finding of likelihood of confusion within the meaning of section 5(2);

(c) that the application for a declaration of invalidity is based on section 5(3)(a) and the earlier trade mark had not yet acquired a reputation within the meaning of section 5(3).]

(3) An application for a declaration of invalidity may be made by any person, and may be made either to the registrar or to the court, except that—

(a) if proceedings concerning the trade mark in question are pending in the court, the application must be made to the court; and

(b) if in any other case the application is made to the registrar, he may at any stage of the proceedings refer the application to the court.

(4) In the case of bad faith in the registration of a trade mark, the registrar himself may apply to the court for a declaration of the invalidity of the registration.

(5) Where the grounds of invalidity exist in respect of only some of the goods or services for which the trade mark is registered, the trade mark shall be declared invalid as regards those goods or services only.

[(5A) An application for a declaration of invalidity may be filed on the basis of one or more earlier trade marks or other earlier rights provided they all belong to the same proprietor.]

(6) Where the registration of a trade mark is declared invalid to any extent, the registration shall to that extent be deemed never to have been made:

Provided that this shall not affect transactions past and closed.

**Effect of acquiescence.**

**48.**—(1) Where the proprietor of an earlier trade mark or other earlier right has acquiesced for a continuous period of five years in the use of a registered trade mark in the United Kingdom, being aware of that use, there shall cease to be any entitlement on the basis of that earlier trade mark or other right— **A1-056**

(a) to apply for a declaration that the registration of the later trade mark is invalid, or

(b) to oppose the use of the later trade mark in relation to the goods or services in relation to which it has been so used.

unless the registration of the later trade mark was applied for in bad faith.

(2) Where subsection (1) applies, the proprietor of the later trade mark is not entitled to oppose the use of the earlier trade mark or, as the case may be, the exploitation of the earlier right, notwithstanding that the earlier trade mark or right may no longer be invoked against his later trade mark.

*Collective marks*

**Collective marks.**

**49.**—[(1) A collective mark is a mark which is described as such when it is applied for and is capable of distinguishing the goods and services of members of the association which is the proprietor of the mark from those of other undertakings. **A1-057**

(1A) The following may be registered as the proprietor of a collective mark—

(a) an association of manufacturers, producers, suppliers of services or traders which has the capacity in its own name to enter into contracts and to sue or be sued; and

(b) a legal person governed by public law.]

(2) The provisions of this Act apply to collective marks subject to the provisions of Schedule 1.

*Certification marks*

**Certification marks.**

**50.**—(1) A certification mark is a mark [which is described as such when the mark is applied for and indicates] that the goods or services in connection with which it is used are certified by the proprietor of the mark in respect of origin, material, mode of manufacture of goods or performance of services, quality, accuracy or other characteristics. **A1-058**

(2) The provisions of this Act apply to certification marks subject to the provisions of Schedule 2.

PART II – [EUROPEAN UNION] TRADE MARKS AND INTERNATIONAL MATTERS

*[European Union] trade marks*

[**Meaning of "European Union trade mark".**

**51.**— In this Act— **A1-059**

"European Union trade mark" has the meaning given by Article 1(1) of the European Union Trade Mark Regulation; and "the European Union Trade Mark Regulation" means [Regulation (EU) 2017/1001 of the European Parliament and of the Council of 14 June 2017 on the European Union Trade Mark.].]

**Power to make provision in connection with [European Union] Trade Mark Regulation.**

A1-060 **52.**—(1) The Secretary of State may by regulation make such provision as he considers appropriate in connection with the operation of the [European Union] Trade Mark Regulation.

(2) Provision may, in particular, be made with respect to—

(a) [...]

(b) the procedures for determining *a posteriori* the invalidity, or liability to revocation, of the registration of a trade mark from which a [European Union] trade mark claims seniority.

(c) the conversion of a [European Union] trade mark, or an application for a [European Union] trade mark, into an application for registration under this Act;

(d) the designation of courts in the United Kingdom having jurisdiction over proceedings arising out of the [European Union] Trade Mark Regulation.

(3) Without prejudice to the generality of subsection (1), provision may be made by regulations under this section—

(a) applying in relation to a [European Union] trade mark the provisions of—

(i) sections 21 to 21F (unjustified threats);]

(ii) sections 89 to 91 (importation of infringing goods, material or articles); and

(iii) sections 92, 93, 95 and 96 (offences); and

(b) making in relation to the list of professional representatives maintained in pursuance of [Article 120] of the [European Union] Trade Mark Regulation and persons on that list, provision corresponding to that made by, or capable of being made under, sections 84 to 88 in relation to the register of [trade mark attorneys and registered trade mark attorneys].

[(3A) The reference in subsections (1) and (2)(d) to the European Union Trade Mark Regulation includes a reference to [Council Regulation (EC) No 207/2009 of 26 February 2009 on the European Union Trade Mark].]

(4) Regulations under this section shall be made by statutory instrument which shall be subject to annulment in pursuance of a resolution of either House of Parliament.

*The Madrid Protocol international registration*

**The Madrid Protocol.**

A1-061 **53.**— In this Act—

"the Madrid Protocol" means the Protocol relating to the Madrid Agreement concerning the International Registration of Marks, adopted at Madrid on 27th June 1989;

"the International Bureau" has the meaning given by Article 2(1) of that Protocol, and ["international trade mark (EC)" means a trade mark which is entitled to protection in the [European Union] under that Protocol ;]

"international trade mark (UK)" means a trade mark which is entitled to protection in the United Kingdom under that Protocol.

**Power to make provision giving effect to Madrid Protocol.**

**54.**—(1) The Secretary of State may by order make such provision as he thinks fit for giving effect in the United Kingdom to the provisions of the Madrid Protocol. **A1-062**

(2) Provision may, in particular, be made with respect to—

(a) the making of application for international registrations by way of the Patent Office as office of origin;

(b) the procedures to be followed where the basic United Kingdom application or registration fails or ceases to be in force;

(c) the procedures to be followed where the Patent Office receives from the International Bureau a request for extension of protection to the United Kingdom;

(d) the effects of a successful request for extension of protection to the United Kingdom;

(e) the transformation of an application for an international registration, or an international registration, into a national application for registration,

(f) the communication of information to the International Bureau.

(g) the payment of fees and amounts prescribed in respect of application for international registrations, extensions of protection and renewals.

(3) Without prejudice to the generality of subsection (1), provision may be made by regulations under this section applying in relation to an international trade mark (UK) the provisions of—

[(a) sections 21 to 21F (unjustified threats);]

(b) sections 89 to 91 (importation of infringing goods, material or articles); and

(c) sections 92, 93, 95 and 96 (offences).

(4) An order under this section shall be made by statutory instrument which shall be subject to annulment in pursuance of a resolution of either House of Parliament.

*The Paris Convention: supplementary provisions*

**The Paris Convention.**

**55.**—(1) In this Act— **A1-063**

(a) "the Paris Convention" means the Paris Convention for the Protection of Industrial Property of March 20th 1883, as revised or amended from time to time ,

[…]

[(aa) "the WTO agreement" means the Agreement establishing the World Trade Organisation signed at Marrakesh on 15th April 1994, and]

(b) a "Convention country" means a country, other than the United Kingdom, which is a party to that Convention [or to that Agreement].

(2) The Secretary of State may by order make such amendments of this Act, and rules made under this Act, as appear to him appropriate in consequence of any revision or amendment of the Parts Convention [or the WTO agreement] after the passing of this Act.

(3) Any such order shall be made by statutory instrument which shall be subject to annulment in pursuance of a resolution of either House of Parliament.

**Protection of well-known trade marks: Article 6bis.**

A1-064 **56.**—(1) References in this Act to a trade mark which is entitled to protection under the Paris Convention[or the WTO agreement] as a well known trade mark are to a mark which is well-known in the United Kingdom as being the mark of a person who—

(a) is a national of a Convention country, or
(b) is domiciled in, or has a real and effective industrial or commercial establishment in, a Convention country.

whether or not that person carries on business, or has any goodwill, in the United Kingdom.

References to the proprietor of such a mark shall be construed accordingly.

(2) The proprietor of a trade mark which is entitled to protection under the Paris Convention[or the WTO agreement] as a well known trade mark is entitled to restrain by injunction the use in the United Kingdom of a trade mark which, or the essential part of which, is identical or similar to his mark, in relation to identical or similar goods or services, where the use is likely to cause confusion.

This right is subject to section 48 (effect of acquiescence by proprietor of earlier trade mark).

(3) Nothing in subsection (2) affects the continuation of any bona fide use of a trade mark begun before the commencement of this section

**National emblems, &c. of Convention countries: Article 6ter.**

A1-065 **57.**—(1) A trade mark which consists of or contains the flag of a Convention country shall not be registered without the authorisation of the competent authorities of that country, unless it appears to the registrar that use of the flag in the manner proposed is permitted without such authorisation.

(2) A trade mark which consists of or contains the armorial bearings or any other state emblem of a Convention country which is protected under the Paris Convention[or the WTO agreement] shall not be registered without the authorisation of the competent authorities of that country.

(3) A trade mark which consists of or contains an official sign or hallmark adopted by a Convention country and indicating control and warranty shall not, where the sign or hallmark is protected under the Paris Convention[or the WTO agreement], be registered in relation to goods or services of the same, or a similar kind, as those in relation to which it indicates control and warranty, without the authorisation of the competent authorities of the country concerned.

(4) The provisions of this section as to national flags and other state emblems, and official signs or hallmarks, apply equally to anything which from a heraldic point of view imitates any such flag or other emblem, or sign or hallmark.

(5) Nothing in this section prevents the registration of a trade mark on the application of a national of a country who is authorised to make use of a state emblem, or official sign or hallmark, of that country, notwithstanding that it is similar to that of another country.

(6) Where by virtue of this section the authorisation of the competent authorities of a Convention country is or would be required for the registration of a trade

mark, those authorities are entitled to restrain by injunction any use of the mark in the United Kingdom without their authorisation.

**Emblems, &c. of certain international organisations: Article 6ter.**

**58.**—(1) This section applies to— A1-066

(a) the armorial bearings, flags or other emblems, and

(b) the abbreviations and names,

of international intergovernmental organisations of which one or more Convention countries are members.

(2) A trade mark which consists of or contains any such emblem, abbreviation or name which is protected under the Paris Convention[or the WTO agreement] shall not be registered without the authorisation of the international organisation concerned, unless it appears to the registrar that the use of the emblem, abbreviation or name in the manner proposed—

(a) is not such as to suggest to the public that a connection exists between the organisation and the trade mark, or

(b) is not likely to mislead the public as to the existence of a connection between the user and the organisation.

(3) The provisions of this section as to emblems of an international organisation apply equally to anything which from a heraldic point of view imitates any such emblem.

(4) Where by virtue of this section the authorisation of an international organisation is or would be required for the registration of a trade mark, that organisation is entitled to restrain by injunction any use of the mark in the United Kingdom without its authorisation.

(5) Nothing in this section affects the rights of a person whose *bona fide* use of the trade mark in question began before 4th January 1962 (when the relevant provisions of the Paris Convention entered into force in relation to the United Kingdom).

**Notification under Article 6ter of the Convention.**

**59.**—(1) For the purposes of section 57 state emblems of a Convention country A1-067
(other than the national flag), and official signs or hallmarks, shall be regarded as protected under the Paris Convention only if, or to the extent that—

(a) the country in question has notified the United Kingdom in accordance with Article 6ter(3) of the Convention that it desires to protect that emblem, sign or hallmark,

(b) the notification remains in force, and

(c) the United Kingdom has not objected to it in accordance with Article 6ter(4) or any such objection has been withdrawn.

(2) For the purposes of section 58 the emblems, abbreviations and names of an international organisation shall be regarded as protected under the Paris Convention only if, or to the extent that—

(a) the organisation in question has notified the United Kingdom in accordance with Article 6ter(3) of the Convention that it desires to protect that emblem, abbreviation or name,

(b) the notification remains in force, and

(c) the United Kingdom has not objected to it in accordance with Article 6ter(4) or any such objection has been withdrawn.

(3) Notification under Article 6ter(3) of the Paris Convention shall have ef-

fect only in relation to applications for registration made more than two months after the receipt of the notification.

(4) The registrar shall keep and make available for public inspection by any person, at all reasonable hours and free of charge, a list of—

(a) the state emblems and official signs or hallmarks, and

(b) the emblems, abbreviations and names of international organisations,

which are for the time being protected under the Paris Convention by virtue of notification under Article 6ter(3).

[(5) Any reference in this section to Article 6ter of the Paris Convention shall be construed as including a reference to that Article as applied by the WTO agreement.]

**Acts of agent or representative: Article 6septies.**

A1-068 […]

**Similarity of goods and services.**

**[60A.**—(1) For the purposes of this Act goods and services—

(a) are not to be regarded as being similar to each other on the ground that they appear in the same class under the Nice Classification;

(b) are not to be regarded as being dissimilar from each other on the ground that they appear in different classes under the Nice Classification.

(2) In subsection (1), the "Nice Classification" means the system of classification under the Nice Agreement Concerning the International Classification of Goods and Services for the Purposes of the Registration of Marks of 15 June 1957, which was last amended on 28 September 1979.]

*Miscellaneous*

A1-069 **61.**— […]

PART III – ADMINISTRATIVE AND OTHER SUPPLEMENTARY PROVISIONS

*The registrar*

**The register.**

A1-070 **62.**— In this Act "the registrar" means the Comptroller-General of Patents, Designs and Trade Marks

*The register*

**The register.**

A1-071 **63.**—(1) The registrar shall maintain a register of trade marks.

References in this Act to "the register" are to that register; and references to registration (in particular, in the expression "registered trade mark") are, unless the context otherwise requires, to registration in that register.

(2) There shall be entered in the register in accordance with this Act—

(a) registered trade marks.

(b) such particulars as may be prescribed of registrable transactions affecting a registered trade mark, and

(c) such other matters relating to registered trade marks as may be prescribed.

(3) The register shall be kept in such manner as may be prescribed, and provision shall in particular be made for—

(a) public inspection of the register, and
(b) the supply of certified or uncertified copies, or extracts, of entries in the register.

**Rectification or correction of the register.**

**64.**—(1) Any person having a sufficient interest may apply for the rectification of an error or omission in the register. **A1-072**

Provided that an application for rectification may not be made in respect of a matter affecting the validity of the registration of a trade mark.

(2) An application for rectification may be made either to the registrar or to the court, except that—

(a) if proceedings concerning the trade mark in question are pending in the court, the application must be made to the court; and
(b) if in any other case the application is made to the registrar, he may at any stage of the proceedings refer the application to the court.

(3) Except where the registrar or the court directs otherwise, the effect of rectification of the register is that the error or omission in question shall be deemed never to have been made.

(4) The registrar may, on request made in the prescribed manner by the proprietor of a registered trade mark, or a licensee, enter any change in his name or address as recorded in the register.

(5) The registrar may remove from the register matter appearing to him to have ceased to have effect.

**Adaptation of entries to new classification.**

**65.**—(1) Provision may be made by rules empowering the registrar to do such things as he considers necessary to implement any amended or substituted classification of goods or services for the purposes of the registration of trade marks. **A1-073**

(2) Provision may in particular be made for the amendment of existing entries on the register so as to accord with the new classification.

(3) Any such power of amendment shall not be exercised so as to extend the rights conferred by the registration, except where it appears to the registrar that compliance with this requirement would involve undue complexity and that any extension would not be substantial and would not adversely affect the rights of any person.

(4) The rules may empower the registrar—

(a) to require the proprietor of a registered trade mark, within such time as may be prescribed, to file a proposal for amendment of the register, and
(b) to cancel or refuse to renew the registration of the trade mark in the event of his failing to do so.

(5) Any such proposal shall be advertised, and may be opposed, in such manner as may be prescribed.

*Powers and duties of the registrar*

**Power to require use of forms.**

A1-074 **66.**—(1) The registrar may require the use of such forms as he may direct for any purpose relating to the registration of a trade mark or any other proceeding before him under this Act.

(2) The forms, and any directions of the registrar with respect to their use, shall be published in the prescribed manner.

**Information about applications and registered trade marks.**

A1-075 **67.**—(1) After publication of an application for registration of a trade mark, the registrar shall on request provide a person with such information and permit him to inspect such documents relating to the application, or to any registered trade mark resulting from it, as may be specified in the request, subject, however, to any prescribed restrictions.

Any request must be made in the prescribed manner and be accompanied by the appropriate fee (if any).

(2) Before publication of an application for registration of a trade mark, documents or information constituting or relating to the application shall not be published by the registrar or communicated by him to any person except—

(a) in such cases and to such extent as may be prescribed, or

(b) with the consent of the applicant;

but subject as follows.

(3) Where a person has been notified that an application for registration of a trade mark has been made, and that the applicant will if the application is granted bring proceedings against him in respect of acts done after publication of the application, he may make a request under subsection (1) notwithstanding that the application has not been published and that subsection shall apply accordingly.

**Costs and security for costs.**

A1-076 **68.**—(1) Provision may be made by rules empowering the registrar, in any proceedings before him under this Act

(a) to award any party such costs as he may consider reasonable, and

(b) to direct how and by what parties they are to be paid

(2) Any such order of the registrar may be enforced—

(a) in England and Wales or Northern Ireland, in the same way as an order of the High Court;

(b) in Scotland, in the same way as a decree for expenses granted by the Court of Session.

(3) Provision may be made by rules empowering the registrar, in such cases as may be prescribed, to require a party to proceedings before him to give security for costs, in relation to those proceedings or to proceedings on appeal, and as to the consequences if security is not given.

**Evidence before registrar.**

A1-077 **69.**— Provision may be made by rules—

(a) as to the giving of evidence in proceedings before the registrar under this Act by affidavit or statutory declaration,

(b) conferring on the registrar the powers of an official referee of the [Senior Courts or of the Court of Judicature] as regards the examination of witnesses on oath and the discovery and production of documents; and

(c) applying in relation to the attendance of witnesses in proceedings before the registrar the rules applicable to the attendance of witnesses before such a referee.

**Exclusion of liability in respect of official acts.**

**70.**—(1) The registrar shall not be taken to warrant the validity of the registration of a trade mark under this Act or under any treaty, convention, arrangement or engagement to which the United Kingdom is a party. **A1-078**

(2) The registrar is not subject to any liability by reason of, or in connection with, any examination required or authorised by this Act, or any such treaty, convention, arrangement or engagement, or any report or other proceedings consequent on such examination.

(3) No proceedings lie against an officer of the registrar in respect of any matter for which, by virtue of this section, the registrar is not liable.

**Registrar's annual report.**

**71.**—(1) The Comptroller-General of Patents, Designs and Trade Marks shall in his annual report under section 121 of the Patents Act 1977 include a report on the execution of this Act, including the discharge of his functions under the Madrid protocol. **A1-079**

(2) The report shall include an account of all money received and paid by him under or by virtue of this Act.

*Legal proceedings and appeals*

**Registration to be prima facie evidence of validity.**

**72.**— In all legal proceedings relating to a registered trade mark (including proceedings for rectification of the register) the registration of a person as proprietor of a trade mark shall be prima facie evidence of the validity of the original registration and of any subsequent assignment or other transmission of it. **A1-080**

**Certificate of validity of contested registration.**

**73.**—(1) If in proceedings before the court the validity of the registration of a trade mark is contested and it is found by the court that the trade mark is validly registered, the court may give a certificate to that effect. **A1-081**

(2) If the court gives such a certificate and in subsequent proceedings—

(a) the validity of the registration is again questioned, and

(b) the proprietor obtains a final order or judgment in his favour,

he is entitled to his costs as between solicitor and client unless the court directs otherwise.

This subsection does not extend to the costs of an appeal in any such proceedings.

**Registrar's appearance in proceedings involving the register.**

**74.**—(1) In proceedings before the court involving an application for— **A1-082**

(a) the revocation of the registration of a trade mark,

(b) a declaration of the invalidity of the registration of a trade mark, or

(c) the rectification of the register,

the registrar is entitled to appear and be heard, and shall appear if so directed by the court.

(2) Unless otherwise directed by the court, the registrar may instead of appearing submit to the court a statement in writing signed by him, giving particulars of

(a) any proceedings before him in relation to the matter in issue,

(b) the grounds of any decision given by him affecting it,

(c) the practice of the Patent Office in like cases, or

(d) such matters relevant to the issues and within his knowledge as registrar as he thinks fit;

and the statement shall be deemed to form part of the evidence in the proceedings.

(3) Anything which the registrar is or may be authorised or required to do under this section may be done on his behalf by a duly authorised officer.

**The court.**

A1-083 **75.—** In this Act, unless the context otherwise requires, "the court" means —

(a) in England and Wales [, the High Court [, or the county court where it has] jurisdiction by virtue of an order made under section 1 of the Courts and Legal Services Act 1990,

[(aa) in] Northern Ireland, the High Court, and]

(b) in Scotland, the Court of Session.

**Appeals from the registrar.**

A1-084 **76.—**(1) An appeal lies from any decision of the registrar under this Act, except as otherwise expressly provided by rules.

For this purpose "decision" includes any act of the registrar in exercise of a discretion vested in him by or under this Act.

(2) Any such appeal may be brought either to an appointed person or to the court

(3) Where an appeal is made to an appointed person, he may refer the appeal to the court if—

(a) it appears to him that a point of general legal importance is involved.

(b) the registrar requests that it be so referred, or

(c) such a request is made by any party to the proceedings before the registrar in which the decision appealed against was made.

Before doing so the appointed person shall give the appellant and any other party to the appeal an opportunity to make representations as to whether the appeal should be referred to the court.

(4) Where an appeal is made to an appointed person and he does not refer it to the court, he shall hear and determine the appeal and his decision shall be final.

(5) The provisions of sections 68 and 69 (costs and security for costs; evidence) apply in relation to proceedings before an appointed person as in relation to proceedings before the registrar.

[(6) In the application of this section to England and Wales, "the court" means the High Court.]

**Persons appointed to hear and determine appeals.**

A1-085 **77.—**(1) For the purposes of section 76 an "appointed person" means a person appointed by the Lord Chancellor to hear and decide appeals under this Act.

(2) A person is not eligible for such appointment unless—

[(a) he satisfies the judicial-appointment eligibility condition on a 5-year basis;]

(b) he is an advocate or solicitor in Scotland of at least [5] years' standing;

(c) he is a member of the Bar of Northern Ireland or [solicitor of the Supreme Court of Northern Ireland] of at least [5] years' standing; or

(d) he has held judicial office.

(3) An appointed person shall hold and vacate office in accordance with his terms of appointment, subject to the following provisions—

(a) there shall be paid to him such remuneration (whether by way of salary or fees), and such allowances, as the Secretary of State with the approval of the Treasury may determine;

(b) he may resign his office by notice in writing to the Lord Chancellor;

(c) the Lord Chancellor may by notice in writing remove him from office if—

(i) he has become bankrupt or [a debt relief order (under Part 7A of the Insolvency Act 1986) has been made in respect of him or he has] made an arrangement with his creditors or, in Scotland, his estate has been sequestrated or he has executed a trust deed for his creditors or entered into a composition contract, or

(ii) he is incapacitated by physical or mental illness,

or if he is in the opinion of the Lord Chancellor otherwise unable or unfit to perform his duties as an appointed person.

(4) The Lord Chancellor shall consult the Lord Advocate before exercising his powers under this section

[(5) The Lord Chancellor may remove a person from office under subsection (3)(c) only with the concurrence of the appropriate senior judge.

(6) The appropriate senior judge is the Lord Chief Justice of England and Wales, unless–

(a) the person to be removed exercises functions wholly or mainly in Scotland, in which case it is the Lord President of the Court of Session, or

(b) the person to be removed exercises functions wholly or mainly in Northern Ireland, in which case it is the Lord Chief Justice of Northern Ireland.]

*Rules, fees, hours of business, &c*

**Power of Secretary of State to make rules.**

**78.**—(1) The Secretary of State may make rules— **A1-086**

(a) for the purposes of any provision of this Act authorising the making of rules with respect to any matter, and

(b) for prescribing anything authorised or required by any provision of this Act to be prescribed,

and generally for regulating practice and procedure under this Act.

(2) Provision may, in particular, be made—

(a) as to the manner of filing of applications and other documents;

(b) requiring and regulating the translation of documents and the filing and authentication of any translation;

(c) as to the service of documents;

(d) authorising the rectification of irregularities of procedure;

(e) prescribing time limits for anything required to be done in connection with any proceeding under this Act;

(f) providing for the extension of any time limit so prescribed, or specified by the registrar, whether or not it has already expired.

(3) Rules under this Act shall be made by statutory instrument which shall be subject to annulment in pursuance of a resolution of either House of Parliament.

**Fees.**

A1-087 **79.**—(1) There shall be paid in respect of applications and registration and other matters under this Act such fees as may be prescribed.

(2) Provision may be made by rules as to—

(a) the payment of a single fee in respect of two or more matters, and
(b) the circumstances (if any) in which a fee may be repaid or remitted.

**Hours of business and business days.**

A1-088 **80.**—(1) The registrar may give directions specifying the hours of business of the Patent Office for the purpose of the transaction by the public of business under this Act, and the days which are business days for that purpose.

(2) Business done on any day after the specified hours of business, or on a day which is not a business day, shall be deemed to have been done on the next business day; and where the time for doing anything under this Act expires on a day which is not a business day, that time shall be extended to the next business day.

(3) Directions under this section may make different provision for different classes of business and shall be published in the prescribed manner.

**The trade marks journal.**

A1-089 **81.**— Provision shall be made by rules for the publication by the registrar of a journal containing particulars of any application for the registration of a trade mark (including a representation of the mark) and such other information relating to trade marks as the registrar thinks fit.

*Trade mark agents*

**Recognition of agents.**

A1-090 **82.**— Except as otherwise provided by rules [and subject to the Legal Services Act 2007], any act required or authorised by this Act to be done by or to a person in connection with the registration of a trade mark, or any procedure relating to a registered trade mark, may be done by or to an agent authorised by that person orally or in writing.

[**The register of trade mark attorneys.**

A1-091 **83.**—(1) There is to continue to be a register of persons who act as agent for others for the purpose of applying for or obtaining the registration of trade marks.

(2) In this Act a registered trade mark attorney means an individual whose name is entered on the register kept under this section.

(3) The register is to be kept by the Institute of Trade Mark Attorneys.

(4) The Secretary of State may, by order, amend subsection (3) so as to require the register to be kept by the person specified in the order.

(5) Before making an order under subsection (4), the Secretary of State must consult the Legal Services Board.

(6) An order under this section must be made by statutory instrument.

(7) An order under this section may not be made unless a draft of it has been laid before, and approved by a resolution of, each House of Parliament.]

[**Regulation of trade mark attorneys.**

**83A.—**(1) The person who keeps the register under section 83 may make regulations which regulate– **A1-092**

(a) the keeping of the register and the registration of persons;

(b) the carrying on of trade mark agency work by registered persons.

(2) Those regulations may, amongst other things, make–

(a) provision as to the educational and training qualifications, and other requirements, which must be satisfied before an individual may be registered or for an individual to remain registered;

(b) provision as to the requirements which must be met by a body (corporate or unincorporate) before it may be registered or for it to remain registered, including provision as to the management and control of the body;

(c) provision as to the educational, training or other requirements to be met by regulated persons;

(d) provision regulating the practice, conduct and discipline of registered persons or regulated persons;

(e) provision authorising in such cases as may be specified in the regulations the erasure from the register of the name of any person registered in it, or the suspension of a person's registration;

(f) provision requiring the payment of such fees as may be specified in or determined in accordance with the regulations;

(g) provision about the provision to be made by registered persons in respect of complaints made against them;

(h) provision about the keeping of records and accounts by registered persons or regulated persons;

(i) provision for reviews of or appeals against decisions made under the regulations;

(j) provision as to the indemnification of registered persons or regulated persons against losses arising from claims in respect of civil liability incurred by them.

(3) Regulations under this section may make different provision for different purposes.

(4) Regulations under this section which are not regulatory arrangements within the meaning of the Legal Services Act 2007 are to be treated as such arrangements for the purposes of that Act.

(5) Before the appointed day, regulations under this section may be made only with the approval of the Secretary of State.

(6) The powers conferred to make regulations under this section are not to be taken to prejudice–

(a) any other power which the person who keeps the register may have to make rules or regulations (however they may be described and whether they are made under an enactment or otherwise);

(b) any rules or regulations made by that person under any such power.

(7) In this section–

"appointed day" means the day appointed for the coming into force of paragraph 1 of Schedule 4 to the Legal Services Act 2007;

"manager", in relation to a body, has the same meaning as in the Legal Services Act 2007 (see section 207);

"registered person" means–

(a) a registered trade mark attorney, or

(b) a body (corporate or unincorporate) registered in the register kept under section 83;

"regulated person" means a person who is not a registered person but is a manager or employee of a body which is a registered person;

"trade mark agency work" means work done in the course of carrying on the business of acting as agent for others for the purpose of–

(a) applying for or obtaining the registration of trade marks in the United Kingdom or elsewhere, or

(b) conducting proceedings before the Comptroller relating to applications for or otherwise in connection with the registration of trade marks.]

**Unregistered persons not to be described as registered trade mark agents.**

A1-093 **84.**—(1) An individual who is not a registered trade mark [attorney] shall not—

(a) carry on a business (otherwise than in partnership) under any name or other description which contains the words "registered trade mark agent" [or registered trade mark attorney]; or

(b) in the course of a business otherwise describe or hold himself out, or permit himself to be described or held out, as a registered trade mark agent [or a registered trade mark attorney].

(2) A partnership [or other unincorporated body] shall not—

(a) carry on a business under any name or other description which contains the words "registered trade mark agent" [or registered trade mark attorney]; or

(b) in the course of a business otherwise describe or hold itself out, or permit itself to be described or held out, as a firm of registered trade mark agents [or registered trade mark attorneys],

unless [the partnership or other body is registered in the register kept under section 83.]

(3) A body corporate shall not—

(a) carry on a business (otherwise than in partnership) under any name or other description which contains the words "registered trade mark agent" [or registered trade mark attorney]; or

(b) in the course of a business otherwise describe or hold itself out, or permit itself to be described or held out, as a registered trade mark agent [or a registered trade mark attorney],

unless [the body corporate is registered in the register kept under section 83.]

(4) A person who contravenes this section commits an offence and is liable on summary conviction to a fine not exceeding level 5 on the standard scale; and proceedings for such an offence may be begun at any time within a year from the date of the offence.

A1-094 **85.**— […]

**Use of the term "trade mark attorney".**

A1-095 **86.**—(1) No offence is committed under the enactments restricting the use of certain expressions in reference to persons not qualified to act as solicitors by the use of the term "trade mark attorney" in reference to a registered trade mark [attorney].

(2) The enactments referred to in subsection (1) are section 21 of the Solicitors Act 1974, section 31 of the Solicitors (Scotland) Act 1980 and Article 22 of the Solicitors (Northern Ireland) Order 1976.

**Privilege for communications with registered trade mark agents.**

**87.**—(1) This section applies to [—

(a)] communications as to any matter relating to the protection of any design or trade mark, or as to any matter involving passing off [, and

(b) documents, material or information relating to any matter mentioned in paragraph (a).]

[(2) Where a trade mark attorney acts for a client in relation to a matter mentioned in subsection (1), any communication, document, material or information to which this section applies is privileged from disclosure in like manner as if the trade mark attorney had at all material times been acting as the client's solicitor.]

(3) In subsection (2) "trade mark [attorney"] means — **A1-096**

(a) a registered trade mark [attorney], or

(b) a partnership entitled to describe itself as a firm of registered trade mark [attorneys], or

(c) [any other unincorporated body or] a body corporate entitled to describe itself as a registered trade mark [attorney]

**Power of registrar to refuse to deal with certain agents.**

**88.**—(1) The Secretary of State may make rules authorising the registrar to refuse to recognise as agent in respect of any business under this Act— **A1-097**

(a) a person who has been convicted of an offence under section 84 (unregistered persons describing themselves as registered trade mark agents);

(b) an individual whose name has been erased from and not restored to, or who is suspended from, the register of trade mark [attorneys] on the ground of misconduct;

(c) a person who is found by the Secretary of State to have been guilty of such conduct as would, in the case of an individual registered in the register of trade mark [attorneys] , render him liable to have his name erased from the register on the ground of misconduct;

(d) a partnership or body corporate of which one of the partners or directors is a person whom the registrar could refuse to recognise under paragraph (a), (b) or (c) above.

(2) The rules may contain such incidental and supplementary provisions as appear to the Secretary of State to be appropriate and may, in particular, prescribe circumstances in which a person is or is not to be taken to have been guilty of misconduct.

*Importation of infringing goods, material or articles*

**Infringing goods, material or articles may be treated as prohibited goods.**

**89.**—(1) The proprietor of a registered trade mark, or a licensee, may give notice in writing to the Commissioners of Customs and Excise— **A1-098**

(a) that he is the proprietor or, as the case may be, a licensee of the registered trade mark,

(b) that, at a time and place specified in the notice, goods which are, in relation to that registered trade mark, infringing goods, material or articles are expected to arrive in the United Kingdom—
  (i) from outside the European Economic Area, or
  (ii) from within that Area but not having been entered for free circulation, and

(c) that he requests the Commissioners to treat them as prohibited goods.

(2) When a notice is in force under this section the importation of the goods to which the notice relates, otherwise than by a person for his private and domestic use, is prohibited; but a person is not by reason of the prohibition liable to any penalty other than forfeiture of the goods.

[(3) This section does not apply to goods placed in, or expected to be placed in, one of the situations referred to in Article 1(1), in respect of which an application may be made under [Article 3 of the European Customs Enforcement Regulation.]]

**Power of Commissioners of Customs and Excise to make regulations.**

A1-099 **90.**—(1) The Commissioners of Customs and Excise may make regulations prescribing the form in which notice is to be given under section 89 and requiring a person giving notice—

(a) to furnish the Commissioners with such evidence as may be specified in the regulations, either on giving notice or when the goods are imported, or at both those times, and

(b) to comply with such other conditions as may be specified in the regulations

(2) The regulations may, in particular, require a person giving such a notice

(a) to pay such fees in respect of the notice as may be specified by the regulations;

(b) to give such security as may be so specified in respect of any liability or expense which the Commissioners may incurring consequence of the notice by reason of the detention of any goods or anything done to goods detained;

(c) to indemnify the Commissioners against any such liability or expense, whether security has been given or not.

(3) The regulations may make different provision as respects different classes of case to which they apply and may include such incidental and supplementary provisions as the Commissioners consider expedient.

(4) Regulations under this section shall be made by statutory instrument which shall be subject to annulment in pursuance of a resolution of either House of Parliament.

(5) [...]

**[Power of Commissioners for Revenue and Customs to disclose information.]**

A1-100 **91.**— Where information relating to infringing goods, material or articles has been obtained [or is held] by [the Commissioners for her Majesty's Revenue and Customs] for the purposes of, or in connection with, the exercise of [functions of Her Majesty's Revenue and Customs] in relation to imported goods, the Commissioners may authorise the disclosure of that information for the purpose of facilitating the exercise by any person of any function in connection with the investigation or prosecution of [an offence under—

(a) section 92 below (unauthorised use of trade mark, &c in relation to goods),
(b) the Trade Descriptions Act 1968,
(c) the Business Protection from Misleading Marketing Regulations 2008, or
(d) the Consumer Protection from Unfair Trading Regulations 2008.]

*Offences*

**Unauthorised use of trade mark, &c. in relation to goods.**

**92.**—(1) A person commits an offence who with a view to gain for himself or another, or with intent to cause loss to another, and without the consent of the proprietor— **A1-101**

(a) applies to goods or their packaging a sign identical to, or likely to be mistaken for, a registered trade mark, or
(b) sells or lets for hire, offers or exposes for sale or hire or distributes goods which bear, or the packaging of which bears, such a sign, or
(c) has in his possession, custody or control in the course of a business any such goods with a view to the doing of anything, by himself or another, which would be an offence under paragraph (b).

(2) A person commits an offence who with a view to gain for himself or another, or with intent to cause loss to another, and without the consent of the proprietor—

(a) applies a sign identical to, or likely to be mistaken for, a registered trade mark to material intended to be used—
  (i) for labelling or packaging goods,
  (ii) as a business paper in relation to goods, or
  (iii) for advertising goods, or
(b) uses in the course of a business material bearing such a sign for labelling or packaging goods, as a business paper in relation to goods, or for advertising goods, or
(c) has in his possession, custody or control in the course of a business any such material with a view to the doing of anything, by himself or another, which would be an offence under paragraph (b).

(3) A person commits an offence who with a view to gain for himself or another, or with intent to cause loss to another, and without the consent of the proprietor—

(a) makes an article specifically designed or adapted for making copies of a sign identical to, or likely to be mistaken for, a registered trade mark, or
(b) has such an article in his possession, custody or control in the course of a business,

knowing or having reason to believe that it has been, or is to be, used to produce goods, or material for labelling or packaging goods, as a business paper in relation to goods, or for advertising goods.

(4) A person does not commit an offence under this section unless—

(a) the goods are goods in respect of which the trade mark is registered, or
(b) the trade mark has a reputation in the United Kingdom and the use of the sign takes or would take unfair advantage of, or is or would be detrimental to, the distinctive character or the repute of the trade mark.

(5) It is a defence for a person charged with an offence under this section to show that he believed on reasonable grounds that the use of the sign in the manner in which it was used, or was to be used, was not an infringement of the registered trade mark.

(6) A person guilty of an offence under this section is liable—

(a) on summary conviction to imprisonment for a term not exceeding six months or a fine not exceeding the statutory maximum, or both;

(b) on conviction on indictment to a fine or imprisonment for a term not exceeding ten years, or both.

[**Search warrants.**

A1-102 **92A.**—(1) Where a justice of the peace (in Scotland, a sheriff or justice of the peace) is satisfied by information on oath given by a constable (in Scotland, by evidence on oath) that there are reasonable grounds for believing—

(a) that an offence under section 92 (unauthorised use of trade mark, etc. in relation to goods) has been or is about to be committed in any premises, and

(b) that evidence that such an offence has been or is about to be committed is in those premises,

he may issue a warrant authorising a constable to enter and search the premises, using such reasonable force as is necessary.

(2) The power conferred by subsection (1) does not, in England and Wales, extend to authorising a search for material of the kinds mentioned in section 9(2) of the Police and Criminal Evidence Act 1984 (c. 60) (certain classes of personal or confidential material).

(3) A warrant under subsection (1)—

(a) may authorise persons to accompany any constable executing the warrant, and

(b) remains in force for three months from the date of its issue.

(4) In executing a warrant issued under subsection (1) a constable may seize an article if he reasonably believes that it is evidence that any offence under section 92 has been or is about to be committed.

(5) In this section "premises" includes land, buildings, fixed or moveable structures, vehicles, vessels, aircraft and hovercraft.]

**Enforcement function of local weights and measures authority.**

A1-103 **93.**—(1) It is the duty of every local weights and measures authority to enforce within their area the provisions of section 92 (unauthorised use of trade mark, &c. in relation to goods).

(2) […]

(3) Subsection (1) above does not apply in relation to the enforcement of section 92 in Northern Ireland, but it is the duty of the Department of Economic Development to enforce that section in Northern Ireland.[…]

[(3A) For the investigatory powers available to a local weights and measures authority or the Department of Enterprise, Trade and Investment in Northern Ireland for the purposes of the duties in this section, see Schedule 5 to the Consumer Rights Act 2015.]

(4) Any enactment which authorises the disclosure of information for the purpose of facilitating the enforcement of the Trade Descriptions Act 1968 shall apply as if section 92 above were contained in that Act and as if the functions of any person in relation to the enforcement of that section were functions under that Act.

(5) Nothing in this section shall be construed as authorising a local weights and measures authority to bring proceedings in Scotland for an offence.

**Falsification of register, &c.**

**94.**—(1) It is an offence for a person to make, or cause to be made, a false entry in the register of trade marks, knowing or having reason to believe that it is false. **A1-104**

(2) It is an offence for a person—

(a) to make or cause to be made anything falsely purporting to be a copy of an entry in the register, or

(b) to produce or tender or cause to be produced or tendered in evidence any such thing,

knowing or having reason to believe that it is false.

(3) A person guilty of an offence under this section is liable—

(a) on conviction on indictment, to imprisonment for a term not exceeding two years or a fine, or both;

(b) on summary conviction, to imprisonment for a term not exceeding six months or a fine not exceeding the statutory maximum, or both.

**Falsely representing trade mark as registered.**

**95.**—(1) It is an offence for a person— **A1-105**

(a) falsely to represent that a mark is a registered trade mark, or

(b) to make a false representation as to the goods or services for which a trade mark is registered

knowing or having reason to believe that the representation is false.

(2) For the purposes of this section, the use in the United Kingdom in relation to a trade mark—

(a) of the word "registered", or

(b) of any other word or symbol importing a reference (express or implied) to registration,

shall be deemed to be a representation as to registration under this Act unless it is shown that the reference is to registration elsewhere than in the United Kingdom and that the trade mark is in fact so registered for the goods or services in question.

(3) A person guilty of an offence under this section is liable on summary conviction to a fine not exceeding level 3 on the standard scale.

**Supplementary provisions as to summary proceedings in Scotland.**

**96.**—(1) Notwithstanding anything in [section 136 of the Criminal Procedure (Scotland) Act 1995] , summary proceedings in Scotland for an offence under this Act may be begun at any time within six months after the date on which evidence sufficient in the Lord Advocate's opinion to justify the proceedings came to his knowledge. **A1-106**

For this purpose a certificate of the Lord Advocate as to the date on which such evidence came to his knowledge is conclusive evidence.

(2) For the purposes of subsection (1) and of any other provision of this Act as to the time within which summary proceedings for an offence may be brought, proceedings in Scotland shall be deemed to be begun on the date on which a warrant to apprehend or to cite the accused is granted, if such warrant is executed without undue delay.

*Forfeiture of counterfeit goods, &c.*

**Forfeiture; England and Wales or Northern Ireland.**

A1-107 **97.**—(1) In England and Wales or Northern Ireland where there has come into the possession of any person in connection with the investigation or prosecution of a relevant offence—

(a) goods which, or the packaging of which, bears a sign identical to or likely to be mistaken for a registered trade mark,

(b) material bearing such a sign and intended to be used for labelling or packaging goods, as a business paper in relation to goods, or for advertising goods, or

(c) articles specifically designed or adapted for making copies of such a sign,

that person may apply under this section for an order for the forfeiture of the goods, material or articles.

(2) An application under this section may be made—

(a) where proceedings have been brought in any court for a relevant offence relating to some or all of the goods, material or articles, to that court;

(b) where no application for the forfeiture of the goods, material or articles has been made under paragraph (a), by way of complaint to a magistrates' court.

(3) On an application under this section the court shall make an order for the forfeiture of any goods, material or articles only if it is satisfied that a relevant offence has been committed in relation to the goods, material or articles.

(4) A court may infer for the purposes of this section that such an offence has been committed in relation to any goods, material or articles if it is satisfied that such an offence has been committed in relation to goods, material or articles which are representative of them (whether by reason of being of the same design or part of the same consignment or batch or otherwise).

(5) Any person aggrieved by an order made under this section by a magistrates court, or by a decision of such a court not to make such an order, may appeal against that order or decision—

(a) in England and Wales, to the Crown Court;

(b) in Northern Ireland, to the county court,

and an order so made may contain such provision as appears to the court to be appropriate for delaying the coming into force of the order pending the making and determination of any appeal (including any application under section 111 of the Magistrates' Courts Act 1980 or Article 146 of the Magistrates' Courts (Northern Ireland) Order 1981 (statement of case))

(6) Subject to subsection (7), where any goods, material or articles are forfeited under this section they shall be destroyed in accordance with such directions as the court may give.

(7) On making an order under this section the court may, if it considers it appropriate to do so, direct that the goods, material or articles to which the order relates shall (instead of being destroyed) be released, to such person as the court may specify, on condition that that person—

(a) causes the offending sign to be erased, removed or obliterated, and

(b) complies with any order to pay costs which has been made against him in the proceedings for the order for forfeiture.

(8) For the purposes of this section a "relevant offence" means
[(a) an offence under section 92 above (unauthorised use of trade mark, &c in relation to goods),
(b) an offence under the Trade Descriptions Act 1968,
(c) an offence under the Business Protection from Misleading Marketing Regulations 2008,
(d) an offence under the Consumer Protection from Unfair Trading Regulations 2008, or
(e) any offence involving dishonesty or deception.]

**Forfeiture; Scotland.**

**98.**—(1) In Scotland the court may make an order for the forfeiture of any— **A1-108**
(a) goods which bear, or the packaging of which bears, a sign identical to or likely to be mistaken for a registered trade mark,
(b) material bearing such a sign and intended to be used for labelling or packaging goods, as a business paper in relation to goods, or for advertising goods, or
(c) articles specifically designed or adapted for making copies of such a sign.

(2) An order under this section may be made—
(a) on an application by the procurator-fiscal made in the manner specified in [section 134 of the Criminal Procedure (Scotland) Act 1995], or
(b) where a person is convicted of a relevant offence, in addition to any other penalty which the court may impose.

(3) On an application under subsection (2)(a), the court shall make an order for the forfeiture of any goods, material or articles only if it is satisfied that a relevant offence has been committed in relation to the goods, material or articles.

(4) The court may infer for the purposes of this section that such an offence has been committed in relation to any goods, material or articles if it is satisfied that such an offence has been committed in relation to goods, material or articles which are representative of them (whether by reason of being of the same design or part of the same consignment or batch or otherwise).

(5) The procurator-fiscal making the application under subsection (2)(a) shall serve on any person appearing to him to be the owner of, or otherwise to have an interest in, the goods, material or articles to which the application relates a copy of the application, together with a notice giving him the opportunity to appear at the hearing of the application to show cause why the goods, material or articles should not be forfeited.

(6) Service under subsection (5) shall be carried out, and such service may be proved, in the manner specified for citation of an accused in summary proceedings under the [Criminal Procedure (Scotland) Act 1995] .

(7) Any person upon whom notice is served under subsection (5) and any other person claiming to be the owner of, or otherwise to have an interest in, goods, material or articles to which an application under this section relates shall be entitled to appear at the hearing of the application to show cause why the goods, material or articles should not be forfeited.

(8) The court shall not make an order following an application under subsection (2)(a)—
(a) if any person on whom notice is served under subsection (5) does not appear, unless service of the notice on that person is proved; or

(b) if no notice under subsection (5) has been served, unless the court is satisfied that in the circumstances it was reasonable not to serve such notice.

(9) Where an order for the forfeiture of any goods, material or articles is made following an application under subsection (2)(a) any person who appeared, or was entitled to appear, to show cause why goods, material or articles should not be forfeited may, within 21 days of the making of the order, appeal to the High Court by Bill of suspension; and [section 182(5)(a) to (e) of the Criminal Procedure (Scotland) Act 1995] shall apply to an appeal under this subsection as it applies to a stated case under Part II of that Act.

(10) An order following an application under subsection (2)(a) shall not take effect—

(a) until the end of the period of 21 days beginning with the day after the day on which the order is made; or

(b) if an appeal is made under subsection (9) above within that period, until the appeal is determined or abandoned

(11) An order under subsection (2)(b) shall not take effect—

(a) until the end of the period within which an appeal against the order could be brought under the [Criminal Procedure (Scotland) Act 1995]; or

(b) if an appeal is made within that period, until the appeal is determined or abandoned.

(12) Subject to subsection (13), goods, material or articles forfeited under this section shall be destroyed in accordance with such directions as the court may give.

(13) On making an order under this section the court may if it considers it appropriate to do so, direct that the goods, material or articles to which the order relates shall (instead of being destroyed) be released, to such person as the court may specify, on condition that that person causes the offending sign to be erased, removed or obliterated

(14) For the purposes of this section—

"relevant offence" means

(a) [an offence under section 92 above (unauthorised use of trade mark, &c in relation to goods),

(b) an offence under the Trade Descriptions Act 1968,

(c) an offence under the Business Protection from Misleading Marketing Regulations 2008,

(d) an offence under the Consumer Protection from Unfair Trading Regulations 2008, or

(e) any offence involving dishonesty or deception;]

"the court" means —

(a) in relation to an order made on an application under subsection (2)(a), the sheriff, and

(b) in relation to an order made unless subsection (2)(b), the court which imposed the penalty.

## Part IV – Miscellaneous and General Provisions

### *Miscellaneous*

**Unauthorised use of Royal arms. &c.**

**99.**—(1) A person shall not without the authority of Her Majesty use in connection with any business the Royal arms (or arms so closely resembling the Royal arms as to be calculated to deceive) in such manner as to be calculated to lead to the belief that he is duly authorised to use the Royal arms. **A1-109**

(2) A person shall not without the authority of Her Majesty or of a member of the Royal family use in connection with any business any device, emblem or title in such a manner as to be calculated to lead to the belief that he is employed by, or supplies goods or services to Her Majesty or that member of the Royal family.

(3) A person who contravenes subsection (1) commits an offence and is liable on summary conviction to a fine not exceeding level 2 on the standard scale.

(4) Contravention of subsection (1) or (2) may be restrained by injunction in proceedings brought by—

(a) any person who is authorised to use the arms, device, emblem or title in question, or

(b) any person authorised by the Lord Chamberlain to take such proceedings

(5) Nothing in this section affects any right of the proprietor of a trade mark containing any such arms, device, emblem or title to use that trade mark.

**Reproduction of trade marks in dictionaries, encyclopaedias etc.**

**[99A.**—(1) Subsection (2) applies if the reproduction of a trade mark in a dictionary, encyclopaedia or similar reference work, in print or electronic form, gives the impression that it constitutes the generic name of the goods or services for which the trade mark is registered. **A1-109.1**

(2) The publisher of the work must, at the request in writing of the proprietor of the trade mark, ensure that the reproduction of the trade mark is accompanied by an indication that it is a registered trade mark.

(3) The action required by subsection (2) must be taken—

(a) without delay, and

(b) in the case of works in printed form, at the latest in the next edition of the publication.

(4) If the publisher fails to take any action required by subsection (2) the court may, on an application by the proprietor—

(a) order the publisher to take the action concerned;

(b) if the work is in printed form, order the publisher to erase or amend the reproduction of the trade mark or secure the destruction of copies of the work in the publisher's possession, custody or control; or

(c) grant such other order as the court in the circumstances considers appropriate.]

**Burden of proving use of trade mark.**

**100.**— If in any civil proceedings under this Act a question arises as to the use to which a registered trade mark has been put, if is for the proprietor to show what use has been made of it. **A1-110**

**Offences committed by partnerships and bodies corporate.**

A1-111 **101.**—(1) Proceedings for an offence under this Act alleged to have been committed by a partnership shall be brought against the partnership in the name of the firm and not in that of the partners; but without prejudice to any liability of the partners under subsection (4) below.

(2) The following provisions apply for the purposes of such proceedings as in relation to a body corporate—

(a) any rules of court relating to the service of documents,
(b) in England and Wales or Northern Ireland, Schedule 3 to the Magistrates' Courts Act 1980 or Schedule 4 to the Magistrates' Courts (Northern Ireland) Order 1981 (procedure on charge of offence).

(3) A fine imposed on a partnership on its conviction in such proceedings shall be paid out of the partnership assets.

(4) Where a partnership is guilty of an offence under this Act, every partner, other than a partner who is proved to have been ignorant of or to have attempted to prevent the commission of the offence, is also guilty of the offence and liable to be proceeded against and punished accordingly.

(5) Where an offence under this Act committed by a body corporate is proved to have been committed with the consent or connivance of a director, manager, secretary or other similar officer of the body, or a person purporting to act in any such capacity, he as well as the body corporate is guilty of the offence and liable to be proceeded against and punished accordingly.

*Interpretation*

**Adaptation of expressions for Scotland.**

A1-112 **102.**— In the application of this Act to Scotland—

"account of profits" means accounting and payment of profits.
"accounts" means count, reckoning and payment.
"assignment" means assignation;
"costs" means expenses;
"declaration" means declarator;
"defendant" means defender;
"delivery up" means delivery;
"injunction" means interdict;
"interlocutory relief" means interim remedy; and
"plaintiff" means pursuer.

**Minor definitions.**

A1-113 **103.**—(1) In this Act—

"business", includes a trade or profession;
"director", in relation to a body corporate whose affairs are managed by its members, means any member of the body;
"infringement proceedings", in relation to a registered trade mark, includes proceedings under section 16 (order for delivery up of infringing goods, &c.);
"publish" means make available to the public, and references to publication—

(a) in relation to an application for registration, are to publication under section 38(1), and

(b) in relation to registration, are to publication under section 40(4);

"statutory provisions", includes provisions of subordinate legislation within the meaning of the Interpretation Act 1978;

"trade", includes any business or profession..

(2) References in this Act to use (or any particular description of use) of a trade mark, or of a sign identical with, similar to, or likely to be mistaken for a trade mark, include use (or that description of use) otherwise than by means of a graphic representation.

(3) References in this Act to [an EU] instrument include references to any instrument amending or replacing that instrument

**Index of defined expressions.**

**104.—** In this Act the expressions listed below are defined by or otherwise fall to be construed in accordance with the provisions indicated— **A1-114**

| | |
|---|---|
| account of profits and accounts (in Scotland) | section 102 |
| appointed person (for purposes of section 76) | section 77 |
| assignment (in Scotland) | section 102 |
| business | section 103(1) |
| certification mark | section 50(1) |
| collective mark | section 49(1) |
| commencement (of this Act) | section 109(2) |
| [... | ...] |
| [... | ...] |
| Convention country | section 55(1)(b) |
| costs (in Scotland) | section 102 |
| the court | section 75 |
| date of application | section 33(2) |
| date of filing | section 33(1) |
| date of registration | section 40(3) |
| defendant (in Scotland) | section 102 |
| delivery up (in Scotland) | section 102 |
| director | section 103(1) |
| earlier right | section 5(4) |
| earlier trade mark | section 6 |
| [European Customs Enforcement Regulation | section 10A] |
| [European Union trade mark] | [section 51] |
| [European Union Trade Mark Regulation] | [section 51] |
| exclusive licence and licensee | section 29(1) |
| infringement (of registered trade mark) | section 9(1) and (2) and 10 |
| infringement proceedings | section 103(1) |

| | |
|---|---|
| infringing articles | section 17 |
| infringing goods | section 17 |
| infringing material | section 17 |
| injunction (in Scotland) | section 102 |
| interlocutory relief (in Scotland) | section 102 |
| the International Bureau | section 53 |
| [international trade mark (EC)] | [section 53] |
| International trade mark (UK) | section 53 |
| Madrid Protocol | section 53 |
| Paris Convention | section 55(1)(a) |
| plaintiff (in Scotland) | section 102 |
| prescribed | section 78(1)(b) |
| protected under the Paris Convention | |
| —well-known trade marks | section 56(1) |
| —state emblems and official signs or hallmarks | section 57(1) |
| —emblems, &c. of international organisations | section 58(2) |
| publish and references to publication | section 103(1) |
| register, registered (and related expressions) | section 63(1) |
| registered trade mark [attorney] | section 83[(2)] |
| registrable transaction | section 25(2) |
| the registrar | section 62 |
| rules | section 78 |
| statutory provisions | section 103(1) |
| trade | section 103(1) |
| trade mark | |
| —generally | section 1(1) |
| —includes collective mark or certification mark | section 1(2) |
| United Kingdom (references include Isle of Man) | section 108(2) |
| use (of trade mark or sign) | section 103(2) |
| well-known trade mark (under Paris Convention) | section 56(1) |

*Other general provisions*

**Transitional provisions.**

A1-115 **105.—** The provisions of Schedule 3 have effect with respect to transitional matters, including the treatment of marks registered under the Trade Marks Act 1938, and applications for registration and other proceedings pending under that Act, on the commencement of this Act.

**Consequential amendments and repeals.**

**106.**—(1) The enactments specified in Schedule 4 are amended in accordance with that Schedule, the amendments being consequential on the provisions of this Act. **A1-116**

(2) The enactments specified in Schedule 5 are repealed to the extent specified

**Territorial waters and the continental shelf.**

**107.**—(1) For the purposes of this Act the territorial waters of the United Kingdom shall be treated as part of the United Kingdom. **A1-117**

(2) This Act applies to things done in the United Kingdom sector of the continental shelf on a structure or vessel which is present there for purposes directly connected with the exploration of the sea bed or subsoil or the exploitation of their natural resources as it applies to things done in the United Kingdom.

(3) The United Kingdom sector of the continental shelf means the areas designated by order under section 1(7) of the Continental Shelf Act 1964.

**Extent.**

**108.**—(1) This Act extends to England and Wales, Scotland and Northern Ireland. **A1-118**

(2) This Act also extends to the Isle of Man, subject to such exceptions and modifications as Her Majesty may specify by Order in Council, and subject to any such Order references in this Act to the United Kingdom shall be construed as including the Isle of Man.

**Commencement**

**109.**—(1) The provisions of this Act come into force on such day as the Secretary of State may appoint by order made by statutory instrument. **A1-119**

Different days may be appointed for different provisions and different purposes.

(2) The references to the commencement of this Act in Schedules 3 and 4 (transitional provisions and consequential amendments) are to the commencement of the main substantive provisions of Parts I and III of this Act and the consequential repeal of the Trade Marks Act 1938. Provision may be made by order under this section identifying the date of that commencement

**Short title.**

**110.**— This Act may be cited as the Trade Marks Act 1994. **A1-120**

*Replace with:*

SCHEDULE 1 **A1-121**

COLLECTIVE MARKS

**Section 49**

*General*

**1.**— The provisions of this Act apply to collective marks subject to the following provisions. **A1-121**

*Signs of which a collective mark may consist*

**2.**— In relation to a collective mark the reference in section 1(1) (signs of which a trade mark may consist) to distinguishing goods or services of one undertaking from those of other undertakings shall **A1-122**

be construed as a reference to distinguishing goods or services of members of the association which is the proprietor of the mark from those of other undertakings.

*Indication of geographical origin*

A1-123 **3.**—(1) Notwithstanding section 3(1)(c), a collective mark may be registered which consists of signs or indications which may serve, in trade, to designate the geographical origin of the goods or services.

(2) However, the proprietor of such a mark is not entitled to prohibit the use of the signs or indications in accordance with honest practices in industrial or commercial matters (in particular, by a person who is entitled to use a geographical name).

*Mark not to be misleading as to character or significance*

A1-124 **4.**—(1) A collective mark shall not be registered if the public is liable to be misled as regards the character or significance of the mark, in particular if it is likely to be taken to be something other than a collective mark.

(2) The registrar may accordingly require that a mark in respect of which application is made for registration include some indication that it is a collective mark.

Notwithstanding section 39(2), an application may be amended so as to comply with any such requirement.

*Regulations governing use of collective mark*

A1-125 **5.**—(1) An applicant for registration of a collective mark must fine with the registrar regulations governing the use of the mark.

(2) The regulations must specify the persons authorised to use the mark, the conditions of membership of the association and, where they exist, the conditions of use of the mark, including any sanctions against misuse.

Further requirements with which the regulations have to comply may be imposed by rules.

(3) Where the regulations govern use of a mark referred to in paragraph 3(1), they must authorise any person whose goods or services originate in the geographical area concerned to become a member of the association which is the proprietor of the mark, provided that the person fulfils all the other conditions of the regulations.

(4) Further requirements with which the regulations have to comply may be imposed by rules.

*Approval of regulations by registrar*

A1-126 **6.**—(1) A collective mark shall not be registered unless the regulations governing the use of the mark—

(a) comply with [paragraph 5(2) and (3)] and any further requirements imposed by rules, and

(b) are not contrary to public policy or to accepted principles of morality

(2) Before the end of the prescribed period after the date of the application for registration of a collective mark, the applicant must file the regulations with the registrar and pay the prescribed fee.

If he does not do so, the application shall be deemed to be withdrawn.

A1-127 **7.**—(1) The registrar shall consider whether the requirements mentioned in paragraph 6(1) are met.

(2) If it appears to the registrar that those requirements are not met, he shall the applicant and give him an opportunity, within such period as the registrar may specify, to make representations or to file amended regulations.

(3) If the applicant fails to satisfy the registrar that those requirements are not, or to file regulations amended so as to meet them, or fails to respond before the end of the specified period, the registrar shall refuse the application.

(4) If it appears to the registrar that those requirements, and the other requirements for registration, are met, he shall accept the application and shall proceed in accordance with section 38 (publication, opposition proceedings and observations).

A1-128 **8.**— The regulations shall be published and notice of opposition may be given, and observations may be made, relating to the matters mentioned in paragraph 6(1).

This is in addition to any other grounds on which the application may be opposed or observations made.

*Regulations to be open to inspection*

A1-129 **9.**— The regulations governing the use of a registered collective mark shall be open to public inspection in the same way as the register.

*Amendment of regulations*

**10.**—(1) An amendment of the regulations governing the use of a registered collective mark is not effective unless and until the amended regulations are filed with the registrar and accepted by him. **A1-130**

(2) Before accepting any amended regulations the registrar may in any case where it appears to him expedient to do so cause them to be published.

(3) If he does so, notice of opposition may be given, and observations may be made, relating to the matters mentioned in paragraph 6(1).

*Infringement rights of authorised users*

**11.**— The following provisions apply in relation to an authorised user of a registered collective mark as in relation to a licensee of a trade mark— **A1-131**

(a) section 10(5) (definition of infringement: unauthorised application of mark to certain material);

(b) section 19(2) (order as to disposal of infringing goods, material or articles adequacy of other remedies);

(c) section 89 (prohibition of importation of infringing goods, material or articles request to Commissioners of Customs and Excise).

**12.**—(1) The following provisions (which correspond to the provisions of section 30 general provisions as to rights of licensees in case of infringement) have effect as regards the rights of an authorised user in relation to infringement of a registered collective mark. **A1-132**

[(2) Subject to any agreement to the contrary between the authorised user and the proprietor, an authorised user may only bring proceedings for infringement of a registered collective mark with the consent of the proprietor.]

(3) [...]

(4) [Where proceedings are brought by an authorised user for infringement of a registered collective mark (with the consent of the proprietor or pursuant to any agreement referred to in sub-paragraph (2))], the authorised user may not, without the leave of the court, proceed with the action unless the proprietor is either joined as a plaintiff or added as a defendant. This does not affect the granting of interlocutory relief on an application by an authorised user alone.

(5) A proprietor who is added as a defendant as mentioned in sub-paragraph (4) shall not be made liable for any costs in the action unless he takes part in the proceedings.

(6) In infringement proceedings brought by the proprietor of a registered collective mark any loss suffered or likely to be suffered by authorised users shall be taken into account; and the court may give such directions as it thinks fit as to the extent to which the plaintiff is to hold the proceeds of any pecuniary remedy on behalf of such users.

[(7) Where the proprietor of a registered collective mark brings infringement proceedings, an authorised user who has suffered loss is entitled to intervene in the proceedings for the purpose of obtaining compensation for that loss.]

**13.**— Apart from the grounds of revocation provided for in section 46, the registration of a collective mark may be revoked on the ground **A1-133**

(a) that the manner in which the mark has been used by the proprietor has caused it to become liable to mislead the public in the manner referred to in paragraph 4(1); or

(b) that the [persons authorised to use it] [has not taken reasonable steps to prevent the mark being used in a manner that is incompatible with the conditions of use laid down in] the regulations governing the use of the mark [(as amended from time to time)], or

(c) that an amendment of the regulations has been made so that the regulations

(i) no longer comply with [paragraph 5(2) and (3)] and any further conditions imposed by rules, or

(ii) are contrary to public policy or to accepted principles of morality.

*Grounds for invalidity of registration*

**14.**— Apart from the grounds of invalidity provided for in section 47, the registration of a collective mark [shall] be declared invalid on the ground that the mark was registered in breach of the provisions of [section 49(1A) (definition of who may be registered as the proprietor of a certification mark) or] paragraph 4(1) or 6(1) [unless the breach was only of paragraph 6(1) and the proprietor of the mark, by amending the regulations governing use, complies with the requirements of paragraph 6(1)]. **A1-134**

## SCHEDULE 2

### CERTIFICATION MARKS

**Section 50**

*General*

**A1-135** **1.—** The provisions of this Act apply to certification marks subject to the following provisions.

*Signs of which a certification mark may consist*

**A1-136** **2.—** In relation to a certification mark the reference in section 1(1) (signs of which a trade mark may consist) to distinguishing goods or services of one undertaking from those of other undertakings shall be construed as a reference to distinguishing goods or services which are certified from those which are not.

*Indication of geographical origin*

**A1-137** **3.**—(1) Notwithstanding section 3(1)(c) a certification mark may be registered which consists of signs or indications which may serve, in trade, to designate the geographical origin of the goods or services.

(2) However, the proprietor of such a mark is not entitled to prohibit the use of the signs or indications in accordance with honest practices in industrial or commercial matters (in particular, by a person who is entitled to use a geographical name).

*Nature of proprietor's business*

**A1-138** **4.**—(1) A certification mark shall not be registered if the proprietor carries on a business involving the supply of goods or services of the kind certified.

*Mark not to be misleading as to character or significance*

**A1-139** **5.**—(1) A certification mark shall not be registered if the public is liable to be misled as regards the character or significance of the mark, in particular if it is likely to be taken to be something other than a certification mark.

(2) The registrar may accordingly require that a mark in respect of which application is made for registration include some indication that it is a certification mark.

Notwithstanding section 39(2); an application may be amended so as to comply with any such requirement.

*Regulations governing use of certification mark*

**A1-140** **6.**—(1) An applicant for registration of a certification mark must file with the registrar regulations governing the use of the mark.

(2) The regulations must indicate who is authorised to use the mark, the characteristics to be certified by the mark, how the certifying body is to test those characteristics and to supervise the use of the mark, the fees (if any) to be paid in connection with the operation of the mark and the procedures for resolving disputes.

Further requirements with which the regulations have to comply may be imposed by rules.

*Approval of regulations, &c.*

**A1-141** **7.**—(1) A certification mark shall not be registered unless—

- (a) the regulations governing the use of the mark—
  - (i) comply with paragraph 6(2) and any further requirements imposed by rules, and
  - (ii) are not contrary to public policy or to accepted principles of morality, and
- (b) the applicant is competent to certify the goods or services for which the mark is to be registered.

(2) Before the end of the prescribed period after the date of the application for registration of a certification mark, the applicant must file the regulations with the registrar and pay the prescribed fee. If he does not do so, the application shall be deemed to be withdrawn.

**A1-142** **8.**—(1) The registrar shall consider whether the requirements mentioned in paragraph 7(1) are met.

(2) If it appears to the registrar that those requirements are not met, he shall inform the applicant and give him an opportunity, within such period as the registrar may specify, to make representations or to file amended regulations.

(3) If the applicant fails to satisfy the registrar that those requirements are met, or to file regulations amended so as to meet them, or fails to respond before the end of the specified period, the registrar shall refuse the application.

(4) If it appears to the registrar that those requirements, and the other requirements for registration, are met, he shall accept the application and shall proceed in accordance with section 38 (publication, opposition proceedings and observations).

**9.—** The regulations shall be published and notice of opposition may be given, and observations may be made, relating to the matters mentioned in paragraph 7(1) **A1-143**

This is in addition to any other grounds on which the application may be opposed or observations made.

*Regulations to be open to inspection*

**10.—** The regulations governing the use of a registered certification mark shall be open to public inspection in the same way as the register. **A1-144**

*Amendment of regulations*

**11.—**(1) An amendment of the regulations governing the use of a registered certification mark is not effective unless and until the amended regulations art filed with the registrar and accepted by him. **A1-145**

(2) Before accepting any amended regulations the registrar may in any case where it appears to him expedient to do so cause them to be published.

(3) If he does so, notice of opposition may be given, and observations may be made, relating to the matters mentioned in paragraph 7(1).

*Consent to assignment of registered certification mark*

**12.—** The assignment or other transmission of a registered certification mark is not effective without the consent of the registrar. **A1-146**

*Infringement rights of authorised users*

**13.—** The following provisions apply in relation to an authorised user of a registered certification mark as in relation to a licensee of a trade mark— **A1-147**

- (a) section 10(5) (definition of infringement unauthorised application of mark to certain material);
- (b) section 19(2) (order as to disposal of infringing goods, material or articles: adequacy of other remedies);
- (c) section 89 (prohibition of importation of infringing goods, material or articles request to Commissioners of Customs and Excise).

**14.—** In infringement proceedings brought by the proprietor of a registered certification mark any loss suffered or likely to be suffered by authorised users shall be taken into account, and the court may give such directions as it thinks fit as to the extent to which the plaintiff is to told the proceeds of any pecuniary remedy on behalf of such users. **A1-148**

*Grounds for revocation of registration*

**15.—** Apart from the grounds of revocation provided for in section 46, the registration of a certification mark may be revoked on the ground— **A1-149**

- (a) that the proprietor has begun to carry on such a business as is mentioned in paragraph 4.
- (b) that the manner in which the mark has been used by the proprietor has caused it to become liable to mislead the public in the manner referred to in paragraph 5(1),
- (c) that the proprietor has failed to observe, or to secure the observance of, the regulations governing the use of the mark,
- (d) that an amendment of the regulations has been made so that the regulations—
  - (i) no longer comply with paragraph 6(2) and any further conditions imposed by rules, or
  - (ii) are contrary to public policy or to accepted principles of morality, or
- (e) that the proprietor is no longer competent to certify the goods or services for which the mark is registered.

*Grounds for invalidity of registration*

**16.—** Apart from the grounds of invalidity provided for in section 47, the registration of a certification mark may be declared invalid on the ground that the mark was registered in breach of the provisions of paragraph 4, 5(1) or 7(1) **A1-150**

## SCHEDULE 3

### TRANSITIONAL PROVISIONS

**Section 105**

*Introductory*

A1-151 **1.**—(1) In this Schedule—

"existing registered mark" means a trade mark, certification trade mark or service mark registered under the 1938 Act immediately before the commencement of this Act;
"the 1938 Act" means the Trade Marks Act 1938; and
"the old law" means that Act and any other enactment or rule of law applying to existing registered marks immediately before the commencement of this Act.

(2) For the purposes of this Schedule—
- (a) an application shall be treated as pending on the commencement of this Act if it was made but not finally determined before commencement, and
- (b) the date on which it was made shall be taken to be the date of filing under the 1938 Act.

*Existing registered marks*

A1-152 **2.**—(1) Existing registered marks (whether registered in Part A or B of the register kept under the 1938 Act shall be transferred on the commencement of this Act to the register kept under this Act and have effect, subject to the provisions of this Schedule, as if registered under this Act.

(2) Existing registered marks registered as a series under section 21(2) of the 1938 Act shall be similarly registered in the new register. Provision may be made by rules for putting such entries in the same form as is required for entries under this Act.

(3) In any other case notes indicating that existing registered marks are associated with other marks shall cease to have effect on the commencement of this Act.

A1-153 **3.**—(1) A condition entered on the former register in relation to an existing registered mark immediately before the commencement of this Act shall cease to have effect on commencement.

Proceedings under section 33 of the 1938 Act (application to expunge or vary registration for breach of condition) which are pending on the commencement of this Act shall be dealt with under the old law and any necessary alteration made to the new register.

(2) A disclaimer or limitation entered on the former register in relation to an existing registered mark immediately before the commencement of this Act shall be transferred to the new register and have effect as if entered on the register in pursuance of section 13 of this Act.

*Effects of registration: Infringement*

A1-154 **4.**—(1) Sections 9 to 12 of this Act (effects of registration) apply in relation to an existing registered mark as from the commencement of this Act and section 14 of this Act (action for infringement) applies in relation to infringement of an existing registered mark committed after the commencement of this Act, subject to sub-paragraph (2) below.

The old law continues to apply in relation to infringements committed before commencement

(2) It is not an infringement of—
- (a) an existing registered mark, or
- (b) a registered trade mark of which the distinctive elements are the same or substantially the same as those of an existing registered mark and which is registered for the same goods or services.

to continue after commencement any use which did not amount to infringement of the existing registered mark under the old law.

*Infringing goods, material or articles*

A1-155 **5.**— Section 16 of this Act (order for delivery up of infringing goods, material or articles) applies to infringing goods, material or articles whether made before or after the commencement of this Act.

*Rights and remedies of licensee or authorised user*

A1-156 **6.**—(1) Section 30 (general provisions as to rights of licensees in case of infringement) of this Act applies to licences granted before the commencement of this Act, but only in relation to infringements committed after commencement

(2) Paragraph 14 of Schedule 2 of this Act(court to take into account loss suffered by authorised users, &c) applies only in relation to infringements committed after commencement.

*Co-ownership of registered mark*

**7.—** The provisions of section 23 of this Act (co-ownership of registered mark) apply as from the commencement of this Act to an existing registered mark of which two or more persons were immediately before commencement registered as joint proprietors. **A1-157**

But so long as the relations between the joint proprietors remain such as are described in section 63 of the 1938 Act (joint ownership) there shall be taken to be an agreement to exclude the operation of subsections (1) and (3) of section 23 of this Act (ownership in undivided shares and right of co-proprietor to make separate use of the mark).

*Assignment. &c. of registered mark*

**8.—**(1) Section 24 of this Act (assignment or other transmission of registered mark) applies to transactions and events occurring after the commencement of this Act in relation to an existing registered mark, and the old law continues to apply in relation to transactions and events occurring before commencement. **A1-158**

(2) Existing entries under section 25 of the 1938 Act (registration of assignments and transmissions) shall be transferred on the commencement of this Act to the register kept under this Act and have effect as if made under section 25 of this Act.

Provision may be made by rules for putting such entries in the same form as is required for entries made under this Act.

(3) An application for registration under section 25 of the 1938 Act which is pending before the registrar on the commencement of this Act shall be treated as an application for registration under section 25 of this Act and shall proceed accordingly.

The registrar may require the applicant to amend his application so as to conform with the requirements of this Act.

(4) An application for registration under section 25 of the 1938 Act which has been determined by the registrar but not finally determined before the commencement of this Act shall be dealt with under the old law; and sub-paragraph (2) above shall apply in relation to any resulting entry in the register.

(5) Where before the commencement of this Act a person has become entitled by assignment or transmission to an existing registered mark but has not registered his title, any application for registration after commencement shall be made under section 25 of this Act.

(6) In cases to which sub-paragraph (3) or (5) applies section 25(3) of the 1938 Act continues to apply (and section 25(3) and (4) of this Act do not apply as regards the consequences of failing to register.

*Licensing of registered mark*

**9.—**(1) Sections 28 and 29(2) of this Act (licensing of registered trade mark; rights of exclusive license against grantor's successor in title) apply only in relation to licences granted after the commencement of this Act; and the old law continues to apply in relation to licences granted before commencement. **A1-159**

(2) Existing entries under section 28 of the 1938 Act (registered users) shall be transferred on the commencement of this Act to the register kept under this Act and have effect as if made under section 25 of this Act.

Provision may be made by rules for putting such entries in the same form as it required for entries made under this Act.

(3) An application for registration as a registered user which is pending before the registrar on the commencement of this Act shall be treated as an application for registration of a licence under section 25(1) of this Act and shall proceed accordingly.

The registrar may require the applicant to amend his application so as to conform with the requirements of this Act.

(4) An application for registration as a registered user which has been determined by the registrar but not finally determined before the commencement of this Act shall be dealt with under the old law; and sub-paragraph (2) above shall apply in relation to any resulting entry in the register.

(5) Any proceedings pending on the commencement of this Act under section 28(8) or (10) of the 1938 Act (variation or cancellation of registration of registered user) shall be dealt with under the old law and any necessary alteration made to the new register.

*Pending applications for registration*

**10.—**(1) An application for registration of a mark under the 1938 Act which is pending on the commencement of this Act shall be dealt with under the old law, subject as mentioned below, and if registered the mark shall be treated for the purposes of this Schedule as an existing registered mark. **A1-160**

(2) The power of the Secretary of State under section 78 of this Act to make rules regulating practice and procedure, and as to the matters mentioned in subsection (2) of that section, is exercisable

in relation to such an application, and different provision may be made for such applications from that made for other applications.

(3) Section 23 of the 1938 Act (provisions as to associated trade marks) shall be disregarded in dealing after the commencement of this Act with an application for registration.

*Conversion of pending application*

A1-161 **11.**—(1) In the case of a pending application for registration which has not been advertised under section 18 of the 1938 Act before the commencement of this Act, the applicant may give notice to the registrar claiming to have the registrability of the mark determined in accordance with the provisions of this Act.

(2) The notice must be in the prescribed form, be accompanied by the appropriate fee and be given no later than six months after the commencement of this Act.

(3) Notice duly given is irrevocable and has the effect that the application shall be treated as if made immediately after the commencement of this Act.

*Trade marks registered according to old classification*

A1-162 **12.**— The registrar may exercise the powers conferred by rules under section 65 of this Act (adaptation of entries to new classification) to secure that any existing registered marks which do not conform to the system of classification prescribed under section 34 of this Act are brought into conformity with that system.

This applies, in particular, to existing registered marks classified according to the pre-1938 classification set out in Schedule 3 to the Trade Marks Rules 1986.

*Claim to priority from overseas application*

A1-163 **13.**— Section 35 of this Act claim to priority of Convention application) applies to an application for registration under this Act made after the commencement of this Act notwithstanding that the Convention application was made before commencement.

A1-164 **14.**—(1) Where before the commencement of this Act a person has duly filed an application for protection of a trade mark in a relevant country within the meaning of section 39A of the 1938 Act which is not a Convention country (a "relevant overseas application"), he, or his successor in title, has a right to priority, for the purposes of registering the same trade mark under this Act for some or all of the same goods or services, for a period of six months from the date of filing of the relevant overseas application.

(2) If the application for registration under this Act is made within that six-month period—

(a) the relevant date for the purposes of establishing which rights take precedence shall be the date of filing of the relevant overseas application, and

(b) the registrability of the trade mark shall not be affected by any use of the mark in the United Kingdom in the period between that date and the date of the application under this Act.

(3) Any filing which in a relevant country is equivalent to a regular national filing, under its domestic legislation or an international agreement, shall be treated as giving rise to the right of priority. A "regular national filing" means a filing which is adequate to establish the date on which the application was filed in that country, whatever may be the subsequent fate of the application.

(4) A subsequent application concerning the same subject as the relevant overseas application, filed in the same country, shall be considered the relevant overseas application (of which the filing date is the starting date of the period of priority), if at the time of the subsequent application—

(a) the previous application has been withdrawn, abandoned or refused, without having been laid open to public inspection and without leaving any rights outstanding, and

(b) it has not yet served as a basis for claiming a right of priority.

The previous application may not thereafter serve as a basis for claiming a right of priority.

(5) Provision may be made by rules as to the manner of claiming a right to priority on the basis of a relevant overseas application.

(6) A right to priority arising as a result of a relevant overseas application may be assigned or otherwise transmitted, either with the application or independently.

The reference in sub-paragraph (1) to the applicant's "successor in title"shall be construed accordingly.

(7) Nothing in this paragraph affects proceedings on an application for registration under the 1938 Act made before the commencement of this Act (see paragraph 10 above).

*Duration and renewal of registration*

A1-165 **15.**—(1) Section 42(1) of this Act (duration of original period of registration) applies in relation to the registration of a mark in pursuance of an application made after the commencement of this Act; and the old law applies in any other case.

(2) Sections 42(2) and 43 of this Act (renewal) apply where the renewal falls due on or after the commencement of this Act; and the old law continues to apply in any other case.

(3) In either case it is immaterial when the fee is paid.

*Pending application for alteration of registered mark*

**16.—** An application under section 35 of the 1938 Act (alternation of registered trade mark) which is pending on the commencement of this Act shall be dealt with under the old law and any necessary alteration made to the new register. **A1-166**

*Revocation for non-use*

**17.—**(1) An application under section 26 of the 1938 Act (removal from register or imposition of limitation on ground of non-use) which is pending on the commencement of this Act shall be dealt with under the old law and any necessary alteration made to the new register. **A1-167**

(2) An application under section 46(1)(a) or (b) of this Act (revocation for non-use) may be made in relation to an existing registered mark at any time after the commencement of this Act.
Provided that no such application for the revocation of the registration of an existing registered mark registered by virtue of section 27 of the 1938 Act (defensive registration of well-known trade marks) may be made until more than five years after the commencement of this Act.

*Application for rectification, &c.*

**18.—**(1) An application under section 32 or 34 of the 1938 Act (rectification or correction of the register) which is pending on the commencement of this Act shall be dealt with under the old law and any necessary alteration made to the new register. **A1-168**

(2) For the purposes of proceedings under section 47 of this Act (grounds for invalidity of registration) as it applies in relation to an existing registered mark, the provisions of this Act shall be deemed to have been in force at all material times.
Provided that no objection to the validity of the registration of an existing registered mark may be taken on the ground specified in subsection (3) of section 5 of this Act (relative grounds for refusal of registration conflict with earlier mark registered for different goods or services).

*Regulations as to use of certification mark*

**19.—**(1) Regulations governing the use of an existing registered certification mark deposited at the Patent Office in pursuance of section 37 of the 1938 Act shall be treated after the commencement of this Act as if filed under paragraph 6 of Schedule 2 to this Act. **A1-169**

(2) Any request for amendment of the regulations which was pending on the commencement of this Act shall be dealt with under the old law.

*Sheffield marks*

**20.—**(1) For the purposes of this Schedule the Sheffield register kept under Schedule 2 to the 1938 Act shall be treated as part of the register of trade marks kept under that Act. **A1-170**

(2) Applications made to the Cutlers' Company in accordance with that Schedule which are pending on the commencement of this Act shall proceed after commencement as if they had been made to the registrar.

*Certificate of validity of contested registration*

**21.—** A certificate given before the commencement of this Act under section 47 of the 1938 Act (certificate of validity of contested registration) shall have effect as if given under section 73(1) of this Act. **A1-171**

*Trade mark agents*

**22.—**(1) Rules in force immediately before the commencement of this Act under section 282 or 283 of the Copyright, Designs and Patents Act 1988 (register of trade mark agents; persons entitled to described themselves as registered) shall continue in force and have effect as if made under section 83 or 85 of this Act. **A1-172**

(2) Rules in force immediately before the commencement of this Act under section 40 of the 1938 Act as to the persons whom the registrar may refuse to recognise as agents for the purposes of business under that Act shall continue in force and have effect as if made under section 88 of this Act.

(3) Rules continued in force under this paragraph may be varied or revoked by further rules made under the relevant provisions of this Act.

## SCHEDULE 4

### CONSEQUENTIAL AMENDMENTS

**Section 106(1)**

*General adaptation of existing references*

**A1-173** **1.**—(1) References in statutory provisions passed or made before the commencement of this Act to trade marks or registered trade marks within the meaning of the Trade Marks Act 1938 shall, unless the context otherwise requires, be construed after the commencement of this Act as references to trade marks or registered trade marks within the meaning of this Act.

(2) Sub-paragraph (1) applies, in particular, to the references in the following provisions—

| | |
|---|---|
| Industrial Organisation and Development Act 1947 | Schedule 1, paragraph 7 |
| Crown Proceedings Act 1947 | section 3(1)(b) |
| [... | ...] |
| Printer's Imprint Act 1961 | section 1(1)(b) |
| [... | ...] |
| [... | ...] |
| Patents Act 1977 | section 19(2) |
| | section 27(4) |
| | section 123(7) |
| Unfair Contract Terms Act 1977 | Schedule 1, paragraph 1(c) |
| Judicature (Northern Ireland) Act 1978 | section 94A(5) |
| State Immunity Act 1978 | section 7(a) and (b). |
| [Senior Courts Act 1981] | section 72(5) |
| | Schedule 1, paragraph 1(i) |
| Civil Jurisdiction and Judgments Act 1982 | Schedule 5, paragraph 2 |
| | Schedule 8, paragraph 2(14) and 4(2) |
| Value Added Tax Act 1983 | Schedule 3, paragraph 1 |
| [... | ... |
| | ...] |
| Law Reform (Miscellaneous Provisions) (Scotland) Act 1985 | section 15(5) |
| Atomic Energy Authority Act 1986 | section 8(2) |
| [... | ... |
| | ... |
| | ...] |
| Consumer Protection Act 1987 | section 2(2)(b) |
| Consumer Protection (Northern Ireland) Order 1987. | article 5(2)(b) |
| Income and Corporation Taxes Act 1988 | section 83(a) |
| Taxation of Chargeable Gains Act 1992 | section 275(h) |
| Tribunals and Inquiries Act 1992 | Schedule 1, paragraph 34. |

*Patents and Designs Act 1907 (c.29)*

**A1-174** **2.**—(1) The Patents and Designs Act 1907 is amended as follows.

(2) In section 62 (the Patent Office)—

(a) in subsection (1) for "this Act and the Trade Marks Act 1905" substitute "the Patents Act 1977 the Registered Designs Act 1949 and the Trade Marks Act 1994", and

(b) In subsections (2) and (3) for "the Board of Trade" substitute "the Secretary of State".

(3) In section 63 (officers and clerks of the Patent Office)—

(a) for "the Board of Trade" in each place where it occurs substitute "the Secretary of State"; and

(b) in subsection (2) omit the words from "and those salaries" to the end.

(4) The repeal by the Patents Act 1949 and the Registered Designs Act 1949 of the whole of the 1907 Act, except certain provisions, shall be deemed not to have extended to the long title, date of enactment or enacting words or to so much of section 99 as provides the Act with its short title.

*Patents, Designs, Copyright and Trade Marks (Emergency) Act 1939 (c.107)*

**3.**—(1) The Patents, Designs, Copyright and Trade Marks (Emergency) Act 1939 is amended as follows. **A1-175**

(2) For section 3 (power of comptroller to suspend rights of enemy or enemy subject) substitute—

**Power of comptroller to suspend trade mark rights of enemy or enemy subject.**

"**3.**—(1) Where on application made by a person proposing to supply goods or services of any description it is made to appear to the comptroller

(a) that it is difficult or impracticable to describe or refer to the goods or services without the use of a registered trade mark, and

(b) that the proprietor of the registered trade mark (whether alone or jointly with another) is an enemy or an enemy subject,

the comptroller may make an order suspending the rights given by the registered trade mark.

(2) An order under this section shall suspend those rights as regards the use of the trade mark—

(a) by the applicant, and

(b) by any person authorised by the applicant to do, for the purposes of or in connection with the supply by the applicant of the goods or services, things which would otherwise infringe the registered trade mark,

to such extent and for such period as the comptroller considers necessary to enable the applicant to render well-known and established some other means of describing or referring to the goods or services in question which does not involves the use of the trade mark.

(3) Where an order has been made under this section; no action for passing off lies on the part of any person interested in the registered trade mark in respect of any use of it which by virtue of the order is not an infringement of the right conferred by it.

(4) An order under this section may be varied or revoked by a subsequent order made by the comptroller".

(3) In each of the following provisions—

(a) section 4(1)(c) (effect of war on registration of trade marks),

(b) section 6(1) (power of comptroller to extend time limits),

(c) section 7(1)(a) (evidence as to nationality, &c.), and

(d) the definition of "the trade comptroller" in section 10(1) (interpretation),

for "the Trade Marks Act 1938" substitute "the Trade Marks Act 1994".

*Trade Descriptions Act 1968 (c.29)*

**4.**— In the Trade Descriptions Act 1968, in section 34 (exemption of trade description contained in pre-1968 trade mark)— **A1-176**

(a) in the opening words, omit "within the meaning of the Trade Marks Act 1938"; and

(b) in paragraph (c) for "a person registered under section 28 of the Trade Marks Act 1938 as a registered user of the trade mark" substitute ", in the case of a registered trade mark, a person licensed to use it".

*Solicitors Act 1974 (c.47)*

**5.**— [...] **A1-177**

*House of Commons Disqualification Act 1975 (c. 24)*

**6.**— In Part III of Schedule 1 to the House of Commons Disqualification Act 1975 (other disqualifying offices), for the entry relating to persons appointed to hear and determine appeals under the Trade Marks Act 1938 substitute— **A1-178**

"Person appointed to hear and determine appeals under the Trade Marks Act 1994.".

*Restrictive Trade Practices Act 1976 (c. 34)*

A1-179 **7.—** In Schedule 3 to the Restrictive Trade Practices Act 1976 (excepted agreements), for paragraph 4 (agreements relating to trade marks) substitute—

"4.—(1) This Act does not apply to an agreement authorising the use of a registered trade mark (other than a collective mark or certification mark) if no such restrictions as are described in section 6(1) or 11(2) above are accepted, and no such information provisions as are described in section 7(1) or 12(2) above are made, except in respect of—

(a) the descriptions of goods bearing the mark which are to be produced or supplied, or the processes of manufacture to be applied to such goods or to goods to which the mark is to be applied, or

(b) the kinds of services in relation to which the mark as to be used which are to be made available or supplied, or the form or manner in which such services are to be made available or supplied, or

(c) the descriptions of goods which are to be produced or supplied in connection with the supply of services in relation to which the mark is to be used, or the process of manufacture to be applied to such goods.

(2) This Act does not apply to an agreement authorising the use of a registered collective mark or certification mark if—

(a) the agreement is made in accordance with regulations approved by the registrar under Schedule 1 or 2 to the Trade Marks Act 1994 and

(b) no such restrictions as are described in section 6(1) or 11(2) above are accepted, and no such information provisions as are described in section 7(1) or 12(2) above are made, except as permitted by those regulations".

*Copyright, Designs and Patents Act 1988 (c.48)*

A1-180 **8.**—(1) The Copyright, Designs and Patents Act 1988 is amended as follows.

(2) In section 114(6), 204(6) and 231(6) (persons regarded as having an interest in infringing copies, &c.), for "section 58C of the Trade Marks Act 1938" substitute "section 19 of the Trade Marks Act 1994".

(3) In section 280(1) (privilege for communications with patent agents), for "trade mark or service mark" substitute "or trade mark".

*Tribunals and Inquiries Act 1992 (c.53)*

A1-181 **9.** In Part 1 of Schedule 1 to the Tribunals and Inquiries Act 1992 (tribunals under direct supervision of Council on Tribunals), for "Patents, designs, trade marks and service marks" substitute "Patents, designs and trade marks".

## SCHEDULE 5

### REPEALS AND REVOCATIONS

**Section 106(2)**

A1-182

| **Chapter or number** | **Short title** | **Extent of repeal or revocation** |
|---|---|---|
| 1891 c. 50. | Commissioners for Oaths Act 1891. | In section 1, the words "or the Patents, Designs and Trade Marks Acts 1883 to 1888". |
| 1907 c. 29. | Patents and Designs Act 1907. | In section 63(2), the words from "and those salaries" to the end. |
| 1938 c. 22. | Trade Marks Act 1938. | The whole Act. |
| 1947 c. 44. | Crown Proceedings Act 1947. | In section 3(1)(b), the words "or registered services mark". |
| 1949 c. 87. | Patents Act 1949. | Section 92(2). |
| 1964 c. 14. | Plant Varieties and Seeds Act 1964. | In section 5A(4), the words "under the Trade Marks Act 1938". |
| 1967 c. 80. | Criminal Justice Act 1967. | In Schedule 3, in Parts I and IV, the |

| Chapter or number | Short title | Extent of repeal or revocation |
|---|---|---|
| | | entries relating to the Trade Marks Act 1938. |
| 1978 c. 23. | Judicature (Northern Ireland) Act 1978. | In Schedule 5, in Part II, the paragraphs amending the Trade Marks Act 1938. |
| 1984 c. 19. | Trade Marks (Amendment) Act 1984. | The whole Act. |
| 1985 c. 6. | Companies Act 1985. | In section 396—<br>(a) in subsection (3A)(a), and<br>(b) in subsection (2)(d)(i) as inserted by the Companies Act 1989, the words "service mark,". |
| 1986 c. 12. | Statute Law (Repeals) Act 1986. | In Schedule 2, paragraph 2. |
| 1986 c. 39. | Patents, Designs and Marks Act 1986. | Section 2. |
| | | Section 4(4). |
| | | In Schedule 1, paragraphs 1 and 2. |
| | | Schedule 2. |
| S.I. 1986/1032. | Companies (Northern Ireland) Order 1986. | In article 403—<br>(a) in paragraph (3A)(a), and<br>(b) in paragraph (2)(d)(i) as inserted by the Companies (No.2) (Northern Ireland) Order 1990, the words "service mark,". |
| 1987 c. 43. | Consumer Protection Act 1987. | In section 45—<br>(a) in subsection (1), the definition of "mark" and "trade mark";<br>(b) subsection (4). |
| S.I. 1987/2049. | Consumer Protection (Northern Ireland) Order 1987. | In article 2—<br>(a) in paragraph (2) the definitions of "mark" and "trade mark",<br>(b) paragraph (3). |
| 1988 c. 1. | Income and Corporation Taxes Act 1988. | In section 83 , the words from "References in this section" to the end. |
| 1988 c. 48. | Copyright, Designs and Patents Act 1988. | Sections 282 to 284. |
| | | In section 286, the definition of "registered trade mark agent". |
| | | Section 300. |
| 1992 c. 12. | Taxation of Chargeable Gains Act 1992. | In section 275(h), the words "service marks" and "service mark". |

**Modifications**

| Provision | Modification | Notes | Further Information |
|---|---|---|---|
| *Whole Document* | Trade Marks Act 1994 (Isle of Man) Order 1996/729, Sch. 1 para. 1 | | |

| Provision | Modification | Notes | Further Information |
|---|---|---|---|
| *Pt I s. 3(4)* | Trade Marks (Isle of Man) Order 2013/2601, Sch. 1 para. 2 | Modified in relation to the Isle of Man | art. 2 |
| *Pt I s. 4(5)* | Olympic Symbol etc. (Protection) Act 1995 c. 32, s. 13(2) | Deemed to be inserted in relation to restrictions on acquisition of competing rights | |
| *Pt I s. 5(3)* | Trade Marks (Isle of Man) Order 2013/2601, Sch. 1 para. 3 | Modified in relation to the Isle of Man | art. 2 |
| *Pt I s. 5(3)(b)* | Trade Marks Act 1994 (Isle of Man) Order 1996/729, Sch. 1 para. 1A | Modified in relation to the Isle of Man | |
| *Pt I s. 6(1)* | Trade Marks (Isle of Man) Order 2013/2601, Sch. 1 para. 4 | Modified in relation to the Isle of Man | art. 2 |
| *Pt I s. 6A* | Trade Marks (International Registration) Order 1996/714, art. 10C(2) | Modifed in relation to the proceedings relating to the opposition to the conferring of protection | |
| | Trade Marks (Isle of Man) Order 2013/2601, Sch. 1 para. 5 | Deemed to be inserted in relation to the Isle of Man | art. 2 |
| | Trade Marks Act 1994 (Isle of Man) Order 1996/729, Sch. 1 para. 1B | Modified in relation to the Isle of Man | |
| *Pt I s. 10(3)* | Trade Marks (Isle of Man) Order 2013/2601, Sch. 1 para. 6 | Modified in relation to the Isle of Man | art. 2 |
| | Trade Marks Act 1994 (Isle of Man) Order 1996/729, Sch. 1 para. 1C(a) | Modified in relation to the Isle of Man | |
| *Pt I s. 10(3)(b)* | Trade Marks Act 1994 (Isle of Man) Order 1996/729, Sch. 1 para. 1C(b) | Modified in relation to the Isle of Man | |
| *Pt I s. 14(2A)* | Trade Marks (Isle of Man) Order 2013/2601, Sch. 1 para. 7 | Deemed to be inserted in relation to the Isle of Man | art. 2 |
| *Pt I s. 14(2B)* | Trade Marks (Isle of Man) Order 2013/2601, Sch. 1 para. 7 | Deemed to be inserted in relation to the Isle of Man | art. 2 |
| *Pt I s. 17(3)* | Trade Marks (Isle of Man) Order 2013/2601, Sch. 1 para. 8 | Modified in relation to the Isle of Man | art. 2 |
| *Pt I s. 18(3)* | Trade Marks Act 1994 (Isle of Man) Order 1996/729, Sch. 1 para. 2 | Modified in relation to the Isle of Man | art. 2 |
| *Pt I s. 18(3)(d)* | Trade Marks (Isle of Man) Order 2013/2601, Sch. 1 para. 9 | Deemed to be inserted in relation to the Isle of Man | art. 2 |
| *Pt I s. 19(6)* | Trade Marks (Isle of Man) Order 2013/2601, Sch. 1 | Modified in relation to the Isle of Man | art. 2 |

| Provision | Modification | Notes | Further Information |
|---|---|---|---|
| | para. 10 | | |
| | Trade Marks Act 1994 (Isle of Man) Order 1996/729, Sch. 1 para. 3 | Modified in relation to the Isle of Man | art. 2 |
| *Pt I s. 20* | Trade Marks Act 1994 (Isle of Man) Order 1996/729, Sch. 1 para. 4 | Modified in relation to the Isle of Man | art. 2 |
| *Pt I s. 21* | Trade Marks (International Registration) Order 1996/714, art. 4(6) | Modified in relation to a protected international trade mark (UK) | |
| *Pt I s. 21(3)* | Community Trade Mark Regulations 1996/1908, reg. 4 | Modifed in relation to an international trade mark (EC) | |
| | Community Trade Mark Regulations 2006/1027, reg. 6(2)(a) | Modified in relation to an international trade mark | |
| *Pt I s. 21(4)* | Community Trade Mark Regulations 1996/1908, reg. 4 | Modifed in relation to an international trade mark (EC) | |
| | Community Trade Mark Regulations 2006/1027, reg. 6(2)(b) | Modified in relation to an international trade mark | |
| | Community Trade Mark Regulations 2006/1027, reg. 6(2)(c) | Modified in relation to an international trade mark | |
| *Pt I s. 22* | Trade Marks (International Registration) Order 1996/714, art. 5 | Modified in relation to an international trade mark (UK) | |
| *Pt I s. 23* | Trade Marks (International Registration) Order 1996/714, art. 5 | Modified in relation to an international trade mark (UK) | |
| *Pt I s. 24(1)* | Trade Marks (International Registration) Order 1996/714, art. 5 | Modified in relation to an international trade mark (UK) | |
| *Pt I s. 24(2)(a)* | Trade Marks (International Registration) Order 1996/714, art. 5 | Modified in relation to an international trade mark (UK) | |
| *Pt I s. 24(3)* | Trade Marks (International Registration) Order 1996/714, art. 5 | Modified in relation to an international trade mark (UK) | |
| *Pt I s. 24(4)* | Trade Marks (International Registration) Order 1996/714, art. 5 | Modified in relation to an international trade mark (UK) | |
| *Pt I s. 24(5)* | Trade Marks (International Registration) Order 1996/714, art. 5 | Modified in relation to an international trade mark (UK) | |
| *Pt I s. 24(6)* | Trade Marks (International Registration) Order 1996/714, art. 5 | Modified in relation to an international trade mark (UK) | |
| *Pt I s. 25* | Trade Marks (International Registration) Order 2008/ | Modified in relation to international trade marks | art. 3(3)(i) |

| Provision | Modification | Notes | Further Information |
| --- | --- | --- | --- |
| | 2206, Sch. 2 para. 1 | | |
| *Pt I s. 25(4)* | Trade Marks (Isle of Man) Order 2013/2601, Sch. 1 para. 11 | Modified in relation to the Isle of Man | art. 2 |
| *Pt I s. 26* | Trade Marks (International Registration) Order 1996/714, art. 5 | Modified in relation to an international trade mark (UK) | |
| *Pt I s. 28* | Trade Marks (International Registration) Order 1996/714, art. 7(1) | Modified in relation to licences to use a protected international trade mark (UK) | |
| *Pt I s. 28(1)* | Trade Marks (International Registration) Order 1996/714, art. 7(2) | Modified in relation to licences to use a protected international trade mark (UK) | |
| *Pt I s. 29* | Trade Marks (International Registration) Order 1996/714, art. 7(1) | Modified in relation to licences to use a protected international trade mark (UK) | |
| *Pt I s. 30* | Trade Marks (International Registration) Order 1996/714, art. 7(1) | Modified in relation to licences to use a protected international trade mark (UK) | |
| *Pt I s. 31* | Trade Marks (International Registration) Order 1996/714, art. 7(1) | Modified in relation to licences to use a protected international trade mark (UK) | |
| *Pt I s. 33(1)* | Trade Marks (International Registration) Order 2008/2206, Sch. 2 para. 2 | Modified in relation to international trade marks | art. 3(3)(i) |
| *Pt I s. 35* | Trade Marks (International Registration) Order 1996/714, art. 8(1) | Modified so as to confer a right to priority in relation to protection of an international registration designating the United Kingdom | |
| *Pt I s. 35(5)* | Trade Marks (International Registration) Order 2008/2206, Sch. 2 para. 3 | Modified in relation to international trade marks | art. 3(3)(i) |
| *Pt I s. 37(3)* | Trade Marks (International Registration) Order 2008/2206, Sch. 2 para. 4 | Modified in relation to international trade marks | art. 3(3)(i) |
| *Pt I s. 37(4)* | Trade Marks (International Registration) Order 2008/2206, Sch. 2 para. 4 | Modified in relation to international trade marks | art. 3(3)(i) |
| *Pt I s. 37(5)* | Trade Marks (International Registration) Order 2008/2206, Sch. 2 para. 4 | Modified in relation to international trade marks | art. 3(3)(i) |
| *Pt I s. 38(2)* | Trade Marks (International Registration) Order 2008/2206, Sch. 2 para. 5 | Modified in relation to international trade marks | art. 3(3)(i) |
| *Pt I s. 39(1)* | Trade Marks (International Registration) Order 2008/ | Modified in relation to international trade marks | art. 3(3)(i) |

| Provision | Modification | Notes | Further Information |
|---|---|---|---|
| | 2206, Sch. 2 para. 7 | | |
| *Pt I s. 40(1)* | Trade Marks (Isle of Man) Order 2013/2601, Sch. 1 para. 12 | Modified in relation to the Isle of Man | art. 2 |
| | Trade Marks Act 1994 (Isle of Man) Order 1996/729, Sch. 1 para. 4A | Modified in relation to the Isle of Man | |
| *Pt I s. 46* | Trade Marks (International Registration) Order 1996/714, art. 13(3) | Modifed to permit the protection of a protected international trade mark (UK) to be revoked, or declared invalid | |
| *Pt I s. 46(1)* | Trade Marks (International Registration) Order 1996/714, art. 13(2) | Modifed to permit the protection of a protected international trade mark (UK) to be revoked, or declared invalid | |
| *Pt I s. 46(2)* | Trade Marks (International Registration) Order 1996/714, art. 13(2) | Modifed to permit the protection of a protected international trade mark (UK) to be revoked, or declared invalid | |
| *Pt I s. 46(5)* | Trade Marks (International Registration) Order 1996/714, art. 13(2) | Modifed to permit the protection of a protected international trade mark (UK) to be revoked, or declared invalid | |
| *Pt I s. 47* | Trade Marks (International Registration) Order 1996/714, art. 13(3) | Modifed to permit the protection of a protected international trade mark (UK) to be revoked, or declared invalid | |
| *Pt I s. 47(2A)* | Trade Marks (Isle of Man) Order 2013/2601, Sch. 1 para. 13 | Deemed to be inserted in relation to the Isle of Man | art. 2 |
| | Trade Marks Act 1994 (Isle of Man) Order 1996/729, Sch. 1 para. 4B | Modified in relation to the Isle of Man | |
| *Pt I s. 47(2B)* | Trade Marks (Isle of Man) Order 2013/2601, Sch. 1 para. 13 | Deemed to be inserted in relation to the Isle of Man | art. 2 |
| | Trade Marks Act 1994 (Isle of Man) Order 1996/729, Sch. 1 para. 4B | Modified in relation to the Isle of Man | |
| *Pt I s. 47(2C)* | Trade Marks (Isle of Man) Order 2013/2601, Sch. 1 para. 13 | Deemed to be inserted in relation to the Isle of Man | art. 2 |
| | Trade Marks Act 1994 (Isle of Man) Order 1996/729, Sch. 1 para. 4B | Modified in relation to the Isle of Man | |
| *Pt I s. 47(2D)* | Trade Marks (Isle of Man) Order 2013/2601, Sch. 1 para. 13 | Deemed to be inserted in relation to the Isle of Man | art. 2 |

| Provision | Modification | Notes | Further Information |
|---|---|---|---|
| | Trade Marks Act 1994 (Isle of Man) Order 1996/729, Sch. 1 para. 4B | Modified in relation to the Isle of Man | |
| *Pt I s. 47(2E)* | Trade Marks (Isle of Man) Order 2013/2601, Sch. 1 para. 13 | Deemed to be inserted in relation to the Isle of Man | art. 2 |
| | Trade Marks Act 1994 (Isle of Man) Order 1996/729, Sch. 1 para. 4B | Modified in relation to the Isle of Man | |
| *Pt I s. 47(2F)* | Trade Marks (Isle of Man) Order 2013/2601, Sch. 1 para. 13 | Deemed to be inserted in relation to the Isle of Man | art. 2 |
| *Pt I s. 47(5)* | Trade Marks (International Registration) Order 1996/714, art. 13(2) | Modifed to permit the protection of a protected international trade mark (UK) to be revoked, or declared invalid | |
| *Pt I s. 48* | Trade Marks (International Registration) Order 1996/714, art. 14 | Modifed where the proprietor of an earlier trade mark has acquiesced for a continuous period of five years in the use of a protected international trade mark (UK) | |
| *Pt II s. 51* | Trade Marks Act 1994 (Isle of Man) Order 1996/729, Sch. 1 para. 5 | Modified in relation to the Isle of Man | art. 2 |
| *Pt II s. 52* | Trade Marks (Isle of Man) Order 2013/2601, Sch. 1 para. 14 | Modified in relation to the Isle of Man | art. 2 |
| | Trade Marks Act 1994 (Isle of Man) Order 1996/729, Sch. 1 para. 5 | Modified in relation to the Isle of Man | art. 2 |
| *Pt II s. 53 definition of "international trade mark EC"* | Trade Marks (Isle of Man) Order 2013/2601, Sch. 1 para. 15 | Deemed to be inserted in relation to the Isle of Man | art. 2 |
| *Pt II s. 55* | Trade Marks (Isle of Man) Order 2013/2601, Sch. 1 para. 16 | Modified in relation to the Isle of Man | art. 2 |
| *Pt II s. 55(1)(aa)* | Trade Marks (Isle of Man) Order 2013/2601, Sch. 1 para. 16(b) | Deemed to be inserted in relation to the Isle of Man | art. 2 |
| *Pt II s. 56(1)* | Trade Marks (Isle of Man) Order 2013/2601, Sch. 1 para. 17 | Modified in relation to the Isle of Man | art. 2 |
| *Pt II s. 56(2)* | Trade Marks (Isle of Man) Order 2013/2601, Sch. 1 para. 17 | Modified in relation to the Isle of Man | art. 2 |
| *Pt II s. 57(2)* | Trade Marks (Isle of Man) Order 2013/2601, Sch. 1 para. 17 | Modified in relation to the Isle of Man | art. 2 |
| *Pt II s. 57(3)* | Trade Marks (Isle of Man) | Modified in relation to the | art. 2 |

| Provision | Modification | Notes | Further Information |
|---|---|---|---|
| | Order 2013/2601, Sch. 1 para. 17 | Isle of Man | |
| *Pt II s. 58(2)* | Trade Marks (Isle of Man) Order 2013/2601, Sch. 1 para. 17 | Modified in relation to the Isle of Man | art. 2 |
| *Pt II s. 59(5)* | Trade Marks (Isle of Man) Order 2013/2601, Sch. 1 para. 18 | Deemed to be inserted in relation to the Isle of Man | art. 2 |
| *Pt II s. 61* | Trade Marks (Isle of Man) Order 2013/2601, Sch. 1 para. 19 | Modified in relation to the Isle of Man | art. 2 |
| *Pt III s. 63* | Trade Marks (International Registration) Order 2008/2206, Sch. 2 para. 8 | Modified in relation to international trade marks | art. 3(3)(i) |
| *Pt III s. 67(2)(a)* | Trade Marks (International Registration) Order 2008/2206, Sch. 2 para. 9 | Modified in relation to international trade marks | art. 3(3)(i) |
| *Pt III s. 68(2)* | Trade Marks Act 1994 (Isle of Man) Order 1996/729, Sch. 1 para. 6 | Modified in relation to the Isle of Man | art. 2 |
| *Pt III s. 68(2)(c)* | Trade Marks (Isle of Man) Order 2013/2601, Sch. 1 para. 20 | Deemed to be inserted in relation to the Isle of Man | art. 2 |
| *Pt III s. 73* | Trade Marks (International Registration) Order 1996/714, art. 15(1) | Modified in relation to proceedings before the court in which the validity of the protection of a protected international trade mark (UK) is contested | |
| *Pt III s. 74* | Trade Marks (International Registration) Order 1996/714, art. 15(2) | Modified in relation to proceedings before the court involving an application for (a) the revocation of the protection of a protected international trade mark (UK); (b) a declaration of the invalidity of the protection of a protected international trade mark (UK); (c) the rectification of the supplementary register | |
| *Pt III s. 75* | Trade Marks (Isle of Man) Order 2013/2601, Sch. 1 para. 21 | Modified in relation to the Isle of Man | art. 2 |
| *Pt III s. 75(aa)* | Trade Marks Act 1994 (Isle of Man) Order 1996/729, Sch. 1 para. 7 | Deemed to be inserted in relation to the Isle of Man | art. 2 |
| *Pt III s. 75(c)* | Trade Marks (Isle of Man) Order 2013/2601, Sch. 1 para. 21(b) | Deemed to be inserted in relation to the Isle of Man | art. 2 |
| *Pt III s. 77* | Transfer of Functions (Lord Advocate and Secretary of State) Order 1999/678, art. | Modified in relation to the transfer of functions of the Lord Advocate to the Secre- | Sch. 1 para. 1 |

| Provision | Modification | Notes | Further Information |
|---|---|---|---|
| | 2(1) | tary of State | |
| | Transfer of Functions (Lord Advocate and Secretary of State) Order 1999/678, Sch. 1 para. 1 | Modified in relation to the transfer of functions to the Secretary of State | |
| *Pt III s. 77(2)(ba)* | Trade Marks (Isle of Man) Order 2013/2601, Sch. 1 para. 22 | Deemed to be inserted in relation to the Isle of Man | art. 2 |
| | Trade Marks Act 1994 (Isle of Man) Order 1996/729, Sch. 1 para. 8 | Deemed to be inserted in relation to the Isle of Man | art. 2 |
| *Pt III s. 83A(7) definition of "trade mark agency work" (a)* | Trade Marks (Isle of Man) Order 2013/2601, Sch. 1 para. 23 | Modified in relation to the Isle of Man | art. 2 |
| *Pt III s. 86* | Trade Marks Act 1994 (Isle of Man) Order 1996/729, Sch. 1 para. 9 | Modified in relation to the Isle of Man | art. 2 |
| *Pt III s. 86(2)* | Trade Marks (Isle of Man) Order 2013/2601, Sch. 1 para. 24 | Modified in relation to the Isle of Man | art. 2 |
| *Pt III s. 87(2)* | Trade Marks (Isle of Man) Order 2013/2601, Sch. 1 para. 25 | Modified in relation to the Isle of Man | art. 2 |
| *Pt III s. 89* | Trade Marks (Isle of Man) Order 2013/2601, Sch. 1 para. 26 | Modified in relation to the Isle of Man | art. 2 |
| | Trade Marks Act 1994 (Isle of Man) Order 1996/729, Sch. 1 para. 10 | Modified in relation to the Isle of Man | art. 2 |
| *Pt III s. 89(3)* | Trade Marks Act 1994 (Isle of Man) Order 1996/729, Sch. 1 para. 10 | Modified in relation to the Isle of Man | |
| *Pt III s. 90* | Trade Marks (Isle of Man) Order 2013/2601, Sch. 1 para. 27 | Modified in relation to the Isle of Man | art. 2 |
| | Trade Marks Act 1994 (Isle of Man) Order 1996/729, Sch. 1 para. 10 | Modified in relation to the Isle of Man | art. 2 |
| *Pt III s. 91* | Trade Marks (Isle of Man) Order 2013/2601, Sch. 1 para. 28 | Modified in relation to the Isle of Man | art. 2 |
| | Trade Marks Act 1994 (Isle of Man) Order 1996/729, Sch. 1 para. 10 | Modified in relation to the Isle of Man | art. 2 |
| *Pt III s. 92* | Trade Marks (International Registration) Order 1996/714, art. 17(2) | Modified in relation to a protected international trade mark (UK) | |
| *Pt III s. 92(6)* | Trade Marks (Isle of Man) Order 2013/2601, Sch. 1 para. 29 | Modified in relation to the Isle of Man | art. 2 |

| Provision | Modification | Notes | Further Information |
| --- | --- | --- | --- |
| *Pt III s. 92(6)(b)* | Trade Marks Act 1994 (Isle of Man) Order 1996/729, Sch. 1 para. 11 | Modified in relation to the Isle of Man | art. 2 |
| *Pt III s. 92A* | Trade Marks (International Registration) Order 1996/714, art. 17(2) | Modified in relation to a protected international trade mark (UK) | |
| *Pt III s. 92A(1)* | Trade Marks Act 1994 (Isle of Man) Order 1996/729, Sch. 1 para. 11A | Modified in relation to the Isle of Man | |
| *Pt III s. 92A(2)* | Trade Marks Act 1994 (Isle of Man) Order 1996/729, Sch. 1 para. 11A | Modified in relation to the Isle of Man | |
| *Pt III s. 92A(2A)* | Trade Marks (Isle of Man) Order 2013/2601, Sch. 1 para. 30(1) | Deemed to be inserted in relation to the Isle of Man | art. 2 |
| *Pt III s. 92A(3)(b)* | Trade Marks (Isle of Man) Order 2013/2601, Sch. 1 para. 30(2) | Modified in relation to the Isle of Man | art. 2 |
| *Pt III s. 93* | Trade Marks (International Registration) Order 1996/714, art. 17(2) | Modified in relation to a protected international trade mark (UK) | |
| | Trade Marks (Isle of Man) Order 2013/2601, Sch. 1 para. 31 | Modified in relation to the Isle of Man | art. 2 |
| | Trade Marks Act 1994 (Isle of Man) Order 1996/729, Sch. 1 para. 12 | Modified in relation to the Isle of Man | art. 2 |
| *Pt III s. 94(3)* | Trade Marks (Isle of Man) Order 2013/2601, Sch. 1 para. 32 | Modified in relation to the Isle of Man | art. 2 |
| *Pt III s. 94(3)(a)* | Trade Marks Act 1994 (Isle of Man) Order 1996/729, Sch. 1 para. 11 | Modified in relation to the Isle of Man | art. 2 |
| *Pt III s. 96* | Trade Marks Act 1994 (Isle of Man) Order 1996/729, Sch. 1 para. 12 | Modified in relation to the Isle of Man | art. 2 |
| *Pt III s. 97* | Olympic Symbol etc. (Protection) Act 1995 c. 32, s. 11 | Modifed in relation to forfeiture in relation to England and Wales of Northern Ireland | |
| | Trade Marks (International Registration) Order 1996/714, art. 17(2) | Modified in relation to a protected international trade mark (UK) | |
| | Trade Marks (Isle of Man) Order 2013/2601, Sch. 1 para. 33 | Modified in relation to the Isle of Man | art. 2 |
| *Pt III s. 97(1)* | Trade Marks Act 1994 (Isle of Man) Order 1996/729, Sch. 1 para. 13(1) | Modified in relation to the Isle of Man | art. 2 |
| *Pt III s. 97(2)(b)* | Trade Marks Act 1994 (Isle of Man) Order 1996/729, Sch. 1 para. 13(2) | Modified in relation to the Isle of Man | art. 2 |

| Provision | Modification | Notes | Further Information |
|---|---|---|---|
| *Pt III s. 97(5)* | Trade Marks Act 1994 (Isle of Man) Order 1996/729, Sch. 1 para. 13(2) | Modified in relation to the Isle of Man | art. 2 |
| | Trade Marks Act 1994 (Isle of Man) Order 1996/729, Sch. 1 para. 13(3)(b) | Modified in relation to the Isle of Man | art. 2 |
| *Pt III s. 97(5)(a)* | Trade Marks Act 1994 (Isle of Man) Order 1996/729, Sch. 1 para. 13(3)(a) | Modified in relation to the Isle of Man | art. 2 |
| *Pt III s. 97(5)(b)* | Trade Marks Act 1994 (Isle of Man) Order 1996/729, Sch. 1 para. 13(3)(a) | Modified in relation to the Isle of Man | art. 2 |
| *Pt III s. 97(5)(c)* | Trade Marks (Isle of Man) Order 2013/2601, Sch. 1 para. 33(3)(b) | Deemed to be inserted in relation to the Isle of Man | art. 2 |
| *Pt III s. 97(8)* | Trade Marks Act 1994 (Isle of Man) Order 1996/729, Sch. 1 para. 13(4) | Modified in relation to the Isle of Man | art. 2 |
| *Pt III s. 98* | Olympic Symbol etc. (Protection) Act 1995 c. 32, s. 12 | Modifed in relation to forfeiture in relation to Scotland | |
| | Trade Marks (International Registration) Order 1996/714, art. 17(2) | Modified in relation to a protected international trade mark (UK) | |
| | Trade Marks Act 1994 (Isle of Man) Order 1996/729, Sch. 1 para. 12 | Modified in relation to the Isle of Man | art. 2 |
| *Pt IV s. 101(2)(b)* | Trade Marks (Isle of Man) Order 2013/2601, Sch. 1 para. 34 | Modified in relation to the Isle of Man | art. 2 |
| | Trade Marks Act 1994 (Isle of Man) Order 1996/729, Sch. 1 para. 14 | Modified in relation to the Isle of Man | art. 2 |
| *Pt IV s. 102* | Trade Marks Act 1994 (Isle of Man) Order 1996/729, Sch. 1 para. 15 | Modified in relation to the Isle of Man | art. 2 |
| *Pt IV s. 103(3)* | Trade Marks (Isle of Man) Order 2013/2601, Sch. 1 para. 35 | Modified in relation to the Isle of Man | art. 2 |
| *Pt IV s. 104* | Trade Marks (Isle of Man) Order 2013/2601, Sch. 1 para. 36 | Modified in relation to the Isle of Man | art. 2 |
| | Trade Marks Act 1994 (Isle of Man) Order 1996/729, Sch. 1 para. 16 | Modified in relation to the Isle of Man | art. 2 |
| *Pt IV s. 106* | Trade Marks (Isle of Man) Order 2013/2601, Sch. 1 para. 37 | Modified in relation to the Isle of Man | art. 2 |
| *Sch. 1 para. 11(c)* | Trade Marks (Isle of Man) Order 2013/2601, Sch. 1 para. 38 | Modified in relation to the Isle of Man | art. 2 |

| Provision | Modification | Notes | Further Information |
|---|---|---|---|
| *Sch. 2 para. 13(c)* | Trade Marks (Isle of Man) Order 2013/2601, Sch. 1 para. 39 | Modified in relation to the Isle of Man | art. 2 |
| *Sch. 4* | Trade Marks (Isle of Man) Order 2013/2601, Sch. 1 para. 37 | Modified in relation to the Isle of Man | art. 2 |
| *Sch. 4 para. 4* | Trade Marks Act 1994 (Isle of Man) Order 1996/729, Sch. 1 para. 17(2) | Modified in relation only to statutory provisions which extend to the Isle of Man | art. 2 |
| *Sch. 5* | Trade Marks (Isle of Man) Order 2013/2601, Sch. 1 para. 37 | Modified in relation to the Isle of Man | art. 2 |
| *Sch. 5 para. 1* | Trade Marks Act 1994 (Isle of Man) Order 1996/729, Sch. 1 para. 17(3) | Modified in relation only to statutory provisions which extend to the Isle of Man | art. 2 |

## Appendix 2

# THE TRADE MARKS RULES 2008

*Replace with:*

A2-001 **SI 2008/1797**

ARRANGEMENT OF RULES

PRELIMINARY

RULE

The Secretary of State makes the following rules in exercise of the powers conferred upon the Secretary of State by sections 4(4), 13(2), 25(1), (5) and (6), 34(1), 35(5), 38(1) and (2), 39(3), 40(4), 41(1) and (3), 43(2), (3), (5) and (6), 44(3), 45(2), 63(2) and (3), 64(4), 65(1) and (2), 66(2), 67(1) and (2), 68(1) and (3), 69, 76(1), 78, 80(3), 81, 82 and 88 of, paragraph 6(2) of Schedule 1 to, and paragraph 7(2) of Schedule 2 to, the Trade Marks Act 1994.

In accordance with section 8 of the Tribunals and Inquiries Act 1992, the Secretary of State has consulted the Administrative Justice and Tribunals Council before making these Rules.

*Preliminary*

**Citation and commencement**

**1.—** These Rules may be cited as the Trade Marks Rules 2008 and shall come into force on 1st October 2008. **A2-001**

**Interpretation**

**2.**—(1) In these Rules— **A2-002**

"the Act" means the Trade Marks Act 1994;

["fast track opposition" means an opposition—

(a) brought solely on grounds under section 5(1) or 5(2) of the Act,

(b) based on no more than 3 earlier trade marks, each of which is registered in the UK or in the EU, or is protected in one or another of those territories as an international trade mark (UK) or (EU),

(c) where proof of use of the earlier marks can be provided with the notice of opposition, and

(d) which the opponent considers may be determined without the need for further evidence and without an oral hearing;]

"the Journal" means the Trade Marks Journal published in accordance with rule 81;

"the "Nice Agreement" means the Nice Agreement Concerning the International Classification of Goods and Services for the Purposes of the Registration of Marks of 15th June 1957, which was last amended on 28th September 1979;

"the "Nice Classification" means the system of classification under the Nice Agreement;

["the Office" means the Patent Office which operates under the name "Intellectual Property Office";]

"send" includes give;

"specification" means the statement of goods or services in respect of which a trade mark is registered or proposed to be registered;

"transformation application" means an application to register a trade mark under the Act where that mark was the subject of an international registration prior to that registration being cancelled.

(2) In these Rules a reference to a section is a reference to that section in the Act and a reference to a form is a reference to that form as published under rule 3.

(3) In these Rules references to the filing of any application, notice or other document, unless the contrary intention appears, are to be construed as references to its being delivered to the registrar at the Office.

**Forms and directions of the registrar; section 66**

**3.**—(1) Any forms required by the registrar to be used for the purpose of registration of a trade mark or any other proceedings before the registrar under the Act pursuant to section 66 and any directions with respect to their use shall be published on the Office website and any amendment or modification of a form or of the directions with respect to its use shall also be published on the Office website. **A2-003**

(2) Except in relation to Forms TM6 and TM7A a requirement under this rule to use a form as published is satisfied by the use either of a replica of that form or

of a form which is acceptable to the registrar and contains the information required by the form as published and complies with any directions as to the use of such a form.

**Requirement as to fees**

A2-004 **4.**—(1) The fees to be paid in respect of any application, registration or any other matter under the Act and these Rules shall be those (if any) prescribed in relation to such matter by rules under section 79 (fees).

(2) Any form required to be filed with the registrar in respect of any specified matter shall be subject to the payment of the fee (if any) prescribed in respect of that matter by those rules.

*Application for registration*

**Application for registration; section 32 (Form TM3)**

A2-005 **5.**—[(1) An application for the registration of a trade mark (other than a transformation application, which shall be filed on Form TM4) shall be filed on Form TM3 or, where the application is filed in electronic form using the filing system provided on the Office website, on Form e-TM3.

(1A) Where an application is filed on Form TM3 (a "standard application") the application shall be subject to the payment of the standard application fee and such class and series fees as may be appropriate.

(1B) Where an application is filed on Form e-TM3 (an "electronic application") the application shall be subject to the payment of the e-filed application fee and such class and series fees as may be appropriate, which shall be payable at the time the electronic application is made and if they are not so paid the application shall be subject to the payment of the standard application fee referred to in paragraph (1A) and such class and series fees as may be appropriate.]

(2) [Subject to paragraph (6) where] an application is for the registration of a single trade mark, an applicant may request the registrar to undertake an expedited examination of the application.

(3) A request for expedited examination shall be made on [Form e-TM3] and shall be subject to payment of the prescribed fee.

(4) Where an applicant makes a request for expedited examination, the application fee and any class fees payable in respect of the application shall be payable at the time the application is made and accordingly rule 13 shall not apply insofar as it relates to the failure of an application to satisfy the requirements of section 32(4).

(5) In this rule and rule 15 a "request for expedited examination" means a request that, following an examination under section 37, the registrar notify the applicant within a period of ten business days (as specified in a direction given by the registrar under section 80) beginning on the business day after the date of filing of the application for registration whether or not it appears to the registrar that the requirements for registration are met.

[(6) The Registrar may at any time—

(a) suspend the right of applicants to file a request for expedited examination under paragraph (2) ("the expedited examination service") for such period as the registrar deems fit; and

(b) resume the expedited examination service.

(7) Where the registrar suspends or resumes the expedited examination service pursuant to paragraph (6), the registrar must publish a notice on the Office website—

(a) of the date from which the expedited examination service is suspended;
(b) of the date upon which the expedited examination service will resume.]

**Claim to priority; sections 35 & 36**

**6.**—(1) Where a right to priority is claimed by reason of an application for protection of a trade mark duly filed in a Convention country under section 35 or in another country or territory in respect of which provision corresponding to that made by section 35 is made under section 36 (an "overseas application"), the application for registration under rule 5 shall specify— **A2-006**

(a) the number accorded to the overseas application by the registering or other competent authority of the relevant country;
(b) the country in which the overseas application was filed; and
(c) the date of filing.

(2) The registrar may, in any particular case, by notice require the applicant to file, within such period of not less than one month as the notice may specify, such documentary evidence as the registrar may require certifying, or verifying to the satisfaction of the registrar, the date of the filing of the overseas application, the country or registering or competent authority, the representation of the mark and the goods or services covered by the overseas application.

**Classification of goods and services; section 34**

**7.**—(1) The prescribed system of classification for the purposes of the registration of trade marks is the Nice Classification. **A2-007**

(2) When a trade mark is registered it shall be classified according to the version of the Nice Classification that had effect on the date of application for registration.

**Application may relate to more than one class and shall specify the class (Form TM3A)**

**8.**—(1) An application may be made in more than one class of the Nice Classification. **A2-008**

(2) Every application shall specify—

(a) the class in the Nice Classification to which it relates; and
(b) the goods or services which are appropriate to the class and they shall be described [with sufficient clarity and precision to enable the registrar and other competent authorities and economic operators, on that sole basis, to determine the extent of the protection sought] and to allow them to be classified in the classes in the Nice Classification.

[(2A) For the purposes of paragraph (2)(b) an application may specify the general indications included in the class headings of the Nice Classification or other general terms provided that they satisfy the requirement that the goods or services be described with sufficient clarity and precision referred to in paragraph (2)(b).

(2B) Where the specification contained in the application describes the goods or services using general terms, including the general indications included in the class headings of the Nice Classification, the application shall be treated as including only the goods or services clearly covered by the literal meaning of the term or indication.]

(3) If the application relates to more than one class in the Nice Classification the specification contained in it shall set out the classes in consecutive numerical order and the specification of the goods or services shall be grouped accordingly.

(4) If the specification contained in the application lists items by reference to a class in the Nice Classification in which they do not fall, the applicant may request, by filing Form TM3A, that the application be amended to include the appropriate class for those items, and upon the payment of such class fee as may be appropriate the registrar shall amend the application accordingly.

[(5) In this rule "economic operators" means any person or group of persons which, in the course of trade, manufactures, supplies, imports, exports or otherwise deals in goods or services.]

**Determination of classification**

A2-009 **9.**—(1) Where an application does not satisfy the requirements of rule 8(2) or (3), the registrar shall send notice to the applicant.

(2) A notice sent under paragraph (1) shall specify a period, of not less than one month, within which the applicant must satisfy those requirements.

(3) Where the applicant fails to satisfy the requirements of rule 8(2) before the expiry of the period specified under paragraph (2), [the registrar must reject] the application for registration, insofar as it relates to any goods or services which failed that requirement, shall be treated as abandoned.

(4) Where the applicant fails to satisfy the requirements of rule 8(3) before the expiry of the period specified under paragraph (2), the application for registration [...].

**Prohibition on registration of mark consisting of arms; section 4**

A2-010 **10.**— Where having regard to matters coming to the notice of the registrar it appears to the registrar that a representation of any arms or insignia as is referred to in section 4(4) appears in a mark, the registrar shall refuse to accept an application for the registration of the mark unless satisfied that the consent of the person entitled to the arms has been obtained.

**Address for service**

A2-011 **11.**—(1) For the purposes of any proceedings under the Act or these Rules, an address for service shall be filed by—

- (a) an applicant for the registration of a trade mark;
- (b) any person who opposes the registration of a trade mark in opposition proceedings;
- (c) any person who applies for revocation, a declaration of invalidity or rectification under the Act;
- (d) the proprietor of the registered trade mark who opposes such an application.

(2) The proprietor of a registered trade mark, or any person who has registered an interest in a registered trade mark, may file an address for service on Form TM33 or, in the case of an assignment of a registered trade mark, on Form TM16.

(3) Where a person has provided an address for service under paragraph (1) or (2), that person may substitute a new address for service by notifying the registrar on Form TM33.

[(4) An address for service filed under this Rule shall be an address in the United Kingdom, another EEA state or the Channel Islands.]

**Failure to provide an address for service**

**12.**—(1) Where— **A2-012**

(a) a person has failed to file an address for service under rule 11(1); and

(b) the registrar has sufficient information enabling the registrar to contact that person, the registrar shall direct that person to file an address for service.

(2) Where a direction has been given under paragraph (1), the person directed shall, before the end of the period of one month [beginning immediately after] the date of the direction, file an address for service.

(3) Paragraph (4) applies where—

(a) a direction was given under paragraph (1) and the period prescribed by paragraph (2) has expired; or

(b) the registrar had insufficient information to give a direction under paragraph (1), and the person has failed to provide an address for service.

(4) Where this paragraph applies—

(a) in the case of an applicant for registration of a trade mark, the application shall be treated as withdrawn;

(b) in the case of a person opposing the registration of a trade mark, that person's opposition shall be treated as withdrawn;

(c) in the case of a person applying for revocation, a declaration of invalidity or rectification, that person's application shall be treated as withdrawn; and

(d) in the case of the proprietor opposing such an application, the proprietor shall be deemed to have withdrawn from the proceedings.

(5) In this rule an "address for service" means an address which complies with the requirements of [rule 11(4)].

**Deficiencies in application; section 32**

**13.**—(1) Where an application for registration of a trade mark does not satisfy the requirements of section 32(2), (3) or (4) or rule 5(1), the registrar shall send notice to the applicant to remedy the deficiencies or, in the case of section 32(4), the default of payment. **A2-013**

(2) A notice sent under paragraph (1) shall specify a period, of not less than [14 days], within which the applicant must remedy the deficiencies or the default of payment.

(3) Where, before the expiry of the period specified under paragraph (2), the applicant—

(a) fails to remedy any deficiency notified to the applicant in respect of section 32(2), the application shall be deemed never to have been made; or

(b) fails to remedy any deficiency notified to the applicant in respect of section 32(3) or rule 5(1) or fails to make payment as required by section 32(4), the application shall be treated as abandoned.

**Notifying results of search**

**14.**—(1) Where, following any search under article 4 of the Trade Marks (Relative Grounds) Order 2007 it appears to the registrar that the requirements for registration mentioned in section 5 are not met, the registrar shall notify this fact to— **A2-014**

(a) the applicant; and
(b) any relevant proprietor.

[(2) In paragraph (1), "relevant proprietor" means the proprietor of a registered trade mark or international trade mark (UK) which is an earlier trade mark in relation to which it appears to the registrar that the conditions set out in section 5(1) or (2) obtain but does not include a proprietor who does not wish to be notified and who has notified the registrar to this effect.]

(3) References in paragraph (2) to the proprietor of a trade mark include a person who has applied for registration of a trade mark which, if registered, would be an earlier trade mark by virtue of section 6(1)(a) or (b).

(4)-(6) […]

(7) Rule 63 shall not apply to any decision made in pursuance of this rule.

(8) No decision made in pursuance of this rule shall be subject to appeal.

**Compliance with request for expedited examination**

A2-015 **15.—** Where the registrar receives a request for expedited examination under rule 5, the date on which the registrar shall be deemed to have notified the applicant whether or not it appears to the registrar that the requirements for registration are met shall be the date on which notice is sent to the applicant.

*Publication, observations, oppositions and registration*

**Publication of application for registration; section 38(1)**

A2-016 **16.—** An application which has been accepted for registration shall be published in the Journal.

**Opposition proceedings: filing of notice of opposition; section 38(2) (Form TM7)**

A2-017 **17.—**(1) [Subject to Rule 17A, any] notice to the registrar of opposition to the registration, including the statement of the grounds of opposition, shall be filed on Form TM7.

(2) Unless paragraph (3) applies, the time prescribed for the purposes of section 38(2) shall be the period of two months [beginning immediately after] the date on which the application was published.

(3) This paragraph applies where a request for an extension of time for the filing of Form TM7 has been made on Form TM7A, before the expiry of the period referred to in paragraph (2) and where this paragraph applies, the time prescribed for the purposes of section 38(2) in relation to any person having filed a Form TM7A (or, in the case of a company, any subsidiary or holding company of that company or any other subsidiary of that holding company) shall be the period of three months [beginning immediately after] the date on which the application was published.

(4) Where a person makes a request for an extension of time under paragraph (3), Form TM7A shall be filed electronically using the filing system provided on the Office website or by such other means as the registrar may permit.

(5) Where the opposition is based on a trade mark which has been registered, there shall be included in the statement of the grounds of opposition a representation of that mark and—

(a) the details of the authority with which the mark is registered;
(b) the registration number of that mark;
(c) the goods and services in respect of which—
  (i) that mark is registered, and
  (ii) the opposition is based; and
(d) where the registration procedure for the mark was completed before the start of the period of five years ending with the [date of application for registration or, if any, the date of priority], a statement detailing whether during the period referred to in section 6A(3)(a) the mark has been put to genuine use in relation to each of the goods and services in respect of which the opposition is based or whether there are proper reasons for non-use (for the purposes of rule 20 this is the "statement of use").

(6) Where the opposition is based on a trade mark in respect of which an application for registration has been made, there shall be included in the statement of the grounds of opposition a representation of that mark and those matters set out in paragraph (5)(a) to (c), with references to registration being construed as references to the application for registration.

(7) Where the opposition is based on an unregistered trade mark or other sign which the person opposing the application claims to be protected by virtue of any rule of law (in particular, the law of passing off), there shall be included in the statement of the grounds of opposition a representation of that mark or sign and the goods and services in respect of which such protection is claimed.

(8) The registrar shall send a copy of Form TM7 to the applicant and the date upon which this is sent shall, for the purposes of rule 18, be the "notification date".

(9) In this rule "subsidiary" and "holding company" have the same meaning as in the Companies Act 2006.

[**Opposition proceedings: filing of notice of fast track opposition; section 38(2) (Form TM7F))**

**17A.**—(1) A notice to the registrar of fast track opposition to the registration, including the statement of the grounds of opposition, may be filed on Form TM7F. **A2-018**

(2) A notice of fast track opposition to the registration filed on Form TM7F and a notice of opposition to the registration filed on Form TM7 shall constitute alternatives and an opponent shall not maintain more than one opposition against the same trade mark application.

(3) Unless paragraph (4) applies, the time prescribed for the purposes of section 38(2) shall be the period of two months beginning immediately after the date on which the application was published.

(4) This paragraph applies where a request for an extension of time for the filing of Form TM7 or TM7F has been made on Form TM7A, before the expiry of the period referred to in paragraph (3) and where this paragraph applies, the time prescribed for the purposes of section 38(2) in relation to any person having filed a Form TM7A (or, in the case of a company, any subsidiary or holding company of that company or any other subsidiary of that holding company) shall be the period of three months beginning immediately after the date on which the application was published.

(5) Forms TM7F and TM7A shall be filed electronically using the filing system provided on the Office website or by such other means as the registrar may permit.

(6) There shall be included in the statement of the grounds of opposition a representation of that mark and—

(a) the details of the authority with which the mark is registered or protected;
(b) the registration number of that mark;
(c) the goods and services in respect of which—
  (i) that mark is registered, and
  (ii) the opposition is based;
(d) the date of completion of the registration procedure or of granting protection to an international trade mark (UK) or (EU); and
(e) where the registration or protection procedure for the mark was completed before the start of the period of five years ending with the [date of application for registration or, if any, the date of priority], a statement detailing whether during the period referred to in section 6A(3)(a) the mark has been put to genuine use in relation to each of the goods and services in respect of which the opposition is based.

(7) Where the earlier mark is subject to proof of use under section 6A of the Act, the proof of use that the opponent wishes to rely upon shall be provided with the notice of fast track opposition.

(8) The registrar shall send a copy of Form TM7F to the applicant and the date upon which this is sent shall, for the purposes of rule 18, be the "notification date".

(9) In this rule "subsidiary" and "holding company" have the same meaning as in the Companies Act 2006.]

**Opposition proceedings: filing of counter-statement and cooling off period (Forms TM8, TM9c & TM9t)**

A2-019 **18.**—(1) The applicant shall, within the relevant period, file a Form TM8, which shall include a counter-statement.

(2) Where the applicant fails to file a Form TM8 or counter-statement within the relevant period, the application for registration, insofar as it relates to the goods and services in respect of which the opposition is directed, shall, unless the registrar otherwise directs, be treated as abandoned.

(3) Unless either paragraph (4), (5) or (6) applies, the relevant period [is the period of two months beginning immediately after the notification date].

(4) This paragraph applies where—
(a) the applicant and the person opposing the registration agree to an extension of time for the filing of Form TM8;
(b) within the period of two months [beginning immediately after] the notification date, either party files Form TM9c requesting an extension of time for the filing of Form TM8; and
(c) during the period beginning on the date Form TM9c was filed and ending nine months after the notification date, no notice to continue on Form TM9t is filed by the person opposing the registration and no request for a further extension of time for the filing of Form TM8 is filed on Form TM9e,

and where this paragraph applies the relevant period [is the period of nine months beginning immediately after the notification date].

(5) This paragraph applies where—
(a) a request for an extension of time for the filing of Form TM8 has been filed on Form TM9c in accordance with paragraph (4)(b);
(b) during the period referred to in paragraph (4)(c), either party files Form TM9e requesting a further extension of time for the filing of Form

TM8 which request includes a statement confirming that the parties are seeking to negotiate a settlement of the opposition proceedings; and

(c) the other party agrees to the further extension of time for the filing of Form TM8,

and where this paragraph applies the relevant period [is the period of eighteen months beginning immediately after the notification date].

(6) This paragraph applies where—

(a) a request for an extension of time for the filing of Form TM8 has been filed on Form TM9c in accordance with paragraph (4)(b); and

(b) the person opposing the registration has filed a notice to continue on Form TM9t,

and where this paragraph applies the relevant period shall begin on the notification date and end one month after the date on which Form TM9t was filed or two months [beginning immediately] after the notification date, whichever is the later.

(7) The registrar shall send a copy of Form TM8 to the person opposing the registration.

**Opposition proceedings: preliminary indication (Form TM53)**

**19.**—(1) This rule applies if— **A2-020**

(a) the opposition or part of it is based on the relative grounds of refusal set out in section 5(1) or (2); and

(b) the registrar has not indicated to the parties that the registrar thinks that it is inappropriate for this rule to apply.

[(1A) This rule shall not apply to fast track oppositions.]

(2) After considering the statement of the grounds of opposition and the counter-statement the registrar shall send notice to the parties ("the preliminary indication") stating whether it appears to the registrar that—

(a) registration of the mark should not be refused in respect of all or any of the goods and services listed in the application on the grounds set out in section 5(1) or (2); or

(b) registration of the mark should be refused in respect of all or any of the goods and services listed in the application on the grounds set out in section 5(1) or (2).

(3) The date upon which the preliminary indication is sent shall be the "indication date".

(4) Where it appeared to the registrar under paragraph (2) that registration of the mark should not be refused in respect of all or any of the goods or services listed in the application on the grounds set out in section 5(1) or (2), the person opposing the registration shall, within one month of the indication date, file a notice of intention to proceed with the opposition based on those grounds by filing a Form TM53, otherwise that person's opposition to the registration of the mark in relation to those goods or services on the grounds set in section 5(1) or (2) shall be deemed to have been withdrawn

(5) Where it appeared to the registrar under paragraph (2) that registration of the mark should be refused in respect of all or any of the goods or services listed in the application on the grounds set out in section 5(1) or (2), the applicant shall, within one month of the indication date, file a notice of intention to proceed on Form TM53, otherwise the applicant shall be deemed to have withdrawn the request to register the mark in respect of the goods or services for which the registrar indicated registration should be refused.

(6) A person who files a Form TM53 shall, at the same time, send a copy to all other parties to the proceedings.

(7) The registrar need not give reasons for the preliminary indication nor shall the preliminary indication be subject to appeal.

**Opposition proceedings: evidence rounds**

A2-021 **20.**—(1) Where—

(a) Form TM53 has been filed by either party;

(b) the opposition or part of it is based on grounds other than those set out in section 5(1) or (2) and the applicant has filed a Form TM8; or

(c) the registrar has indicated to the parties that it is inappropriate for rule 19 to apply,

the registrar shall specify the periods within which evidence and submissions may be filed by the parties.

(2) Where—

(a) the opposition is based on an earlier trade mark of a kind falling within section 6(1)(c); or

(b) the opposition or part of it is based on grounds other than those set out in section 5(1) or (2); or

(c) the truth of a matter set out in the statement of use is either denied or not admitted by the applicant,

the person opposing the registration ("the opposer") shall file evidence supporting the opposition.

(3) Where the opposer files no evidence under paragraph (2), the opposer shall be deemed to have withdrawn the opposition to the registration to the extent that it is based on—

(a) the matters in paragraph (2)(a) or (b); or

(b) an earlier trade mark which has been registered and which is the subject of the statement of use referred to in paragraph (2)(c).

(4) The registrar may, at any time, give leave to either party to file evidence upon such terms as the registrar thinks fit.

[(5) Paragraphs (1)-(3) of this Rule shall not apply to fast track oppositions but paragraph (4) shall apply.]

**Procedure for intervention**

A2-022 **21.**—(1) If the opposition or part of it is based on the relative grounds for refusal set out in section 5(1), (2) or (3), any person in paragraph (3) may file an application to the registrar on Form TM27 for leave to intervene and the registrar may, after hearing the parties concerned if so required, refuse such leave or grant leave upon such terms and conditions (including any undertaking as to costs) as the registrar thinks fit.

(2) Any person granted leave to intervene shall, subject to any terms and conditions imposed in respect of the intervention, be treated as a party to the proceedings for the purposes of the application of the provisions of rules 19, 20 and 62 to 73.

(3) The persons referred to in paragraph (1) are—

(a) where the opposition is based on an earlier trade mark, a licensee of that mark; and

(b) where the opposition is based on an earlier collective mark or certification mark, an authorised user of that mark.

**Observations on application to be sent to applicant; section 38(3)**

**22.—** The registrar shall send to the applicant a copy of any document containing observations made under section 38(3). **A2-023**

**Publication of registration; section 40**

**23.—** On the registration of the trade mark the registrar shall publish the registration on the Office website, specifying the date upon which the trade mark was entered in the register. **A2-024**

*Amendment of application*

**Amendment of application; section 39 (Form TM21)**

**24.—** A request for an amendment of an application to correct an error or to change the name or address of the applicant or in respect of any amendment requested after publication of the application shall be made on Form TM21. **A2-025**

**Amendment of application after publication; section 39 (Form TM7)**

**25.—**(1) Where, pursuant to section 39, a request is made for amendment of an application which has been published in the Journal and the amendment affects the representation of the trade mark or the goods or services covered by the application, the amendment or a statement of the effect of the amendment shall also be published in the Journal. **A2-026**

(2) Any person claiming to be affected by the amendment may, within one month of the date on which the amendment or a statement of the effect of the amendment was published under paragraph (1), give notice to the registrar of objection to the amendment on Form TM7 which shall include a statement of the grounds of objection which shall, in particular, indicate why the amendment would not fall within section 39(2).

(3) The registrar shall send a copy of Form TM7 to the applicant and the procedure in rules 17, 18 and 20 shall apply to the proceedings relating to the objection to the amendment as they apply to proceedings relating to opposition to an application for registration, but with the following modifications—

(a) any reference to—

  (i) an application for registration shall be construed as a reference to a request for amendment of an application,

  (ii) the person opposing the registration shall be construed as a reference to the person objecting to the amendment of an application,

  (iii) the opposition shall be construed as a reference to the objection;

(b) the relevant period, referred to in rule 18(1), shall for these purposes be the period of two months [beginning immediately after] the date upon which the registrar sent a copy of Form TM7 to the applicant; and

(c) rules 18(3) to (6), 20(2) and (3) shall not apply.

*Division, merger and series of marks*

### Division of application; section 41(Form TM12)

A2-027 **26.**—(1) At any time before registration an applicant may send to the registrar a request on Form TM12 [to divide the specification] of the application for registration (the original application) into two or more separate applications (divisional applications), indicating for each division the specification of goods or services.

(2) Each divisional application shall be treated as a separate application for registration with the same filing date as the original application.

(3) Where the request to divide an application is sent after publication of the application, any objections in respect of, or opposition to, the original application shall be taken to apply to each divisional application and shall be proceeded with accordingly.

(4) Upon division of an original application in respect of which notice has been given to the registrar of particulars relating to the grant of a licence, or a security interest or any right in or under it, the notice and the particulars shall be deemed to apply in relation to each of the applications into which the original application has been divided.

### [Division of registration; section 41 (Form TM12R)

A2-027.1 **26A.**—(1) The proprietor of a trade mark may send to the registrar a request on Form TM12R to divide the specification of the registration (the original registration) into two or more separate trade marks (divisional registrations), indicating for each divisional registration the specification of goods or services.

(2) Each divisional registration must be treated as a separate registration with the same date of registration as the original registration.

(3) No request under paragraph (1) may be granted in respect of the registration of a trade mark which is the subject of proceedings for its revocation or invalidation, where the request would introduce a division amongst the goods or services in respect of which the proceedings are directed.

(4) Where the original registration is subject to a disclaimer or limitation, the divisional registrations must also be restricted accordingly.

(5) Where the original registration has had registered in relation to it particulars relating to—

- (a) the grant of a licence;
- (b) a security interest;
- (c) any right in or under that original registration; or
- (d) any memorandum or statement of the effect of a memorandum;

the registrar must enter in the register the same particulars in relation to each of the divisional registrations into which the original registration has been divided.]

### Merger of separate applications or registrations; section 41(Form TM17)

A2-028 **27.**—(1)-(2) [...]

(3) The proprietor of two or more registrations of a trade mark [, the applications relating to which were filed on the same date,] may request the registrar on Form TM17 to merge them into a single registration and the registrar shall, if satisfied that the registrations are in respect of the same trade mark, merge them into a single registration.

[(3A) No application under paragraph (3) may be granted in respect of the registration of a trade mark which—

(a) is the subject of proceedings for its revocation or invalidation; or
(b) is the subject of an international registration within the meaning of article 2 of the Trade Marks (International Registration) Order 2008 which has not become independent of the trade mark as provided for in accordance with Article 6 of the Madrid Protocol.]

(4) Where any registration of a trade mark to be merged under paragraph (3) is subject to a disclaimer or limitation, the merged registration shall also be restricted accordingly.

(5) Where any registration of a trade mark to be merged under paragraph (3) has had registered in relation to it particulars relating to the grant of a licence or a security interest or any right in or under it, or of any memorandum or statement of the effect of a memorandum, the registrar shall enter in the register the same particulars in relation to the merged registration.

(6) The date of registration of the merged registration shall, where the separate registrations bear different dates of registration, be the latest of those dates.

### Registration of a series of trade marks; section 41 (Form TM12)

**28.**—[(1) An application may be made in accordance with rule 5 for the registration of a series of trade marks in a single registration provided that the series comprises of no more than six trade marks. **A2-029**

(1A) Where an application for registration of a series of trade marks comprises three or more trade marks, the application shall be subject to the payment of the prescribed fee for each trade mark in excess of two trade marks.]

(2) Following an application under paragraph (1) the registrar shall, if satisfied that the marks constitute a series, accept the application.

(3)-(4) [...]

(5) At any time the applicant for registration of a series of trade marks or the proprietor of a registered series of trade marks may request the deletion of a mark in that series and, following such request, the registrar shall delete the mark accordingly.

(6) Where under paragraph (5) the registrar deletes a trade mark from an application for registration, the application, in so far as it relates to the deleted mark, shall be treated as withdrawn.

(7) [...]

*Collective and certification marks*

### Filing of regulations for collective and certification marks; Schedules 1 & 2 (Form TM35)

**29.**— Where an application for registration of a collective or certification mark is filed, the applicant shall, within such period of not less than three months as the registrar may specify, file Form TM35 accompanied by a copy of the regulations governing the use of the mark. **A2-030**

### Amendment of regulations of collective and certification marks; Schedule 1 paragraph 10 and Schedule 2 paragraph 11 (Forms TM36 & TM7)

**30.**—(1) An application for the amendment of the regulations governing the use of a registered collective or certification mark shall be filed on Form TM36. **A2-031**

(2) Where it appears to be expedient to the registrar that the amended regula-

tions should be made available to the public the registrar shall publish a notice in the Journal indicating where copies of the amended regulations may be inspected.

(3) Any person may, within two months of the date of publication of the notice under paragraph (2), make observations to the registrar on the amendments relating to the matters referred to in paragraph 6(1) of Schedule 1 to the Act in relation to a collective mark, or paragraph 7(1) of Schedule 2 to the Act in relation to a certification mark and the registrar shall send a copy of those observations to the proprietor.

(4) Any person may, within two months of the date on which the notice was published under paragraph (2), give notice to the registrar of opposition to the amendment on Form TM7 which shall include a statement of the grounds of opposition indicating why the amended regulations do not comply with the requirements of paragraph 6(1) of Schedule 1 to the Act, or, as the case may be, paragraph 7(1) of Schedule 2 to the Act.

(5) The registrar shall send a copy of Form TM7 to the proprietor and the procedure in rules 18 and 20 shall apply to the proceedings relating to the opposition to the amendment as they apply to proceedings relating to opposition to an application for registration, but with the following modifications—

- (a) any reference to—
  - (i) the applicant shall be construed as a reference to the proprietor,
  - (ii) an application for registration shall be construed as a reference to an application for the amendment of the regulations,
  - (iii) the person opposing the registration shall be construed as a reference to the person opposing the amendment of the regulations;
- (b) the relevant period, referred to in rule 18(1), shall for these purposes be the period of two months [beginning immediately after] the date upon which the registrar sent a copy of Form TM7 to the proprietor;
- (c) rules 18(3) to (6), 20(2) and (3) shall not apply.

**Registration subject to disclaimer or limitation; section 13**

A2-032 **31.—** Where the applicant for registration of a trade mark or the proprietor by notice in writing sent to the registrar—

- (a) disclaims any right to the exclusive use of any specified element of the trade mark; or
- (b) agrees that the rights conferred by the registration shall be subject to a specified territorial or other limitation,

the registrar shall make the appropriate entry in the register and publish such disclaimer or limitation.

**Alteration of registered trade marks; section 44 (Forms TM25 & TM7)**

A2-033 **32.—**(1) The proprietor of a registered trade mark may request the registrar on Form TM25 for such alteration of the mark as is permitted under section 44 and following such request the registrar may require evidence as to the circumstances in which the application is made.

(2) Where, upon the request of the proprietor, the registrar proposes to allow such alteration, the registrar shall publish the mark as altered in the Journal.

(3) Any person claiming to be affected by the alteration may, within two months of the date on which the mark as altered was published under paragraph (2), give notice to the registrar of objection to the alteration on Form TM7 which shall include a statement of the grounds of objection.

(4) The registrar shall send a copy of Form TM7 to the proprietor and the procedure in rules 18 and 20 shall apply to the proceedings relating to the objection to the alteration as they apply to proceedings relating to opposition to an application for registration, but with the following modifications—

(a) any reference to—

(i) the applicant shall be construed as a reference to the proprietor,

(ii) an application for registration shall be construed as a reference to a request for alteration,

(iii) the person opposing the registration shall be construed as a reference to the person objecting to the alteration,

(iv) the opposition shall be construed as a reference to the objection;

(b) the relevant period, referred to in rule 18(1), shall for these purposes be the period of two months [beginning immediately after] the date upon which the registrar sent a copy of Form TM7 to the proprietor;

(c) rules 18(3) to (6), 20(2) and (3) shall not apply.

**Surrender of registered trade mark; section 45 (Forms TM22 & TM23)**

**33.**—(1) Subject to paragraph (2), the proprietor may surrender a registered trade mark, by sending notice to the registrar— **A2-034**

(a) on Form TM22 in respect of all the goods or services for which it is registered; or

(b) on Form TM23, in respect only of those goods or services specified by the proprietor in the notice.

(2) A notice under paragraph (1) shall be of no effect unless the proprietor in that notice—

(a) gives the name and address of any person having a registered interest in the mark; and

(b) certifies that any such person—

(i) has been sent not less than three months' notice of the proprietor's intention to surrender the mark, or

(ii) is not affected or if affected consents to the surrender.

(3) The registrar shall, upon the surrender taking effect, make the appropriate entry in the register and publish the date of surrender on the Office website.

*Renewal and restoration*

**Reminder of renewal of registration; section 43**

**34.**—(1) Subject to paragraph (2) below, [at least six months] before the expiration of the last registration of a trade mark, the registrar shall [...] send to the registered proprietor notice of the approaching expiration and inform the proprietor at the same time that the registration may be renewed in the manner described in rule 35. **A2-035**

(2) If it appears to the registrar that a trade mark may be registered under section 40 at any time within six months before or at any time on or after the date on which renewal would be due (by reference to the date of application for registration), the registrar shall be taken to have complied with paragraph (1) if the registrar sends to the applicant notice to that effect within one month following the date of actual registration.

[(2A) The registrar is not subject to any liability by reason of any failure to notify the proprietor in accordance with paragraph (1) and no proceedings lie against any officer of the registrar in respect of any such failure.]

**Renewal of registration; section 43 (Form TM11)**

**A2-036** **35.—** Renewal of registration shall be effected by filing a request for renewal on Form TM11 at any time within the period of six months ending on the date of the expiration of the registration [or following receipt of a notice from the registrar pursuant to rule 34(1)].

**Delayed renewal and removal of registration; section 43 (Form TM11)**

**A2-037** **36.**—(1) If on the expiration of the last registration of a trade mark the renewal fee has not been paid, the registrar shall publish that fact.

(2) If, within six months from the date of the expiration of the last registration, a request for renewal is filed on Form TM11 accompanied by the appropriate renewal fee and additional renewal fee, the registrar shall renew the registration without removing the mark from the register.

(3) Where no request for renewal is filed, the registrar shall, subject to rule 37, remove the mark from the register.

(4) Where a mark is due to be registered after the date on which it is due for renewal (by reference to the date of application for registration), the request for renewal shall be filed together with the renewal fee and additional renewal fee within six months after the date of actual registration.

(5) The removal of the registration of a trade mark shall be published on the Office website.

**Restoration of registration; section 43 (Form TM13)**

**A2-038** **37.**—(1) Where the registrar has removed the mark from the register for failure to renew its registration in accordance with rule 36, the registrar may, following receipt of a request filed on Form TM13 within six months of the date of the removal of the mark accompanied by the appropriate renewal fee and appropriate restoration fee—

(a) restore the mark to the register; and

(b) renew its registration,

[if the registrar is satisfied that the failure to renew was unintentional].

[(1A) Where a mark is restored to the register, the proprietor of the mark may not bring an action for infringement against a third party who, in good faith, has put goods on the market or supplied services under a sign which is identical with or similar to the mark in respect of the period beginning with the date of expiration of the registration and ending on the date its restoration is published in accordance with paragraph (2).]

(2) The restoration of the registration, including the date of restoration, shall be published on the Office website.

*Revocation, invalidation and rectification*

### Application for revocation (on the grounds of non-use); section 46(1)(a) or (b) (Forms TM8(N) & TM26(N))

**38.**—(1) An application to the registrar for revocation of a trade mark under section 46, on the grounds set out in section 46(1)(a) or (b), shall be made on Form TM26(N). **A2-039**

(2) The registrar shall send a copy of Form TM26(N) to the proprietor.

(3) The proprietor shall, within two months of the date on which he was sent a copy of Form TM26(N) by the registrar, file a Form TM8(N), which shall include a counter-statement.

(4) Where the proprietor fails to file evidence of use of the mark or evidence supporting the reasons for non-use of the mark within the period specified in paragraph (3) above the registrar shall specify a further period of not less than two months within which the evidence shall be filed.

(5) The registrar shall send a copy of Form TM8(N) and any evidence of use, or evidence supporting reasons for non-use, filed by the proprietor to the applicant.

(6) Where the proprietor fails to file a Form TM8(N) within the period specified in paragraph (3) the registration of the mark shall, unless the registrar directs otherwise, be revoked.

(7) Where the proprietor fails to file evidence within the period specified under paragraph (3) or any further period specified under paragraph (4), the registrar may treat the proprietor as not opposing the application and the registration of the mark shall, unless the registrar directs otherwise, be revoked.

(8) The registrar may, at any time, give leave to either party to file evidence upon such terms as the registrar thinks fit.

### Application for revocation (on grounds other than non-use); section 46(1)(c) or (d) (Forms TM8 & TM26(O))

**39.**—(1) An application to the registrar for revocation of a trade mark under section 46, on the grounds set out in section 46(1)(c) or (d), shall be made on Form TM26(O) and shall include a statement of the grounds on which the application is made and be accompanied by a statement of truth. **A2-040**

(2) The registrar shall send a copy of Form TM26(O) and the statement of the grounds on which the application is made to the proprietor.

(3) The proprietor shall, within two months of the date on which he was sent a copy of Form TM26(O) and the statement by the registrar, file a Form TM8 which shall include a counter-statement, otherwise the registrar may treat the proprietor as not opposing the application and the registration of the mark shall, unless the registrar directs otherwise, be revoked.

(4) The registrar shall send a copy of Form TM8 to the applicant.

### Application for revocation (on grounds other than non-use): evidence rounds

**40.**—(1) Where the [proprietor] has filed a Form TM8, the registrar shall specify the periods within which further evidence may be filed by the parties. **A2-041**

(2) Where the applicant files no further evidence in support of the application the applicant, shall, unless the registrar otherwise directs, be deemed to have withdrawn the application.

(3) The registrar shall notify the proprietor of any direction given under paragraph (2).

(4) The registrar may, at any time give leave to either party to file evidence upon such terms as the registrar thinks fit.

**Application for invalidation: filing of application and counter-statement; section 47 (Forms TM8 & TM26(I))**

A2-042 **41.**—(1) An application to the registrar for a declaration of invalidity under section 47 shall be filed on Form TM26(I) and shall include a statement of the grounds on which the application is made and be accompanied by a statement of truth.

(2) Where the application is based on a trade mark which has been registered, there shall be included in the statement of the grounds on which the application is made a representation of that mark and—

- (a) the details of the authority with which the mark is registered;
- (b) the registration number of that mark;
- (c) the goods and services in respect of which—
  - (i) that mark is registered, and
  - (ii) the application is based; and
- (d) where neither section 47(2A)(a) nor (b) applies to the mark, a statement detailing whether during the period referred to in section 47(2B)(a) it has been put to genuine use in relation to each of the goods and services in respect of which the application is based or whether there are proper reasons for non-use (for the purposes of rule 42 this is the "statement of use").

(3) Where the application is based on a trade mark in respect of which an application for registration has been made, there shall be included in the statement of the grounds on which the application is made a representation of that mark and those matters set out in paragraph (2)(a) to (c), with references to registration being construed as references to the application for registration.

(4) Where the application is based on an unregistered trade mark or other sign which the applicant claims to be protected by virtue of any rule of law (in particular, the law of passing off), there shall be included in the statement of the grounds on which the application is made a representation of that mark or sign and the goods and services in respect of which such protection is claimed.

(5) The registrar shall send a copy of Form TM26(I) and the statement of the grounds on which the application is made to the proprietor.

(6) The proprietor shall, within two months of the date on which a copy of Form TM26(I) and the statement was sent by the registrar, file a Form TM8, which shall include a counter-statement, otherwise the registrar may treat the proprietor as not opposing the application and registration of the mark shall, unless the registrar otherwise directs, be declared invalid.

(7) The registrar shall send a copy of Form TM8 to the applicant.

**Application for invalidation: evidence rounds**

A2-043 **42.**—(1) Where the proprietor has filed Form TM8, the registrar shall send notice to the applicant inviting the applicant to file evidence in support of the grounds on which the application is made and any submissions and to send a copy to all the other parties.

(2) The registrar shall specify the periods within which evidence and submissions may be filed by the parties.

(3) Where—

- (a) the application is based on an earlier trade mark of a kind falling within section 6(1)(c); or

(b) the application or part of it is based on grounds other than those set out in section 5(1) or (2); or

(c) the truth of a matter set out in the statement of use is either denied or not admitted by the proprietor,

the applicant shall file evidence supporting the application.

(4) Where the applicant files no evidence under paragraph (3), the applicant shall be deemed to have withdrawn the application to the extent that it is based on—

(a) the matters in paragraph (3)(a) or (b); or

(b) an earlier trade mark which has been registered and is the subject of the statement of use referred to in paragraph (3)(c).

(5) The registrar may, at any time give leave to either party to file evidence upon such terms as the registrar thinks fit.

**Setting aside cancellation of application or revocation or invalidation of registration; (Form TM29)**

**43.**—(1) This rule applies where— **A2-044**

(a) an application for registration is treated as abandoned under rule 18(2);

(b) the registration of a mark is revoked under rule 38(6) or rule 39(3); or

(c) the registration of a mark is declared invalid under rule 41(6),

and the applicant or the proprietor (as the case may be) claims that the decision of the registrar to treat the application as abandoned or revoke the registration of the mark or declare the mark invalid (as the case may be) ("the original decision") should be set aside on the grounds set out in paragraph (3).

(2) Where this rule applies, the applicant or the proprietor shall, within a period of six months [beginning immediately after] the date that the application was refused or the register was amended to reflect the revocation or the declaration of invalidity (as the case may be), file an application on Form TM29 to set aside the decision of the registrar and shall include evidence in support of the application and shall copy the form and the evidence to the other party to the original proceedings under the rules referred to in paragraph (1).

(3) Where the applicant or the proprietor demonstrates to the reasonable satisfaction of the registrar that the failure to file Form TM8 within the period specified in the rules referred to in paragraph (1) was due to a failure to receive Form TM7, Form TM26(N), Form TM26(O) or Form TM26(I) (as the case may be), the original decision may be set aside on such terms and conditions as the registrar thinks fit.

(4) In considering whether to set aside the original decision the matters to which the registrar must have regard include whether the person seeking to set aside the decision made an application to do so promptly upon becoming aware of the original decision and any prejudice which may be caused to the other party to the original proceedings if the original decision were to be set aside.

**Procedure on application for rectification; section 64 (Form TM26(R))**

**44.**—(1) An application for rectification of an error or omission in the register **A2-045**
under section 64(1) shall be made on Form TM26(R) together with:

(a) a statement of the grounds on which the application is made; and

(b) any evidence to support those grounds.

(2) Where any application is made under paragraph (1) by a person other than the proprietor of the registered trade mark the registrar—

(a) shall send a copy of the application and the statement, together with any evidence filed, to the proprietor; and

(b) may give such direction with regard to the filing of subsequent evidence and upon such terms as the registrar thinks fit.

**Procedure for intervention**

A2-046 **45.**—(1) Any person, other than the registered proprietor, claiming to have an interest in proceedings on an application under rule 38, 39, 41 or 44, may file an application to the registrar on Form TM27 for leave to intervene, stating the nature of the person's interest and the registrar may, after hearing the parties concerned if they request a hearing, refuse leave or grant leave upon such terms and conditions (including any undertaking as to costs) as the registrar thinks fit.

(2) Any person granted leave to intervene shall, subject to any terms and conditions imposed in respect of the intervention, be treated as a party to the proceedings for the purposes of the application of the provisions of rules 38 to 40, 41 and 42 or 44 (as appropriate) and rules 62 to 73.

*The register*

**Form of register; section 63(1)**

A2-047 **46.**— The register required to be maintained by the registrar under section 63(1) need not be kept in documentary form.

**Entry in register of particulars of registered trade marks; section 63(2) (Form TM24)**

A2-048 **47.**— In addition to the entries in the register of registered trade marks required to be made by section 63(2)(a), there shall be entered in the register in respect of each trade mark the following particulars—

(a) the date of registration as determined in accordance with section 40(3) (that is to say, the date of the filing of the application for registration);

(b) the date of completion of the registration procedure;

(c) the priority date (if any) to be accorded pursuant to a claim to a right to priority made under section 35 or 36;

(d) the name and address of the proprietor;

(e) the address for service (if any) filed under rule 11;

(f) any disclaimer or limitation of rights under section 13(1)(a) or (b);

(g) any memorandum or statement of the effect of any memorandum relating to a trade mark of which the registrar has been notified on Form TM24;

(h) the goods or services in respect of which the mark is registered;

(i) where the mark is a collective or certification mark, that fact;

(j) where the mark is registered pursuant to section 5(5) with the consent of the proprietor of an earlier trade mark or other earlier right, that fact;

(k) where the mark is registered pursuant to a transformation application,

(i) the number of the international registration, and

(ii) either:—

(aa) the date accorded to the international registration under Article 3(4), or

(bb) the date of recordal of the request for extension to the United Kingdom of the international registration under Article 3*ter*, as the case may be, of the Madrid Protocol;

(l) where the mark arises from the conversion of a [European Union] trade mark or an application for a [European Union] trade mark, the number of any other registered trade mark from which the [European Union] trade mark or the application for a [European Union] trade mark claimed seniority and the earliest seniority date.

[(m) where the mark is a collective mark and amended regulations have been accepted by the registrar, that fact, including the date of that entry.]

**Entry in register of particulars of registrable transactions; section 25**

**48.—** Upon application made to the registrar by such person as is mentioned in section 25(1)(a) or (b) there shall be entered in the register in respect of each trade mark the following particulars of registrable transactions together with the date on which the entry is made— **A2-049**

(a) in the case of an assignment of a registered trade mark or any right in it—
  (i) the name and address of the assignee,
  (ii) the date of the assignment, and
  (iii) where the assignment is in respect of any right in the mark, a description of the right assigned;

(b) in the case of the grant of a licence under a registered trade mark—
  (i) the name and address of the licensee,
  (ii) where the licence is an exclusive licence, that fact,
  (iii) where the licence is limited, a description of the limitation, and
  (iv) the duration of the licence if the same is or is ascertainable as a definite period;

(c) in the case of the grant of any security interest over a registered trade mark or any right in or under it—
  (i) the name and address of the grantee,
  (ii) the nature of the interest (whether fixed or floating), and
  (iii) the extent of the security and the right in or under the mark secured;

(d) in the case of the making by personal representatives of an assent in relation to a registered trade mark or any right in or under it—
  (i) the name and address of the person in whom the mark or any right in or under it vests by virtue of the assent, and
  (ii) the date of the assent;

(e) in the case of a court or other competent authority transferring a registered trade mark or any right in or under it—
  (i) the name and address of the transferee,
  (ii) the date of the order, and
  (iii) where the transfer is in respect of a right in the mark, a description of the right transferred; and

(f) in the case of any amendment of the registered particulars relating to a licence under a registered trade mark or a security interest over a registered trade mark or any right in or under it, particulars to reflect such amendment.

**Application to register or give notice of transaction; sections 25 & 27(3) (Form TM16, TM24, TM50 & TM51)**

A2-050 **49.**—(1) An application to register particulars of a transaction to which section 25 applies or to give notice to the registrar of particulars of a transaction to which section 27(3) applies shall be made—

(a) relating to an assignment or transaction other than a transaction referred to in sub-paragraphs (b) to (d) below, on Form TM16;

(b) relating to a grant of a licence, on Form TM50;

(c) relating to an amendment to, or termination of a licence, on Form TM51;

(d) relating to the grant, amendment or termination of any security interest, on Form TM24; and

(e) relating to the making by personal representatives of an assent or to an order of a court or other competent authority, on Form TM24.

(2) An application under paragraph (1) shall—

(a) where the transaction is an assignment, be signed by or on behalf of the parties to the assignment;

(b) where the transaction falls within sub-paragraphs (b), (c) or (d) of paragraph (1), be signed by or on behalf of the grantor of the licence or security interest,

or be accompanied by such documentary evidence as suffices to establish the transaction.

(3) Where an application to give notice to the registrar has been made of particulars relating to an application for registration of a trade mark, upon registration of the trade mark, the registrar shall enter those particulars in the register.

**Public inspection of register; section 63(3)**

A2-051 **50.**—(1) The register shall be open for public inspection at the Office during the hours of business of the Office as published in accordance with rule 80.

(2) Where any portion of the register is kept otherwise than in documentary form, the right of inspection is a right to inspect the material on the register.

**Supply of certified copies etc; section 63(3) (Form TM31R)**

A2-052 **51.**— The registrar shall supply a certified copy or extract or uncertified copy or extract, as requested on Form TM31R, of any entry in the register.

**Request for change of name or address in register; section 64(4) (Form TM21)**

A2-053 **52.**— The registrar shall, on a request made on Form TM21 by the proprietor of a registered trade mark or a licensee or any person having an interest in or charge on a registered trade mark which has been registered under rule 48 ("the applicant"), enter a change in the applicant's name or address as recorded in the register.

**Removal of matter from register; sections 25(5)(b) and 64(5) (Form TM7)**

A2-054 **53.**—(1) Where it appears to the registrar that any matter in the register has ceased to have effect, before removing it from the register—

(a) the registrar may publish in the Journal the fact that it is intended to remove that matter, and

(b) where any person appears to the registrar to be affected by the removal, notice of the intended removal shall be sent to that person.

(2) Within two months of the date on which the intention to remove the matter is published, or notice of the intended removal is sent, as the case may be—

(a) any person may file notice of opposition to the removal on form TM7; and

(b) the person to whom a notice is sent under paragraph (1)(b) may file in writing their objections, if any, to the removal,

and where such opposition or objections are made, rule 63 shall apply.

(3) If the registrar is satisfied after considering any objections or opposition to the removal that the matter has not ceased to have effect, the registrar shall not remove it.

(4) Where there has been no response to the registrar's notice the registrar may remove the matter and where representations objecting to the removal of the entry have been made the registrar may, if after considering the objections the registrar is of the view that the entry or any part of it has ceased to have effect, remove it or the appropriate part of it.

*Change of classification*

**Change of classification; sections 65(2) & 76(1)**

**54.**—(1) The registrar may at any time amend an entry in the register which **A2-055**
relates to the classification of a registered trade mark so that it accords with the version of the Nice Classification that has effect at that time.

(2) Before making any amendment to the register under paragraph (1) the registrar shall give the proprietor of the mark written notice of the proposed amendments and shall at the same time advise the proprietor that—

(a) the proprietor may make written objections to the proposals, within two months of the date of the notice, stating the grounds of those objections; and

(b) if no written objections are received within the period specified the registrar shall publish the proposals and the proprietor shall not be entitled to make any objections to the proposals upon such publication.

(3) If the proprietor makes no written objections within the period specified in paragraph (2)(a) or at any time before the expiration of that period decides not to make any objections and gives the registrar written notice to this effect, the registrar shall as soon as practicable after the expiration of that period or upon receipt of the notice publish the proposals in the Journal.

(4) Where the proprietor makes written objections within the period specified in paragraph (2)(a), the registrar shall, as soon as practicable after having considered the objections, publish the proposals in the Journal or, where the registrar has amended the proposals, publish the proposals as amended in the Journal; and the registrar's decision shall be final and not subject to appeal.

**Opposition to proposals; sections 65(3), (5) & 76(1) (Form TM7)**

**55.**—(1) Any person may, within two months of the date on which the propos- **A2-056**
als were published under rule 54, give notice to the registrar of opposition to the proposals on Form TM7 which shall include a statement of the grounds of opposition which shall, in particular, indicate why the proposed amendments would be contrary to section 65(3).

(2) If no notice of opposition under paragraph (1) is filed within the time specified, or where any opposition has been determined, the registrar shall make the amendments as proposed and shall enter in the register the date when they were made; and the registrar's decision shall be final and not subject to appeal.

*Request for information, inspection of documents and confidentiality*

**Request for information; section 67(1) (Form TM31C)**

A2-057 **56.—** A request for information relating to an application for registration or to a registered trade mark shall be made on Form TM31C.

**Information available before publication; section 67(2)**

A2-058 **57.—**(1) Before publication of an application for registration the registrar shall make available for inspection by the public the application and any amendments made to it and any particulars contained in a notice given to the registrar under rule 49.

(2) Nothing in section 67(2) relating to publication of information shall be construed as preventing the publication of decisions on cases relating to trade marks decided by the registrar.

**Inspection of documents; sections 67 & 76(1)**

A2-059 **58.—**(1) Subject to paragraphs (2) and (3), the registrar shall permit all documents filed or kept at the Office in relation to a registered mark or, where an application for the registration of a trade mark has been published, in relation to that application, to be inspected.

(2) The registrar shall not be obliged to permit the inspection of any such document as is mentioned in paragraph (1) until the completion of any procedure, or the stage in the procedure which is relevant to the document in question, which the registrar is required or permitted to carry out under the Act or these Rules.

(3) The right of inspection under paragraph (1) does not apply to—

(a) any document prepared in the Office solely for its own use;

(b) any document sent to the Office, whether at its request or otherwise, for inspection and subsequent return to the sender;

(c) any request for information under rule 56;

(d) any document received by the Office which the registrar considers should be treated as confidential;

(e) any document in respect of which the registrar issues directions under rule 59 that it be treated as confidential.

(4) Nothing in paragraph (1) shall be construed as imposing on the registrar any duty of making available for public inspection—

(a) any document or part of a document which in the registrar's opinion disparages any person in a way likely to cause damage to that person; or

(b) any document or information filed at or sent to or by the Office before 31st October 1994; or

(c) any document or information filed at or sent to or by the Office after 31st October 1994 relating to an application for registration of a trade mark under the Trade Marks Act 1938.

(5) No appeal shall lie from a decision of the registrar under paragraph (4) not to make any document or part of a document available for public inspection.

**Confidential documents**

**59.**—(1) Where a document (other than a form required by the registrar and published in accordance with rule 3) is filed at the Office and the person filing it requests at the time of filing that it or a specified part of it be treated as confidential, giving reasons for the request, the registrar may direct that it or part of it, as the case may be, be treated as confidential, and the document shall not be open to public inspection while the matter is being determined by the registrar. **A2-060**

(2) Where such direction has been given and not withdrawn, nothing in this rule shall be taken to authorise or require any person to be allowed to inspect the document or part of it to which the direction relates except by leave of the registrar.

(3) The registrar shall not withdraw any direction given under this rule without prior consultation with the person at whose request the direction was given, unless the registrar is satisfied that such prior consultation is not reasonably practical.

(4) The registrar may where the registrar considers that any document issued by the Office should be treated as confidential so direct, and upon such direction that document shall not be open to public inspection except by leave of the registrar.

(5) Where a direction is given under this rule for a document to be treated as confidential a record of the fact shall be filed with the document.

*Agents*

**Proof of authorisation of agent may be required; section 82 (Form TM33)**

**60.**—(1) Where an agent has been authorised under section 82, the registrar may in a particular case require the personal signature or presence of the agent or the person authorising the agent to act as agent. **A2-061**

(2) Subject to paragraph (3), where a person appoints an agent for the first time or appoints one agent in substitution for another, the newly appointed agent shall file Form TM33.

(3) Where after a person has become a party to proceedings involving a third party before the registrar, the person appoints an agent for the first time or appoints one agent in substitution for another, the newly appointed agent shall file Form TM33P.

(4) Any act required or authorised by the Act in connection with the registration of a trade mark or any procedure relating to a trade mark may not be done by or to the newly appointed agent until on or after the date on which the newly appointed agent files Form TM33 or TM33P as appropriate.

(5) The registrar may by notice in writing require an agent to produce evidence of his authority under section 82.

**Registrar may refuse to deal with certain agents; section 88**

**61.**— The registrar may refuse to recognise as agent in respect of any business under the Act— **A2-062**

(a) a person who has been convicted of an offence under section 84;
(b) an individual whose name has been erased from and not restored to, or who is suspended from, the register of trade mark agents on the ground of misconduct;

(c) a person who is found by the Secretary of State to have been guilty of such conduct as would, in the case of an individual registered in that register, render that person liable to have their name erased from it on the ground of misconduct;

(d) a partnership or body corporate of which one of the partners or directors is a person whom the registrar could refuse to recognise under paragraph (a), (b) or (c).

*Proceedings before and decision of registrar, evidence and costs*

**General powers of registrar in relation to proceedings**

A2-063 **62.**—(1) Except where the Act or these Rules otherwise provide, the registrar may give such directions as to the management of any proceedings as the registrar thinks fit, and in particular may—

(a) require a document, information or evidence to be filed within such period as the registrar may specify;

(b) require a translation of any document;

(c) require a party or a party's legal representative to attend a hearing;

(d) hold a hearing by telephone or by using any other method of direct oral communication;

[(e) allow a statement of case to be amended, provided that—

(i) where an application is made to add grounds of opposition other than under subsections 5(1) or (2) of the Act, the application shall be made on Form TM7G; and

(ii) in the case of fast track oppositions the registrar may only permit a statement of case to be amended to add additional or alternative earlier registered or protected trade marks as additional grounds of opposition under subsections 5(1) or 5(2) of the Act, provided that the total number of earlier trade marks relied upon may not exceed three;]

(f) stay the whole, or any part, of the proceedings either generally or until a specified date or event;

[(g) consolidate proceedings provided that where a fast track opposition is consolidated with other non-fast track proceedings, it shall no longer be treated as a fast track opposition;]

(h) direct that part of any proceedings be dealt with as separate proceedings;

(i) exclude any evidence which the registrar considers to be inadmissible [;]

[(j) direct that with effect from the date specified in the direction opposition proceedings which have been commenced on Form TM7F as a fast track opposition but which do not satisfy the criteria for a fast track opposition may continue as if the opposition proceedings were an opposition to the registration commenced under Rule 17 on Form TM7.]

(2) The registrar may control the evidence by giving directions as to—

(a) the issues on which evidence is required; and

(b) the way in which the evidence is to be placed before the registrar.

(3) When the registrar gives directions under any provision of these Rules, the registrar may—

(a) make them subject to conditions; and

(b) specify the consequences of failure to comply with the directions or a condition.

(4) The registrar may at any stage of any proceedings direct that the parties to the proceedings attend a case management conference or pre-hearing review.

[(5) In the case of a fast track opposition—

(a) proceedings shall be held orally only if the Office requests it or if either party to the proceedings requests it and the registrar considers that oral proceedings are necessary to deal with the case justly and at proportionate cost; and

(b) the parties shall be given at least fourteen days' notice beginning on the date on which the notice is sent, of the time when the oral proceedings are to take place unless each party to the proceedings consents to shorter notice.

(6) In the case of a fast track opposition, where no oral hearing is held, the registrar shall give the parties the opportunity to provide arguments in writing before reaching a decision that is adverse to either party.]

**Decisions of registrar to be taken after hearing**

**63.**—(1) Without prejudice to any provisions of the Act or these Rules requiring the registrar to hear any party to proceedings under the Act or these Rules, or to give such party an opportunity to be heard, the registrar shall, before taking any decision on any matter under the Act or these Rules which is or may be adverse to any party to any proceedings, give that party an opportunity to be heard. **A2-064**

(2) The registrar shall give that party at least fourteen days' notice, beginning on the date on which notice is sent, of the time when the party may be heard unless the party consents to shorter notice.

[(3) This Rule shall not apply to fast track opposition proceedings.]

**Evidence in proceedings before the registrar; section 69**

**64.**—(1) Subject to rule 62(2) and as follows, evidence filed in any proceedings under the Act or these Rules may be given— **A2-065**

(a) by witness statement, affidavit, statutory declaration; or

(b) in any other form which would be admissible as evidence in proceedings before the court.

(2) A witness statement may only be given in evidence if it includes a statement of truth.

(3) The general rule is that evidence at hearings is to be by witness statement unless the registrar or any enactment requires otherwise.

(4) For the purposes of these Rules, a statement of truth—

(a) means a statement that the person making the statement believes that the facts stated in a particular document are true; and

(b) shall be dated and signed by—

(i) in the case of a witness statement, the maker of the statement,

(ii) in any other case, the party or legal representative of such party.

(5) In these Rules, a witness statement is a written statement signed by a person that contains the evidence which that person would be allowed to give orally.

(6) Under these Rules, evidence shall only be considered filed when—

(a) it has been received by the registrar; and

(b) it has been sent to all other parties to the proceedings.

**Registrar to have power of an official referee; section 69**

A2-066 **65.—** The registrar shall have the powers of an official referee of the Supreme Court as regards—

(a) the attendance of witnesses and their examination on oath; and

(b) the discovery and production of documents,

but the registrar shall have no power to punish summarily for contempt.

**Hearings before registrar to be in public**

A2-067 **66.—**(1) The hearing before the registrar of any dispute between two or more parties relating to any matter in connection with an application for the registration of a mark or a registered mark shall be in public unless the registrar, after consultation with those parties who appear in person or are represented at the hearing, otherwise directs.

(2) […]

**Costs of proceedings; section 68**

A2-068 **67.—** The registrar may, in any proceedings under the Act or these Rules, by order award to any party such costs as the registrar may consider reasonable, and direct how and by what parties they are to be paid.

**Security for costs; section 68**

A2-069 **68.—**(1) The registrar may require any person who is a party in any proceedings under the Act or these Rules to give security for costs in relation to those proceedings; and may also require security for the costs of any appeal from the registrar's decision.

(2) In default of such security being given, the registrar, in the case of the proceedings before the registrar, or in the case of an appeal, the person appointed under section 76 may treat the party in default as having withdrawn their application, opposition, objection or intervention, as the case may be.

**Decision of registrar (Form TM5)**

A2-070 **69.—**(1) The registrar shall send to each party to the proceedings written notice of any decision made in any proceedings before the registrar stating the reasons for that decision and for the purposes of any appeal against that decision, subject to paragraph (2), the date on which the notice is sent shall be taken to be the date of the decision.

(2) Where a statement of the reasons for the decision is not included in the notice sent under paragraph (1), any party may, within one month of the date on which the notice was sent to that party, request the registrar on Form TM5 to send a statement of the reasons for the decision and upon such request the registrar shall send such a statement, and the date on which that statement is sent shall be deemed to be the date of the registrar's decision for the purpose of any appeal against it.

*Appeals*

**Decisions subject to appeal; section 76(1)**

A2-071 **70.—**(1) Except as otherwise expressly provided by these Rules an appeal lies from any decision of the registrar made under these Rules relating to a dispute between two or more parties in connection with a trade mark, including a decision which terminates the proceedings as regards one of the parties or a decision awarding costs to any party ("a final decision") or a decision which is made at any point in the proceedings prior to a final decision ("an interim decision").

(2) An interim decision (including a decision refusing leave to appeal under this paragraph) may only be appealed against independently of any appeal against a final decision with the leave of the registrar.

**Appeal to person appointed; section 76**

**71.**—(1) [Subject to paragraph (1A), notice] of appeal to the person appointed under section 76 shall be filed on Form TM55 which shall include the appellant's grounds of appeal and his case in support of the appeal. **A2-072**

[(1A) Where the appeal arises in proceedings between two or more parties, notice of appeal to the person appointed under section 76 shall be filed on Form TM55P, which shall include the appellant's grounds of appeal and his case in support of the appeal.]

[(2) Forms TM55 or TM55P shall be filed within the period of 28 days beginning immediately after the date of the registrar's decision which is the subject of the appeal ("the original decision").]

(3) The registrar shall send the notice and the statement to the person appointed.

(4) Where any person other than the appellant was a party to the proceedings before the registrar in which the original decision was made ("the respondent"), the registrar shall send to the respondent a copy of the notice and the statement and the respondent may, within the period of 21 days [beginning immediately after] the date on which the notice and statement was sent, file a notice responding to the notice of appeal.

(5) The respondent's notice shall specify any grounds on which the respondent considers the original decision should be maintained where these differ from or are additional to the grounds given by the registrar in the original decision.

(6) The registrar shall send a copy of the respondent's notice to the person appointed and a copy to the appellant.

**Determination whether appeal should be referred to court; section 76(3)**

**72.**—(1) Within 28 days of the date on which the notice of appeal is sent to the respondent by the registrar under rule 71(4); **A2-073**

(a) the registrar; or
(b) any person who was a party to the proceedings in which the decision appealed against was made,

may request that the person appointed refer the appeal to the court.

(2) Where the registrar requests that the appeal be referred to the court, the registrar shall send a copy of the request to each party to the proceedings.

(3) A request under paragraph (1)(b) shall be sent to the registrar following which the registrar shall send it to the person appointed and shall send a copy of the request to any other party to the proceedings.

(4) Within 28 days of the date on which a copy of a request is sent by the registrar under paragraph (2) or (3), the person to whom it is sent may make representations as to whether the appeal should be referred to the court.

(5) In any case where it appears to the person appointed that a point of general legal importance is involved in the appeal, the person appointed shall send to the registrar and to every party to the proceedings in which the decision appealed against was made, notice to that effect.

(6) Within 28 days of the date on which a notice is sent under paragraph (5), the person to whom it was sent may make representations as to whether the appeal should be referred to the court.

**Hearing and determination of appeal; section 76(4)**

A2-074 **73.**—(1) Where the person appointed does not refer the appeal to the court, the person appointed shall send written notice of the time and place appointed for the oral hearing of the appeal—

(a) where no person other than the appellant was a party to the proceedings in which the decision appealed against was made, to the registrar and to the appellant; and

(b) in any other case, to the registrar and to each person who was a party to those proceedings.

(2) The person appointed shall send the notice at least fourteen days before the time appointed for the oral hearing.

(3) If all the persons notified under paragraph (1) inform the person appointed that they do not wish to make oral representations then—

(a) the person appointed may hear and determine the case on the basis of any written representations; and

(b) the time and place appointed for the oral hearing may be vacated.

(4) Rules 62, 65, 67 and 68 shall apply to the person appointed and to proceedings before the person appointed as they apply to the registrar and to proceedings before the registrar.

(5) If there is an oral hearing of the appeal then rule 66 shall apply to the person appointed and to proceedings before the person appointed as it applies to the registrar and to proceedings before the registrar.

(6) A copy of the decision of the appointed person shall be sent, with a statement of the reasons for the decision, to the registrar and to each person who was a party to the appeal.

*Correction of irregularities, calculation and extension of time*

**Correction of irregularities in procedure**

A2-075 **74.**—(1) Subject to rule 77, the registrar may authorise the rectification of any irregularity in procedure (including the rectification of any document filed) connected with any proceeding or other matter before the registrar or the Office.

(2) Any rectification made under paragraph (1) shall be made—

(a) after giving the parties such notice; and

(b) subject to such conditions,

as the registrar may direct.

**Interrupted day**

A2-076 **75.**—(1) The registrar may certify any day as an interrupted day where—

(a) there is an event or circumstance causing an interruption in the normal operation of the Office; or

(b) there is a general interruption or subsequent dislocation in the postal services of the United Kingdom.

(2) Any certificate of the registrar made under paragraph (1) shall be displayed in the Office and published on the Office website.

(3) The registrar shall, where the time for doing anything under these Rules

expires on an interrupted day, extend that time to the next following day not being an interrupted day (or an excluded day).

(4) In this rule—

"excluded day" means a day which is not a business day as specified in a direction given by the registrar under section 80; and

"interrupted day" means a day which has been certified as such under paragraph (1).

**Delays in communication services**

**76.**—(1) The registrar shall extend any time limit in these Rules where the registrar is satisfied that the failure to do something under these Rules was wholly or mainly attributed to a delay in, or failure of, a communication service. **A2-077**

(2) Any extension under paragraph (1) shall be—

(a) made after giving the parties such notice; and

(b) subject to such conditions,

as the registrar may direct.

(3) In this rule "communication service" means a service by which documents may be sent and delivered and includes post, facsimile, email and courier.

**Alteration of time limits (Form TM9)**

**77.**—(1) Subject to paragraphs (4) and (5), the registrar may, at the request of the person or party concerned or at the registrar's own initiative extend a time or period prescribed by these Rules or a time or period specified by the registrar for doing any act and any extension under this paragraph shall be made subject to such conditions as the registrar may direct. **A2-078**

(2) A request for extension under this rule may be made before or after the time or period in question has expired and shall be made—

(a) where the application for registration has not been published and the request for an extension [relates to a time or period other than one specified under rule 13 and] is made before the time or period in question has expired, in writing; and

(b) in any other case, on Form TM9.

(3) Where an extension under paragraph (1) is requested in relation to proceedings before the registrar, the party seeking the extension shall send a copy of the request to every other person who is a party to the proceedings.

(4) The registrar shall extend a flexible time limit, except a time or period which applies in relation to proceedings before the registrar or the filing of an appeal to the Appointed Person under rule 71, where—

(a) the request for extension is made before the end of the period of two months [beginning immediately after] the date the relevant time or period expired; and

(b) no previous request has been made under this paragraph.

(5) A time limit listed in Schedule 1 (whether it has already expired or not) may be extended under paragraph (1) if, and only if—

(a) the irregularity or prospective irregularity is attributable, wholly or in part, to a default, omission or other error by the registrar, the Office or the International Bureau; and

(b) it appears to the registrar that the irregularity should be rectified.

(6) In this rule—

"flexible time limit" means—

(a) a time or period prescribed by these Rules, except a time or period prescribed by the rules listed in Schedule 1, or
(b) a time or period specified by the registrar for doing any act or taking any proceedings; and

"proceedings before the registrar" means any dispute between two or more parties relating to a matter before the registrar in connection with a trade mark.

*Filing of documents, hours of business, Trade Marks Journal and translations*

**Filing of documents by electronic means**

A2-079 **78.—** The registrar may permit as an alternative to the sending by post or delivery of the application, notice or other document in legible form the filing of the application, notice or other document by electronic means subject to such terms or conditions as the registrar may specify either generally by published notice or in any particular case by written notice to the person desiring to file any such documents by such means.

**Electronic communications**

A2-080 **79.**—(1) The delivery using electronic communications to any person by the registrar of any document is deemed to be effected, unless the registrar has otherwise specified, by transmitting an electronic communication containing the document to an address provided or made available to the registrar by that person as an address for the receipt of electronic communications; and unless the contrary is proved such delivery is deemed to be effected immediately upon the transmission of the communication.

(2) In this rule "electronic communication" has the same meaning as in the Electronic Communications Act 2000.

**Directions on hours of business; section 80**

A2-081 **80.—** Any directions given by the registrar under section 80 specifying the hours of business of the Office and business days of the Office shall be published on the Office website.

**Trade Marks Journal; section 81**

A2-082 **81.—** The registrar shall publish a journal, entitled "The Trade Marks Journal" containing such information as is required to be published in the Journal under these Rules and such other information as the registrar thinks fit.

**Translations**

A2-083 **82.**—(1) Where any document or part thereof which is in a language other than English is filed or sent to the registrar in pursuance of the Act or these Rules, the registrar may require that there be furnished a translation into English of the document or that part, verified to the satisfaction of the registrar as corresponding to the original text.

(2) The registrar may refuse to accept any translation which the registrar considers to be inaccurate in which event there shall be furnished another translation of the document in question verified in accordance with paragraph (1).

*Transitional provisions and revocations*

**Revocation of previous rules and proceedings commenced under previous rules**

**83.**—(1) The instruments set out in Schedule 2 ("the previous rules") are revoked to the extent specified. **A2-084**

(2) Where immediately before these Rules come into force, any time or period prescribed by the previous rules has effect in relation to any act or proceeding and has not expired, the time or period prescribed by the previous rules and not by these Rules shall apply to that act or proceeding.

(3) Except as provided by paragraph (4) where a new step is to be taken on or after 1st October 2008 in relation to any proceedings commenced under the previous rules these Rules shall apply to such proceedings from that date.

(4) Subject to paragraph (5) where prior to the entry into force of these Rules–

(a) a Form TM8 and counter-statement have been filed in–

(i) opposition proceedings, or

(ii) proceedings for the revocation of a trade mark on the grounds set out in section 46(1)(c) or (d); or

(iii) invalidation proceedings; or

(b) an application for revocation of a trade mark on the grounds set out in section 46(1)(a) or (b) has been filed,

the previous rules shall apply with regard to the filing of any evidence in relation to those proceedings.

(5) Where proceedings as described in paragraph (4) are consolidated with proceedings commenced on or after 1st October 2008 these Rules shall apply with regard to the filing of any evidence in relation to those consolidated proceedings.

*Baroness Morgan of Drefelin*

Parliamentary Under Secretary of State for Intellectual Property and Quality Department for Innovation, Universities and Skills

7th July 2008

SCHEDULE 1

EXTENSION OF TIME LIMITS

**Rule 77**

**A2-085**

rule 17(2) (filing notice of opposition)
rule 17(3) (filing notice of opposition: request for extension of time)
rule 18(1) (counter-statement in opposition proceedings)
rule 19(4) (responding to preliminary indication)
rule 25(2) (opposition to amendment after publication)
rule 30(4) (opposition to amendment of regulations of collective and certification marks)
rule 32(3) (opposition to alteration of mark)
rule 35 (renewal of registration)
rule 36(2) (delayed renewal)
rule 37(1) (restoration of registration)
rule 38(3) (counter-statement for revocation on grounds of non-use)
rule 39(3) (counter-statement for revocation on grounds other than non-use)
rule 41(6) (counter-statement for invalidity)
rule 43(2) (setting aside cancellation of application or revocation or invalidation of registration)

rule 53(2) (opposition to removal of matter from register)
rule 55(1) (opposition to proposals for change of classification)
rule 77(4) (period for making a retrospective request to extend a flexible time period).

## SCHEDULE 2

### REVOCATIONS

**Rule 83**

**A2-086**

| **Rules revoked** | **References** | **Extent of Revocation** |
|---|---|---|
| The Trade Marks Rules 2000 | SI 2000/136 | The whole rules |
| The Trade Marks (Amendment) Rules 2001 | SI 2001/3832 | The whole rules |
| The Trade Marks (Amendment) Rules 2004 | SI 2004/947 | The whole rules |
| The Patents, Trade Marks and Designs (Address for Service and Time Limits etc.) Rules 2006 | SI 2006/760 | Rules 15 to 20 |
| The Trade Marks and Designs (Address for Service) (Amendment) Rules 2006 | SI 2006/1029 | The whole rules |
| The Trade Marks (Amendment) Rules 2006 | SI 2006/3039 | The whole rules |
| The Trade Marks (Amendment) Rules 2007 | SI 2007/2076 | The whole rules |
| The Trade Marks and Trade Marks (Fees) (Amendment) Rules 2008 | SI 2008/11 | Rules 2 to 4 |

## THE COMMUNITY TRADE MARK REGULATIONS 2006

*Replace with:*

The Secretary of State makes the following Regulations in exercise of the powers conferred by section 52 of the Trade Marks Act 1994: A9-001

### Citation, commencement, extent and revocations

**1.**—(1) These Regulations may be cited as the Community Trade Mark Regulations 2006 and shall come into force on 29th April 2006. A9-001

(2) These Regulations extend to England and Wales, Scotland and Northern Ireland.

(3) The instruments set out in the Schedule (revocations) shall be revoked to the extent specified.

### Interpretation

**2.**—(1) In these Regulations— A9-002

["EU trade mark court" means a court designated by regulation 12;]

"international application" means an application to the International Bureau for registration of a trade mark in the International Register;

"international application designating the European [Union]" means an international application in which a request has been made for extension of protection to [the European Union] under Article 3ter (1) of the Madrid Protocol;

"International Register" means the register of trade marks maintained by the International Bureau for the purposes of the Madrid Protocol;

"international registration" means the registration of a trade mark in the International Register;

"international registration designating the European [Union]" means an international registration in relation to which a request has been made (either in the relevant international application or subsequently) for extension of protection to the European [Union] under Article 3ter (1) or (2) of the Madrid Protocol.

(2) In regulations 3 to 9, a reference to a [European Union trade mark] includes a reference to an international trade mark (EC), and in that case—

- (a) a reference to a revocation or declaration of invalidity of the mark is a reference to a revocation or declaration of invalidity of the protection of the mark;
- (b) a reference to the goods or services for which the mark is registered is a reference to the goods or services in respect of which the mark is protected.

(3) In these Regulations "the Act" means the Trade Marks Act 1994, and any reference to a section is, unless the context otherwise requires, a reference to a section of that Act.

**Determination of invalidity and liability to revocation in relation to claims of seniority**

A9-003 **3.**—(1) Where the proprietor of a [European Union trade mark] claims the seniority of a registered trade mark which—

(a) has been removed from the register under section 43, or

(b) has been surrendered under section 45, any person may apply to the registrar or to the court for the declaration set out in paragraph (3).

(2) Where such a proprietor claims the seniority of an international trade mark (UK) which has been removed from the International Register or surrendered, any person may apply to the registrar or to the court for the declaration set out in paragraph (3).

(3) The declaration is that if the trade mark had not been so removed or surrendered, it would have been liable [as at the date of such removal or surrender] to be revoked under section 46 or declared invalid under section 47.

(4) An address for service in the United Kingdom shall be filed by—

(a) the person making an application under paragraph (1) or (2); and

(b) the proprietor of the [European Union trade mark],

unless in a particular case the registrar otherwise directs.

(5) Where the trade mark has been surrendered in respect of some only of the goods or services for which it is registered (or protected), paragraph (1) or (2) shall apply in relation to those goods or services only.

**Procedure for declaration that trade mark would have been liable to be revoked or declared invalid**

A9-004 **4.**—(1) In proceedings on an application under regulation 3(1) or (2) the registration of a person as proprietor of a trade mark shall be prima facie evidence of the validity of the original registration.

(2) In the case of such proceedings before the registrar, the provisions of [rules 38 to 43, 45, 62 to 79 and 82 of the Trade Marks Rules 2008], with necessary modifications, shall apply.

(3) In the case of such proceedings before the court, the registrar is entitled to appear and be heard, and shall appear if so directed by the court.

(4) Unless otherwise directed by the court, the registrar may instead of appearing submit to the court a statement in writing signed by him, giving particulars of—

(a) any proceedings before him in relation to the matter in issue,

(b) the grounds of any decision given by him affecting it,

(c) he practice of the Patent Office in like cases, or

(d) such matters relevant to the issues and within his knowledge as registrar as he thinks fit;

and the statement shall be deemed to form part of the evidence in the proceedings.

(5) Anything which the registrar is or may be authorised or required to do under this regulation may be done on his behalf by a duly authorised officer.

**Remedies in infringement proceedings**

A9-005 **5.**—(1) This regulation is without prejudice to the duties of the [EU trade mark court] under [Article 130(1)] of the [European Union Trade Mark Regulation].

(2) In an action for infringement of a [European Union trade mark] all such relief by way of damages, injunctions, accounts or otherwise is available to the proprietor of the [European Union trade mark] as is available in respect of the infringement of any other property right.

(3) The provisions of sections 15 to 19 apply in relation to a [European Union trade mark] as they apply to a registered trade mark; and any reference to the court shall be construed as meaning the [EU trade mark court].

### [Unjustified threats]

**6.**—(1) The provisions of [sections 21 to 21D and section 21F] apply in relation to a [European Union trade mark] as they apply to a registered trade mark. **A9-006**

[(1A) In the application of sections 21 and 21B in relation to a European Union trade mark, references to a registered trade mark are to be treated as references to a European Union trade mark in respect of which an application has been published in accordance with Article 39 of the European Union Trade Mark Regulation.

(1B) In the application of section 21C in relation to a European Union trade mark in a case where the threat of infringement proceedings is made after an application has been published (but before registration) the reference in section 21C(2) to "the registered trade mark" is to be treated as a reference to the European Union trade mark registered in pursuance of that application.]

[(2) In the application of sections 21 and 21B in relation to an international trade mark (EC), references to a registered trade mark are to be treated as references to an international trade mark (EC) in respect of which particulars of an international registration designating the European Union have been published in accordance with Article 152 of the European Union Trade Mark Regulation.

(3) In the application of section 21C in relation to an international trade mark (EC) in a case where the threat of infringement proceedings is made after particulars have been published (but before registration) the reference in section 21C(2) to "the registered trade mark" is to be treated as a reference to the international trade mark (EC) registered in pursuance of those particulars.]

### Importation of infringing goods, material or articles

**7.**—(1) The provisions of— **A9-007**

(a) section 89 (infringing goods, material or articles may be treated as prohibited goods);

(b) section 90 and section 91 (power of Commissioners of Customs and Excise to disclose information), apply in relation to a [European Union trade mark] as they apply in relation to a registered trade mark.

(2) The Trade Marks (Customs) Regulations 1994 shall apply in relation to notices given under section 89 as applied by paragraph (1).

### Offences and forfeiture

**8.**—(1) The provisions of— **A9-008**

(a) section 92 (unauthorised use of trade mark, etc, in relation to goods);

(b) section 92A (search warrants);

(c) section 93 (enforcement function of local weights and measures authority);

(d) section 97 (forfeiture: England and Wales or Northern Ireland); and

(e) section 98 (forfeiture: Scotland),

apply in relation to a [European Union trade mark] as they apply in relation to a registered trade mark.

(2) For the purposes of those provisions, references to goods in respect of which a trade mark is registered shall include goods in respect of which an international trade mark (EC) confers protection in [the European Union].

**Falsely representing trade mark as a [European Union trade mark]**

A9-009 **9.**—(1) It is an offence for a person—

(a) falsely to represent that a mark is a [European Union trade mark], or

(b) to make a false representation as to the goods or services for which a [European Union trade mark] is registered,

knowing or having reason to believe that the representation is false.

(2) A person guilty of an offence under this regulation is liable on summary conviction to a fine not exceeding level 3 on the standard scale.

**Conversion**

A9-010 **10.**—(1) This regulation applies where, pursuant to [Article 139] of the [European Union Trade Mark Regulation] —

(a) the applicant for or the proprietor of a [European Union trade mark] requests the conversion of his [European Union trade mark] application or [European Union trade mark] into an application for registration of a trade mark under the Act; or

(b) the holder of an international registration designating [the European Union] requests (in accordance with [Article 202(1)(a)] of that Regulation) the conversion of that designation into an application for registration of a trade mark under the Act.

(2) Where the request has been transmitted to the registrar under [Article 140(5)] of the [European Union Trade Mark Regulation], it shall be treated as an application for registration of a trade mark under the Act.

(3) A decision of the registrar in relation to the request shall be treated as a decision of the registrar under the Act.

**Privilege for communications with those on the list of professional trade marks representatives**

A9-011 **11.**—(1) This regulation applies to communications as to any matter relating to the protection of any trade mark or as to any matter involving passing off.

(2) Any such communication—

(a) between a person and his professional trade marks representative, or

(b) for the purposes of obtaining, or in response to a request for, information which a person is seeking for the purpose of instructing his professional trade marks representative,

is privileged from, or in Scotland protected against, disclosure in legal proceedings in the same way as a communication between a person and his solicitor or, as the case may be, a communication for the purpose of obtaining, or in response to a request for, information which a person is seeking for the purpose of instructing his solicitor.

(3) In paragraph (2) a person's "professional trade marks representative" means a person who is retained by him and is on the special list of professional representatives for trade marks matters referred to in [Article 120] of the [European Union Trade Mark Regulation].

**Designation of [EU trade mark courts]**

**12.**—(1) [For the purposes of [Article 123(1)] of the European Union Trade Mark Regulation, the following courts are designated as EU trade mark courts] — **A9-012**

(a) in England and Wales—
  (i) the High Court; [and]
  (ii) [...]
  (iii) the county courts listed in paragraph (2);
(b) in Scotland, the Court of Session; and
(c) in Northern Ireland, the High Court.

(2) The county courts referred to in paragraph (1)(a)(iii) are the county courts at—

(a) Birmingham;
(b) Bristol;
(c) Cardiff;
(d) Leeds;
(e) Liverpool;
(f) Manchester; and
(g) Newcastle upon Tyne.

(3) For the purpose of hearing appeals from judgments of the courts designated by paragraph (1), the following courts are also designated as Community trade mark courts—

(a) in England and Wales, the Court of Appeal;
(b) in Scotland, the Court of Session; and
(c) in Northern Ireland, the Court of Appeal.

*Barry Gardiner*

Minister for Competitiveness Department of Trade and Industry

5th April 2006

APPENDIX 10

## REGULATION (EU) NO.1151/2012 OF THE EUROPEAN PARLIAMENT AND OF THE COUNCIL

*Replace with:*

A10-001 **of 21 November 2012**

**on quality schemes for agricultural products and foodstuffs**

Retained and amended EU legislation:

THE EUROPEAN PARLIAMENT AND THE COUNCIL OF THE EUROPEAN UNION,

Having regard to the Treaty on the Functioning of the European Union, and in particular Article 43(2) and the first paragraph of Article 118 thereof,

Having regard to the proposal from the European Commission,

After transmission of the draft legislative act to the national parliaments,

Having regard to the opinion of the European Economic and Social Committee[1],

Having regard to the opinion of the Committee of the Regions[2],

Acting in accordance with the ordinary legislative procedure[3],

Whereas:

**(1)** The quality and diversity of the Union's agricultural, fisheries and aquaculture production is one of its important strengths, giving a competitive advantage to the Union's producers and making a major contribution to its living cultural and gastronomic heritage. This is due to the skills and determination of Union farmers and producers who have kept traditions alive while taking into account the developments of new production methods and material.

**(2)** Citizens and consumers in the Union increasingly demand quality as well as traditional products. They are also concerned to maintain the diversity of the agricultural production in the Union. This generates a demand for agricultural products or foodstuffs with identifiable specific characteristics, in particular those linked to their geographical origin.

**(3)** Producers can only continue to produce a diverse range of quality products if they are rewarded fairly for their effort. This requires that they are able to communicate to buyers and consumers the characteristics of their product under conditions of fair competition. It also requires them to be able to correctly identify their products on the marketplace.

---

1 OJ C 218, 23.7.2011, p. 114.

2 OJ C 192, 1.7.2011, p. 28.

3 Position of the European Parliament of 13 September 2012 (not yet published in the Official Journal) and decision of the Council of 13 November 2012.

**(4)** Operating quality schemes for producers which reward them for their efforts to produce a diverse range of quality products can benefit the rural economy. This is particularly the case in less favoured areas, in mountain areas and in the most remote regions, where the farming sector accounts for a significant part of the economy and production costs are high. In this way quality schemes are able to contribute to and complement rural development policy as well as market and income support policies of the common agricultural policy (CAP). In particular, they may contribute to areas in which the farming sector is of greater economic importance and, especially, to disadvantaged areas.
**(5)** The Europe 2020 policy priorities as set out in the Commission Communication entitled 'Europe 2020: A strategy for smart, sustainable and inclusive growth', include the aims of achieving a competitive economy based on knowledge and innovation and fostering a high-employment economy delivering social and territorial cohesion. Agricultural product quality policy should therefore provide producers with the right tools to better identify and promote those of their products that have specific characteristics while protecting those producers against unfair practices.
**(6)** The set of complementary measures envisaged should respect the principles of subsidiarity and proportionality.
**(7)** Agricultural product quality policy measures are laid down in Council Regulation (EEC) No 1601/91 of 10 June 1991 laying down general rules on the definition, description and presentation of aromatized wines, aromatized wine-based drinks and aromatized wine-product cocktails[4]; Council Directive 2001/110/EC of 20 December 2001 relating to honey[5] and in particular in Article 2 thereof, Council Regulation (EC) No 247/2006 of 30 January 2006 laying down specific measures for agriculture in the outermost regions of the Union[6] and in particular in Article 14 thereof; Council Regulation (EC) No 509/2006 of 20 March 2006 on agricultural products and foodstuffs as traditional specialities guaranteed[7]; Council Regulation (EC) No 510/2006 of 20 March 2006 on the protection of geographical indications and designations of origin for agricultural products and foodstuffs[8]; Council Regulation (EC) No 1234/2007 of 22 October 2007 establishing a common organisation of agricultural markets and on specific provisions for certain agricultural products (Single CMO Regulation)[9] and in particular in Part II, Title II, Chapter I, Section I and in Section Ia, Subsection I thereof; Council Regulation (EC) No 834/2007 of 28 June 2007 on organic production and labelling of organic products[10]; and Regulation (EC) No 110/2008 of the European Parliament and of the Council of 15 January 2008 on the definition, description, presentation, labelling and the protection of geographical indications of spirit drinks[11].
**(8)** The labelling of agricultural products and foodstuffs should be subject to the general rules laid down in Directive 2000/13/EC of the European Parliament and of the Council of 20 March 2000 on the approximation of the laws of the Member

---

[4] OJ L 149, 14.6.1991, p. 1.
[5] OJ L 10, 12.1.2002, p. 47.
[6] OJ L 42, 14.2.2006, p. 1.
[7] OJ L 93, 31.3.2006, p. 1.
[8] OJ L 93, 31.3.2006, p. 12.
[9] OJ L 299, 16.11.2007, p. 1.
[10] OJ L 189, 20.7.2007, p. 1.
[11] OJ L 39, 13.2.2008, p. 16.

States relating to the labelling, presentation and advertising of foodstuffs[12], and in particular the provisions aimed at preventing labelling that may confuse or mislead consumers.

**(9)** The Communication from the Commission to the European Parliament, the Council, the European Economic and Social Committee and the Committee of the Regions on agricultural product quality policy identified the achievement of a greater overall coherence and consistency of agricultural product quality policy as a priority.

**(10)** The geographical indications scheme for agricultural products and foodstuffs and the traditional specialities guaranteed scheme have certain common objectives and provisions.

**(11)** The Union has for some time been pursuing an approach that aims to simplify the regulatory framework of the CAP. This approach should also be applied to regulations in the field of agricultural product quality policy, without, in so doing, calling into question the specific characteristics of those products.

**(12)** Some regulations that form part of the agricultural product quality policy have been reviewed recently but are not yet fully implemented. As a result, they should not be included in this Regulation. However, they may be incorporated at a later stage, once the legislation has been fully implemented.

**(13)** In the light of the aforementioned considerations, the following provisions should be amalgamated into a single legal framework comprising the new or updated provisions of Regulations (EC) No 509/2006 and (EC) No 510/2006 and those provisions of Regulations (EC) No 509/2006 and (EC) No 510/2006 that are maintained.

**(14)** In the interests of clarity and transparency, Regulations (EC) No 509/2006 and (EC) No 510/2006 should therefore be repealed and replaced by this Regulation.

**(15)** The scope of this Regulation should be limited to the agricultural products intended for human consumption listed in Annex I to the Treaty and to a list of products outside the scope of that Annex that are closely linked to agricultural production or to the rural economy.

**(16)** The rules provided for in this Regulation should apply without affecting existing Union legislation on wines, aromatised wines, spirit drinks, product of organic farming, or outermost regions.

**(17)** The scope for designations of origin and geographical indications should be limited to products for which an intrinsic link exists between product or foodstuff characteristics and geographical origin. The inclusion in the current scheme of only certain types of chocolate as confectionery products is an anomaly that should be corrected.

**(18)** The specific objectives of protecting designations of origin and geographical indications are securing a fair return for farmers and producers for the qualities and characteristics of a given product, or of its mode of production, and providing clear information on products with specific characteristics linked to geographical origin, thereby enabling consumers to make more informed purchasing choices.

**(19)** Ensuring uniform respect throughout the Union for the intellectual property rights related to names protected in the Union is a priority that can be achieved more effectively at Union level.

---

12 OJ L 109, 6.5.2000, p. 29.

**(20)** A Union framework that protects designations of origin and geographical indications by providing for their inclusion on a register facilitates the development of those instruments, since the resulting, more uniform, approach ensures fair competition between the producers of products bearing such indications and enhances the credibility of the products in the consumers' eyes. Provision should be made for the development of designations of origin and geographical indications at Union level and for promoting the creation of mechanisms for their protection in third countries in the framework of the World Trade Organisation (WTO) or multilateral and bilateral agreements, thereby contributing to the recognition of the quality of products and of their model of production as a factor that adds value.
**(21)** In the light of the experience gained from the implementation of Council Regulation (EEC) No 2081/92 of 14 July 1992 on the protection of geographical indications and designations of origin for agricultural products and foodstuffs[13] and Regulation (EC) No 510/2006, there is a need to address certain issues, to clarify and simplify some rules and to streamline the procedures of this scheme.
**(22)** In the light of existing practice, the two different instruments for identifying the link between the product and its geographical origin, namely the protected designation of origin and the protected geographical indication, should be further defined and maintained. Without changing the concept of those instruments, some modifications to the definitions should be adopted in order to better take into account the definition of geographical indications laid down in the Agreement on Trade-Related Aspects of Intellectual Property Rights and to make them simpler and clearer for operators to understand.
**(23)** An agricultural product or foodstuff bearing such a geographical description should meet certain conditions set out in a specification, such as specific requirements aimed at protecting the natural resources or landscape of the production area or improving the welfare of farm animals.
**(24)** To qualify for protection in the territories of Member States, designations of origin and geographical indications should be registered only at Union level. With effect from the date of application for such registration at Union level, Member States should be able to grant transitional protection at national level without affecting intra-Union or international trade. The protection afforded by this Regulation upon registration, should be equally available to designations of origin and geographical indications of third countries that meet the corresponding criteria and that are protected in their country of origin.
**(25)** The registration procedure at Union level should enable any natural or legal person with a legitimate interest from a Member State, other than the Member State of the application, or from a third country, to exercise their rights by notifying their opposition.
**(26)** Entry in the register of protected designations of origin and protected geographical indications should also provide information to consumers and to those involved in trade.
**(27)** The Union negotiates international agreements, including those concerning the protection of designations of origin and geographical indications, with its trade partners. In order to facilitate the provision to the public of information about the names so protected, and in particular to ensure protection and control of the use to which those names are put, the names may be entered in the register of protected

---

[13] OJ L 208, 24.7.1992, p. 1.

designations of origin and protected geographical indications. Unless specifically identified as designations of origin in such international agreements, the names should be entered in the register as protected geographical indications.

**(28)** In view of their specific nature, special provisions concerning labelling should be adopted in respect of protected designations of origin and protected geographical indications that require producers to use the appropriate Union symbols or indications on packaging. In the case of Union names, the use of such symbols or indications should be made obligatory in order to make this category of products, and the guarantees attached to them, better known to consumers and in order to permit easier identification of these products on the market, thereby facilitating checks. Taking into account the requirements of the WTO, the use of such symbols or indications should be made voluntary for third-country geographical indications and designations of origin.

**(29)** Protection should be granted to names included in the register with the aim of ensuring that they are used fairly and in order to prevent practices liable to mislead consumers. In addition, the means of ensuring that geographical indications and designations of origin are protected should be clarified, particularly as regards the role of producer groups and competent authorities of Member States.

**(30)** Provision should be made for specific derogations that permit, for transitional periods, the use of a registered name alongside other names. Those derogations should be simplified and clarified. In certain cases, in order to overcome temporary difficulties and with the long-term objective of ensuring that all producers comply with the specifications, those derogations may be granted for a period of up to 10 years.

**(31)** The scope of the protection granted under this Regulation should be clarified, in particular with regard to those limitations on registration of new trade marks set out in Directive 2008/95/EC of the European Parliament and of the Council of 22 October 2008 to approximate the laws of the Member States relating to trade marks[14] that conflict with the registration of protected designations of origin and protected geographical indications as is already the case for the registration of new trade marks at Union level. Such clarification is also necessary with regard to the holders of prior rights in intellectual property, in particular those concerning trade marks and homonymous names registered as protected designations of origin or as protected geographical indications.

**(32)** Protection of designations of origin and geographical indications should be extended to the misuse, imitation and evocation of the registered names on goods as well as on services in order to ensure a high level of protection and to align that protection with that which applies to the wine sector. When protected designations of origin or protected geographical indications are used as ingredients, the Commission Communication entitled 'Guidelines on the labelling of foodstuffs using protected designations of origin (PDOs) or protected geographical indications (PGIs) as ingredients' should be taken into account.

**(33)** The names already registered under Regulation (EC) No 510/2006 on 3 January 2013 should continue to be protected under this Regulation and they should be automatically included in the register.

**(34)** The specific objective of the scheme for traditional specialities guaranteed is to help the producers of traditional products to communicate to consumers the

[14] OJ L 299, 8.11.2008, p. 25.

value-adding attributes of their product. However, as only a few names have been registered, the current scheme for traditional specialities guaranteed has failed to realise its potential. Current provisions should therefore be improved, clarified and sharpened in order to make the scheme more understandable, operational and attractive to potential applicants.

**(35)** The current scheme provides the option to register a name for identification purposes without reservation of the name in the Union. As this option has not been well understood by stakeholders and since the function of identifying traditional products can be better achieved at Member State or regional level in application of the principle of subsidiarity, this option should be discontinued. In the light of experience, the scheme should only deal with the reservation of names across the Union.

**(36)** To ensure that names of genuine traditional products are registered under the scheme, the criteria and conditions for registration of a name should be adapted, in particular those concerning the definition of 'traditional', which should cover products that have been produced for a significant period of time.

**(37)** To ensure that traditional specialities guaranteed comply with their specification and are consistent, producers organised into groups should themselves define the product in a specification. The option of registering a name as a traditional speciality guaranteed should be open to third-country producers.

**(38)** To qualify for reservation, traditional specialities guaranteed should be registered at Union level. The entry in the register should also provide information to consumers and to those involved in the trade.

**(39)** In order to avoid creating unfair conditions of competition, any producer, including a third-country producer, should be able to use a registered name of a traditional speciality guaranteed, provided that the product concerned complies with the requirements of the relevant specification and the producer is covered by a system of controls. For traditional specialities guaranteed produced within the Union, the Union symbol should be indicated on the labelling and it should be possible to associate it with the indication 'traditional speciality guaranteed'.

**(40)** In order to protect registered names from misuse, or from practices that might mislead consumers, their use should be reserved.

**(41)** For those names already registered under Regulation (EC) No 509/2006 that, on 3 January 2013, would otherwise not be covered by the scope of this Regulation, the terms of use laid down in Regulation (EC) No 509/2006 should continue to apply for a transitional period.

**(42)** A procedure should be introduced for registering names that are registered without reservation of name pursuant to Regulation (EC) No 509/2006, enabling them to be registered with reservation of name.

**(43)** Provision should also be made for transitional measures applicable to registration applications received by the Commission before 3 January 2013.

**(44)** A second tier of quality systems, based on quality terms which add value, which can be communicated on the internal market and which are to be applied voluntarily, should be introduced. Those optional quality terms should refer to specific horizontal characteristics, with regard to one or more categories of products, farming methods or processing attributes which apply in specific areas. The optional quality term 'mountain product' has met the conditions up to now and will add value to the product on the market. In order to facilitate the application of Directive 2000/13/EC where the labelling of foodstuffs may give rise to consumer confusion in relation to optional quality terms, including in particular 'mountain products', the Commission may adopt guidelines.

**(45)** In order to provide mountain producers with an effective tool to better market their product and to reduce the actual risks of consumer confusion as to the mountain provenance of products in the market place, provision should be made for the definition at Union level of an optional quality term for mountain products. The definition of mountain areas should build on the general classification criteria employed to identify a mountain area in Council Regulation (EC) No 1257/1999 of 17 May 1999 on support for rural development from the European Agricultural Guidance and Guarantee Fund (EAGGF)[15].

**(46)** The added value of the geographical indications and traditional specialities guaranteed is based on consumer trust. It is only credible if accompanied by effective verification and controls. Those quality schemes should be subject to a monitoring system of official controls, in line with the principles set out in Regulation (EC) No 882/2004 of the European Parliament and of the Council of 29 April 2004 on official controls performed to ensure the verification of compliance with feed and food law, animal health and animal welfare rules[16], and should include a system of checks at all stages of production, processing and distribution. In order to help Member States to better apply provisions of Regulation (EC) No 882/2004 for the controls of geographical indications and traditional specialities guaranteed, references to the most relevant articles should be mentioned in this Regulation.

**(47)** To guarantee to the consumer the specific characteristics of geographical indications and traditional specialities guaranteed, operators should be subject to a system that verifies compliance with the product specification.

**(48)** In order to ensure that they are impartial and effective, the competent authorities should meet a number of operational criteria. Provisions on delegating some competences of performing specific control tasks to control bodies should be envisaged.

**(49)** European standards (EN standards) developed by the European Committee for Standardisation (CEN) and international standards developed by the International Organisation for Standardisation (ISO) should be used for the accreditation of the control bodies as well as by those bodies for their operations. The accreditation of those bodies should take place in accordance with Regulation (EC) No 765/2008 of the European Parliament and of the Council of 9 July 2008 setting out the requirements for accreditation and market surveillance relating to the marketing of products[17].

**(50)** Information on control activities for geographical indications and traditional specialities guaranteed should be included in the multiannual national control plans and annual report prepared by the Member States in accordance with Regulation (EC) No 882/2004.

**(51)** Member States should be authorised to charge a fee to cover the costs incurred.

**(52)** Existing rules concerning the continued use of names that are generic should be clarified so that generic terms that are similar to or form part of a name or term that is protected or reserved should retain their generic status.

**(53)** The date for establishing the seniority of a trade mark and of a designation of origin or a geographical indication should be that of the date of application of the trade mark for registration in the Union or in the Member States and the date

---

15 OJ L 160, 26.6.1999, p. 80.

16 OJ L 165, 30.4.2004, p. 1.

17 OJ L 218, 13.8.2008, p. 30.

of application for protection of a designation of origin or a geographical indication to the Commission.

**(54)** The provisions dealing with the refusal or coexistence of a designation of origin or a geographical indication on the ground of conflict with a prior trade mark should continue to apply.

**(55)** The criteria by which subsequent trade marks should be refused or, if registered, invalidated on the ground that they conflict with a prior designation of origin or geographical indication should correspond to the scope of protection of designation of origin or a geographical indication laid down.

**(56)** The provisions of systems establishing intellectual property rights, and particularly of those established by the quality scheme for designations of origin and geographical indications or those established under trade mark law, should not be affected by the reservation of names and the establishment of indications and symbols pursuant to the quality schemes for traditional specialities guaranteed and for optional quality terms.

**(57)** The role of groups should be clarified and recognised. Groups play an essential role in the application process for the registration of names of designations of origin and geographical indications and traditional specialities guaranteed, as well as in the amendment of specifications and cancellation requests. The group can also develop activities related to the surveillance of the enforcement of the protection of the registered names, the compliance of the production with the product specification, the information and promotion of the registered name as well as, in general, any activity aimed at improving the value of the registered names and effectiveness of the quality schemes. Moreover, it should monitor the position of the products on the market. Nevertheless, these activities should not facilitate nor lead to anti-competitive conduct incompatible with Articles 101 and 102 of the Treaty.

**(58)** To ensure that registered names of designations of origin and geographical indications and traditional specialities guaranteed meet the conditions laid down by this Regulation, applications should be examined by the national authorities of the Member State concerned, in compliance with minimum common provisions, including a national opposition procedure. The Commission should subsequently scrutinise applications to ensure that there are no manifest errors and that Union law and the interests of stakeholders outside the Member State of application have been taken into account.

**(59)** Registration as designations of origin, geographical indications and traditional specialities guaranteed should be open to names that relate to products originating in third countries and that satisfy the conditions laid down by this Regulation.

**(60)** The symbols, indications and abbreviations identifying participation in a quality scheme, and the rights therein pertaining to the Union, should be protected in the Union as well as in third countries with the aim of ensuring that they are used on genuine products and that consumers are not misled as to the qualities of products. Furthermore, in order for the protection to be effective, the Commission should have recourse to reasonable budget resources on a centralised basis within the framework of Council Regulation (EC) No 1698/2005 of 20 September 2005 on support for rural development by the European Agricultural Fund for Rural

Development (EAFRD)[18] and in accordance with Article 5 of Council Regulation (EC) No 1290/2005 of 21 June 2005 on the financing of the common agricultural policy[19].

**(61)** The registration procedure for protected designations of origin, protected geographical indications and traditional specialities guaranteed, including the scrutiny and the opposition periods, should be shortened and improved, in particular as regards decision making. The Commission, in certain circumstances acting with the assistance of Member States, should be responsible for decision-making on registration. Procedures should be laid down to allow the amendment of product specifications after registration and the cancellation of registered names, in particular if the product no longer complies with the corresponding product specification or if a name is no longer used in the market place.

**(62)** In order to facilitate cross-border applications for joint registration of protected designations of origin, protected geographical indications or traditional specialities guaranteed, provision should be made for appropriate procedures.

**(63)** In order to supplement or amend certain non-essential elements of this Regulation, the power to adopt acts in accordance with Article 290 of the Treaty should be delegated to the Commission in respect of supplementing the list of products set out in Annex I to this Regulation; establishing the restrictions and derogations with regard to the sourcing of feed in the case of a designation of origin; establishing restrictions and derogations with regard to the slaughtering of live animals or with regard to the sourcing of raw materials; laying down rules which limit the information contained in the product specification; establishing the Union symbols; laying down additional transitional rules in order to protect the rights and legitimate interests of producers or stakeholders concerned; laying down further details on the eligibility criteria for the names of traditional specialities guaranteed; laying down detailed rules relating to the criteria for optional quality terms; reserving an additional optional quality term, laying down its conditions of use and amending those conditions; laying down derogations to the use of the term 'mountain product' and establishing the methods of production, and other criteria relevant for the application of that optional quality term, in particular, laying down the conditions under which raw materials or feedstuffs are permitted to come from outside the mountain areas; laying down additional rules for determining the generic status of terms in the Union; laying down rules for determining the use of the name of a plant variety or of an animal breed; defining the rules for carrying out the national objection procedure for joint applications concerning more than one national territory; and for complementing the rules of the application process, the opposition process, the amendment application process and the cancellation process in general. It is of particular importance that the Commission carry out appropriate consultations during its preparatory work, including at expert level. The Commission, when preparing and drawing up delegated acts, should ensure a simultaneous, timely and appropriate transmission of relevant documents to the European Parliament and to the Council.

**(64)** In order to ensure uniform conditions for the implementation of this Regulation, implementing powers should be conferred on the Commission as regards laying down rules on the form of the product specification; laying down detailed rules on the form and content of the register of protected designations of origin and

---

18 OJ L 277, 21.10.2005, p. 1.
19 OJ L 209, 11.8.2005, p. 1.

protected geographical indications; defining the technical characteristics of the Union symbols and indications as well as the rules on their use on products, including the appropriate linguistic versions to be used; granting and extending transitional periods for temporary derogations for use of protected designations of origin and protected geographical indication; laying down detailed rules on the form and content of the register of traditional specialities guaranteed; laying down rules for the protection of traditional specialities guaranteed; laying down all measures relating to forms, procedures and other technical details for the application of Title IV; laying down rules for the use of optional quality terms; laying down rules for the uniform protection of indications, abbreviations and symbols referring to the quality schemes; laying down detailed rules on the procedure, form and presentation of applications for registration and of oppositions; rejecting the application; deciding on the registration of a name if an agreement has not been reached; laying down detailed rules on the procedure, form and presentation of an amendment application; cancelling the registration of a protected designation of origin, a protected geographical indication or a traditional speciality guaranteed; and laying down detailed rules on the procedure and form of the cancellation process and on the presentation of the requests for cancellation. Those powers should be exercised in accordance with Regulation (EU) No 182/2011 of the European Parliament and of the Council of 16 February 2011 laying down the rules and general principles concerning mechanisms for control by Member States of the Commission's exercise of implementing powers[20].

**(65)** In respect of establishing and maintaining registers of protected designations of origin, protected geographical indications and traditional specialties guaranteed, recognised under this scheme; defining the means by which the name and address of product certification bodies are to be made public; and registering a name if there is no notice of opposition or no admissible reasoned statement of opposition or in the case there is one the agreement has been reached, the Commission should be empowered to adopt implementing acts without applying Regulation (EU) No 182/2011,

HAVE ADOPTED THIS REGULATION:

## TITLE I

## GENERAL PROVISIONS

### *Article 1*

### Objectives

**1.** This Regulation aims to help producers of agricultural products and foodstuffs to communicate the product characteristics and farming attributes of those products and foodstuffs to buyers and consumers, thereby ensuring: **A10-002**

(a) fair competition for farmers and producers of agricultural products and foodstuffs having value-adding characteristics and attributes;
(b) the availability to consumers of reliable information pertaining to such products; and

[20] OJ L 55, 28.2.2011, p. 13.

(c) respect for intellectual property rights;

The measures set out in this Regulation are intended to support agricultural and processing activities and the farming systems associated with high quality products, thereby contributing to the achievement of rural development policy objectives.

**2.** This Regulation establishes quality schemes which provide the basis for the identification and, where appropriate, protection of names and terms that, in particular, indicate or describe agricultural products with:

(a) value-adding characteristics; or

(b) value-adding attributes as a result of the farming or processing methods used in their production, or of the place of their production or marketing.

*Article 2*

**Scope**

**A10-003** **1.** This Regulation covers agricultural products intended for human consumption listed in Annex I to the Treaty and other agricultural products and foodstuffs listed in Annex I to this Regulation.

In order to take into account international commitments or new production methods or material, the Secretary of State may make regulations supplementing the list of products set out in Annex I to this Regulation. Such products shall be closely linked to agricultural products or to the rural economy.

**2.** This Regulation shall not apply to spirit drinks, aromatised wines or grapevine products as defined in Part 2 of Annex 7 to Regulation 1308/2013, with the exception of wine-vinegars.

**3.** This Regulation shall apply without prejudice to other specific provisions in retained EU law relating to the placing of products on the market and, in particular, to provisions in, or under, Regulation 1308/2013 and provisions relating to food labelling.

*Article 3*

**Definitions**

**A10-004** For the purposes of this Regulation the following definitions shall apply:

(1) 'quality schemes' means the schemes established under Titles II, III and IV;

(2) 'group' means any association, irrespective of its legal form, mainly composed of producers or processors working with the same product;

(3) 'traditional' means proven usage on the domestic market for a period that allows transmission between generations; this period is to be at least 30 years;

(4) 'labelling' means any words, particulars, trade marks, brand name, pictorial matter or symbol relating to a foodstuff and placed on any packaging, document, notice, label, ring or collar accompanying or referring to such foodstuff;

(5) 'specific character' in relation to a product means the characteristic production attributes which distinguish a product clearly from other similar products of the same category;

(6) 'generic terms ' means the names of products which, although relating to the place, region or country where the product was originally produced or

marketed, have become the common name of a product in the United Kingdom;

(7) 'production step' means production, processing or preparation;

(8) 'processed products' means foodstuffs resulting from the processing of unprocessed products. Processed products may contain ingredients that are necessary for their manufacture or to give them specific characteristics.

[(9) 'the EUWA' means the European Union (Withdrawal) Act 2018;

(10) 'EU Regulation 1151/2012' means Regulation (EU) No 1151/2012 of the European Parliament and of the Council on quality schemes for agricultural products and foodstuffs as it had effect in EU law immediately before exit day;

(11) 'Regulation 1308/2013' means Regulation (EU) No 1308/2013 of the European Parliament and of the Council establishing a common organisation of the markets in agricultural products;

(12) 'Regulation 664/2014' means Commission Delegated Regulation (EU) No 664/2014 supplementing Regulation (EU) No 1151/2012 of the European Parliament and of the Council with regard to the establishment of the Union symbols for protected designations of origin, protected geographical indications and traditional specialities guaranteed and with regard to certain rules on sourcing, certain procedural rules and certain additional transitional rules;

(13) 'the Quality Schemes Regulations' means the Quality Schemes (Agricultural Products and Foodstuffs) Regulations 2018;

(14) 'the competent authority', in relation to the United Kingdom, means the person specified in regulation 3(1) of the Quality Schemes Regulations;

(15) 'the designated authority' means:

(a) unless point (b) or (c) applies, the person specified in regulation 3(2) of the Quality Schemes Regulations as the person responsible for carrying out the relevant function;

(b) in a case where an official control has been delegated to a control body in accordance with Article 39, the control body to which the function has been delegated;

(c) in a case where an enforcement authority has been appointed to carry out the function under regulation 6 of the Quality Schemes Regulations, the appointed enforcement authority;

(16) 'domestic law' means the means the law of England and Wales, Scotland and Northern Ireland;

(17) 'enactment' includes:

(a) enactments of the type specified in paragraphs (a) to (f) of the definition of "enactment" in section 20(1) of the EUWA, and

(b) except in Article 28, retained direct EU legislation;

(18) 'established protected designation of origin' means a designation of origin shown as a United Kingdom registered designation of origin on the register maintained by the European Commission pursuant to Article 11 of EU Regulation 1151/2012 as that register stood immediately before exit day;

(19) 'established protected geographical indication' means a geographical indication shown as a registered United Kingdom geographical indication on the register maintained by the European Commission pursuant to Article 11 of EU Regulation 1151/2012 as that register stood immediately before exit day;

(20) 'established protected traditional speciality guaranteed' means a traditional

speciality guaranteed shown as a registered United Kingdom traditional speciality guaranteed on the register maintained by the European Commission pursuant to Article 22 of EU Regulation 1151/2012 as that register stood immediately before exit day;

(21) 'FTT' means the First-tier Tribunal;

(22) 'third country' means any country, other than the United Kingdom, and includes:

(a)the Bailiwick of Guernsey;

(b)the Bailiwick of Jersey;

(c)the Isle of Man.]

## TITLE II

## PROTECTED DESIGNATIONS OF ORIGIN AND PROTECTED GEOGRAPHICAL INDICATIONS

*Article 4*

### Objective

A10-005 A scheme for protected designations of origin and protected geographical indications is established in order to help producers of products linked to a geographical area by:

(a) securing fair returns for the qualities of their products;

(b) ensuring uniform protection of the names as an intellectual property right in the territory of the United Kingdom;

(c) providing clear information on the value-adding attributes of the product to consumers.

*Article 5*

### Requirements for designations of origin and geographical indications

A10-006 **1.** For the purpose of this Regulation, 'designation of origin' is a name which identifies a product:

(a) originating in a specific place, region or, in exceptional cases, a country;

(b) whose quality or characteristics are essentially or exclusively due to a particular geographical environment with its inherent natural and human factors; and

(c) the production steps of which all take place in the defined geographical area.

**2.** For the purpose of this Regulation, 'geographical indication' is a name which identifies a product:

(a) originating in a specific place, region or country;

(b) whose given quality, reputation or other characteristic is essentially attributable to its geographical origin; and

(c) at least one of the production steps of which take place in the defined geographical area.

**3.** Notwithstanding paragraph 1, certain names shall be treated as designations of origin even though the raw materials for the products concerned come from a geographical area larger than, or different from, the defined geographical area, provided that:

(a) the production area of the raw materials is defined;
(b) special conditions for the production of the raw materials exist;
(c) there are control arrangements to ensure that the conditions referred to in point (b) are adhered to; and
(d) the designations of origin in question were recognised as designations of origin in the country of origin before 1 May 2004.

Only live animals, meat and milk may be considered as raw materials for the purposes of this paragraph.

**4.** In order to take into account the specific character of production of products of animal origin, the Secretary of State may make regulations concerning restrictions and derogations with regard to the sourcing of feed in the case of a designation of origin.

In addition, in order to take into account the specific character of certain products or areas, the Secretary of State may make regulations concerning restrictions and derogations with regard to the slaughtering of live animals or with regard to the sourcing of raw materials.

These restrictions and derogations shall, based on objective criteria, take into account quality or usage and recognised know-how or natural factors.

*Article 6*

**Generic nature, conflicts with names of plant varieties and animal breeds, with homonyms and trade marks**

**1.** Generic terms shall not be registered as protected designations of origin or protected geographical indications. **A10-007**

**2.** A name may not be registered as a designation of origin or geographical indication where it conflicts with a name of a plant variety or an animal breed and is likely to mislead the consumer as to the true origin of the product.

**3.** A name proposed for registration that is wholly or partially homonymous with a name already entered in the register established under Article 11 may not be registered unless there is sufficient distinction in practice between the conditions of local and traditional usage and presentation of the homonym registered subsequently and the name already entered in the register, taking into account the need to ensure equitable treatment of the producers concerned and that consumers are not misled.

A homonymous name which misleads the consumer into believing that products come from another territory shall not be registered even if the name is accurate as far as the actual territory, region or place of origin of the products in question is concerned.

**4.** A name proposed for registration as a designation of origin or geographical indication shall not be registered where, in the light of a trade mark's reputation and renown and the length of time it has been used, registration of the name proposed as the designation of origin or geographical indication would be liable to mislead the consumer as to the true identity of the product.

*Article 7*

**Product specification**

A10-008 **1.** A protected designation of origin or a protected geographical indication shall comply with a specification which shall include at least:

(a) the name to be protected as a designation of origin or geographical indication, as it is used, whether in trade or in common language, and only in the languages which are or were historically used to describe the specific product in the defined geographical area;

(b) a description of the product, including the raw materials, if appropriate, as well as the principal physical, chemical, microbiological or organoleptic characteristics of the product;

(c) the definition of the geographical area delimited with regard to the link referred to in point (f)(i) or (ii) of this paragraph, and, where appropriate, details indicating compliance with the requirements of Article 5(3);

(d) evidence that the product originates in the defined geographical area referred to in Article 5(1) or (2);

(e) a description of the method of obtaining the product and, where appropriate, the authentic and unvarying local methods as well as information concerning packaging, if the applicant group so determines and gives sufficient product-specific justification as to why the packaging must take place in the defined geographical area to safeguard quality, to ensure the origin or to ensure control;

(f) details establishing the following:

(i) the link between the quality or characteristics of the product and the geographical environment referred to in Article 5(1); or

(ii) where appropriate, the link between a given quality, the reputation or other characteristic of the product and the geographical origin referred to in Article 5(2);

(g) the name and address of the authorities or, if available, the name and address of bodies verifying compliance with the provisions of the product specification pursuant to Article 37 and their specific tasks;

(h) any specific labelling rule for the product in question.

**2.** In order to ensure that product specifications provide relevant and succinct information, the Secretary of State may make regulations laying down rules which limit the information contained in the specification referred to in paragraph 1 of this Article, where such a limitation is necessary to avoid excessively voluminous applications for registration.

The Secretary of State may make regulations laying down rules on the form of the specification.

*Article 8*

**Content of application for registration**

A10-009 **1.** An application for registration of a designation of origin or geographical indication pursuant to Article 49 shall include at least:

(a) the name and address of the applicant group and of the authorities or, if available, bodies verifying compliance with the provisions of the product specification;

(b) the product specification provided for in Article 7;
(c) a single document setting out the following:
(i) the main points of the product specification: the name, a description of the product, including, where appropriate, specific rules concerning packaging and labelling, and a concise definition of the geographical area;
(ii) a description of the link between the product and the geographical environment or geographical origin referred to in Article 5(1) or (2), as the case may be, including, where appropriate, the specific elements of the product description or production method justifying the link.

An application as referred to in Article 49(5) shall, in addition, include proof that the name of the product is protected in its country of origin.

*Article 10*

**Grounds for opposition**

**1.** A reasoned statement of opposition as referred to in Article 51(2) shall be admissible only if it is received by the Secretary of State within the time limit set out in that paragraph and if it: **A10-011**
(a) shows that the conditions referred to in Article 5 and Article 7(1) are not complied with;
(b) shows that the registration of the name proposed would be contrary to Article 6(2), (3) or (4);
(c) shows that the registration of the name proposed would jeopardise the existence of an entirely or partly identical name or of a trade mark or the existence of products which have been legally on the market for at least five years preceding the date of the publication provided for in point (a) of Article 50(2); or
(d) gives details from which it can be concluded that the name for which registration is requested is a generic term.

**2.** The grounds for opposition shall be assessed in relation to the territory of the United Kingdom.

*Article 11*

**Register of protected designations of origin and protected geographical indications**

**1.** The Secretary of State must establish and maintain a publicly accessible updated register of protected designations of origin and protected geographical indications recognised under this scheme. **A10-012**

**2.** Geographical indications pertaining to products of third countries that are protected in the United Kingdom under an international agreement to which the United Kingdom is a contracting party may be entered in the register. Unless specifically identified in the said agreement as protected designations of origin under this Regulation, such names shall be entered in the register as protected geographical indications.

**3.** The Secretary of State may make regulations laying down detailed rules on the form and content of the register.

**4.** The Secretary of State shall make public and regularly update the list of the international agreements referred to in paragraph 2 as well as the list of geographical indications protected under those agreements.

*Article 12*

## Names, symbols and indications

A10-013 **1.** Protected designations of origin and protected geographical indications may be used by any operator marketing a product conforming to the corresponding specification.

**2.** Symbols designed to publicise protected designations of origin and protected geographical indications shall be established.

**3.** In the case of products originating in the Union that are marketed under a protected designation of origin or a protected geographical indication registered in accordance with the procedures laid down in this Regulation, the Union symbols associated with them shall appear on the labelling. In addition, the registered name of the product should appear in the same field of vision. The indications 'protected designation of origin' or 'protected geographical indication' or the corresponding abbreviations 'PDO' or 'PGI' may appear on the labelling.

**4.** In addition, the following may also appear on the labelling: depictions of the geographical area of origin, as referred to in Article 5, and text, graphics or symbols referring to the United Kingdom or third country, as relevant, in which that geographical area of origin is located and/or region in which that geographical area of origin is located.

**5.** Without prejudice to Regulation (EU) No 1169/2011 of the European Parliament and of the Council on the provision of food information to consumers, the collective geographical marks registered under the Trade Marks Act 1994 may be used on labels, together with the protected designation of origin or protected geographical indication.

**6.** In the case of products originating in third countries marketed under a name entered in the register, the indications referred to in paragraph 3 or the symbols associated with them may appear on the labelling.

**7.** In order to ensure that the appropriate information is communicated to the consumer, the Secretary of State may make regulations establishing the symbols.

The Secretary of State may make regulations defining the technical characteristics of the symbols and indications as well as the rules of their use on the products marketed under a protected designation of origin or a protected geographical indication, including rules concerning the appropriate linguistic versions to be used.

*Article 13*

## Protection

A10-014 **1.** Registered names shall be protected against:

(a) any direct or indirect commercial use of a registered name in respect of products not covered by the registration where those products are comparable to the products registered under that name or where using the name exploits the reputation of the protected name, including when those products are used as an ingredient;

(b) any misuse, imitation or evocation, even if the true origin of the products or services is indicated or if the protected name is translated or accompanied by an expression such as 'style', 'type', 'method', 'as produced in', 'imitation' or similar, including when those products are used as an ingredient;

(c) any other false or misleading indication as to the provenance, origin, nature or essential qualities of the product that is used on the inner or outer packaging, advertising material or documents relating to the product concerned, and the packing of the product in a container liable to convey a false impression as to its origin;

(d) any other practice liable to mislead the consumer as to the true origin of the product.

Where a protected designation of origin or a protected geographical indication contains within it the name of a product which is considered to be generic, the use of that generic name shall not be considered to be contrary to points (a) or (b) of the first subparagraph.

**2.** Protected designations of origin and protected geographical indications shall not become generic.

**3.** The designated authority shall take appropriate administrative and judicial steps to prevent or stop the unlawful use of protected designations of origin and protected geographical indications, as referred to in paragraph 1, that are produced or marketed in the United Kingdom.

These authorities shall offer adequate guarantees of objectivity and impartiality, and shall have at their disposal the qualified staff and resources necessary to carry out their functions.

*Article 14*

**Relations between trade marks, designations of origin and geographical indications**

**1.** Where a designation of origin or a geographical indication is registered under this Regulation, the registration of a trade mark the use of which would contravene Article 13(1) and which relates to a product of the same type shall be refused if the application for registration of the trade mark is submitted after the date of submission of the registration application in respect of the designation of origin or the geographical indication to the Secretary of State. **A10-015**

Trade marks registered in breach of the first subparagraph shall be invalidated.

The provisions of this paragraph shall apply notwithstanding the provisions of the Trade Marks Act 1994.

**2.** Without prejudice to Article 6(4), a trade mark the use of which contravenes Article 13(1) which has been applied for, registered, or established by use if that possibility is provided for by the legislation concerned, in good faith within the territory of the Union, before the date on which the application for protection of the designation of origin or geographical indication is submitted to the Commission, may continue to be used and renewed for that product notwithstanding the registration of a designation of origin or geographical indication, provided that no grounds for its invalidity or revocation exist under Council Regulation (EC) No 207/2009 of 26 February 2009 on the Community trade mark[21] or under Directive 2008/95/EC. In such cases, the use of the protected designation of origin or protected geographical indication shall be permitted as well as use of the relevant trade marks.

*Article 15*

**Transitional periods for use of protected designations of origin and protected geographical indications**

A10-016 **1.** Without prejudice to Article 14, the Secretary of State may, by regulations, make provision for a transitional period of up to five years to apply to enable products the designation of which consists of or contains a name that contravenes Article 13(1) to continue to use the designation under which it was marketed if the Secretary of State is satisfied that an admissible statement of opposition under Article 51 shows that:

(a) the registration of the name would jeopardise the existence of an entirely or partly identical name; or

(b) such products have been legally marketed with that name in the territory concerned for at least five years preceding the date of the publication provided for point (a) of Article 50(2).

**2.** Without prejudice to Article 14, if the Secretary of State is satisfied that:

(a) the designation referred to in paragraph 1 of this Article has been in legal use consistently and fairly for at least 25 years before the application for registration was submitted to the Secretary of State;

(b) the purpose of using the designation referred to in paragraph 1 of this Article has not, at any time, been to profit from the reputation of the registered name and it is shown that the consumer has not been nor could have been misled as to the true origin of the product.

**3.** When using a designation referred to in paragraphs 1 and 2, the indication of country of origin shall clearly and visibly appear on the labelling.

**4.** To overcome temporary difficulties with the long-term objective of ensuring that all producers in the area concerned comply with the specification, nothing in this Regulation prevents the Secretary of State from using any power the Secretary of State has to make regulations to provide for a transitional period of up to 10 years to apply, with effect from the date on which the application is lodged with the Secretary of State, on condition that the operators concerned have legally marketed the products in question, using the names concerned continuously for at least the five years prior to the lodging of the application and have made that point in the national opposition procedure referred to in Article 51.

The first subparagraph shall apply mutatis mutandis to a protected geographical indication or protected designation of origin referring to a geographical area situated in a third country, with the exception of the opposition procedure.

Such transitional periods shall be indicated in the application submitted under Article 8(1).

---

21 OJ L 78, 24.3.2009, p. 1.

*Article 16*

**Transitional provisions**

**1.** The Secretary of State must enter the names of established protected designations of origin and established protected geographical indications on the register referred to in Article 11 of this Regulation. The corresponding specifications shall be deemed to be the specifications referred to in Article 7 of this Regulation. Any specific transitional provisions associated with such registrations under EU Regulation 1151/2012 (2) shall continue to apply. **A10-017**
**2.** In order to protect the rights and legitimate interests of producers or stakeholders concerned, the Secretary of State may make regulations concerning additional transitional rules.
**3.** In relation to established protected designations of origin and established protected geographical indications, this Regulation shall apply without prejudice to any right of coexistence recognised under Regulation (EC) No 510/2006, as that Regulation had effect in the United Kingdom immediately before it was repealed by EU Regulation 1151/2012, in respect of designations of origin and geographical indications, on the one hand, and trade marks, on the other.
**4.** In paragraph 1, in relation to an established protected designation of origin and an established protected geographical indication, 'corresponding specifications' means the product specification for the relevant designation of origin or geographical indication as the specification stood immediately before exit day.

Fn (2) OJ No. L 343, 14.12.2012, p. 1, to which there are amendments not relevant to these Regulations.

**TITLE III**

**TRADITIONAL SPECIALITIES GUARANTEED**

*Article 17*

**Objective**

A scheme for traditional specialities guaranteed is established to safeguard traditional methods of production and recipes by helping producers of traditional product in marketing and communicating the value-adding attributes of their traditional recipes and products to consumers. **A10-018**

*Article 18*

**Criteria**

**1.** A name shall be eligible for registration as a traditional speciality guaranteed where it describes a specific product or foodstuff that: **A10-019**

(a) results from a mode of production, processing or composition corresponding to traditional practice for that product or foodstuff; or
(b) is produced from raw materials or ingredients that are those traditionally used.

**2.** For a name to be registered as a traditional speciality guaranteed, it shall:
(a) have been traditionally used to refer to the specific product; or

(b) identify the traditional character or specific character of the product.

**3.** If it is demonstrated in the opposition procedure under Article 51 that the name is also used in another country, in order to distinguish comparable products or products that share an identical or similar name, the decision on registration taken in accordance with Article 52(3) may provide that the name of the traditional speciality guaranteed is to be accompanied by the claim 'made following the tradition of' immediately followed by the name of a country or a region thereof.

**4.** A name may not be registered if it refers only to claims of a general nature used for a set of products, or to claims provided for by particular retained EU law.

**5.** In order to ensure the smooth functioning of the scheme, the Secretary of State may make regulations concerning further details of the eligibility criteria laid down in this Article.

*Article 19*

**Product specification**

A10-020 **1.** A traditional speciality guaranteed shall comply with a specification which shall comprise:

(a) the name proposed for registration;

(b) a description of the product including its main physical, chemical, microbiological or organoleptic characteristics, showing the product's specific character;

(c) a description of the production method that the producers must follow, including, where appropriate, the nature and characteristics of the raw materials or ingredients used, and the method by which the product is prepared; and

(d) the key elements establishing the product's traditional character.

**2.** In order to ensure that product specifications provide relevant and succinct information, the Secretary of State may make regulations laying down rules which limit the information contained in the specification referred to in paragraph 1 of this Article, where such a limitation is necessary to avoid excessively voluminous applications for registration.

The Commission may adopt implementing acts laying down rules on the form of the specification.

*Article 20*

**Content of application for registration**

A10-021 **1.** An application for registration of a name as a traditional speciality guaranteed referred to in Article 49 shall comprise:

(a) the name and address of the applicant group;

(b) the product specification as provided for in Article 19.

*Article 21*

**Grounds for opposition**

A10-022 **1.** A reasoned statement of opposition as referred to in Article 51(2) shall be admissible only if it is received by the Secretary of State before expiry of the time limit and if it:

(a) gives duly substantiated reasons why the proposed registration is incompatible with the terms of this Regulation; or
(b) shows that use of the name is lawful, renowned and economically significant for similar agricultural products or foodstuffs.

**2.** The criteria referred to in point (b) of paragraph 1 shall be assessed in relation to the territory of the United Kingdom.

*Article 22*

**Register of traditional specialities guaranteed**

**1.** The Secretary of State must establish and maintain a publicly accessible updated register of traditional specialties guaranteed recognised under this scheme. **A10-023**
**2.** The Secretary of State may make regulations laying down detailed rules on the form and content of the register.

*Article 23*

**Names, symbol and indication**

**1.** A name registered as a traditional speciality guaranteed may be used by any operator marketing a product that conforms to the corresponding specification. **A10-024**
**2.** A symbol shall be established in order to publicise the traditional specialities guaranteed.
**3.** In the case of the products originating in the Union that are marketed under a traditional speciality guaranteed that is registered in accordance with this Regulation, the symbol referred to in paragraph 2 shall, without prejudice to paragraph 4, appear on the labelling. In addition, the name of the product should appear in the same field of vision. The indication 'traditional speciality guaranteed' or the corresponding abbreviation 'TSG' may also appear on the labelling.

The symbol shall be optional on the labelling of traditional specialities guaranteed which are produced outside the Union.

**4.** In order to ensure that the appropriate information is communicated to the consumer, the Secretary of State may make regulations establishing the symbol.

The Secretary of State may make regulations defining the technical characteristics of the symbol and indication, as well as the rules of their use on the products bearing the name of a traditional speciality guaranteed.

*Article 24*

**Restriction on use of registered names**

**1.** Registered names shall be protected against any misuse, imitation or evocation, or against any other practice liable to mislead the consumer. **A10-025**
**2.** The designated authority shall ensure that sales descriptions used in the United Kingdom do not give rise to confusion with names that are registered.
**3.** The Secretary of State may make regulationslaying down rules for the protection of traditional specialities guaranteed.

*Article 25*

**Transitional provisions**

A10-026 **1.** The Secretary of State must enter the names of established protected traditional specialities guaranteed on the register referred to in Article 22 of this Regulation. The corresponding specifications shall be deemed to be the specifications referred to in Article 19 of this Regulation. Any specific transitional provisions associated with such registrations under EU Regulation 1151/2012 as it had effect in the United Kingdom immediately before exit day shall continue to apply.

**3.** In order to protect the rights and legitimate interests of producers or stakeholders concerned, the Secretary of State may make regulations laying down additional transitional rules relating to the entries to be made on the register referred to in Article 22 under paragraph 1.

**4.** In paragraph 1, in relation to an established protected traditional speciality guaranteed, 'corresponding specifications' means the product specification for the traditional speciality guaranteed as the specification stood immediately before exit day.

## TITLE IV

## OPTIONAL QUALITY TERMS

*Article 27*

**Objective**

A10-028 A scheme for optional quality terms is established in order to facilitate the communication within the United Kingdom of the value-adding characteristics or attributes of agricultural products by the producers thereof.

[*Article 28*

**Existing enactments**

A10-029 **1.** Nothing in this Regulation prevents the maintenance of enactments on optional quality terms that are not covered by this Regulation and are in force immediately before exit day, provided that they comply with retained EU law.

**2.** In paragraph 1, 'maintenance' includes repeal and replacement, and revocation and replacement, without, in both cases, any substantive modification.]

*Article 29*

**Optional quality terms**

A10-030 **1.** Optional quality terms shall satisfy the following criteria:

(a) the term relates to a characteristic of one or more categories of products, or to a farming or processing attribute which applies in specific areas;

(b) the use of the term adds value to the product as compared to products of a similar type; and

(c) the term has a United Kingdom dimension.

**2.** Optional quality terms that describe technical product qualities with the purpose of putting into effect compulsory marketing standards and are not intended to inform consumers about those product qualities shall be excluded from this scheme.
**3.** Optional quality terms shall exclude optional reserved terms which support and complement specific marketing standards determined on a sectoral or product category basis.
**4.** In order to take into account the specific character of certain sectors as well as consumer expectations, the Secretary of State may make regulations laying down detailed rules relating to the criteria referred to in paragraph 1 of this Article.
**5.** The Secretary of State may make regulations laying down all measures related to forms, procedures or other technical details, necessary for the application of this Title.
**6.** When making regulations in accordance with paragraphs 4 and 5 of this Article, the Secretary of State shall take account of any relevant international standards.

*Article 30*

**Reservation and amendment**

**1.** In order to take account of the expectations of consumers, developments in scientific and technical knowledge, the market situation, and developments in marketing standards and in international standards, the Secretary of State may make regulations reserving an additional optional quality term and laying down its conditions of use. **A10-031**
**2.** In duly justified cases and in order to take into account the appropriate use of the additional optional quality term, the Secretary of State may make regulations laying down amendments to the conditions of use referred to in paragraph 1 of this Article.

*Article 31*

**Mountain product**

**1.** The term 'mountain product' is established as an optional quality term. **A10-032**

This term shall only be used to describe products intended for human consumption listed in Annex I to the Treaty in respect of which:

(a) both the raw materials and the feedstuffs for farm animals come essentially from mountain areas;
(b) in the case of processed products, the processing also takes place in mountain areas.

**2.** For the purposes of this Article, mountain areas within the United Kingdom are those delimited pursuant to Article 18(1) of Regulation (EC) No 1257/1999. For third-country products, mountain areas include areas officially designated as mountain areas by the third country or that meet criteria equivalent to those set out in Article 18(1) of Regulation (EC) No 1257/1999.
**3.** In duly justified cases and in order to take into account natural constraints affecting agricultural production in mountain areas, the Secretary of State may make regulations laying down derogations from the conditions of use referred to in paragraph 1 of this Article. In particular, the Secretary of State may make regulations laying down the conditions under which raw materials or feedstuffs are permitted to come from outside the mountain areas, the conditions under which the

processing of products is permitted to take place outside of the mountain areas in a geographical area to be defined, and the definition of that geographical area.
**4.** In order to take into account natural constraints affecting agricultural production in mountain areas, the Secretary of State may make regulations concerning the establishment of the methods of production, and other criteria relevant for the application of the optional quality term established in paragraph 1 of this Article.

*Article 33*

**Restrictions on use**

A10-034 **1.** An optional quality term may only be used to describe products that comply with the corresponding conditions of use.
**2.** The Secretary of State may make regulations laying down rules for the use of optional quality terms.

*Article 34*

**Monitoring**

A10-035 The designated authority shall undertake checks, based on a risk analysis, to ensure compliance with the requirements of this Title and, in the event of breach, shall apply appropriate administrative penalties.

## TITLE V

## COMMON PROVISIONS

## CHAPTER I

## OFFICIAL CONTROLS OF PROTECTED DESIGNATIONS OF ORIGIN, PROTECTED GEOGRAPHICAL INDICATIONS AND TRADITIONAL SPECIALITIES GUARANTEED

*Article 35*

**Scope**

A10-036 The provisions of this Chapter shall apply in respect of the quality schemes set out in Title II and Title III.

*Article 36*

**Official controls**

A10-037 **1.** Procedures and requirements of Regulation (EC) No 882/2004 shall apply mutatis mutandis to the official controls carried out to verify compliance with the legal requirement related to the quality schemes for all products covered by Annex I to this Regulation.
**2.** The competent authorities shall offer adequate guarantees of objectivity and impartiality, and shall have at their disposal the qualified staff and resources necessary to carry out their functions.
**3.** Official controls shall cover:

(a) verification that a product complies with the corresponding product specification; and
(b) monitoring of the use of registered names to describe product placed on the market, in conformity with Article 13 for names registered under Title II and in conformity with Article 24 for names registered under Title III.

*Article 37*

**Verification of compliance with product specification**

**1.** In respect of protected designations of origin, protected geographical indications and traditional specialities guaranteed that designate products originating within the United Kingdom, verification of compliance with the product specification, before placing the product on the market, shall be carried out by: **A10-038**

(a) the competent authority; and/or
(b) one or more of the control bodies within the meaning of point (5) of Article 2 of Regulation (EC) No 882/2004 operating as a product certification body.

The costs of such verification of compliance with the specifications may be borne by the operators that are subject to those controls. The Secretary of State may also contribute to these costs.

**2.** In respect of designations of origin, geographical indications and traditional specialities guaranteed that designate products originating in a third country, the verification of compliance with the specifications before placing the product on the market shall be carried out by:

(a) one or more of the public authorities designated by the third country; and/or
(b) one or more of the product certification bodies.

**3.** The Secretary of State shall make public the name and address of the authorities and bodies referred to paragraph 1 of this Article, and update that information periodically.

The Secretary of State shall make public the name and address of the authorities and bodies referred to in paragraph 2 of this Article and update that information periodically. The Secretary of State may make the information specified in the first and second subparagraphs public, and update that information periodically, in such manner as appears appropriate to the Secretary of State from time to time.

*Article 38*

**Surveillance of the use of the name in the market place**

The designated authority shall carry out checks, based on a risk analysis, to ensure compliance with the requirements of this Regulation and, in the event of breaches, that authority shall take all necessary measures. **A10-039**

*Article 39*

**Delegation by competent authorities to control bodies**

**1.** Competent authorities may delegate, in accordance with Article 5 of Regulation (EC) No 882/2004, specific tasks related to official controls of the quality schemes to one or more control bodies. **A10-040**

**2.** Such control bodies shall be accredited in accordance with European Standard EN 45011 or ISO/IEC Guide 65 (General requirements for bodies operating product certification systems).
**3.** Accreditation referred to in paragraph 2 of this Article may only be performed by:

(a) a national accreditation body in the United Kingdom in accordance with the provisions of Regulation (EC) No 765/2008; or
(b) an accreditation body outside the United Kingdom that is a signatory of a multilateral recognition arrangement under the auspices of the International Accreditation Forum.

*Article 40*

**Planning and reporting of control activities**

A10-041 **1.** The Secretary of State shall ensure that activities for the control of obligations under this Chapter are specifically included in a separate section within the multi-annual national control plans in accordance with Articles 41, 42 and 43 of Regulation (EC) No 882/2004.
**2.** The annual reports concerning the control of the obligations established by this Regulation shall include a separate section comprising the information laid down in Article 44 of Regulation (EC) No 882/2004.

## CHAPTER II

## EXCEPTIONS FOR CERTAIN PRIOR USES

*Article 41*

**Generic terms**

A10-042 **1.** Without prejudice to Article 13, this Regulation shall not affect the use of terms that are generic in the United Kingdom, even if the generic term is part of a name that is protected under a quality scheme.
**2.** To establish whether or not a term has become generic, account shall be taken of all relevant factors, in particular:

(a) the existing situation in areas of consumption;
(b) any relevant enactment.

**3.** In order to fully protect the rights of interested parties, the Secretary of State may make regulations laying down additional rules for determining the generic status of terms referred to in paragraph 1 of this Article.

*Article 42*

**Plant varieties and animal breeds**

A10-043 **1.** This Regulation shall not prevent the placing on the market of products the labelling of which includes a name or term protected or reserved under a quality scheme described in Title II, Title III, or Title IV that contains or comprises the name of a plant variety or animal breed, provided that the following conditions are met:

(a) the product in question comprises or is derived from the variety or breed indicated;
(b) consumers are not misled;
(c) the usage of the name of the variety or breed name constitutes fair competition;
(d) the usage does not exploit the reputation of the protected term; and
(e) in the case of the quality scheme described in Title II, production and marketing of the product had spread beyond its area of origin prior to the date of application for registration of the geographical indication.

**2.** In order to further clarify the extent of rights and freedoms of food business operators to use the name of a plant variety or of an animal breed referred to in paragraph 1 of this Article, the Secretary of State may make regulations concerning rules for determining the use of such names.

*Article 43*

### Relation to intellectual property

The quality schemes described in Titles III and IV shall apply without prejudice to retained EU law and any other enactments governing intellectual property, and in particular to those concerning designations of origin and geographical indications and trade marks, and rights granted under such law and those enactments. **A10-044**

## CHAPTER III

## QUALITY SCHEME INDICATIONS AND SYMBOLS AND ROLE OF PRODUCERS

*Article 44*

### Protection of indications and symbols

**1.** Indications, abbreviations and symbols referring to the quality schemes may only be used in connection with products produced in conformity with the rules of the quality scheme to which they apply. This applies in particular to the following indications, abbreviations and symbols: **A10-045**

(a) 'protected designation of origin', 'protected geographical indication', 'geographical indication', 'PDO', 'PGI', and the associated symbols, as provided for in Title II;
(b) 'traditional speciality guaranteed', 'TSG', and the associated symbol, as provided for in Title III;
(c) 'mountain product', as provided for in Title IV.

**3.** The Secretary of State may make regulations laying down rules for the uniform protection of the indications, abbreviations and symbols referred to in paragraph 1 of this Article.

*Article 45*

**Role of groups**

A10-046 **1.** Without prejudice to specific provisions on producer organisations and interbranch organisations as laid down in Regulation (EC) No 1308/2013, a group is entitled to:

(a) contribute to ensuring that the quality, reputation and authenticity of their products are guaranteed on the market by monitoring the use of the name in trade and, if necessary, by informing the competent authority or any designated authority within the framework of Article 13(3);

(b) take action to ensure adequate legal protection of the protected designation of origin or protected geographical indication and of the intellectual property rights that are directly connected with them;

(c) develop information and promotion activities aiming at communicating the value-adding attributes of the product to consumers;

(d) develop activities related to ensuring compliance of a product with its specification;

(e) take action to improve the performance of the scheme, including developing economic expertise, carrying out economic analyses, disseminating economic information on the scheme and providing advice to producers;

(f) take measures to enhance the value of products and, where necessary, take steps to prevent or counter any measures which are, or risk being, detrimental to the image of those products.

**2.** The Secretary of State may encourage the formation and functioning of groups in the United Kingdom by administrative means. The Secretary of State must publish the names and addresses of the groups referred to in Article 3(2) in such manner as appears appropriate to the Secretary of State from time to time.

*Article 46*

**Right to use the schemes**

A10-047 **1.** The Secretary of State shall ensure that any operator complying with the rules of a quality scheme set out in Titles II and III is entitled to be covered by the verification of compliance established pursuant to Article 37.

**2.** Operators who prepare and store a product marketed under the traditional speciality guaranteed, protected designation of origin or protected geographical indication schemes or who place such products on the market shall also be subject to the controls laid down in Chapter I of this Title.

**3.** The Secretary of State shall ensure that operators willing to adhere to the rules of a quality scheme set out in Titles III and IV are able to do so and do not face obstacles to participation that are discriminatory or otherwise not objectively founded.

## CHAPTER IV

## APPLICATION AND REGISTRATION PROCESSES FOR DESIGNATIONS OF ORIGIN, GEOGRAPHICAL INDICATIONS, AND TRADITIONAL SPECIALITIES GUARANTEED

*Article 48*

### Scope of application processes

The provisions of this Chapter shall apply in respect of the quality schemes set out in Title II and Title III. **A10-049**

*Article 49*

### Application for registration of names

**1.** Applications for registration of names under the quality schemes referred to in Article 48 may be submitted to the Secretary of State". They may only be submitted by groups who work with the products with the name to be registered. In the case of a 'protected designations of origin' or 'protected geographical indications' name that designates a trans-border geographical area or in the case of a 'traditional specialities guaranteed' name, several groups from the United Kingdom and a third country, or from more than one country, as relevant, may lodge a joint application for registration. **A10-050**

A single natural or legal person may be treated as a group where it is shown that both of the following conditions are fulfilled:

(a) the person concerned is the only producer willing to submit an application;

(b) with regard to protected designations of origin and protected geographical indications, the defined geographical area possesses characteristics which differ appreciably from those of neighbouring areas or the characteristics of the product are different from those produced in neighbouring areas.

**5.** Where the application under the scheme set out in Title II relates to a geographical area in a third country, or where an application under the scheme set out in Title III is prepared by a group established in a third country, the application shall be lodged with the Secretary of State, either directly or via the authorities of the third country concerned.

**6.** The documents referred to in this Article which are sent to the Secretary of State shall be in one of the official languages of the Union.

**7.** The Secretary of State may make regulationslaying down detailed rules on procedures, form and presentation of applications, including for applications concerning more than one national territory.

*Article 50*

### Scrutiny by the Secretary of State and publication for opposition

**1.** The Secretary of State shall scrutinise by appropriate means any application received pursuant to Article 49, in order to check that it is justified and that it meets the conditions of the respective scheme. This scrutiny should not exceed a period **A10-051**

of six months. Where this period is exceeded, the Secretary of State shall indicate in writing to the applicant the reasons for the delay.

The Secretary of State shall, at least each month, make public, in such manner as appears appropriate to the Secretary of State from time to time, the list of names for which registration applications have been submitted to the Secretary of State, as well as their date of submission.

**2.** Where, based on the scrutiny carried out pursuant to the first subparagraph of paragraph 1, the Secretary of State considers that the conditions laid down in this Regulation are fulfilled, the Secretary of State shall publish in such manner as appears appropriate to the Secretary of State from time to time:

(a) for applications under the scheme set out in Title II, the single document and product specification;

(b) for applications under the scheme set out in Title III, the specification.

*Article 51*

## Opposition procedure

A10-052 **1.** Within three months from the date of publication of the documents published by virtue of Article 50(2), the authorities of a third country, or a natural or legal person having a legitimate interest may lodge a notice of opposition with the Secretary of State.

The Secretary of State shall forward the notice of opposition to the authority or body that lodged the application without delay.

**2.** If a notice of opposition is lodged with the Secretary of State and is followed within two months by a reasoned statement of opposition, the Secretary of State shall check the admissibility of this reasoned statement of opposition.

**3.** Within two months after the receipt of an admissible reasoned statement of opposition, the Secretary of State shall invite the authority or person that lodged the opposition and the authority or body that lodged the application to engage in appropriate consultations for a reasonable period that shall not exceed three months.

The authority or person that lodged the opposition and the authority or body that lodged the application shall start such appropriate consultations without undue delay. They shall provide each other with the relevant information to assess whether the application for registration complies with the conditions of this Regulation. If no agreement is reached, this information shall also be provided to the Secretary of State.

At any time during these three months, the Secretary of State may, at the request of the applicant extend the deadline for the consultations by a maximum of three months.

**4.** Where, following the appropriate consultations referred to in paragraph 3 of this Article, the details published in accordance with Article 50(2) have been substantially amended, the Secretary of State shall repeat the scrutiny referred to in Article 50.

**5.** The notice of opposition, the reasoned statement of opposition and the related documents which are sent to the Secretary of State in accordance with paragraphs 1 to 4 of this Article shall be in one of the official languages of the Union.

**6.** In order to establish clear procedures and deadlines for opposition, the Secretary of State may make regulations complementing the rules of the opposition procedure.

The Secretary of State may make regulations laying down detailed rules on procedures, form and presentation of the oppositions.

*Article 52*

**Decision on registration**

**1.** Where, on the basis of the information available to the Secretary of State from the scrutiny carried out pursuant to the first subparagraph of Article 50(1), the Secretary of State considers that the conditions for registration are not fulfilled, the Secretary of State must reject the application. **A10-053**

**2.** If the Secretary of State receives no notice of opposition or no admissible reasoned statement of opposition under Article 51, the Secretary of State must register the name.

**3.** If the Secretary of State receives an admissible reasoned statement of opposition, the Secretary of State shall, following the appropriate consultations referred to in Article 51(3), and taking into account the results thereof, either:

- (a) if an agreement has been reached, register the name; or
- (b) if an agreement has not been reached, decide whether to register the name.

**4.** After making a decision under this Article, the Secretary of State must publish in such manner as appears appropriate to the Secretary of State from time to time:

- (a) a notice informing the applicant and the public of the decision made in relation to the application, and
- (b) where the application is approved, a copy of the approved product specification.

**5.** An implementing act to which paragraph 6 applies is revoked.

**6.** This paragraph applies to an implementing act adopted by the European Commission under Article 52 of EU Regulation 1151/2012 and incorporated into domestic law by section 3 of the European Union (Withdrawal) Act 2018.

[*Article 52a*

**Applications pending on exit day**

**1.** An application made under EU Regulation 1151/2012 before exit day to which paragraph 2 applies is deemed to be an application made under Article 49(1) of this Regulation for which scrutiny under Article 50(1) of this Regulation has not been commenced. Unless requested not to do so in writing by the applicant who submitted the application, the Secretary of State must scrutinise the application under Article 50(1) of this Regulation. The six month period specified in Article 50(1) starts from the day on which exit day falls. **A10-053.1**

**2.** This paragraph applies to an application submitted to the Secretary of State on or after 1st January 2019 or the Secretary of State or the Department for Environment Food and Rural Affairs before that date:

- (a) to register:
  - (i) a name of a geographical area in, or partly in, the United Kingdom as a designation of origin,
  - (ii) a name of a geographical area in, or partly in, the United Kingdom as a geographical indication, or
  - (iii) a name as a traditional speciality guaranteed, and
- (b) that has not been scrutinised under Article 49(2) of EU Regulation 1151/

2012 before exit day or has been subject to scrutiny under Article 49(2) before exit day but for which no decision has been taken as to whether it meets the relevant conditions of EU Regulation 1151/2012 or is justified.

**3.** An application made under EU Regulation 1151/2012 before exit day to which paragraph 4 applies is deemed to be an application made under Article 49(1) of this Regulation that has been found by the Secretary of State, for the purpose of Article 50(2), to fulfil the conditions laid down in this Regulation but for which the documents specified in Article 50(2) have not been published. In the case of an application to register the name of a designation of origin or geographical indication, the Secretary of State must, unless requested not to do so in writing by the applicant who submitted the application, publish the single document and product specification submitted with the application made under EU Regulation 1151/2012 as soon as reasonably practicable after exit day. In the case of an application to register the name of a traditional speciality guaranteed, the Secretary of State must, unless requested not to do so in writing by the applicant who submitted the application, publish the product specification submitted with the application made under EU Regulation 1151/2012 as soon as reasonably practicable after exit day. The publication of the documents specified in the second or third subparagraph by the Secretary of State initiates the opposition procedure to which Article 51 of this Regulation applies in relation to the application.

**4.** This paragraph applies to an application submitted to the Secretary of State on or after 1st January 2019 or the Secretary of State or the Department for Environment Food and Rural Affairs before that date:

(a) to register:

(i) the name of a geographical area in, or partly in, the United Kingdom as a designation of origin,

(ii) the name of a geographical area in, or partly in, the United Kingdom as a geographical indication, or

(iii) a name as a traditional speciality guaranteed, and

(b) that has been scrutinised under Article 49(2) of EU Regulation 1151/2012 and been found by the Secretary of State to meet the conditions of, and to be justified under, EU Regulation 1151/2012 before exit day but for which the Commission has not adopted an implementing act under Article 52 of EU Regulation 1151/2012 before exit day.]

### *Article 53*

### Amendment to a product specification

A10-054 **1.** A group having a legitimate interest may apply for approval of an amendment to a product specification.

Applications shall describe and give reasons for the amendments requested.

**2.** Where the amendment involves one or more amendments to the specification that are not minor, the amendment application shall follow the procedure laid down in Articles 49 to 52.

However, if the proposed amendments are minor, the Secretary of State shall approve or reject the application. In the event of the approval of amendments implying a modification of the elements referred to in Article 50(2), the Secretary of State shall publish those elements in such manner as appears appropriate to the Secretary of State from time to time.

For an amendment to be regarded as minor in the case of the quality scheme described in Title II, it shall not:

(a) relate to the essential characteristics of the product;
(b) alter the link referred to in point (f)(i) or (ii) of Article 7(1);
(c) include a change to the name, or to any part of the name of the product;
(d) affect the defined geographical area; or
(e) represent an increase in restrictions on trade in the product or its raw materials.

For an amendment to be regarded as minor in the case of the quality scheme described in Title III, it shall not:

(a) relate to the essential characteristics of the product;
(b) introduce essential changes to the production method; or
(c) include a change to the name, or to any part of the name of the product.

The scrutiny of the application shall focus on the proposed amendment.

**3.** In order to facilitate the administrative process of an amendment application, including where the amendment does not involve any change to the single document and where it concerns a temporary change in the specification resulting from the imposition of obligatory sanitary or phytosanitary measures by the public authorities, the Secretary of State may make regulations complementing the rules of the amendment application process.

The Secretary of State may make regulations laying down detailed rules on procedures, form and presentation of an amendment application.

**4.** An implementing act to which paragraph 5 applies is revoked.

**5.** This paragraph applies to an implementing act relating to an amendment to a product specification adopted by the European Commission pursuant to Article 53 of EU Regulation 1151/2012 and incorporated into domestic law by section 3 of the EUWA.

*Article 54*

## Cancellation

**1.** The Secretary of State may, on the Secretary of State's own initiative or at the request of any natural or legal person having a legitimate interest, to cancel the registration of a protected designation of origin or of a protected geographical indication or of a traditional speciality guaranteed in the following cases: **A10-055**

(a) where compliance with the conditions of the specification is not ensured;
(b) where no product is placed on the market under the traditional speciality guaranteed, the protected designation of origin or the protected geographical indication for at least seven years.

The Secretary of State may, at the request of the producers of product marketed under the registered name, cancel the corresponding registration.

**2.** In order to ensure legal certainty that all parties have the opportunity to defend their rights and legitimate interests, the Secretary of State may make regulations complementing the rules regarding the cancellation process.

The Secretary of State may make regulations laying down detailed rules on procedures and form of the cancellation process, as well as on the presentation of the requests referred to in paragraph 1 of this Article.

**3.** An implementing act to which paragraph 4 applies is revoked.

**4.** This paragraph applies to an implementing act adopted by the European Commission under Article 54 of EU Regulation 1151/2012 and incorporated into domestic law by section 3 of the EUWA

## [TITLE 5A

## APPEALS

### *Article 54a*

### Appeals: general

A10-055.1 **1.** An appeal may be made to the FTT against a decision of the Secretary of State specified in the first column of the table in Annex 3.

**2.** Such an appeal may be made:

(a) in all cases, by a person specified in the corresponding entry in the second column of the table in Annex 3;

(b) in the case of a decision affecting an application submitted by the authorities of a third country, the authorities of that third country.

**3.** In determining such an appeal the FTT:

(a) must consider the decision appealed against afresh, and

(b) may take into account evidence that was not available to the Secretary of State.

**4.** The FTT may:

(a) dismiss the appeal, or

(b) if it allows the appeal, exercise any power specified in the corresponding entry in the third column of the table in Annex 3.

**5.** The Secretary of State may consider a decision specified in the first column of the table in Annex 3 afresh if evidence becomes available to the Secretary of State after making the original decision that was not available to the Secretary of State at the time of the original decision.

**6.** Paragraph 5 applies even though an appeal has been made to the FTT in respect of the original decision.

**7.** Where the Secretary of State decides to consider an original decision afresh in a case where an appeal has been made to the FTT in respect of that decision, the appeal to the FTT is suspended until such time as the Secretary of State has made a fresh decision in relation to the matter.

**8.** If the Secretary of State makes the same decision again, the appeal to the FTT restarts. If the Secretary of State makes a different decision, the appeal to the FTT ceases unless the FTT directs otherwise.

### *Article 54b*

### Appeals: applications to register designations of origin, geographical indications and traditional specialities guaranteed

A10-055.2 **1.** Where an appeal is made to the FTT relating to a decision to approve an application to register a designation of origin, geographical indication or traditional speciality guaranteed, and the Secretary of State has made an entry in the relevant register pursuant to Article 52 relating to that registration, the entry in the register is to be maintained but is in suspense and must be marked to indicate that it is in

suspense until the FTT has determined the appeal and any necessary consequent action or decision has been taken by the Secretary of State.
**2.** Where an appeal is made to the FTT relating to a decision to approve an application to register a designation of origin, geographical indication or traditional speciality guaranteed, and the Secretary of State has not made an entry in the register, the Secretary of State must not make an entry in the register until the FTT has determined the appeal and any necessary consequent action or decision has been taken by the Secretary of State.

*Article 54c*

**Appeals: applications to amend product specifications**

**1.** Paragraph 2 applies where an appeal is made to the FTT relating to a decision **A10-056**
by the Secretary of State to approve an application of the type specified in Article 53(2) to amend a product specification relating to a protected designation of origin, protected geographical indication or traditional speciality guaranteed and the Secretary of State has not updated the entry in the relevant register relating to it pursuant to Article 14(3) of Commission Implementing Regulation (EU) 668/2014 by replacing the copy of the product specification attached to the relevant register with the amended version of the product specification.
**2.** Until the FTT has determined the appeal and any necessary consequent action or decision has been taken by the Secretary of State, the existing copy of the product specification attached to the entry in the relevant register relating to the protected designation of origin, protected geographical indication or traditional speciality guaranteed applies without amendment but the entry in the relevant register must be marked to indicate that an appeal relating to the amendment of the product specification is pending.
**3.** Paragraph 4 applies where an appeal is made to the FTT relating to a decision by the Secretary of State to approve an application of the type specified in Article 53(2) in relation to the amendment of a product specification relating to a protected designation of origin, protected geographical indication or traditional speciality guaranteed and the Secretary of State has updated the entry in the relevant register relating to the protected designation of origin, protected geographical indication or traditional speciality guaranteed by replacing the copy of the product specification with the approved amended version.
**4.** Until the FTT has determined the appeal and any necessary consequent action or decision has been taken by the Secretary of State, the previous copy of the product specification attached to the entry in the relevant register is to be restored but the entry in the relevant register must be marked to indicate that an appeal relating to the amendment of the product specification is pending.
**5.** Paragraph 6 applies where an appeal is made to the FTT relating to a decision by the Secretary of State to reject an application of the type specified in Article 53(2) to amend a product specification relating to a protected designation of origin, protected geographical indication or traditional speciality guaranteed.
**6.** Until the FTT has determined the appeal and any necessary consequent action or decision has been taken by the Secretary of State, the existing copy of the product specification attached to the entry in the relevant register is to be maintained but the entry in the register must be marked to indicate that an appeal relating to an application to amend the product specification is pending.

**7.** Paragraph 8 applies where an appeal is made to the FTT relating to a decision by the Secretary of State to approve an application of the type specified in Article 6(4) and (4)(a) of Regulation 664/2014 to amend a product specification relating to a protected designation of origin, protected geographical indication or traditional speciality guaranteed on a temporary basis and the Secretary of State has not included an entry in the relevant register relating to the temporary amendment of the product specification pursuant to Article 14(3b) of Commission Implementing Regulation (EU) 668/2014.
**8.** Until the FTT has determined the appeal and any necessary consequent action or decision has been taken by the Secretary of State, the existing copy of the product specification attached to the entry in the relevant register applies without amendment but the entry in the register must be marked to indicate that an appeal relating to the temporary amendment of the product specification is pending.
**9.** Paragraph 10 applies where an appeal is made to the FTT relating to a decision by the Secretary of State to approve an application of the type specified in Article 6(4) of Regulation 664/2014 in relation to the temporary amendment of a product specification relating to a protected designation of origin, protected geographical indication or traditional speciality guaranteed and the Secretary of State has updated the entry in the relevant register by including an entry relating to the temporary amendment of the product specification.
**10.** Until the FTT has determined the appeal and any necessary consequent action or decision has been taken by the Secretary of State, the copy of the product specification attached to the entry in the relevant register applies and the entry in the relevant register relating to the temporary amendment must be marked to indicate that an appeal relating to the temporary amendment of the product specification is pending.
**11.** Paragraph 12 applies where an appeal is made to the FTT relating to a decision by the Secretary of State to reject an application of the type specified in Article 6(4) and (4)(a) of Regulation 664/2014 to amend a product specification relating to a protected designation of origin, protected geographical indication or traditional speciality guaranteed on a temporary basis.
**12.** Until the FTT has determined the appeal and any necessary consequent action or decision has been taken by the Secretary of State, the copy of the product specification attached to the entry in the relevant register applies but the entry in the register must be marked to indicate that an appeal relating to an application to amend the product specification on a temporary basis is pending.

*Article 54d*

**Appeals: applications to cancel registered designations of origin, geographical indications and traditional specialities guaranteed**

A10-057 **1.** Paragraph 2 applies where an appeal is made to the FTT relating to a decision of the Secretary of State to cancel the registration of a protected designation of origin, protected geographical indication or traditional speciality guaranteed under Article 54 and the Secretary of State has not removed the entry in the relevant register.
**2.** Until the FTT has determined the appeal and any necessary consequent action or decision has been taken by the Secretary of State, the entry in the relevant register is to be maintained but must be marked to indicate that an appeal relating to its cancellation is pending.

**3.** Paragraph 4 applies where an appeal has been made to the FTT relating to a decision of the Secretary of State to cancel the registration of a protected designation of origin, protected geographical indication or traditional speciality guaranteed and the Secretary of State has removed the entry in the relevant register.
**4.** Until the FTT has determined the appeal and any necessary consequent action or decision has been taken by the Secretary of State, the entry in the register must be restored but must be marked to indicate that an appeal relating to its cancellation is pending.
**5.** Paragraph 6 applies where an appeal has been made to the FTT relating to a decision of the Secretary of State not to cancel the registration of a protected designation of origin, protected geographical indication or traditional speciality guaranteed.
**6.** Until the FTT has determined the appeal and any necessary consequent action or decision has been taken by the Secretary of State, the entry in the relevant register relating to the protected designation of origin, protected geographical indication or traditional speciality guaranteed must be marked to indicate that an appeal relating to the cancellation of the entry is pending.]

## TITLE VI

## PROCEDURAL AND FINAL PROVISIONS

## CHAPTER II

## PROCEDURAL RULES

[*Article 56*

### Regulations

**1.** Any power to make regulations conferred on the Secretary of State by this Regulation is exercisable by statutory instrument. **A10-058**
**2.** Such regulations may:

(a) contain supplementary, incidental, consequential, transitional or saving provision (including provision amending, repealing or revoking enactments);
(b) make different provision for different purposes.

**3.** Except as specified in paragraph 4, a statutory instrument containing regulations under this Regulation is subject to annulment in pursuance of a resolution of either House of Parliament.
**4.** A statutory instrument containing regulations made under the second subparagraph of Article 2(1) or Article 18(5), 30(1) or 41(3) may not be made unless a draft of the instrument has been laid before, and approved by a resolution of, each House of Parliament.
**5.** Before making any regulations under this Regulation, the Secretary of State must consult:

(a) such bodies or persons as appear to the Secretary of State to be representative of the interests likely to be substantially affected by the regulations;
(b) such other bodies or persons as the Secretary of State may consider appropriate.]

## CHAPTER III
## REPEAL AND FINAL PROVISIONS

*Article 58*

### Repeal

A10-059 **1.** Regulations (EC) No 509/2006 and (EC) No 510/2006 are hereby repealed.

**2.** References to the repealed Regulations shall be construed as references to this Regulation and be read in accordance with the correlation table in Annex II to this Regulation.

*Article 59*

### Entry into force

A10-060 This Regulation shall enter into force on the twentieth day following that of its publication in the *Official Journal of the European Union*.

Done at Strasbourg, 21 November 2012.

For the European Parliament
The President
M. SCHULZ
For the Council
The President
A. D. MAVROYIANNIS

*ANNEX I*

### Agricultural Products and Foodstuffs Referred to in Article 2(1)

I. DESIGNATIONS OF ORIGIN AND GEOGRAPHICAL INDICATIONS

— beer,
— chocolate and derived products,
— bread, pastry, cakes, confectionery, biscuits and other baker's wares,
— beverages made from plant extracts,
— pasta,
— salt,
— natural gums and resins,
— mustard paste,
— hay,
— essential oils,
— cork,
— cochineal,
— flowers and ornamental plants,
— cotton,
— wool,
— wicker,
— scutched flax,
— leather,

— fur,
— feather.

II. **TRADITIONAL SPECIALITIES GUARANTEED**

— prepared meals,
— beer,
— chocolate and derived products,
— bread, pastry, cakes, confectionery, biscuits and other baker's wares,
— beverages made from plant extracts,
— pasta,
— salt.

*ANNEX II*

**Correlation Table Referred to in Article 58(2)**

A10-062

| *Regulation (EC) No 509/2006* | *This Regulation* |
|---|---|
| Article 1(1) | Article 2(1) |
| Article 1(2) | Article 2(3) |
| Article 1(3) | Article 2(4) |
| Article 2(1), point (a) | Article 3, point (5) |
| Article 2(1), point (b) | Article 3, point (3) |
| Article 2(1), point (c) | — |
| Article 2(1), point (d) | Article 3, point (2) |
| Article 2(2), first to third subparagraph | — |
| Article 2(2), fourth subparagraph | — |
| Article 3 | Article 22(1) |
| Article 4(1), first subparagraph | Article 18(1) |
| Article 4(2) | Article 18(2) |
| Article 4(3), first subparagraph | — |
| Article 4(3), second subparagraph | Article 18(4) |
| Article 5(1) | Article 43 |
| Article 5(2) | Article 42(1) |
| Article 6(1) | Article 19(1) |
| Article 6(1), point (a) | Article 19(1), point (a) |
| Article 6(1), point (b) | Article 19(1), point (b) |
| Article 6(1), point (c) | Article 19(1), point (c) |
| Article 6(1), point (d) | — |
| Article 6(1), point (e) | Article 19(1), point (d) |
| Article 6(1), point (f) | — |
| Article 7(1) and (2) | Article 49(1) |
| Article 7(3), points (a) and (b) | Article 20(1), points (a) and (b) |
| Article 7(3), point (c) | — |
| Article 7(3), point (d) | — |

| *Regulation (EC) No 509/2006* | *This Regulation* |
|---|---|
| Article 7(4) | Article 49(2) |
| Article 7(5) | Article 49(3) |
| Article 7(6), points (a), (b) and (c) | Article 49(4) |
| Article 7(6), point (d) | Article 20(2) |
| Article 7(7) | Article 49(5) |
| Article 7(8) | Article 49(6) |
| Article 8(1) | Article 50(1) |
| Article 8(2), first subparagraph | Article 50(2), point (b) |
| Article 8(2), second subparagraph | Article 52(1) |
| Article 9(1) and (2) | Article 51(1) |
| Article 9(3) | Article 21(1) and (2) |
| Article 9(4) | Article 52(2) |
| Article 9(5) | Article 52(3) and (4) |
| Article 9(6) | Article 51(5) |
| Article 10 | Article 54 |
| Article 11 | Article 53 |
| Article 12 | Article 23 |
| Article 13(1) | — |
| Article 13(2) | — |
| Article 13(3) | — |
| Article 14(1) | Article 36(1) |
| Article 14(2) | Article 46(1) |
| Article 14(3) | Article 37(3), second subparagraph |
| Article 15(1) | Article 37(1) |
| Article 15(2) | Article 37(2) |
| Article 15(3) | Article 39(2) |
| Article 15(4) | Article 36(2) |
| Article 16 | — |
| Article 17(1) and (2) | Article 24(1) |
| Article 17(3) | Article 24(2) |
| Article 18 | Article 57 |
| Article 19(1), point (a) | — |
| Article 19(1), point (b) | Article 49(7), second subparagraph |
| Article 19(1), point (c) | Article 49(7), first subparagraph |
| Article 19(1), point (d) | Article 22(2) |
| Article 19(1), point (e) | Article 19(1), point (f) |
| Article 51(6) | Article 54(1) |
| Article 19(1), point (g) | Article 23(4) |
| Article 19(1), point (h) | — |
| Article 19(1), point (i) | — |
| Article 19(2) | Article 25(1) |

| *Regulation (EC) No 509/2006* | *This Regulation* |
|---|---|
| Article 19(3), point (a) | — |
| Article 19(3), point (b) | Article 25(2) |
| Article 20 | Article 47 |
| Article 21 | Article 58 |
| Article 22 | Article 59 |
| Annex I | Annex I (Part II) |

| *Regulation (EC) No 510/2006* | *This Regulation* |
|---|---|
| Article 1(1) | Article 2(1) and (2) |
| Article 1(2) | Article 2(3) |
| Article 1(3) | Article 2(4) |
| Article 2 | Article 5 |
| Article 3(1), first subparagraph | Article 6(1) |
| Article 3(1), second and third subparagraph | Article 41(1), (2) and (3) |
| Article 3(2), (3) and (4) | Article 6(2), (3) and (4) |
| Article 4 | Article 7 |
| Article 5(1) | Article 3, point (2), and Article 49(1) |
| Article 5(2) | Article 49(1) |
| Article 5(3) | Article 8(1) |
| Article 5(4) | Article 49(2) |
| Article 5(5) | Article 49(3) |
| Article 5(6) | Article 9 |
| Article 5(7) | Article 8(2) |
| Article 5(8) | — |
| Article 5(9), first subparagraph | — |
| Article 5(9), second subparagraph | Article 49(5) |
| Article 5(10) | Article 49(6) |
| Article 5(11) | — |
| Article 6(1), first subparagraph | Article 50(1) |
| Article 6(2), first subparagraph | Article 50(2), point (a) |
| Article 6(2), second subparagraph | Article 52(1) |
| Article 7(1) | Article 51(1), first subparagraph |
| Article 7(2) | Article 51(1), second subparagraph |
| Article 7(3) | Article 10 |
| Article 7(4) | Article 52(2) and (4) |
| Article 7(5) | Article 51(3) and Article 52(3) and (4) |
| Article 7(6) | Article 11 |
| Article 7(7) | Article 51(5) |
| Article 8 | Article 12 |
| Article 9 | Article 53 |

| *Regulation (EC) No 510/2006* | *This Regulation* |
|---|---|
| Article 10(1) | Article 36(1) |
| Article 10(2) | Article 46(1) |
| Article 10(3) | Article 37(3), second subparagraph |
| Article 11(1) | Article 37(1) |
| Article 11(2) | Article 37(2) |
| Article 11(3) | Article 39(2) |
| Article 11(4) | Article 36(2) |
| Article 12 | Article 54 |
| Article 13(1) | Article 13(1) |
| Article 13(2) | Article 13(2) |
| Article 13(3) | Article 15(1) |
| Article 13(4) | Article 15(2) |
| Article 14 | Article 14 |
| Article 15 | Article 57 |
| Article 16, point (a) | Article 5(4), second subparagraph |
| Article 16, point (b) | — |
| Article 16, point (c) | — |
| Article 16, point (d) | Article 49(7) |
| Article 16, point (e) | — |
| Article 16, point (f) | Article 51(6) |
| Article 16, point (g) | Article 12(7) |
| Article 16, point (h) | — |
| Article 16, point (i) | Article 11(3) |
| Article 16, point (j) | — |
| Article 16, point (k) | Article 54(2) |
| Article 17 | Article 16 |
| Article 18 | Article 47 |
| Article 19 | Article 58 |
| Article 20 | Article 59 |
| Annex I and Annex II | Annex I (Part I) |

[*ANNEX 3*

**Appeals**

| *Decision* | *Persons who may appeal against the decision* | *FTT powers* |
|---|---|---|
| Decision of the Secretary of State to approve an application made under Article 49 to register a designation of origin, geographical indication or | The persons are: (a) a person who submitted a reasoned statement of opposition under Article 51(2); (b) a person marketing a | Power to: (a) quash the decision and direct the Secretary of State to reject the application and (if appropriate) restore the register; |

| *Decision* | *Persons who may appeal against the decision* | *FTT powers* |
|---|---|---|
| traditional speciality guaranteed | product that is, or may be, affected by the registration of the designation of origin, geographical indication or traditional speciality guaranteed. | (b) remit the matter to the Secretary of State with a direction to repeat the scrutiny of the application and (if appropriate) to restore the register in the meantime. |
| Decision of the Secretary of State to reject an application made under Article 49 to register a designation of origin, geographical indication or traditional speciality guaranteed | The persons are:<br>(a) the person who submitted the application to register the designation of origin, geographical indication or traditional speciality guaranteed;<br>(b) a person marketing a product that is, or may be, affected by the decision not to register the designation of origin, geographical indication or traditional speciality guaranteed. | Power to:<br>(a) quash the decision and direct the Secretary of State to approve the application and register the designation of origin, geographical indication or traditional speciality guaranteed;<br>(b) remit the matter to the Secretary of State with a direction to repeat the scrutiny of the application. |
| Decision of the Secretary of State to approve an application made under Article 53 to make an amendment to a product specification relating to a protected designation of origin, protected geographical indication or protected traditional speciality guaranteed | The persons are:<br>(a) a person who submitted a reasoned statement of opposition under Article 51(2), as read with the first subparagraph of Article 53(2), in relation to the application;<br>(b) a person marketing a product that is, or may be, affected by the amendment of the product specification. | Power to:<br>(a) quash the decision and direct the Secretary of State to reject the application and (if appropriate) restore the register;<br>(b) remit the matter to the Secretary of State with a direction to repeat the scrutiny of the application and (if appropriate) to restore the register in the meantime. |
| Decision of the Secretary of State to reject an application made under Article 53 to make an amendment to a product specification relating to a protected designation of origin, protected geographical indication or protected traditional speciality guaranteed | The persons are:<br>(a) the person who submitted the application to amend the product specification;<br>(b) a person marketing a product that is, or may be, affected by the decision not to approve the application to amend the product specification. | Power to:<br>(a) quash the decision and direct the Secretary of State to approve the application and attach a copy of the amended product specification to the register;<br>(b) remit the matter to the Secretary of State with a direction to repeat the |

| *Decision* | *Persons who may appeal against the decision* | *FTT powers* |
|---|---|---|
| | | scrutiny of the application. |
| Decision of the Secretary of State under Article 54 to cancel the registration of a protected designation of origin, protected geographical indication or protected traditional speciality guaranteed on thc Secretary of State's initiative | The persons are: (a) a person who submitted a reasoned statement of opposition under Article 51(2) as read with Article 7(1) and (4) of Regulation 664/2014; (b) a person marketing a product that is, or may be, affected by the cancellation of the registration of the protected designation of origin, protected geographical indication or protected traditional speciality guaranteed. | Power to: (a) quash the decision and direct the Secretary of State (if appropriate) to restore the register; (b) remit the matter to the Secretary of State with a direction to repeat the scrutiny relating to the cancellation and (if appropriate) to restore the register in the meantime. |
| Decision of the Secretary of State to approve an application made under Article 54 to cancel the registration of a protected designation of origin, protected geographical indication or protected traditional speciality guaranteed | The persons are: (a) a person who submitted a reasoned statement of opposition under Article 51(2) as read with Article 7(1) and (4) of Regulation 664/2014; (b) a person marketing a product that is, or may be, affected by the cancellation of the registration of the protected designation of origin, protected geographical indication or protected traditional speciality guaranteed. | Power to: (a) quash the decision and direct the Secretary of State to (if appropriate) restore the register, or (b) remit the matter to the Secretary of State with a direction to repeat the scrutiny of the application and (if appropriate) to rectify the register in the meantime. |
| Decision of the Secretary of State to reject an application made under Article 54 to cancel the registration of a protected designation of origin, protected geographical indication or protected traditional speciality guaranteed | The persons are: (a) the person who submitted the application to cancel the registration of the protected designation of origin, protected geographical indication or protected traditional speciality guaranteed; (b) a person marketing a product that is, or may be, affected by the decision | Power to: (a) quash the decision and direct the Secretary of State to cancel the registration; (b) remit the matter to the Secretary of State with a direction to repeat the scrutiny of the application.] |

| *Decision* | *Persons who may appeal against the decision* | *FTT powers* |
|---|---|---|
| | not to cancel the registration the protected designation of origin, protected geographical indication or protected traditional speciality guaranteed. | |

## APPENDIX 15

# THE TRADE MARKS (INTERNATIONAL REGISTRATION) ORDER 2008

*Replace Schedules with:*

A15-009 SCHEDULE 1

PROVISIONS OF THE ACT AND TRADE MARKS RULES WHICH DO NOT APPLY TO INTERNATIONAL TRADE MARKS (UK) OR REQUESTS FOR EXTENSION

**Article 3(3)**

PART 1

A15-009 section 24(2)(b) (assignment or other transmission in relation to use of the trade mark in a particular manner or locality)
section 32(1), (2) and (4) (application for registration)
section 33(1) (date of filing )
section 34 (classification of trade marks)
section 39(2) (withdrawal, restriction or amendment of application)
section 40 (registration)
section 41 (registration: supplementary provisions)
section 42 (duration of registration)
section 43 (renewal of registration)
section 44 (alteration of registered trade mark)
section 45 (surrender of registered trade mark)
section 64(4) (change of name and address by proprietor or licensee)
section 65 (adaptation of entries to new classification)
section 79 (fees)
section 94 (falsification of register)

PART 2

A15-010 trade marks rule 6 (claim to priority; sections 35 & 36)

trade marks rule 8 (application may relate to more than one class and shall specify the class (Form TM31C))

trade marks rule 9 (determination of classification) trade marks rule 12(4)(a) (failure to provide an address for service)

trade marks rule 13 (deficiencies in application; section 32)

[trade marks rule 28 (registration of a series of trade marks; section 41) (Form TM12)]

trade marks rule 46 (form of register; section 63(1))

trade marks rule 47 (entry in register of particulars of registered trade marks; section 63(2) (Form TM24))

trade marks rule 56 (request for information; s.67(1) (Form TM31C))

SCHEDULE 2

MODIFICATIONS TO PROVISIONS OF THE ACT APPLIED TO INTERNATIONAL TRADE MARKS (UK)

**Article 3(3)(i)**

A15-011 **1.**—(1) Section 25 (registration of transactions affecting registered trade mark) is modified as follows.

(2) Omit paragraph (a) of subsection (1) and substitute—

> "(a) a person claiming to be entitled to any security interest (whether fixed or floating) over a protected international trade mark (UK) or any right in or under it, or".

(3) Omit paragraphs (a), (b) and (c) of subsection (2) and substitute—

"(a) a change to the ownership of a registration recorded by the International Bureau in the International Register pursuant to article 9 of the Madrid Protocol;

(b) the grant of a licence recorded by the International Bureau in the International Register pursuant to rule 20bis of the Common Regulations;".

(4) After subsection (2)(e) insert—

"(f) any matter other than as is referred to in paragraphs (a) and (b) above that is recorded in the International Register pursuant to article 9bis of the Madrid Protocol.".

(5) In subsection (3) omit "Until an application has been made for registration of the prescribed particulars of a registrable transaction" and substitute "Until an application for registration of a matter in the supplementary register pursuant to subsection (1) has been made or an application for registration of a registrable transaction in the International Register (in accordance with Article 9bis of the Madrid Protocol and rule 20bis of the Common Regulations) has been made".

(6) In subsection (4)(a) omit "the prescribed particulars of the transaction" and substitute "a transaction in the International Register (in accordance with Article 9bis of the Madrid Protocol and rule 20bis of the Common Regulations)".

**2.** In section 33 (date of filing), for subsection (1), substitute— A15-012

"**33.**—(1) The date of filing of a request for extension shall be the date of the international registration except—

(a) where at the time protection is conferred on an international trade mark (UK) there is a concurrent registered trade mark, the date of filing shall be the date of filing of the registered trade mark; and

(b) where a request for extension is made in accordance with Article 3ter(2) of the Madrid Protocol, the date of filing shall be the date that the request for extension was recorded in the International Register.".

**3.** In section 35 (claim to priority of convention application), for subsection (5), substitute— A15-013

"(5) The manner of claiming priority shall be determined in accordance with the Madrid Protocol and the Common Regulations.".

**4.** In section 37 (examination of application) omit subsections (3) to (5) and substitute— A15-014

"(3) If it appears to the registrar that the requirements for registration are not met, the registrar shall give notice of provisional refusal to the International Bureau.

(4) Where the International Bureau notifies the registrar or the registrar considers that a particular term used to indicate any of the goods or services included in the international registration is—

(a) too vague for the purposes of classification; or

(b) incomprehensible or linguistically incorrect,

the registrar may give notice of provisional refusal to the International Bureau in respect of that term.

(5) Where a decision of the registrar has been notified to the International Bureau pursuant to subsection (3) or (4), the registrar shall give the holder of the international registration an opportunity, within such period as the registrar may specify, to make representations or amend the request for extension by limiting the goods and services.".

**5.** In section 38(2) (publication, opposition proceedings and observations) after "opposition to the registration" insert "in which event the registrar shall give notice of provisional refusal to the International Bureau". A15-015

**6.** After section 38, insert— A15-016

**Notices of provisional refusal**

"**38A.**(1) A notice of provisional refusal must set out the matters required by Article 5 of the Madrid Protocol and Rule 17 of the Common Regulations.

(2) Except as provided in subsection (3), a notice of provisional refusal may not be given after the expiry of the relevant period.

(3) Where before the expiry of the relevant period the registrar has given notice to the International Bureau—

(a) that the period prescribed for the purposes of section 38(2) expires after the end of the relevant period; or

(b) that the period prescribed for the purposes of section 38(2) expires less than one month before the end of the relevant period;

a notice of provisional refusal may be given after the expiry of the relevant period provided that it is given before the end of the period of one month beginning immediately after the period prescribed for the purposes of section 38(2).

(4) Where the registrar sends the International Bureau a notice of provisional refusal, the registrar must notify the International Bureau as to the final decision (meaning a decision from which no appeal may be brought) on whether the refusal should be upheld.

(5) The relevant period is the period of 18 months [beginning immediately after] the date the International Bureau sent the registrar the request for extension.

**Protection**

**38B.**(1) Where no notice of provisional refusal is given to the International Bureau following publication under section 38(1), the international registration which is the subject of the request for extension shall be protected as a protected international trade mark (UK) with effect from the first day immediately following the end of the period prescribed for the purposes of section 38(2).

(2) Where notice of provisional refusal is given following publication under section 38(1), the international registration which is the subject of the request for extension shall be protected as a protected international trade mark (UK) with effect from the date on which the registrar notifies the International Bureau that the final decision is that the provisional refusal should not be upheld in accordance with section 38A(4).

(3) The reference to the completion of the registration procedure in [sections 6A, 11A, 46(1) and 47(2A)] shall be construed as a reference to the conferring of protection on an international registration in accordance with this section.

(4) When an international registration becomes protected as a protected international trade mark (UK), the registrar shall—

(a) notify the International Bureau that the international registration is protected in the United Kingdom; and

(b) publish a notice specifying the number of the international registration in respect of that trade mark, the date on which protection is conferred and the date and place of publication of the request for extension under section 38(1) in relation to that trade mark.".

**A15-017** **7.** In section 39 (Withdrawal, restriction or amendment of application) for subsection (1) substitute—

"(1) The goods and services covered by a request for extension may be restricted at any time by the applicant provided that if the request for extension has been published, the restriction must also be published in the Journal [...] .".

**A15-018** **8.**—(1) Section 63 (the register) shall be modified as follows.

(2) For subsection (1) substitute—

"(1) The registrar shall maintain a register for the purpose of entering transactions under section 25(1) (as modified by paragraph 1 of Schedule 2 to the Trade Marks International Registration) Order 2008) and disclaimers and limitations relating to international trade marks (UK).".

(3) In subsection (3) for the words "shall be kept in such manner as may be prescribed" substitute "need not be kept in documentary form".

(4) After subsection (3) insert—

"(4) Following notification from the International Bureau under rule 28(2) of the Common Regulations the registrar may correct an error or omission in the information entered in the register required to be maintained under subsection (1).".

**A15-019** **9.** In section 67(2)(a) (Information about applications and registered trade marks) before "in such cases" insert "any information recorded in the International Register or".

## SCHEDULE 3

### INTERNATIONAL APPLICATIONS ORIGINATING IN THE UNITED KINGDOM

**Article 4**

**Application for international registration at the Patent Office**

**1.**—(1) An applicant for the registration of a trade mark, or the proprietor of a registered trade mark, may, subject to the provisions of this paragraph, apply by way of the Patent Office as office of origin for the international registration of the trade mark. **A15-020**

(2) For the purposes of this paragraph an applicant shall be—

(a) a British citizen, a British overseas territories citizen, a British overseas citizen, a British subject or a British protected person;

(b) an individual domiciled in the United Kingdom;

(c) a body incorporated under the law of a part of the United Kingdom; or

(d) a person who has a real and effective industrial or commercial establishment in the United Kingdom.

(3) Where the registrar has reasonable doubts about whether an applicant is eligible, the registrar—

(a) must inform the applicant of the reason for those doubts; and

(b) may require that applicant to file evidence in support of his eligibility.

(4) Where—

(a) the registrar has no doubts or is satisfied as to the applicant's eligibility; and

(b) the particulars appearing in the application for an international registration correspond with the particulars at that time in the basic application or, as the case may be, the basic registration,

the registrar must submit the application to the International Bureau.

(5) In this Schedule—

(a) "basic application" means an application for registration of a trade mark in the United Kingdom in respect of which application is made for international registration;

(b) "basic registration" means a trade mark registered in the United Kingdom in respect of which application is made for international registration.

**Termination of basic application or basic registration**

**2.**—(1) This paragraph applies where the registrar submits an application to the International Bureau in accordance with paragraph 1 and the basic application or basic registration is terminated. **A15-021**

(2) Where, before the end of the relevant period, a basic application or basic registration is terminated, the registrar shall request that the International Bureau cancel the International Registration.

(3) A basic application is terminated where it is—

(a) not accepted;

(b) refused; or

(c) withdrawn (including deemed as such).

(4) A basic registration is terminated where the rights in the registered trade mark cease to have effect.

(5) Where a basic application or basic registration is terminated in respect of some only of the goods or services for which the trade mark is registered (or is sought to be registered), the request must relate only to those goods and services.

(6) The relevant period is the period of 5 years [beginning immediately after] the date of the international registration.

(7) But if during that period the registrar becomes aware of proceedings which may result in the termination of the basic application or basic registration, the registrar must notify the International Bureau accordingly, stating that no final decision has been made.

(8) On completion of the proceedings referred to in paragraph (7) the registrar must promptly notify the International Bureau of their outcome.

**Division or merger of basic application or basic registration**

**3.**—(1) This paragraph applies where the registrar submits an application to the International Bureau in accordance with paragraph 1 and— **A15-022**

(a) the basic application is divided into two or more applications; or

(b) two or more basic applications or basic registrations are merged into a single application or registration.

(2) Where, before the end of the relevant period, a basic application is divided or two or more basic applications or basic registrations are merged, the registrar shall notify the International Bureau and shall indicate—

(a) the number of the international registration or, where the mark has not been registered, the number of the basic application;

(b) the name of the applicant or the holder of the relevant trade mark; and

(c) the number of each application resulting from the division or the number of the application or registration resulting from the merger.

(3) The relevant period is the period of 5 years [beginning immediately after] the date of the international registration.

## SCHEDULE 4

### TRANSFORMATION APPLICATIONS AND CONCURRENT REGISTRATIONS

**Article 5**

**Transformation applications**

A15-023 **1.**—(1) A transformation application is an application to register a trade mark under the Act where—

(a) the mark was the subject of an international registration and the international registration was the subject of a request for extension; and

(b) the international registration was cancelled at the request of the Office of origin under Article 6(4) of the Madrid Protocol.

(2) But an application shall only be treated as a transformation application where the goods and services cited in it are identical to some or all of the goods and services included in the international registration.

(3) Any application made under the Act which is a transformation application shall state that it is made by way of transformation.

(4) Such an application may only be made before the end of the period of three months [beginning immediately after] the date on which the international registration was cancelled.

(5) A transformation application may only be made by the person who was the holder of the international registration immediately before it was cancelled.

(6) Where on or before the date the transformation application was made, the trade mark is protected as an international trade mark (UK), the mark shall be registered under the Act; and it shall have the date of filing of the cancelled international trade mark (UK).

(7) Where on that date the trade mark is not so protected, the transformation application shall be treated as an application to register under the Act and it shall have the date of filing of the request for extension relating to that mark.

(8) Where in relation to the international registration a right of priority was claimed on the basis of a Convention application, the transformation application shall have the same right of priority.

**Concurrent registrations**

A15-024 **2.**—(1) This paragraph applies where at the time protection is conferred on an international trade mark (UK) there is a concurrent registered trade mark.

(2) A registration is concurrent where—

(a) the proprietor of the registered trade mark is the holder of the protected international trade mark (UK);

(b) the registered trade mark is the same as the protected international trade mark (UK);

(c) the goods and services in relation to which protection is conferred by the international trade mark (UK) include all those for which the registered trade mark is registered.

(3) The protected international trade mark (UK) shall be treated as being registered under the Act as of the date of registration of the registered trade mark.

(4) The priorities claimed in respect of the registered trade mark may also be claimed in respect of the international trade mark (UK).

(5) The provisions of this paragraph shall continue to apply after the registered trade mark lapses or is surrendered, but shall cease to apply if or to the extent that it is revoked or declared invalid.

(6) On the application of the holder of the protected international trade mark (UK) the registrar shall note the international registration in the register against the registered trade mark.

(7) For the purposes of paragraph (6), the holder of the international trade mark (UK) shall make an application to the registrar using Form TM28.

## SCHEDULE 5

### MISCELLANEOUS AND GENERAL PROVISIONS

**Article 6**

**Correction of international registration**

**1.**—(1) Where the International Bureau notifies the registrar that it has corrected an international registration and the correction either— **A15-025**

(a) substantially affects the identity of the trade mark; or

(b) alters the goods or services covered by the international registration, the registrar may treat the notification as a new request for extension.

(2) Where paragraph (1)(a) applies, any earlier request for protection shall be deemed to have been withdrawn and any resulting protection granted to the international trade mark (UK) shall be treated as having been declared invalid.

(3) Where paragraph (1)(b) applies and—

(a) the correction extends the goods and services covered by the request for extension, the new request for extension shall apply only to the additional goods and services; or

(b) the correction restricts the goods and services covered by the international registration, to the extent it relates to goods and service outside the restriction, an earlier request for protection shall be treated as having been withdrawn, and any resulting protection granted to the international trade mark (UK) shall be treated as having been declared invalid.

**Assignment**

**2.**—(1) A protected international trade mark (UK) may only be assigned to an eligible person. **A15-026**

(2) An eligible person is—

(a) a national of any country which is a party to the Madrid Protocol;

(b) an individual domiciled in such a country;

(c) a body incorporated under the law of such a country; and

(d) a person who has a real and effective industrial or commercial establishment in such a country.

**Judicial notice**

**3.**—(1) Judicial notice shall be taken of the following— **A15-027**

(a) the Madrid Protocol and the Common Regulations;

(b) copies issued by the International Bureau of entries in the International Register;

(c) copies of the periodical gazette published by the International Bureau in accordance with rule 32 of the Common Regulations.

(2) Any document mentioned in paragraph (1)(b) or (c) shall be admissible as evidence of any instrument or other act of the International Bureau so communicated.

(3) Where in relation to the international registration a right of priority was claimed on the basis of a Convention application, the transformation application shall have the same right of priority.

**Revocation**

**4.** Where the protection of a protected international trade mark (UK) is revoked or declared invalid to any extent, the registrar shall notify the International Bureau, and— **A15-028**

(a) in the case of a revocation, the rights of the proprietor shall be deemed to have ceased to exist to that extent as from—

(i) the date of the application for revocation, or

(ii) if the registrar or court is satisfied that the grounds for revocation existed at an earlier date, that date;

(b) in the case of a declaration of invalidity, the trade mark shall to that extent be deemed never to have been a protected international trade mark (UK).

**Requests for Information**

**5.** A request for information relating to a protected international trade mark (UK) must be made on Form TM31M. **A15-029**

**Communication of information to the International Bureau**

A15-030 **6.** Notwithstanding any other enactment or rule of law, the registrar may communicate to the International Bureau any information which the United Kingdom is required to communicate by virtue of this Order or pursuant to the Madrid Protocol or Common Regulations.

**Transmission of fees to the International Bureau**

A15-031 **7.** The registrar may accept for transmission to the International Bureau fees payable to the International Bureau in respect of an application for international registration originating in the United Kingdom or a renewal of such an international registration, subject to such terms and conditions as the registrar may specify, either generally by published notice, or in any particular case by written notice to the applicant desiring to make payment by such means.

SCHEDULE 6

FEES

**Article 7**

A15-032

| **Matter in respect of which fee payable** | **Amount** |
|---|---|
| Notice of opposition to the conferring of protection on an international registration (trade marks rule 17) | £200 |
| [Notice of opposition to the conferring of protection on an international registration where the grounds of opposition are based solely on either or both of sub-sections 5(1) and (2) of the Trade Marks Act 1994 | £100 |
| Notice of fast track opposition to the conferring of protection on an international registration (trade marks rule 17A) | £100 |
| Application to add grounds, other than under section 5(1) or 5(2) of the Act, to an opposition to the conferring of protection on an international registration (trade marks rule 62(1)(e)) | £100] |
| Request for the revocation of a protected international trade mark (UK) (on grounds other than non-use) (trade marks rule 39) | £200 |
| Request for the revocation of a protected international trade mark (UK) (on grounds of non-use) (trade marks rule 38) | £200 |
| Request for the invalidation of a protected international trade mark (UK) (trade marks rule 41) | £200 |
| Submission fee for an international application (Schedule 3, paragraph 1) | £40 |
| Handling fee for the transmission by the Patent Office of fees payable to the International Bureau for renewal of an international registration (Schedule 5, paragraph 7) | £20 |
| Request to the Registrar for a statement of reasons for his decision (trade mark rule 69(2)) | £20 |
| Request for an extension of time (trade marks rule 77(2)) | [£100] |
| Request for information in relation to an international mark (UK) | £50 |
| Filing of regulations governing the use of a certification or collective mark (trade mark rules 29) | £200 |
| Request to amend regulations governing the use of a certification or collective mark (trade mark rules 30) | £100 |
| Notice of opposition to the amendment of regulations relating to a certification or collective mark (trademark rules 30(4)) | £200 |
| [Request to enter details in the supplementary register relating to the grant, amendment or termination of any security interest (trade marks rule 49(1)(d)) | £50] |
| [Appeal to the person appointed under section 76 in proceedings between two or more parties (trade marks rule 71(1A)) | £250] |

## SCHEDULE 7

### REVOCATIONS

**Article 8**

A15-033

| Title and number |
|---|
| The Trade Marks (International Registration) Order 1996 (SI 1996/714) |
| Trade Marks (International Registration) (Amendment) Order 2000 (SI 2000/138) |
| Trade Marks (International Registration) (Amendment) Order 2002 (SI 2002/692) |
| Trade Marks (International Registration) (Amendment) Order 2004 (SI 2004/948) |
| Trade Marks (International Registration) (Amendment) Order 2006 (SI 2006/763) |
| Trade Marks (International Registration) (Amendment No 2) Order 2006 (SI 2006/1080) |

# REPLACEMENT APPENDICES

*Replace Appendix 5:*

## Appendix 5

# DIRECTIVE (EU) 2015/2436 OF THE EUROPEAN PARLIAMENT AND OF THE COUNCIL

## of 16 December 2015

## to approximate the laws of the Member States relating to trade marks (Recast) (Text with EEA relevance)

**A5-001** THE EUROPEAN PARLIAMENT AND THE COUNCIL OF THE EUROPEAN UNION,

Having regard to the Treaty on the Functioning of the European Union, and in particular Article 114(1) thereof,

Having regard to the proposal from the European Commission,

After transmission of the draft legislative act to the national parliaments,

Having regard to the opinion of the European Economic and Social Committee,

Acting in accordance with the ordinary legislative procedure,

Whereas:

**(1)** A number of amendments should be made to Directive 2008/95/EC of the European Parliament and of the Council. In the interests of clarity, that Directive should be recast.

**(2)** Directive 2008/95/EC has harmonised central provisions of substantive trade mark law which at the time of adoption were considered as most directly affecting the functioning of the internal market by impeding the free movement of goods and the freedom to provide services in the Union.

**(3)** Trade mark protection in the Member States coexists with protection available at Union level through European Union trade marks ('EU trade marks') which are unitary in character and valid throughout the Union as laid down in Council Regulation (EC) No 207/2009. The coexistence and balance of trade mark systems at national and Union level in fact constitutes a cornerstone of the Union's approach to intellectual property protection.

**(4)** Further to the Commission's communication of 16 July 2008 on an industrial property rights strategy for Europe, the Commission carried out a comprehensive evaluation of the overall functioning of the trade mark system in Europe as a whole, covering Union and national levels and the interrelation between the two.

**(5)** In its conclusions of 25 May 2010 on the future revision of the trade mark system in the European Union, the Council called on the Commission to present proposals for the revision of Regulation (EC) No 207/2009 and Directive 2008/95/EC. The revision of that Directive should include measures to make it more consistent with Regulation (EC) No 207/2009, which would thus reduce the areas of divergence within the trade mark system in Europe as a whole, while maintaining national trade mark protection as an attractive option for applicants. In this context, the complementary relationship between the EU trade mark system and national trade mark systems should be ensured.

**(6)** The Commission concluded in its communication of 24 May 2011 entitled 'A single market for intellectual property rights' that in order to meet increased demands from stakeholders for faster, higher quality, more streamlined trade mark registration systems, which are also more consistent, user friendly, publicly accessible and technologically up to date, there is a necessity to modernise the trade mark system in the Union as a whole and adapt it to the internet era.

**(7)** Consultation and evaluation for the purpose of this Directive has revealed that, in spite of the previous partial harmonisation of national laws, there remain areas where further harmonisation could have a positive impact on competitiveness and growth.

**(8)** In order to serve the objective of fostering and creating a well-functioning internal market and to facilitate acquiring and protecting trade marks in the Union, to the benefit of the growth and the competitiveness of European businesses, in particular small and medium-sized enterprises, it is necessary to go beyond the limited scope of approximation achieved by Directive 2008/95/EC and extend approximation to other aspects of substantive trade mark law governing trade marks protected through registration pursuant to Regulation (EC) No 207/2009.

**(9)** For the purpose of making trade mark registrations throughout the Union easier to obtain and administer, it is essential to approximate not only provisions of substantive law but also procedural rules. Therefore, the principal procedural rules in the area of trade mark registration in the Member States and in the EU trade mark system should be aligned. As regards procedures under national law, it is sufficient to lay down general principles, leaving the Member States free to establish more specific rules.

**(10)** It is essential to ensure that registered trade marks enjoy the same protection under the legal systems of all the Member States. In line with the extensive protection granted to EU trade marks which have a reputation in the Union, extensive protection should also be granted at national level to all registered trade marks which have a reputation in the Member State concerned.

**(11)** This Directive should not deprive the Member States of the right to continue to protect trade marks acquired through use but should take them into account only with regard to their relationship with trade marks acquired by registration.

**(12)** Attainment of the objectives of this approximation of laws requires that the conditions for obtaining and continuing to hold a registered trade mark be, in general, identical in all Member States.

**(13)** To this end, it is necessary to list examples of signs which are capable of constituting a trade mark, provided that such signs are capable of distinguishing the goods or services of one undertaking from those of other undertakings. In order to fulfil the objectives of the registration system for trade marks, namely to ensure legal certainty and sound administration, it is also essential to require that the sign is capable of being represented in a manner which is clear, precise, self-contained, easily accessible, intelligible, durable and objective. A sign should therefore be permitted to be represented in any appropriate form using generally available technology, and thus not necessarily by graphic means, as long as the representation offers satisfactory guarantees to that effect.

**(14)** Furthermore, the grounds for refusal or invalidity concerning the trade mark itself, including the absence of any distinctive character, or concerning conflicts between the trade mark and earlier rights, should be listed in an exhaustive manner, even if some of those grounds are listed as an option for the Member States which should therefore be able to maintain or introduce them in their legislation.

**(15)** In order to ensure that the levels of protection afforded to geographical indications by Union legislation and national law are applied in a uniform and exhaustive manner in the examination of absolute and relative grounds for refusal throughout the Union, this Directive should include the same provisions in relation to geographical indications as contained in Regulation (EC) No 207/2009. Furthermore, it is appropriate to ensure that the scope of absolute grounds is extended to also cover protected traditional terms for wine and traditional specialties guaranteed.

**(16)** The protection afforded by the registered trade mark, the function of which is in particular to guarantee the trade mark as an indication of origin, should be absolute in the event of there being identity between the mark and the corresponding sign and the goods or services. The protection should apply also in the case of similarity between the mark and the sign and the goods or services. It is indispensable to give an interpretation of the concept of similarity in relation to the likelihood of confusion. The likelihood of confusion, the appreciation of which depends on numerous elements and, in particular, on the recognition of the trade mark on the market, the association which can be made with the used or registered sign, the degree of similarity between the trade mark and the sign and between the goods or services identified, should constitute the specific condition for such protection. The ways in which a likelihood of confusion can be established, and in particular the onus of proof in that regard, should be a matter for national procedural rules which should not be prejudiced by this Directive.

**(17)** In order to ensure legal certainty and full consistency with the principle of priority, under which a registered earlier trade mark takes precedence over later registered trade marks, it is necessary to provide that the enforcement of rights which are conferred by a trade mark should be without prejudice to the rights of proprietors acquired prior to the filing or priority date of the trade mark. Such an approach is in conformity with Article 16(1) of the Agreement on trade-related aspects of intellectual property rights of 15 April 1994 ('TRIPS Agreement').

**(18)** It is appropriate to provide that an infringement of a trade mark can only be established if there is a finding that the infringing mark or sign is used in the course of trade for the purposes of distinguishing goods or services. Use of the sign for purposes other than for distinguishing goods or services should be subject to the provisions of national law.

**(19)** The concept of infringement of a trade mark should also comprise the use of the sign as a trade name or similar designation, as long as such use is made for the purposes of distinguishing goods or services.

**(20)** In order to ensure legal certainty and full consistency with specific Union legislation, it is appropriate to provide that the proprietor of a trade mark should be entitled to prohibit a third party from using a sign in comparative advertising where such comparative advertising is contrary to Directive 2006/114/EC of the European Parliament and of the Council.

**(21)** In order to strengthen trade mark protection and combat counterfeiting more effectively, and in line with international obligations of the Member States under the World Trade Organisation (WTO) framework, in particular Article V of the General Agreement on Tariffs and Trade on freedom of transit and, as regards generic medicines, the 'Declaration on the TRIPS Agreement and public health' adopted by the Doha WTO Ministerial Conference on 14 November 2001, the proprietor of a trade mark should be entitled to prevent third parties from bringing goods, in the course of trade, into the Member State where the trade mark is registered without being released for free circulation there, where such goods come from third countries and bear without authorisation a trade mark which is identical or essentially identical with the trade mark registered in respect of such goods.

**(22)** To this effect, it should be permissible for trade mark proprietors to prevent the entry of infringing goods and their placement in all customs situations, including, in particular transit, transhipment, warehousing, free zones, temporary storage, inward processing or temporary admission, also when such goods are not intended to be placed on the market of the Member State concerned. In performing customs controls, the customs authorities should make use of the powers and procedures laid down in Regulation (EU) No 608/2013 of the European Parliament and of the Council, also at the request of the right holders. In particular, the customs authorities should carry out the relevant controls on the basis of risk analysis criteria.

**(23)** In order to reconcile the need to ensure the effective enforcement of trade mark rights with the necessity to avoid hampering the free flow of trade in legitimate goods, the entitlement of the proprietor of the trade mark should lapse where, during the subsequent proceedings initiated before the judicial or other authority competent to take a substantive decision on whether the registered trade mark has been infringed, the declarant or the holder of the goods is able to prove that the proprietor of the registered trade mark is not entitled to prohibit the placing of the goods on the market in the country of final destination.

**(24)** Article 28 of Regulation (EU) No 608/2013 provides that a right holder is to be liable for damages towards the holder of the goods where, inter alia, the goods in question are subsequently found not to infringe an intellectual property right.

**(25)** Appropriate measures should be taken with a view to ensuring the smooth transit of generic medicines. With respect to international non-proprietary names (INN) as globally recognised generic names for active substances in pharmaceutical preparations, it is vital to take due account of the existing limitations on the effect of trade mark rights. Consequently, the proprietor of a trade mark should not have the right to prevent a third party from bringing goods into a Member State where the trade mark is registered without being released for free circulation there based upon similarities between the INN for the active ingredient in the medicines and the trade mark.

**(26)** In order to enable proprietors of registered trade marks to combat counterfeiting more effectively, they should be entitled to prohibit the affixing of an infringing trade mark to goods, and certain preparatory acts carried out prior to such affixing.

**(27)** The exclusive rights conferred by a trade mark should not entitle the proprietor to prohibit the use of signs or indications by third parties which are used fairly and thus in accordance with honest practices in industrial and commercial matters. In order to create equal conditions for trade names and trade marks against the background that trade names are regularly granted unrestricted protection against later trade marks, such use should only be considered to include the use of the personal name of the third party. Such use should further permit the use of descriptive or non-distinctive signs or indications in general. Furthermore, the proprietor should not be entitled to prevent the fair and honest use of the mark for the purpose of identifying or referring to the goods or services as those of the proprietor. Use of a trade mark by third parties to draw the consumer's attention to the resale of genuine goods that were originally sold by, or with the consent of, the proprietor of the trade mark in the Union should be considered as being fair as long as it is at the same time in accordance with honest practices in industrial and commercial matters. Use of a trade mark by third parties for the purpose of artistic expression should be considered as being fair as long as it is at the same time in accordance with honest practices in industrial and commercial matters. Furthermore, this Directive should be applied in a way that ensures full respect for fundamental rights and freedoms, and in particular the freedom of expression.

**(28)** It follows from the principle of free movement of goods that the proprietor of a trade mark should not be entitled to prohibit its use by a third party in relation to goods which have been put into circulation in the Union, under the trade mark, by him or with his consent, unless the proprietor has legitimate reasons to oppose further commercialisation of the goods.

**(29)** It is important, for reasons of legal certainty to provide that, without prejudice to his interests as a proprietor of an earlier trade mark, the latter may no longer request a declaration of invalidity or oppose the use of a trade mark subsequent to his own trade mark, of which he has knowingly tolerated the use for a substantial length of time, unless the application for the subsequent trade mark was made in bad faith.

**(30)** In order to ensure legal certainty and safeguard legitimately acquired trade mark rights, it is appropriate and necessary to provide that, without prejudice to the principle that the later trade mark cannot be enforced against the earlier trade mark, proprietors of earlier trade marks should not be entitled to obtain refusal or invalidation or to oppose the use of a later trade mark if the later trade mark was acquired at a time when the earlier trade mark was liable to be declared invalid or revoked, for example because it had not yet acquired distinctiveness through use, or if the earlier trade mark could not be enforced against the later trade mark because the necessary conditions were not applicable, for example when the earlier mark had not yet obtained a reputation.

**(31)** Trade marks fulfil their purpose of distinguishing goods or services and allowing consumers to make informed choices only when they are actually used on the market. A requirement of use is also necessary in order to reduce the total number of trade marks registered and protected in the Union and, consequently, the number of conflicts which arise between them. It is therefore essential to require that registered trade marks actually be used in connection with the goods or services for which they are registered, or, if not used in that connection within five years of the date of the completion of the registration procedure, be liable to be revoked.

**(32)** Consequently, a registered trade mark should only be protected in so far as it is actually used and a registered earlier trade mark should not enable its proprietor to oppose or invalidate a later trade mark if that proprietor has not put his trade mark to genuine use. Furthermore, Member States should provide that a trade mark may not be successfully invoked in infringement proceedings if it is established, as a result of a plea, that the trade mark could be revoked or, when the action is brought against a later right, could have been revoked at the time when the later right was acquired.

**(33)** It is appropriate to provide that, where the seniority of a national mark or a trade mark registered under international arrangements having effect in the Member State has been claimed for an EU trade mark and the mark providing the basis for the seniority claim has thereafter been surrendered or allowed to lapse, the validity of that mark can still be challenged. Such a challenge should be limited to situations where the mark could have been declared invalid or revoked at the time it was removed from the register.

**(34)** For reasons of coherence and in order to facilitate the commercial exploitation of trade marks in the Union, the rules applicable to trade marks as objects of property should be aligned to the extent appropriate with those already in place for EU trade marks, and should include rules on assignment and transfer, licensing, rights in rem and levy of execution.

**(35)** Collective trade marks have proven a useful instrument for promoting goods or services with specific common properties. It is therefore appropriate to subject national collective trade marks to rules similar to the rules applicable to European Union collective marks.

**(36)** In order to improve and facilitate access to trade mark protection and to increase legal certainty and predictability, the procedure for the registration of trade marks in the Member States should be efficient and transparent and should follow rules similar to those applicable to EU trade marks.

**(37)** In order to ensure legal certainty with regard to the scope of trade mark rights and to facilitate access to trade mark protection, the designation and classification of goods and services covered by a trade mark application should follow the same rules in all Member States and should be aligned to those applicable to EU trade marks. In order to enable the competent authorities and economic operators to determine the extent of the trade mark protection sought on the basis of the application alone, the designation of goods and services should be sufficiently clear and precise. The use of general terms should be interpreted as including only goods and services clearly covered by the literal meaning of a term. In the interest of clarity and legal certainty, the Member States' central industrial property offices and the Benelux Office for Intellectual Property should, in cooperation with each other, endeavour to compile a list reflecting their respective administrative practices with regard to the classification of goods and services.

**(38)** For the purpose of ensuring effective trade mark protection, Member States should make available an efficient administrative opposition procedure, allowing at least the proprietor of earlier trade mark rights and any person authorised under the relevant law to exercise the rights arising from a protected designation of origin or a geographical indication to oppose the registration of a trade mark application. Furthermore, in order to offer efficient means of revoking trademarks or declaring them invalid, Member States should provide for an administrative procedure for revocation or declaration of invalidity within the longer transposition period of seven years, after the entry into force of this Directive.

**(39)** It is desirable that Member States' central industrial property offices and the Benelux Office for Intellectual Property cooperate with each other and with the European Union Intellectual Property Office in all fields of trade mark registration and administration in order to promote convergence of practices and tools, such as the creation and updating of common or connected databases and portals for consultation and search purposes. The Member States should further ensure that their offices cooperate with each other and with the European Union Intellectual Property Office in all other areas of their activities which are relevant for the protection of trade marks in the Union.

**(40)** This Directive should not exclude the application to trade marks of provisions of law of the Member States other than trade mark law, such as provisions relating to unfair competition, civil liability or consumer protection.

**(41)** Member States are bound by the Paris Convention for the Protection of Industrial Property ('the Paris Convention') and the TRIPS Agreement. It is necessary that this Directive be entirely consistent with that Convention and that Agreement. The obligations of the Member States resulting from that Convention and that Agreement should not be affected by this Directive. Where appropriate, the second paragraph of Article 351 of the Treaty on the Functioning of the European Union should apply.

**(42)** Since the objectives of this Directive, namely to foster and create a well-functioning internal market and to facilitate the registration, administration and protection of trade marks in the Union to the benefit of growth and competitiveness, cannot be sufficiently achieved by the Member States but can rather, by reason of its scale and effects, be better achieved at Union level, the Union may adopt measures, in accordance with the principle of subsidiarity as set out in Article 5 of the Treaty on European Union. In accordance with the principle of proportionality as set out in that Article, this Directive does not go beyond what is necessary in order to achieve those objectives.

**(43)** Directive 95/46/EC of the European Parliament and of the Council governs the processing of personal data carried out in the Member States in the context of this Directive.

**(44)** The European Data Protection Supervisor was consulted in accordance with Article 28(2) of Regulation (EC) No 45/2001 of the European Parliament and of the Council and delivered an opinion on 11 July 2013.

**(45)** The obligation to transpose this Directive into national law should be confined to those provisions which represent a substantive amendment as compared with the earlier Directive. The obligation to transpose the provisions which are unchanged arises under the earlier Directive.

**(46)** This Directive should be without prejudice to the obligations of the Member States under Directive 2008/95/EC relating to the time limit for transposition of Council Directive 89/104/EEC9 into national law as set out in Part B of Annex I to Directive 2008/95/EC,

HAVE ADOPTED THIS DIRECTIVE:

## CHAPTER 1

## GENERAL PROVISIONS

### *Article 1*

### Scope

This Directive applies to every trade mark in respect of goods or services which is the subject of registration or of an application for registration in a Member State as an individual trade mark, a guarantee or certification mark or a collective mark, or which is the subject of a registration or an application for registration in the Benelux Office for Intellectual Property or of an international registration having effect in a Member State.

### *Article 2*

### Definitions

For the purpose of this Directive, the following definitions apply:

(a) 'office' means the central industrial property office of the Member State or the Benelux Office for Intellectual Property, entrusted with the registration of trade marks;

(b) 'register' means the register of trade marks kept by an office.

# CHAPTER 2

# SUBSTANTIVE LAW ON TRADE MARKS

## SECTION 1

## Signs of which a trade mark may consist

### *Article 3*

### Signs of which a trade mark may consist

A trade mark may consist of any signs, in particular words, including personal names, or designs, letters, numerals, colours, the shape of goods or of the packaging of goods, or sounds, provided that such signs are capable of:

(a) distinguishing the goods or services of one undertaking from those of other undertakings; and

(b) being represented on the register in a manner which enables the competent authorities and the public to determine the clear and precise subject matter of the protection afforded to its proprietor.

## SECTION 2

## Grounds for refusal or invalidity

### *Article 4*

### Absolute grounds for refusal or invalidity

**1.** The following shall not be registered or, if registered, shall be liable to be declared invalid:

(a) signs which cannot constitute a trade mark;

(b) trade marks which are devoid of any distinctive character;

(c) trade marks which consist exclusively of signs or indications which may serve, in trade, to designate the kind, quality, quantity, intended purpose, value, geographical origin, or the time of production of the goods or of rendering of the service, or other characteristics of the goods or services;

(d) trade marks which consist exclusively of signs or indications which have become customary in the current language or in the bona fide and established practices of the trade;

(e) signs which consist exclusively of:

(i) the shape, or another characteristic, which results from the nature of the goods themselves;

(ii) the shape, or another characteristic, of goods which is necessary to obtain a technical result;

(iii) the shape, or another characteristic, which gives substantial value to the goods;

(f) trade marks which are contrary to public policy or to accepted principles of morality;

(g) trade marks which are of such a nature as to deceive the public, for instance, as to the nature, quality or geographical origin of the goods or service;

(h) trade marks which have not been authorised by the competent authorities and are to be refused or invalidated pursuant to Article 6ter of the Paris Convention;

(i) trade marks which are excluded from registration pursuant to Union legislation or the national law of the Member State concerned, or to international agreements to which the Union or the Member State concerned is party, providing for protection of designations of origin and geographical indications;

(j) trade marks which are excluded from registration pursuant to Union legislation or international agreements to which the Union is party, providing for protection of traditional terms for wine;

(k) trade marks which are excluded from registration pursuant to Union legislation or international agreements to which the Union is party, providing for protection of traditional specialities guaranteed;

(l) trade marks which consist of, or reproduce in their essential elements, an earlier plant variety denomination registered in accordance with Union legislation or the national law of the Member State concerned, or international agreements to which the Union or the Member State concerned is party, providing protection for plant variety rights, and which are in respect of plant varieties of the same or closely related species.

**2.** A trade mark shall be liable to be declared invalid where the application for registration of the trade mark was made in bad faith by the applicant. Any Member State may also provide that such a trade mark is not to be registered.

**3.** Any Member State may provide that a trade mark is not to be registered or, if registered, is liable to be declared invalid where and to the extent that:

(a) the use of that trade mark may be prohibited pursuant to provisions of law other than trade mark law of the Member State concerned or of the Union;

(b) the trade mark includes a sign of high symbolic value, in particular a religious symbol;

(c) the trade mark includes badges, emblems and escutcheons other than those covered by Article 6ter of the Paris Convention and which are of public interest, unless the consent of the competent authority to their registration has been given in conformity with the law of the Member State.

**4.** A trade mark shall not be refused registration in accordance with paragraph 1(b), (c) or (d) if, before the date of application for registration, following the use which has been made of it, it has acquired a distinctive character. A trade mark shall not be declared invalid for the same reasons if, before the date of application for a declaration of invalidity, following the use which has been made of it, it has acquired a distinctive character.

**5.** Any Member State may provide that paragraph 4 is also to apply where the distinctive character was acquired after the date of application for registration but before the date of registration.

*Article 5*

**Relative grounds for refusal or invalidity**

**1.** A trade mark shall not be registered or, if registered, shall be liable to be declared invalid where:

(a) it is identical with an earlier trade mark, and the goods or services for which the trade mark is applied for or is registered are identical with the goods or services for which the earlier trade mark is protected;

(b) because of its identity with, or similarity to, the earlier trade mark and the identity or similarity of the goods or services covered by the trade marks, there exists a likelihood of confusion on the part of the public; the likelihood of confusion includes the likelihood of association with the earlier trade mark.

**2.** 'Earlier trade marks' within the meaning of paragraph 1 means:

(a) trade marks of the following kinds with a date of application for registration which is earlier than the date of application for registration of the trade mark, taking account, where appropriate, of the priorities claimed in respect of those trade marks:

(i) EU trade marks;

(ii) trade marks registered in the Member State concerned or, in the case of Belgium, Luxembourg or the Netherlands, at the Benelux Office for Intellectual Property;

(iii) trade marks registered under international arrangements which have effect in the Member State concerned;

(b) EU trade marks which validly claim seniority, in accordance with Regulation (EC) No 207/2009, of a trade mark referred to in points (a)(ii) and (iii), even when the latter trade mark has been surrendered or allowed to lapse;

(c) applications for the trade marks referred to in points (a) and (b), subject to their registration;

(d) trade marks which, on the date of application for registration of the trade mark, or, where appropriate, of the priority claimed in respect of the application for registration of the trade mark, are well known in the Member State concerned, in the sense in which the words 'well-known' are used in Article 6bis of the Paris Convention.

**3.** Furthermore, a trade mark shall not be registered or, if registered, shall be liable to be declared invalid where:

(a) it is identical with, or similar to, an earlier trade mark irrespective of whether the goods or services for which it is applied or registered are identical with, similar to or not similar to those for which the earlier trade mark is registered, where the earlier trade mark has a reputation in the Member State in respect of which registration is applied for or in which the trade mark is registered or, in the case of an EU trade mark, has a reputation in the Union and the use of the later trade mark without due cause would take unfair advantage of, or be detrimental to, the distinctive character or the repute of the earlier trade mark;

(b) an agent or representative of the proprietor of the trade mark applies for registration thereof in his own name without the proprietor's authorisation, unless the agent or representative justifies his action;

(c) and to the extent that, pursuant to Union legislation or the law of the

Member State concerned providing for protection of designations of origin and geographical indications:

(i) an application for a designation of origin or a geographical indication had already been submitted in accordance with Union legislation or the law of the Member State concerned prior to the date of application for registration of the trade mark or the date of the priority claimed for the application, subject to its subsequent registration;

(ii) that designation of origin or geographical indication confers on the person authorised under the relevant law to exercise the rights arising therefrom the right to prohibit the use of a subsequent trade mark.

**4.** Any Member State may provide that a trade mark is not to be registered or, if registered, is liable to be declared invalid where, and to the extent that:

(a) rights to a non-registered trade mark or to another sign used in the course of trade were acquired prior to the date of application for registration of the subsequent trade mark, or the date of the priority claimed for the application for registration of the subsequent trade mark, and that non-registered trade mark or other sign confers on its proprietor the right to prohibit the use of a subsequent trade mark;

(b) the use of the trade mark may be prohibited by virtue of an earlier right, other than the rights referred to in paragraph 2 and point (a) of this paragraph, and in particular:

(i) a right to a name;

(ii) a right of personal portrayal;

(iii) a copyright;

(iv) an industrial property right;

(c) the trade mark is liable to be confused with an earlier trade mark protected abroad, provided that, at the date of the application, the applicant was acting in bad faith.

**5.** The Member States shall ensure that in appropriate circumstances there is no obligation to refuse registration or to declare a trade mark invalid where the proprietor of the earlier trade mark or other earlier right consents to the registration of the later trade mark.

**6.** Any Member State may provide that, by way of derogation from paragraphs 1 to 5, the grounds for refusal of registration or invalidity in force in that Member State prior to the date of the entry into force of the provisions necessary to comply with Directive 89/104/EEC are to apply to trade marks for which an application has been made prior to that date.

*Article 6*

**Establishment a posteriori of invalidity or revocation of a trade mark**

Where the seniority of a national trade mark or of a trade mark registered under international arrangements having effect in the Member State, which has been surrendered or allowed to lapse, is claimed for an EU trade mark, the invalidity or revocation of the trade mark providing the basis for the seniority claim may be established a posteriori, provided that the invalidity or revocation could have been declared at the time the mark was surrendered or allowed to lapse. In such a case, the seniority shall cease to produce its effects.

*Article 7*

## Grounds for refusal or invalidity relating to only some of the goods or services

Where grounds for refusal of registration or for invalidity of a trade mark exist in respect of only some of the goods or services for which that trade mark has been applied or registered, refusal of registration or invalidity shall cover those goods or services only.

*Article 8*

## Lack of distinctive character or of reputation of an earlier trade mark precluding a declaration of invalidity of a registered trade mark

An application for a declaration of invalidity on the basis of an earlier trade mark shall not succeed at the date of application for invalidation if it would not have been successful at the filing date or the priority date of the later trade mark for any of the following reasons:

(a) the earlier trade mark, liable to be declared invalid pursuant to Article 4(1)(b), (c) or (d), had not yet acquired a distinctive character as referred to in Article 4(4);

(b) the application for a declaration of invalidity is based on Article 5(1)(b) and the earlier trade mark had not yet become sufficiently distinctive to support a finding of likelihood of confusion within the meaning of Article 5(1)(b);

(c) the application for a declaration of invalidity is based on Article 5(3)(a) and the earlier trade mark had not yet acquired a reputation within the meaning of Article 5(3)(a).

*Article 9*

## Preclusion of a declaration of invalidity due to acquiescen

**1.** Where, in a Member State, the proprietor of an earlier trade mark as referred to in Article 5(2) or Article 5(3)(a) has acquiesced, for a period of five successive years, in the use of a later trade mark registered in that Member State while being aware of such use, that proprietor shall no longer be entitled on the basis of the earlier trade mark to apply for a declaration that the later trade mark is invalid in respect of the goods or services for which the later trade mark has been used, unless registration of the later trade mark was applied for in bad faith.

**2.** Member States may provide that paragraph 1 of this Article is to apply to the proprietor of any other earlier right referred to in Article 5(4)(a) or (b).

**3.** In the cases referred to in paragraphs 1 and 2, the proprietor of a later registered trade mark shall not be entitled to oppose the use of the earlier right, even though that right may no longer be invoked against the later trade mark.

## SECTION 3
## Rights conferred and limitations

*Article 10*

### Rights conferred by a trade mark

**1.** The registration of a trade mark shall confer on the proprietor exclusive rights therein.
**2.** Without prejudice to the rights of proprietors acquired before the filing date or the priority date of the registered trade mark, the proprietor of that registered trade mark shall be entitled to prevent all third parties not having his consent from using in the course of trade, in relation to goods or services, any sign where:
(a) the sign is identical with the trade mark and is used in relation to goods or services which are identical with those for which the trade mark is registered;
(b) the sign is identical with, or similar to, the trade mark and is used in relation to goods or services which are identical with, or similar to, the goods or services for which the trade mark is registered, if there exists a likelihood of confusion on the part of the public; the likelihood of confusion includes the likelihood of association between the sign and the trade mark;
(c) the sign is identical with, or similar to, the trade mark irrespective of whether it is used in relation to goods or services which are identical with, similar to, or not similar to, those for which the trade mark is registered, where the latter has a reputation in the Member State and where use of that sign without due cause takes unfair advantage of, or is detrimental to, the distinctive character or the repute of the trade mark.
**3.** The following, in particular, may be prohibited under paragraph 2:
(a) affixing the sign to the goods or to the packaging thereof;
(b) offering the goods or putting them on the market, or stocking them for those purposes, under the sign, or offering or supplying services thereunder;
(c) importing or exporting the goods under the sign;
(d) using the sign as a trade or company name or part of a trade or company name;
(e) using the sign on business papers and in advertising;
(f) using the sign in comparative advertising in a manner that is contrary to Directive 2006/114/EC.
**4.** Without prejudice to the rights of proprietors acquired before the filing date or the priority date of the registered trade mark, the proprietor of that registered trade mark shall also be entitled to prevent all third parties from bringing goods, in the course of trade, into the Member State where the trade mark is registered, without being released for free circulation there, where such goods, including the packaging thereof, come from third countries and bear without authorisation a trade mark which is identical with the trade mark registered in respect of such goods, or which cannot be distinguished in its essential aspects from that trade mark.

The entitlement of the trade mark proprietor pursuant to the first subparagraph shall lapse if, during the proceedings to determine whether the registered trade mark has been infringed, initiated in accordance with Regulation (EU) No 608/2013, evidence is provided by the declarant or the holder of the goods that the proprietor of the registered trade mark is not entitled to prohibit the placing of the goods on the market in the country of final destination.

**5.** Where, under the law of a Member State, the use of a sign under the conditions referred to in paragraph 2 (b) or (c) could not be prohibited before the date of entry into force of the provisions necessary to comply with Directive 89/104/EEC in the Member State concerned, the rights conferred by the trade mark may not be relied on to prevent the continued use of the sign.

**6.** Paragraphs 1, 2, 3 and 5 shall not affect provisions in any Member State relating to the protection against the use of a sign other than use for the purposes of distinguishing goods or services, where use of that sign without due cause takes unfair advantage of, or is detrimental to, the distinctive character or the repute of the trade mark.

*Article 11*

## The right to prohibit preparatory acts in relation to the use of packaging or other means

Where the risk exists that the packaging, labels, tags, security or authenticity features or devices, or any other means to which the trade mark is affixed, could be used in relation to goods or services and that use would constitute an infringement of the rights of the proprietor of a trade mark under Article 10(2) and (3), the proprietor of that trade mark shall have the right to prohibit the following acts if carried out in the course of trade:

(a) affixing a sign identical with, or similar to, the trade mark on packaging, labels, tags, security or authenticity features or devices, or any other means to which the mark may be affixed;

(b) offering or placing on the market, or stocking for those purposes, or importing or exporting, packaging, labels, tags, security or authenticity features or devices, or any other means to which the mark is affixed.

*Article 12*

## Reproduction of trade marks in dictionaries

If the reproduction of a trade mark in a dictionary, encyclopaedia or similar reference work, in print or electronic form, gives the impression that it constitutes the generic name of the goods or services for which the trade mark is registered, the publisher of the work shall, at the request of the proprietor of the trade mark, ensure that the reproduction of the trade mark is, without delay, and in the case of works in printed form at the latest in the next edition of the publication, accompanied by an indication that it is a registered trade mark.

*Article 13*

**Prohibition of the use of a trade mark registered in the name of an agent or representative**

**1.** Where a trade mark is registered in the name of the agent or representative of a person who is the proprietor of that trade mark, without the proprietor's consent, the latter shall be entitled to do either or both of the following:

(a) oppose the use of the trade mark by his agent or representative;

(b) demand the assignment of the trade mark in his favour.

**2.** Paragraph 1 shall not apply where the agent or representative justifies his action.

*Article 14*

**Limitation of the effects of a trade mark**

**1.** A trade mark shall not entitle the proprietor to prohibit a third party from using, in the course of trade:

(a) the name or address of the third party, where that third party is a natural person;

(b) signs or indications which are not distinctive or which concern the kind, quality, quantity, intended purpose, value, geographical origin, the time of production of goods or of rendering of the service, or other characteristics of goods or services;

(c) the trade mark for the purpose of identifying or referring to goods or services as those of the proprietor of that trade mark, in particular, where the use of the trade mark is necessary to indicate the intended purpose of a product or service, in particular as accessories or spare parts.

**2.** Paragraph 1 shall only apply where the use made by the third party is in accordance with honest practices in industrial or commercial matters.

**3.** A trade mark shall not entitle the proprietor to prohibit a third party from using, in the course of trade, an earlier right which only applies in a particular locality, if that right is recognised by the law of the Member State in question and the use of that right is within the limits of the territory in which it is recognised.

*Article 15*

**Exhaustion of the rights conferred by a trade mark**

**1.** A trade mark shall not entitle the proprietor to prohibit its use in relation to goods which have been put on the market in the Union under that trade mark by the proprietor or with the proprietor's consent.

**2.** Paragraph 1 shall not apply where there exist legitimate reasons for the proprietor to oppose further commercialisation of the goods, especially where the condition of the goods is changed or impaired after they have been put on the market.

*Article 16*

**Use of trade marks**

**1.** If, within a period of five years following the date of the completion of the registration procedure, the proprietor has not put the trade mark to genuine use in the Member State in connection with the goods or services in respect of which it is registered, or if such use has been suspended during a continuous five-year period, the trade mark shall be subject to the limits and sanctions provided for in Article 17, Article 19(1), Article 44(1) and (2), and Article 46(3) and (4), unless there are proper reasons for non-use.

**2.** Where a Member State provides for opposition proceedings following registration, the five-year period referred to in paragraph 1 shall be calculated from the date when the mark can no longer be opposed or, in the event that an opposition has been lodged, from the date when a decision terminating the opposition proceedings became final or the opposition was withdrawn.

**3.** With regard to trade marks registered under international arrangements and having effect in the Member State, the five-year period referred to in paragraph 1 shall be calculated from the date when the mark can no longer be rejected or opposed. Where an opposition has been lodged or when an objection on absolute or relative grounds has been notified, the period shall be calculated from the date when a decision terminating the opposition proceedings or a ruling on absolute or relative grounds for refusal became final or the opposition was withdrawn.

**4.** The date of commencement of the five-year period, as referred to in paragraphs 1 and 2, shall be entered in the register.

**5.** The following shall also constitute use within the meaning of paragraph 1:

(a) use of the trade mark in a form differing in elements which do not alter the distinctive character of the mark in the form in which it was registered, regardless of whether or not the trade mark in the form as used is also registered in the name of the proprietor;

(b) affixing of the trade mark to goods or to the packaging thereof in the Member State concerned solely for export purposes.

**6.** Use of the trade mark with the consent of the proprietor shall be deemed to constitute use by the proprietor.

*Article 17*

**Non-use as defence in infringement proceedings**

The proprietor of a trade mark shall be entitled to prohibit the use of a sign only to the extent that the proprietor's rights are not liable to be revoked pursuant to Article 19 at the time the infringement action is brought. If the defendant so requests, the proprietor of the trade mark shall furnish proof that, during the five-year period preceding the date of bringing the action, the trade mark has been put to genuine use as provided in Article 16 in connection with the goods or services in respect of which it is registered and which are cited as justification for the action, or that there are proper reasons for non-use, provided that the registration procedure of the trade mark has at the date of bringing the action been completed for not less than five years.

### *Article 18*

### Intervening right of the proprietor of a later registered trade mark as defence in infringement proceedings

**1.** In infringement proceedings, the proprietor of a trade mark shall not be entitled to prohibit the use of a later registered mark where that later trade mark would not be declared invalid pursuant to Article 8, Article 9(1) or (2) or Article 46(3).
**2.** In infringement proceedings, the proprietor of a trade mark shall not be entitled to prohibit the use of a later registered EU trade mark where that later trade mark would not be declared invalid pursuant to Article 53(1), (3) or (4), 54(1) or (2) or 57(2) of Regulation (EC) No 207/2009.
**3.** Where the proprietor of a trade mark is not entitled to prohibit the use of a later registered trade mark pursuant to paragraph 1 or 2, the proprietor of that later registered trade mark shall not be entitled to prohibit the use of the earlier trade mark in infringement proceedings, even though that earlier right may no longer be invoked against the later trade mark.

## SECTION 4

## Revocation of trade mark rights

### *Article 19*

### Absence of genuine use as ground for revocation

**1.** A trade mark shall be liable to revocation if, within a continuous five-year period, it has not been put to genuine use in the Member State in connection with the goods or services in respect of which it is registered, and there are no proper reasons for non-use.
**2.** No person may claim that the proprietor's rights in a trade mark should be revoked where, during the interval between expiry of the five-year period and filing of the application for revocation, genuine use of the trade mark has been started or resumed.
**3.** The commencement or resumption of use within the three-month period preceding the filing of the application for revocation which began at the earliest on expiry of the continuous five-year period of non-use shall be disregarded where preparations for the commencement or resumption occur only after the proprietor becomes aware that the application for revocation may be filed.

### *Article 20*

### Trade mark having become generic or misleading indication as grounds for revocation

A trade mark shall be liable to revocation if, after the date on which it was registered:

(a) as a result of acts or inactivity of the proprietor, it has become the common name in the trade for a product or service in respect of which it is registered;
(b) as a result of the use made of it by the proprietor of the trade mark or with the proprietor's consent in respect of the goods or services for which it is registered, it is liable to mislead the public, particularly as to the nature, quality or geographical origin of those goods or services.

*Article 21*

**Revocation relating to only some of the goods or services**

Where grounds for revocation of a trade mark exist in respect of only some of the goods or services for which that trade mark has been registered, revocation shall cover those goods or services only.

## SECTION 5

## Trade marks as objects of property

*Article 22*

**Transfer of registered trade marks**

**1.** A trade mark may be transferred, separately from any transfer of the undertaking, in respect of some or all of the goods or services for which it is registered.
**2.** A transfer of the whole of the undertaking shall include the transfer of the trade mark except where there is agreement to the contrary or circumstances clearly dictate otherwise. This provision shall apply to the contractual obligation to transfer the undertaking.
**3.** Member States shall have procedures in place to allow for the recordal of transfers in their registers.

*Article 23*

**Rights in rem**

**1.** A trade mark may, independently of the undertaking, be given as security or be the subject of rights in rem.
**2.** Member States shall have procedures in place to allow for the recordal of rights in rem in their registers.

*Article 24*

**Levy of execution**

**1.** A trade mark may be levied in execution.
**2.** Member States shall have procedures in place to allow for the recordal of levy of execution in their registers.

*Article 25*

**Licensing**

**1.** A trade mark may be licensed for some or all of the goods or services for which it is registered and for the whole or part of the Member State concerned. A licence may be exclusive or non-exclusive.
**2.** The proprietor of a trade mark may invoke the rights conferred by that trade mark against a licensee who contravenes any provision in his licensing contract with regard to:

(a) its duration;
(b) the form covered by the registration in which the trade mark may be used;

(c) the scope of the goods or services for which the licence is granted;
(d) the territory in which the trade mark may be affixed; or
(e) the quality of the goods manufactured or of the services provided by the licensee.

**3.** Without prejudice to the provisions of the licensing contract, the licensee may bring proceedings for infringement of a trade mark only if its proprietor consents thereto. However, the holder of an exclusive licence may bring such proceedings if the proprietor of the trade mark, after formal notice, does not himself bring infringement proceedings within an appropriate period.

**4.** A licensee shall, for the purpose of obtaining compensation for damage suffered by him, be entitled to intervene in infringement proceedings brought by the proprietor of the trade mark.

**5.** Member States shall have procedures in place to allow for the recordal of licences in their registers.

*Article 26*

**Applications for a trade mark as an object of property**

Articles 22 to 25 shall apply to applications for trade marks.

## SECTION 6

## Guarantee or certification marks and collective marks

*Article 27*

**Definitions**

For the purposes of this Directive, the following definitions apply:

(a) 'guarantee or certification mark' means a trade mark which is described as such when the mark is applied for and is capable of distinguishing goods or services which are certified by the proprietor of the mark in respect of material, mode of manufacture of goods or performance of services, quality, accuracy or other characteristics, from goods and services which are not so certified;
(b) 'collective mark' means a trade mark which is described as such when the mark is applied for and is capable of distinguishing the goods or services of the members of an association which is the proprietor of the mark from the goods or services of other undertakings.

*Article 28*

**Guarantee or certification marks**

**1.** Member States may provide for the registration of guarantee or certification marks.

**2.** Any natural or legal person, including institutions, authorities and bodies governed by public law, may apply for guarantee or certification marks provided that such person does not carry on a business involving the supply of goods or services of the kind certified.

Member States may provide that a guarantee or certification mark is not to be registered unless the applicant is competent to certify the goods or services for which the mark is to be registered.

**3.** Member States may provide that guarantee or certification marks are not to be registered, or are to be revoked or declared invalid, on grounds other than those specified in Articles 4, 19 and 20, where the function of those marks so requires.

**4.** By way of derogation from Article 4(1)(c), Member States may provide that signs or indications which may serve, in trade, to designate the geographical origin of the goods or services may constitute guarantee or certification marks. Such a guarantee or certification mark shall not entitle the proprietor to prohibit a third party from using in the course of trade such signs or indications, provided that third party uses them in accordance with honest practices in industrial or commercial matters. In particular, such a mark may not be invoked against a third party who is entitled to use a geographical name.

**5.** The requirements laid down in Article 16 shall be satisfied where genuine use of a guarantee or certification mark in accordance with Article 16 is made by any person who has the authority to use it.

*Article 29*

**Collective marks**

**1.** Member States shall provide for the registration of collective marks.

**2.** Associations of manufacturers, producers, suppliers of services or traders, which, under the terms of the law governing them, have the capacity in their own name to have rights and obligations, to make contracts or accomplish other legal acts, and to sue and be sued, as well as legal persons governed by public law, may apply for collective marks.

**3.** By way of derogation from Article 4(1)(c), Member States may provide that signs or indications which may serve, in trade, to designate the geographical origin of the goods or services may constitute collective marks. Such a collective mark shall not entitle the proprietor to prohibit a third party from using, in the course of trade, such signs or indications, provided that third party uses them in accordance with honest practices in industrial or commercial matters. In particular, such a mark may not be invoked against a third party who is entitled to use a geographical name.

*Article 30*

**Regulations governing use of a collective mark**

**1.** An applicant for a collective mark shall submit the regulations governing its use to the office.

**2.** The regulations governing use shall specify at least the persons authorised to use the mark, the conditions of membership of the association and the conditions of use of the mark, including sanctions. The regulations governing use of a mark referred to in Article 29(3) shall authorise any person whose goods or services originate in the geographical area concerned to become a member of the association which is the proprietor of the mark, provided that the person fulfils all the other conditions of the regulations.

*Article 31*

**Refusal of an application**

**1.** In addition to the grounds for refusal of a trade mark application provided for in Article 4, where appropriate with the exception of Article 4(1)(c) concerning signs or indications which may serve, in trade, to designate the geographical origin of the goods or services, and Article 5,and without prejudice to the right of an office not to undertake examination ex officio of relative grounds, an application for a collective mark shall be refused where the provisions of point (b) of Article 27, Article 29 or Article 30 are not satisfied, or where the regulations governing use of that collective mark are contrary to public policy or to accepted principles of morality.
**2.** An application for a collective mark shall also be refused if the public is liable to be misled as regards the character or the significance of the mark, in particular if it is likely to be taken to be something other than a collective mark.
**3.** An application shall not be refused if the applicant, as a result of amendment of the regulations governing use of the collective mark, meets the requirements referred to in paragraphs 1 and 2.

*Article 32*

**Use of collective marks**

The requirements of Article 16 shall be satisfied where genuine use of a collective mark in accordance with that Article is made by any person who has authority to use it.

*Article 33*

**Amendments to the regulations governing use of a collective mark**

**1.** The proprietor of a collective mark shall submit to the office any amended regulations governing use.
**2.** Amendments to the regulations governing use shall be mentioned in the register unless the amended regulations do not satisfy the requirements of Article 30 or involve one of the grounds for refusal referred to in Article 31.
**3.** For the purposes of this Directive, amendments to the regulations governing use shall take effect only from the date of entry of the mention of those amendments in the register.

*Article 34*

**Persons entitled to bring an action for infringement**

**1.** Article 25(3) and (4) shall apply to every person who has the authority to use a collective mark.
**2.** The proprietor of a collective mark shall be entitled to claim compensation on behalf of persons who have authority to use the mark where those persons have sustained damage as a result of unauthorised use of the mark.

*Article 35*

**Additional grounds for revocation**

In addition to the grounds for revocation provided for in Articles 19 and 20, the rights of the proprietor of a collective mark shall be revoked on the following grounds:

(a) the proprietor does not take reasonable steps to prevent the mark being used in a manner that is incompatible with the conditions of use laid down in the regulations governing use, including any amendments thereto mentioned in the register;

(b) the manner in which the mark has been used by authorised persons has caused it to become liable to mislead the public in the manner referred to in Article 31(2);

(c) an amendment to the regulations governing use of the mark has been mentioned in the register in breach of Article 33(2), unless the proprietor of the mark, by further amending the regulations governing use, complies with the requirements of that Article.

*Article 36*

**Additional grounds for invalidity**

In addition to the grounds for invalidity provided for in Article 4, where appropriate with the exception of Article 4(1)(c) concerning signs or indications which may serve, in trade, to designate the geographical origin of the goods or services, and Article 5, a collective mark which is registered in breach of Article 31 shall be declared invalid unless the proprietor of the mark, by amending the regulations governing use, complies with the requirements of Article 31.

## CHAPTER 3

## PROCEDURES

### SECTION 1

### Application and registration

*Article 37*

**Application requirements**

**1.** An application for registration of a trade mark shall contain at least all of the following:

(a) a request for registration;

(b) information identifying the applicant;

(c) a list of the goods or services in respect of which the registration is requested;

(d) a representation of the trade mark, which satisfies the requirements set out in point (b) of Article 3.

**2.** The application for a trade mark shall be subject to the payment of a fee determined by the Member State concerned.

*Article 38*

**Date of filing**

**1.** The date of filing of a trade mark application shall be the date on which the documents containing the information specified in Article 37(1) are filed with the office by the applicant.
**2.** Member States may, in addition, provide that the accordance of the date of filing is to be subject to the payment of a fee as referred to in Article 37(2).

*Article 39*

**Designation and classification of goods and services**

**1.** The goods and services in respect of which trade mark registration is applied for shall be classified in conformity with the system of classification established by the Nice Agreement Concerning the International Classification of Goods and Services for the Purposes of the Registration of Marks of 15 June 1957 ('the Nice Classification').
**2.** The goods and services for which protection is sought shall be identified by the applicant with sufficient clarity and precision to enable the competent authorities and economic operators, on that sole basis, to determine the extent of the protection sought.
**3.** For the purposes of paragraph 2, the general indications included in the class headings of the Nice Classification or other general terms may be used, provided that they comply with the requisite standards of clarity and precision set out in this Article.
**4.** The office shall reject an application in respect of indications or terms which are unclear or imprecise, where the applicant does not suggest an acceptable wording within a period set by the office to that effect.
**5.** The use of general terms, including the general indications of the class headings of the Nice Classification, shall be interpreted as including all the goods or services clearly covered by the literal meaning of the indication or term. The use of such terms or indications shall not be interpreted as comprising a claim to goods or services which cannot be so understood.
**6.** Where the applicant requests registration for more than one class, the applicant shall group the goods and services according to the classes of the Nice Classification, each group being preceded by the number of the class to which that group of goods or services belongs, and shall present them in the order of the classes.
**7.** Goods and services shall not be regarded as being similar to each other on the ground that they appear in the same class under the Nice Classification. Goods and services shall not be regarded as being dissimilar from each other on the ground that they appear in different classes under the Nice Classification.

*Article 40*

**Observations by third parties**

**1.** Member States may provide that prior to registration of a trade mark, any natural or legal person and any group or body representing manufacturers, producers, suppliers of services, traders or consumers may submit to the office written observations, explaining on which grounds the trade mark should not be registered ex officio.

Persons and groups or bodies, as referred to in the first subparagraph, shall not be parties to the proceedings before the office.

**2.** In addition to the grounds referred to in paragraph 1 of this Article, any natural or legal person and any group or body representing manufacturers, producers, suppliers of services, traders or consumers may submit to the office written observations based on the particular grounds on which the application for a collective mark should be refused under Article 31(1) and (2). This provision may be extended to cover certification and guarantee marks where regulated in Member States.

*Article 41*

**Division of applications and registrations**

The applicant or proprietor may divide a national trade mark application or registration into two or more separate applications or registrations by sending a declaration to the office and indicating for each divisional application or registration the goods or services covered by the original application or registration which are to be covered by the divisional applications or registrations.

*Article 42*

**Class fees**

Member States may provide that the application and renewal of a trade mark is to be subject to an additional fee for each class of goods and services beyond the first class.

## SECTION 2

## Procedures for opposition, revocation and invalidity

*Article 43*

**Opposition procedure**

**1.** Member States shall provide for an efficient and expeditious administrative procedure before their offices for opposing the registration of a trade mark application on the grounds provided for in Article 5.

**2.** The administrative procedure referred to in paragraph 1 of this Article shall at least provide that the proprietor of an earlier trade mark as referred to in Article 5(2) and Article 5(3)(a), and the person authorised under the relevant law to exercise the rights arising from a protected designation of origin or geographical indication as referred to in Article 5(3)(c) shall be entitled to file a notice of opposition. A notice of opposition may be filed on the basis of one or more earlier rights, provided that they all belong to the same proprietor, and on the basis of part or the totality of the goods or services in respect of which the earlier right is protected or applied for, and may be directed against part or the totality of the goods or services in respect of which the contested mark is applied for.

**3.** The parties shall be granted, at their joint request, a minimum of two months in the opposition proceedings in order to allow for the possibility of a friendly settlement between the opposing party and the applicant.

*Article 44*

**Non-use as defence in opposition proceedings**

**1.** In opposition proceedings pursuant to Article 43, where at the filing date or date of priority of the later trade mark, the five-year period within which the earlier trade mark must have been put to genuine use as provided for in Article 16 had expired, at the request of the applicant, the proprietor of the earlier trade mark who has given notice of opposition shall furnish proof that the earlier trade mark has been put to genuine use as provided for in Article 16 during the five-year period preceding the filing date or date of priority of the later trade mark, or that proper reasons for non-use existed. In the absence of proof to this effect, the opposition shall be rejected.
**2.** If the earlier trade mark has been used in relation to only part of the goods or services for which it is registered, it shall, for the purpose of the examination of the opposition as provided for in paragraph 1, be deemed to be registered in respect of that part of the goods or services only.
**3.** Paragraphs 1 and 2 of this Article shall also apply where the earlier trade mark is an EU trade mark. In such a case, the genuine use of the EU trade mark shall be determined in accordance with Article 15 of Regulation (EC) No 207/2009.

*Article 45*

**Procedure for revocation or declaration of invalidity**

**1.** Without prejudice to the right of the parties to appeal to the courts, Member States shall provide for an efficient and expeditious administrative procedure before their offices for the revocation or declaration of invalidity of a trade mark.
**2.** The administrative procedure for revocation shall provide that the trade mark is to be revoked on the grounds provided for in Articles 19 and 20.
**3.** The administrative procedure for invalidity shall provide that the trade mark is to be declared invalid at least on the following grounds:

(a) the trade mark should not have been registered because it does not comply with the requirements provided for in Article 4;
(b) the trade mark should not have been registered because of the existence of an earlier right within the meaning of Article 5(1) to (3).

**4.** The administrative procedure shall provide that at least the following are to be entitled to file an application for revocation or for a declaration of invalidity:

(a) in the case of paragraph 2 and paragraph 3(a), any natural or legal person and any group or body set up for the purpose of representing the interests of manufacturers, producers, suppliers of services, traders or consumers, and which, under the terms of the law governing it, has the capacity to sue in its own name and to be sued;
(b) in the case of paragraph 3(b) of this Article, the proprietor of an earlier trade mark as referred to in Article 5(2) and Article 5(3)(a), and the person authorised under the relevant law to exercise the rights arising from a protected designation of origin or geographical indication as referred to in Article 5(3)(c).

**5.** An application for revocation or for a declaration of invalidity may be directed against a part or the totality of the goods or services in respect of which the contested mark is registered.

**6.** An application for a declaration of invalidity may be filed on the basis of one or more earlier rights, provided they all belong to the same proprietor.

*Article 46*

### Non-use as a defence in proceedings seeking a declaration of invalidity

**1.** In proceedings for a declaration of invalidity based on a registered trade mark with an earlier filing date or priority date, if the proprietor of the later trade mark so requests, the proprietor of the earlier trade mark shall furnish proof that, during the five-year period preceding the date of the application for a declaration of invalidity, the earlier trade mark has been put to genuine use, as provided for in Article 16, in connection with the goods or services in respect of which it is registered and which are cited as justification for the application, or that there are proper reasons for non-use, provided that the registration process of the earlier trade mark has at the date of the application for a declaration of invalidity been completed for not less than five years.
**2.** Where, at the filing date or date of priority of the later trade mark, the five-year period within which the earlier trade mark was to have been put to genuine use, as provided for in Article 16, had expired, the proprietor of the earlier trade mark shall, in addition to the proof required under paragraph 1 of this Article, furnish proof that the trade mark was put to genuine use during the five-year period preceding the filing date or date of priority, or that proper reasons for non-use existed.
**3.** In the absence of the proof referred to in paragraphs 1 and 2, an application for a declaration of invalidity on the basis of an earlier trade mark shall be rejected.
**4.** If the earlier trade mark has been used in accordance with Article 16 in relation to only part of the goods or services for which it is registered, it shall, for the purpose of the examination of the application for a declaration of invalidity, be deemed to be registered in respect of that part of the goods or services only.
**5.** Paragraphs 1 to 4 of this Article shall also apply where the earlier trade mark is an EU trade mark. In such a case, genuine use of the EU trade mark shall be determined in accordance with Article 15 of Regulation (EC) No 207/2009.

*Article 47*

### Consequences of revocation and invalidity

**1.** A registered trade mark shall be deemed not to have had, as from the date of the application for revocation, the effects specified in this Directive, to the extent that the rights of the proprietor have been revoked. An earlier date, on which one of the grounds for revocation occurred, may be fixed in the decision on the application for revocation, at the request of one of the parties.

**2.** A registered trade mark shall be deemed not to have had, as from the outset, the effects specified in this Directive, to the extent that the trade mark has been declared invalid.

## SECTION 3
## Duration and renewal of registration

*Article 48*

### Duration of registration

**1.** Trade marks shall be registered for a period of 10 years from the date of filing of thc application.
**2.** Registration may be renewed in accordance with Article 49 for further 10-year periods.

*Article 49*

### Renewal

**1.** Registration of a trade mark shall be renewed at the request of the proprietor of the trade mark or any person authorised to do so by law or by contract, provided that the renewal fees have been paid. Member States may provide that receipt of payment of the renewal fees is to be deemed to constitute such a request.
**2.** The office shall inform the proprietor of the trade mark of the expiry of the registration at least six months before the said expiry. The office shall not be held liable if it fails to give such information.
**3.** The request for renewal shall be submitted and the renewal fees shall be paid within a period of at least six months immediately preceding the expiry of the registration. Failing that, the request may be submitted within a further period of six months immediately following the expiry of the registration or of the subsequent renewal thereof. The renewal fees and an additional fee shall be paid within that further period.
**4.** Where the request is submitted or the fees paid in respect of only some of the goods or services for which the trade mark is registered, registration shall be renewed for those goods or services only.
**5.** Renewal shall take effect from the day following the date on which the existing registration expires. The renewal shall be recorded in the register.

## SECTION 4
## Communication with the office

*Article 50*

### Communication with the office

Parties to the proceedings or, where appointed, their representatives, shall designate an official address for all official communication with the office. Member States shall have the right to require that such an official address be situated in the European Economic Area.

## CHAPTER 4

## ADMINISTRATIVE COOPERATION

*Article 51*

### Cooperation in the area of trade mark registration and administration

The offices shall be free to cooperate effectively with each other and with the European Union Intellectual Property Office in order to promote convergence of practices and tools in relation to the examination and registration of trade marks.

*Article 52*

### Cooperation in other areas

The offices shall be free to cooperate effectively with each other and with the European Union Intellectual Property Office in all areas of their activities other than those referred to in Article 51 which are of relevance for the protection of trade marks in the Union.

## CHAPTER 5

## FINAL PROVISIONS

*Article 53*

### Data protection

The processing of any personal data carried out in the Member States in the framework of this Directive shall be subject to national law implementing Directive 95/46/EC.

*Article 54*

### Transposition

**1.** Member States shall bring into force the laws, regulations and administrative provisions necessary to comply with Articles 3 to 6, Articles 8 to 14, Articles 16, 17 and 18, Articles 22 to 39, Article 41, Articles 43 to 50 by 14 January 2019. Member States shall bring into force the laws, regulations and administrative provisions to comply with Article 45 by 14 January 2023. They shall immediately communicate the text of those measures to the Commission.

When Member States adopt those measures, they shall contain a reference to this Directive or be accompanied by such a reference on the occasion of their official publication. They shall also include a statement that references in existing laws, regulations and administrative provisions to the Directive repealed by this Directive shall be construed as references to this Directive. Member States shall determine how such reference is to be made and how that statement is to be formulated.

**2.** Member States shall communicate to the Commission the text of the main provisions of national law which they adopt in the field covered by this Directive.

*Article 55*

**Repeal**

Directive 2008/95/EC is repealed with effect from 15 January 2019, without prejudice to the obligations of the Member States relating to the time limit for the transposition into national law of Directive 89/104/EEC set out in Part B of Annex I to Directive 2008/95/EC.

References to the repealed Directive shall be construed as references to this Directive and shall be read in accordance with the correlation table in the Annex.

*Article 56*

**Entry into Force**

This Directive shall enter into force on the twentieth day following that of its publication in the Official Journal of the European Union.

Articles 1, 7, 15, 19, 20, 21 and 54 to 57 shall apply from 15 January 2019.

*Article 57*

**Addressees**

This Directive is addressed to the Member States.

Done at Strasbourg, 16 December 2015.

For the European Parliament
The President
M. SCHULZ
For the Council
The President
N. SCHMIT

*ANNEX*

**Correlation table**

| *Directive 2008/95/EC* | *This Directive* |
|---|---|
| Article 1 | Article 1 |
| — | Article 2 |
| Article 2 | Article 3 |
| Article 3(1)(a) to (h) | Article 4(1)(a) to (h) |
| — | Article 4(1)(i) to (l) |
| Article 3(2)(a) to (c) | Article 4(3)(a) to (c) |
| Article 3(2)(d) | Article 4(2) |
| Article 3(3), first sentence | Article 4(4), first sentence |
| — | Article 4(4), second sentence |
| Article 3(3), second sentence | Article 4(5) |
| Article 3(4) | — |
| Article 4(1) and (2) | Article 5(1) and (2) |

| *Directive 2008/95/EC* | *This Directive* |
|---|---|
| Article 4(3) and (4)(a) | Article 5(3)(a) |
| — | Article 5(3)(b) |
| — | Article 5(3)(c) |
| Article 4(4)(b) and (c) | Article 5(4)(a) and (b) |
| Article 4(4)(d) to (f) | — |
| Article 4(4)(g) | Article 5(4)(c) |
| Article 4(5) and (6) | Article 5(5) and (6) |
| — | Article 8 |
| Article 5(1), first sentence | Article 10(1) |
| Article 5(1), second sentence, introductory part | Article 10(2), introductory part of the sentence |
| Article 5(1)(a) and (b) | Article 10(2)(a) and (b) |
| Article 5(2) | Article 10(2)(c) |
| Article 5(3)(a) to (c) | Article 10(3)(a) to (c) |
| — | Article 10(3)(d) |
| Article 5(3)(d) | Article 10(3)(e) |
| — | Article 10(3)(f) |
| — | Article 10(4) |
| Article 5(4) and (5) | Article 10(5) and (6) |
| — | Article 11 |
| — | Article 12 |
| — | Article 13 |
| Article 6(1)(a) to (c) | Article 14(1)(a) to (c), and (2) |
| Article 6(2) | Article 14(3) |
| Article 7 | Article 15 |
| Article 8(1) and (2) | Article 25(1) and (2) |
| — | Article 25(3) to (5) |
| Article 9 | Article 9 |
| Article 10(1), first subparagraph | Article 16(1) |
| — | Article 16(2) to (4) |
| Article 10(1), second subparagraph | Article 16(5) |
| Article 10(2) | Article 16(6) |
| Article 10(3) | — |
| Article 11(1) | Article 46(1) to (3) |
| Article 11(2) | Article 44(1) |
| Article 11(3) | Article 17 |
| Article 11(4) | Articles 17, 44(2) and Article 46(4) |
| — | Article 18 |
| Article 12(1), first subparagraph | Article 19(1) |
| Article 12(1), second subparagraph | Article 19(2) |
| Article 12(1), third subparagraph | Article 19(3) |
| Article 12(2) | Article 20 |

| *Directive 2008/95/EC* | *This Directive* |
|---|---|
| Article 13 | Article 7 and Article 21 |
| Article 14 | Article 6 |
| — | Articles 22 to 24 |
| — | Article 26 |
| — | Article 27 |
| Article 15(1) | Article 28(1) and (3) |
| Article 15(2) | Article 28(4) |
| — | Article 28(2) and (5) |
| — | Articles 29 to 54(1) |
| Article 16 | Article 54(2) |
| Article 17 | Article 55 |
| Article 18 | Article 56 |
| Article 19 | Article 57 |

*Replace Appendix 7:*

## Appendix 7

# COMMISSION IMPLEMENTING REGULATION (EU) 2018/626 of 5 March 2018

**laying down detailed rules for implementing certain provisions of Regulation (EU) 2017/1001 of the European Parliament and of the Council on the European Union trade mark, and repealing Implementing Regulation (EU) 2017/1431 (Retained EU Legislation)** A7-001

THE EUROPEAN COMMISSION,

Having regard to the Treaty on the Functioning of the European Union,

Having regard to Regulation (EU) 2017/1001 of the European Parliament and of the Council of 14 June 2017 on the European Union trade mark, and in particular Article 20(6), Article 31(4), Article 35(2), Article 38(4), Article 39(6), Article 44(5), Article 50(9), Article 51(3), the second subparagraph of Article 54(3), the second subparagraph of Article 55(1), Article 56(8), Article 57(5), Article 75(3), Article 84(3), the first subparagraph of Article 109(2), Article 116(4), Article 117(3), Article 140(6), Article 146(11), the second subparagraph of Article 161(2), Article 184(9), Article 186(2), Article 187(2), Article 192(6), Article 193(8), Article 198(4), Article 202(10) and Article 204(6) thereof,

Whereas:

**(1)** Council Regulation (EC) No 40/94, which was codified as Regulation (EC) No 207/2009, created a system specific to the Union for the protection of trade marks to be obtained at the level of the Union on the basis of an application to the European Union Intellectual Property Office ('the Office').

**(2)** Regulation (EU) 2015/2424 of the European Parliament and the Council aligned the powers conferred upon the Commission under Regulation (EC) No 207/2009 with Articles 290 and 291 of the Treaty on the Functioning of the European Union. In order to conform with the new legal framework resulting from that alignment, Commission Delegated Regulation (EU) 2017/1430 and Commission Implementing Regulation (EU) 2017/1431 were adopted.

**(3)** Council Regulation (EC) No 207/2009 was codified as Regulation (EU) 2017/1001. For reasons of clarity and simplification, the references contained in an Implementing Regulation should reflect the renumbering of Articles resulting from such a codification of the relevant basic act. Implementing Regulation (EU) 2017/1431 should therefore be repealed and the provisions of that Implementing Regulation should be laid down, with updated references to Regulation (EU) 2017/1001, in this Regulation.

**(4)** In the interest of clarity, legal certainty and efficiency, and with a view to facilitating the filing of EU trade mark applications, it is of essential importance to specify, in a clear and exhaustive manner while avoiding unnecessary administrative burdens, the mandatory and optional particulars to be contained in an application for an EU trade mark.

**(5)** Regulation (EU) 2017/1001 no longer requires the representation of a mark to be graphic, as long as it enables the competent authorities and the public to determine with clarity and precision the subject matter of protection. It is therefore necessary, in order to ensure legal certainty, to clearly affirm that the precise subject matter of the exclusive right conferred by the registration is defined by the representation. The representation should, where appropriate, be complemented by an indication of the type of the mark concerned. It may be complemented by a description of the sign in appropriate cases. Such an indication or description should accord with the representation.

**(6)** Moreover, in order to ensure consistency in the process of filing an EU trade mark application and in order to enhance the effectiveness of clearance searches, it is appropriate to establish general principles to which the representation of every mark must conform, as well as lay down specific rules and requirements for the representation of certain types of trade mark, in accordance with the trade mark's specific nature and attributes.

**(7)** The introduction of technical alternatives to graphic representation, in line with new technologies, derives from the necessity of modernisation, bringing the registration process closer to technical developments. At the same time, the technical specifications for filing a representation of the trade mark, including representations filed electronically, should be laid down with a view to ensuring that the EU trade mark system remains interoperable with the system established by the Protocol relating to the Madrid Agreement concerning the international registration of marks, adopted at Madrid on 27 June 1989 (Madrid Protocol). In accordance with Regulation (EU) 2017/1001, and for the sake of increased flexibility and quicker adaptation to technological advances, it should be left to the Executive Director of the Office to lay down the technical specifications for marks filed electronically.

**(8)** It is appropriate to streamline proceedings so as to reduce administrative burdens in the filing and process of priority and seniority claims. It should therefore not be necessary any more to submit certified copies of the previous application or registration. Furthermore, the Office should no longer be required to include a copy of the prior trade mark application in the file in the case of a priority claim.

**(9)** Following the abolition of the requirement of a graphic representation of a trade mark, certain types of trade marks can be represented in electronic format and accordingly, their publication using conventional means is no longer suitable. In order to guarantee the publication of all the information concerning an application, which is required for reasons of transparency and legal certainty, access to the representation of the trade mark by way of a link to the Office's electronic Register should be recognised as a valid form of representation of the sign for publication purposes.

**(10)** For the same reasons, it should also be permissible for the Office to issue certificates of registration in which the reproduction of the trade mark is substituted by an electronic link. Furthermore, for certificates issued after the registration, and to cater for requests made at a time when registration particulars may have changed, it is appropriate to provide for the possibility of issuing updated versions of the certificate, where relevant subsequent entries in the Register are indicated.

**(11)** Practical experience in applying the former regime revealed the need to clarify certain provisions, in particular in relation to partial transfers and partial surrenders, in order to ensure clarity and legal certainty.
**(12)** In order to ensure legal certainty, while keeping a certain level of flexibility, it is necessary to establish a minimum content of the regulations governing the use of EU collective marks and of EU certification marks submitted pursuant to Regulation (EU) 2017/1001, with the purpose of enabling market operators to avail themselves of this new type of trade mark protection.
**(13)** Maximum rates for representation costs incurred by the successful party to proceedings before the Office should be specified, taking into account the need to ensure that the obligation to bear the costs may not be misused, inter alia, for tactical reasons by the other party.
**(14)** For reasons of efficiency, electronic publications by the Office should be allowed.
**(15)** It is necessary to ensure an effective and efficient exchange of information between the Office and the authorities of the Member States in the context of administrative cooperation, taking appropriate account of the restrictions to which the inspection of files is subject.
**(16)** The requirements concerning requests for conversion should ensure a smooth and effective interface between the EU trade mark system and the national trade mark systems.
**(17)** In order to streamline proceedings before the Office, it should be possible to limit the submission of translations to those parts of documents that are relevant to the proceedings. For the same purpose, the Office should be authorised to require proof that a translation corresponds to the original only in the event of doubt.
**(18)** For reasons of efficiency, certain decisions of the Office in relation to oppositions or applications for the revocation or a declaration of invalidity of an EU trade mark should be taken by a single member.
**(19)** Due to the accession of the Union to the Madrid Protocol, it is necessary that the detailed requirements governing the procedures concerning the international registration of marks be entirely consistent with the rules of that Protocol.
**(20)** Implementing Regulation (EU) 2017/1431 replaced the rules previously laid down in Commission Regulation (EC) No 2868/95 which was therefore repealed. Notwithstanding that repeal, certain proceedings initiated before the date of applicability of Implementing Regulation (EU) 2017/1431 should continue to be governed until their conclusion by specific provisions of Regulation (EC) No 2868/95.
**(21)** The measures provided for in this Regulation are in accordance with the opinion of the Committee on Implementation Rules,

HAS ADOPTED THIS REGULATION:

*Article 1*

**Subject matter**

This Regulation lays down rules specifying:

(a) the details to be contained in an application for an EU trade mark to be filed at the European Union Intellectual Property Office ('the Office');
(b) the documentation required to claim the priority of a previous application and to claim seniority, and the evidence to be filed to claim an exhibition priority;

(c) the details to be contained in the publication of an application for an EU trade mark;
(d) the content of a declaration of division of an application, how the Office has to process such a declaration, and the details to be contained in the publication of the divisional application;
(e) the content and form of the certificate of registration;
(f) the content of a declaration of division of a registration and how the Office has to process such a declaration;
(g) the details to be contained in requests for alteration and for the change of name or address;
(h) the content of an application for registration of a transfer, the documentation required to establish a transfer, and how to process applications for partial transfers;
(i) the details to be contained in a declaration of surrender and the required documentation to establish a third party's agreement;
(j) the details to be contained in the regulations governing use of an EU collective mark and those governing use of an EU certification mark;
(k) the maximum rates for costs essential to proceedings and actually incurred;
(l) certain details concerning publications in the European Union Trade Marks Bulletin and the Official Journal of the Office;
(m) the detailed arrangements as to how the Office and the authorities of the Member States are to exchange information between each other and open files for inspection;
(n) the details to be contained in requests for conversion and in the publication of a request for conversion;
(o) the extent to which supporting documents to be used in written proceedings before the Office may be filed in any official language of the Union, the need to supply a translation and the requisite standards of translations;
(p) the decisions to be taken by single members of the Opposition and Cancellation Divisions;
(q) concerning the international registration of marks:
   (i) the form to be used for the filing of an international application;
   (ii) the facts and decisions of invalidity to be notified to the International Bureau of the World Intellectual Property Organisation ('the International Bureau') and the relevant time of such notification;
   (iii) the detailed requirements regarding requests for territorial extension subsequent to international registration;
   (iv) the details to be contained in a seniority claim for an international registration and the details of the information to be notified to the International Bureau;
   (v) the details to be contained in the notification of ex officio provisional refusal of protection to be sent to the International Bureau;
   (vi) the details to be contained in the final grant or refusal of protection;
   (vii) the details to be contained in the notification of invalidation;
   (viii) the details to be contained in the requests for conversion of an international registration and in the publication of such requests;
   (ix) the details to be contained in an application for transformation.

*Article 2*

**Content of the application**

**1.** The application for an EU trade mark shall contain:

(a) a request for registration of the trade mark as an EU trade mark;

(b) the name and address of the applicant and the State in which that applicant is domiciled or has a seat or an establishment. Names of natural persons shall be indicated by the person's family name(s) and given name(s). Names of legal entities, as well as bodies falling under Article 3 of Regulation (EU) 2017/1001, shall be indicated by their official designation and include the legal form of the entity, which may be abbreviated in a customary manner. The company's national identification number may also be specified if available. The Office may require the applicant to provide telephone numbers or other contact details for communication by electronic means as defined by the Executive Director. Only one address shall, in principle, be indicated for each applicant. Where several addresses are indicated, only the address mentioned first shall be taken into account, except where the applicant designates one of the addresses as an address for service. Where an identification number has already been given by the Office, it shall be sufficient for the applicant to indicate that number and the name of the applicant;

(c) a list of the goods or services for which the trade mark is to be registered, in accordance with Article 33(2) of Regulation (EU) 2017/1001. That list may be selected, in whole or in part, from a database of acceptable terms made available by the Office;

(d) a representation of the trade mark in accordance with Article 3 of this Regulation;

(e) where the applicant has appointed a representative, the name and business address of that representative or the identification number in accordance with point (b); where the representative has more than one business address or where there are two or more representatives with different business addresses, only the first-mentioned address shall be taken into account as an address for service unless the application indicates which address is to be used as an address for service;

(f) where the priority of a previous application is claimed pursuant to Article 35 of Regulation (EU) 2017/1001, a declaration to that effect, stating the date on which and the country in or for which the previous application was filed;

(g) where exhibition priority is claimed pursuant to Article 38 of Regulation (EU) 2017/1001, a declaration to that effect, stating the name of the exhibition and the date of the first display of the goods or services;

(h) where the seniority of one or more earlier trade marks, registered in a Member State, including a trade mark registered in the Benelux countries or registered under international arrangements having effect in a Member State, as referred to in Article 39(1) of Regulation (EU) 2017/1001, is claimed together with the application, a declaration to that effect, stating the Member State or Member States in or for which the earlier trade mark is registered, the date from which the relevant registration was effective, the number of the relevant registration, and the goods or services for which the trade mark is registered. Such declaration may also be made within the period referred to in Article 39(2) of Regulation (EU) 2017/1001;

(i) where applicable, a statement that the application is for registration of an EU collective mark pursuant to Article 74 of Regulation (EU) 2017/1001 or for registration of an EU certification mark pursuant to Article 83 of Regulation (EU) 2017/1001;

(j) specification of the language in which the application has been filed, and of the second language pursuant to Article 146(3) of Regulation (EU) 2017/1001;

(k) the signature of the applicant or the applicant's representative in accordance with Article 63(1) of Commission Delegated Regulation (EU) 2018/625;

(l) where applicable, the request of a search report referred to in Article 43(1) or (2) of Regulation (EU) 2017/1001.

**2.** The application may include a claim that the sign has acquired distinctive character through use within the meaning of Article 7(3) of Regulation (EU) 2017/1001, as well as an indication of whether this claim is meant as a principal or subsidiary one. Such claim may also be made within the period referred to in Article 42(2), second sentence, of Regulation (EU) 2017/1001.

**3.** The application for an EU collective mark or an EU certification mark may include the regulations governing its use. Where such regulations are not included with the application, they shall be submitted within the period referred to in Article 75(1) and Article 84(1) of Regulation (EU) 2017/1001.

**4.** If there is more than one applicant, the application may contain the appointment of one applicant or representative as common representative.

### *Article 3*

### Representation of the trade mark

**1.** The trade mark shall be represented in any appropriate form using generally available technology, as long as it can be reproduced on the Register in a clear, precise, self-contained, easily accessible, intelligible, durable and objective manner so as to enable the competent authorities and the public to determine with clarity and precision the subject matter of the protection afforded to its proprietor.

**2.** The representation of the trade mark shall define the subject matter of the registration. Where the representation is accompanied by a description pursuant to paragraph 3(d), (e), (f)(ii), (h) or paragraph 4, such description shall accord with the representation and shall not extend its scope.

**3.** Where the application concerns any of the trade mark types listed in points (a) to (j), it shall contain an indication to that effect. Without prejudice to paragraphs 1 or 2, the type of the trade mark and its representation shall accord with each other as follows:

(a) in the case of a trade mark consisting exclusively of words or letters, numerals, other standard typographic characters or a combination thereof (word mark), the mark shall be represented by submitting a reproduction of the sign in standard script and layout, without any graphic feature or colour;

(b) in the case of a trade mark where non-standard characters, stylisation or layout, or a graphic feature or a colour are used (figurative mark), including marks that consist exclusively of figurative elements or of a combination of verbal and figurative elements, the mark shall be represented by submitting a reproduction of the sign showing all its elements and, where applicable, its colours;

(c) in the case of a trade mark consisting of, or extending to, a three-dimensional shape, including containers, packaging, the product itself or their appearance (shape mark), the mark shall be represented by submitting either a graphic reproduction of the shape, including computer-generated imaging, or a photographic reproduction. The graphic or photographic reproduction may contain different views. Where the representation is not provided electronically, it may contain up to six different views;

(d) in the case of a trade mark consisting of the specific way in which the mark is placed or affixed on the goods (position mark), the mark shall be represented by submitting a reproduction which appropriately identifies the position of the mark and its size or proportion with respect to the relevant goods. The elements which do not form part of the subject matter of the registration shall be visually disclaimed preferably by broken or dotted lines. The representation may be accompanied by a description detailing how the sign is affixed on the goods;

(e) in the case of a trade mark consisting exclusively of a set of elements which are repeated regularly (pattern mark), the mark shall be represented by submitting a reproduction showing the pattern of repetition. The representation may be accompanied by a description detailing how its elements are repeated regularly;

(f) in the case of a colour mark,

   (i) where the trade mark consists exclusively of a single colour without contours, the mark shall be represented by submitting a reproduction of the colour and an indication of that colour by reference to a generally recognised colour code;

   (ii) where the trade mark consists exclusively of a combination of colours without contours, the mark shall be represented by submitting a reproduction that shows the systematic arrangement of the colour combination in a uniform and predetermined manner and an indication of those colours by reference to a generally recognised colour code. A description detailing the systematic arrangement of the colours may also be added;

(g) in the case of a trade mark consisting exclusively of a sound or combination of sounds (sound mark), the mark shall be represented by submitting an audio file reproducing the sound or by an accurate representation of the sound in musical notation;

(h) in the case of a trade mark consisting of, or extending to, a movement or a change in the position of the elements of the mark (motion mark), the mark shall be represented by submitting a video file or by a series of sequential still images showing the movement or change of position. Where still images are used, they may be numbered or accompanied by a description explaining the sequence;

(i) in the case of a trade mark consisting of, or extending to, the combination of image and sound (multimedia mark), the mark shall be represented by submitting an audiovisual file containing the combination of the image and the sound;

(j) in the case of a trade mark consisting of elements with holographic characteristics (hologram mark), the mark shall be represented by submitting a video file or a graphic or photographic reproduction containing the views which are necessary to sufficiently identify the holographic effect in its entirety.

**4.** Where the trade mark is not covered by any of the types listed in paragraph 3, its representation shall comply with the standards set out in paragraph 1 and may be accompanied by a description.

**5.** Where the representation is provided electronically, the Executive Director of the Office shall determine the formats and size of the electronic file as well as any other relevant technical specifications.

**6.** Where the representation is not provided electronically, the trade mark shall be reproduced on a single sheet of paper separate from the sheet on which the text of the application appears. The single sheet on which the mark is reproduced shall contain all the relevant views or images and shall not exceed DIN A4 size (29,7 cm high, 21 cm wide). A margin of at least 2,5 cm shall be left all around.

**7.** Where the correct orientation of the mark is not obvious, it shall be indicated by adding the word 'top' to each reproduction.

**8.** The reproduction of the mark shall be of such quality as to enable it to be:

(a) reduced to a size of not less than 8 cm wide by 8 cm high; or

(b) enlarged to a size of not more than 8 cm wide by 8 cm high.

**9.** The filing of a sample or a specimen shall not constitute a proper representation of a trade mark.

*Article 4*

**Claiming priority**

**1.** Where the priority of one or more previous applications is claimed together with the application pursuant to Article 35 of Regulation (EU) 2017/1001, the applicant shall indicate the file number of the previous application and file a copy of it within three months of the filing date. That copy shall state the date of filing of the previous application.

**2.** Where the language of the previous application for which priority is claimed is not one of the languages of the Office, the applicant shall, if required by the Office, provide the Office with a translation of the previous application into the language of the Office used as the first or second language of the application, within a period specified by the Office.

**3.** Paragraphs 1 and 2 shall apply *mutatis mutandis* where the priority claim relates to one or more previous registrations.

*Article 5*

**Exhibition priority**

Where an exhibition priority is claimed together with the application pursuant to Article 38(1) of Regulation (EU) 2017/1001, the applicant shall, within three months of the filing date, file a certificate issued at the exhibition by the authority responsible for the protection of industrial property at the exhibition. That certificate shall attest that the mark was used for the goods or services covered by the application. It shall also state the opening date of the exhibition and the date of first public use, if different from the opening date of the exhibition. The certificate shall be accompanied by an identification of the actual use of the mark, duly certified by the authority.

*Article 6*

**Claiming seniority of a national trade mark before registration of the EU trade mark**

Where the seniority of an earlier registered trade mark, as referred to in Article 39(1) of Regulation (EU) 2017/1001, is claimed pursuant to Article 39(2) of Regulation (EU) 2017/1001, the applicant shall submit a copy of the relevant registration within three months of the receipt of the seniority claim by the Office.

*Article 7*

**Content of the publication of an application**

The publication of the application shall contain:

(a) the applicant's name and address;

(b) where applicable, the name and business address of the representative appointed by the applicant other than a representative falling within the first sentence of Article 119(3) of Regulation (EU) 2017/1001. Where there is more than one representative with the same business address, only the name and business address of the first-named representative shall be published and it shall be followed by the words 'and others'. Where there are two or more representatives with different business addresses, only the address for service determined pursuant to Article 2(1)(e) of this Regulation shall be published. Where an association of representatives is appointed in accordance with Article 74(8) of Delegated Regulation (EU) 2018/625, only the name and business address of the association shall be published;

(c) the representation of the mark, together with the elements and descriptions referred to in Article 3 where applicable. Where the representation has been provided in the form of an electronic file, it shall be made accessible by means of a link to that file;

(d) the list of goods or services, grouped according to the classes of the Nice Classification, each group being preceded by the number of the class of that classification to which that group of goods or services belongs, and presented in the order of the classes of that classification;

(e) the date of filing and the file number;

(f) where applicable, particulars of the claim of priority filed by the applicant pursuant to Article 35 of Regulation (EU) 2017/1001;

(g) where applicable, particulars of the claim of exhibition priority filed by the applicant pursuant to Article 38 of Regulation (EU) 2017/1001;

(h) where applicable, particulars of the claim of seniority filed by the applicant pursuant to Article 39 of Regulation (EU) 2017/1001;

(i) where applicable, a statement pursuant to Article 7(3) of Regulation (EU) 2017/1001 that the mark has become distinctive in relation to the goods or services for which registration is requested in consequence of the use which has been made of it;

(j) where applicable, a statement that the application is for an EU collective mark or an EU certification mark;

(k) an indication of the language in which the application was filed and of the second language which the applicant has indicated pursuant to Article 146(3) of Regulation (EU) 2017/1001;

(l) where applicable, a statement that the application results from a transformation of an international registration designating the Union pursuant to Article 204(2) of Regulation (EU) 2017/1001, together with the date of the international registration pursuant to Article 3(4) of the Madrid Protocol or the date on which the territorial extension to the Union made subsequently to the international registration pursuant to Article 3*ter* (2) of the Madrid Protocol was recorded in the international register and, where applicable, the priority date of the international registration.

*Article 8*

**Division of the application**

**1.** A declaration of the division of the application pursuant to Article 50 of Regulation (EU) 2017/1001 shall contain:

(a) the file number of the application;

(b) the name and address of the applicant in accordance with Article 2(1)(b) of this Regulation;

(c) the list of goods or services subject to the divisional application, or, where the division into more than one divisional application is sought, the list of goods or services for each divisional application;

(d) the list of goods or services which are to remain in the original application.

**2.** The Office shall establish a separate file for each divisional application, which shall consist of a complete copy of the file of the original application, including the declaration of division and the correspondence relating thereto. The Office shall assign a new application number to each divisional application.

**3.** The publication of each divisional application shall contain the indications and elements laid down in Article 7.

*Article 9*

**Certificate of registration**

The certificate of registration issued in accordance with Article 51(2) of Regulation (EU) 2017/1001 shall contain the entries in the Register listed in Article 111(2) of Regulation (EU) 2017/1001 and a statement to the effect that those entries have been recorded in the Register. Where the representation of the mark is provided in the form of an electronic file, the relevant entry shall be made accessible by means of a link to that file. The certificate shall be complemented, where applicable, by an extract showing all entries to be recorded in the Register in accordance with Article 111(3) of Regulation (EU) 2017/1001 and a statement to the effect that those entries have been recorded in the Register.

*Article 10*

**Content of the request for alteration of a registration**

A request for alteration of a registration pursuant to Article 54(2) of Regulation (EU) 2017/1001 shall contain:

(a) the registration number of the EU trade mark;
(b) the name and the address of the proprietor of the EU trade mark in accordance with Article 2(1)(b) of this Regulation;
(c) an indication of the element in the representation of the EU trade mark to be altered and that element in its altered version in accordance with Article 54(3) of Regulation (EU) 2017/1001;
(d) a representation of the EU trade mark as altered, in accordance with Article 3 of this Regulation.

*Article 11*

**Declaration of the division of a registration**

**1.** A declaration of the division of a registration pursuant to Article 56(1) of Regulation (EU) 2017/1001 shall contain:
(a) the registration number of the EU trade mark;
(b) the name and address of the proprietor of the EU trade mark in accordance with Article 2(1)(b) of this Regulation;
(c) the list of goods or services which are to form the divisional registration, or, where the division into more than one divisional registration is sought, the list of goods or services for each divisional registration;
(d) the list of goods or services which are to remain in the original registration.

**2.** The Office shall establish a separate file for the divisional registration, which shall consist of a complete copy of the file of the original registration, including the declaration of division and the correspondence relating thereto. The Office shall assign a new registration number to the divisional registration.

*Article 12*

**Content of a request for the change of the name or address of the proprietor of an EU trade mark or of the applicant for an EU trade mark**

A request for the change of the name or address of the proprietor of a registered EU trade mark pursuant to Article 55(1) of Regulation (EU) 2017/1001 shall contain:
(a) the registration number of the EU trade mark;
(b) the name and the address of the proprietor of the EU trade mark as recorded in the Register, unless an identification number has already been given by the Office to the proprietor, in which case it shall be sufficient for the applicant to indicate that number and the proprietor's name;
(c) the indication of the new name or address of the proprietor of the EU trade mark, in accordance with Article 2(1)(b) of this Regulation.

Points (b) and (c) of the first subparagraph shall apply *mutatis mutandis* for the purposes of a request for the change of the name or address of the applicant for an EU trade mark. Such a request shall also contain the application number.

*Article 13*

**Application for registration of a transfer**

**1.** An application for registration of a transfer under Article 20(5) of Regulation (EU) 2017/1001 shall contain:

(a) the registration number of the EU trade mark;
(b) particulars of the new proprietor in accordance with Article 2(1)(b) of this Regulation;
(c) where not all the registered goods or services are included in the transfer, particulars of the registered goods or services to which the transfer relates;
(d) evidence duly establishing the transfer in accordance with Article 20(2) and (3) of Regulation (EU) 2017/1001;
(e) where applicable, the name and business address of the representative of the new proprietor, to be set out in accordance with Article 2(1)(e) of this Regulation.

**2.** Points (b) to (e) of paragraph 1 shall apply *mutatis mutandis* for the purposes of an application for the recording of a transfer of an EU trade mark application.

**3.** For the purposes of paragraph 1(d), any of the following shall constitute sufficient evidence of transfer:
(a) the signing of the application for registration of the transfer by the registered proprietor or a representative of that proprietor, and by the successor in title or a representative of that successor;
(b) where the application is submitted by the registered proprietor or a representative of that proprietor, a declaration signed by the successor in title or a representative of that successor agreeing to the registration of the transfer;
(c) where the application for registration is submitted by the successor in title, a declaration, signed by the registered proprietor or a representative of that proprietor, that the registered proprietor agrees to the registration of the successor in title;
(d) the signing of a completed transfer form or document, as laid down in Article 65(1)(e) of Delegated Regulation (EU) 2018/625, by the registered proprietor or a representative of that proprietor and by the successor in title or a representative of that successor.

*Article 14*

## Processing of applications for partial transfer

**1.** Where the application for registration of a transfer relates only to some of the goods or services for which the mark is registered, the applicant shall distribute the goods or services in the original registration between the remaining registration and the application for partial transfer so that the goods or services in the remaining registration and the new registration do not overlap.

**2.** The Office shall establish a separate file for the new registration, which shall consist of a complete copy of the file of the original registration, including the application for registration of the partial transfer and the correspondence relating thereto. The Office shall assign a new registration number to the new registration.

**3.** Paragraphs 1 and 2 shall apply *mutatis mutandis* for the purposes of an application to record a transfer of an EU trade mark application. The Office shall assign a new application number to the new EU trade mark application.

*Article 15*

**Surrender**

**1.** A declaration of surrender pursuant to Article 57(2) of Regulation (EU) 2017/1001 shall contain:

(a) the registration number of the EU trade mark;

(b) the name and address of the proprietor in accordance with Article 2(1)(b) of this Regulation;

(c) where surrender is declared only for some of the goods or services for which the mark is registered, an indication of the goods or services for which the mark is to remain registered.

**2.** Where a right of a third party relating to the EU trade mark is entered in the Register, a declaration of consent to the surrender, signed by the proprietor of that right or a representative of that proprietor, shall be sufficient proof of the third party's agreement to the surrender.

*Article 16*

**Content of regulations governing the use of EU collective marks**

The regulations governing EU collective marks referred to in Article 75(1) of Regulation (EU) 2017/1001 shall specify:

(a) the name of the applicant;

(b) the object of the association or the object for which the legal person governed by public law is constituted;

(c) the bodies authorised to represent the association or the legal person governed by public law;

(d) in the case of an association, the conditions for membership;

(e) the representation of the EU collective mark;

(f) the persons authorised to use the EU collective mark;

(g) where appropriate, the conditions governing use of the EU collective mark, including sanctions;

(h) the goods or services covered by the EU collective mark including, where appropriate, any limitation introduced as a consequence of the application of Article 7(1)(j), (k) or (l) of Regulation (EU) 2017/1001;

(i) where appropriate, the authorisation referred to in the second sentence of Article 75(2) of Regulation (EU) 2017/1001.

*Article 17*

**Content of regulations governing the use of EU certification marks**

The regulations governing use of EU certification marks referred to in Article 84 of Regulation (EU) 2017/1001 shall specify:

(a) the name of the applicant;

(b) a declaration that the applicant complies with the requirements laid down in Article 83(2) of Regulation (EU) 2017/1001;

(c) the representation of the EU certification mark;

(d) the goods or services covered by the EU certification mark;

(e) the characteristics of the goods or services to be certified by the EU certification mark, such as the material, mode of manufacture of goods or performance of services, quality or accuracy;

(f) the conditions governing the use of the EU certification mark, including sanctions;

(g) the persons authorised to use the EU certification mark;

(h) how the certifying body is to test those characteristics and to supervise the use of the EU certification mark.

### *Article 18*

### **Maximum rates for costs**

**1.** Costs referred to in the first subparagraph of Article 109(2) of Regulation (EU) 2017/1001 shall be borne by the losing party on the basis of the following maximum rates:

(a) where the successful party is not represented, the travel and subsistence costs of that party for one person for the outward and return journey between the place of residence or the place of business and the place where oral proceedings are held pursuant to Article 49 of Delegated Regulation (EU) 2018/625, as follows:

(i) the cost of the first-class rail fare including usual transport supplements where the total distance by rail does not exceed 800 km or the cost of the tourist-class airfare where the total distance by rail exceeds 800 km or the route includes a sea crossing;

(ii) subsistence costs as laid down in Article 13 of Annex VII to the Staff Regulations of Officials of the Union and the Conditions of Employment of Other Servants of the Union, laid down in Council Regulation (EEC, Euratom, ECSC) No 259/68;

(b) travel costs of representatives pursuant to Article 120(1) of Regulation (EU) 2017/1001, at the rates provided for in point (a)(i) of this paragraph;

(c) costs of representation, within the meaning of Article 120(1) of Regulation (EU) 2017/1001, incurred by the successful party, as follows:

(i) in opposition proceedings: EUR 300;

(ii) in proceedings relating to the revocation or invalidity of an EU trade mark: EUR 450;

(iii) in appeal proceedings: EUR 550;

(iv) where oral proceedings have taken place to which the parties have been summoned pursuant to Article 49 of Delegated Regulation (EU) 2018/625, the amount referred to in points (i), (ii) or (iii) increased by EUR 400.

**2.** Where there are several applicants or proprietors of the EU trade mark application or registration or where there are several opposing parties or applicants for revocation or a declaration of invalidity that have filed the opposition or application for revocation or a declaration of invalidity jointly, the losing party shall bear the costs referred to in paragraph 1(a) for one such person only.

**3.** Where the successful party is represented by more than one representative within the meaning of Article 120(1) of Regulation (EU) 2017/1001, the losing party shall bear the costs referred to in paragraph 1(b) and (c) of this Article for one such person only.

**4.** The losing party shall not be obliged to reimburse the successful party for any costs, expenses and fees relating to proceedings before the Office other than those referred to in paragraphs 1, 2 and 3.

*Article 19*

**Periodical publications**

**1.** Where particulars are published in the European Union Trade Marks Bulletin in accordance with Regulation (EU) 2017/1001, Delegated Regulation (EU) 2018/625 or this Regulation, the date of issue shown in the European Union Trade Marks Bulletin shall be taken as the date of publication of the particulars.
**2.** To the extent that the entries regarding the registration of a trade mark contain no changes as compared to the publication of the application, the publication of such entries shall be made by way of a reference to the particulars contained in the publication of the application.
**3.** The Office may make editions of the Official Journal of the Office publicly available by electronic means.

*Article 20*

**Exchange of information between the Office and the authorities of the Member States**

**1.** Without prejudice to Article 152 of Regulation (EU) 2017/1001, the Office and the central industrial property offices of the Member States, including the Benelux Office for Intellectual Property, shall, upon request, communicate to each other relevant information about the filing of applications for EU trade marks or national marks and about proceedings relating to such applications and the marks registered as a result thereof.
**2.** The Office and the courts or authorities of the Member States shall exchange information for the purposes of Regulation (EU) 2017/1001 directly or through the central industrial property offices of the Member States.
**3.** Expenditure in respect of communications under paragraphs 1 and 2 shall be chargeable to the authority making the communications. Such communications shall be exempt from fees.

*Article 21*

**Opening of files for inspection**

**1.** Inspection of files relating to EU trade mark applications or registered EU trade marks by courts or authorities of the Member States shall be of the original documents or of copies thereof, or of technical means of storage if the files are stored in this way.
**2.** The Office shall, at the time of transmission of files relating to EU trade marks applied for or registered, or copies thereof, to the courts or public prosecutors' offices of the Member States, indicate the restrictions to which the inspection of those files is subject pursuant to Article 114 of Regulation (EU) 2017/1001.
**3.** Courts or public prosecutors' offices of the Member States may, in the course of proceedings before them, open files or copies thereof transmitted to them by the

Office to inspection by third parties. Such inspection shall be subject to Article 114 of Regulation (EU) 2017/1001.

*Article 22*

**Content of a request for conversion**

A request for conversion of an EU trade mark application or a registered EU trade mark into a national trade mark application pursuant to Article 139 of Regulation (EU) 2017/1001 shall contain:

(a) the name and the address of the applicant for conversion in accordance with Article 2(1)(b) of this Regulation;

(b) the filing number of the EU trade mark application or the registration number of the EU trade mark;

(c) an indication of the ground for conversion in accordance with Article 139(1)(a) or (b) of Regulation (EU) 2017/1001;

(d) an indication of the Member State or the Member States in respect of which conversion is requested;

(e) where the request does not relate to all of the goods or services for which the application has been filed or for which the EU trade mark has been registered, an indication of the goods or services for which conversion is requested, and, where conversion is requested in respect of more than one Member State and the list of goods or services is not the same for all Member States, an indication of the respective goods or services for each Member State;

(f) where conversion is requested, pursuant to Article 139(6) of Regulation (EU) 2017/1001, on the grounds that an EU trade mark has ceased to have effect as a result of a decision of an EU trade mark court, an indication of the date on which that decision became final, and a copy of the decision, which may be submitted in the language in which the decision was given.

*Article 23*

**Content of the publication of a request for conversion**

The publication of a request for conversion in accordance with Article 140(2) of Regulation (EU) 2017/1001 shall contain:

(a) the filing number or the registration number of the EU trade mark in respect of which conversion is requested;

(b) a reference to the previous publication of the request or to the registration in the European Union Trade Marks Bulletin;

(c) an indication of the Member State or Member States in respect of which conversion has been requested;

(d) where the request does not relate to all of the goods or services for which the application has been filed or for which the EU trade mark has been registered, an indication of the goods or services for which conversion is requested;

(e) where conversion is requested in respect of more than one Member State and the list of goods or services is not the same for all Member States, an indication of the respective goods or services for each Member State;

(f) the date of the request for conversion.

*Article 24*

## Filing of supporting documents in written proceedings

Unless otherwise provided for in this Regulation or in Delegated Regulation (EU) 2018/625, supporting documents to be used in written proceedings before the Office may be filed in any official language of the Union. Where the language of such documents is not the language of the proceedings as determined in accordance with Article 146 of Regulation (EU) 2017/1001, the Office may, of its own motion or upon reasoned request by the other party, require that a translation be supplied, within a period specified by it, in that language.

*Article 25*

## Standard of translations

**1.** Where a translation of a document is to be filed with the Office, the translation shall identify the document to which it refers and reproduce the structure and contents of the original document. Where a party has indicated that only parts of the document are relevant, the translation may be limited to those parts.

**2.** Unless otherwise provided for in Regulation (EU) 2017/1001, in Delegated Regulation (EU) 2018/625 or in this Regulation, a document for which a translation is to be filed shall be deemed not to have been received by the Office in the following cases:

(a) where the translation is received by the Office after the expiry of the relevant period for submitting the original document or the translation;

(b) where the certificate referred to in Article 26 of this Regulation is not filed within the period specified by the Office.

*Article 26*

## Legal authenticity of translations

In the absence of evidence or indications to the contrary, the Office shall assume that a translation corresponds to the relevant original text. In the event of doubt, the Office may require the filing, within a specific period, of a certificate that the translation corresponds to the original text.

*Article 27*

## Decisions of an Opposition Division or a Cancellation Division taken by a single member

Pursuant to Article 161(2) or Article 163(2) of Regulation (EU) 2017/1001, a single member of an Opposition Division or of a Cancellation Division shall take the following types of decisions:

(a) decisions on the apportionment of costs;

(b) decisions to fix the amount of the costs to be paid pursuant to the first sentence of Article 109(7) of Regulation (EU) 2017/1001;

(c) decisions to discontinue the proceedings or decisions confirming that there is no need to proceed to a decision on merits;

(d) decisions to reject an opposition as inadmissible before expiry of the period referred to in Article 6(1) of Delegated Regulation (EU) 2018/625;

(e) decisions to stay proceedings;
(f) decisions to join or separate multiple oppositions pursuant to Article 9(1) of Delegated Regulation (EU) 2018/625.

*Article 28*

**Form to be used for the filing of an international application**

The form made available by the Office for the filing of an international application, as referred to in Article 184(1) of Regulation (EU) 2017/1001 shall include all the elements of the official form provided by the International Bureau. Applicants may also use the official form provided by the International Bureau.

*Article 29*

**Facts and decisions on invalidity to be notified to the International Bureau**

**1.** The Office shall notify the International Bureau within a period of five years of the date of the international registration in the following cases:
(a) where the EU trade mark application on which the international registration was based has been withdrawn, is deemed to be withdrawn or has been refused by a final decision, in respect of all or some of the goods or services listed in the international registration;
(b) where the EU trade mark on which the international registration was based has ceased to have effect because it has been surrendered, has not been renewed, has been revoked, or has been declared invalid by the Office by a final decision or, on the basis of a counterclaim in infringement proceedings, by an EU trade mark court, in respect of all or some of the goods or services listed in the international registration;
(c) where the EU trade mark application or the EU trade mark on which the international registration was based has been divided into two applications or registrations.

**2.** The notification referred to in paragraph 1 shall include:
(a) the number of the international registration;
(b) the name of the holder of the international registration;
(c) the facts and decisions affecting the basic application or registration, as well as the effective date of those facts and decisions;
(d) in the case referred to in paragraph 1(a) or (b), the request to cancel the international registration;
(e) where the act referred to in paragraph 1(a) or (b) affects the basic application or basic registration only with respect to some of the goods or services, those goods or services, or the goods or services which are not affected;
(f) in the case referred to in paragraph 1(c), the number of each EU trade mark application or registration concerned.

**3.** The Office shall notify the International Bureau at the end of a period of five years of the date of the international registration in the following cases:
(a) where an appeal is pending against a decision of an examiner to refuse the EU trade mark application on which the international registration was based pursuant to Article 42 of Regulation (EU) 2017/1001;
(b) where an opposition is pending against the EU trade mark application on which the international registration was based;

(c) where an application for revocation or an application for a declaration of invalidity is pending against the EU trade mark on which the international registration was based;

(d) where mention has been made in the Register of EU trade marks that a counterclaim for revocation or for declaration of invalidity has been filed before an EU trade mark court against the EU trade mark on which the international registration was based, but no mention has yet been made in the Register of the decision of the EU trade mark court on the counterclaim.

**4.** Once the proceedings referred to in paragraph 3 have been concluded by means of a final decision or an entry in the Register, the Office shall notify the International Bureau in accordance with paragraph 2.

**5.** For the purposes of paragraphs 1 and 3, an EU trade mark on which the international registration was based shall include an EU trade mark registration resulting from an EU trade mark application on which the international application was based.

*Article 30*

## Request for territorial extension subsequent to international registration

**1.** A request for territorial extension filed at the Office pursuant to Article 187(1) of Regulation (EU) 2017/1001 shall meet the following requirements:

(a) it is filed using one of the forms referred to in Article 31 of this Regulation and contains all the indications and information required by the form used;

(b) it indicates the number of the international registration to which it relates;

(c) the list of goods or services is covered by the list of goods or services contained in the international registration;

(d) the applicant is entitled, based on the indications made in the international form, to make a designation subsequent to the international registration through the Office in accordance with Article 2(1)(ii), and Article 3*ter* (2) of the Madrid Protocol.

**2.** Where a request for territorial extension does not meet all of the requirements laid down in paragraph 1, the Office shall invite the applicant to remedy the deficiencies within such time limit as it may specify.

*Article 31*

## Form to be used for a request for territorial extension

The form made available by the Office for a request for territorial extension subsequent to international registration, as referred to in Article 187(1) of Regulation (EU) 2017/1001, shall include all the elements of the official form provided by the International Bureau. Applicants may also use the official form provided by the International Bureau.

*Article 32*

## Seniority claims before the Office

**1.** Without prejudice to Article 39(7) of Regulation (EU) 2017/1001, a seniority claim pursuant to Article 192(1) of Regulation (EU) 2017/1001 shall contain:

(a) the registration number of the international registration;

(b) the name and address of the holder of the international registration in accordance with Article 2(1)(b) of this Regulation;
(c) an indication of the Member State or Member States in or for which the earlier trade mark is registered;
(d) the number and the filing date of the relevant registration;
(e) an indication of the goods or services for which the earlier trade mark is registered and those in respect of which seniority is claimed;
(f) a copy of the relevant registration certificate.

**2.** Where the holder of the international registration is obliged to be represented in proceedings before the Office pursuant to Article 119(2) of Regulation (EU) 2017/1001, the seniority claim shall contain the appointment of a representative within the meaning of Article 120(1) of Regulation (EU) 2017/1001.

**3.** Where the Office has accepted the seniority claim, it shall inform the International Bureau accordingly by communicating the following:
(a) the number of the international registration concerned;
(b) the name of the Member State or Member States in or for which the earlier trade mark is registered;
(c) the number of the relevant registration;
(d) the date from which the relevant registration was effective.

*Article 33*

### Notification of ex officio provisional refusals to the International Bureau

**1.** The notification of an ex officio provisional refusal of protection of the international registration in whole or in part to be issued to the International Bureau pursuant to Article 193(2) and (5) of Regulation (EU) 2017/1001 shall, without prejudice to the requirements laid down in Article 193(3) and (4) of that Regulation, contain the following:
(a) the number of the international registration;
(b) a reference to the provisions of Regulation (EU) 2017/1001 which are relevant for the provisional refusal;
(c) an indication that the provisional refusal of protection will be confirmed by a decision of the Office if the holder of the international registration does not overcome the grounds for refusal by submitting observations to the Office within a time limit of two months of the date on which the Offices issues the provisional refusal;
(d) where the provisional refusal relates to only part of the goods or services, an indication of those goods or services.

**2.** In respect of each notification of an *ex officio* provisional refusal to the International Bureau, and provided that the time limit for entering an opposition has expired and that no notification of provisional refusal based on an opposition has been issued pursuant to Article 78(1) of Delegated Regulation (EU) 2018/625, the Office shall inform the International Bureau of the following:
(a) where as a result of the proceedings before the Office the provisional refusal has been withdrawn, the fact that the mark is protected in the Union;
(b) where a decision to refuse protection of the mark has become final, if applicable, following an appeal under Article 66 of Regulation (EU) 2017/1001 or an action under Article 72 of Regulation (EU) 2017/1001, the fact that protection of the mark is refused in the Union;

(c) where the refusal pursuant to point (b) concerns only part of the goods or services, the goods or services for which the mark is protected in the Union.

*Article 34*

**Notification of invalidation of the effects of an international registration to the International Bureau**

The notification referred to in Article 198(3) of Regulation (EU) 2017/1001 shall bear a date and shall contain:

(a) the indication that the invalidation has been pronounced by the Office, or the indication of the EU trade mark court which has pronounced the invalidation;

(b) an indication of whether invalidation has been pronounced in the form of revocation of the rights of the holder of the international registration, of a declaration that the trade mark is invalid on absolute grounds, or of a declaration that the trade mark is invalid on relative grounds;

(c) a statement to the effect that the invalidation is no longer subject to appeal;

(d) the number of the international registration;

(e) the name of the holder of the international registration;

(f) where the invalidation does not concern all the goods or services, an indication of the goods or services in respect of which the invalidation has been pronounced or those in respect of which the invalidation has not been pronounced;

(g) the date on which the invalidation was pronounced, together with an indication of the date from when the invalidation became effective.

*Article 35*

**Request for conversion of an international registration into a national trade mark application or into a designation of Member States**

**1.** A request for conversion of an international registration designating the Union into a national trade mark application or into a designation of Member States pursuant to Articles 139 and 202 of Regulation (EU) 2017/1001 shall, without prejudice to the requirements laid down in Article 202(4) to (7) of that Regulation, contain:

(a) the registration number of the international registration;

(b) the date of the international registration or the date of the designation of the Union made subsequently to the international registration pursuant to Article 3ter (2) of the Madrid Protocol and, where applicable, particulars of the claim to priority for the international registration pursuant to Article 202(2) of Regulation (EU) 2017/1001, and particulars of the claim to seniority pursuant to Articles 39, 40 or 191 of Regulation (EU) 2017/1001;

(c) the indications and elements referred to in Article 140(1) of Regulation (EU) 2017/1001 and Article 22(a), (c) and (d) of this Regulation.

**2.** The publication of a request for conversion referred to in paragraph 1 shall contain the details laid down in Article 23.

*Article 36*

**Transformation of an international registration designating the Union into an EU trade mark application**

An application for transformation pursuant to Article 204(3) of Regulation (EU) 2017/1001 shall contain, in addition to the indications and elements referred to in Article 2 of this Regulation, the following:

(a) the number of the international registration which has been cancelled;

(b) the date on which the international registration was cancelled by the International Bureau;

(c) as appropriate, the date of the international registration pursuant to Article 3(4) of the Madrid Protocol or the date of recordal of the territorial extension to the Union made subsequently to the international registration pursuant to Article 3*ter* (2) of the Madrid Protocol;

(d) where applicable, the date of priority claimed in the international application as entered in the international register kept by the International Bureau.

*Article 37*

**Transitional measures**

The provisions of Regulation (EC) No 2868/95 shall continue to apply to ongoing proceedings where this Regulation does not apply in accordance with its Article 39, until such proceedings are concluded.

*Article 38*

**Repeal**

Implementing Regulation (EU) 2017/1431 is repealed.

*Article 39*

**Entry into force and application**

**1.** This Regulation shall enter into force on the twentieth day following that of its publication in the *Official Journal of the European Union*.

**2.** It shall apply from the date of entry into force referred to in paragraph 1, subject to the following exceptions:

(a) Title II shall not apply to applications for an EU trade mark entered before 1 October 2017, as well as to international registrations for which the designation of the Union was made before that date;

(b) Article 9 shall not apply to EU trade marks registered before 1 October 2017;

(c) Article 10 shall not apply to requests for alteration entered before 1 October 2017;

(d) Article 11 shall not apply to declarations of division entered before 1 October 2017;

(e) Article 12 shall not apply to requests for the change of name or address entered before 1 October 2017;

(f) Title IV shall not apply to applications for registration of a transfer entered before 1 October 2017;

(g) Title V shall not apply to declarations of surrender entered before 1 October 2017;
(h) Title VI shall not apply to applications for EU collective marks or EU certification marks entered before 1 October 2017, as well as to international registrations for which the designation of the Union was made before that date;
(i) Title VII shall not apply to costs incurred in proceedings initiated before 1 October 2017;
(j) Title VIII shall not apply to publications made before 1 October 2017;
(k) Title IX shall not apply to requests for information or inspection entered before 1 October 2017;
(l) Title X shall not apply to requests for conversion entered before 1 October 2017;
(m) Title XI shall not apply to supporting documents or translations entered before 1 October 2017;
(n) Title XII shall not apply to decisions taken before 1 October 2017;
(o) Title XIII shall not apply to international applications, notifications of facts and decisions on invalidity of the EU trade mark application or registration on which the international registration was based, requests for territorial extension, seniority claims, notification of ex officio provisional refusals, notifications of invalidation of the effects of an international registration, requests for conversion for an international registration into a national trade mark application and applications for transformation of an international registration designating the Union into an EU trade mark application entered or made before 1 October 2017, as the case may be.

Signatures

This Regulation shall be binding in its entirety and directly applicable in all Member States.

Done at Brussels, 5 March 2018.

For the Commission
The President
Jean-Claude JUNCKER

*Replace Appendix 8:*

## Appendix 8

# COMMISSION DELEGATED REGULATION (EU) 2018/625
# of 5 March 2018

A8-001 **supplementing Regulation (EU) 2017/1001 of the European Parliament and of the Council on the European Union trade mark, and repealing Delegated Regulation (EU) 2017/1430**

THE EUROPEAN COMMISSION,

Having regard to the Treaty on the Functioning of the European Union,

Having regard to Regulation (EU) 2017/1001 of the European Parliament and of the Council of 14 June 2017 on the European Union trade mark (1), and in particular Article 48, Article 49(3), Article 65, Article 73, Article 96(4), Article 97(6), Article 98(5), Article 100(2), Article 101(5), Article 103(3), Article 106(3), Article 121, Article 168, Article 194(3) and Article 196(4) thereof,

Whereas:

**(1)** Council Regulation (EC) No 40/94 (2), which was codified as Council Regulation (EC) No 207/2009 (3), created a system specific to the Union for the protection of trade marks to be obtained at the level of the Union on the basis of an application to the European Union Intellectual Property Office ('the Office').

**(2)** Regulation (EU) 2015/2424 of the European Parliament and of the Council (4) amending Regulation (EC) No 207/2009 aligned the powers conferred therein upon the Commission with Articles 290 and 291 of the Treaty on the Functioning of the European Union. In order to conform with the new legal framework resulting from that alignment, Commission Delegated Regulation (EU) 2017/1430 (5) and Commission Implementing Regulation (EU) 2017/1431 (6) were adopted.

**(3)** Regulation (EC) No 207/2009 was codified as Regulation (EU) 2017/1001. For reasons of clarity and simplification, the references contained in a Delegated Regulation should reflect the renumbering of articles resulting from such a codification of the relevant basic act. Delegated Regulation (EU) 2017/1430 should therefore be repealed and the provisions of that Delegated Regulation should be laid down, with updated references to Regulation (EU) 2017/1001, in this Regulation.

**(4)** The procedural rules on opposition should ensure an effective, efficient and expeditious examination and registration of EU trade mark applications by the Office using a procedure which is transparent, thorough, fair and equitable. In order to enhance legal certainty and clarity, those opposition rules should take account of the extended relative grounds for refusal laid down in Regulation (EU) 2017/1001, in particular as regards the requirements for admissibility and substantiation of opposition proceedings, and be adjusted to better reflect the case-law of the Court of Justice of the European Union and to codify the practice of the Office.

**(5)** In order to allow for a more flexible, consistent and modern trade mark system in the Union, while ensuring legal certainty, it is appropriate to reduce the administrative burden for the parties in inter partes proceedings by relaxing the requirements for the substantiation of earlier rights in cases where the content of the relevant evidence is accessible online from a source recognised by the Office, as well as the requirement of submitting evidence in the language of the proceedings.

**(6)** In the interest of clarity and legal certainty, it is important to specify the requirements for amending an application for an EU trade mark in a clear and exhaustive manner.

**(7)** The procedural rules governing the revocation and declaration of invalidity of an EU trade mark should ensure that an EU trade mark can be revoked or declared invalid in an effective and efficient way by means of transparent, thorough, fair and equitable procedures. For the sake of greater clarity, consistency as well as efficiency and legal certainty, the procedural rules governing the revocation and declaration of invalidity of an EU trade mark should be aligned with those applicable to opposition proceedings, retaining only those differences which are required due to the specific nature of revocation and declaration of invalidity proceedings. Furthermore, requests for assignment of an EU trade mark registered in the name of an unauthorised agent should follow the same procedural path as invalidity proceedings, serving in practice as an alternative to invalidating the mark.

**(8)** According to settled case-law of the Court of Justice (7), unless otherwise provided, the Office enjoys discretionary powers when examining belated evidence, submitted for the purpose of either substantiating an opposition or proving genuine use of the earlier mark in the context of opposition or invalidity proceedings. In order to ensure legal certainty the relevant boundaries of such discretion should be accurately reflected in the rules governing opposition proceedings or proceedings for the declaration of invalidity of EU trade marks.

**(9)** In order to allow for an effective, efficient and, within the scope of the appeal defined by the parties, complete review of decisions taken by the Office in the first instance by means of a transparent, thorough, fair and impartial appeal procedure suited to the specific nature of intellectual property law and taking into account the principles laid down in Regulation (EU) 2017/1001, it is appropriate to reinforce legal certainty and predictability by clarifying and specifying the procedural rules and the parties' procedural guarantees, in particular where a defendant makes use of the right to file a cross appeal.

**(10)** In order to ensure an effective and efficient organisation of the Boards of Appeal, the President, the chairpersons and the members of the Boards of Appeal should, in the exercise of their respective functions conferred upon them by Regulation (EU) 2017/1001 and by this Regulation, be required to ensure a high quality and consistency of the decisions taken independently by the Boards on appeal as well as the efficiency of the appeal proceedings.

**(11)** In order to ensure the independence of the President, the chairpersons and the members of the Boards of Appeal as provided in Article 166 of Regulation (EU) 2017/1001, the Management Board should take the latter Article into account when adopting appropriate implementing rules to give effect to the Staff Regulations and the Conditions of Employment of Other Servants in accordance with Article 110 of the Staff Regulations.

**(12)** In order to enhance the transparency and predictability of the appeal proceedings, the rules of procedure of the Boards of Appeal originally laid down in Commission Regulation (EC) No 2868/95 (8) and Commission Regulation (EC) No 216/96 (9), should be set out in a single text and properly interlinked with the procedural rules applicable to the instances of the Office whose decisions are subject to appeals.

**(13)** For the sake of clarity and legal certainty, it is required to codify and clarify certain procedural rules governing oral proceedings, in particular relating to the language of such proceedings. It is further appropriate to provide greater efficiency and flexibility by introducing the possibility of taking part in oral proceedings by technical means and of substituting the minutes of oral proceedings by their recording.

**(14)** In order to further streamline proceedings and render them more consistent, it is appropriate to set out the basic structure and format of evidence to be submitted to the Office in all proceedings, as well as the consequences of not submitting evidence in accordance with that structure and format.

**(15)** In order to modernise the trade mark system in the Union by adapting it to the internet era, it is further appropriate to provide for a definition of 'electronic means' in the context of notifications and for forms of notification that are not obsolete.

**(16)** In the interest of efficiency, transparency and user-friendliness, the Office should make available standard forms in all the official languages of the Office for communication in proceedings before the Office, which may be completed online.

**(17)** For the purposes of greater clarity, consistency and efficiency, a provision on the suspension of opposition, revocation, invalidity and appeal proceedings should be introduced, laying down also the maximum duration of a suspension requested by both parties.

**(18)** The rules governing the calculation and duration of time limits, the procedures for the revocation of a decision or for cancellation of an entry in the Register, the detailed arrangements for the resumption of proceedings, and the details on representation before the Office need to ensure a smooth, effective and efficient operation of the EU trade mark system.

**(19)** It is necessary to ensure the effective and efficient registration of international trade marks in a manner that is fully consistent with the rules of the Protocol relating to the Madrid Agreement concerning the international registration of marks.

**(20)** Implementing Regulation (EU) 2017/1431 and Delegated Regulation (EU) 2017/1430 replaced the rules previously laid down in Regulations (EC) No 2868/95 and (EC) No 216/96 which were therefore repealed. Notwithstanding that repeal, it is necessary to continue to apply specific provisions of Regulations (EC) No 2868/95 and (EC) No 216/96 to certain proceedings that had been initiated before the date of applicability of Regulation (EU) 2017/1430 until the conclusion of those proceedings,

HAS ADOPTED THIS REGULATION:

## TITLE I

## GENERAL PROVISIONS

*Article 1*

### Subject matter

This Regulation lays down rules specifying:

(a) the details of the procedure for filing and examining an opposition to the registration of an EU trade mark at the European Union Intellectual Property Office ('the Office');
(b) the details of the procedure governing the amendment of an application for an EU trade mark;
(c) the details governing the revocation and declaration of invalidity of an EU trade mark, as well as the transfer of an EU trade mark registered in the name of an unauthorised agent;
(d) the formal content of a notice of appeal and the procedure for the filing and the examination of an appeal, the formal content and form of the Boards of Appeal's decisions and the reimbursement of the appeal fee, the details concerning the organisation of the Boards of Appeal, and the conditions under which decisions on appeals are to be taken by a single member;
(e) the detailed arrangements for oral proceedings and for the taking of evidence;
(f) the detailed arrangements for notification by the Office and the rules on the means of communication with the Office;
(g) the details regarding the calculation and duration of time limits;
(h) the procedure for the revocation of a decision or for the cancellation of an entry in the Register of EU trade marks;
(i) the detailed arrangements for the resumption of proceedings before the Office;
(j) the conditions and the procedure for the appointment of a common representative, the conditions under which employees and professional representatives shall file an authorisation, and the content of that authorisation, and the circumstances in which a person may be removed from the list of admitted professional representatives;
(k) the details of the procedure concerning international registrations based on a basic application or basic registration relating to a collective mark, certification mark or guarantee mark, and the procedure for the filing and examination of an opposition to an international registration.

## TITLE II

## PROCEDURE FOR OPPOSITION AND PROOF OF USE

*Article 2*

### Notice of opposition

**1.** A notice of opposition may be entered on the basis of one or more earlier marks or other rights within the meaning of Article 8 of Regulation (EU) 2017/1001, provided that the proprietors or authorised persons entering the notice pursuant to Article 46 of Regulation (EU) 2017/1001 are entitled to do so for all the earlier marks or rights. Where an earlier mark has more than one proprietor ('co-ownership') or where an earlier right may be exercised by more than one person, an opposition pursuant to Article 46 of Regulation (EU) 2017/1001 may be filed by any or all of the proprietors or authorised persons.

**2.** The notice of opposition shall contain:

(a) the file number of the application against which opposition is entered and the name of the applicant for the EU trade mark;

(b) a clear identification of the earlier mark or right on which the opposition is based, namely:

(i) where the opposition is based on an earlier mark within the meaning of Article 8(2)(a) or (b) of Regulation (EU) 2017/1001, the file number or registration number of the earlier mark, an indication of whether the earlier mark is registered or an application for registration of that mark, as well as an indication of the Member States including, where applicable, the Benelux, in or for which the earlier mark is protected, or, if applicable, the indication that it is an EU trade mark;

(ii) where the opposition is based on a well-known mark within the meaning of Article 8(2)(c) of Regulation (EU) 2017/1001, the indication of the Member State(s) where the mark is well known and a representation of the mark;

(iii) where the opposition is based on the absence of the proprietor's consent as referred to in Article 8(3) of Regulation (EU) 2017/1001, an indication of the territory in which the earlier trade mark is protected, the representation of the mark and, if applicable, an indication whether the earlier mark is an application or a registration, in which case the filing or registration number shall be provided;

(iv) where the opposition is based on an earlier mark or another sign within the meaning of Article 8(4) of Regulation (EU) 2017/1001, an indication of its kind or nature, a representation of the earlier mark or sign, and an indication of whether the right to the earlier mark or sign exists in the whole Union or in one or more Member States, and if so, an indication of those Member States;

(v) where the opposition is based on an earlier designation of origin or geographical indication within the meaning of Article 8(6) of Regulation (EU) 2017/1001, an indication of its nature, a representation of the earlier designation of origin or geographical indication, and an indication of whether it is protected in the whole Union or in one or more Member States, and if so, an indication of those Member States;

(c) the grounds on which the opposition is based by means of a statement to the effect that the requirements under Article 8(1), (3), (4), (5) or (6) of Regulation (EU) 2017/1001 in respect of each of the earlier marks or rights invoked by the opposing party are fulfilled;

(d) in the case of an earlier trade mark application or registration, the filing date and, where available, the registration date and the priority date of the earlier mark;

(e) in the case of earlier rights pursuant to Article 8(6) of Regulation (EU) 2017/1001, the date of application for registration or, if that date is not available, the date from which protection is granted;

(f) in the case of an earlier trade mark application or registration, a representation of the earlier mark as registered or applied for; if the earlier mark is in colour, the representation shall be in colour;

(g) an indication of the goods or services on which each of the grounds of the opposition is based;

(h) as concerns the opposing party:

 (i) the identification of the opposing party in accordance with Article 2(1)(b) of Implementing Regulation (EU) 2018/626 (10);

 (ii) where the opposing party has appointed a representative, or where representation is mandatory pursuant to Article 119(2) of Regulation (EU) 2017/1001, the name and business address of the representative in accordance with Article 2(1)(e) of Implementing Regulation (EU) 2018/626;

 (iii) where the opposition is entered by a licensee or by a person who is entitled under the relevant Union legislation or national law to exercise an earlier right, a statement to that effect and indications concerning the authorisation or the entitlement to file the opposition;

(i) an indication of the goods or services against which the opposition is directed; in the absence of such an indication, the opposition shall be considered to be directed against all of the goods or services of the opposed EU trade mark application.

**3.** Where the opposition is based on more than one earlier mark or earlier right, paragraph 2 shall apply for each of those marks, signs, designations of origin or geographical indications.

**4.** The notice of opposition may also contain a reasoned statement on the grounds, the facts and arguments on which the opposition relies, and supporting evidence.

*Article 3*

**Use of languages in opposition proceedings**

The opposing party or the applicant may, before the date on which the adversarial part of the opposition proceedings is deemed to commence pursuant to Article 6(1), inform the Office that the applicant and the opposing party have agreed on a different language for the opposition proceedings pursuant to Article 146(8) of Regulation (EU) 2017/1001. Where the notice of opposition has not been filed in that language, the applicant may request that the opposing party file a translation in that language. Such a request must be received by the Office not later than the date on which the adversarial part of the opposition proceedings is deemed to commence. The Office shall specify a time limit for the opposing party to file a translation. Where that translation is not filed or filed late, the language of the proceedings as determined in accordance with Article 146 of Regulation (EU) 2017/1001 ('language of proceedings') shall remain unchanged.

*Article 4*

**Information to the parties to opposition proceedings**

The notice of opposition and any document submitted by the opposing party, as well as any communication addressed to one of the parties by the Office prior to the finding on admissibility shall be sent by the Office to the other party for purposes of informing of the introduction of an opposition.

*Article 5*

**Admissibility of the opposition**

**1.** Where the opposition fee has not been paid within the opposition period laid down in Article 46(1) of Regulation (EU) 2017/1001, the opposition shall be deemed not to have been entered. Where the opposition fee has been paid after the expiry of the opposition period, it shall be refunded to the opposing party.
**2.** Where the notice of opposition has been filed after the expiry of the opposition period, the Office shall reject the opposition as inadmissible.
**3.** Where the notice of opposition has been filed in a language which is not one of the languages of the Office as required under Article 146(5) of Regulation (EU) 2017/1001, or where it does not comply with Article 2(2)(a), (b) or (c) of this Regulation, and where those deficiencies have not been remedied before the expiry of the opposition period, the Office shall reject the opposition as inadmissible.
**4.** Where the opposing party does not submit a translation as required under Article 146(7) of Regulation (EU) 2017/1001, the opposition shall be rejected as inadmissible. Where the opposing party submits an incomplete translation, the part of the notice of opposition that has not been translated shall not be taken into account in the examination of admissibility.
**5.** Where the notice of opposition does not comply with the provisions of Article 2(2)(d) to (h), the Office shall inform the opposing party accordingly and shall invite it to remedy the deficiencies noted within a period of two months. If the deficiencies are not remedied before the time limit expires, the Office shall reject the opposition as inadmissible.
**6.** The Office shall notify the applicant of any finding pursuant to paragraph 1 that the notice of opposition is deemed not to have been entered and of any decision to reject the opposition on the grounds of inadmissibility under paragraphs 2, 3, 4 or 5. Where an opposition is rejected in its entirety as inadmissible pursuant to paragraphs 2, 3, 4 or 5, prior to the notification of Article 6(1), no decision on costs shall be taken.

*Article 6*

**Commencement of the adversarial part of the opposition proceedings and prior closure of the proceedings**

**1.** Where the opposition is found admissible pursuant to Article 5, the Office shall send a communication to the parties informing them that the adversarial part of the opposition proceedings shall be deemed to commence two months after receipt of the communication. That period may be extended to a total of 24 months if both parties request an extension before the two-month period expires.
**2.** Where, within the period referred to in paragraph 1, the application is withdrawn or restricted to goods or services against which the opposition is not directed, or the Office is informed about a settlement between the parties, or the application is rejected in parallel proceedings, the opposition proceedings shall be closed.
**3.** Where, within the period referred to in paragraph 1, the applicant restricts the application by deleting some of the goods or services against which the opposition is directed, the Office shall invite the opposing party to state, within such a period as it may specify, whether it maintains the opposition, and if so, against

which of the remaining goods or services. Where the opposing party withdraws the opposition in light of the restriction, the opposition proceedings shall be closed.

**4.** Where, before the expiry of the period referred to in paragraph 1, the opposition proceedings are closed pursuant to paragraphs 2 or 3, no decision on costs shall be taken.

**5.** Where, before the expiry of the period referred to in paragraph 1, the opposition proceedings are closed following a withdrawal or restriction of the application pursuant to paragraph 2 or following a withdrawal of the opposition pursuant to paragraph 3, the opposition fee shall be refunded.

*Article 7*

**Substantiation of the opposition**

**1.** The Office shall give the opposing party the opportunity to submit the facts, evidence and arguments in support of the opposition or to complete any facts, evidence or arguments that have already been submitted pursuant to Article 2(4). For that purpose, the Office shall specify a time limit which shall be at least two months, starting on the date on which the adversarial part of the opposition proceedings is deemed to commence in accordance with Article 6(1).

**2.** Within the period referred to in paragraph 1, the opposing party shall also file evidence of the existence, validity and scope of protection of its earlier mark or right, as well as evidence proving its entitlement to file the opposition. In particular, the opposing party shall provide the following evidence:

(a) where the opposition is based on an earlier trade mark within the meaning of Article 8(2)(a) and (b) of Regulation (EU) 2017/1001, which is not an EU trade mark, evidence of its filing or registration, by submitting:

(i) a copy of the relevant filing certificate or an equivalent document from the administration with which the trade mark application was filed, if the trade mark is not yet registered; or

(ii) where the earlier trade mark is registered, a copy of the relevant registration certificate and, if applicable, of the latest renewal certificate, showing that the term of protection of the trade mark extends beyond the time limit referred to in paragraph 1 or any extension thereof, or equivalent documents from the administration by which the trade mark was registered;

(b) where the opposition is based on a well-known mark within the meaning of Article 8(2)(c) of Regulation (EU) 2017/1001, evidence showing that that mark is well known in the relevant territory for the goods or services indicated in accordance with Article 2(2)(g) of this Regulation;

(c) where the opposition is based on the absence of the proprietor's consent as referred to in Article 8(3) of Regulation (EU) 2017/1001, evidence of the opposing party's proprietorship of the prior trade mark and of its relationship with the agent or representative;

(d) where the opposition is based on an earlier right within the meaning of Article 8(4) of Regulation (EU) 2017/1001, evidence showing use of that right in the course of trade of more than mere local significance, as well as evidence of its acquisition, continued existence and scope of protection including, where the earlier right is invoked pursuant to the law of a Member State, a clear identification of the content of the national law relied upon by adducing publications of the relevant provisions or jurisprudence;

(e) where the opposition is based on an earlier designation of origin or geographical indication within the meaning of Article 8(6) of Regulation (EU) 2017/1001, evidence of its acquisition, continued existence and scope of protection including, where the earlier designation of origin or geographical indication is invoked pursuant to the law of a Member State, a clear identification of the content of the national law relied upon by adducing publications of the relevant provisions or jurisprudence;

(f) if the opposition is based on a mark with a reputation within the meaning of Article 8(5) of Regulation (EU) 2017/1001, in addition to the evidence referred to in point (a) of this paragraph, evidence showing that the mark has a reputation in the Union or in the Member State concerned for the goods or services indicated in accordance with Article 2(2)(g) of this Regulation, as well as evidence or arguments showing that use without due cause of the trade mark applied for would take unfair advantage of, or be detrimental to, the distinctive character or the repute of the earlier trade mark.

**3.** Where the evidence concerning the filing or registration of the earlier rights referred to in paragraph 2(a) or, where applicable, paragraph 2(d) or (e), or the evidence concerning the content of the relevant national law, is accessible online from a source recognised by the Office, the opposing party may provide such evidence by making reference to that source.

**4.** Any filing, registration or renewal certificates or equivalent documents referred to in paragraph 2(a), (d) or (e), as well as any provisions of the applicable national law governing the acquisition of rights and their scope of protection as referred to in paragraph 2(d) and (e), including evidence accessible online as referred to in paragraph 3, shall be in the language of the proceedings or shall be accompanied by a translation into that language. The translation shall be submitted by the opposing party of its own motion within the time limit specified for submitting the original document. Any other evidence submitted by the opposing party to substantiate the opposition shall be subject to Article 24 of Implementing Regulation (EU) 2018/626. Translations submitted after the expiry of the relevant time limits shall not be taken into account.

**5.** The Office shall not take into account written submissions, or parts thereof, which have not been submitted in or not been translated into the language of the proceedings within the time limit set by the Office in accordance with paragraph 1.

*Article 8*

**Examination of the opposition**

**1.** Where, until the expiry of the period referred to in Article 7(1), the opposing party has not provided any evidence, or where the evidence provided is manifestly irrelevant or manifestly insufficient to meet the requirements laid down in Article 7(2) for any of the earlier rights, the opposition shall be rejected as unfounded.

**2.** Where the opposition is not rejected pursuant to paragraph 1, the Office shall communicate the submission of the opposing party to the applicant and shall invite it to file its observations within a period specified by the Office.

**3.** Where the applicant submits no observations, the Office shall base its ruling on the opposition on the evidence before it.

**4.** The observations submitted by the applicant shall be communicated to the opposing party who shall be invited, if the Office considers it necessary, to reply within a period specified by the Office.
**5.** Where, after the expiry of the period referred to in Article 7(1), the opposing party submits facts or evidence that supplement relevant facts or evidence provided within that period and that relate to the same requirement laid down in Article 7(2), the Office shall exercise its discretion under Article 95(2) of Regulation (EU) 2017/1001 in deciding whether to accept these supplementing facts or evidence. For that purpose, the Office shall take into account, in particular, the stage of proceedings and whether the facts or evidence are, prima facie, likely to be relevant for the outcome of the case and whether there are valid reasons for the late submission of the facts or evidence.
**6.** The Office shall invite the applicant to submit further observations in response if it deems it appropriate under the circumstances.
**7.** Where the opposition has not been rejected pursuant to paragraph 1 and the evidence submitted by the opposing party is not sufficient to substantiate the opposition in accordance with Article 7 for any of the earlier rights, the opposition shall be rejected as unfounded.
**8.** Article 6(2) and (3) shall apply mutatis mutandis after the date on which the adversarial part of the opposition proceedings is deemed to commence. Where the applicant wishes to withdraw or restrict the contested application, it shall do so by way of a separate document.
**9.** In appropriate cases, the Office may invite the parties to limit their observations to particular issues, in which case it shall allow them to raise the other issues at a later stage of the proceedings. The Office shall not be required to inform a party of the possibility of producing certain relevant facts or evidence which that party previously failed to produce.

### *Article 9*

### **Multiple oppositions**

**1.** Where a number of oppositions have been entered in respect of the same application for the registration of an EU trade mark, the Office may examine them in one set of proceedings. The Office may subsequently decide to examine those oppositions separately.
**2.** Where a preliminary examination of one or more oppositions reveals that the EU trade mark for which an application for registration has been filed may be ineligible for registration in respect of some or all of the goods or services for which registration is sought, the Office may suspend the other opposition proceedings relating to that application. The Office shall inform the opposing parties affected by the suspension of any relevant decisions taken in the context of those proceedings which are ongoing.
**3.** Once a decision rejecting an application as referred to in paragraph 1 has become final, the oppositions for which proceedings have been suspended in accordance with paragraph 2 shall be deemed to have been disposed of and the opposing parties concerned shall be informed accordingly. Such a disposition shall be considered to constitute a case which has not proceeded to judgment within the meaning of Article 109(5) of Regulation (EU) 2017/1001.
**4.** The Office shall refund 50 % of the opposition fee paid by each opposing party whose opposition is deemed to have been disposed of in accordance with paragraph

3, provided that the suspension of the proceedings relating to that opposition took place before the commencement of the adversarial part of the proceedings.

*Article 10*

**Proof of use**

**1.** A request for proof of use of an earlier mark pursuant to Article 47(2) or (3) of Regulation (EU) 2017/1001 shall be admissible if it is submitted as an unconditional request in a separate document within the period specified by the Office pursuant to Article 8(2) of this Regulation.

**2.** Where the applicant has made a request for proof of use of an earlier mark which complies with the requirements of Article 47(2) or (3) of Regulation (EU) 2017/1001, the Office shall invite the opposing party to provide the proof required within a time limit specified by the Office. Where the opposing party does not provide any evidence or reasons for non-use before the time limit expires or where the evidence or reasons provided are manifestly irrelevant or manifestly insufficient, the Office shall reject the opposition in so far as it is based on that earlier mark.

**3.** The indications and evidence of use shall establish the place, time, extent and nature of use of the opposing trade mark for the goods or services in respect of which it is registered and on which the opposition is based.

**4.** The evidence referred to in paragraph 3 shall be filed in accordance with Article 55(2) and Articles 63 and 64 and shall be limited to the submission of supporting documents and items such as packages, labels, price lists, catalogues, invoices, photographs, newspaper advertisements, and statements in writing as referred to in Article 97(1)(f) of Regulation (EU) 2017/1001.

**5.** A request for proof of use may be filed at the same time as observations on the grounds on which the opposition is based. Such observations may also be filed together with the observations in reply to the proof of use.

**6.** Where the evidence supplied by the opposing party is not in the language of the opposition proceedings, the Office may require the opposing party to submit a translation of that evidence in that language pursuant to Article 24 of Implementing Regulation (EU) 2018/626.

**7.** Where after the expiry of the time limit referred to in paragraph 2, the opposing party submits indications or evidence that supplement relevant indications or evidence already submitted before expiry of that time limit and relate to the same requirement laid down in paragraph 3, the Office shall exercise its discretion under Article 95(2) of Regulation (EU) 2017/1001 in deciding whether to accept those supplementary indications or evidence. For that purpose, the Office shall take into account, in particular, the stage of proceedings and whether the indications or evidence are, prima facie, likely to be relevant for the outcome of the case and whether there are valid reasons for the late submission of the indications or evidence.

# TITLE III

# AMENDMENT OF THE APPLICATION

*Article 11*

## Amendment of the application

**1.** A request for amendment of an application pursuant to Article 49(2) of Regulation (EU) 2017/1001 shall contain:

(a) the file number of the application;

(b) the name and address of the applicant in accordance with Article 2(1)(b) of Implementing Regulation (EU) 2018/626;

(c) an indication of the element of the application to be amended, and that element in its amended version;

(d) where the amendment relates to the representation of the mark, a representation of the mark as amended, in accordance with Article 3 of Implementing Regulation (EU) 2018/626.

**2.** Where the requirements for the amendment of the application are not fulfilled, the Office shall communicate the deficiency to the applicant and shall specify a time limit for remedying the deficiency. Where the applicant does not remedy the deficiency within the specified time limit, the Office shall reject the request for amendment.

**3.** Where the amended trade mark application is published pursuant to Article 49(2) of Regulation (EU) 2017/1001, Articles 2 to 10 of this Regulation shall apply mutatis mutandis.

**4.** A single request for amendment may be made for the amendment of the same element in two or more applications by the same applicant.

**5.** Paragraphs 1, 2 and 4 shall apply mutatis mutandis for applications to correct the name or the business address of a representative appointed by the applicant.

# TITLE IV

# REVOCATION AND INVALIDITY OR ASSIGNMENT

*Article 12*

## Application for revocation or for a declaration of invalidity

**1.** An application to the Office for revocation or for a declaration of invalidity pursuant to Article 63 of Regulation (EU) 2017/1001 shall contain:

(a) the registration number of the EU trade mark in respect of which revocation or a declaration of invalidity is sought and the name of its proprietor;

(b) the grounds on which the application is based by means of a statement that the respective requirements laid down in Articles 58, 59, 60, 81, 82, 91 or 92 of Regulation (EU) 2017/1001 are fulfilled;

(c) as concerns the applicant:

(i) the identification of the applicant in accordance with Article 2(1)(b) of Implementing Regulation (EU) 2018/626;

(ii) where the applicant has appointed a representative or where representation is mandatory within the meaning of Article 119(2) of Regulation (EU) 2017/1001, the name and business address of the representative, in accordance with Article 2(1)(e) of Implementing Regulation (EU) 2018/626;

(d) an indication of the goods or services in respect of which revocation or a declaration of invalidity is sought, in the absence of which the application shall be deemed to be directed against all the goods or services covered by the contested EU trade mark.

**2.** In addition to the requirements laid down in paragraph 1, an application for a declaration of invalidity based on relative grounds shall contain the following:

(a) in the case of an application pursuant to Article 60(1) of Regulation (EU) 2017/1001, an identification of the earlier right on which the application is based, in accordance with Article 2(2)(b) of this Regulation, which shall apply mutatis mutandis to such an application;

(b) in the case of an application pursuant to Article 60(2) of Regulation (EU) 2017/1001, an indication of the nature of the earlier right on which the application is based, its representation and an indication of whether this earlier right exists in the whole of the Union or in one or more Member States, and if so, an indication of those Member States;

(c) particulars pursuant to Article 2(2)(d) to (g) of this Regulation, which apply mutatis mutandis to such an application;

(d) where the application is entered by a licensee or by a person who is entitled under the relevant Union legislation or national law to exercise an earlier right, an indication concerning the authorisation or entitlement to file the application.

**3.** Where the application for a declaration of invalidity pursuant to Article 60 of Regulation (EU) 2017/1001 is based on more than one earlier mark or earlier right, paragraphs 1(b) and 2 of this Article shall apply for each of those marks or rights.

**4.** The application may contain a reasoned statement on the grounds setting out the facts and arguments on which it is based and supporting evidence.

*Article 13*

**Languages used in revocation or invalidity proceedings**

The applicant for revocation or for a declaration of invalidity or the proprietor of the EU trade mark may inform the Office before the expiry of a period of two months of receipt by the EU trade mark proprietor of the communication referred to in Article 17(1), that a different language of proceedings has been agreed pursuant to Article 146(8) of Regulation (EU) 2017/1001. Where the application has not been filed in that language, the proprietor may request that the applicant file a translation in that language. Such a request shall be received by the Office before the expiry of the period of two months of receipt by the EU trade mark proprietor of the communication referred to in Article 17(1). The Office shall specify a time limit for the applicant to file such a translation. Where that translation is not filed or filed late, the language of the proceedings shall remain unchanged.

*Article 14*

**Information to the parties concerning an application for revocation or for a declaration of invalidity**

An application for revocation or for a declaration of invalidity and any document submitted by the applicant, as well as any communication addressed to one of the parties by the Office prior to the finding on admissibility shall be sent by the

Office to the other party for the purposes of informing of the introduction of an application for revocation or for a declaration of invalidity.

*Article 15*

**Admissibility of an application for revocation or for a declaration of invalidity**

**1.** Where the fee required under Article 63(2) of Regulation (EU) 2017/1001 has not been paid, the Office shall invite the applicant to pay the fee within a period specified by it. Where the required fee is not paid within the specified period, the Office shall inform the applicant that the application for revocation or for a declaration of invalidity is deemed not to have been entered. Where the fee has been paid after the expiry of the specified period, it shall be refunded to the applicant.
**2.** Where the application has been filed in a language which is not one of the languages of the Office as required under Article 146(5) of Regulation (EU) 2017/1001, or it does not comply with Article 12(1)(a) or (b) or, where applicable, Article 12(2)(a) or (b) of this Regulation, the Office shall reject the application as inadmissible.
**3.** Where the translation required under the second subparagraph of Article 146(7) Regulation (EU) 2017/1001 is not filed within a period of one month of the date of filing an application for revocation or a declaration of invalidity, the Office shall reject the application for revocation or for a declaration of invalidity as inadmissible.
**4.** Where the application does not comply with the provisions laid down in Article 12(1)(c), Article 12(2)(c) or (d), the Office shall inform the applicant accordingly and shall invite the applicant to remedy the deficiencies noted within a period of two months. If the deficiencies are not remedied before the time limit expires, the Office shall reject the application as inadmissible.
**5.** The Office shall notify the applicant and the proprietor of the EU trade mark of any finding pursuant to paragraph 1 that the application for revocation or a declaration of invalidity is deemed not to have been entered and of any decision to reject the application for revocation or a declaration of invalidity on the grounds of inadmissibility under paragraphs 2, 3 or 4. Where an application for revocation or a declaration of invalidity is rejected in its entirety as inadmissible pursuant to paragraphs 2, 3 or 4, prior to the notification of Article 17(1), no decision on costs shall be taken.

*Article 16*

**Substantiation of an application for revocation or for a declaration of invalidity**

**1.** The applicant shall present the facts, evidence and arguments in support of the application up to the closure of the adversarial part of revocation or invalidity proceedings. In particular, the applicant shall provide the following:

(a) in the case of an application pursuant to Article 58(1)(b) or (c) or Article 59 of Regulation (EU) 2017/1001, facts, arguments and evidence to support the grounds on which the application for revocation or a declaration of invalidity is based;

(b) in the case of an application pursuant to Article 60(1) of Regulation (EU)

2017/1001, the evidence required by Article 7(2) of this Regulation and the provisions of Article 7(3) shall apply mutatis mutandis;

(c) in the case of an application pursuant to Article 60(2) of Regulation (EU) 2017/1001, evidence of acquisition, continued existence and scope of protection of the relevant earlier right as well as evidence proving that the applicant is entitled to file the application, including, where the earlier right is invoked pursuant to the law of a Member State, a clear identification of the content of the national law relied upon by adducing publications of the relevant provisions or jurisprudence. Where the evidence concerning the filing or registration of an earlier right under Article 60(2)(d) of Regulation (EU) 2017/1001 or the evidence concerning the contents of the relevant national law is accessible online from a source recognised by the Office, the applicant may provide such evidence by making reference to that source.

**2.** Evidence concerning the filing, registration or renewal of earlier rights or, where applicable, the content of the relevant national law, including evidence accessible online, as referred to in paragraph 1(b) and (c), shall be filed in the language of the proceedings or shall be accompanied by a translation into that language. The translation shall be submitted by the applicant of the applicant's own motion within one month from the filing of such evidence. Any other evidence submitted by the applicant to substantiate the application or, in case of an application for revocation under Article 58(1)(a) of Regulation (EU) 2017/1001, by the proprietor of the contested EU trade mark, shall be subject to Article 24 of Implementing Regulation (EU) 2018/626. Translations submitted after the expiry of the relevant time limits shall not be taken into account.

*Article 17*

**Examination on the merits of an application for revocation or for a declaration of invalidity**

**1.** Where the application is found admissible pursuant to Article 15, the Office shall send a communication to the parties informing them that the adversarial part of the revocation or invalidity proceedings has commenced and inviting the proprietor of the EU trade mark to file observations within a specified period.

**2.** Where the Office has invited a party in accordance with Article 64(1) of Regulation (EU) 2017/1001 to file observations within a specified period and that party does not submit any observations within that period, the Office shall close the adversarial part of the proceedings and base its ruling on the revocation or invalidity on the basis of the evidence before it.

**3.** Where the applicant has not submitted the facts, arguments or evidence required to substantiate the application, the application shall be rejected as unfounded.

**4.** Without prejudice to Article 62, all observations filed by the parties shall be sent to the other party concerned.

**5.** Where the proprietor surrenders the EU trade mark subject to an application as referred to in Article 12 to cover only goods or services against which the application is not directed, or the EU trade mark is revoked or declared invalid in parallel proceedings, or expires, the proceedings shall be closed except where Article 57(2) of Regulation (EU) 2017/1001 shall apply or the applicant shows a legitimate interest in obtaining a decision on the merits.

**6.** Where the proprietor partially surrenders the EU trade mark by deleting some of the goods or services against which the application is directed, the Office shall

invite the applicant to state, within such a period as it may specify, whether it maintains the application and if so, against which of the remaining goods or services. Where the applicant withdraws the application in light of the surrender, or the Office is informed about a settlement between the parties, the proceedings shall be closed.
**7.** Where the proprietor wishes to surrender the contested EU trade mark, it shall do so by way of a separate document.
**8.** Article 8(9) shall apply mutatis mutandis.

*Article 18*

**Multiple applications for revocation or for a declaration of invalidity**

**1.** Where a number of applications for revocation or for a declaration of invalidity have been filed relating to the same EU trade mark, the Office may examine them in one set of proceedings. The Office may subsequently decide to examine those applications separately.
**2.** Article 9(2), (3) and (4) shall apply mutatis mutandis.

*Article 19*

**Proof of use in relation to an application for revocation or for a declaration of invalidity**

**1.** In the case of an application for revocation based on Article 58(1)(a) of Regulation (EU) 2017/1001, the Office shall invite the proprietor of the EU trade mark to provide proof of genuine use of that mark or of proper reasons for non-use, within such period as it shall specify. Where the proprietor does not provide any evidence of genuine use or of reasons for non-use before the time limit expires or the evidence or reasons provided are manifestly irrelevant or manifestly insufficient, the EU trade mark shall be revoked. Article 10(3), (4), (6) and (7) of this Regulation shall apply mutatis mutandis.
**2.** A request for proof of use pursuant to Article 64(2) or (3) of Regulation (EU) 2017/1001 shall be admissible if the proprietor of the EU trade mark submits it as an unconditional request in a separate document within the period specified by the Office pursuant to Article 17(1) of this Regulation. Where the proprietor of the EU trade mark has made a request for proof of use of an earlier mark or of proper reasons for non-use which complies with the requirements of Article 64(2) or (3) of Regulation (EU) 2017/1001, the Office shall invite the applicant for a declaration of invalidity to provide the proof required within a time limit specified by the Office. Where the applicant for a declaration of invalidity does not provide any evidence of genuine use or of reasons for non-use before the time limit expires or the evidence or reasons provided are manifestly irrelevant or manifestly insufficient, the Office shall reject the application for a declaration of invalidity in so far as it is based on that earlier mark. Article 10(3) to (7) of this Regulation shall apply mutatis mutandis.

*Article 20*

**Request for assignment**

1. Where the proprietor of a trade mark requests, in accordance with Article 21(1) and (2)(a) of Regulation (EU) 2017/1001, an assignment instead of a declaration of invalidity, the provisions of Articles 12 to 19 of this Regulation shall apply mutatis mutandis.

2. Where a request for assignment pursuant to Article 21(2) of Regulation (EU) 2017/1001 is partially or totally granted by the Office or by an EU trade mark court and the decision or judgment has become final, the Office shall ensure that the resulting partial or total transfer of the EU trade mark is entered in the Register and published.

## TITLE V

## APPEALS

*Article 21*

**Notice of appeal**

1. A notice of appeal filed in accordance with Article 68(1) of Regulation (EU) 2017/1001 shall contain the following:

(a) the name and address of the appellant in accordance with Article 2(1)(b) of Implementing Regulation (EU) 2018/626;
(b) where the appellant has appointed a representative, the name and the business address of the representative in accordance with Article 2(1)(e) of Implementing Regulation (EU) 2018/626;
(c) where representation of the appellant is mandatory pursuant to Article 119(2) of Regulation (EU) 2017/1001, the name and the business address of the representative in accordance with Article 2(1)(e) of Implementing Regulation (EU) 2018/626;
(d) a clear and unambiguous identification of the decision subject to appeal indicating the date on which it was issued and the file number of the proceedings to which the decision subject to appeal relates;
(e) where the decision subject to appeal is only contested in part, a clear and unambiguous identification of the goods or services in respect of which the decision subject to appeal is contested.

2. Where the notice of appeal is filed in another official language of the Union than the language of proceedings, the appellant shall provide a translation thereof within four months of the date of notification of the decision subject to appeal.

3. Where in ex parte proceedings the decision subject to appeal has been taken in an official language other than the language of proceedings, the appellant may file the notice of appeal either in the language of the proceedings or in the language in which the decision subject to appeal was taken; in either case, the language used for the notice of appeal shall become the language of the appeal proceedings and paragraph 2 shall not apply.

4. As soon as the notice of appeal has been filed in inter partes proceedings, it shall be notified to the defendant.

*Article 22*

**Statement of grounds**

**1.** A statement setting out the grounds of appeal filed pursuant to the fourth sentence of Article 68(1) of Regulation (EU) 2017/1001 shall contain a clear and unambiguous identification of the following:

(a) the appeal proceedings to which it refers by indicating either the corresponding appeal number or the decision subject to appeal in accordance with the requirements laid down in Article 21(1)(d) of this Regulation;

(b) the grounds of appeal on which the annulment of the contested decision is requested within the extent identified in accordance with Article 21(1)(e) of this Regulation;

(c) the facts, evidence and arguments in support of the grounds invoked, submitted in accordance with the requirements set out in Article 55(2).

**2.** The statement of grounds shall be filed in the language of the appeal proceedings as determined in accordance with Article 21(2) and (3). Where the statement of grounds is filed in another official language of the Union, the appellant shall provide a translation thereof within one month of the date of the submission of the original statement.

*Article 23*

**Admissibility of an appeal**

**1.** The Board of Appeal shall reject an appeal as inadmissible in any of the following events:

(a) where the notice of appeal has not been filed within two months of the date of notification of the decision subject to appeal;

(b) where the appeal does not comply with Articles 66 and 67 of Regulation (EU) 2017/1001, or with those laid down in Article 21(1)(d) and Article 21(2) and (3) of this Regulation, unless those deficiencies are remedied within four months of the date of notification of the decision subject to appeal;

(c) where the notice of appeal does not comply with the requirements laid down in Article 21(1)(a), (b), (c) and (e), and the appellant has, despite having been informed thereof by the Board of Appeal, not remedied those deficiencies within the time limit specified by the Board of Appeal to that effect;

(d) where the statement of grounds has not been filed within four months of the date of notification of the decision subject to appeal;

(e) where the statement of grounds does not comply with the requirements laid down in Article 22(1)(a) and (b), and the appellant has, despite having been informed thereof by the Board of Appeal, not remedied those deficiencies within the time limit specified by the Board of Appeal to that effect or has not submitted the translation of the statement of grounds within one month of the date of the submission of the original statement in accordance with Article 22(2).

**2.** Where the appeal appears to be inadmissible, the chairperson of the Board of Appeal to which the case has been allocated pursuant to Article 35(1) may request the Board of Appeal to decide without delay on the admissibility of the appeal prior

to the notification to the defendant of the notice or of the statement of grounds, as the case may be.
**3.** The Board of Appeal shall declare an appeal as deemed not to have been filed where the appeal fee has been paid after the expiry of the time limit set out in the first sentence of Article 68(1) of Regulation (EU) 2017/1001. In such a case, paragraph 2 of this Article shall apply.

*Article 24*

## Response

**1.** In inter partes proceedings, the defendant may file a response within two months of the date of notification of the appellant's statement of grounds. In exceptional circumstances, that time limit may be extended upon reasoned request by the defendant.
**2.** The response shall contain the name and address of the defendant in accordance with Article 2(1)(b) of Implementing Regulation (EU) 2018/626 and shall comply, mutatis mutandis, with the conditions laid down in Article 21(1)(b), (c) and (d), Article 22(1)(a) and (c) and Article 22(2) of this Regulation.

*Article 25*

## Cross appeal

**1.** Where the defendant seeks a decision annulling or altering the contested decision on a point not raised in the appeal, pursuant to Article 68(2) of Regulation (EU) 2017/1001, that cross appeal shall be filed within the time limit for filing a response in accordance with Article 24(1) of this Regulation.
**2.** A cross appeal shall be submitted by a document separate from the response.
**3.** The cross appeal shall contain the name and address of the defendant in accordance with Article 2(1)(b) of Implementing Regulation (EU) 2018/626 and shall comply mutatis mutandis with the conditions laid down in Article 21(1)(b) to (e) and Article 22 of this Regulation.
**4.** A cross appeal shall be rejected as inadmissible in any of the following events:

(a) where it has not been filed within the time limit laid down in paragraph 1;
(b) where it has not been filed in observance of the requirements laid down either in paragraph 2 or Article 21(1)(d);
(c) where it does not comply with the requirements referred to in paragraph 3, and the defendant has, despite having been informed thereof by the Board of Appeal, not remedied these deficiencies within the time limit specified by the Board of Appeal to that effect or has not submitted the translation of the cross appeal and the corresponding statement of grounds within one month of the date of submission of the original.

**5.** The appellant shall be invited to submit observations on the defendant's cross appeal within two months of the date of notification to the appellant. In exceptional circumstances, that time limit may be extended by the Board of Appeal upon the reasoned request of the appellant. Article 26 shall apply mutatis mutandis.

*Article 26*

**Reply and rejoinder in inter partes proceedings**

**1.** Upon the appellant's reasoned request filed within two weeks of the notification of the response, the Board of Appeal may, pursuant to Article 70(2) of Regulation (EU) 2017/1001, authorise the appellant to supplement the statement of grounds with a reply within a period specified by the Board of Appeal.

**2.** In such a case, the Board of Appeal shall also authorise the defendant to supplement the response with a rejoinder within a period specified by the Board of Appeal.

*Article 27*

**Examination of the appeal**

**1.** In ex parte proceedings, and with respect to those goods or services which form part of the subject matter of the appeal, the Board of Appeal, in compliance with Article 45(3) of Regulation (EU) 2017/1001, shall proceed in accordance with Article 42 of Regulation (EU) 2017/1001 where it raises a ground for refusal of the trade mark application which had not already been invoked in the decision subject to appeal in application of that provision.

**2.** In inter partes proceedings, the examination of the appeal and, as the case may be, the cross appeal, shall be restricted to the grounds invoked in the statement of grounds and, as the case may be, in the cross appeal. Matters of law not raised by the parties shall be examined by the Board of Appeal only where they concern essential procedural requirements or where it is necessary to resolve them in order to ensure a correct application of Regulation (EU) 2017/1001 having regard to the facts, evidence and arguments presented by the parties.

**3.** The examination of the appeal shall include the following claims or requests provided that they have been raised in the statement of grounds of the appeal or, as the case may be, in the cross appeal and provided that they were raised in due time in the proceedings before the instance of the Office which adopted the decision subject to appeal:

- (a) distinctiveness acquired through use as referred to in Article 7(3) and Article 59(2) of Regulation (EU) 2017/1001;
- (b) recognition of the earlier trade mark on the market acquired through use for the purposes of Article 8(1)(b) of Regulation (EU) 2017/1001;
- (c) proof of use pursuant to Article 47(2) and (3) of Regulation (EU) 2017/1001 or Article 64(2) and (3) of Regulation (EU) 2017/1001.

**4.** In accordance with Article 95(2) of Regulation (EU) 2017/1001, the Board of Appeal may accept facts or evidence submitted for the first time before it only where those facts or evidence meet the following requirements:

- (a) they are, on the face of it, likely to be relevant for the outcome of the case; and
- (b) they have not been produced in due time for valid reasons, in particular where they are merely supplementing relevant facts and evidence which had already been submitted in due time, or are filed to contest findings made or examined by the first instance of its own motion in the decision subject to appeal.

**5.** The Board of Appeal shall, at the latest in its decision on the appeal and, as the case may be, the cross appeal, decide on requests for restriction, division or partial surrender of the contested mark declared during the appeal proceedings by the applicant or the proprietor in accordance with Articles 49, 50 or 57 of Regulation (EU) 2017/1001. Where the Board of Appeal accepts the restriction, division or partial surrender, it shall without delay inform the department in charge of the Register and the departments dealing with parallel proceedings involving the same mark accordingly.

*Article 28*

**Communications by the Board of Appeal**

**1.** Communications by the Board of Appeal in the course of the examination of the appeal or with a view to facilitating an amicable settlement of proceedings shall be prepared by the rapporteur and shall be signed by the rapporteur on behalf of the Board of Appeal, in agreement with the chairperson of the Board of Appeal.
**2.** Where a Board of Appeal communicates with the parties regarding its provisional opinion on matters of fact or law, it shall state that it is not bound by such a communication.

*Article 29*

**Comments on questions of general interest**

The Board of Appeal may, on its own initiative or upon the written, reasoned request of the Executive Director of the Office, invite the Executive Director to comment on questions of general interest which arise in the course of proceedings pending before it. The parties shall be entitled to submit their observations on the Executive Director's comments.

*Article 30*

**Reopening of the examination of absolute grounds**

**1.** Where, in ex parte proceedings, the Board of Appeal considers that an absolute ground for refusal may be applicable to goods or services listed in the trade mark application which do not form part of the subject matter of the appeal, it shall inform the examiner competent for examining that application who may decide to reopen the examination pursuant to Article 45(3) of Regulation (EU) 2017/1001 with respect to those goods or services.
**2.** Where a decision of the Opposition Division is subject to an appeal, the Board of Appeal may, by means of a reasoned interim decision and without prejudice to Article 66(1) of Regulation (EU) 2017/1001, suspend the appeal proceedings and remit the contested application to the examiner competent for examining that application with a recommendation to reopen the examination pursuant to Article 45(3) of Regulation (EU) 2017/1001, where it considers that an absolute ground for refusal shall apply to some or all of the goods or services listed in the trade mark application.
**3.** Where the contested application has been remitted in application of paragraph 2, the examiner shall inform the Board of Appeal without delay whether or not the examination of the contested application has been reopened. Where the examina-

tion has been reopened, the appeal proceedings shall remain suspended until the examiner's decision has been taken and, where the contested application is rejected in whole or in part, until the examiner's decision to this effect has become final.

*Article 31*

**Examination of an appeal as a matter of priority**

**1.** Upon reasoned request of the appellant or of the defendant and after hearing the other party, the Board of Appeal may decide, having regard to the particular urgency and the circumstances of the case, to examine the appeal as a matter of priority, without prejudice to the provisions in Articles 23 and 26, including the provisions on time limits.
**2.** The request for the examination of the appeal as a matter of priority may be filed at any time in the course of the appeal proceedings. It shall be filed in a separate document and shall be supported by evidence as to the urgency and the particular circumstances of the case.

*Article 32*

**Formal content of the Board of Appeal's decision**

The Board of Appeal's decision shall contain:
(a) a statement that it is delivered by the Boards of Appeal;
(b) the date when the decision was taken;
(c) the names of the parties and of their representatives;
(d) the number of the appeal to which it refers and an identification of the decision subject to appeal in accordance with the requirements laid down in Article 21(1)(d);
(e) an indication as to the formation of the Board of Appeal;
(f) the name and, without prejudice to Article 39(5), the signature of the chairperson and members who took part in the decision, including an indication of who acted as rapporteur in the case, or, where the decision is delivered by a single member, the name and signature of the member who took the decision;
(g) the name and the signature of the Registrar or, as the case may be, of the member of the Registry signing on the Registrar's behalf;
(h) a summary of the facts and of the arguments submitted by the parties;
(i) a statement of the reasons for which the decision has been taken;
(j) the order of the Board of Appeal, including, where necessary, a decision on costs.

*Article 33*

**Reimbursement of the appeal fee**

The appeal fee shall be reimbursed by order of the Board of Appeal in either of the following events:
(a) where the appeal is not deemed to have been filed in accordance with the second sentence of Article 68(1) of Regulation (EU) 2017/1001;
(b) where the decision-making instance of the Office which adopted the contested decision grants revision pursuant to Article 69(1) of Regulation

(EU) 2017/1001 or revokes the contested decision in application of Article 103 of Regulation (EU) 2017/1001;

(c) where, following reopening of the examination proceedings within the meaning of Article 45(3) of Regulation (EU) 2017/1001 upon the Board of Appeal's recommendation pursuant to Article 30(2) of this Regulation, the contested application has been rejected by final decision of the examiner and the appeal has become devoid of purpose as a consequence thereof;

(d) where the Board of Appeal considers such reimbursement equitable by reason of a substantial procedural violation.

*Article 34*

**Revision and revocation of the decision subject to appeal**

**1.** Where, in ex parte proceedings, the appeal is not rejected pursuant to Article 23(1), the Board of Appeal shall submit the notice of appeal and the statement of grounds of appeal to the instance of the Office which adopted the contested decision for the purposes of Article 69 of Regulation (EU) 2017/1001.

**2.** Where the instance of the Office which adopted the decision subject to appeal decides to grant revision pursuant to Article 69(1) of Regulation (EU) 2017/1001, it shall inform the Board of Appeal thereof without delay.

**3.** Where the instance of the Office which adopted the decision subject to appeal has initiated the procedure for revoking the decision subject to appeal pursuant to Article 103(2) of Regulation (EU) 2017/1001, it shall inform the Board of Appeal thereof without delay for the purposes of Article 71 of this Regulation. It shall also inform the Board of Appeal without delay about the final outcome of that procedure.

*Article 35*

**Allocation of an appeal to a Board and designation of a rapporteur**

**1.** As soon as the notice of appeal has been filed, the President of the Boards shall allocate the case to a Board of Appeal according to the objective criteria determined by the Presidium of the Boards of Appeal referred to in Article 166(4)(c) of Regulation (EU) 2017/1001.

**2.** For each case allocated to a Board of Appeal pursuant to paragraph 1, its chairperson shall designate a member of that Board of Appeal, or the chairperson, as rapporteur.

**3.** Where a case falls under the authority of a single member pursuant to Article 36(1), the Board of Appeal handling a case shall designate the rapporteur as single member pursuant to Article 165(5) of Regulation (EU) 2017/1001.

**4.** Where a decision of a Board of Appeal on a case has been annulled or altered by a final ruling of the General Court or, as the case may be, of the Court of Justice, the President of the Boards of Appeal shall, with a view to complying with that ruling in accordance with Article 72(6) of Regulation (EU) 2017/1001, reallocate the case pursuant to paragraph 1 of this Article to a Board of Appeal, which shall not comprise those members who had adopted the annulled decision, except where the case is referred to the enlarged Board of Appeal ('Grand Board') or where the annulled decision had been taken by the Grand Board.

**5.** Where several appeals are filed against the same decision, those appeals shall be considered in the same proceedings. Where appeals involving the same parties are filed against separate decisions concerning the same mark, or have other relevant factual or legal elements in common, those appeals may be considered in joined proceedings with the consent of the parties.

*Article 36*

**Cases falling under the authority of a single member**

**1.** The Board of Appeal handling the case may designate a single member within the meaning of Article 165(2) of Regulation (EU) 2017/1001 for the purposes of the following decisions:

(a) decisions pursuant to Article 23;
(b) decisions closing the appeal proceedings following withdrawal, rejection, surrender or cancellation of the contested or the earlier mark;
(c) decisions closing the appeal proceedings following withdrawal of the opposition, of the request for revocation or for a declaration of invalidity or of the appeal;
(d) decisions on measures pursuant to Article 102(1) and Article 103(2) of Regulation (EU) 2017/1001, provided that the correction or, as the case may be, the revocation of the decision on the appeal concerns a decision taken by a single member;
(e) decisions pursuant to Article 104(4) of Regulation (EU) 2017/1001;
(f) decisions pursuant to Article 109(4), (5) and (8) of Regulation (EU) 2017/1001;
(g) decisions on appeals against decisions in ex parte proceedings taken on the grounds laid down in Article 7 of Regulation (EU) 2017/1001, which are either manifestly unfounded or manifestly well founded.

**2.** Where the single member considers that the conditions set out in paragraph 1 or in Article 165(5) of Regulation (EU) 2017/1001 are not, or no longer, met, the single member shall refer the case back to the Board of Appeal in its composition of three members by submitting a draft decision pursuant to Article 41 of this Regulation.

*Article 37*

**Referral to the Grand Board**

**1.** Without prejudice to the faculty to refer a case to the Grand Board under Article 165(3) of Regulation (EU) 2017/1001, a Board of Appeal shall refer a case allocated to it to the Grand Board if it considers that it must deviate from an interpretation of the relevant legislation given in an earlier decision of the Grand Board, or if it observes that the Boards of Appeal have issued diverging decisions on a point of law which is liable to affect the outcome of the case.

**2.** All decisions on referrals of appeal cases to the Grand Board shall state the reasons for which the referring Board of Appeal or, as the case may be, the Presidium of the Boards of Appeal considers that this is justified, shall be communicated to the parties to the case and shall be published in the Official Journal of the Office.

**3.** The Grand Board shall, without delay, refer the case back to the Board of Appeal to which it was originally allocated if it believes that the conditions for the original referral are not, or no longer, met.

**4.** Requests for a reasoned opinion on questions on a point of law pursuant to Article 157(4)(l) of Regulation (EU) 2017/1001 shall be referred to the Grand Board in writing, shall state the questions of law of which the interpretation is sought, and may also state the Executive Director's view on the different possible interpretations as well as on their respective legal and practical consequences. The request shall be published in the Official Journal of the Office.
**5.** Where a Board of Appeal has to decide, in a case pending before it, on the same point in law that has already been raised in a referral to the Grand Board pursuant to Article 165(3) or Article 157(4)(l) of Regulation (EU) 2017/1001, it shall suspend the proceedings until the Grand Board has taken its decision or delivered its reasoned opinion.
**6.** Groups or bodies representing manufacturers, producers, suppliers of services, traders or consumers which can establish an interest in the result of a case on appeal or a request for a reasoned opinion brought before the Grand Board, may submit written observations within two months following the publication in the Official Journal of the Office of the decision of referral or, as the case may be, the request for a reasoned opinion. They shall not be parties to the proceedings before the Grand Board and shall bear their own costs.

*Article 38*

**Change in the composition of a Board**

**1.** Where, after oral proceedings, the composition of a Board of Appeal is changed pursuant to Article 43(2) and (3), all parties to the proceedings shall be informed that, at the request of any party, fresh oral proceedings shall be held before the Board of Appeal in its new composition. Fresh oral proceedings shall also be held if the new member so requests and provided that the other members of the Board of Appeal have given their agreement.
**2.** The new member of a Board of Appeal shall be bound to the same extent as the other members by any interim decision which has already been taken.

*Article 39*

**Deliberation, voting and signing of decisions**

**1.** The rapporteur shall submit to the other members of the Board of Appeal a draft of the decision to be taken and shall set a reasonable time limit within which to oppose it or to ask for changes.
**2.** The Board of Appeal shall meet to deliberate on the decision to be taken if it appears that its members are not all of the same opinion. Only members of the Board of Appeal shall participate in the deliberations; the chairperson of the Board of Appeal may, however, authorise other officers such as the Registrar or interpreters to attend. Deliberations shall be and remain secret.
**3.** During the deliberations between members of a Board of Appeal, the opinion of the rapporteur shall be heard first, and, if the rapporteur is not the chairperson, the opinion of the chairperson shall be heard last.
**4.** If voting is necessary, votes shall be taken in the same sequence, save that the chairperson shall always vote last. Abstentions shall not be permitted.
**5.** All members of the Board of Appeal taking the decision shall sign it. However, where the Board of Appeal has already reached a final decision and a member is

unable to act, that member shall not be replaced and the chairperson shall sign the decision on the member's behalf. Where the chairperson is unable to act, the most senior member of the Board of Appeal as determined in accordance with Article 43(1) shall sign the decision on behalf of the chairperson.

**6.** Paragraphs 1 to 5 shall not apply where a decision is to be taken by a single member pursuant to Article 165(2) of Regulation (EU) 2017/1001 and Article 36(1) of this Regulation. In such cases, decisions shall be signed by the single member.

*Article 40*

### Chairperson of a Board of Appeal

A chairperson shall preside over a Board of Appeal and shall have the following duties:

(a) designate a member of the Board of Appeal, or himself or herself, as rapporteur for each case allocated to that Board of Appeal in accordance with Article 35(2);

(b) designate, on behalf of the Board of Appeal, the rapporteur as single member pursuant to Article 165(2) of Regulation (EU) 2017/1001;

(c) request the Board of Appeal to decide on the admissibility of the appeal in accordance with Article 23(2) of this Regulation;

(d) direct the preparatory examination of the case carried out by the rapporteur in accordance with Article 41 of this Regulation;

(e) preside over, and sign the minutes of, oral hearings and the taking of evidence.

*Article 41*

### Rapporteur to a Board of Appeal

**1.** The rapporteur shall carry out a preliminary study of the appeal assigned to the rapporteur, prepare the case for examination and deliberation by the Board of Appeal, and draft the decision to be taken by the Board of Appeal.

**2.** To that effect, the rapporteur shall, where necessary and subject to the direction of the chairperson of the Board of Appeal, have the following duties:

(a) invite the parties to file observations in accordance with Article 70(2) of Regulation (EU) 2017/1001;

(b) decide on requests for the extension of time limits and, as the case may be, set time limits within the meaning of Article 24(1), Article 25(5) and Article 26 of this Regulation, and on suspensions pursuant to Article 71;

(c) prepare communications in accordance with Article 28 and the oral hearing;

(d) sign the minutes of oral proceedings and of the taking of evidence.

*Article 42*

### Registry

**1.** A Registry shall be set up at the Boards of Appeal. It shall be responsible for the receipt, dispatch, safekeeping and notification of all documents relating to the proceedings before the Boards of Appeal, and for the compilation of the relevant files.

**2.** The Registry shall be headed by a Registrar. The Registrar shall fulfil the tasks referred to in this Article under the authority of the President of the Boards of Appeal, without prejudice to the provisions in paragraph 3.
**3.** The Registrar shall ensure that all formal requirements and time limits, laid down in Regulation (EU) 2017/1001, in this Regulation or in decisions of the Presidium of the Boards of Appeal adopted in accordance with Article 166(4)(c) and (d) of Regulation (EU) 2017/1001 are respected. To this effect, the Registrar shall have the following duties:

(a) sign the decisions taken by the Boards of Appeal in respect of appeals;
(b) take and sign the minutes of oral proceedings and of the taking of evidence;
(c) provide, either of its own motion or upon request from the Board of Appeal, reasoned opinions to the Board of Appeal on procedural and formal requirements including on irregularities pursuant to Article 23(2) of this Regulation;
(d) submit the appeal, in accordance with Article 34(1) of this Regulation, to the instance of the Office which adopted the contested decision;
(e) order, on behalf of the Board of Appeal, in the cases referred to in Article 33(a) and (b) of this Regulation, the reimbursement of the appeal fee.

**4.** The Registrar shall, upon delegation of the President of the Boards of Appeal, have the following duties:

(a) allocate cases in accordance with Article 35(1) and (4);
(b) implement, pursuant to Article 166(4)(b) of Regulation (EU) 2017/1001, decisions of the Presidium of the Boards of Appeal relating to the conduct of proceedings before the Boards of Appeal.

**5.** The Registrar may, upon delegation of the Presidium of the Boards of Appeal made upon proposal of the President of the Boards of Appeal, perform other tasks relating to the conduct of appeal proceedings before the Boards of Appeal and the organisation of their work.
**6.** The Registrar may delegate the tasks referred to in this Article to a member of the Registry.
**7.** Where the Registrar is prevented from acting within the meaning of Article 43(4), or where the post of Registrar is vacant, the President of the Boards of Appeal shall appoint a member of the Registry who shall perform the tasks of the Registrar in the Registrar's absence.
**8.** The members of the Registry shall be managed by the Registrar.

*Article 43*

### Order of seniority and replacement of members and chairpersons

**1.** The seniority of chairpersons and members shall be calculated according to the date on which they took up their duties as specified in the instrument of appointment or, failing that, as fixed by the Management Board of the Office. Where there is equal seniority on that basis, the order of seniority shall be determined by age. Chairpersons and members whose term of office is renewed shall retain their former seniority.
**2.** Where the chairperson of a Board of Appeal is prevented from acting, that chairperson shall be replaced, on the basis of seniority as determined in accordance with paragraph 1, by the most senior member of that Board of Appeal, or, where no member of that Board of Appeal is available, by the most senior of the other members of the Boards of Appeal.

**3.** Where a member of a Board of Appeal is prevented from acting, that member shall be replaced, on the basis of seniority as determined in accordance with paragraph 1, by the most senior member of that Board of Appeal, or, where no member of that Board of Appeal is available, by the most senior of the other members of the Boards of Appeal.
**4.** For the purposes of paragraphs 2 and 3, chairpersons and members of the Boards of Appeal shall be considered to be prevented from acting in case of leave, sickness, inescapable commitments and exclusion pursuant to Article 169 of Regulation (EU) 2017/1001 and Article 35(4) of this Regulation. A chairperson shall also be considered to be prevented from acting where that chairperson acts ad interim as President of the Boards of Appeal pursuant to Article 47(2) of this Regulation. Where the post of chairperson or member is vacant, their respective functions shall be exercised ad interim pursuant to the provisions in paragraphs 2 and 3 of this Article concerning replacement.
**5.** Any members considering themselves prevented from acting shall without delay inform the chairperson of the Board of Appeal concerned. Any chairpersons considering themselves prevented from acting shall without delay inform simultaneously that chairperson's alternate determined in accordance with paragraph 2 and the President of the Boards of Appeal.

*Article 44*

**Exclusion and objection**

**1.** Before a decision is taken by a Board of Appeal pursuant to Article 169(4) of Regulation (EU) 2017/1001, the chairperson or member concerned shall be invited to present comments as to whether there is a reason for exclusion or objection.
**2.** Where the Board of Appeal obtains knowledge, from a source other than the member concerned or a party to the proceedings, of a possible reason for exclusion or objection under Article 169(3) of Regulation (EU) 2017/1001, the procedure laid down in Article 169(4) of Regulation (EU) 2017/1001 shall be applied.
**3.** The proceedings concerned shall be suspended until a decision is taken on the action to be taken pursuant to Article 169(4) of Regulation (EU) 2017/1001.

*Article 45*

**Grand Board**

**1.** The list comprising the names of all members of the Boards of Appeal other than the President of the Boards of Appeal and the chairpersons of the Boards of Appeal for the purposes of drawing in rotation the members of the Grand Board referred to in Article 167(2) of Regulation (EU) 2017/1001 shall be drawn up in the order of seniority determined in accordance with Article 43(1) of this Regulation. Where an appeal has been referred to the Grand Board pursuant to Article 165(3)(b) of Regulation (EU) 2017/1001, the Grand Board shall comprise the rapporteur designated prior to the referral.
**2.** Article 40 shall apply to the President of the Boards of Appeal acting in the capacity of chairperson of the Grand Board. Article 41 shall apply to the rapporteur to the Grand Board.
**3.** Where the President of the Boards of Appeal is prevented from acting as chairperson of the Grand Board, the President of the Boards of Appeal shall be

replaced in that function and, as the case may be, as rapporteur to the Grand Board, on the basis of seniority as determined in accordance with Article 43(1), by the most senior chairperson of the Boards of Appeal. Where a member of the Grand Board is prevented from acting, that member shall be replaced by another member of the Boards of Appeal to be designated pursuant to Article 167(2) of Regulation (EU) 2017/1001 and paragraph 1 of this Article. Article 43(4) and (5) of this Regulation shall apply mutatis mutandis.

**4.** The Grand Board shall not deliberate or vote on cases, and oral proceedings shall not take place before the Grand Board unless seven of its members are present, including its chairperson and the rapporteur.

**5.** Article 39(1) to (5) shall apply to the deliberations and voting of the Grand Board. In the event of a tie, the vote of the chairperson shall be decisive.

**6.** Article 32 shall apply to decisions of the Grand Board and mutatis mutandis to its reasoned opinions within the meaning of Article 157(4)(l) of Regulation (EU) 2017/1001.

*Article 46*

**Presidium of the Boards of Appeal**

**1.** The Presidium of the Boards of Appeal shall have the following duties:

(a) decide on the constitution of Boards of Appeal;

(g) determine the objective criteria for the allocation of appeal cases to the Boards of Appeal and rule on any conflict as regards the application thereof;

(c) upon proposal of the President of the Boards of Appeal, establish the Boards of Appeal's expenditure requirements with a view to drawing up the Office's expenditure estimates;

(d) lay down its internal rules;

(e) lay down rules for the processing of excluding and objecting to members pursuant to Article 169 of Regulation (EU) 2017/1001;

(f) lay down the working instructions for the Registry;

(g) take any other measure for the purpose of exercising its functions of laying down the rules and of organising the work of the Boards of Appeal pursuant to Article 165(3)(a) and Article 166(4)(a) of Regulation (EU) 2017/1001.

**2.** The Presidium may validly deliberate only if at least two thirds of its members, including the chairperson of the Presidium and half of the chairpersons of the Boards of Appeal, rounded up if necessary, are present. Decisions of the Presidium shall be taken by a majority vote. In the event of a tie, the vote of the chairperson shall be decisive.

**3.** The decisions adopted by the Presidium pursuant to Article 43(1), to Article 45(1), and to paragraph 1(a) and (b) of this Article shall be published in the Official Journal of the Office.

*Article 47*

**President of the Boards of Appeal**

**1.** Where the President of the Boards of Appeal is prevented from acting within the meaning of Article 43(4), the managerial and organisational functions conferred upon the President of the Boards of Appeal by Article 166(4) of Regulation (EU)

2017/1001 shall be exercised, on the basis of seniority as determined in accordance with Article 43(1) of this Regulation, by the most senior chairperson of the Boards of Appeal.

**2.** Where the post of the President of the Boards of Appeal is vacant, the functions of that president shall be exercised ad interim, on the basis of seniority as determined in accordance with Article 43(1), by the most senior chairperson of the Boards of Appeal.

*Article 48*

**Applicability to appeal proceedings of provisions relating to other proceedings**

Unless otherwise provided in this title, the provisions relating to proceedings before the instance of the Office which adopted the decision subject to appeal shall be applicable to appeal proceedings mutatis mutandis.

## TITLE VI

## ORAL PROCEEDINGS AND TAKING OF EVIDENCE

*Article 49*

**Summons to oral proceedings**

**1.** The parties shall be summoned to oral proceedings provided for in Article 96 of Regulation (EU) 2017/1001 and their attention shall be drawn to paragraph 3 of this Article.

**2.** When issuing the summons, the Office shall request, where necessary, that the parties provide all relevant information and documents before the hearing. The Office may invite the parties to concentrate on one or more specified issues during the oral proceedings. It may also offer to the parties the possibility to take part in the oral proceedings by videoconference or other technical means.

**3.** If a party who has been duly summoned to oral proceedings before the Office does not appear as summoned, the proceedings may continue without that party.

**4.** The Office shall ensure that the case is ready for decision at the conclusion of the oral proceedings, unless there are special reasons to the contrary.

*Article 50*

**Languages of oral proceedings**

**1.** Oral proceedings shall be conducted in the language of the proceedings unless the parties agree to use a different official language of the Union.

**2.** The Office may communicate in oral proceedings in another official language of the Union and it may, upon request, authorise a party to do so provided that simultaneous interpretation into the language of proceedings can be made available. The costs of providing simultaneous interpretation shall be borne by the party making the request or by the Office as the case may be.

*Article 51*

**Oral evidence of parties, witnesses or experts and inspection**

**1.** Where the Office considers it necessary to hear the oral evidence of parties, witnesses or experts or to carry out an inspection, it shall take an interim decision to that end, stating the means by which it intends to obtain the evidence, the relevant facts to be proved and the date, time and place of hearing or inspection. Where the hearing of oral evidence of witnesses or experts is requested by a party, the Office shall determine in its decision the period within which that party must make known to the Office the names and addresses of the witnesses or experts.
**2.** The summons of parties, witnesses or experts to give evidence shall contain:

(a) an extract from the decision referred to in paragraph 1, indicating the date, time and place of the hearing ordered and stating the facts regarding which the parties, witnesses and experts are to be heard;
(b) the names of the parties to the proceedings and particulars of the rights which the witnesses or experts may invoke under Article 54(2) to (5).

The summons shall also offer to the parties, witnesses or experts being summoned the possibility to take part in the oral proceedings by videoconference or other technical means.
**3.** Article 50(2) shall apply mutatis mutandis.

*Article 52*

**Commissioning of and opinions by experts**

**1.** The Office shall decide in what form an opinion is to be submitted by an expert.
**2.** The terms of reference of the expert shall include:
(a) a precise description of the expert's task;
(b) the time limit laid down for the submission of the expert opinion;
(c) the names of the parties to the proceedings;
(d) particulars of the rights which the expert may invoke pursuant to Article 54(2), (3) and (4).
**3.** Where an expert is appointed, the expert opinion shall be submitted in the language of the proceedings or accompanied by a translation into that language. A copy of any written opinion, and of the translation if needed, shall be sent to the parties.
**4.** The parties may object to the appointment of an expert on grounds of incompetence or on the same grounds as those on which objection may be made against an examiner or against a member of a Division or Board of Appeal pursuant to Article 169(1) and (3) of Regulation (EU) 2017/1001. Any objection to the appointment of an expert shall be submitted in the language of the proceedings, or accompanied by a translation into that language. The department of the Office concerned shall rule on the objection.

*Article 53*

**Minutes of oral proceedings**

**1.** Minutes of oral proceedings or the taking of oral evidence shall be drawn up, containing:

(a) the number of the case to which the oral proceedings relate and the date of the oral proceedings;
(b) the names of the officials of the Office, the parties, their representatives, and of the witnesses and experts who are present;
(c) the submissions and requests made by the parties;
(d) the means of giving or obtaining evidence;
(e) where applicable, the orders or the decision issued by the Office.

**2.** The minutes shall become part of the file of the relevant EU trade mark application or registration. They shall be notified to the parties.

**3.** Where oral proceedings or the taking of evidence before the Office are recorded, the recording shall replace the minutes and paragraph 2 shall apply mutatis mutandis.

*Article 54*

**Costs of taking of evidence in oral proceedings**

**1.** The taking of evidence by the Office may be made conditional upon deposit with it, by the party who has requested the evidence to be taken, of a sum which shall be fixed by reference to an estimate of the costs.

**2.** Witnesses and experts who are summoned by and appear before the Office shall be entitled to reimbursement of reasonable expenses for travel and subsistence where such expenses are incurred. An advance for such expenses may be granted to them by the Office.

**3.** Witnesses entitled to reimbursement pursuant to paragraph 2 shall also be entitled to appropriate compensation for loss of earnings, and experts to fees for their work. That compensation shall be paid to the witnesses and experts after they have fulfilled their duties or tasks, where such witnesses and experts have been summoned by the Office of its own initiative.

**4.** The amounts and advances for expenses to be paid pursuant to paragraphs 1, 2 and 3 shall be determined by the Executive Director and shall be published in the Official Journal of the Office. The amounts shall be calculated on the same basis as laid down in the Staff Regulations of the Officials of the Union and the Conditions of Employment of Other Servants of the Union, laid down in Council Regulation (EEC, Euratom, ECSC) No 259/68 (11) and Annex VII thereto.

**5.** Liability for the amounts due or paid pursuant to paragraphs 1 to 4 shall lie with:
(a) the Office where it, at its own initiative, has summoned the witnesses or experts;
(b) the party concerned where that party has requested the giving of oral evidence by witnesses or experts, subject to the decision on apportionment and fixing of costs pursuant to Articles 109 and 110 of Regulation (EU) 2017/1001 and Article 18 of Implementing Regulation (EU) 2018/626. Such party shall reimburse the Office for any advances duly paid.

*Article 55*

**Examination of written evidence**

**1.** The Office shall examine any evidence given or obtained in any proceedings before it to the extent necessary to take a decision in the proceedings in question.

**2.** The documents or other items of evidence shall be contained in annexes to a submission which shall be numbered consecutively. The submission shall include an index indicating, for each document or item of evidence annexed:

(a) the number of the annex;

(b) a short description of the document or item and, if applicable, the number of pages;

(c) the page number of the submission where the document or item is mentioned.

The submitting party may also indicate, in the index of annexes, which specific parts of a document it relies upon in support of its arguments.

**3.** Where the submission or the annexes do not comply with the requirements set out in paragraph 2, the Office may invite the submitting party to remedy any deficiency, within a period specified by the Office.

**4.** Where the deficiency is not remedied within the period specified by the Office, and where it is still not possible for the Office to clearly establish to which ground or argument a document or item of evidence refers, that document or item shall not be taken into account.

## TITLE VII

## NOTIFICATIONS BY THE OFFICE

*Article 56*

### General provisions on notifications

**1.** In proceedings before the Office, notifications to be made by the Office shall be in accordance with Article 94(2) of Regulation (EU) 2017/1001 and shall consist in the transmission of the document to be notified to the parties concerned. Transmission may be effected by providing electronic access to that document.

**2.** Notifications shall be made by one of the following means:

(a) electronic means pursuant to Article 57;

(b) post or courier pursuant to Article 58;

(c) public notification pursuant to Article 59.

**3.** Where the addressee has indicated contact details for communicating with the addressee through electronic means, the Office shall have the choice between those means and notification by post or courier.

*Article 57*

### Notification by electronic means

**1.** Notification by electronic means covers transmissions by wire, by radio, by optical means or by other electromagnetic means, including the internet.

**2.** The Executive Director shall determine the details regarding the specific electronic means to be used, the manner in which electronic means will be used, and the time limit for notification by electronic means.

*Article 58*

**Notification by post or courier**

**1.** Notwithstanding Article 56(3), decisions subject to a time limit for appeal, summons and other documents as determined by the Executive Director shall be notified by courier service or registered post, in both cases with advice of delivery. All other notifications shall be either by courier service or registered post, whether or not with advice of delivery, or by ordinary post.

**2.** Notwithstanding Article 56(3), notifications in respect of addressees having neither their domicile nor their principal place of business or a real and effective industrial or commercial establishment in the European Economic Area ('EEA') and who have not appointed a representative as required by Article 119(2) of Regulation (EU) 2017/1001 shall be effected by posting the document requiring notification by ordinary post.

**3.** Where notification is effected by courier service or registered post, whether or not with advice of delivery, it shall be deemed to be delivered to the addressee on the tenth day following that of its posting, unless the letter has failed to reach the addressee or has reached the addressee at a later date. In the event of any dispute, it shall be for the Office to establish that the letter has reached its destination or to establish the date on which it was delivered to the addressee, as the case may be.

**4.** Notification by courier service or registered post shall be deemed to have been effected even if the addressee refuses to accept the letter.

**5.** Notification by ordinary post shall be deemed to have been effected on the 10th day following that of its posting.

*Article 59*

**Notification by public notice**

Where the address of the addressee cannot be established or where after at least one attempt at notification in accordance with Article 56(2)(a) and (b) has proved impossible, notification shall be effected by public notice.

*Article 60*

**Notification to representatives**

**1.** Where a representative has been appointed or where the applicant first named in a common application is considered to be the common representative pursuant to Article 73(1), notifications shall be addressed to that appointed or common representative.

**2.** Where a single party has appointed several representatives, notification shall be effected in accordance with Article 2(1)(e) of Implementing Regulation (EU) 2018/626. Where several parties have appointed a common representative, notification of a single document to the common representative shall be sufficient.

**3.** A notification or other communication addressed by the Office to the duly authorised representative shall have the same effect as if it had been addressed to the represented person.

*Article 61*

**Irregularities in notification**

Where a document has reached the addressee and where the Office is unable to prove that it has been duly notified or where provisions relating to its notification have not been observed, the document shall be deemed to have been notified on the date established as the date of receipt.

*Article 62*

**Notification of documents in the case of several parties**

Documents emanating from parties shall be notified to the other parties as a matter of course. Notification may be dispensed with where the document contains no new pleadings and the matter is ready for decision.

## TITLE VIII

## WRITTEN COMMUNICATIONS AND FORMS

*Article 63*

**Communications to the Office in writing or by other means**

**1.** Applications for the registration of an EU trade mark as well as any other application provided for in Regulation (EU) 2017/1001 and all other communications addressed to the Office shall be submitted as follows:

(a) by transmitting a communication by electronic means, in which case the indication of the name of the sender shall be deemed to be equivalent to the signature;
(b) by submitting a signed original of the document in question to the Office by post or courier.

**2.** In proceedings before the Office, the date on which a communication is received by the Office shall be considered to be its date of filing or submission.

**3.** Where a communication received by electronic means is incomplete or illegible or where the Office has reasonable doubts as to the accuracy of the transmission, the Office shall inform the sender accordingly and shall invite the sender, within a period to be specified by the Office, to retransmit the original or to submit it in accordance with paragraph (1)(b). Where that request is complied with within the period specified, the date of receipt of the retransmission or of the original shall be deemed to be the date of the receipt of the original communication. However, where the deficiency concerns the granting of a filing date for an application to register a trade mark, the provisions on the filing date shall apply. Where the request is not complied with within the period specified, the communication shall be deemed not to have been received.

*Article 64*

**Annexes to communications by post or courier**

**1.** Annexes to communications may be submitted on data carriers in accordance with the technical specifications determined by the Executive Director.
**2.** Where a communication with annexes is submitted in accordance with Article 63(1)(b) by a party to proceedings involving more than one party, the party shall submit as many copies of the annexes as there are parties to the proceedings. Annexes shall be indexed in accordance with the requirements laid down in Article 55(2).

*Article 65*

**Forms**

**1.** The Office shall make forms available to the public free of charge, which may be completed online, for the purposes of:
- (a) filing an application for an EU trade mark, including, where appropriate, requests for the search reports;
- (b) entering an opposition;
- (c) applying for revocation of rights;
- (d) applying for a declaration of invalidity or the assignment of an EU trade mark;
- (e) applying for the registration of a transfer and the transfer form or document referred to in Article 13(3)(d) of Implementing Regulation (EU) 2018/626;
- (f) applying for the registration of a licence;
- (g) applying for the renewal of an EU trade mark;
- (h) making an appeal;
- (i) authorising a representative, in the form of an individual authorisation or a general authorisation;
- (j) submitting an international application or a subsequent designation pursuant to the Protocol relating to the Madrid Agreement concerning the international registration of marks, adopted at Madrid on 27 June 1989 (12) to the Office.

**2.** Parties to the proceedings before the Office may also use:
- (a) forms established under the Trademark Law Treaty or pursuant to recommendations of the Assembly of the Paris Union for the Protection of Industrial Property;
- (b) with the exception of the form referred to in point (i) of paragraph 1, forms with the same content and format as those referred to in paragraph 1.

**3.** The Office shall make the forms referred to in paragraph 1 available in all the official languages of the Union.

*Article 66*

**Communications by representatives**

Any communication addressed to the Office by the duly authorised representative shall have the same effect as if it originated from the represented person.

## TITLE IX

## TIME LIMITS

*Article 67*

### Calculation and duration of time limits

**1.** The calculation of a time limit shall start on the day following the day on which the relevant event occurred, either a procedural step or the expiry of another time limit. Where that procedural step is a notification, the event shall be the receipt of the document notified, unless otherwise provided for.
**2.** Where a time limit is expressed as one year or a certain number of years, it shall expire on the relevant subsequent year in the month having the same name and on the day having the same number as the month and the day on which the relevant event occurred. Where the relevant month has no day with the same number, the time limit shall expire on the last day of that month.
**3.** Where a time limit is expressed as one month or a certain number of months, it shall expire on the relevant subsequent month on the day which has the same number as the day on which the relevant event occurred. Where the relevant subsequent month has no day with the same number, the time limit shall expire on the last day of that month.
**4.** Where a time limit is expressed as one week or a certain number of weeks, it shall expire on the relevant subsequent week on the day having the same name as the day on which the said event occurred.

*Article 68*

### Extension of time limits

Subject to specific or maximum time limits laid down in Regulation (EU) 2017/1001, Implementing Regulation (EU) 2018/626 or this Regulation, the Office may grant an extension of a time limit upon reasoned request. Such request shall be submitted by the party concerned before the time limit in question expires. Where there are two or more parties, the Office may subject the extension of a time limit to the agreement of the other parties.

*Article 69*

### Expiry of time limits in special cases

**1.** Where a time limit expires on a day on which the Office is not open for receipt of documents or on which, for reasons other than those referred to in paragraph 2, ordinary post is not delivered in the locality in which the Office is located, the time limit shall be extended until the first day thereafter on which the Office is open for receipt of documents and on which ordinary mail is delivered.
**2.** Where a time limit expires on a day on which there is a general interruption in the delivery of mail in the Member State where the Office is located, or, if and to the extent that the Executive Director has allowed communications to be sent by electronic means pursuant to Article 100(1) of Regulation (EU) 2017/1001, on which there is an actual interruption of the Office's connection to those electronic means of communication, the time limit shall be extended until the first day

thereafter on which the Office is open for receipt of documents and on which ordinary mail is delivered or the Office's connection to those electronic means of communication is restored.

## TITLE X

## REVOCATION OF A DECISION

*Article 70*

### Revocation of a decision or entry in the Register

**1.** Where the Office finds of its own motion or pursuant to corresponding information provided by the parties to the proceedings that a decision or entry in the Register is subject to revocation pursuant to Article 103 of Regulation (EU) 2017/1001, it shall inform the affected party about the intended revocation.
**2.** The affected party shall submit observations on the intended revocation within a time limit specified by the Office.
**3.** Where the affected party agrees to the intended revocation or does not submit any observations within the time limit, the Office shall revoke the decision or entry. If the affected party does not agree to the intended revocation, the Office shall take a decision on the intended revocation.
**4.** Where the intended revocation is likely to affect more than one party, paragraphs 1, 2 and 3 shall apply mutatis mutandis. In those cases the observations submitted by one of the parties pursuant to paragraph 3 shall always be communicated to the other party or parties with an invitation to submit observations.
**5.** Where the revocation of a decision or an entry in the Register affects a decision or entry that has been published, the revocation shall also be published.
**6.** Competence for revocation pursuant to paragraphs 1 to 4 shall lie with the department or unit which took the decision.

## TITLE XI

## SUSPENSION OF PROCEEDINGS

*Article 71*

### Suspension of proceedings

**1.** As regards opposition, revocation and declaration of invalidity and appeal proceedings, the competent department or Board of Appeal may suspend proceedings:

(a) of its own motion where a suspension is appropriate under the circumstances of the case;
(b) at the reasoned request of one of the parties in inter partes proceedings where a suspension is appropriate under the circumstances of the case, taking into account the interests of the parties and the stage of the proceedings.

**2.** At the request of both parties in inter partes proceedings, the competent department or Board of Appeal shall suspend the proceedings for a period which shall not exceed six months. That suspension may be extended upon a request of both parties up to a total maximum of two years.

**3.** Any time limits related to the proceedings in question, other than the time limits for the payment of the applicable fee, shall be interrupted as from the date of suspension. Without prejudice to Article 170(5) of Regulation (EU) 2017/1001, the time limits shall be recalculated to begin in full as from the day on which the proceedings are resumed.

**4.** Where appropriate under the circumstances of the case, the parties may be invited to submit their observations as regards the suspension or resumption of the proceedings.

## TITLE XII

## INTERRUPTION OF PROCEEDINGS

*Article 72*

### Resumption of proceedings

**1.** Where proceedings before the Office have been interrupted pursuant to Article 106(1) of Regulation (EU) 2017/1001, the Office shall be informed of the identity of the person authorised to continue the proceedings before it pursuant to Article 106(2) of Regulation (EU) 2017/1001. The Office shall communicate to that person and to any interested third parties that the proceedings shall be resumed as from a date to be fixed by the Office.

**2.** Where, three months after the beginning of the interruption of the proceedings pursuant to Article 106(1)(c) of Regulation (EU) 2017/1001, the Office has not been informed of the appointment of a new representative, it shall inform the applicant for or proprietor of the EU trade mark that:

(a) where Article 119(2) of Regulation (EU) 2017/1001 shall apply, the EU trade mark application shall be deemed to be withdrawn if the information is not submitted within two months after the communication is notified;

(b) where Article 119(2) of Regulation (EU) 2017/1001 does not apply, the proceedings will be resumed with the applicant for or proprietor of the EU trade mark as from the date on which this communication is notified.

**3.** The time limits in force as regards the applicant for or proprietor of the EU trade mark at the date of interruption of the proceedings, other than the time limit for paying the renewal fees, shall begin again as from the day on which the proceedings are resumed.

## TITLE XIII

## REPRESENTATION

*Article 73*

### Appointment of a common representative

**1.** Where there is more than one applicant and the application for an EU trade mark does not name a common representative, the first applicant named in the application having its domicile or principal place of business or a real and effective industrial or commercial establishment in the EEA, or its representative if appointed, shall be considered to be the common representative. Where all of the applicants are obliged to appoint a professional representative, the professional representative who is named first in the application shall be considered to be the common representative. This shall apply mutatis mutandis to third parties acting jointly in filing notice of opposition or applying for revocation or for a declaration of invalidity and to joint proprietors of an EU trade mark.

**2.** Where, during the course of proceedings, transfer is made to more than one person and those persons have not appointed a common representative, paragraph 1 shall apply. Where such an appointment is not possible, the Office shall require those persons to appoint a common representative within two months. If that request is not complied with, the Office shall appoint the common representative.

*Article 74*

**Authorisations**

**1.** Employees who represent natural or legal persons within the meaning of Article 119(3) of Regulation (EU) 2017/1001, as well as legal practitioners and professional representatives entered on the list maintained by the Office pursuant to Article 120(2) of Regulation (EU) 2017/1001, shall file a signed authorisation with the Office for insertion in the files pursuant to Article 119(3) and Article 120(1) of Regulation (EU) 2017/1001 only where the Office expressly requires it or where there are several parties to the proceedings in which the representative acts before the Office and the other party expressly asks for it.

**2.** Where it is required, pursuant to Article 119(3) or Article 120(1) of Regulation (EU) 2017/1001, that a signed authorisation be filed, such an authorisation may be filed in any official language of the Union. It may cover one or more applications or registered trade marks or may be in the form of a general authorisation authorising the representative to act in respect of all proceedings before the Office to which the person giving the authorisation is a party.

**3.** The Office shall specify a time limit within which such an authorisation shall be filed. Where the authorisation is not filed in due time, proceedings shall be continued with the represented person. Any procedural steps taken by the representative other than the filing of the application shall be deemed not to have been taken if the represented person does not approve them within a time limit specified by the Office.

**4.** Paragraphs 1 and 2 shall apply mutatis mutandis to a document withdrawing an authorisation.

**5.** Any representative who has ceased to be authorised shall continue to be regarded as the representative until the termination of that representative's authorisation has been communicated to the Office.

**6.** Subject to any provisions to the contrary contained therein, an authorisation shall not automatically cease to be valid vis-à-vis the Office upon the death of the person who gave it.

**7.** Where the appointment of a representative is communicated to the Office, the name and the business address of the representative shall be indicated in accordance with Article 2(1)(e) of Implementing Regulation (EU) 2018/626. Where a representative who has already been appointed appears before the Office, that representative shall indicate the name and the identification number attributed to the representative by the Office. Where several representatives are appointed by the same party, they may, notwithstanding any provisions to the contrary in their authorisations, act either jointly or singly.

**8.** The appointment or authorisation of an association of representatives shall be deemed to be an appointment or authorisation of any representative who practises within that association.

*Article 75*

**Amendment of the list of professional representatives**

**1.** Pursuant to Article 120(5) of Regulation (EU) 2017/1001, the entry of a professional representative shall be deleted automatically:

(a) in the event of the death or legal incapacity of the professional representative;
(b) where the professional representative is no longer a national of one of the Member States of the EEA, unless the Executive Director has granted an exemption under Article 120(4)(b) of Regulation (EU) 2017/1001;
(c) where the professional representative no longer has a place of business or employment in the EEA;
(d) where the professional representative no longer possesses the entitlement referred to in the first sentence of Article 120(2)(c) of Regulation (EU) 2017/1001.

**2.** The entry of a professional representative shall be suspended of the Office's own motion where the representative's entitlement to represent natural or legal persons before the Benelux Office for Intellectual Property or the central industrial property office of a Member State as referred to in the first sentence of Article 120(2)(c) of Regulation (EU) 2017/1001 has been suspended.
**3.** Where the conditions for deletion no longer exist, a person whose entry has been deleted shall, upon request, accompanied by a certificate pursuant to Article 120(3) of Regulation (EU) 2017/1001, be reinstated in the list of professional representatives.
**4.** The Benelux Office for Intellectual Property and the central industrial property offices of the Member States concerned shall, where they are aware of any relevant events referred to in paragraphs 1 and 2, promptly inform the Office thereof.

**TITLE XIV**

**PROCEDURES CONCERNING THE INTERNATIONAL REGISTRATION OF MARKS**

*Article 76*

**Collective and certification marks**

**1.** Without prejudice to Article 193 of Regulation (EU) 2017/1001, where an international registration designating the Union is dealt with as an EU collective mark or as an EU certification mark pursuant to Article 194(1) of Regulation (EU) 2017/1001, a notification of an ex officio provisional refusal shall also be issued in accordance with Article 33 of Implementing Regulation (EU) 2018/626 in the following cases:

(a) where one of the grounds for refusal provided for in Article 76(1) or (2) of Regulation (EU) 2017/1001, in conjunction with paragraph 3 of that Article,

or in Article 85(1) or (2) of Regulation (EU) 2017/1001, in conjunction with paragraph 3 of that Article exists;
(b) where the regulations governing use of the mark have not been submitted in accordance with Article 194(2) of Regulation (EU) 2017/1001.

**2.** Notice of amendments to the regulations governing the use of the mark pursuant to Articles 79 and 88 of Regulation (EU) 2017/1001 shall be published in the European Union Trade Marks Bulletin.

*Article 77*

**Opposition proceedings**

**1.** Where an opposition is entered against an international registration designating the Union pursuant to Article 196 of Regulation (EU) 2017/1001, the notice of opposition shall contain:
(a) the number of the international registration against which opposition is entered;
(b) an indication of the goods or services listed in the international registration against which opposition is entered;
(c) the name of the holder of the international registration;
(d) the requirements laid down in Article 2(2)(b) to (h) of this Regulation.

**2.** Article 2(1), (3) and (4) and Articles 3 to 10 of this Regulation shall apply for the purposes of opposition proceedings relating to international registrations designating the Union, subject to the following conditions:
(a) any reference to an application for registration of the EU trade mark shall be read as a reference to an international registration;
(b) any reference to a withdrawal of the application for registration of the EU trade mark shall be read as a reference to the renunciation of the international registration in respect of the Union;
(c) any reference to the applicant shall be read as a reference to the holder of the international registration.

**3.** Where the notice of opposition is filed before the expiry of the period of one month referred to in Article 196(2) of Regulation (EU) 2017/1001, the notice of opposition shall be deemed to have been filed on the first day following the expiry of the period of one month.

**4.** Where the holder of the international registration is obliged to be represented in proceedings before the Office pursuant to Article 119(2) of Regulation (EU) 2017/1001, and where the holder of the international registration has not already appointed a representative within the meaning of Article 120(1) of Regulation (EU) 2017/1001, the communication of the opposition to the holder of the international registration pursuant to Article 6(1) of this Regulation shall contain a request for the appointment of a representative within the meaning of Article 120(1) of Regulation (EU) 2017/1001 within a time limit of two months of the date of notification of the communication.

Where the holder of the international registration fails to appoint a representative within that time limit, the Office shall take a decision refusing the protection of the international registration.

**5.** The opposition procedure shall be stayed where an ex officio provisional refusal of protection is issued pursuant to Article 193 of Regulation (EU) 2017/1001. Where the ex officio provisional refusal has led to a decision to refuse protection of the mark which has become final, the Office shall not proceed to a decision and refund the opposition fee and no decision on the apportionment of costs shall be taken.

*Article 78*

**Notification of provisional refusals based on an opposition**

**1.** Where a notice of opposition against an international registration is entered at the Office pursuant to Article 196(2) of Regulation (EU) 2017/1001, or where an opposition is deemed to have been entered pursuant to Article 77(3) of this Regulation, the Office shall issue a notification of provisional refusal of protection based on an opposition to the International Bureau of the World Intellectual Property Organisation ('the International Bureau').

**2.** The notification of provisional refusal of protection based on an opposition shall contain:

(a) the number of the international registration;

(b) the indication that the refusal is based on the fact that an opposition has been filed, together with a reference to the provisions of Article 8 of Regulation (EU) 2017/1001 upon which the opposition relies;

(c) the name and the address of the opposing party.

**3.** Where the opposition is based on a trade mark application or registration, the notification referred to in paragraph 2 shall contain the following indications:

(a) the filing date, the registration date and the priority date, if any;

(b) the filing number and, the registration number, if different;

(c) the name and address of the owner;

(d) a reproduction of the mark;

(e) the list of goods or services upon which the opposition is based.

**4.** Where the provisional refusal relates to only part of the goods or services, the notification referred to in paragraph 2 shall indicate those goods or services.

**5.** The Office shall inform the International Bureau of the following:

(a) where as a result of the opposition proceedings the provisional refusal has been withdrawn, the fact that the mark is protected in the Union;

(b) where a decision to refuse protection of the mark has become final following an appeal pursuant to Article 66 of Regulation (EU) 2017/1001 or an action pursuant to Article 72 of Regulation (EU) 2017/1001, the fact that protection of the mark is refused in the Union;

(c) where the refusal referred to in point (b) concerns only part of the goods or services, the goods or services for which the mark is protected in the Union.

**6.** Where more than one provisional refusal has been issued for one international registration pursuant to Article 193(2) of Regulation (EU) 2017/1001 or paragraph 1 of this Article, the communication referred to in paragraph 5 of this Article shall relate to the total or partial refusal of protection of the mark pursuant to Articles 193 and 196 of Regulation (EU) 2017/1001.

*Article 79*

**Statement of grant of protection**

**1.** Where the Office has not issued an ex officio provisional notification of refusal pursuant to Article 193 of Regulation (EU) 2017/1001 and no opposition has been received by the Office within the opposition period referred to in Article 196(2) of Regulation (EU) 2017/1001 and the Office has not issued an ex officio provisional refusal as a result of the third party observations submitted, the Office shall send a statement of grant of protection to the International Bureau indicating that the mark is protected in the Union.

**2.** For the purposes of Article 189(2) of Regulation (EU) 2017/1001, the statement of grant of protection referred to in paragraph 1 of this Article shall have the same effect as a statement by the Office that a notice of refusal has been withdrawn.

## TITLE XV

## FINAL PROVISIONS

*Article 80*

### Transitional measures

The provisions of Regulations (EC) No 2868/95 and (EC) No 216/96 shall continue to apply to ongoing proceedings where this Regulation does not apply in accordance with its Article 82, until such proceedings are concluded.

*Article 81*

### Repeal

Commission Delegated Regulation (EU) 2017/1430 is repealed.

*Article 82*

### Entry into force and application

**1.** This Regulation shall enter into force on the twentieth day following that of its publication in the Official Journal of the European Union.

**2.** It shall be applicable from the date of entry into force referred to in paragraph 1, subject to the following exceptions:

(a) Articles 2 to 6 shall not apply to notices of opposition entered before 1 October 2017;

(b) Articles 7 and 8 shall not apply to opposition proceedings, the adversarial part of which has started before 1 October 2017;

(c) Article 9 shall not apply to suspensions made before 1 October 2017;

(d) Article 10 shall not apply to requests for proof of use made before 1 October 2017;

(e) Title III shall not apply to requests for amendment entered before 1 October 2017;

(f) Articles 12 to 15 shall not apply to applications for revocation or for a declaration of invalidity or requests for assignment entered before 1 October 2017;

(g) Articles 16 and 17 shall not apply to proceedings, the adversarial part of which has started before 1 October 2017;

(h) Article 18 shall not apply to suspensions made before 1 October 2017;

(i) Article 19 shall not apply to requests for proof of use made before 1 October 2017;
(j) Title V shall not apply to appeals entered before 1 October 2017;
(k) Title VI shall not apply to oral proceedings initiated before 1 October 2017 or to written evidence where the period for its presentation has started before that date;
(l) Title VII shall not apply to notifications made before 1 October 2017;
(m) Title VIII shall not apply to communications received and to forms made available before 1 October 2017;
(n) Title IX shall not apply to time limits set before 1 October 2017;
(o) Title X shall not apply to revocations of decisions taken or entries in the Register made before 1 October 2017;
(p) Title XI shall not apply to suspensions requested by the partics or imposed by the Office before 1 October 2017;
(q) Title XII shall not apply to proceedings interrupted before 1 October 2017;
(r) Article 73 shall not apply to EU trade mark applications received before 1 October 2017;
(s) Article 74 shall not apply to representatives appointed before 1 October 2017;
(t) Article 75 shall not apply to entries on the list of professional representatives made before 1 October 2017;
(u) Title XIV shall not apply to designations of the EU trade mark made before 1 October 2017.

This Regulation shall be binding in its entirety and directly applicable in all Member States.

Done at Brussels, 5 March 2018.

For the Commission
The President
Jean-Claude JUNCKER

*Replace Appendix 19:*

APPENDIX 19

# REGULATION (EU) NO 608/2013 OF THE EUROPEAN PARLIAMENT AND OF THE COUNCIL OF 12 JUNE 2013

## concerning customs enforcement of intellectual property rights and repealing Council Regulation (EC) No 1383/2003 A19-001

THE EUROPEAN PARLIAMENT AND THE COUNCIL OF THE EUROPEAN UNION,

Having regard to the Treaty on the Functioning of the European Union, and in particular Article 207 thereof,

Having regard to the proposal from the European Commission,

After transmission of the draft legislative act to the national parliaments,

Acting in accordance with the ordinary legislative procedure[1],

Whereas:

**(1)** The Council requested, in its Resolution of 25 September 2008 on a comprehensive European anti-counterfeiting and anti-piracy plan, that Council Regulation (EC) No 1383/2003 of 22 July 2003 concerning customs action against goods suspected of infringing certain intellectual property rights and the measures to be taken against goods found to have infringed such rights[2], be reviewed.

**(2)** The marketing of goods infringing intellectual property rights does considerable damage to right-holders, users or groups of producers, and to law-abiding manufacturers and traders. Such marketing could also be deceiving consumers, and could in some cases be endangering their health and safety. Such goods should, in so far as is possible, be kept off the Union market and measures should be adopted to deal with such unlawful marketing without impeding legitimate trade.

**(3)** The review of Regulation (EC) No 1383/2003 showed that, in the light of economic, commercial and legal developments, certain improvements to the legal framework are necessary to strengthen the enforcement of intellectual property rights by customs authorities, as well as to ensure appropriate legal certainty.

**(4)** The customs authorities should be competent to enforce intellectual property rights with regard to goods, which, in accordance with Union customs legislation, are liable to customs supervision or customs control, and to carry out adequate

1 Position of the European Parliament of 3 July 2012 (not yet published in the Official Journal) and position of the Council at first reading of 16 May 2013 (not yet published in the Official Journal). Position of the European Parliament of 11 June 2013 (not yet published in the Official Journal).

2 OJ L 196, 2.8.2003, p. 7.

controls on such goods with a view to preventing operations in breach of intellectual property rights laws. Enforcing intellectual property rights at the border, wherever the goods are, or should have been, under customs supervision or customs control is an efficient way to quickly and effectively provide legal protection to the right-holder as well as the users and groups of producers. Where the release of goods is suspended or goods are detained by customs authorities at the border, only one legal proceeding should be required, whereas several separate proceedings should be required for the same level of enforcement for goods found on the market, which have been disaggregated and delivered to retailers. An exception should be made for goods released for free circulation under the end-use regime, as such goods remain under customs supervision, even though they have been released for free circulation. This Regulation should not apply to goods carried by passengers in their personal luggage provided that those goods are for their own personal use and there are no indications that commercial traffic is involved.

**(5)** Regulation (EC) No 1383/2003 does not cover certain intellectual property rights and certain infringements are excluded from its scope. In order to strengthen the enforcement of intellectual property rights, customs intervention should be extended to other types of infringements not covered by Regulation (EC) No 1383/2003. This Regulation should therefore, in addition to the rights already covered by Regulation (EC) No 1383/2003, also include trade names in so far as they are protected as exclusive property rights under national law, topographies of semiconductor products and utility models and devices which are primarily designed, produced or adapted for the purpose of enabling or facilitating the circumvention of technological measures.

**(6)** Infringements resulting from so-called illegal parallel trade and overruns are excluded from the scope of Regulation (EC) No 1383/2003. Goods subject to illegal parallel trade, namely goods that have been manufactured with the consent of the right-holder but placed on the market for the first time in the European Economic Area without his consent, and overruns, namely goods that are manufactured by a person duly authorised by a right-holder to manufacture a certain quantity of goods, in excess of the quantities agreed between that person and the right-holder, are manufactured as genuine goods and it is therefore not appropriate that customs authorities focus their efforts on such goods. Illegal parallel trade and overruns should therefore also be excluded from the scope of this Regulation.

**(7)** Member States should, in cooperation with the Commission, provide appropriate training for customs officials, in order to ensure the correct implementation of this Regulation.

**(8)** This Regulation, when fully implemented, will further contribute to an internal market which ensures right-holders a more effective protection, fuels creativity and innovation and provides consumers with reliable and high-quality products, which should in turn strengthen cross-border transactions between consumers, businesses and traders.

**(9)** Member States face increasingly limited resources in the field of customs. Therefore, the promotion of risk management technologies and strategies to maximise resources available to customs authorities should be supported.

**(10)** This Regulation solely contains procedural rules for customs authorities. Accordingly, this Regulation does not set out any criteria for ascertaining the existence of an infringement of an intellectual property right.

**(11)** Under the 'Declaration on the TRIPS Agreement and Public Health' adopted by the Doha WTO Ministerial Conference on 14 November 2001, the Agreement on Trade-Related Aspects of Intellectual Property Rights (TRIPS Agreement) can and should be interpreted and implemented in a manner supportive of WTO Members' right to protect public health and, in particular, to promote access to medicines for all. Consequently, in line with the Union's international commitments and its development cooperation policy, with regard to medicines, the passage of which across the customs territory of the Union, with or without transhipment, warehousing, breaking bulk, or changes in the mode or means of transport, is only a portion of a complete journey beginning and terminating beyond the territory of the Union, customs authorities should, when assessing a risk of infringement of intellectual property rights, take account of any substantial likelihood of diversion of such medicines onto the market of the Union.

**(12)** This Regulation should not affect the provisions on the competence of courts, in particular, those of Regulation (EU) No 1215/2012 of the European Parliament and of the Council of 12 December 2012 on jurisdiction and the recognition and enforcement of judgments in civil and commercial matters[3].

**(13)** Persons, users, bodies or groups of producers, who are in a position to initiate legal proceedings in their own name with respect to a possible infringement of an intellectual property right, should be entitled to submit an application.

**(14)** In order to ensure that intellectual property rights are enforced throughout the Union, it is appropriate to allow persons or entities seeking enforcement of Union-wide rights to apply to the customs authorities of a single Member State. Such applicants should be able to request that those authorities decide that action be taken to enforce the intellectual property right both in their own Member State and in any other Member State.

**(15)** In order to ensure the swift enforcement of intellectual property rights, it should be provided that, where the customs authorities suspect, on the basis of reasonable indications, that goods under their supervision infringe intellectual property rights, they may suspend the release of or detain the goods whether at their own initiative or upon application, in order to enable a person or entity entitled to submit an application to initiate proceedings for determining whether an intellectual property right has been infringed.

**(16)** Regulation (EC) No 1383/2003 allowed Member States to provide for a procedure allowing the destruction of certain goods without there being any obligation to initiate proceedings to establish whether an intellectual property right has been infringed. As recognised in the European Parliament Resolution of 18 December 2008 on the impact of counterfeiting on international trade[4], such procedure has proved very successful in the Member States where it has been available. Therefore, the procedure should be made compulsory with regard to all infringements of intellectual property rights and should be applied, where the declarant or the holder of the goods agrees to destruction. Furthermore, the procedure should provide that customs authorities may deem that the declarant or the holder of the goods has agreed to the destruction of the goods where he has not explicitly opposed destruction within the prescribed period.

---

[3] OJ L 351, 20.12.2012, p. 1.

[4] OJ C 45 E, 23.2.2010, p. 47.

**(17)** In order to reduce the administrative burden and costs to a minimum, a specific procedure should be introduced for small consignments of counterfeit and pirated goods, which should allow for such goods to be destroyed without the explicit agreement of the applicant in each case. However, a general request made by the applicant in the application should be required in order for that procedure to be applied. Furthermore, customs authorities should have the possibility to require that the applicant covers the costs incurred by the application of that procedure.

**(18)** For further legal certainty, it is appropriate to modify the timelines for suspending the release of or detaining goods suspected of infringing an intellectual property right and the conditions in which information about detained goods is to be passed on to persons and entities concerned by customs authorities, as provided for in Regulation (EC) No 1383/2003.

**(19)** Taking into account the provisional and preventive character of the measures adopted by the customs authorities when applying this Regulation and the conflicting interests of the parties affected by the measures, some aspects of the procedures should be adapted to ensure the smooth application of this Regulation, whilst respecting the rights of the concerned parties. Thus, with respect to the various notifications envisaged by this Regulation, the customs authorities should notify the relevant person, on the basis of the documents concerning the customs treatment or of the situation in which the goods are placed. Furthermore, since the procedure for destruction of goods implies that both the declarant or the holder of the goods and the holder of the decision should communicate their possible objections to destruction in parallel, it should be ensured that the holder of the decision is given the possibility to react to a potential objection to destruction by the declarant or the holder of the goods. It should therefore be ensured that the declarant or the holder of the goods is notified of the suspension of the release of the goods or their detention before, or on the same day as, the holder of the decision.

**(20)** Customs authorities and the Commission are encouraged to cooperate with the European Observatory on Infringements of Intellectual Property Rights in the framework of their respective competences.

**(21)** With a view to eliminating international trade in goods infringing intellectual property rights, the TRIPS Agreement provides that WTO Members are to promote the exchange of information between customs authorities on such trade. Accordingly, it should be possible for the Commission and the customs authorities of the Member States to share information on suspected breaches of intellectual property rights with the relevant authorities of third countries, including on goods which are in transit through the territory of the Union and originate in or are destined for those third countries.

**(22)** In the interest of efficiency, the provisions of Council Regulation (EC) No 515/97 of 13 March 1997 on mutual assistance between the administrative authorities of the Member States and cooperation between the latter and the Commission to ensure the correct application of the law on customs or agricultural matters[5], should apply.

**(23)** The liability of the customs authorities should be governed by the legislation of the Member States, though the granting by the customs authorities of an application should not entitle the holder of the decision to compensation in the event

---

5 OJ L 82, 22.3.1997, p. 1.

that goods suspected of infringing an intellectual property right are not detected by the customs authorities and are released or no action is taken to detain them.

**(24)** Given that customs authorities take action upon application, it is appropriate to provide that the holder of the decision should reimburse all the costs incurred by the customs authorities in taking action to enforce his intellectual property rights. Nevertheless, this should not preclude the holder of the decision from seeking compensation from the infringer or other persons that might be considered liable under the legislation of the Member State where the goods were found. Such persons might include intermediaries, where applicable. Costs and damages incurred by persons other than customs authorities as a result of a customs action, where the release of goods is suspended or the goods are detained on the basis of a claim of a third party based on intellectual property, should be governed by the specific legislation applicable in each particular case.

**(25)** This Regulation introduces the possibility for customs authorities to allow goods which are to be destroyed to be moved, under customs supervision, between different places within the customs territory of the Union. Customs authorities may furthermore decide to release such goods for free circulation with a view to further recycling or disposal outside commercial channels including for awareness-raising, training and educational purposes.

**(26)** Customs enforcement of intellectual property rights entails the exchange of data on decisions relating to applications. Such processing of data covers also personal data and should be carried out in accordance with Union law, as set out in Directive 95/46/EC of the European Parliament and of the Council of 24 October 1995 on the protection of individuals with regard to the processing of personal data and on the free movement of such data[6] and Regulation (EC) No 45/2001 of the European Parliament and of the Council of 18 December 2000 on the protection of individuals with regard to the processing of personal data by Community institutions and bodies and on the free movement of such data[7].

**(27)** The exchange of information relating to decisions on applications and to customs actions should be made via a central electronic database. The entity which will control and manage that database and the entities in charge of ensuring the security of the processing of the data contained in the database should be defined. Introducing any type of possible interoperability or exchange should first and foremost comply with the purpose limitation principle, namely that data should be used for the purpose for which the database has been established, and no further exchange or interconnection should be allowed other than for that purpose.

**(28)** In order to ensure that the definition of small consignments can be adapted if it proves to be impractical, taking into account the need to ensure the effective operation of the procedure, or where necessary to avoid any circumvention of this procedure as regards the composition of consignments, the power to adopt acts in accordance with Article 290 of the Treaty on the Functioning of the European Union should be delegated to the Commission in respect of amending the non-essential elements of the definition of small consignments, namely the specific quantities set out in that definition. It is of particular importance that the Commission carry out appropriate consultations during its preparatory work, including at expert level. The Commission, when preparing and drawing up delegated acts, should ensure a

---

6 OJ L 281, 23.11.1995, p. 31.

7 OJ L 8, 12.1.2001, p. 1.

simultaneous, timely and appropriate transmission of relevant documents to the European Parliament and to the Council.

**(29)** In order to ensure uniform conditions for the implementation of the provisions concerning defining the elements of the practical arrangements for the exchange of data with third countries and the provisions concerning the forms for the application and for requesting the extension of the period during which customs authorities are to take action, implementing powers should be conferred on the Commission, namely to define those elements of the practical arrangements and to establish standard forms. Those powers should be exercised in accordance with Regulation (EU) No 182/2011 of the European Parliament and of the Council of 16 February 2011 laying down the rules and general principles concerning mechanisms for control by Member States of the Commission's exercise of implementing powers[8]. For establishing the standard forms, although the subject of the provisions of this Regulation to be implemented falls within the scope of the common commercial policy, given the nature and impacts of those implementing acts, the advisory procedure should be used for their adoption, because all details of what information to include in the forms follows directly from the text of this Regulation. Those implementing acts will therefore only establish the format and structure of the form and will have no further implications for the common commercial policy of the Union.

**(30)** Regulation (EC) No 1383/2003 should be repealed.

**(31)** The European Data Protection Supervisor was consulted in accordance with Article 28(2) of Regulation (EC) No 45/2001 and delivered an opinion on 12 October 2011[9],

HAVE ADOPTED THIS REGULATION:

## CHAPTER I

## SUBJECT MATTER, SCOPE AND DEFINITIONS

*Article 1*

### Subject matter and scope

**1.** This Regulation sets out the conditions and procedures for action by the customs authorities where goods suspected of infringing an intellectual property right are, or should have been, subject to customs supervision or customs control [...], particularly goods in the following situations:

(a) when declared for release for free circulation, export or re-export;

(b) when entering or leaving the customs territory of the [United Kingdom];

(c) when placed under a suspensive procedure or in a free zone or free warehouse.

**2.** In respect of the goods subject to customs supervision or customs control, and without prejudice to Articles 17 and 18, the customs authorities shall carry out adequate customs controls and shall take proportionate identification measures as provided for in Article 13(1) and Article 72 of Regulation (EEC) No 2913/92 in accordance with risk analysis criteria with a view to preventing acts in breach of intel-

---

8 OJ L 55, 28.2.2011, p. 13.

9 OJ C 363, 13.12.2011, p. 3.

lectual property laws applicable in the territory of the [United Kingdom] and in order to cooperate with third countries on the enforcement of intellectual property rights.

**3.** This Regulation shall not apply to goods that have been released for free circulation under the end-use regime.

**4.** This Regulation shall not apply to goods of a non-commercial nature contained in travellers' personal luggage.

**5.** This Regulation shall not apply to goods that have been manufactured with the consent of the right-holder or to goods manufactured, by a person duly authorised by a right-holder to manufacture a certain quantity of goods, in excess of the quantities agreed between that person and the right-holder.

**6.** This Regulation shall not affect [the law on intellectual property]. in relation to criminal procedures.

*Article 2*

**Definitions**

For the purposes of this Regulation:

[(A1) References to "the customs authorities" or "the competent customs department" shall be read as references to the Commissioners for Her Majesty's Revenue and Customs;]

(1) 'intellectual property right' means:

(a) a trade mark;

(b) a design;

(c) a copyright or any related right as provided for by [...] law;

(d) a geographical indication;

(e) a patent as provided for by [...] law;

(f) a supplementary protection certificate for medicinal products [which is recognised in law];

(g) a supplementary protection certificate for plant protection products as provided for in Regulation (EC) No 1610/96 of the European Parliament and of the Council of 23 July 1996 concerning the creation of a supplementary protection certificate for plant protection products[10];

(h) [...];

(i) a plant variety right [which is recognised in] law;

(j) a topography of semiconductor product as provided for by [...] law;

(k) [...]

(l) a trade name in so far as it is protected as an exclusive intellectual property right by [...] law;

[(2) "trade mark" means a trade mark registered in the United Kingdom or under international arrangements which has effect in the United Kingdom;

(3) "design" means a design registered in the United Kingdom or under international arrangements which has effect in the United Kingdom;]

[(4) "geographical indication" means a geographical indication for products in so far as it is established as an exclusive intellectual property right by law;]

(5) 'counterfeit goods' means:

---

[10] OJ L 198, 8.8.1996, p. 30.

a. goods which are the subject of an act infringing a trade mark in the [United Kingdom] and bear without authorisation a sign which is identical to the trade mark validly registered in respect of the same type of goods, or which cannot be distinguished in its essential aspects from such a trade mark;
b. goods which are the subject of an act infringing a geographical indication in the [United Kingdom] and, bear or are described by, a name or term protected in respect of that geographical indication;
c. any packaging, label, sticker, brochure, operating instructions, warranty document or other similar item, even if presented separately, which is the subject of an act infringing a trade mark or a geographical indication, which includes a sign, name or term which is identical to a validly registered trade mark or protected geographical indication, or which cannot be distinguished in its essential aspects from such a trade mark or geographical indication, and which can be used for the same type of goods as that for which the trade mark or geographical indication has been registered;

(6) 'pirated goods' means goods which are the subject of an act infringing a copyright or related right or a design in the [United Kingdom] and which are, or contain copies, made without the consent of the holder of a copyright or related right or a design, or of a person authorised by that holder in the country of production;
(7) 'goods suspected of infringing an intellectual property right' means goods with regard to which there are reasonable indications that, in the [United Kingdom], they are prima facie:

a. goods which are the subject of an act infringing an intellectual property right [...];
b. devices, products or components which are primarily designed, produced or adapted for the purpose of enabling or facilitating the circumvention of any technology, device or component that, in the normal course of its operation, prevents or restricts acts in respect of works which are not authorised by the holder of any copyright or any right related to copyright and which relate to an act infringing those rights [...];
c. any mould or matrix which is specifically designed or adapted for the manufacture of goods infringing an intellectual property right, if such moulds or matrices relate to an act infringing an intellectual property right [...];

(8) 'right-holder' means the holder of an intellectual property right;
(9) 'application' means a request made to the competent customs department for customs authorities to take action with respect to goods suspected of infringing an intellectual property right;
(10) 'national application' means an application requesting the customs authorities of [the United Kingdom to take action];
(11) [...]
(12) 'applicant' means the person or entity in whose name an application is submitted;
(13) 'holder of the decision' means the holder of a decision granting an application;
(14) 'holder of the goods' means the person who is the owner of the goods suspected of infringing an intellectual property right or who has a similar right of disposal, or physical control, over such goods;

(15) 'declarant' means the declarant as defined in section 159(4B)(a) or (b) of the Customs and Excise Management Act 1979[11];
(16) 'destruction' means the physical destruction, recycling or disposal of goods outside commercial channels, in such a way as to preclude damage to the holder of the decision;
(17) [...]
(18) 'release of the goods' means the release of the goods [within the meaning of paragraph 17(6) of Schedule 1 to the Taxation (Cross-border Trade) Act 2018[12]];
(19) 'small consignment' means a postal or express courier consignment, which:

a. contains three units or less; or
b. has a gross weight of less than two kilograms.

For the purpose of point (a), 'units' means goods as classified under the [Harmonized Commodity Description and Coding System ("the Harmonized System") provided for under the International Convention on the Harmonized System as done in Brussels on 14 June 1983 and as amended from time to time][13] if unpackaged, or the package of such goods intended for retail sale to the ultimate consumer.

For the purpose of this definition, separate goods falling in the same [Harmonized System] code shall be considered as different units and goods presented as sets classified in one [Harmonized System] code shall be considered as one unit;
(20) 'perishable goods' means goods considered by customs authorities to deteriorate by being kept for up to 20 days from the date of their suspension of release or detention;
(21) 'exclusive licence' means a licence (whether general or limited) authorising the licensee to the exclusion of all other persons, including the person granting the licence, to use an intellectual property right in the manner authorised by the licence.

## CHAPTER II

## APPLICATIONS

### SECTION 1

### Submission of applications

*Article 3*

#### Entitlement to submit an application

The following persons and entities shall, to the extent they are entitled to initiate proceedings, in order to determine whether an intellectual property right has been infringed, in the [United Kingdom], be entitled to submit [an application]:
[(1) right-holders;
(2) intellectual property rights management collective bodies;

---

11 1979 c. 2. Subsection (4B) was inserted by paragraph 107(3) of Schedule 7 to the Taxation (Cross-border Trade) Act 2018.

12 2018 c. 22.

13 Available from *www.wcoomd.org/en/topics/nomenclature/instrument-and-tools/hs_nomenclature_previous_editions/hs_nomenclature_table_2012.aspx*. A copy may be inspected free of charge by arrangement with HM Revenue and Customs at 100 Parliament Street, London SW1A 2BQ..

(3) persons or entities authorised to use intellectual property rights, which have been authorised formally by the right-holder to initiate proceedings in order to determine whether the intellectual property right has been infringed.]

*Article 4*

**Intellectual property rights covered by Union applications**

[…][14]

*Article 5*

**Submission of applications**

**1.** […]
**2.** Applications shall be submitted to the competent customs department. The applications shall be completed using the form referred to in Article 6 and shall contain the information required therein.
**3.** Where an application is submitted after notification by the customs authorities of the suspension of the release or detention of the goods in accordance with Article 18(3), that application shall comply with the following:
(a) it is submitted to the competent customs department within four working days of the notification of the suspension of the release or detention of the goods;
(b) […]
(c) it contains the information referred to in Article 6(3). The applicant may, however, omit the information referred to in point (g), (h) or (i) of that paragraph.
**4.** Only one application may be submitted for the same intellectual property right..
**5.** […]
**6.** Where computerised systems are available for the purpose of receiving and processing applications, applications as well as attachments shall be submitted using electronic data-processing techniques. […].

*Article 6*

**Application form**

**1.** [The Commissioners for Her Majesty's Revenue and Customs shall establish an application form.]
**2.** The application form shall specify the information that has to be provided to the data subject pursuant to [Regulation (EU) 2016/679 of the European Parliament and of the Council of 27 April 2016 on the protection of natural persons with regard to the processing of personal data and on the free movement of such data and repealing Directive 95/46/EC (General Data Protection Regulation)].
**3.** The […] following information is required of the applicant in the application form:
(a) details concerning the applicant;
(b) the status, within the meaning of Article 3, of the applicant;

14 OJ L 157, 30.4.2004, p. 45.

(c) documents providing evidence to satisfy the competent customs department that the applicant is entitled to submit the application;
(d) where the applicant submits the application by means of a representative, details of the person representing him and evidence of that person's powers to act as representative, in accordance with the legislation of the [United Kingdom];
(e) the intellectual property right or rights to be enforced;
(f) [...]
(g) specific and technical data on the authentic goods, including markings such as bar-coding and images where appropriate;
(h) the information needed to enable the customs authorities to readily identify the goods in question;
(i) information relevant to the customs authorities' analysis and assessment of the risk of infringement of the intellectual property right or the intellectual property rights concerned, such as the authorised distributors;
(j) whether information provided in accordance with point (g), (h) or (i) of this paragraph is to be marked for restricted handling [...];
(k) the details of any representative designated by the applicant to take charge of legal and technical matters;
(l) an undertaking by the applicant to notify the competent customs department of any of the situations laid down in Article 15;
(m) an undertaking by the applicant to forward and update any information relevant to the customs authorities' analysis and assessment of the risk of infringement of the intellectual property right(s) concerned;
(n) an undertaking by the applicant to assume liability under the conditions laid down in Article 28;
(o) an undertaking by the applicant to bear the costs referred to in Article 29 under the conditions laid down in that Article;
(p) an agreement by the applicant that the data provided by him may be processed by the [United Kingdom];
(q) whether the applicant requests the use of the procedure referred to in Article 26 and, where requested by the customs authorities, agrees to cover the costs related to destruction of goods under that procedure.

## SECTION 2

## Decisions on applications

### *Article 7*

### Processing of incomplete applications

**1.** Where, on receipt of an application, the competent customs department considers that the application does not contain all the information required by Article 6(3), the competent customs department shall request the applicant to supply the missing information within 10 working days of notification of the request.

In such cases, the time-limit referred to in Article 9(1) shall be suspended until the relevant information is received.

**2.** Where the applicant does not provide the missing information within the period referred to in the first subparagraph of paragraph 1, the competent customs department shall reject the application.

### *Article 8*

### Fees

The applicant shall not be charged a fee to cover the administrative costs resulting from the processing of the application.

### *Article 9*

### Notification of decisions granting or rejecting applications

**1.** The competent customs department shall notify the applicant of its decision granting or rejecting the application within 30 working days of the receipt of the application. In the event of rejection, the competent customs department shall provide reasons for its decision and include information on the appeal procedure.

**2.** If the applicant has been notified of the suspension of the release or the detention of the goods by the customs authorities before the submission of an application, the competent customs department shall notify the applicant of its decision granting or rejecting the application within two working days of the receipt of the application.

### *Article 10*

### Decisions concerning applications

**1.** [A decision granting an application and any decision revoking it or amending it shall take effect in the United Kingdom from the day following the date of adoption.]

A decision extending the period during which customs authorities are to take action shall take effect in the [United Kingdom] in which the national application was submitted on the day following the date of expiry of the period to be extended.

[…]

### *Article 11*

### Period during which the customs authorities are to take action

**1.** When granting an application, the competent customs department shall specify the period during which the customs authorities are to take action.

That period shall begin on the day the decision granting the application takes effect, pursuant to Article 10, and shall not exceed one year from the day following the date of adoption.

**2.** Where an application submitted after notification by the customs authorities of the suspension of the release or detention of the goods in accordance with Article 18(3) does not contain the information referred to in point (g), (h) or (i) of Article 6(3), it shall be granted only for the suspension of the release or detention of those goods, unless that information is provided within 10 working days after the notification of the suspension of the release or detention of the goods.

**3.** Where an intellectual property right ceases to have effect or where the applicant ceases for other reasons to be entitled to submit an application, no action shall be taken by the customs authorities. The decision granting the application shall be revoked or amended accordingly by the competent customs department that granted the decision.

*Article 12*

**Extension of the period during which the customs authorities are to take action**

**1.** On expiry of the period during which the customs authorities are to take action, and subject to the prior discharge by the holder of the decision of any debt owed to the customs authorities under this Regulation, the competent customs department which adopted the initial decision may, at the request of the holder of the decision, extend that period.

**2.** Where the request for extension of the period during which the customs authorities are to take action is received by the competent customs department less than 30 working days before the expiry of the period to be extended, it may refuse that request.

**3.** The competent customs department shall notify its decision on the extension to the holder of the decision within 30 working days of the receipt of the request referred to in paragraph 1. The competent customs department shall specify the period during which the customs authorities are to take action.

**4.** The extended period during which the customs authorities are to take action shall run from the day following the date of expiry of the previous period and shall not exceed one year.

**5.** Where an intellectual property right ceases to have effect or where the applicant ceases for other reasons to be entitled to submit an application, no action shall be taken by the customs authorities. The decision granting the extension shall be revoked or amended accordingly by the competent customs department that granted the decision.

**6.** The holder of the decision shall not be charged a fee to cover the administrative costs resulting from the processing of the request for extension.

**7.** [The Commissioners for Her Majesty's Revenue and Customs shall establish an extension request form.]

*Article 13*

**Amending the decision with regard to intellectual property rights.**

The competent customs department that adopted the decision granting the application may, at the request of the holder of that decision, modify the list of intellectual property rights in that decision.

Where a new intellectual property right is added, the request shall contain the information referred to in points (c), (e), (g), (h) and (i) of Article 6(3).

[...]

*Article 14*

**Notification obligations of the competent customs department**

**1.** The competent customs department to which a national application has been submitted shall forward the following decisions to the customs offices [...], immediately after their adoption:

(a) decisions granting the application;
(b) decisions revoking decisions granting the application;
(c) decisions amending decisions granting the application;
(d) decisions extending the period during which the customs authorities are to take action.

**2.** […]

**3.** […]

**4.** The competent customs department shall forward its decision suspending the actions of the customs authorities under […] Article 16(2) to the customs offices […], immediately after its adoption.

*Article 15*

**Notification obligations of the holder of the decision**

The holder of the decision shall immediately notify the competent customs department that granted the application of any of the following:
(a) an intellectual property right covered by the application ceases to have effect;
(b) the holder of the decision ceases for other reasons to be entitled to submit the application;
(c) modifications to the information referred to in Article 6(3).

*Article 16*

**Failure of the holder of the decision to fulfil his obligations**

**1.** Where the holder of the decision uses the information provided by the customs authorities for purposes other than those provided for in Article 21, the competent customs department […] may:
(a) revoke any decision adopted by it granting [an] application to that holder of the decision, and refuse to extend the period during which the customs authorities are to take action;
(b) […]

**2.** The competent customs department may decide to suspend the actions of the customs authorities until the expiry of the period during which those authorities are to take action, where the holder of the decision:
(a) does not fulfil the notification obligations set out in Article 15;
(b) does not fulfil the obligation on returning samples set out in Article 19(3);
(c) does not fulfil the obligations on costs and translation set out in Article 29(1) and (3);
(d) without valid reason does not initiate proceedings as provided for in Article 23(3) or Article 26(9).

[…].

# CHAPTER III

# ACTION BY THE CUSTOMS AUTHORITIES

## SECTION 1

## Suspension of the release or detention of goods suspected of infringing an intellectual property right

*Article 17*

### Suspension of the release or detention of the goods following the grant of an application

**1.** Where the customs authorities identify goods suspected of infringing an intellectual property right covered by a decision granting an application, they shall suspend the release of the goods or detain them.

**2.** Before suspending the release of or detaining the goods, the customs authorities may ask the holder of the decision to provide them with any relevant information with respect to the goods. The customs authorities may also provide the holder of the decision with information about the actual or estimated quantity of goods, their actual or presumed nature and images thereof, as appropriate.

**3.** The customs authorities shall notify the declarant or the holder of the goods of the suspension of the release of the goods or the detention of the goods within one working day of that suspension or detention.

Where the customs authorities opt to notify the holder of the goods and two or more persons are considered to be the holder of the goods, the customs authorities shall not be obliged to notify more than one of those persons.

The customs authorities shall notify the holder of the decision of the suspension of the release of the goods or the detention on the same day as, or promptly after, the declarant or the holder of the goods is notified.

The notifications shall include information on the procedure set out in Article 23.

**4.** The customs authorities shall inform the holder of the decision and the declarant or the holder of the goods of the actual or estimated quantity and the actual or presumed nature of the goods, including available images thereof, as appropriate, whose release has been suspended or which have been detained. The customs authorities shall also, upon request and where available to them, inform the holder of the decision of the names and addresses of the consignee, the consignor and the declarant or the holder of the goods, of the customs procedure and of the origin, provenance and destination of the goods whose release has been suspended or which have been detained.

*Article 18*

### Suspension of the release or detention of the goods before the grant of an application

**1.** Where the customs authorities identify goods suspected of infringing an intellectual property right, which are not covered by a decision granting an application, they may, except for in the case of perishable goods, suspend the release of those goods or detain them.

**2.** Before suspending the release of or detaining the goods suspected of infringing an intellectual property right, the customs authorities may, without disclosing any information other than the actual or estimated quantity of goods, their actual or presumed nature and images thereof, as appropriate, request any person or entity potentially entitled to submit an application concerning the alleged infringement of the intellectual property rights to provide them with any relevant information.

**3.** The customs authorities shall notify the declarant or the holder of the goods of the suspension of the release of the goods or their detention within one working day of that suspension or detention.

Where the customs authorities opt to notify the holder of the goods and two or more persons are considered to be the holder of the goods, the customs authorities shall not be obliged to notify more than one of those persons.

The customs authorities shall notify persons or entities entitled to submit an application concerning the alleged infringement of the intellectual property rights, of the suspension of the release of the goods or their detention on the same day as, or promptly after, the declarant or the holder of the goods is notified.

The customs authorities may consult the competent public authorities in order to identify the persons or entities entitled to submit an application.

The notifications shall include information on the procedure set out in Article 23.

**4.** The customs authorities shall grant the release of the goods or put an end to their detention immediately after completion of all customs formalities in the following cases:

(a) where they have not identified any person or entity entitled to submit an application concerning the alleged infringement of intellectual property rights within one working day from the suspension of the release or the detention of the goods;

(b) where they have not received an application in accordance with Article 5(3), or where they have rejected such an application.

**5.** Where an application has been granted, the customs authorities shall, upon request and where available to them, inform the holder of the decision of the names and addresses of the consignee, the consignor and the declarant or the holder of the goods, of the customs procedure and of the origin, provenance and destination of the goods whose release has been suspended or which have been detained.

### *Article 19*

### Inspection and sampling of goods whose release has been suspended or which have been detained

**1.** The customs authorities shall give the holder of the decision and the declarant or the holder of the goods the opportunity to inspect the goods whose release has been suspended or which have been detained.

**2.** The customs authorities may take samples that are representative of the goods. They may provide or send such samples to the holder of the decision, at the holder's request and strictly for the purposes of analysis and to facilitate the subsequent procedure in relation to counterfeit and pirated goods. Any analysis of those samples shall be carried out under the sole responsibility of the holder of the decision.

**3.** The holder of the decision shall, unless circumstances do not allow, return the samples referred to in paragraph 2 to the customs authorities on completion of the analysis, at the latest before the goods are released or their detention is ended.

*Article 20*

**Conditions for storage**

**1.** The conditions of storage of goods during a period of suspension of release or detention shall be determined by the customs authorities.

*Article 21*

**Permitted use of certain information by the holder of the decision**

Where the holder of the decision has received the information referred to in Article 17(4), Article 18(5), Article 19 or Article 26(8), he may disclose or use that information only for the following purposes:

(a) to initiate proceedings to determine whether an intellectual property right has been infringed and in the course of such proceedings;

(b) in connection with criminal investigations related to the infringement of an intellectual property right and undertaken by public authorities in the [United Kingdom];

(c) to initiate criminal proceedings and in the course of such proceedings;

(d) to seek compensation from the infringer or other persons;

(e) to agree with the declarant or the holder of the goods that the goods be destroyed in accordance with Article 23(1);

(f) to agree with the declarant or the holder of the goods of the amount of the guarantee referred to in point (a) of Article 24(2).

*Article 22*

**Sharing of information and data between customs authorities**

**1.** Without prejudice to applicable provisions on data protection in the [United Kingdom] and for the purpose of contributing to eliminating international trade in goods infringing intellectual property rights, [...] the customs authorities of the [United Kingdom] may share certain data and information available to them with the relevant authorities in third countries according to the practical arrangements referred to in paragraph 3.

**2.** The data and information referred to in paragraph 1 shall be exchanged to swiftly enable effective enforcement against shipments of goods infringing an intellectual property right. Such data and information may relate to seizures, trends and general risk information, including on goods which are in transit [...] and which have originated in or are destined for the territory of third countries concerned. Such data and information may include, where appropriate, the following:

(a) nature and quantity of goods;

(b) suspected intellectual property right infringed;

(c) origin, provenance and destination of the goods;

(d) information on movements of means of transport, in particular:

- (i) name of vessel or registration of means of transport;
- (ii) reference numbers of freight bill or other transport document;
- (iii) number of containers;
- (iv) weight of load;
- (v) description and/or coding of goods;
- (vi) reservation number;

(vii) seal number;
(viii) place of first loading;
(ix) place of final unloading;
(x) places of transhipment;
(xi) expected date of arrival at place of final unloading;

(e) information on movements of containers, in particular:
(i) container number;
(ii) container loading status;
(iii) date of movement;
(iv) type of movement (loaded, unloaded, transhipped, entered, left, etc.);
(v) name of vessel or registration of means of transport;
(vi) number of voyage/journey;
(vii) place;
(viii) freight bill or other transport document.

**3.** [The Commissioners for Her Majesty's Revenue and Customs shall make the necessary practical arrangements concerning the exchange of data and information referred to in paragraphs 1 and 2 of this Article.]

## SECTION 2

## Destruction of goods, initiation of proceedings and early release of goods

### *Article 23*

### Destruction of goods and initiation of proceedings

**1.** Goods suspected of infringing an intellectual property right may be destroyed under customs control, without there being any need to determine whether an intellectual property right has been infringed under the law of the [United Kingdom], where all of the following conditions are fulfilled:

(a) the holder of the decision has confirmed in writing to the customs authorities, within 10 working days, or three working days in the case of perishable goods, of notification of the suspension of the release or the detention of the goods, that, in his conviction, an intellectual property right has been infringed;

(b) the holder of the decision has confirmed in writing to the customs authorities, within 10 working days, or three working days in the case of perishable goods, of notification of the suspension of the release or the detention of the goods, his agreement to the destruction of the goods;

(c) the declarant or the holder of the goods has confirmed in writing to the customs authorities, within 10 working days, or three working days in the case of perishable goods, of notification of the suspension of the release or the detention of the goods, his agreement to the destruction of the goods. Where the declarant or the holder of the goods has not confirmed his agreement to the destruction of the goods nor notified his opposition thereto to the customs authorities, within those deadlines, the customs authorities may deem the declarant or the holder of the goods to have confirmed his agreement to the destruction of those goods.

The customs authorities shall grant the release of the goods or put an end to their detention, immediately after completion of all customs formalities, where within the periods referred to in points (a) and (b) of the first subparagraph, they have not received both the written confirmation from the holder of the decision that, in his conviction, an intellectual property right has been infringed and his agreement to destruction, unless those authorities have been duly informed about the initiation of proceedings to determine whether an intellectual property right has been infringed.

**2.** The destruction of the goods shall be carried out under customs control and under the responsibility of the holder of the decision [...]. Samples may be taken by competent authorities prior to the destruction of the goods. Samples taken prior to destruction may be used for educational purposes.

**3.** Where the declarant or the holder of the goods has not confirmed his agreement to the destruction in writing and where the declarant or the holder of the goods has not been deemed to have confirmed his agreement to the destruction, in accordance with point (c) of the first subparagraph of paragraph 1 within the periods referred to therein, the customs authorities shall immediately notify the holder of the decision thereof. The holder of the decision shall, within 10 working days, or three working days in the case of perishable goods, of notification of the suspension of the release or the detention of the goods, initiate proceedings to determine whether an intellectual property right has been infringed.

**4.** Except in the case of perishable goods the customs authorities may extend the period referred to in paragraph 3 by a maximum of 10 working days upon a duly justified request by the holder of the decision in appropriate cases.

**5.** The customs authorities shall grant the release of the goods or put an end to their detention, immediately after completion of all customs formalities, where, within the periods referred to in paragraphs 3 and 4, they have not been duly informed, in accordance with paragraph 3, on the initiation of proceedings to determine whether an intellectual property right has been infringed.

*Article 24*

**Early release of goods**

**1.** Where the customs authorities have been notified of the initiation of proceedings to determine whether a design, patent, [...] topography of semiconductor product or plant variety has been infringed, the declarant or the holder of the goods may request the customs authorities to release the goods or put an end to their detention before the completion of those proceedings.

**2.** The customs authorities shall release the goods or put an end to their detention only where all the following conditions are fulfilled:

(a) the declarant or the holder of the goods has provided a guarantee that is of an amount sufficient to protect the interests of the holder of the decision;

(b) the authority competent to determine whether an intellectual property right has been infringed has not authorised precautionary measures;

(c) all customs formalities have been completed.

**3.** The provision of the guarantee referred to in point (a) of paragraph 2 shall not affect the other legal remedies available to the holder of the decision.

*Article 25*

**Goods for destruction**

**1.** Goods to be destroyed under Article 23 or 26 shall not be:

(a) released for free circulation, unless customs authorities, with the agreement of the holder of the decision, decide that it is necessary in the event that the goods are to be recycled or disposed of outside commercial channels, including for awareness-raising, training and educational purposes. The conditions under which the goods can be released for free circulation shall be determined by the customs authorities;
(b) brought out of the customs territory of the [United Kingdom];
(c) exported;
(d) re-exported;
(e) placed under a suspensive procedure;
(f) placed in a free zone or free warehouse.

**2.** The customs authorities may allow the goods referred to in paragraph 1 to be moved under customs supervision between different places within the customs territory of the [United Kingdom] with a view to their destruction under customs control.

*Article 26*

**Procedure for the destruction of goods in small consignments**

**1.** This Article shall apply to goods where all of the following conditions are fulfilled:
(a) the goods are suspected of being counterfeit or pirated goods;
(b) the goods are not perishable goods;
(c) the goods are covered by a decision granting an application;
(d) the holder of the decision has requested the use of the procedure set out in this Article in the application;
(e) the goods are transported in small consignments.

**2.** When the procedure set out in this Article is applied, Article 17(3) and (4) and Article 19(2) and (3) shall not apply.

**3.** The customs authorities shall notify the declarant or the holder of the goods of the suspension of the release of the goods or their detention within one working day of the suspension of the release or of the detention of the goods. The notification of the suspension of the release or the detention of the goods shall include the following information:
(a) that the customs authorities intend to destroy the goods;
(b) the rights of the declarant or the holder of the goods under paragraphs 4, 5 and 6.

**4.** The declarant or the holder of the goods shall be given the opportunity to express his point of view within 10 working days of notification of the suspension of the release or the detention of the goods.

**5.** The goods concerned may be destroyed where, within 10 working days of notification of the suspension of the release or the detention of the goods, the declarant or the holder of the goods has confirmed to the customs authorities his agreement to the destruction of the goods.

**6.** Where the declarant or the holder of the goods has not confirmed his agreement to the destruction of the goods nor notified his opposition thereto to the customs authorities, within the period referred to in paragraph 5, the customs authorities may deem the declarant or the holder of the goods to have confirmed his agreement to the destruction of the goods.

**7.** The destruction shall be carried out under customs control. The customs authorities shall, upon request and as appropriate, provide the holder of the decision with information about the actual or estimated quantity of destroyed goods and their nature.
**8.** Where the declarant or the holder of the goods has not confirmed his agreement to the destruction of the goods and where the declarant or the holder of the goods has not been deemed to have confirmed such agreement, in accordance with paragraph 6, the customs authorities shall immediately notify the holder of the decision thereof and of the quantity of goods and their nature, including images thereof, where appropriate. The customs authorities shall also, upon request and where available to them, inform the holder of the decision of the names and addresses of the consignee, the consignor and the declarant or the holder of the goods, of the customs procedure and of the origin, provenance and destination of the goods whose release has been suspended or which have been detained.
**9.** The customs authorities shall grant the release of the goods or put an end to their detention immediately after completion of all customs formalities where they have not received information from the holder of the decision on the initiation of proceedings to determine whether an intellectual property right has been infringed within 10 working days of the notification referred to in paragraph 8.
**10.** […].

## CHAPTER IV

## LIABILITY, COSTS AND PENALTIES

*Article 27*

### Liability of the customs authorities

[The] decision granting an application shall not entitle the holder of that decision to compensation in the event that goods suspected of infringing an intellectual property right are not detected by a customs office and are released, or no action is taken to detain them.

*Article 28*

### Liability of the holder of the decision

Where a procedure duly initiated pursuant to this Regulation is discontinued owing to an act or omission on the part of the holder of the decision, where samples taken pursuant to Article 19(2) are either not returned or are damaged and beyond use owing to an act or omission on the part of the holder of the decision, or where the goods in question are subsequently found not to infringe an intellectual property right, the holder of the decision shall be liable towards any holder of the goods or declarant, who has suffered damage in that regard, in accordance with specific applicable legislation.

*Article 29*

**Cos ts**

**1.** Where requested by the customs authorities, the holder of the decision shall reimburse the costs incurred by the customs authorities, or other parties acting on behalf of customs authorities, from the moment of detention or suspension of the release of the goods, including storage and handling of the goods, in accordance with Article 17(1), Article 18(1) and Article 19(2) and (3), and when using corrective measures such as destruction of goods in accordance with Articles 23 and 26.

The holder of a decision to whom the suspension of release or detention of goods has been notified shall, upon request, be given information by the customs authorities on where and how those goods are being stored and on the estimated costs of storage referred to in this paragraph. The information on estimated costs may be expressed in terms of time, products, volume, weight or service depending on the circumstances of storage and the nature of the goods.

**2.** This Article shall be without prejudice to the right of the holder of the decision to seek compensation from the infringer or other persons in accordance with the legislation applicable.

**3.** […]

*Article 30*

**Penalties**

[…]

## CHAPTER V

## EXCHANGE OF INFORMATION

*Article 31*

**Exchange of data on decisions relating to applications and detentions between [the United Kingdom]** and the Commission

**1.** The competent customs departments [may notify] the Commission of the following:

(a) decisions granting applications, including the application and its attachments;

(b) decisions extending the period during which the customs authorities are to take action or decisions revoking the decision granting the application or amending it;

(c) the suspension of a decision granting the application.

**2.** [Where] the release of the goods is suspended or the goods are detained, the customs authorities [may] transmit to the Commission any relevant information, except personal data, including information on the quantity and type of the goods, value, intellectual property rights, customs procedures, countries of provenance, origin and destination, and transport routes and means.

**3.** […]

**4.** […].

**5.** [Upon request by the Commission, the customs authorities may share such information with the Commission as they consider necessary for the application of this Regulation.]
**6.** […]
**7.** […]

*Article 32*

**Establishment of a central database**

[…]

*Article 33*

**Data protection provisions**

**1.** […]
**2.** [Processing of personal data by the Commissioners for Her Majesty's Revenue and Customs shall be carried out in accordance with Regulation (EU) 2016/679 of the European Parliament and of the Council of 27 April 2016 on the protection of natural persons with regard to the processing of personal data and on the free movement of such data and repealing Directive 95/46/EC (General Data Protection Regulation).]
**3.** Personal data shall be collected and used solely for the purposes of this Regulation. Personal data so collected shall be accurate and shall be kept up to date.
**4.** […]
**5.** […]
**6.** […]
**7.** Personal data shall not be kept longer than six months from the date the relevant decision granting the application has been revoked or the relevant period during which the customs authorities are to take action has expired.
**8.** Where the holder of the decision has initiated proceedings in accordance with Article 23(3) or Article 26(9) and has notified the customs authorities of the initiation of such proceedings, personal data shall be kept for six months after proceedings have determined in a final way whether an intellectual property right has been infringed.

## CHAPTER VI

## COMMITTEE, DELEGATION AND FINAL PROVISIONS

*Article 34*

**Committee procedure**

[…]

*Article 35*

**Exercise of the delegation**

[…]

*Article 36*

**Mutual administrative assistance**

[…]

*Article 37*

**Reporting**

[…]

*Article 38*

**Repeal**

Regulation (EC) No 1383/2003 is repealed with effect from 1 January 2014.

References to the repealed Regulation shall be construed as references to this Regulation and shall be read in accordance with the correlation table set out in the Annex.

*Article 39*

**Transitional provisions**

Applications granted in accordance with Regulation (EC) No 1383/2003 shall remain valid for the period specified in the decision granting the application during which the customs authorities are to take action and shall not be extended.

*Article 40*

**Entry into force and application**

**1.** This Regulation shall enter into force on the twentieth day following that of its publication in the Official Journal of the European Union.
**2.** It shall apply from 1 January 2014, with the exception of:
(a) Article 6, Article 12(7) and Article 22(3), which shall apply from 19 July 2013;
(b) Article 31(1) and (3) to (7) and Article 33, which shall apply from the date on which the central database referred to in Article 32 is in place. The Commission shall make that date public.

[…]

Done at Strasbourg, 12 June 2013.

For the European Parliament
The President
M. SCHULZ
For the Council
The President
L. CREIGHTON

*ANNEX*

## Correlation table

| *Regulation (EC) No 1383/2003* | *This Regulation* |
|---|---|
| Article 1 | Article 1 |
| Article 2 | Article 2 |
| Article 3 | Article 1 |
| Article 4 | Article 18 |
| Article 5 | Articles 3 to 9 |
| Article 6 | Articles 6 and 29 |
| Article 7 | Article 12 |
| Article 8 | Articles 10, 11, 12, 14 and 15 |
| Article 9 | Articles 17 and 19 |
| Article 10 | — |
| Article 11 | Article 23 |
| Article 12 | Articles 16 and 21 |
| Article 13 | Article 23 |
| Article 14 | Article 24 |
| Article 15 | Article 20 |
| Article 16 | Article 25 |
| Article 17 | — |
| Article 18 | Article 30 |
| Article 19 | Articles 27 and 28 |
| Article 20 | Articles 6, 12, 22 and 26 |
| Article 21 | Article 34 |
| Article 22 | Articles 31 and 36 |
| Article 23 | — |
| Article 24 | Article 38 |
| Article 25 | Article 40 |

# NEW APPENDICES

*After Appendix 1, add new Appendix 1A:*

APPENDIX 1A

# TRADE MARKS ACT 1994

**A1A-001** (1994 CHAPTER 26)

An Act to make new provision for registered trade marks, implementing Council Directive No. 89/104/EEC of 21st December 1988 to approximate the laws of the Member States relating to trade marks; to make provision in connection with Council Regulation (EC) No. 40/94 of 20th December 1993 on the Community trade mark; to give effect to the Madrid Protocol Relating to the International Registration of Marks of 27th June 1989, and to certain provisions of the Paris Convention for the Protection of Industrial Property of 20th March 1883, as revised and amended; and for connected purposes.

[21st July 1994]

BE IT ENACTED by the Queen's most Excellent Majesty, by and with the advice and consent of the Lords Spiritual and Temporal, and Commons, in this present Parliament assembled, and by the authority of the same, as follows:—

ARRANGEMENT OF SECTIONS

PART I REGISTERED TRADE MARKS

*Introductory*

## PART I – – REGISTERED TRADE MARKS

*Introductory*

### Trade marks.

**1.**—[(1) In this Act "trade mark" means any sign which is capable—

(a) of being represented in the register in a manner which enables the registrar and other competent authorities and the public to determine the clear and precise subject matter of the protection afforded to the proprietor, and

(b) of distinguishing goods or services of one undertaking from those of other undertakings.

A trade mark may, in particular, consist of words (including personal names), designs, letters, numerals, colours, sounds or the shape of goods or their packaging.]

(2) References in this Act to a trade mark include, unless the context otherwise requires, references to a collective mark (see section 49) or certification mark (see section 50).

### Registered trade marks.

**2**—(1) A registered trade mark is a property right obtained by the registration of the trade mark under this Act and the proprietor of a registered trade mark has the rights and remedies provided by this Act.

(2) No proceedings lie to prevent or recover damages for the infringement of an unregistered trade mark as such; but nothing in this Act affects the law relating to passing off.

*Grounds for refusal of registration*

### Absolute grounds for refusal of registration.

**3.**—(1) The following shall not be registered—

(a) signs which do not satisfy the requirements of section 1(1).

(b) trade marks which are devoid of any distinctive character.

(c) trade marks which consist exclusively of signs or indications which may serve, in trade, to designate the kind, quality, quantity, intended purpose, value, geographical origin, the time of production of goods or of rendering of services, or other characteristics of goods or services,

(d) trade marks which consist exclusively of signs or indications which have become customary in the current language or in the bona fide and established practices of the trade:

Provided that, a trade mark shall not be refused registration by virtue of paragraph (b), (c) or (d) above if, before the date of application for registration, it has in fact acquired a distinctive character as a result of the use made of it.

(2) A sign shall not be registered as a trade mark if it consists exclusively of—

(a) the shape [, or another characteristic,] which results from the nature of the goods themselves,

(b) the shape [, or another characteristic,] of goods which is necessary to obtain a technical result, or

(c) the shape [, or another characteristic,] which gives substantial value to the goods.

(3) A trade mark shall not be registered if it is—

(a) contrary to public policy or to accepted principles of morality, or

(b) of such a nature as to deceive the public (for instance as to the nature, quality or geographical origin of the goods or service).

(4) A trade mark shall not be registered if or to the extent that its use is prohibited in the United Kingdom by any enactment or rule of law [...] [other than law relating to trade marks].

[(4A) A trade mark is not to be registered if its registration is prohibited by or under—

(a) any enactment or rule of law, [or]

(b) [...]

(c) any international agreement to which the United Kingdom [...] is a party,

providing for the protection of designations of origin or geographical indications.

(4B) [...]

(4C) A trade mark is not to be registered if it—

(a) consists of, or reproduces in its essential elements, an earlier plant variety denomination registered as mentioned in subsection (4D), and

(b) is in respect of plant varieties of the same or closely related species.

(4D) Subsection (4C)(a) refers to registration in accordance with any—

(a) enactment or rule of law, [or]

(b) [...]

(c) international agreement to which the United Kingdom [...] is a party,

providing for the protection of plant variety rights.]

(5) A trade mark shall not be registered in the cases specified, or referred to, in section 4 (specially protected emblems).

(6) A trade mark shall not be registered if or to the extent that the application is made in bad faith.

**Specially protected emblems.**

**4.**—(1) A trade mark which consists of or contains—

(a) the Royal arms, or any of the principal armorial bearings of the Royal arms, or any insignia or device so nearly resembling the Royal arms or any such armorial bearing as to be likely to be mistaken for them or it,

(b) a representation of the Royal crown or any of the Royal flags,

(c) a representation of Her Majesty or any member of the Royal family, or any colourable imitation thereof, or

(d) words, letters or devices likely to lead persons to think that the applicant either has or recently has had Royal patronage or authorisation,

shall not be registered unless it appears to the registrar that consent has been given by or on behalf of Her Majesty or, as the case may be, the relevant member of the Royal family.

(2) A trade mark which consists of or contains a representation of—

(a) the national flag of the United Kingdom (commonly known as the Union Jack), or

(b) the flag of England, Wales, Scotland, Northern Ireland or the Isle of Man,

shall not be registered if it appears to the registrar that the use of the trade mark would be misleading or grossly offensive.

Provision may be made by rules identifying the flags to which paragraph (b) applies.

(3) A trade mark shall not be registered in the cases specified in—

section 57 (national emblems, &c. of Convention countries), or section 58 (emblems, &c. of certain international organisations).

(4) Provision may be made by rules prohibiting in such cases as may be prescribed the registration of a trade mark which consists of or contains—

(a) arms to which a person is entitled by virtue of a grant of arms by the Crown, or

(b) insignia so nearly resembling such arms as to be likely to be mistaken for them,

unless it appears to the registrar that consent has been given by or on behalf of that person. Where such a mark is registered, nothing in this Act shall be construed as authorising its use in any way contrary to the laws of arms.

(5) A trade mark which consists of or contains a controlled representation within the meaning of the Olympic Symbol etc. (Protection) Act 1995 shall not be registered unless it appears to the registrar—

(a) that the application is made by the person for the time being appointed under section 1(2) of the Olympic Symbol etc (Protection) Act 1995 (power of Secretary of State to appoint a person as the proprietor of the Olympics association right), or

(b) that consent has been given by or on behalf of the person mentioned in paragraph (a) above.

**Relative grounds for refusal of registration.**

**5.**—(1) A trade mark shall not be registered if it is identical with an earlier trade mark and the goods or services for which the trade mark is applied for are identical with the goods or services for which the earlier trade mark is protected.

(2) A trade mark shall not be registered if because—

(a) it is identical with an earlier trade mark and is to be registered for goods or services similar to those for which the earlier trade mark is protected, or

(b) it is similar to an earlier trade mark and is to be registered for goods or services identical with or similar to those for which the earlier trade mark is protected,

there exists a likelihood of confusion of the part of the public, which includes the likelihood of association with the earlier trade mark.

(3) A trade mark which—

(a) is identical with or similar to an earlier trade mark, [...]

(b) [...]

shall not be registered if, or to the extent that, the earlier trade mark has a reputation in the United Kingdom [...] and the use of the later mark without due cause would take unfair advantage of, or be detrimental to, the distinctive character or the repute of the earlier trade mark.

[(3A) Subsection (3) applies irrespective of whether the goods and services for which the trade mark is to be registered are identical with, similar to or not similar to those for which the earlier trade mark is protected.]

(4) A trade mark shall not be registered if, or to the extent that, its use in the United Kingdom is liable to be prevented—

(a) by virtue of any rule of law (in particular, the law of passing off) protecting an unregistered trade mark or other sign used in the course of trade, [where the condition in subsection (4A) is met,]

[(aa) by virtue of [...] any enactment or rule of law, providing for protection of designations of origin or geographical indications, where the condition in subsection (4B) is met,] or

(b) by virtue of an earlier right other than those referred to in subsections (1) to (3) or paragraph (a) [or (aa)] above, in particular by virtue of the law of copyright [or the law relating to industrial property rights].

A person thus entitled to prevent the use of a trade mark is referred to in this Act as the proprietor of an "earlier right" in relation to the trade mark.

[(4A) The condition mentioned in subsection (4)(a) is that the rights to the unregistered trade mark or other sign were acquired prior to the date of application for registration of the trade mark or date of the priority claimed for that application.

(4B) The condition mentioned in subsection 4(aa) is that—

(a) an application for a designation of origin or a geographical indication has been submitted prior to the date of application for registration of the trade mark or the date of the priority claimed for that application, and

(b) the designation of origin or (as the case may be) geographical indication is subsequently registered.]

(5) Nothing in this section prevents the registration of a trade mark where the proprietor of the earlier trade mark or other earlier right consents to the registration.

[(6) Where an agent or representative ("R") of the proprietor of a trade mark applies, without the proprietor's consent, for the registration of the trade mark in R's own name, the application is to be refused unless R justifies that action.]

[**Grounds for refusal relating to only some of the goods or services.**

**5A.** Where grounds for refusal of an application for registration of a trade mark exist in respect of only some of the goods or services in respect of which the trade mark is applied for, the application is to be refused in relation to those goods and services only.]

**Meaning of "earlier trade mark".**

**6.**—(1) In this Act an "earlier trade mark" means —

(a) a registered trade mark [or] international trade mark (UK), [...] which has a date of application for registration earlier than that of the trade mark in question, taking account (where appropriate) of the priorities claimed in respect of the trade marks, [(aa) a comparable trade mark (EU) or a trade mark registered pursuant to an application made under paragraph 25 of Schedule 2A which has a valid claim to seniority of an earlier registered trade mark or protected international trade mark (UK) even where the earlier trade mark has been surrendered or its registration has expired;]

[(ab) a comparable trade mark (IR) or a trade mark registered pursuant to an application made under paragraph 28, 29 or 33 of Schedule 2B which has a valid claim to seniority of an earlier registered trade mark or protected international trade mark (UK) even where the earlier trade mark has been surrendered or its registration has expired;]

[(b) [...]]

(ba) a registered trade mark or international trade mark (UK) which–

(i) [prior to IP complction day] has been converted from a [European Union] trade mark or international trade mark (EC) which itself had a valid claim to seniority [of an earlier registered trade mark or protected international trade mark (UK) even where the earlier trade mark has been surrendered or its registration has expired], and

(ii) accordingly has the same claim to seniority, or

(b) a trade mark which, at the date of application for registration of the trade mark in question or (where appropriate) of the priority claimed in respect of the application, was entitled to protection under the Parts Convention [or the WTO agreement] as a well known trade mark.

[(1A) In subsection (1), "protected international trade mark (UK)" has the same meaning as in the Trade Marks (International Registration) Order 2008.]

(2) References in this Act to an earlier trade mark include a trade mark in respect of which an application for registration has been made and which, if registered, would be an earlier trade mark by virtue of subsection (1)(a) [...], subject to its being so registered [(taking account of subsection (2C))].

[(2A) References in this Act to an earlier trade mark include a trade mark in respect of which an application for registration has been made pursuant to paragraph 25 of Schedule 2A and which if registered would be an earlier trade mark by virtue of subsection (1)(aa), subject to its being so registered.]

[(2B) References in this Act to an earlier trade mark include a trade mark in respect of which an application for registration has been made pursuant to paragraph 28, 29 or 33 of Schedule 2B and which if registered would be an earlier trade mark by virtue of subsection (1)(ab), subject to its being so registered.

(2C) Where an application for registration of a trade mark has been made pursuant to paragraph 25 of Schedule 2A or paragraph 28, 29 or 33 of Schedule 2B, subsection (l)(a) is to apply as if the date of application for registration of the trade mark were—

(a) in the case of an application made pursuant to paragraph 25 of Schedule 2A, the relevant date referred to in paragraph 25(2) in respect of that application;

(b) in the case of an application made pursuant to paragraph 28 of Schedule 2B, the relevant date referred to in paragraph 28(2) in respect of that application (taking account of paragraph 28(5));

(c) in the case of an application made pursuant to paragraph 29 of Schedule 2B, the relevant date referred to in paragraph 29(2) in respect of that application (taking account of paragraph 29(4));

(d) in the case of an application made pursuant to paragraph 33 of Schedule 2B, the relevant date referred to in paragraph 33(2) or (3) (as the case may be) in respect of that application (taking account of paragraph 33(4)).]

(3) […].

[**Raising of relative grounds in opposition proceedings in case of non-use.**

**6A.**—(1) This section applies where–

(a) an application for registration of a trade mark has been published,

(b) there is an earlier trade mark [of a kind falling within section 6(1)(a), [aa] or (ba)] in relation to which the conditions set out in section 5(1), (2) or (3) obtain, and

(c) the registration procedure for the earlier trade mark was completed before the start of the [relevant period].

[(1A) In this section "the relevant period" means the period of 5 years ending with the date of the application for registration mentioned in subsection (1)(a) or (where applicable) the date of the priority claimed for that application.]

(2) In opposition proceedings, the registrar shall not refuse to register the trade mark by reason of the earlier trade mark unless the use conditions are met.

(3) The use conditions are met if–

(a) within the [relevant period] the earlier trade mark has been put to genuine use in the United Kingdom by the proprietor or with his consent in relation to the goods or services for which it is registered, or

(b) the earlier trade mark has not been so used, but there are proper reasons for non-use.

(4) For these purposes–

(a) use of a trade mark includes use in a form [(the "variant form")] differing in elements which do not alter the distinctive character of the mark in the form in which it was registered [(regardless of whether or not the trade mark in the variant form is also registered in the name of the proprietor)], and

(b) use in the United Kingdom includes affixing the trade mark to goods or to the packaging of goods in the United Kingdom solely for export purposes.

(5) […]

[(5A) […]]

(6) Where an earlier trade mark satisfies the use conditions in respect of some only of the goods or services for which it is registered, it shall be treated for the purposes of this section as if it were registered only in respect of those goods or services.

(7) Nothing in this section affects–

(a) the refusal of registration on the grounds mentioned in section 3 (absolute grounds for refusal) or section 5(4)(relative grounds of refusal on the basis of an earlier right), or

(b) the making of an application for a declaration of invalidity under section 47(2) (application on relative grounds where no consent to registration).]

**Raising of relative grounds in case of honest concurrent use.**

**7.**—(1) This section applies where on an application for the registration of a trade mark it appears to the registrar—

(a) that there is an earlier trade mark in relation to which the conditions set out in section 5(1), (2) or (3) obtain, or

(b) that there is an earlier right in relation to which the condition set out in section 5(4) is satisfied,

but the applicant shows to the satisfaction of the registrar that there has been honest concurrent use of the trade mark for which registration is sought.

(2) In that case the registrar shall not refuse the application by reason of the earlier trade mark or other earlier right unless objection on that ground is raised in opposition proceedings by the proprietor of that earlier trade mark or other earlier right.

(3) For the purposes of this section "honest concurrent use" means such use in the United Kingdom, by the applicant or with his consent, as would formerly have amounted to honest concurrent use for the purposes of section 12(2) of the Trade Marks Act 1938.

(4) Nothing in this section affects—

(a) the refusal of registration on the grounds mentioned in section 3 (absolute grounds for refusal), or

(b) the making of an application for a declaration of invalidity under section 47(2) (application on relative grounds where no consent to registration).

(5) This section does not apply when there is an order in force under section 8 below.

**Power to require that relative grounds be raised in opposition proceedings.**

**8.**—(1) The Secretary of State may by order provide that in any case a trade mark shall not be refused registration on a ground mentioned in section 5 (relative grounds for refusal) unless objection on that ground is raised in opposition proceedings by the proprietor of the earlier trade mark or other earlier right.

(2) The order may make such consequential provision as appears to the Secretary of State appropriate—

(a) with respect to the carrying out by the registrar of searches of earlier trade marks, and

(b) as to the persons by whom an application for a declaration of invalidity may be made on the grounds specified in section 47(2) (relative grounds).

(3) An order making such provision as is mentioned in subsection (2)(a) may direct that so much of section 37 (examination of application) as requires a search to be carried out shall cease to have effect.

(4) An order making such provision as is mentioned in subsection (2)(b) may provide that so much of section 47(3) as provides that any person may make an application for a declaration of invalidity shall have effect subject to the provisions of the order.

(5) An order under this section shall be made by statutory instrument, and no order shall be made unless a draft of it has been laid before and approved by a resolution of each House of Parliament. No such draft of an order making such provision as is mentioned in subsection (1) shall be laid before Parliament until after the end of the period of ten years beginning with the day on which applications for

Community trade marks may first be filed in pursuance of [Council Regulation (EC) No 40/94 of 20th December 1993 on the Community trade mark].

(6) An order under this section may contain such transitional provisions as appear to the Secretary of State to be appropriate.

*Effects of registered trade mark*

**Rights conferred by registered trade mark.**

**9.**—(1) The proprietor of a registered trade mark has exclusive rights in the trade mark which are infringed by use of the trade mark in the United Kingdom without his consent.

The acts amounting to infringement, if done without the consent of the proprietor, are specified in [subsections (1) to (3) of] section 10.

[(1A) See subsection (3B) of section 10 for provision about certain other acts amounting to infringement of a registered trade mark.

(1B) Subsection (1) is without prejudice to the rights of proprietors acquired before the date of filing of the application for registration or (where applicable) the date of the priority claimed in respect of that application.]

(2) References in this Act to the infringement of a registered trade mark are to any [...] infringement of the rights of the proprietor [such as is mentioned in subsection (1) or (1A)].

(3) The rights of the proprietor have effect from the date of registration (which in accordance with section 40(3) is the date of filing of the application for registration):

Provided that—

(a) no infringement proceedings may be begun before the date on which the trade mark is in fact registered; and

(b) no offence under section 92 (unauthorised use of trade mark, &c. in relation to goods) is committed by anything done before the date of publication of the registration.

**Infringement of registered trade mark.**

**10.**—(1) A person infringes a registered trade mark if he uses in the course of trade a sign which is identical with the trade mark in relation to goods or services which are identical with those for which it is registered.

(2) A person infringes a registered trade mark if he uses in the course of trade a sign where because—

(a) the sign is identical with the trade mark and is used in relation to goods or services similar to those for which the trade mark is registered, or

(b) the sign is similar to the trade mark and is used in relation to goods or services identical with or similar to those for which the trade mark is registered,

there exists a likelihood of confusion on the part of the public, which includes the likelihood of association with the trade mark.

(3) A person infringes a registered trade mark if he uses in the course of trade [, in relation to goods or services,] a sign which—

(a) is identical with or similar to the trade mark, [...]

(b) [...]

where the trade mark has a reputation in the United Kingdom and the use of the sign, being without due cause, takes unfair advantage of, or is detrimental to, the distinctive character or the repute of the trade mark.

[(3A) Subsection (3) applies irrespective of whether the goods and services in relation to which the sign is used are identical with, similar to or not similar to those for which the trade mark is registered.

(3B) Where the risk exists that the packaging, labels, tags, security or authenticity features or devices, or any other means to which the trade mark is affixed could be used in relation to goods or services and that use would constitute an infringement of the rights of the proprietor of the trade mark, a person infringes a registered trade mark if the person carries out in the course of trade any of the following acts—

(a) affixing a sign identical with, or similar to, the trade mark on packaging, labels, tags, security or authenticity features or devices, or any other means to which the mark may be affixed; or

(b) offering or placing on the market, or stocking for those purposes, or importing or exporting, packaging, labels, tags, security or authenticity features or devices, or any other means to which the mark is affixed.]

(4) For the purposes of this section a person uses a sign if, in particular, he—

(a) affixes it to goods or the packaging thereof;

(b) offers or exposes goods for sale, puts them on the market or stocks them for those purposes under the sign, or offers or supplies services under the sign;

(c) imports or exports goods under the sign; […]

[(ca) uses the sign as a trade or company name or part of a trade or company name;]

(d) uses the sign on business papers or in advertising [; [and]]

(e) uses the sign in comparative advertising in a manner that is contrary to the Business Protection from Misleading Marketing Regulations 2008.

(5) […]

(6) […]

[**Right to prevent goods entering the UK without being released for free circulation**

**10A.**—(1) The proprietor of a registered trade mark is entitled to prevent third parties from bringing goods into the United Kingdom in the course of trade without being released for free circulation if they are goods for which the trade mark is registered which—

(a) come from outside the customs territory of the [United Kingdom]; and

(b) bear without authorisation a sign which is identical with the trade mark or cannot be distinguished in its essential aspects from the trade mark.

(2) In subsection (1) the reference to goods for which the trade mark is registered includes a reference to the packaging of goods for which the trade mark is registered.

(3) Subsection (1) is without prejudice to the rights of proprietors acquired before the date of application for registration of the trade mark, or (where applicable) the date of the priority claimed in respect of that application.

(4) The entitlement of the proprietor under subsection (1) is to lapse if—

(a) proceedings are initiated in accordance with the European Customs Enforcement Regulation to determine whether the trade mark has been infringed; and

(b) during those proceedings evidence is provided by the declarant or the holder of the goods that the proprietor of the trade mark is not entitled to prohibit the placing of the goods on the market in the country of final destination.

(5) References in this Act to the "European Customs Enforcement Regulation" are references to Regulation (EU) No 608/2013 of the European Parliament and of the Council of 12 June 2013 concerning customs enforcement of intellectual property rights [as amended from time to time].]

[**Prohibition on the use of a trade mark registered in the name of an agent or representative**

**10B.**—(1) Subsection (2) applies where a trade mark is registered in the name of an agent or representative of a person ("P") who is the proprietor of the trade mark, without P's consent.

(2) Unless the agent or representative justifies the action mentioned in subsection (1), P may do either or both of the following—

(a) prevent the use of the trade mark by the agent or representative (notwithstanding the rights conferred by this Act in relation to a registered trade mark);

(b) apply for the rectification of the register so as to substitute P's name as the proprietor of the registered trade mark.]

**Limits on effect of registered trade mark.**

**11.**—(1) A registered trade mark is not infringed by the use of [a later registered trade mark where that later registered trade mark would not be declared invalid pursuant to section 47(2A) or (2G) or section 48(1)].

[(1A) [...].

(1B) Where subsection (1) [...] applies, the later registered trade mark is not infringed by the use of the earlier trade mark even though the earlier trade mark may no longer be invoked against the later registered trade mark.]

(2) A registered trade mark is not infringed by—

(a) the use by [an individual]of his own name or address,

(b) the use of [signs or indications which are not distinctive or which concern]the kind, quality, quantity, intended purpose, value, geographical origin, the time of production of goods or of rendering of services, or other characteristics of goods or services, or

(c) the use of the trade mark [for the purpose of identifying or referring to goods or services as those of the proprietor of that trade mark, in particular where that use]is necessary to indicate the intended purpose of a product or service (in particular, as accessories or spare parts),

provided the use is in accordance with honest practices in industrial or commercial matters.

(3) A registered trade mark is not infringed by the use in the course of trade in a particular locality of an earlier right which applies only in that locality.

For this purpose an "earlier right" means an unregistered trade mark or other sign continuously used in relation to goods or services by a person or a predecessor in title of his from a date prior to whichever is the earlier of—

(a) the use of the first-mentioned trade mark in relation to those goods or services by the proprietor or a predecessor in title of his, or

(b) the registration of the first-mentioned trade mark in respect of those goods or services in the name of the proprietor or a predecessor in title of his;

and an earlier right shall be regarded as applying in a locality if, or to the extent that, its use in that locality is protected by virtue of any rule of law (in particular, the law of passing off).

**[Non-use as defence in infringement proceedings**

**11A.**—(1) The proprietor of a trade mark is entitled to prohibit the use of a sign only to the extent that the registration of the trade mark is not liable to be revoked pursuant to section 46(1)(a) or (b) (revocation on basis of non-use) at the date the action for infringement is brought.

(2) Subsection (3) applies in relation to an action for infringement of a registered trade mark where the registration procedure for the trade mark was completed before the start of the period of five years ending with the date the action is brought.

(3) If the defendant so requests, the proprietor of the trade mark must furnish proof—

(a) that during the five-year period preceding the date the action for infringement is brought, the trade mark has been put to genuine use in the United Kingdom by or with the consent of the proprietor in relation to the goods and services for which it is registered and which are cited as justification for the action, or

(b) that there are proper reasons for non-use.

(4) Nothing in subsections (2) and (3) overrides any provision of section 46, as applied by subsection (1) (including the words from "Provided that" to the end of subsection (3)).]

**Exhaustion of rights conferred by registered trade mark.**

**12.**—(1) A registered trade mark is not infringed by the use of the trade mark in relation to goods which have been put on the market in [the United Kingdom or] the European Economic Area under that trade mark by the proprietor or with his consent.

(2) Subsection (1) does not apply where there exist legitimate reasons for the proprietor to oppose further dealings in the goods (in particular, where the condition of the goods has been changed or impaired after they have been put on the market).

**Registration subject to disclaimer or limitation.**

**13.**—(1) An applicant for registration of a trade mark, or the proprietor of a registered trade mark, may—

(a) disclaim any right to the exclusive use of any specified element of the trade mark, or

(b) agree that the rights conferred by the registration shall be subject to a specified territorial or other limitation;

and where the registration of a trade mark is subject to a disclaimer or limitation, the rights conferred by section 9 (rights conferred by registered trade mark) are restricted accordingly.

(2) Provision shall be made by rules as to the publication and entry in the register of a disclaimer or limitation.

*Infringement proceedings*

**Action for infringement.**

**14.**—(1) An infringement of a registered trade mark is actionable by the proprietor of the trade mark.

(2) In an action for infringement all such relief by way of damages, injunctions, accounts or otherwise is available to him as is available in respect of the infringement of any other property right.

**Order for erasure &c. of offending sign.**

**15.**—(1) Where a person is found to have infringed a registered trade mark, the court may make an order requiring him—

(a) to cause the offending sign to be erased, removed or obliterated from any infringing goods, material or articles in his possession, custody or control, or

(b) if it is not reasonably practicable for the offending sign to be erased, removed or obliterated, to secure the destruction of the infringing goods, material or articles in question.

(2) If an order under subsection (1) is not complied with, or it appears to the court likely that such an order would not be complied with, the court may order that the infringing goods, material or articles be delivered to such person as the court may direct for erasure, removal or obliteration of the sign, or for destruction, as the case may be.

**Order for delivery up of infringing goods, material or articles.**

**16.**—(1) The proprietor of a registered trade mark may apply to the court for an order for the delivery up to him, or such other person as the court may direct, of any infringing goods, material or articles which a person has in his possession, custody or control in the course of a business.

(2) An application shall not be made after the end of the period specified in section 18 (period after which remedy of delivery up not available), and no order shall be made unless the court also makes, or it appears to the court that there are grounds for making, an order under section 19 (order as to disposal of infringing goods, &c.).

(3) A person to whom any infringing goods, material or articles are delivered up in pursuance of an order under this section shall, if an order under section 19 is not made, retain them pending the making of an order, or the decision not to make an order, under that section.

(4) Nothing in this section affects any other power of the court.

**Meaning of "infringing goods, material or articles".**

**17.**—(1) In this Act the expressions "infringing goods", "infringing material" and "infringing articles" shall be construed as follows

(2) Goods are "infringing goods", in relation to a registered trade mark, if they or their packaging bear a sign identical or similar to that mark and—

(a) the application of the sign to the goods or their packaging was an infringement of the registered trade mark, or

(b) the goods are proposed to be imported into the United Kingdom and the application of the sign in the United Kingdom to them or their packaging would be an infringement of the registered trade mark, or

(c) the sign has otherwise been used in relation to the goods in such a way as to infringe the registered trade mark.

(3) Nothing in subsection (2) shall be construed as affecting the importation of goods which may lawfully be imported into the United Kingdom by virtue of [anything which forms part of retained EU law as a result of section 3 or 4 of the European Union (Withdrawal) Act 2018].

(4) Material is "infringing material", in relation to a registered trade mark if it bears a sign identical or similar to that mark and either—

(a) it is used for labelling or packaging goods, as a business paper, or for advertising goods or services, in such a way as to infringe the registered trade mark, or

(b) it is intended to be so used and such use would infringe the registered trade mark.

(5) "Infringing articles", in relation to a registered trade mark, means articles—

(a) which are specifically designed or adapted for making copies of a sign identical or similar to that mark, and

(b) which a person has in his possession, custody or control, knowing or having reason to believe that they have been or are to be used to produce infringing goods or material.

**Period after which remedy of delivery up not available.**

**18.**—(1) An application for an order under section 16 (order for delivery up of infringing goods, material or articles) may not be made after the end of the period of six years from—

(a) in the case of infringing goods, the date on which the trade mark was applied to the goods or their packaging,

(b) in the case of infringing material, the date on which the trade mark was applied to the material, or

(c) in the case of infringing articles, the date on which they were made,

except as mentioned in the following provisions.

(2) If during the whole or part of that period the proprietor of the registered trade mark—

(a) is under a disability, or

(b) is prevented by fraud or concealment from discovering the facts entitling him to apply for an order.

an application may be made at any time before the end of the period of six years from the date on which he ceased to be under a disability or, as the case may be, could with reasonable diligence have discovered those facts.

(3) In subsection (2) "disability"—

(a) in England and Wales, has the same meaning as in the Limitation Act 1980;

(b) in Scotland, means legal disability within the meaning of the Prescription and Limitation (Scotland) Act 1973,

(c) in Northern Ireland, has the same meaning as in the Limitation (Northern Ireland) Order 1989.

**Order as to disposal of infringing goods, material or articles.**

**19.**—(1) Where infringing goods, material or articles have been delivered up in pursuance of an order under section 16, an application may be made to the court—

(a) for an order that they be destroyed or forfeited to such person as the court may think fit, or
(b) for a decision that no such order should be made.

(2) In considering what order (if any) should be made, the court shall consider whether other remedies available in an action for infringement of the registered trade mark would be adequate to compensate the proprietor and any licensee and protect their interests.

(3) Provision shall be made by rules of court as to the service of notice on persons having an interest in the goods, material or articles, and any such person is entitled—
(a) to appear in proceedings for an order under this section, whether or not he was served with notice, and
(b) to appeal against any order made, whether or not he appeared;
and an order shall not take effect until the end of the period within which notice of an appeal may be given or, if before the end of that period notice of appeal is duly given, until the final determination or abandonment of the proceedings on the appeal.

(4) Where there is more than one person interested in the goods, material or articles, the court shall make such order as it thinks just.

(5) If the court decides that no order should be made under this section, the person in whose possession, custody or control the goods, material or articles were before being delivered up is entitled to their return.

(6) References in this section to a person having an interest in goods, material or articles include any person in whose favour an order could be made [...]
[(a) under this section [...];
(b) under section 24D of the Registered Designs Act 1949;
(c) under section 114, 204 or 231 of the Copyright, Designs and Patents Act 1988; or
(d) under regulation 1C of the Community Design Regulations 2005 (SI 2005/2339).]

**Jurisdiction of sheriff court or county court in Northern Ireland.**

**20.**— Proceedings for an order under section 16 (order for delivery up of infringing goods, material or articles) or section 19 (order as to disposal of infringing goods, &c.) may be brought—
(a) in the sheriff court in Scotland, or
(b) in a county court in Northern Ireland.
This does not affect the jurisdiction of the Court of Session or the High Court in Northern Ireland.

*Unjustified threats*

[**Threats of infringement proceedings.**

**21.**—(1) A communication contains a "threat of infringement proceedings" if a reasonable person in the position of a recipient would understand fom the communication that—
(a) a registered trade mark exists, and
(b) a person intends to bring proceedings (whether in a court in the United Kingdom or elsewhere) against another person for infringement of the registered trade mark by—

(i) an act done in the United Kingdom, or

(ii) an act which, if done, would be done in the United Kingdom.

(2) References in this section and in section 21C to a "recipient" include, in the case of a communication directed to the public or a section of the public, references to a person to whom the communication is directed.

(a) a declaration that the threats are unjustifiable,

(b) an injunction against the continuance of the threats,

(c) damages in respect of any loss he has sustained by the threats;

and the plaintiff is entitled to such relief unless the defendant shows that the acts in respect of which proceedings were threatened constitute (or if done would constitute) an infringement of the registered trade mark concerned.

(3) If that is shown by the defendant, the plaintiff is nevertheless entitled to relief if he shows that the registration of the trade mark is invalid or liable to be revoked in a relevant respect.

(4) The mere notification that a trade mark is registered, or that an application for registration has been made, does not constitute a threat of proceedings for the purposes of this section

**Actionable threats.**

**21A.**—(1) Subject to subsections (2) to (6), a threat of infringement proceedings made by any person is actionable by any person aggrieved by the threat.

(2) A threat of infringement proceedings is not actionable if the infringement is alleged to consist of—

(a) applying, or causing another person to apply, a sign to goods or their packaging,

(b) importing, for disposal, goods to which, or to the packaging of which, a sign has been applied, or

(c) supplying services under a sign.

(3) A threat of infringement proceedings is not actionable if the infringement is alleged to consist of an act which, if done, would constitute an infringement of a kind mentioned in subsection (2)(a), (b) or (c).

(4) A threat of infringement proceedings is not actionable if the threat—

(a) is made to a person who has done, or intends to do, an act mentioned in subsection (2)(a) or (b) in relation to goods or their packaging, and

(b) is a threat of proceedings for an infringement alleged to consist of doing anything else in relation to those goods or their packaging.

(5) A threat of infringement proceedings is not actionable if the threat—

(a) is made to a person who has done, or intends to do, an act mentioned in subsection (2)(c) in relation to services, and

(b) is a threat of proceedings for an infringement alleged to consist of doing anything else in relation to those services.

(6) A threat of infringement proceedings which is not an express threat is not actionable if it is contained in a permitted communication.

(7) In sections 21C and 21D "an actionable threat" means a threat of infringement proceedings that is actionable in accordance withi this section.

**Permitted communications.**

**21B.**—(1) For the purposes of section 21A(6), a communication containing a threat of infringement proceedings is a "permitted communication" if—

(a) the communication, so far as it contains information that relates to the threat, is made for a permitted purpose;

(b) all of the information that relates to the threat is information that—
(i) is necessary for that purpose (see subsection (5)(a) to (c) for some examples of necessary information), and
(ii) the person making the communication reasonably believes is true.

(2) Each of the following is a "permitted purpose"—
(a) giving notice that a registered trade mark exists;
(b) discovering whether, or by whom, a registered trade mark has been infringed by an act mentioned in section 21A(2)(a), (b) or (c);
(c) giving notice that a person has a right in or under a registered trade mark, where another person's awareness of the right is relevant to any proceedings that may be brought in respect of the registered trade mark.

(3) The court may, having regard to the nature of the purposes listed in subsection (2)(a) to (c), treat any other purpose as a "permitted purpose" if it considers that it is in the interests of justice to do so.

(4) But the following may not be treated as a "permitted purpose"—
(a) requesting a person to cease using, in the course of trade, a sign in relation to goods goods or services,
(b) requesting a person to deliver up or destroy goods, or
(c) requesting a person to give an undertaking relating to the use of a sign in relation to goods or services.

(5) If any of the following information is included in a communication made for a permitted purpose, it is information that is "necessary for that purpose" (see subsection (1)(b)(i))—
(a) a statement that a registered trade mark exists and is in force or that an application for the registration of a trade mark has been made;
(b) details of the registered trade mark, or of a right in or under the registered trade mark, which—
(i) are accurate in all material respects, and
(ii) are not misleading in any material respect; and
(c) information enabling the identification of the goods or their packaging, or the services, in relation to which it is alleged that the use of a sign constitutes an infringement of the registered trade mark.

**Remedies and defences.**

**21C.**—(1) Proceedings in respect of an actionable threat may be brought against the person who made th threat for—
(a) a declaration that the threat is unjustified;
(b) an injunction against the continuance of the threat;
(c) damages in respect of any loss sustained by the aggrieved person by reason of the threat.

(2) It is a defence for the person who made the threat to show that the act in respect of which proceedings were threatened constitutes (or if done would constitute) an infringement of the registered trade mark.

(3) It is a defence for the person who made the threat to show—
(a) that, despite having taken reasonable steps, the person has not identified anyone who has done an act mentioned in section 21A(2)(a), (b) or (c) in relation to the goods or their packaging or the services which are the subject of the threat, and

(b) that the person notified the recipient, before or at the time of making the threat, of the steps taken.

**Professional advisers.**

**21D.**—(1) Proceedings in respect of an actionable threat may not be brought against a professional adviser (or any person vicariously liable for the actions of that professional adviser) if the conditions in subsection (3) are met.

(2) In this section "professional adviser" means a person who, in relation to the making of the communication containing the threat—

(a) is acting in a professional capacity in providing legal services or the services of a trade mark attorney or a patent attorney, and

(b) is regulated in the provision of legal services, or the services of a trade mark attorney or a patent attorney, by one or more regulatory bodies (whether through membership of a regulatory body, the issue of a licence to practise or any other means).

(3) The conditions are that—

(a) in making the communication the professional adviser is acting on the instructions of another person, and

(b) when the communication is made the professional adviser identifies the person on whose instructions the adviser is acting.

(4) This section does not affect any liability of the person on whose instructions the professional adviser is acting.

(5) It is for a person asserting that subsection (1) applies to prove (if required) that at the material time—

(a) the person concerned was acting as a professional adviser, and

(b) the conditions in subsection (3) were met.

**Supplementary: pending registration.**

**21E.**—(1) In sections 21 and 21B references to a registered trade mark include references to a trade mark in respect of which an application for registration has been published under section 38.

(2) Where the threat of infringement proceedings is made after an application for registration has been published (but before registration) the reference in section 21C(2) to "the registered trade mark" is to be treated as a reference to the trade mark registered in pursuance of that application.

**Supplementary: proceedings for delivery up etc.**

**21F.**— In section 21(1)(b) the reference to proceedings for infringement of a registered trade mark includes a reference to—

(a) proceedings for an order under section 16 (order for delivery up of infringing goods, material or articles), and

(b) proceedings for an order under section 19 (order as to disposal of infringing goods, material or articles).]

*Registered trade mark as object of property*

**Nature of registered trade mark.**

**22.**— A registered trade mark is personal property (in Scotland, incorporeal moveable property).

**Co-ownership of registered trade mark.**

**23.**—(1) Where a registered trade mark is granted to two or more persons jointly, each of them is entitled, subject to an agreement to the contrary, to an equal undivided share in the registered trade mark.

(2) The following provisions apply where two or more persons are co-proprietors of a registered trade mark, by virtue of subsection (1) or otherwise.

(3) Subject to any agreement to the contrary, each co-proprietor is entitled, by himself or his agents, to do for his own benefit and without the consent of or the need to account to the other or others, any act which would otherwise amount to an infringement of the registered trade mark

(4) One co-proprietor may not without the consent of the other or others—

- (a) grant a licence to use the registered trade mark, or
- (b) assign or charge his share in the registered trade mark (or, in Scotland, cause or permit security to be granted over it).

(5) Infringement proceedings may be brought by any co-proprietor, but he may not, without the leave of the court, proceed with the action unless the other, or each of the others, is either joined as a plaintiff or added as a defendant.

A co-proprietor who is thus added as a defendant shall not be made liable for any costs in the action unless he takes part in the proceedings.

Nothing in this subsection affects the granting of interlocutory relief on the application of a single co-proprietor.

(6) Nothing in this section affects the mutual rights and obligations of trustees or personal representatives, or their rights and obligations as such.

**Assignment, &c. of registered trade mark.**

**24.**—(1) A registered trade mark is transmissible by assignment, testamentary disposition or operation of law in the same way as other personal or moveable property.

It is so transmissible either in connection with the goodwill of a business or independently.

[(1A) A contractual obligation to transfer a business is to be taken to include an obligation to transfer any registered trade mark, except where there is agreement to the contrary or it is clear in all the circumstances that this presumption should not apply.]

(2) An assignment or other transmission of a registered trade mark may be partial, that is, limited so as to apply—

- (a) in relation to some but not all of the goods or services for which the trade mark is registered, or
- (b) in relation to use of the trade mark in a particular manner or a particular locality.

(3) An assignment of a registered trade mark, or an assent relating to a registered trade mark, is not effective unless it is in writing signed by or on behalf of the assignor or, as the case may be, a personal representative.

Except in Scotland, this requirement may be satisfied in a case where the assignor or personal representative is a body corporate by the affixing of its seal.

(4) The above provisions apply to assignment by way of security as in relation to any other assignment.

(5) A registered trade mark may be the subject of a charge (in Scotland, security) in the same way as other personal or moveable property.

(6) Nothing in this Act shall be construed as affecting the assignment or other transmission of an unregistered trade mark as part of the goodwill of a business.

**Registration of transactions affecting registered trade mark.**

**25.**—(1) On application being made to the registrar by—

(a) a person claiming to be entitled to an interest in or under a registered trade mark by virtue of a registrable transaction, or

(b) any other person claiming to be affected by such a transaction,

the prescribed particulars of the transaction shall be entered in the register.

(2) The following are registrable transactions—

(a) an assignment of a registered trade mark or any right in it;

(b) the grant of a licence under a registered trade mark;

(c) the granting of any security interest (whether fixed or floating) over a registered trade mark or any right in or under it;

(d) the making by personal representatives of an assent in relation to a registered trade mark or any right in or under it;

(e) an order of a court or other competent authority transferring a registered trade mark or any right in or under it.

(3) Until an application has been made for registration of the prescribed particulars of a registrable transaction—

(a) the transaction is ineffective as against a person acquiring a conflicting interest in or under the registered trade mark in ignorance of it, and

(b) a person claiming to be a licensee by virtue of the transaction does not have the protection of section 30 or 31 (rights and remedies of licensee in relation to infringement).

(4) Where a person becomes the proprietor or a licensee of a registered trade mark by virtue of a registrable transaction [and the mark is infringed before the prescribed particulars of the transaction are registered, in proceedings for such an infringement, the court shall not award him costs unless—

(a) an application for registration of the prescribed particulars of the transaction is made before the end of the period of six months beginning with its date, or

(b) the court is satisfied that it was not practicable for such an application to be made before the end of that period and that an application was made as soon as practicable thereafter.]

(5) Provision may be made by rules as to—

(a) the amendment of registered particulars relating to a licence so as to reflect any alteration of the terms of the licence, and

(b) the removal of such particulars from the register—

(i) where it appears from the registered particulars that the licence was granted for a fixed period and that period has expired, or

(ii) where no such period is indicated and, after such period as may be prescribed, the registrar has notified the parties of his intention to remove the particulars from the register.

(6) Provision may also be made by rules as to the amendment or removal from the register of particulars relating to a security interest on the application of, or with the consent of, the person entitled to the benefit of that interest.

**Trusts and equities.**

**26.**—(1) No notice of any trust (express, implied or constructive) shall be entered in the register; and the registrar shall not be affected by any such notice.

(2) Subject to the provisions of this Act, equities (in Scotland, rights) in respect of a registered trade mark may be enforced in like manner as in respect of other personal or moveable property.

**Application for registration of trade mark as an object of property.**

**27.**—(1) The provisions of sections 22 to 26 (which relate to a registered trade mark as an object of property) [and sections 28 to 31 (which relate to licensing)] apply, with the necessary modifications, in relation to an application for the registration of a trade mark as in relation to a registered trade mark.

(2) In section 23 (co-ownership of registered trade mark) as it applies in relation to an application for registration the reference in subsection (1) to the granting of the registration shall be construed as a reference to the making of the application.

(3) In section 25 (registration of transactions affecting registered trade marks) as it applies in relation to a transaction affecting an application for the registration of a trade mark, the references to the entry of particulars in the register, and to the making of an application to register particulars, shall be construed as references to the giving of notice to the registrar of those particulars.

*Licensing*

**Licensing of registered trade mark.**

**28.**—(1) A licence to use a registered trade mark may be general or limited. A limited licence may, in particular, apply—

(a) in relation to some but not all of the goods or services for which the trade mark is registered, or

(b) in relation to use of the trade mark in a particular manner or a particular locality.

(2) A licence is not effective unless it is in writing signed by or on behalf of the grantor. Except in Scotland, this requirement may be satisfied in a case where the grantor is a body corporate by the affixing of its seal.

(3) Unless the licence provides otherwise, it is binding on a successor in title to the grantor's interest. References in this Act to doing anything with, or without, the consent of the proprietor of a registered trade mark shall be construed accordingly.

(4) Where the licence so provides, a sub-licence may be granted by the licensee; and references in this Act to a licence or licensee include a sub-licence or sub-licensee.

(5) The proprietor of a registered trade mark may invoke the rights conferred by that trade mark against a licensee who contravenes any provision in the licence with regard to—

(a) its duration,

(b) the form covered by the registration in which the trade mark may be used,

(c) the scope of the goods or services for which the licence is granted,

(d) the territory in which the trade mark may be affixed, or

(e) the quality of the goods manufactured or of the services provided by the licensee.

**Exclusive licences.**

**29.**—(1) In this Act an "exclusive licence" means a licence (whether general or limited) authorising the licensee to the exclusion of all other persons, including the person granting the licence, to use a registered trade mark in the manner authorised by the licence.

The expression "exclusive licensee"shall be construed accordingly

(2) An exclusive licensee has the same rights against a successor in title who is bound by the licence as he has against the person granting the licence.

**General provisions as to rights of licensees in case of infringement.**

**30.**—(1) This section has effect with respect to the rights of a licensee in relation to infringement of a registered trade mark.

The provisions of this section do not apply where or to the extent that, by virtue of section 31(1) below (exclusive licensee having rights and remedies of assignee), the licensee has a right to bring proceedings in his own name.

[(1A) Except so far as the licence provides otherwise a licensee may only bring proceedings for infringement of the registered trade mark with the consent of the proprietor (but see subsections (2) and (3)).]

(2) [An exclusive licensee may] call on the proprietor of the registered trade mark to take infringement proceedings in respect of any matter which affects his interests.

(3) If the proprietor[mentioned in subsection (2)]—

(a) refuses to do so, or

(b) fails to do so within two months after being called upon.

the [exclusive] licensee may bring the proceedings in his own name as if he were the proprietor.

(4) Where infringement proceedings are brought by a licensee by virtue of this section [or with the consent of the proprietor or pursuant to the licence] the licensee may not, without the leave of the court, proceed with the action unless the proprietor is either joined as a plaintiff or added as a defendant.

This does not affect the granting of interlocutory relief on an application by a licensee alone.

(5) A proprietor who is added as a defendant as mentioned in subsection (4) shall not be made liable for any costs in the action unless he takes part in the proceedings.

(6) In infringement proceedings brought by the proprietor of a registered trade mark any loss suffered or likely to be suffered by licensees shall be taken into account; and the court may give such directions as it thinks fit as to the extent to which the plaintiff is to hold the proceeds of any pecuniary remedy on behalf of licensees.

[(6A) Where the proprietor of a registered trade mark brings infringement proceedings, a licensee who has suffered loss is entitled to intervene in the proceedings for the purpose of obtaining compensation for that loss.]

(7) The provisions of this section apply in relation to an exclusive licensee if or to the extent that he has, by virtue of section 31(1), the rights and remedies of an assignee as if he were the proprietor of the registered trade mark.

**Exclusive licensee having rights and remedies of assignee.**

**31.**—(1) An exclusive licence may provide that the licensee shall have, to such extent as may be provided by the licence, the same rights and remedies in respect of matters occurring after the grant of the licence as if the licence had been an assignment.

Where or to the extent that such provision is made, the licensee is entitled, subject to the provisions of the licence and to the following provisions of this section, to bring infringement proceedings, against any person other than the proprietor, in his own name.

(2) Any such rights and remedies of an exclusive licensee are concurrent with those of the proprietor of the registered trade mark, and references to the proprietor of a registered trade mark in the provisions of this Act relating to infringement shall be construed accordingly.

(3) In an action brought by an exclusive licensee by virtue of this section a defendant may avail himself of any defence which would have been available to him if the action had been brought by the proprietor of the registered trade mark.

(4) Where proceedings for infringement of a registered trade mark brought by the proprietor or an exclusive licensee relate wholly or partly to an infringement in respect of which they have concurrent rights of action, the proprietor or, as the case may be, the exclusive licensee may not, without the leave of the court, proceed with the action unless the other is either joined as a plaintiff or added as a defendant.

This does not affect the granting of interlocutory relief on an application by a proprietor or exclusive licensee alone.

(5) A person who is added as a defendant as mentioned in subsection (4) shall not be made liable for any costs in the action unless he takes part in the proceedings.

(6) Where an action for infringement of a registered trade mark is brought which relates wholly or partly to an infringement in respect of which the proprietor and an exclusive licensee have or had concurrent rights of action—

- (a) the court shall in assessing damages take into account—
  - (i) the terms of the licence, and
  - (ii) any pecuniary remedy already awarded or available to either of them in respect of the infringement;
- (b) no account of profits shall be directed if an award of damages has been made, or an account of profits has been directed, in favour of the other of them in respect of the infringement; and
- (c) the court shall if an account of profits is directed apportion the profits between them as the court considers just, subject to any agreement between them.

The provisions of this subsection apply whether or not the proprietor and the exclusive licensee are both parties to the action, and if they are not both parties the court may give such directions as it thinks fit as to the extent to which the party to the proceedings is to hold the proceeds of any pecuniary remedy on behalf of the other.

(7) The proprietor of a registered trade mark shall notify any exclusive licensee who has a concurrent right of action before applying for an order under section 16 (order for delivery up), and the court may on the application of the licensee make such order under that section as it thinks fit having regard to the terms of the licence.

(8) The provisions of subsections (4) to (7) above have effect subject to any agreement to the contrary between the exclusive licensee and the proprietor.

*Application for registered trade mark*

**Application for registration.**

**32.**—(1) An application for registration of a trade mark shall be made to the registrar.

(2) The application shall contain—

(a) a request for registration of a trade mark,
(b) the name and address of the applicant,
(c) a statement of the goods or services in relation to which it is sought to register the trade mark, and
(d) a representation of the trade mark[, which is capable of being represented in the register in a manner which enables the registrar and other competent authorities and the public to determine the clear and precise subject matter of the protection afforded to the proprietor].

(3) The application shall state that the trade mark is being used, by the applicant or with his consent, in relation to those goods or services, or that he has a bona fide intention that it should be so used.

(4) The application shall be subject to the payment of the application fee and such class fees as may be appropriate

**Date of filing.**

**33.**—(1) The date of filing of an application for registration of a trade mark is the date on which documents containing everything required by section 32(2) are furnished to the registrar by the applicant.

If the documents are furnished on different days, the date of filing is the last of those days.

(2) References in this Act to the date of application for registration are to the date of filing of the application.

**Classification of trade marks.**

**34.**—(1) Goods and services shall be classified for the purposes of the registration of trade marks according to a prescribed system of classification.

(2) Any question arising as to the class within which any goods or services fall shall be determined by the registrar, whose decision shall be final.

*Priority*

**Claim to priority of Convention application.**

**35.**—(1) A person who has duly filed an application for protection of a trade mark in a Convention country (a "Convention application"), or his successor in title, has a right to priority, for the purposes of registering the same trade mark under this Act for some or all of the same goods or services, for a period of six months from the date of filing of the first such application.

(2) If the application for registration under this Act is made within that six-month period—

(a) the relevant date for the purposes of establishing which rights take precedence shall be the date of filing of the first Convention application, and
(b) the registrability of the trade mark shall not be affected by any use of the mark in the United Kingdom in the period between that date and the date of the application under this Act.

(3) Any filing which in a Convention country is equivalent to a regular national filing, under its domestic legislation or an international agreement, shall be treated as giving rise to the right of priority.

A "regular national filing" means a filing which is adequate to establish the date on which the application was filed in that country, whatever may be the subsequent fate of the application.

(4) A subsequent application concerning the same subject as the first Convention application, filed in the same Convention country, shall be considered the first Convention application (of which the filing date is the starting date of the period of priority), if at the time of the subsequent application—

(a) the previous application has been withdrawn, abandoned or refused, without having been laid open to public inspection and without leaving any rights outstanding, and

(b) it has not yet served as a basis for claiming a right of priority.

The previous application may not thereafter serve as a basis for claiming a right of priority.

(5) Provision may be made by rules as to the manner of claiming a right to priority on the basis of a Convention application.

(6) A right to priority arising as a result of a Convention application may be assigned or otherwise transmitted, either with the application or independently.

The reference in subsection (1) to the applicant's "successor in title" shall be construed accordingly.

**Claim to priority from other relevant overseas application.**

**36.**—(1) Her Majesty may by Order in Council make provision for conferring on a person who has duly filed an application for protection of a trade mark in—

(a) any of the Channel Islands or a colony, or

(b) a country or territory in relation to which Her Majesty's Government in the United Kingdom have entered into a treaty, convention, arrangement or engagement for the reciprocal protection of trade marks,

a right to priority, for the purpose of registering the same trade mark under this Act for some or all of the same goods or services, for a specified period from the date of filing of that application.

(2) An Order in Council under this section may make provision corresponding to that made by section 35 in relation to Convention countries or such other provision as appears to Her Majesty to be appropriate.

(3) A statutory instrument containing an Order in Council under this section shall be subject to annulment in pursuance of a resolution of either House of Parliament.

*Registration procedure*

**Examination of application.**

**37.**—(1) The registrar shall examine whether an application for registration of a trade mark satisfies the requirements of this Act (including any requirements imposed by rules)

(2) [...]

(3) If it appears to the registrar that the requirements for registration are not met, he shall inform the applicant and give him an opportunity, within such period as the registrar may specify, to make representations or to amend the application.

(4) If the applicant fails to satisfy the registrar that those requirements are met, or to amend the application so as to meet them, or fails to respond before the end of the specified period, the registrar shall refuse to accept the application.

(5) If it appears to the registrar that the requirements for registration are met, he shall accept the application.

**Publication, opposition proceedings and observations.**

**38.**—(1) When an application for registration has been accepted, the registrar shall cause the application to be published in the prescribed manner

(2) Any person may, within the prescribed time from the date of the publication of the application, give notice to the registrar of opposition to the registration.

The notice shall be given in writing in the prescribed manner, and shall include a statement of the grounds of opposition.

[(2A) Where a notice of opposition is filed on the basis of one or more earlier trade marks or other earlier rights—

(a) the rights (if plural) must all belong to the same proprietor;

(b) the notice may be filed on the basis of part, or the totality, of the goods or services in respect of which the earlier right is protected or applied for.

(2B) A notice of opposition may be directed against part or the totality of the goods or services in respect of which the contested mark is applied for.]

(3) Where an application has been published, any person may, at any time before the registration of the trade mark, make observations in writing to the registrar as to whether the trade mark should be registered; and the registrar shall inform the applicant of any such observations.

A person who makes observations does not thereby become a party to the proceedings on the application.

**Withdrawal, restriction or amendment of application.**

**39.**—(1) The applicant may at any time withdraw his application or restrict the goods or services covered by the application.

If the application has been published, the withdrawal or restriction shall also be published.

(2) In other respects, an application may be amended, at the request of the applicant, only by correcting—

(a) the name or address of the applicant,

(b) errors of wording or of copying, or

(c) obvious mistakes,

and then only where the correction does not substantially affect the identity of the trade mark or extend the goods or services covered by the application

(3) Provision shall be made by rules for the publication of any amendment which affects the representation of the trade mark, or the goods or services covered by the application, and for the making of objections by any person claiming to be affected by it.

**Registration.**

**40.**—(1) Where an application has been accepted and—

(a) no notice of opposition is given within the period referred to in section 38(2), or

(b) all opposition proceedings are withdrawn or decided in favour of the applicant,

the registrar shall register the trade mark, unless it appears to him having regard to matters coming to his notice [since the application was accepted that the registration requirements (other than those mentioned in section 5(1), (2) or (3)) were not met at that time.]

(2) A trade mark shall not be registered unless any fee prescribed for the registration is paid within the prescribed period.

If the fee is not paid within that period, the application shall be deemed to be withdrawn.

(3) A trade mark when registered shall be registered as of the date of filing of the application for registration, and that date shall be deemed for the purposes of this Act to be the date of registration.

(4) On the registration of a trade mark the registrar shall publish the registration in the prescribed manner and issue to the applicant a certificate of registration.

**Registration: supplementary provisions.**

**41.**—(1) Provision may be made by rules as to—

(a) the division of an application for the registration of a trade mark into several applications;

[(aa) the division of a registration of a trade mark into several registrations;]

(b) the merging of separate applications or registrations;

(c) the registration of a series of trade marks.

(2) A series of trade marks means a number of trade marks which resemble each other as to their material particulars and differ only as to matters of a non-distinctive character not substantially affecting the identity of the trade mark.

(3) Rules under this section may include provision as to—

(a) the circumstances in which, and conditions subject to which, division, merger or registration of a series is permitted, and

(b) the purposes for which an application [or registration] to which the rules apply is to be treated as a single application [or registration] and those for which it is to be treated as a number of separate applications [or registrations].

*Duration, renewal and alteration of registered trade mark*

**Duration of registration.**

**42.**—(1) A trade mark shall be registered for a period of ten years from the date of registration.

(2) Registration may be renewed in accordance with section 43 for further periods of ten years.

**Renewal of registration.**

**43.**—(1) The registration of a trade mark may be renewed at the request of the proprietor, subject to payment of a renewal fee.

(2) Provision shall be made by rules for the registrar to inform the proprietor of a registered trade mark, before the expiry of the registration, of the date of expiry and the manner in which the registration may be renewed.

(3) A request for renewal must be made, and the renewal fee paid, before the expiry of the registration.

Failing this, the request may be made and the fee paid within such further period (of not less than six months) as may be prescribed, in which case an additional renewal fee must also be paid within that period.

[(3A) If a request for renewal is made or the renewal fee is paid in respect of only some of the goods or services for which the trade mark is registered, the registration is to be renewed for those goods or services only.]

(4) Renewal shall take effect from the expiry of the previous registration.

(5) If the registration is not renewed in accordance with the above provisions, the registrar shall remove the trade mark from the register.

Provision may be made by rules for the restoration of the registration of a trade mark which has been removed from the register, subject to such condition (if any) as may be prescribed.

(6) The renewal or restoration of the registration of a trade mark shall be published in the prescribed manner.

**Alteration of registered trade mark.**

**44.**—(1) A registered trade mark shall not be altered in the register, during the period of registration or on renewal.

(2) Nevertheless, the registrar may, at the request of the proprietor, allow the alteration of a registered trade mark where the mark includes the proprietor's name or address and the alteration is limited to alteration of that name or address and does not substantially affect the identity of the mark.

(3) Provision shall be made by rules for the publication of any such alteration and the making of objections by any person claiming to be affected by it.

*Surrender, revocation and invalidity*

**Surrender of registered trade mark.**

**45.**—(1) A registered trade mark may be surrendered by the proprietor in respect of some or all of the goods or services for which it is registered.

(2) Provision may be made by rules—

(a) as to the manner and effect of a surrender, and

(b) for protecting the interests of other persons having a right in the registered trade mark.

**Revocation of registration.**

**46.**—(1) The registration of a trade mark may be revoked on any of the following grounds—

(a) that within the period of five years following the date of completion of the registration procedure it has not been put to genuine use in the United Kingdom, by the proprietor or with his consent, in relation to the goods or services for which it is registered, and there are no proper reasons for non-use;

(b) that such use has been suspended for an uninterrupted period of five years, and there are no proper reasons for non-use;

(c) that, in consequence of acts or inactivity of the proprietor, it has become the common name in the trade for a product or service for which it is registered;

(d) that in consequence of the use made of it by the proprietor or with his consent in relation to the goods or services for which it is registered, it is liable to mislead the public, particularly as to the nature, quality or geographical origin of those goods or services.

(2) For the purposes of subsection (1) use of a trade mark includes use in a

form[(the "variant form")] differing in elements which do not alter the distinctive character of the mark in the form in which it was registered[(regardless of whether or not the trade mark in the variant form is also registered in the name of the proprietor)], and use in the United Kingdom includes affixing the trade mark to goods or to the packaging of goods in the United Kingdom solely for export purposes.

(3) The registration of a trade mark shall not be revoked on the ground mentioned in subsection (1)(a) or (b) if such use as is referred to in that paragraph is commenced or resumed after the expiry of the five year period and before the application for revocation is made:

Provided that, any such commencement or resumption of use after the expiry of the five year period but within the period of three months before the making of the application shall be disregarded unless preparation for the commencement or resumption began before the proprietor became aware that the application might be made.

(4) An application for revocation may be made by any person, and may be made either to the registrar or to the court, except that—

(a) if proceedings concerning the trade mark in question are pending in the court, the application must be made to the court; and

(b) if in any other case the application is made to the registrar, he may at any stage of the proceedings refer the application to the court.

(5) Where grounds for revocation exist in respect of only some of the goods or services for which the trade mark is registered, revocation shall relate to those goods or services only.

(6) Where the registration of a trade mark is revoked to any extent, the rights of the proprietor shall be deemed to have ceased to that extent as from—

(a) the date of the application for revocation, or

(b) if the registrar or court is satisfied that the grounds for revocation existed at an earlier date, that date.

**Grounds for invalidity of registration.**

**47.**—(1) The registration of a trade mark may be declared invalid on the ground that the trade mark was registered in breach of section 3 or any of the provisions referred to in that section (absolute grounds for refusal of registration).

Where the trade mark was registered in breach of subsection (1)(b), (c) or (d) of that section, it shall not be declared invalid if, in consequence of the use which has been made of it, it has after registration acquired a distinctive character in relation to the goods or services for which it is registered.

(2) [Subject to subsections (2A) and (2G), the]registration of a trade mark may be declared invalid on the ground—

(a) that there is an earlier trade mark in relation to which the conditions set out in section 5(1), (2) or (3) obtain, or

(b) that there is an earlier right in relation to which the condition set out in section 5(4) is satisfied,

unless the proprietor of that earlier trade mark or other earlier right has consented to the registration.

[(2ZA) The registration of a trade mark may be declared invalid on the ground that the trade mark was registered in breach of section 5(6).]

[(2A) [The]registration of a trade mark may not be declared invalid on the ground that there is an earlier trade mark unless–

(a) the registration procedure for the earlier trade mark was completed within the period of five years ending with the date of the application for the declaration,

(b) the registration procedure for the earlier trade mark was not completed before that date, or

(c) the use conditions are met.

(2B) The use conditions are met if–

[(a) the earlier trade mark has been put to genuine use in the United Kingdom by the proprietor or with their consent in relation to the goods or services for which it is registered—

(i) within the period of 5 years ending with the date of application for the declaration, and

(ii) within the period of 5 years ending with the date of filing of the application for registration of the later trade mark or (where applicable) the date of the priority claimed in respect of that application where, at that date, the five year period within which the earlier trade mark should have been put to genuine use as provided in section 46(1)(a) has expired, or]

(b) it has not been so used, but there are proper reasons for non-use.

(2C) For these purposes–

(a) use of a trade mark includes use in a form [(the "variant form")] differing in elements which do not alter the distinctive character of the mark in the form in which it was registered [(regardless of whether or not the trade mark in the variant form is also registered in the name of the proprietor)], and

(b) use in the United Kingdom includes affixing the trade mark to goods or to the packaging of goods in the United Kingdom solely for export purposes.

(2D) [...].

[(2DA) [...]]

(2E) Where an earlier trade mark satisfies the use conditions in respect of some only of the goods or services for which it is registered, it shall be treated for the purposes of this section as if it were registered only in respect of those goods or services.]

[(2F) Subsection (2A) does not apply where the earlier trade mark is a trade mark within section 6(1)(c).]

[(2G) An application for a declaration of invalidity on the basis of an earlier trade mark must be refused if it would have been refused, for any of the reasons set out in subsection (2H), had the application for the declaration been made on the date of filing of the application for registration of the later trade mark or (where applicable) the date of the priority claimed in respect of that application.

(2H) The reasons referred to in subsection (2G) are—

(a) that on the date in question the earlier trade mark was liable to be declared invalid by virtue of section 3(1)(b), (c) or (d), (and had not yet acquired a distinctive character as mentioned in the words after paragraph (d) in section 3(1));

(b) that the application for a declaration of invalidity is based on section 5(2) and the earlier trade mark had not yet become sufficiently distinctive to support a finding of likelihood of confusion within the meaning of section 5(2);

(c) that the application for a declaration of invalidity is based on section 5(3)(a) and the earlier trade mark had not yet acquired a reputation within the meaning of section 5(3).]

(3) An application for a declaration of invalidity may be made by any person, and may be made either to the registrar or to the court, except that—

(a) if proceedings concerning the trade mark in question are pending in the court, the application must be made to the court; and

(b) if in any other case the application is made to the registrar, he may at any stage of the proceedings refer the application to the court.

(4) In the case of bad faith in the registration of a trade mark, the registrar himself may apply to the court for a declaration of the invalidity of the registration.

(5) Where the grounds of invalidity exist in respect of only some of the goods or services for which the trade mark is registered, the trade mark shall be declared invalid as regards those goods or services only.

[(5A) An application for a declaration of invalidity may be filed on the basis of one or more earlier trade marks or other earlier rights provided they all belong to the same proprietor.]

(6) Where the registration of a trade mark is declared invalid to any extent, the registration shall to that extent be deemed never to have been made:

Provided that this shall not affect transactions past and closed.

**Effect of acquiescence.**

**48.**—(1) Where the proprietor of an earlier trade mark or other earlier right has acquiesced for a continuous period of five years in the use of a registered trade mark in the United Kingdom, being aware of that use, there shall cease to be any entitlement on the basis of that earlier trade mark or other right—

(a) to apply for a declaration that the registration of the later trade mark is invalid, or

(b) to oppose the use of the later trade mark in relation to the goods or services in relation to which it has been so used.

unless the registration of the later trade mark was applied for in bad faith.

(2) Where subsection (1) applies, the proprietor of the later trade mark is not entitled to oppose the use of the earlier trade mark or, as the case may be, the exploitation of the earlier right, notwithstanding that the earlier trade mark or right may no longer be invoked against his later trade mark.

*Collective marks*

**Collective marks.**

**49.**—[(1) A collective mark is a mark which is described as such when it is applied for and is capable of distinguishing the goods and services of members of the association which is the proprietor of the mark from those of other undertakings.

(1A) The following may be registered as the proprietor of a collective mark—

(a) an association of manufacturers, producers, suppliers of services or traders which has the capacity in its own name to enter into contracts and to sue or be sued; and

(b) a legal person governed by public law.]

(2) The provisions of this Act apply to collective marks subject to the provisions of Schedule 1.

*Certification marks*

**Certification marks.**

**50.**—(1) A certification mark is a mark [which is described as such when the mark is applied for and indicates]that the goods or services in connection with which it is used are certified by the proprietor of the mark in respect of origin, material, mode of manufacture of goods or performance of services, quality, accuracy or other characteristics.

(2) The provisions of this Act apply to certification marks subject to the provisions of Schedule 2.

PART II -- [EUROPEAN UNION] TRADE MARKS AND INTERNATIONAL MATTERS

[*European Union*] *trade marks*

**[Meaning of "European Union trade mark".**

**51.**— In this Act—

"European Union trade mark" has the meaning given by Article 1(1) of the European Union Trade Mark Regulation; and

"the European Union Trade Mark Regulation" means [Regulation (EU) 2017/1001 of the European Parliament and of the Council of 14 June 2017 on the European Union Trade Mark[(as it had effect immediately before [IP completion day)].]]

**Power to make provision in connection with [European Union] Trade Mark Regulation.**

**52.**— […].

**Certain trade marks registered as European Union trade marks to be treated as registered trade marks**

**52A.** Schedule 2A makes provision for European Union trade marks (including certain expired and removed marks) to be treated as registered trade marks with effect from IP completion day and about certain applications for a European Union trade mark made before [IP completion day.]

(b) the conversion of a [European Union] trade mark, or an application for a [European Union] trade mark, into an application for registration under this Act;

(c) the designation of courts in the United Kingdom having jurisdiction over proceedings arising out of the [European Union] Trade Mark Regulation.

(2) Without prejudice to the generality of subsection (1), provision may be made by regulations under this section—

(a) applying in relation to a [European Union] trade mark the provisions of—

(i) sections 21 to 21F (unjustified threats);]

(ii) sections 89 to 91 (importation of infringing goods, material or articles); and

(iii) sections 92, 93, 95 and 96 (offences); and

(b) making in relation to the list of professional representatives maintained in pursuance of [Article 120] of the [European Union] Trade Mark Regulation and persons on that list, provision corresponding to that made by, or capable of being made under, sections 84 to 88 in relation to the register of [trade mark attorneys and registered trade mark attorneys].

[(3A) The reference in subsections (1) and (2)(d) to the European Union Trade Mark Regulation includes a reference to [Council Regulation (EC) No 207/2009 of 26 February 2009 on the European Union Trade Mark].]

(3) Regulations under this section shall be made by statutory instrument which shall be subject to annulment in pursuance of a resolution of either House of Parliament.

*The Madrid Protocol international registration*

**The Madrid Protocol.**

**53.—** In this Act—

"the Madrid Protocol" means the Protocol relating to the Madrid Agreement concerning the International Registration of Marks, adopted at Madrid on 27th June 1989;

"the International Bureau" has the meaning given by Article 2(1) of that Protocol, and

["international trade mark (EC)" means a trade mark which is entitled to protection in the [European Union] under that Protocol ;]

[…].

**Power to make provision giving effect to Madrid Protocol.**

**54.**—(1) The Secretary of State may by order make such provision as he thinks fit for giving effect in the United Kingdom to the provisions of the Madrid Protocol.

(2) Provision may, in particular, be made with respect to—

(a) the making of application for international registrations by way of the Patent Office as office of origin;

(b) the procedures to be followed where the basic United Kingdom application or registration fails or ceases to be in force;

(c) the procedures to be followed where the Patent Office receives from the International Bureau a request for extension of protection to the United Kingdom;

(d) the effects of a successful request for extension of protection to the United Kingdom;

(e) the transformation of an application for an international registration, or an international registration, into a national application for registration,

(f) the communication of information to the International Bureau.

(g) the payment of fees and amounts prescribed in respect of application for international registrations, extensions of protection and renewals.

(3) Without prejudice to the generality of subsection (1), provision may be made by regulations under this section applying in relation to an international trade mark (UK) the provisions of—

[(a) sections 21 to 21F (unjustified threats);]

(b) sections 89 to 91 (importation of infringing goods, material or articles); and

(c) sections 92, 93, 95 and 96 (offences).

(4) An order under this section shall be made by statutory instrument which shall be subject to annulment in pursuance of a resolution of either House of Parliament.

**[Certain international trade marks protected in the European Union to be treated as registered trade marks**

**54A.** Schedule 2B makes provision for international trade marks protected in the European Union (including certain expired marks) to be treated as registered trade marks with effect from IP completion day and about certain applications for the protection of an international trade mark in the European Union and transformation applications made before IP completion day.]

*The Paris Convention: supplementary provisions*

**The Paris Convention.**

**55.**—(1) In this Act—

(a) "the Paris Convention" means the Paris Convention for the Protection of Industrial Property of March 20th 1883, as revised or amended from time to time,

[…]

[(aa) "the WTO agreement" means the Agreement establishing the World Trade Organisation signed at Marrakesh on 15th April 1994, and]

(b) a "Convention country" means a country, other than the United Kingdom, which is a party to that Convention [or to that Agreement].

(2) The Secretary of State may by order make such amendments of this Act, and rules made under this Act, as appear to him appropriate in consequence of any revision or amendment of the Parts Convention [or the WTO agreement] after the passing of this Act.

(3) Any such order shall be made by statutory instrument which shall be subject to annulment in pursuance of a resolution of either House of Parliament.

**Protection of well-known trade marks: Article 6bis.**

**56.**—(1) References in this Act to a trade mark which is entitled to protection under the Paris Convention [or the WTO agreement] as a well known trade mark are to a mark which is well-known in the United Kingdom as being the mark of a person who—

(a) is a national of a Convention country, or

(b) is domiciled in, or has a real and effective industrial or commercial establishment in, a Convention country.

whether or not that person carries on business, or has any goodwill, in the United Kingdom.

References to the proprietor of such a mark shall be construed accordingly.

(2) The proprietor of a trade mark which is entitled to protection under the Paris Convention [or the WTO agreement] as a well known trade mark is entitled to restrain by injunction the use in the United Kingdom of a trade mark which, or the essential part of which, is identical or similar to his mark, in relation to identical or similar goods or services, where the use is likely to cause confusion.

This right is subject to section 48 (effect of acquiescence by proprietor of earlier trade mark).

(3) Nothing in subsection (2) affects the continuation of any bona fide use of a trade mark begun before the commencement of this section

**National emblems, &c. of Convention countries: Article 6ter.**

**57.**—(1) A trade mark which consists of or contains the flag of a Convention country shall not be registered without the authorisation of the competent authorities of that country, unless it appears to the registrar that use of the flag in the manner proposed is permitted without such authorisation.

(2) A trade mark which consists of or contains the armorial bearings or any other state emblem of a Convention country which is protected under the Paris Convention [or the WTO agreement] shall not be registered without the authorisation of the competent authorities of that country.

(3) A trade mark which consists of or contains an official sign or hallmark adopted by a Convention country and indicating control and warranty shall not, where the sign or hallmark is protected under the Paris Convention [or the WTO agreement], be registered in relation to goods or services of the same, or a similar kind, as those in relation to which it indicates control and warranty, without the authorisation of the competent authorities of the country concerned.

(4) The provisions of this section as to national flags and other state emblems, and official signs or hallmarks, apply equally to anything which from a heraldic point of view imitates any such flag or other emblem, or sign or hallmark.

(5) Nothing in this section prevents the registration of a trade mark on the application of a national of a country who is authorised to make use of a state emblem, or official sign or hallmark, of that country, notwithstanding that it is similar to that of another country.

(6) Where by virtue of this section the authorisation of the competent authorities of a Convention country is or would be required for the registration of a trade mark, those authorities are entitled to restrain by injunction any use of the mark in the United Kingdom without their authorisation.

**Emblems, &c. of certain international organisations: Article 6ter.**

**58.**—(1) This section applies to—

(a) the armorial bearings, flags or other emblems, and

(b) the abbreviations and names,

of international intergovernmental organisations of which one or more Convention countries are members.

(2) A trade mark which consists of or contains any such emblem, abbreviation or name which is protected under the Paris Convention [or the WTO agreement] shall not be registered without the authorisation of the international organisation concerned, unless it appears to the registrar that the use of the emblem, abbreviation or name in the manner proposed—

(a) is not such as to suggest to the public that a connection exists between the organisation and the trade mark, or

(b) is not likely to mislead the public as to the existence of a connection between the user and the organisation.

(3) The provisions of this section as to emblems of an international organisation apply equally to anything which from a heraldic point of view imitates any such emblem.

(4) Where by virtue of this section the authorisation of an international organisation is or would be required for the registration of a trade mark, that

organisation is entitled to restrain by injunction any use of the mark in the United Kingdom without its authorisation.

(5) Nothing in this section affects the rights of a person whose bona fide use of the trade mark in question began before 4th January 1962 (when the relevant provisions of the Paris Convention entered into force in relation to the United Kingdom).

**Notification under Article 6ter of the Convention.**

**59.**—(1) For the purposes of section 57 state emblems of a Convention country (other than the national flag), and official signs or hallmarks, shall be regarded as protected under the Paris Convention only if, or to the extent that—

(a) the country in question has notified the United Kingdom in accordance with Article 6ter(3) of the Convention that it desires to protect that emblem, sign or hallmark,

(b) the notification remains in force, and

(c) the United Kingdom has not objected to it in accordance with Article 6ter(4) or any such objection has been withdrawn.

(2) For the purposes of section 58 the emblems, abbreviations and names of an international organisation shall be regarded as protected under the Paris Convention only if, or to the extent that—

(a) the organisation in question has notified the United Kingdom in accordance with Article 6ter(3) of the Convention that it desires to protect that emblem, abbreviation or name,

(b) the notification remains in force, and

(c) the United Kingdom has not objected to it in accordance with Article 6ter(4) or any such objection has been withdrawn.

(3) Notification under Article 6ter(3) of the Paris Convention shall have effect only in relation to applications for registration made more than two months after the receipt of the notification.

(4) The registrar shall keep and make available for public inspection by any person, at all reasonable hours and free of charge, a list of—

(a) the state emblems and official signs or hallmarks, and

(b) the emblems, abbreviations and names of international organisations,

which are for the time being protected under the Paris Convention by virtue of notification under Article 6ter(3).

[(5) Any reference in this section to Article 6ter of the Paris Convention shall be construed as including a reference to that Article as applied by the WTO agreement.]

**Acts of agent or representative: Article 6septies.**

**60.**— [...]

[**Similarity of goods and services.**

**60A.**—(1) For the purposes of this Act goods and services—

(a) are not to be regarded as being similar to each other on the ground that they appear in the same class under the Nice Classification;

(b) are not to be regarded as being dissimilar from each other on the ground that they appear in different classes under the Nice Classification.

(2) In subsection (1), the "Nice Classification" means the system of classifica-

tion under the Nice Agreement Concerning the International Classification of Goods and Services for the Purposes of the Registration of Marks of 15 June 1957, which was last amended on 28 September 1979.]

*Miscellaneous*

**61.—** […]

PART III – – ADMINISTRATIVE AND OTHER SUPPLEMENTARY PROVISIONS

*The registrar*

**The register.**

**62.—** In this Act "the registrar" means the Comptroller-General of Patents, Designs and Trade Marks

*The register*

**The register.**

**63.—**(1) The registrar shall maintain a register of trade marks.

References in this Act to "the register" are to that register; and references to registration (in particular, in the expression "registered trade mark") are, unless the context otherwise requires, to registration in that register.

(2) There shall be entered in the register in accordance with this Act—

(a) registered trade marks.

(b) such particulars as may be prescribed of registrable transactions affecting a registered trade mark, and

(c) such other matters relating to registered trade marks as may be prescribed.

(3) The register shall be kept in such manner as may be prescribed, and provision shall in particular be made for—

(a) public inspection of the register, and

(b) the supply of certified or uncertified copies, or extracts, of entries in the register.

**Rectification or correction of the register.**

**64.—**(1) Any person having a sufficient interest may apply for the rectification of an error or omission in the register.

Provided that an application for rectification may not be made in respect of a matter affecting the validity of the registration of a trade mark.

(2) An application for rectification may be made either to the registrar or to the court, except that—

(a) if proceedings concerning the trade mark in question are pending in the court, the application must be made to the court; and

(b) if in any other case the application is made to the registrar, he may at any stage of the proceedings refer the application to the court.

(3) Except where the registrar or the court directs otherwise, the effect of rectification of the register is that the error or omission in question shall be deemed never to have been made.

(4) The registrar may, on request made in the prescribed manner by the proprietor of a registered trade mark, or a licensee, enter any change in his name or address as recorded in the register.

(5) The registrar may remove from the register matter appearing to him to have ceased to have effect.

**Adaptation of entries to new classification.**

**65.**—(1) Provision may be made by rules empowering the registrar to do such things as he considers necessary to implement any amended or substituted classification of goods or services for the purposes of the registration of trade marks.

(2) Provision may in particular be made for the amendment of existing entries on the register so as to accord with the new classification.

(3) Any such power of amendment shall not be exercised so as to extend the rights conferred by the registration, except where it appears to the registrar that compliance with this requirement would involve undue complexity and that any extension would not be substantial and would not adversely affect the rights of any person.

(4) The rules may empower the registrar—

(a) to require the proprietor of a registered trade mark, within such time as may be prescribed, to file a proposal for amendment of the register, and

(b) to cancel or refuse to renew the registration of the trade mark in the event of his failing to do so.

(5) Any such proposal shall be advertised, and may be opposed, in such manner as may be prescribed.

*Powers and duties of the registrar*

**Power to require use of forms.**

**66.**—(1) The registrar may require the use of such forms as he may direct for any purpose relating to the registration of a trade mark or any other proceeding before him under this Act.

(2) The forms, and any directions of the registrar with respect to their use, shall be published in the prescribed manner.

**Information about applications and registered trade marks.**

**67.**—(1) After publication of an application for registration of a trade mark, the registrar shall on request provide a person with such information and permit him to inspect such documents relating to the application, or to any registered trade mark resulting from it, as may be specified in the request, subject, however, to any prescribed restrictions.

Any request must be made in the prescribed manner and be accompanied by the appropriate fee (if any).

(2) Before publication of an application for registration of a trade mark, documents or information constituting or relating to the application shall not be published by the registrar or communicated by him to any person except—

(a) in such cases and to such extent as may be prescribed, or

(b) with the consent of the applicant;

but subject as follows.

(3) Where a person has been notified that an application for registration of a trade mark has been made, and that the applicant will if the application is granted bring proceedings against him in respect of acts done after publication of the ap-

plication, he may make a request under subsection (1) notwithstanding that the application has not been published and that subsection shall apply accordingly.

**Costs and security for costs.**

**68.**—(1) Provision may be made by rules empowering the registrar, in any proceedings before him under this Act

(a) to award any party such costs as he may consider reasonable, and

(b) to direct how and by what parties they are to be paid

(2) Any such order of the registrar may be enforced—

(a) in England and Wales or Northern Ireland, in the same way as an order of the High Court;

(b) in Scotland, in the same way as a decree for expenses granted by the Court of Session.

(3) Provision may be made by rules empowering the registrar, in such cases as may be prescribed, to require a party to proceedings before him to give security for costs, in relation to those proceedings or to proceedings on appeal, and as to the consequences if security is not given.

**Evidence before registrar.**

**69.**— Provision may be made by rules—

(a) as to the giving of evidence in proceedings before the registrar under this Act by affidavit or statutory declaration,

(b) conferring on the registrar the powers of an official referee of the [Senior Courts or of the Court of Judicature] as regards the examination of witnesses on oath and the discovery and production of documents; and

(c) applying in relation to the attendance of witnesses in proceedings before the registrar the rules applicable to the attendance of witnesses before such a referee.

**Exclusion of liability in respect of official acts.**

**70.**—(1) The registrar shall not be taken to warrant the validity of the registration of a trade mark under this Act or under any treaty, convention, arrangement or engagement to which the United Kingdom is a party.

(2) The registrar is not subject to any liability by reason of, or in connection with, any examination required or authorised by this Act, or any such treaty, convention, arrangement or engagement, or any report or other proceedings consequent on such examination.

(3) No proceedings lie against an officer of the registrar in respect of any matter for which, by virtue of this section, the registrar is not liable.

**Registrar's annual report.**

**71.**—(1) The Comptroller-General of Patents, Designs and Trade Marks shall in his annual report under section 121 of the Patents Act 1977 include a report on the execution of this Act, including the discharge of his functions under the Madrid protocol.

(2) The report shall include an account of all money received and paid by him under or by virtue of this Act.

*Legal proceedings and appeals*

**Registration to be prima facie evidence of validity.**

**72.**— In all legal proceedings relating to a registered trade mark (including proceedings for rectification of the register) the registration of a person as proprietor of a trade mark shall be prima facie evidence of the validity of the original registration and of any subsequent assignment or other transmission of it.

**Certificate of validity of contested registration.**

**73.**—(1) If in proceedings before the court the validity of the registration of a trade mark is contested and it is found by the court that the trade mark is validly registered, the court may give a certificate to that effect.

(2) If the court gives such a certificate and in subsequent proceedings—

(a) the validity of the registration is again questioned, and

(b) the proprietor obtains a final order or judgment in his favour,

he is entitled to his costs as between solicitor and client unless the court directs otherwise.

This subsection does not extend to the costs of an appeal in any such proceedings.

**Registrar's appearance in proceedings involving the register.**

**74.**—(1) In proceedings before the court involving an application for—

(a) the revocation of the registration of a trade mark,

(b) a declaration of the invalidity of the registration of a trade mark, or

(c) the rectification of the register,

the registrar is entitled to appear and be heard, and shall appear if so directed by the court.

(2) Unless otherwise directed by the court, the registrar may instead of appearing submit to the court a statement in writing signed by him, giving particulars of

(a) any proceedings before him in relation to the matter in issue,

(b) the grounds of any decision given by him affecting it,

(c) the practice of the Patent Office in like cases, or

(d) such matters relevant to the issues and within his knowledge as registrar as he thinks fit;

and the statement shall be deemed to form part of the evidence in the proceedings.

(3) Anything which the registrar is or may be authorised or required to do under this section may be done on his behalf by a duly authorised officer.

**The court.**

**75.**— In this Act, unless the context otherwise requires, "the court" means—

(a) in England and Wales [, the High Court [, or the county court where it has] jurisdiction by virtue of an order made under section 1 of the Courts and Legal Services Act 1990,

[(aa) in] Northern Ireland, the High Court, and]

(b) in Scotland, the Court of Session.

**Appeals from the registrar.**

**76.**—(1) An appeal lies from any decision of the registrar under this Act, except as otherwise expressly provided by rules.

For this purpose "decision" includes any act of the registrar in exercise of a discretion vested in him by or under this Act.

(2) Any such appeal may be brought either to an appointed person or to the court

(3) Where an appeal is made to an appointed person, he may refer the appeal to the court if—

(a) it appears to him that a point of general legal importance is involved.

(b) the registrar requests that it be so referred, or

(c) such a request is made by any party to the proceedings before the registrar in which the decision appealed against was made.

Before doing so the appointed person shall give the appellant and any other party to the appeal an opportunity to make representations as to whether the appeal should be referred to the court.

(4) Where an appeal is made to an appointed person and he does not refer it to the court, he shall hear and determine the appeal and his decision shall be final.

(5) The provisions of sections 68 and 69 (costs and security for costs; evidence) apply in relation to proceedings before an appointed person as in relation to proceedings before the registrar.

[(6) In the application of this section to England and Wales, "the court" means the High Court.]

**Persons appointed to hear and determine appeals.**

**77.—**(1) For the purposes of section 76 an "appointed person" means a person appointed by the Lord Chancellor to hear and decide appeals under this Act.

(2) A person is not eligible for such appointment unless—

[(a) he satisfies the judicial-appointment eligibility condition on a 5-year basis;]

(b) he is an advocate or solicitor in Scotland of at least [5] years' standing;

(c) he is a member of the Bar of Northern Ireland or [solicitor of the Supreme Court of Northern Ireland] of at least [5] years' standing; or

(d) he has held judicial office.

(3) An appointed person shall hold and vacate office in accordance with his terms of appointment, subject to the following provisions—

(a) there shall be paid to him such remuneration (whether by way of salary or fees), and such allowances, as the Secretary of State with the approval of the Treasury may determine;

(b) he may resign his office by notice in writing to the Lord Chancellor;

(c) the Lord Chancellor may by notice in writing remove him from office if—

(i) he has become bankrupt or [a debt relief order (under Part 7A of the Insolvency Act 1986) has been made in respect of him or he has] made an arrangement with his creditors or, in Scotland, his estate has been sequestrated or he has executed a trust deed for his creditors or entered into a composition contract, or

(ii) he is incapacitated by physical or mental illness,

or if he is in the opinion of the Lord Chancellor otherwise unable or unfit to perform his duties as an appointed person.

(4) The Lord Chancellor shall consult the Lord Advocate before exercising his powers under this section

[(5) The Lord Chancellor may remove a person from office under subsection (3)(c) only with the concurrence of the appropriate senior judge.

(6) The appropriate senior judge is the Lord Chief Justice of England and Wales, unless—

(a) the person to be removed exercises functions wholly or mainly in Scotland, in which case it is the Lord President of the Court of Session, or

(b) the person to be removed exercises functions wholly or mainly in Northern Ireland, in which case it is the Lord Chief Justice of Northern Ireland.]

*Rules, fees, hours of business, &c*

**Power of Secretary of State to make rules.**

**78.**—(1) The Secretary of State may make rules—

(a) for the purposes of any provision of this Act authorising the making of rules with respect to any matter, and

(b) for prescribing anything authorised or required by any provision of this Act to be prescribed,

and generally for regulating practice and procedure under this Act.

(2) Provision may, in particular, be made—

(a) as to the manner of filing of applications and other documents;

(b) requiring and regulating the translation of documents and the filing and authentication of any translation;

(c) as to the service of documents;

(d) authorising the rectification of irregularities of procedure;

(e) prescribing time limits for anything required to be done in connection with any proceeding under this Act;

(f) providing for the extension of any time limit so prescribed, or specified by the registrar, whether or not it has already expired.

(3) Rules under this Act shall be made by statutory instrument which shall be subject to annulment in pursuance of a resolution of either House of Parliament.

**Fees.**

**79.**—(1) There shall be paid in respect of applications and registration and other matters under this Act such fees as may be prescribed.

(2) Provision may be made by rules as to—

(a) the payment of a single fee in respect of two or more matters, and

(b) the circumstances (if any) in which a fee may be repaid or remitted.

**Hours of business and business days.**

**80.**—(1) The registrar may give directions specifying the hours of business of the Patent Office for the purpose of the transaction by the public of business under this Act, and the days which are business days for that purpose.

(2) Business done on any day after the specified hours of business, or on a day which is not a business day, shall be deemed to have been done on the next business day; and where the time for doing anything under this Act expires on a day which is not a business day, that time shall be extended to the next business day.

(3) Directions under this section may make different provision for different classes of business and shall be published in the prescribed manner.

**The trade marks journal.**

**81.—** Provision shall be made by rules for the publication by the registrar of a journal containing particulars of any application for the registration of a trade mark (including a representation of the mark) and such other information relating to trade marks as the registrar thinks fit.

*Trade mark agents*

**Recognition of agents.**

**82.—** Except as otherwise provided by rules [and subject to the Legal Services Act 2007] , any act required or authorised by this Act to be done by or to a person in connection with the registration of a trade mark, or any procedure relating to a registered trade mark, may be done by or to an agent authorised by that person orally or in writing.

[**The register of trade mark attorneys.**

**83.**—(1) There is to continue to be a register of persons who act as agent for others for the purpose of applying for or obtaining the registration of trade marks.

(2) In this Act a registered trade mark attorney means an individual whose name is entered on the register kept under this section.

(3) The register is to be kept by the Institute of Trade Mark Attorneys.

(4) The Secretary of State may, by order, amend subsection (3) so as to require the register to be kept by the person specified in the order.

(5) Before making an order under subsection (4), the Secretary of State must consult the Legal Services Board.

(6) An order under this section must be made by statutory instrument.

(7) An order under this section may not be made unless a draft of it has been laid before, and approved by a resolution of, each House of Parliament.]

[**Regulation of trade mark attorneys.**

**83A.**—(1) The person who keeps the register under section 83 may make regulations which regulate—

(a) the keeping of the register and the registration of persons;

(b) the carrying on of trade mark agency work by registered persons.

(2) Those regulations may, amongst other things, make—

(a) provision as to the educational and training qualifications, and other requirements, which must be satisfied before an individual may be registered or for an individual to remain registered;

(b) provision as to the requirements which must be met by a body (corporate or unincorporate) before it may be registered or for it to remain registered, including provision as to the management and control of the body;

(c) provision as to the educational, training or other requirements to be met by regulated persons;

(d) provision regulating the practice, conduct and discipline of registered persons or regulated persons;

(e) provision authorising in such cases as may be specified in the regulations the erasure from the register of the name of any person registered in it, or the suspension of a person's registration;

(f) provision requiring the payment of such fees as may be specified in or determined in accordance with the regulations;
(g) provision about the provision to be made by registered persons in respect of complaints made against them;
(h) provision about the keeping of records and accounts by registered persons or regulated persons;
(i) provision for reviews of or appeals against decisions made under the regulations;
(j) provision as to the indemnification of registered persons or regulated persons against losses arising from claims in respect of civil liability incurred by them.

(3) Regulations under this section may make different provision for different purposes.

(4) Regulations under this section which are not regulatory arrangements within the meaning of the Legal Services Act 2007 are to be treated as such arrangements for the purposes of that Act.

(5) Before the appointed day, regulations under this section may be made only with the approval of the Secretary of State.

(6) The powers conferred to make regulations under this section are not to be taken to prejudice—
(a) any other power which the person who keeps the register may have to make rules or regulations (however they may be described and whether they are made under an enactment or otherwise);
(b) any rules or regulations made by that person under any such power.

(7) In this section—

"appointed day" means the day appointed for the coming into force of paragraph 1 of Schedule 4 to the Legal Services Act 2007;

"manager", in relation to a body, has the same meaning as in the Legal Services Act 2007 (see section 207);

"registered person" means—
(a) a registered trade mark attorney, or
(b) a body (corporate or unincorporate) registered in the register kept under section 83;

"regulated person" means a person who is not a registered person but is a manager or employee of a body which is a registered person;

"trade mark agency work" means work done in the course of carrying on the business of acting as agent for others for the purpose of—
(a) applying for or obtaining the registration of trade marks in the United Kingdom or elsewhere, or
(b) conducting proceedings before the Comptroller relating to applications for or otherwise in connection with the registration of trade marks.]

**Unregistered persons not to be described as registered trade mark agents.**

**84.**—(1) An individual who is not a registered trade mark [attorney] shall not—
(a) carry on a business (otherwise than in partnership) under any name or other description which contains the words "registered trade mark agent" [or registered trade mark attorney]; or

(b) in the course of a business otherwise describe or hold himself out, or permit himself to be described or held out, as a registered trade mark agent [or a registered trade mark attorney].

(2) A partnership [or other unincorporated body] shall not—

(a) carry on a business under any name or other description which contains the words "registered trade mark agent" [or registered trade mark attorney]; or

(b) in the course of a business otherwise describe or hold itself out, or permit itself to be described or held out, as a firm of registered trade mark agents [or registered trade mark attorneys],

unless [the partnership or other body is registered in the register kept under section 83.]

(3) A body corporate shall not—

(a) carry on a business (otherwise than in partnership) under any name or other description which contains the words "registered trade mark agent" [or registered trade mark attorney]; or

(b) in the course of a business otherwise describe or hold itself out, or permit itself to be described or held out, as a registered trade mark agent [or a registered trade mark attorney],

unless [the body corporate is registered in the register kept under section 83.]

(4) A person who contravenes this section commits an offence and is liable on summary conviction to a fine not exceeding level 5 on the standard scale; and proceedings for such an offence may be begun at any time within a year from the date of the offence.

**85.—** […]

**Use of the term "trade mark attorney".**

**86.—**(1) No offence is committed under the enactments restricting the use of certain expressions in reference to persons not qualified to act as solicitors by the use of the term "trade mark attorney" in reference to a registered trade mark [attorney].

(2) The enactments referred to in subsection (1) are section 21 of the Solicitors Act 1974, section 31 of the Solicitors (Scotland) Act 1980 and Article 22 of the Solicitors (Northern Ireland) Order 1976.

**Privilege for communications with registered trade mark agents.**

**87.—**(1) This section applies to[—

(a)] communications as to any matter relating to the protection of any design or trade mark, or as to any matter involving passing off[, and

(b) documents, material or information relating to any matter mentioned in paragraph (a).]

[(2) Where a trade mark attorney acts for a client in relation to a matter mentioned in subsection (1), any communication, document, material or information to which this section applies is privileged from disclosure in like manner as if the trade mark attorney had at all material times been acting as the client's solicitor.]

(3) In subsection (2) "trade mark [attorney"] means —

(a) a registered trade mark [attorney], or

(b) a partnership entitled to describe itself as a firm of registered trade mark [attorneys], or

(c) [any other unincorporated body or] a body corporate entitled to describe itself as a registered trade mark [attorney] [or] [(d) a person whose name appears on the list of professional representatives for trade mark matters maintained by the European Union Intellectual Property Office referred to in Article 120 of the European Union Trade Mark Regulation.]

[(4) Where a trade mark attorney is a person falling within subsection (3)(d), subsection (2) applies as if the reference to a matter mentioned in subsection (1) were a reference to a matter relating to the protection of a trade mark.]

**Power of registrar to refuse to deal with certain agents.**

**88.**—(1) The Secretary of State may make rules authorising the registrar to refuse to recognise as agent in respect of any business under this Act—

(a) a person who has been convicted of an offence under section 84 (unregistered persons describing themselves as registered trade mark agents);

(b) an individual whose name has been erased from and not restored to, or who is suspended from, the register of trade mark [attorneys] on the ground of misconduct;

(c) a person who is found by the Secretary of State to have been guilty of such conduct as would, in the case of an individual registered in the register of trade mark [attorneys], render him liable to have his name erased from the register on the ground of misconduct;

(d) a partnership or body corporate of which one of the partners or directors is a person whom the registrar could refuse to recognise under paragraph (a), (b) or (c) above.

(2) The rules may contain such incidental and supplementary provisions as appear to the Secretary of State to be appropriate and may, in particular, prescribe circumstances in which a person is or is not to be taken to have been guilty of misconduct.

*Importation of infringing goods, material or articles*

**Infringing goods, material or articles may be treated as prohibited goods.**

**89.**—(1) The proprietor of a registered trade mark, or a licensee, may give notice in writing to the Commissioners of Customs and Excise—

(a) that he is the proprietor or, as the case may be, a licensee of the registered trade mark,

(b) that, at a time and place specified in the notice, goods which are, in relation to that registered trade mark, infringing goods, material or articles are expected to arrive in the United Kingdom—

(i) from outside the European Economic Area, or

(ii) from within that Area but not having been entered for free circulation, and

(c) that he requests the Commissioners to treat them as prohibited goods.

(2) When a notice is in force under this section the importation of the goods to which the notice relates, otherwise than by a person for his private and domestic use, is prohibited; but a person is not by reason of the prohibition liable to any penalty other than forfeiture of the goods.

[(3) This section does not apply to goods placed in, or expected to be placed in, one of the situations referred to in Article 1(1), in respect of which an application may be made under [Article 3 of the European Customs Enforcement Regulation.]

**Power of Commissioners of Customs and Excise to make regulations.**

**90.**—(1) The Commissioners of Customs and Excise may make regulations prescribing the form in which notice is to be given under section 89 and requiring a person giving notice—

(a) to furnish the Commissioners with such evidence as may be specified in the regulations, either on giving notice or when the goods are imported, or at both those times, and

(b) to comply with such other conditions as may be specified in the regulations

(2) The regulations may, in particular, require a person giving such a notice

(a) to pay such fees in respect of the notice as may be specified by the regulations;

(b) to give such security as may be so specified in respect of any liability or expense which the Commissioners may incurring consequence of the notice by reason of the detention of any goods or anything done to goods detained;

(c) to indemnify the Commissioners against any such liability or expense, whether security has been given or not.

(3) The regulations may make different provision as respects different classes of case to which they apply and may include such incidental and supplementary provisions as the Commissioners consider expedient.

(4) Regulations under this section shall be made by statutory instrument which shall be subject to annulment in pursuance of a resolution of either House of Parliament.

(5) [...]

[**Power of Commissioners for Revenue and Customs to disclose information.**]

**91.**— Where information relating to infringing goods, material or articles has been obtained [or is held] by [the Commissioners for her Majesty's Revenue and Customs] for the purposes of, or in connection with, the exercise of [functions of Her Majesty's Revenue and Customs] in relation to imported goods, the Commissioners may authorise the disclosure of that information for the purpose of facilitating the exercise by any person of any function in connection with the investigation or prosecution of [an offence under—

(a) section 92 below (unauthorised use of trade mark, &c in relation to goods),

(b) the Trade Descriptions Act 1968,

(c) the Business Protection from Misleading Marketing Regulations 2008, or

(d) the Consumer Protection from Unfair Trading Regulations 2008.]

*Offences*

**Unauthorised use of trade mark, &c. in relation to goods.**

**92.**—(1) A person commits an offence who with a view to gain for himself or another, or with intent to cause loss to another, and without the consent of the proprietor—

(a) applies to goods or their packaging a sign identical to, or likely to be mistaken for, a registered trade mark, or
(b) sells or lets for hire, offers or exposes for sale or hire or distributes goods which bear, or the packaging of which bears, such a sign, or
(c) has in his possession, custody or control in the course of a business any such goods with a view to the doing of anything, by himself or another, which would be an offence under paragraph (b).

(2) A person commits an offence who with a view to gain for himself or another, or with intent to cause loss to another, and without the consent of the proprietor—
(a) applies a sign identical to, or likely to be mistaken for, a registered trade mark to material intended to be used—
(i) for labelling or packaging goods,
(ii) as a business paper in relation to goods, or
(iii) for advertising goods, or
(b) uses in the course of a business material bearing such a sign for labelling or packaging goods, as a business paper in relation to goods, or for advertising goods, or
(c) has in his possession, custody or control in the course of a business any such material with a view to the doing of anything, by himself or another, which would be an offence under paragraph (b).

(3) A person commits an offence who with a view to gain for himself or another, or with intent to cause loss to another, and without the consent of the proprietor—
(a) makes an article specifically designed or adapted for making copies of a sign identical to, or likely to be mistaken for, a registered trade mark, or
(b) has such an article in his possession, custody or control in the course of a business,

knowing or having reason to believe that it has been, or is to be, used to produce goods, or material for labelling or packaging goods, as a business paper in relation to goods, or for advertising goods.

(4) A person does not commit an offence under this section unless—
(a) the goods are goods in respect of which the trade mark is registered, or
(b) the trade mark has a reputation in the United Kingdom and the use of the sign takes or would take unfair advantage of, or is or would be detrimental to, the distinctive character or the repute of the trade mark.

(5) It is a defence for a person charged with an offence under this section to show that he believed on reasonable grounds that the use of the sign in the manner in which it was used, or was to be used, was not an infringement of the registered trade mark.

(6) A person guilty of an offence under this section is liable—
(a) on summary conviction to imprisonment for a term not exceeding six months or a fine not exceeding the statutory maximum, or both;
(b) on conviction on indictment to a fine or imprisonment for a term not exceeding ten years, or both.

[**Search warrants.**

**92A.**—(1) Where a justice of the peace (in Scotland, a sheriff or justice of the peace) is satisfied by information on oath given by a constable (in Scotland, by evidence on oath) that there are reasonable grounds for believing—

(a) that an offence under section 92 (unauthorised use of trade mark, etc. in relation to goods) has been or is about to be committed in any premises, and

(b) that evidence that such an offence has been or is about to be committed is in those premises,

he may issue a warrant authorising a constable to enter and search the premises, using such reasonable force as is necessary.

(2) The power conferred by subsection (1) does not, in England and Wales, extend to authorising a search for material of the kinds mentioned in section 9(2) of the Police and Criminal Evidence Act 1984 (c. 60) (certain classes of personal or confidential material).

(3) A warrant under subsection (1)—

(a) may authorise persons to accompany any constable executing the warrant, and

(b) remains in force for three months from the date of its issue.

(4) In executing a warrant issued under subsection (1) a constable may seize an article if he reasonably believes that it is evidence that any offence under section 92 has been or is about to be committed.

(5) In this section "premises" includes land, buildings, fixed or moveable structures, vehicles, vessels, aircraft and hovercraft.]

**Enforcement function of local weights and measures authority.**

**93.**—(1) It is the duty of every local weights and measures authority to enforce within their area the provisions of section 92 (unauthorised use of trade mark, &c. in relation to goods).

(2) [...]

(3) Subsection (1) above does not apply in relation to the enforcement of section 92 in Northern Ireland, but it is the duty of the Department of Economic Development to enforce that section in Northern Ireland.[...]

[(3A) For the investigatory powers available to a local weights and measures authority or the Department of Enterprise, Trade and Investment in Northern Ireland for the purposes of the duties in this section, see Schedule 5 to the Consumer Rights Act 2015.]

(4) Any enactment which authorises the disclosure of information for the purpose of facilitating the enforcement of the Trade Descriptions Act 1968 shall apply as if section 92 above were contained in that Act and as if the functions of any person in relation to the enforcement of that section were functions under that Act.

(5) Nothing in this section shall be construed as authorising a local weights and measures authority to bring proceedings in Scotland for an offence.

**Falsification of register, &c.**

**94.**—(1) It is an offence for a person to make, or cause to be made, a false entry in the register of trade marks, knowing or having reason to believe that it is false.

(2) It is an offence for a person—

(a) to make or cause to be made anything falsely purporting to be a copy of an entry in the register, or

(b) to produce or tender or cause to be produced or tendered in evidence any such thing,

knowing or having reason to believe that it is false.

(3) A person guilty of an offence under this section is liable—

(a) on conviction on indictment, to imprisonment for a term not exceeding two years or a fine, or both;

(b) on summary conviction, to imprisonment for a term not exceeding six months or a fine not exceeding the statutory maximum, or both.

**Falsely representing trade mark as registered.**

**95.**—(1) It is an offence for a person—

(a) falsely to represent that a mark is a registered trade mark, or

(b) to make a false representation as to the goods or services for which a trade mark is registered

knowing or having reason to believe that the representation is false.

(2) For the purposes of this section, the use in the United Kingdom in relation to a trade mark—

(a) of the word "registered", or

(b) of any other word or symbol importing a reference (express or implied) to registration,

shall be deemed to be a representation as to registration under this Act unless it is shown that the reference is to registration elsewhere than in the United Kingdom and that the trade mark is in fact so registered for the goods or services in question.

(3) A person guilty of an offence under this section is liable on summary conviction to a fine not exceeding level 3 on the standard scale.

**Supplementary provisions as to summary proceedings in Scotland.**

**96.**—(1) Notwithstanding anything in [section 136 of the Criminal Procedure (Scotland) Act 1995] , summary proceedings in Scotland for an offence under this Act may be begun at any time within six months after the date on which evidence sufficient in the Lord Advocate's opinion to justify the proceedings came to his knowledge.

For this purpose a certificate of the Lord Advocate as to the date on which such evidence came to his knowledge is conclusive evidence.

(2) For the purposes of subsection (1) and of any other provision of this Act as to the time within which summary proceedings for an offence may be brought, proceedings in Scotland shall be deemed to be begun on the date on which a warrant to apprehend or to cite the accused is granted, if such warrant is executed without undue delay.

*Forfeiture of counterfeit goods, &c.*

**Forfeiture; England and Wales or Northern Ireland.**

**97.**—(1) In England and Wales or Northern Ireland where there has come into the possession of any person in connection with the investigation or prosecution of a relevant offence—

(a) goods which, or the packaging of which, bears a sign identical to or likely to be mistaken for a registered trade mark,

(b) material bearing such a sign and intended to be used for labelling or packaging goods, as a business paper in relation to goods, or for advertising goods, or

(c) articles specifically designed or adapted for making copies of such a sign,

that person may apply under this section for an order for the forfeiture of the goods, material or articles.

(2) An application under this section may be made—

(a) where proceedings have been brought in any court for a relevant offence relating to some or all of the goods, material or articles, to that court;

(b) where no application for the forfeiture of the goods, material or articles has been made under paragraph (a), by way of complaint to a magistrates' court.

(3) On an application under this section the court shall make an order for the forfeiture of any goods, material or articles only if it is satisfied that a relevant offence has been committed in relation to the goods, material or articles.

(4) A court may infer for the purposes of this section that such an offence has been committed in relation to any goods, material or articles if it is satisfied that such an offence has been committed in relation to goods, material or articles which are representative of them (whether by reason of being of the same design or part of the same consignment or batch or otherwise).

(5) Any person aggrieved by an order made under this section by a magistrates court, or by a decision of such a court not to make such an order, may appeal against that order or decision—

(a) in England and Wales, to the Crown Court;

(b) in Northern Ireland, to the county court,

and an order so made may contain such provision as appears to the court to be appropriate for delaying the coming into force of the order pending the making and determination of any appeal (including any application under section 111 of the Magistrates' Courts Act 1980 or Article 146 of the Magistrates' Courts (Northern Ireland) Order 1981 (statement of case))

(6) Subject to subsection (7), where any goods, material or articles are forfeited under this section they shall be destroyed in accordance with such directions as the court may give.

(7) On making an order under this section the court may, if it considers it appropriate to do so, direct that the goods, material or articles to which the order relates shall (instead of being destroyed) be released, to such person as the court may specify, on condition that that person—

(a) causes the offending sign to be erased, removed or obliterated, and

(b) complies with any order to pay costs which has been made against him in the proceedings for the order for forfeiture.

(8) For the purposes of this section a "relevant offence" means

[(a) an offence under section 92 above (unauthorised use of trade mark, &c in relation to goods),

(b) an offence under the Trade Descriptions Act 1968,

(c) an offence under the Business Protection from Misleading Marketing Regulations 2008,

(d) an offence under the Consumer Protection from Unfair Trading Regulations 2008, or

(e) any offence involving dishonesty or deception.]

**Forfeiture; Scotland.**

**98.**—(1) In Scotland the court may make an order for the forfeiture of any—

(a) goods which bear, or the packaging of which bears, a sign identical to or likely to be mistaken for a registered trade mark,

(b) material bearing such a sign and intended to be used for labelling or packaging goods, as a business paper in relation to goods, or for advertising goods, or

(c) articles specifically designed or adapted for making copies of such a sign.

(2) An order under this section may be made—

(a) on an application by the procurator-fiscal made in the manner specified in [section 134 of the Criminal Procedure (Scotland) Act 1995], or

(b) where a person is convicted of a relevant offence, in addition to any other penalty which the court may impose.

(3) On an application under subsection (2)(a), the court shall make an order for the forfeiture of any goods, material or articles only if it is satisfied that a relevant offence has been committed in relation to the goods, material or articles.

(4) The court may infer for the purposes of this section that such an offence has been committed in relation to any goods, material or articles if it is satisfied that such an offence has been committed in relation to goods, material or articles which are representative of them (whether by reason of being of the same design or part of the same consignment or batch or otherwise).

(5) The procurator-fiscal making the application under subsection (2)(a) shall serve on any person appearing to him to be the owner of, or otherwise to have an interest in, the goods, material or articles to which the application relates a copy of the application, together with a notice giving him the opportunity to appear at the hearing of the application to show cause why the goods, material or articles should not be forfeited.

(6) Service under subsection (5) shall be carried out, and such service may be proved, in the manner specified for citation of an accused in summary proceedings under the [Criminal Procedure (Scotland) Act 1995].

(7) Any person upon whom notice is served under subsection (5) and any other person claiming to be the owner of, or otherwise to have an interest in, goods, material or articles to which an application under this section relates shall be entitled to appear at the hearing of the application to show cause why the goods, material or articles should not be forfeited.

(8) The court shall not make an order following an application under subsection (2)(a)—

(a) if any person on whom notice is served under subsection (5) does not appear, unless service of the notice on that person is proved; or

(b) if no notice under subsection (5) has been served, unless the court is satisfied that in the circumstances it was reasonable not to serve such notice.

(9) Where an order for the forfeiture of any goods, material or articles is made following an application under subsection (2)(a) any person who appeared, or was entitled to appear, to show cause why goods, material or articles should not be forfeited may, within 21 days of the making of the order, appeal to the High Court by Bill of suspension; and [section 182(5)(a) to (e) of the Criminal Procedure (Scotland) Act 1995] shall apply to an appeal under this subsection as it applies to a stated case under Part II of that Act.

(10) An order following an application under subsection (2)(a) shall not take effect—

(a) until the end of the period of 21 days beginning with the day after the day on which the order is made; or

(b) if an appeal is made under subsection (9) above within that period, until the appeal is determined or abandoned

(11) An order under subsection (2)(b) shall not take effect—

(a) until the end of the period within which an appeal against the order could be brought under the [Criminal Procedure (Scotland) Act 1995]; or

(b) if an appeal is made within that period, until the appeal is determined or abandoned.

(12) Subject to subsection (13), goods, material or articles forfeited under this section shall be destroyed in accordance with such directions as the court may give.

(13) On making an order under this section the court may if it considers it appropriate to do so, direct that the goods, material or articles to which the order relates shall (instead of being destroyed) be released, to such person as the court may specify, on condition that that person causes the offending sign to be erased, removed or obliterated

(14) For the purposes of this section—

"relevant offence" means

(a) [an offence under section 92 above (unauthorised use of trade mark, &c in relation to goods),

(b) an offence under the Trade Descriptions Act 1968,

(c) an offence under the Business Protection from Misleading Marketing Regulations 2008,

(d) an offence under the Consumer Protection from Unfair Trading Regulations 2008, or

(e) any offence involving dishonesty or deception;]

"the court" means —

(a) in relation to an order made on an application under subsection (2)(a), the sheriff, and

(b) in relation to an order made unless subsection (2)(b), the court which imposed the penalty.

## PART IV— – MISCELLANEOUS AND GENERAL PROVISIONS

### *Miscellaneous*

**Unauthorised use of Royal arms. &c.**

**99.—**(1) A person shall not without the authority of Her Majesty use in connection with any business the Royal arms (or arms so closely resembling the Royal arms as to be calculated to deceive) in such manner as to be calculated to lead to the belief that he is duly authorised to use the Royal arms.

(2) A person shall not without the authority of Her Majesty or of a member of the Royal family use in connection with any business any device, emblem or title in such a manner as to be calculated to lead to the belief that he is employed by, or supplies goods or services to Her Majesty or that member of the Royal family.

(3) A person who contravenes subsection (1) commits an offence and is liable on summary conviction to a fine not exceeding level 2 on the standard scale.

(4) Contravention of subsection (1) or (2) may be restrained by injunction in proceedings brought by—

(a) any person who is authorised to use the arms, device, emblem or title in question, or

(b) any person authorised by the Lord Chamberlain to take such proceedings

(5) Nothing in this section affects any right of the proprietor of a trade mark containing any such arms, device, emblem or title to use that trade mark.

[**Reproduction of trade marks in dictionaries, encyclopaedias etc.**

**99A.**—(1) Subsection (2) applies if the reproduction of a trade mark in a dictionary, encyclopaedia or similar reference work, in print or electronic form, gives the impression that it constitutes the generic name of the goods or services for which the trade mark is registered.

(2) The publisher of the work must, at the request in writing of the proprietor of the trade mark, ensure that the reproduction of the trade mark is accompanied by an indication that it is a registered trade mark.

(3) The action required by subsection (2) must be taken—

(a) without delay, and

(b) in the case of works in printed form, at the latest in the next edition of the publication.

(4) If the publisher fails to take any action required by subsection (2) the court may, on an application by the proprietor—

(a) order the publisher to take the action concerned;

(b) if the work is in printed form, order the publisher to erase or amend the reproduction of the trade mark or secure the destruction of copies of the work in the publisher's possession, custody or control; or

(c) grant such other order as the court in the circumstances considers appropriate.]

**Burden of proving use of trade mark.**

**100.**— If in any civil proceedings under this Act a question arises as to the use to which a registered trade mark has been put, if is for the proprietor to show what use has been made of it.

**Offences committed by partnerships and bodies corporate.**

**101.**—(1) Proceedings for an offence under this Act alleged to have been committed by a partnership shall be brought against the partnership in the name of the firm and not in that of the partners; but without prejudice to any liability of the partners under subsection (4) below.

(2) The following provisions apply for the purposes of such proceedings as in relation to a body corporate—

(a) any rules of court relating to the service of documents,

(b) in England and Wales or Northern Ireland, Schedule 3 to the Magistrates' Courts Act 1980 or Schedule 4 to the Magistrates' Courts (Northern Ireland) Order 1981 (procedure on charge of offence).

(3) A fine imposed on a partnership on its conviction in such proceedings shall be paid out of the partnership assets.

(4) Where a partnership is guilty of an offence under this Act, every partner, other than a partner who is proved to have been ignorant of or to have attempted to prevent the commission of the offence, is also guilty of the offence and liable to be proceeded against and punished accordingly.

(5) Where an offence under this Act committed by a body corporate is proved to have been committed with the consent or connivance of a director, manager, secretary or other similar officer of the body, or a person purporting to act in any such capacity, he as well as the body corporate is guilty of the offence and liable to be proceeded against and punished accordingly.

*Interpretation*

**Adaptation of expressions for Scotland.**

**102.—** In the application of this Act to Scotland—

"account of profits" means accounting and payment of profits.
"accounts" means count, reckoning and payment.
"assignment" means assignation;
"costs" means expenses;
"declaration" means declarator;
"defendant" means defender;
"delivery up" means delivery;
"injunction" means interdict;
"interlocutory relief" means interim remedy; and
"plaintiff" means pursuer.

**Minor definitions.**

**103.—**(1) In this Act—

"business" includes a trade or profession;
"director", in relation to a body corporate whose affairs are managed by its members, means any member of the body;
"infringement proceedings", in relation to a registered trade mark, includes proceedings under section 16 (order for delivery up of infringing goods, &c.);
"publish" means make available to the public, and references to publication—

(a) in relation to an application for registration, are to publication under section 38(1), and
(b) in relation to registration, are to publication under section 40(4);

"statutory provisions" includes provisions of subordinate legislation within the meaning of the Interpretation Act 1978;
"trade" includes any business or profession..

(2) References in this Act to use (or any particular description of use) of a trade mark, or of a sign identical with, similar to, or likely to be mistaken for a trade mark, include use (or that description of use) otherwise than by means of a graphic representation.

(3) […]

**Index of defined expressions.**

**104.—** In this Act the expressions listed below are defined by or otherwise fall to be construed in accordance with the provisions indicated—

| | |
|---|---|
| account of profits and accounts (in Scotland) | section 102 |
| appointed person (for purposes of section 76) | section 77 |
| assignment (in Scotland) | section 102 |
| business | section 103(1) |
| certification mark | section 50(1) |
| collective mark | section 49(1) |

| | |
|---|---|
| commencement (of this Act) | section 109(2) |
| [comparable trade mark (EU) | Schedule 2A, paragraph 1(2)] |
| [... | ...] |
| [... | ...] |
| [comparable trade mark (IR) | Schedule 2B, paragraph 1(4)] |
| Convention country | section 55(1)(b) |
| costs (in Scotland) | section 102 |
| the court | section 75 |
| date of application | section 33(2) |
| date of application (comparable trade mark (EU)) | Schedule 2A, paragraph 1(8)(b)] |
| [date of application (comparable trade mark (IR)) | Schedule 2B, paragraph 1(10)(b)] |
| date of filing | section 33(1) |
| [date of filing (comparable trade mark (EU)) | Schedule 2A, paragraph 1(8)(a)] |
| [date of filing (comparable trade mark (IR)) | Schedule 2B, paragraph 1(10)(a)] |
| date of registration | section 40(3) |
| [date of registration (comparable trade mark (EU)) | Schedule 2A, paragraph 1(4)] |
| [date of registration (comparable trade mark (IR)) | Schedule 2B, paragraph 1(6)] |
| defendant (in Scotland) | section 102 |
| delivery up (in Scotland) | section 102 |
| director | section 103(1) |
| earlier right | section 5(4) |
| earlier trade mark | section 6 |
| [European Customs Enforcement Regulation | section 10A] |
| [European Union trade mark] | [section 51] |
| [European Union Trade Mark Regulation] | [section 51] |
| exclusive licence and licensee | section 29(1) |
| infringement (of registered trade mark) | section 9(1) and (2) and 10 |
| infringement proceedings | section 103(1) |
| infringing articles | section 17 |
| infringing goods | section 17 |
| infringing material | section 17 |
| injunction (in Scotland) | section 102 |
| interlocutory relief (in Scotland) | section 102 |
| the International Bureau | section 53 |
| [...] | |

| | |
|---|---|
| International trade mark (UK) | section 53 |
| Madrid Protocol | section 53 |
| Paris Convention | section 55(1)(a) |
| plaintiff (in Scotland) | section 102 |
| prescribed | section 78(1)(b) |
| protected under the Paris Convention | |
| —well-known trade marks | section 56(1) |
| —state emblems and official signs or hallmarks | section 57(1) |
| —emblems, &c. of international organisations | section 58(2) |
| publish and references to publication | section 103(1) |
| register, registered (and related expressions) | section 63(1) |
| registered trade mark [attorney] | section 83[(2)] |
| registrable transaction | section 25(2) |
| the registrar | section 62 |
| rules | section 78 |
| statutory provisions | section 103(1) |
| trade | section 103(1) |
| trade mark | |
| —generally | section 1(1) |
| —includes collective mark or certification mark | section 1(2) |
| United Kingdom (references include Isle of Man) | section 108(2) |
| use (of trade mark or sign) | section 103(2) |
| well-known trade mark (under Paris Convention) | section 56(1) |

*Other general provisions*

**Transitional provisions.**

**105.—** The provisions of Schedule 3 have effect with respect to transitional matters, including the treatment of marks registered under the Trade Marks Act 1938, and applications for registration and other proceedings pending under that Act, on the commencement of this Act.

**Consequential amendments and repeals.**

**106.—**(1) The enactments specified in Schedule 4 are amended in accordance with that Schedule, the amendments being consequential on the provisions of this Act.

(2) The enactments specified in Schedule 5 are repealed to the extent specified

**Territorial waters and the continental shelf.**

**107.**—(1) For the purposes of this Act the territorial waters of the United Kingdom shall be treated as part of the United Kingdom.

(2) This Act applies to things done in the United Kingdom sector of the continental shelf on a structure or vessel which is present there for purposes directly connected with the exploration of the sea bed or subsoil or the exploitation of their natural resources as it applies to things done in the United Kingdom.

(3) The United Kingdom sector of the continental shelf means the areas designated by order under section 1(7) of the Continental Shelf Act 1964.

**Extent.**

**108.**—(1) This Act extends to England and Wales, Scotland and Northern Ireland.

(2) This Act also extends to the Isle of Man, subject to such exceptions and modifications as Her Majesty may specify by Order in Council, and subject to any such Order references in this Act to the United Kingdom shall be construed as including the Isle of Man.

**Commencement.**

**109.**—(1) The provisions of this Act come into force on such day as the Secretary of State may appoint by order made by statutory instrument.

Different days may be appointed for different provisions and different purposes.

(2) The references to the commencement of this Act in Schedules 3 and 4 (transitional provisions and consequential amendments) are to the commencement of the main substantive provisions of Parts I and III of this Act and the consequential repeal of the Trade Marks Act 1938. Provision may be made by order under this section identifying the date of that commencement

**Short title.**

**110.**— This Act may be cited as the Trade Marks Act 1994.

## SCHEDULE 1

### COLLECTIVE MARKS

**Section 49**

*General*

**1.**— The provisions of this Act apply to collective marks subject to the following provisions.

*Signs of which a collective mark may consist*

**2.**— In relation to a collective mark the reference in section 1(1) (signs of which a trade mark may consist) to distinguishing goods or services of one undertaking from those of other undertakings shall be construed as a reference to distinguishing goods or services of members of the association which is the proprietor of the mark from those of other undertakings.

*Indication of geographical origin*

**3.**—(1) Notwithstanding section 3(1)(c), a collective mark may be registered which consists of signs or indications which may serve, in trade, to designate the geographical origin of the goods or services.

(2) However, the proprietor of such a mark is not entitled to prohibit the use of the signs or indications in accordance with honest practices in industrial or commercial matters (in particular, by a person who is entitled to use a geographical name).

*Mark not to be misleading as to character or significance*

**4.**—(1) A collective mark shall not be registered if the public is liable to be misled as regards the character or significance of the mark, in particular if it is likely to be taken to be something other than a collective mark.

(2) The registrar may accordingly require that a mark in respect of which application is made for registration include some indication that it is a collective mark.

Notwithstanding section 39(2), an application may be amended so as to comply with any such requirement.

*Regulations governing use of collective mark*

**5.**—(1) An applicant for registration of a collective mark must fine with the registrar regulations governing the use of the mark.

(2) The regulations must specify the persons authorised to use the mark, the conditions of membership of the association and, where they exist, the conditions of use of the mark, including any sanctions against misuse.

(3) Where the regulations govern use of a mark referred to in paragraph 3(1), they must authorise any person whose goods or services originate in the geographical area concerned to become a member of the association which is the proprietor of the mark, provided that the person fulfils all the other conditions of the regulations.

(4) Further requirements with which the regulations have to comply may be imposed by rules.

*Approval of regulations by registrar*

**6.**—(1) A collective mark shall not be registered unless the regulations governing the use of the mark—

(a) comply with [paragraph 5(2) and (3)] and any further requirements imposed by rules, and

(b) are not contrary to public policy or to accepted principles of morality

(2) Before the end of the prescribed period after the date of the application for registration of a collective mark, the applicant must file the regulations with the registrar and pay the prescribed fee.

If he does not do so, the application shall be deemed to be withdrawn.

**7.**—(1) The registrar shall consider whether the requirements mentioned in paragraph 6(1) are met.

(2) If it appears to the registrar that those requirements are not met, he shall the applicant and give him an opportunity, within such period as the registrar may specify, to make representations or to file amended regulations.

(3) If the applicant fails to satisfy the registrar that those requirements are not, or to file regulations amended so as to meet them, or fails to respond before the end of the specified period, the registrar shall refuse the application.

(4) If it appears to the registrar that those requirements, and the other requirements for registration, are met, he shall accept the application and shall proceed in accordance with section 38 (publication, opposition proceedings and observations).

**8.**— The regulations shall be published and notice of opposition may be given, and observations may be made, relating to the matters mentioned in paragraph 6(1).

This is in addition to any other grounds on which the application may be opposed or observations made.

*Regulations to be open to inspection*

**9.**— The regulations governing the use of a registered collective mark shall be open to public inspection in the same way as the register.

*Amendment of regulations*

**10.**—(1) An amendment of the regulations governing the use of a registered collective mark is not effective unless and until the amended regulations are filed with the registrar and accepted by him.

(2) Before accepting any amended regulations the registrar may in any case where it appears to him expedient to do so cause them to be published.

(3) If he does so, notice of opposition may be given, and observations may be made, relating to the matters mentioned in paragraph 6(1).

*Infringement rights of authorised users*

**11.**— The following provisions apply in relation to an authorised user of a registered collective mark as in relation to a licensee of a trade mark—

(a) section 10(5) (definition of infringement: unauthorised application of mark to certain material);
(b) section 19(2) (order as to disposal of infringing goods, material or articles adequacy of other remedies);
(c) section 89 (prohibition of importation of infringing goods, material or articles request to Commissioners of Customs and Excise).

**12.**—(1) The following provisions (which correspond to the provisions of section 30 general provisions as to rights of licensees in case of infringement) have effect as regards the rights of an authorised user in relation to infringement of a registered collective mark.

[(2) Subject to any agreement to the contrary between the authorised user and the proprietor, an authorised user may only bring proceedings for infringement of a registered collective mark with the consent of the proprietor.]

(3) […]

(4) [Where proceedings are brought by an authorised user for infringement of a registered collective mark (with the consent of the proprietor or pursuant to any agreement referred to in sub-paragraph (2))], the authorised user may not, without the leave of the court, proceed with the action unless the proprietor is either joined as a plaintiff or added as a defendant. This does not affect the granting of interlocutory relief on an application by an authorised user alone.

(5) A proprietor who is added as a defendant as mentioned in sub-paragraph (4) shall not be made liable for any costs in the action unless he takes part in the proceedings.

(6) In infringement proceedings brought by the proprietor of a registered collective mark any loss suffered or likely to be suffered by authorised users shall be taken into account; and the court may give such directions as it thinks fit as to the extent to which the plaintiff is to hold the proceeds of any pecuniary remedy on behalf of such users.

[(7) Where the proprietor of a registered collective mark brings infringement proceedings, an authorised user who has suffered loss is entitled to intervene in the proceedings for the purpose of obtaining compensation for that loss.]

**13.** Apart from the grounds of revocation provided for in section 46, the registration of a collective mark may be revoked on the ground

(a) that the manner in which the mark has been used by the proprietor has caused it to become liable to mislead the public in the manner referred to in paragraph 4(1); or
(b) that the [persons authorised to use it] [has not taken reasonable steps to prevent the mark being used in a manner that is incompatible with the conditions of use laid down in] the regulations governing the use of the mark [(as amended from time to time)], or
(c) that an amendment of the regulations has been made so that the regulations
   (i) no longer comply with [paragraph 5(2) and (3)]4 and any further conditions imposed by rules, or
   (ii) are contrary to public policy or to accepted principles of morality.

**14.** Apart from the grounds of invalidity provided for in section 47, the registration of a collective mark [shall] be declared invalid on the ground that the mark was registered in breach of the provisions of [section 49(1A) (definition of who may be registered as the proprietor of a certification mark) or] paragraph 4(1) or 6(1)[unless the breach was only of paragraph 6(1) and the proprietor of the mark, by amending the regulations governing use, complies with the requirements of paragraph 6(1)].

## SCHEDULE 2

### CERTIFICATION MARKS

**Section 50**

*General*

**1.**— The provisions of this Act apply to certification marks subject to the following provisions.

*Signs of which a certification mark may consist*

**2.**— In relation to a certification mark the reference in section 1(1) (signs of which a trade mark may consist) to distinguishing goods or services of one undertaking from those of other undertakings shall be construed as a reference to distinguishing goods or services which are certified from those which are not.

*Indication of geographical origin*

**3.**—(1) Notwithstanding section 3(1)(c) a certification mark may be registered which consists of signs or indications which may serve, in trade, to designate the geographical origin of the goods or services.

(2) However, the proprietor of such a mark is not entitled to prohibit the use of the signs or indications in accordance with honest practices in industrial or commercial matters (in particular, by a person who is entitled to use a geographical name).

*Nature of proprietor's business*

**4.**—(1) A certification mark shall not be registered if the proprietor carries on a business involving the supply of goods or services of the kind certified.

*Mark not to be misleading as to character or significance*

**5.**—(1) A certification mark shall not be registered if the public is liable to be misled as regards the character or significance of the mark, in particular if it is likely to be taken to be something other than a certification mark.

(2) The registrar may accordingly require that a mark in respect of which application is made for registration include some indication that it is a certification mark.

Notwithstanding section 39(2); an application may be amended so as to comply with any such requirement.

*Regulations governing use of certification mark*

**6.**—(1) An applicant for registration of a certification mark must file with the registrar regulations governing the use of the mark.

(2) The regulations must indicate who is authorised to use the mark, the characteristics to be certified by the mark, how the certifying body is to test those characteristics and to supervise the use of the mark, the fees (if any) to be paid in connection with the operation of the mark and the procedures for resolving disputes.

Further requirements with which the regulations have to comply may be imposed by rules.

*Approval of regulations, &c.*

**7.**—(1) A certification mark shall not be registered unless—

(a) the regulations governing the use of the mark—

(i) comply with paragraph 6(2) and any further requirements imposed by rules, and

(ii) are not contrary to public policy or to accepted principles of morality, and

(b) the applicant is competent to certify the goods or services for which the mark is to be registered.

(2) Before the end of the prescribed period after the date of the application for registration of a certification mark, the applicant must file the regulations with the registrar and pay the prescribed fee.

If he does not do so, the application shall be deemed to be withdrawn.

**8.**—(1) The registrar shall consider whether the requirements mentioned in paragraph 7(1) are met.

(2) If it appears to the registrar that those requirements are not met, he shall inform the applicant and give him an opportunity, within such period as the registrar may specify, to make representations or to file amended regulations.

(3) If the applicant fails to satisfy the registrar that those requirements are met, or to file regulations amended so as to meet them, or fails to respond before the end of the specified period, the registrar shall refuse the application.

(4) If it appears to the registrar that those requirements, and the other requirements for registration, are met, he shall accept the application and shall proceed in accordance with section 38 (publication, opposition proceedings and observations).

**9.**— The regulations shall be published and notice of opposition may be given, and observations may be made, relating to the matters mentioned in paragraph 7(1)

This is in addition to any other grounds on which the application may be opposed or observations made.

*Regulations to be open to inspection*

**10.**— The regulations governing the use of a registered certification mark shall be open to public inspection in the same way as the register.

*Amendment of regulations*

**11.**—(1) An amendment of the regulations governing the use of a registered certification mark is not effective unless and until the amended regulations art filed with the registrar and accepted by him.

(2) Before accepting any amended regulations the registrar may in any case where it appears to him expedient to do so cause them to be published.

(3) If he does so, notice of opposition may be given, and observations may be made, relating to the matters mentioned in paragraph 7(1).

*Consent to assignment of registered certification mark*

**12.—** The assignment or other transmission of a registered certification mark is not effective without the consent of the registrar.

*Infringement rights of authorised users*

**13.—** The following provisions apply in relation to an authorised user of a registered certification mark as in relation to a licensee of a trade mark—

(a) section 10(5) (definition of infringement unauthorised application of mark to certain material);

(b) section 19(2) (order as to disposal of infringing goods, material or articles: adequacy of other remedies);

(c) section 89 (prohibition of importation of infringing goods, material or articles request to Commissioners of Customs and Excise).

**14.—** In infringement proceedings brought by the proprietor of a registered certification mark any loss suffered or likely to be suffered by authorised users shall be taken into account, and the court may give such directions as it thinks fit as to the extent to which the plaintiff is to told the proceeds of any pecuniary remedy on behalf of such users.

*Grounds for revocation of registration*

**15.—** Apart from the grounds of revocation provided for in section 46, the registration of a certification mark may be revoked on the ground—

(a) that the proprietor has begun to carry on such a business as is mentioned in paragraph 4.

(b) that the manner in which the mark has been used by the proprietor has caused it to become liable to mislead the public in the manner referred to in paragraph 5(1),

(c) that the proprietor has failed to observe, or to secure the observance of, the regulations governing the use of the mark,

(d) that an amendment of the regulations has been made so that the regulations—

(i) no longer comply with paragraph 6(2) and any further conditions imposed by rules, or

(ii) are contrary to public policy or to accepted principles of morality, or

(e) that the proprietor is no longer competent to certify the goods or services for which the mark is registered.

*Grounds for invalidity of registration*

**16.—** Apart from the grounds of invalidity provided for in section 47, the registration of a certification mark may be declared invalid on the ground that the mark was registered in breach of the provisions of paragraph 4, 5(1) or 7(1)

[SCHEDULE 2A

EUROPEAN UNION TRADE MARKS

**(Section 52A)**

PART 1

EXISTING EUROPEAN UNION TRADE MARKS

**A trade mark registered as an existing EUTM to be treated as registered under this Act**

**1.—**(1) A trade mark which is registered in the EUTM Register immediately before IP completion day (an "existing EUTM") is to be treated on and after IP completion day as if an application had been made, and the trade mark had been registered, under this Act in respect of the same goods or services as the existing EUTM is registered in the EUTM Register.

(2) A registered trade mark which comes into being by virtue of sub-paragraph (1) is referred to in this Act as a comparable trade mark (EU).

(3) This Act applies to a comparable trade mark (EU) as it applies to other registered trade marks except as otherwise provided in this Schedule.

(4) A comparable trade mark (EU) is deemed for the purposes of this Act to be registered as of the filing date accorded pursuant to Article 32 to the application which resulted in the registration of

the corresponding EUTM and that date is deemed for the purposes of this Act to be the date of registration.

(5) Section 40(3) and (4) does not apply to the registration of a comparable trade mark (EU) under this Part.

(6) Section 67(1) applies in relation to the provision of information and the inspection of documents relating to a comparable trade mark (EU) notwithstanding that there will have been no application under this Act for the registration of the trade mark (and so no publication of an application).

(7) Nothing in this Act authorises the imposition of a fee, or the making of provision by rules or regulations which authorises the imposition of a fee, in respect of any matter relating to a comparable trade mark (EU) (see instead provision made by regulations under Schedule 4 to the European Union (Withdrawal) Act 2018).

(8) For the purposes of this Act—

(a) the date of filing of an application for registration of a comparable trade mark (EU) is the filing date accorded pursuant to Article 32 to the application which resulted in the registration of the corresponding EUTM;

(b) references to the date of application for registration of a comparable trade mark (EU) are to the date of filing of the application;

(c) where an earlier trade mark is a comparable trade mark (EU), references to the completion of the registration procedure for the earlier trade mark are to the completion of the registration procedure in respect of the corresponding EUTM.

(9) In this Schedule—

(a) "corresponding EUTM" , in relation to a comparable trade mark (EU), means the existing EUTM from which the comparable trade mark (EU) derives;

(b) "the EUTM Register" means the register of European Union trade marks maintained by the European Union Intellectual Property Office.

**Opt out**

**2.**—(1) Subject to sub-paragraph (2), the proprietor of an existing EUTM may, at any time on or after IP completion day, serve notice on the registrar that the trade mark is not to be treated as if the trade mark had been registered under this Act (an "opt out notice").

(2) An opt out notice may not be served where on or after IP completion day—

(a) the comparable trade mark (EU) has been put to use in the United Kingdom by the proprietor or with the proprietor's consent (which use includes affixing the trade mark to goods or to the packaging of goods in the United Kingdom solely for export purposes);

(b) the comparable trade mark (EU) (or any right in or under it) has been made the subject of an assignment, licence, security interest or any other agreement or document except for an assent by personal representatives in relation to the comparable trade mark (EU); or

(c) proceedings based on the comparable trade mark (EU) have been initiated by the proprietor or with the proprietor's consent.

(3) An opt out notice must—

(a) identify the existing EUTM; and

(b) include the name and address of any person having an interest in the existing EUTM which had effect before IP completion day in the United Kingdom, and in respect of which an entry was recorded in the EUTM Register.

(4) An opt out notice is of no effect unless the proprietor in that notice certifies that any such person—

(a) has been given not less than three months' notice of the proprietor's intention to serve an opt out notice; or

(b) is not affected or if affected, consents to the opt out.

(5) Where a notice has been served in accordance with this paragraph—

(a) the comparable trade mark (EU) which derives from the existing EUTM ceases with effect from IP completion day to be treated as if it had been registered under this Act; and

(b) the registrar must, where particulars of the comparable trade mark (EU) have been entered in the register, remove the comparable trade mark (EU) from the register.

**Entries to be made in the register in relation to a comparable trade mark (EU)**

**3.**—(1) The registrar must as soon as reasonably practicable after IP completion day enter a comparable trade mark (EU) in the register.

(2) The particulars of the goods or services in respect of which the comparable trade mark (EU) is treated as if it had been registered must be taken from the English language version of the entry for the corresponding EUTM in the EUTM Register.

(3) Where—

(a) the application for registration of the corresponding EUTM was not filed in English; or
(b) the second language indicated by the applicant pursuant to Article 146(3) was a language other than English,

a person having a sufficient interest who considers that the English language version is inaccurate may apply to the registrar for rectification of the register by the substitution of an English translation of the relevant authentic text (as determined in accordance with Article 147(3)) verified to the satisfaction of the registrar as corresponding to the authentic text.

**Comparable trade mark (EU) which derives from an EU Collective Mark or EU Certification Mark**

**4.**—(1) This paragraph applies where the European Union trade mark from which a comparable trade mark (EU) derives is an EU collective mark or an EU certification mark.

(2) The comparable trade mark (EU) is to be treated as either a collective mark or a certification mark, as the case may be.

(3) The proprietor of the comparable trade mark (EU) must, following notice from the registrar, file with the registrar regulations governing the use of the European Union trade mark, submitted pursuant to the European Union Trade Mark Regulation, which had effect immediately before IP completion day.

(4) Where the regulations referred to in sub-paragraph (3) are in a language other than English they must be filed together with a translation into English verified to the satisfaction of the registrar as corresponding to the original text.

(5) Paragraph 9 of Schedule 1 and paragraph 10 of Schedule 2 apply in relation to the translation referred to in sub-paragraph (4) as they apply in relation to the regulations referred to in sub-paragraph (3).

(6) Where the regulations or any translation are not filed in accordance with the above provisions—

(a) the registrar must remove the comparable trade mark (EU) from the register; and
(b) the rights of the proprietor shall be deemed to have ceased as from the date of removal.

**Renewal of a comparable trade mark (EU) which expires within six months after IP completion day**

**5.**—(1) This paragraph applies to the renewal of the registration of a comparable trade mark (EU) which expires within the period beginning with IP completion day and ending with the end of the relevant period (and accordingly section 43(1) to (3A) does not apply).

(2) The registration of the comparable trade mark (EU) may be renewed at the request of the proprietor before the expiry of the registration.

(3) Where the registration of the comparable trade mark (EU) is not renewed in accordance with sub-paragraph (2)—

(a) on, or as soon as reasonably practicable after, the expiry of the registration, the registrar must notify the proprietor that the registration has expired and of the manner in which the registration may be renewed; and
(b) a request for renewal must be made within the period of six months beginning with the date of the notice.

(4) If a request for renewal is made in respect of only some of the goods or services for which the comparable trade mark (EU) is registered, the registration is to be renewed for those goods or services only.

(5) If the registration is not renewed in accordance with the above provisions, the registrar must remove the comparable trade mark (EU) from the register.

(6) Section 43(4) and (6) applies to the registration of a comparable trade mark (EU) which is renewed in accordance with the above provisions.

(7) In paragraph (1), the "relevant period" means the period of six months beginning with the day after that on which IP completion day falls.

**Restoration of a comparable trade mark (EU)**

**6.** Where a comparable trade mark (EU) is removed from the register pursuant to paragraph 5, the rules relating to the restoration of the registration of a trade mark (referred to in section 43(5)) apply in relation to the restoration of the comparable trade mark (EU) to the register.

**Raising of relative grounds in opposition proceedings in case of non-use**

**7.**—(1) Section 6A applies where an earlier trade mark is a comparable trade mark (EU), subject to the modifications set out below.

(2) Where the relevant period referred to in section 6A(3)(a) (the "five-year period") has expired before IP completion day—

(a) the references in section 6A(3) and (6) to the earlier trade mark are to be treated as references to the corresponding EUTM; and

(b) the references in section 6A(3) and (4) to the United Kingdom include the European Union.

(3) Where IP completion day falls within the five-year period, in respect of that part of the five-year period which falls before IP completion day—

(a) the references in section 6A(3) and (6) to the earlier trade mark are to be treated as references to the corresponding EUTM ; and

(b) the references in section 6A to the United Kingdom include the European Union.

**Non-use as defence in infringement proceedings and revocation of registration of a comparable trade mark (EU)**

**8.**—(1) Sections 11A and 46 apply in relation to a comparable trade mark (EU), subject to the modifications set out below.

(2) Where the period of five years referred to in sections 11A(3)(a) and 46(1)(a) or (b) (the "five-year period") has expired before IP completion day—

(a) the references in sections 11A(3) and (insofar as they relate to use of a trade mark) 46 to a trade mark are to be treated as references to the corresponding EUTM; and

(b) the references in sections 11A and 46 to the United Kingdom include the European Union.

(3) Where IP completion day falls within the five-year period, in respect of that part of the five-year period which falls before IP completion day—

(a) the references in sections 11A(3) and (insofar as they relate to use of a trade mark) 46 to a trade mark, are to be treated as references to the corresponding EUTM ; and

(b) the references in sections 11A and 46 to the United Kingdom include the European Union.

**Grounds for invalidity of registration of a trade mark based upon an earlier comparable trade mark (EU)**

**9.**—(1) Section 47 applies where an earlier trade mark is a comparable trade mark (EU), subject to the modifications set out below.

(2) Where the period of five years referred to in sections 47(2A)(a) and 47(2B) (the "five-year period") has expired before IP completion day—

(a) the references in section 47(2B) and (2E) to the earlier trade mark are to be treated as references to the corresponding EUTM; and

(b) the references in section 47 to the United Kingdom include the European Union.

(3) Where IP completion day falls within the five-year period, in respect of that part of the five-year period which falls before IP completion day—

(a) the references in section 47(2B) and (2E) to the earlier trade mark are to be treated as references to the corresponding EUTM; and

(b) the references in section 47 to the United Kingdom include the European Union.

**Reputation of a comparable trade mark (EU)**

**10.**—(1) Sections 5 and 10 apply in relation to a comparable trade mark (EU), subject to the modifications set out below.

(2) Where the reputation of a comparable trade mark (EU) falls to be considered in respect of any time before IP completion day, references in sections 5(3) and 10(3) to—

(a) the reputation of the mark are to be treated as references to the reputation of the corresponding EUTM; and

(b) the United Kingdom include the European Union.

**Rights conferred by registered trade mark**

**11.** Section 9 applies in relation to a comparable trade mark (EU) but as if—

(a) the words in brackets in subsection (3) referring to section 40(3) were replaced with a reference to paragraph 1(4) of this Schedule; and

(b) the proviso in subsection (3) were omitted.

**Effect of claim of priority**

**12.**—(1) This paragraph applies where—

(a) the proprietor of an existing EUTM has claimed a right of priority in accordance with Article 35; and

(b) immediately before IP completion day there is an entry in the EUTM Register containing particulars of that claim of priority (a "claim of priority").

(2) The proprietor of the comparable trade mark (EU) which derives from the existing EUTM is to be treated on and after IP completion day as having the same claim of priority.

(3) Accordingly, the relevant date for the purposes of establishing, in relation to the comparable trade mark (EU), which rights take precedence is the date of filing of the application for a trade mark in a Convention country which formed the basis for the claim of priority.

**Effect of seniority claim**

**13.**—(1) This paragraph applies where immediately before IP completion day an existing EUTM has a valid claim to seniority of a trade mark which trade mark (the "senior mark") is a registered trade mark or a protected international trade mark (UK).

(2) The comparable trade mark (EU) which derives from the existing EUTM is to be treated on and after IP completion day as if it had a valid claim to seniority of the senior mark.

(3) Accordingly, where the proprietor of the comparable trade mark (EU) surrenders the senior mark or allows it to lapse (whether wholly or partially), subject to paragraph 14, the proprietor of the comparable trade mark (EU) is deemed to continue to have the same rights as the proprietor would have had if the senior mark had continued to be registered in respect of all the goods or services for which it was registered prior to the surrender or lapse.

(4) An existing EUTM has a valid claim to seniority of a trade mark where—

(a) a claim has been filed in accordance with Article 39 or 40; and

(b) the seniority claimed for the existing EUTM has not lapsed in the circumstances referred to in Article 39.

**Determination of invalidity and liability to revocation in relation to claims of seniority**

**14.**—(1) Where pursuant to paragraph 13 a comparable trade mark (EU) is treated as if it had a valid claim to seniority of a registered trade mark which has been—

(a) removed from the register under section 43; or

(b) surrendered under section 45,

any person may apply to the registrar or to the court for the declaration set out in sub-paragraph (2).

(2) The declaration is that if the trade mark had not been so removed or surrendered, the registration of the trade mark would have been liable to be revoked under section 46 with effect from a date specified in the declaration or declared invalid under section 47.

(3) Where the declaration is that had the trade mark not been so removed or surrendered the registration of it would have been liable to be—

(a) revoked under section 46 with effect from a date prior to—

(i) the filing date accorded pursuant to Article 32 to the application which resulted in the registration of the existing EUTM from which the comparable trade mark (EU) derives where there has been no claim of priority; or

(ii) the priority date (if any) accorded pursuant to a right of priority claimed pursuant to Article 35 in respect of the existing EUTM from which the comparable trade mark (EU) derives where there has been a claim of priority; or

(b) declared invalid under section 47,

the seniority claimed for the comparable trade mark (EU) is to be treated as if it never had effect.

(4) Where pursuant to paragraph 13 a comparable trade mark (EU) is treated as if it had a valid claim to seniority of a protected international trade mark (UK) which has been—

(a) removed from the register of trade marks maintained by the International Bureau for the purposes of the Madrid Protocol; or

(b) surrendered under the Madrid Protocol,

any person may apply to the registrar or to the court for the declaration set out in sub-paragraph (5).

(5) The declaration is that, if the trade mark had not been so removed or surrendered, the protection of the mark in the United Kingdom would have been liable to be revoked under section 46 with effect from a date specified in the declaration or declared invalid under section 47.

(6) Where the declaration is that had the trade mark not been so removed or surrendered the protection of the mark in the United Kingdom would have been liable to be—

(a) revoked under section 46 with effect from a date prior to—

(i) the filing date accorded pursuant to Article 32 to the application which resulted in the registration of the existing EUTM from which the comparable trade mark (EU) derives where there has been no claim of priority; or

(ii) the priority date (if any) accorded pursuant to a right of priority claimed pursuant to Article 35 in respect of the existing EUTM from which the comparable trade mark (EU) derives where there has been a claim of priority; or

(b) declared invalid under section 47,

the seniority claimed for the comparable trade mark (EU) is to be treated as if it never had effect.

(7) References in sub-paragraphs (5) and (6) to sections 46 and 47 are to those sections as they apply to a protected international trade mark (UK) under an order made pursuant to section 54.

(8) Where a trade mark has been surrendered or allowed to lapse in respect of some only of the goods or services for which it is registered, the declaration in sub-paragraphs (2) and (5) is that if the goods or services had not been removed from the registration, the registration of the trade mark would have been liable to be revoked under section 46 with effect from a date specified in the declaration or declared invalid under section 47 and sub-paragraphs (3) and (6) shall be construed accordingly.

**Procedure for declaration that trade mark would have been liable to be revoked or declared invalid**

**15.**—(1) In the case of proceedings on an application under paragraph 14 before the registrar, the rules relating to applications for and proceedings relating to the revocation or invalidation of a trade mark apply, with necessary modifications.

(2) In the case of proceedings on an application under paragraph 14 before the court, section 74 applies to the proceedings as it applies to proceedings involving an application of the type referred to in section 74(1)(a) to (c).

**Assignment of an existing EUTM not registered on IP completion day**

**16.**—(1) This paragraph applies where before IP completion day an existing EUTM (or any right in it) is the subject of an assignment (a "relevant assignment") which immediately before IP completion day is not recorded in the EUTM Register.

(2) Section 25 applies in relation to a relevant assignment as if it were a registrable transaction affecting a comparable trade mark (EU), subject to the modification set out below.

(3) An application under section 25(1) may only be made by—

(a) a person claiming to be entitled to an interest in or under a comparable trade mark (EU) by virtue of a relevant assignment of the corresponding EUTM; or

(b) the proprietor of the comparable trade mark (EU).

**Effect of a licence of an existing EUTM**

**17.**—(1) This paragraph applies where immediately before IP completion day an existing EUTM is the subject of a licence (a "relevant licence") which—

(a) authorises the doing of acts in the United Kingdom which would otherwise infringe the European Union trade mark; and

(b) does not expire on IP completion day.

(2) Subject to any agreement to the contrary between the licensee and the licensor, a relevant licence continues to authorise the doing of acts in the United Kingdom which would otherwise infringe the comparable trade mark (EU) which derives from the existing EUTM.

(3) Sub-paragraph (2) is subject to—

(a) the terms on which the relevant licence was granted; and

(b) such modifications to the terms referred to in paragraph (a) as are necessary for their application in the United Kingdom.

(4) Section 25 applies in relation to a relevant licence as if it were a registrable transaction affecting a comparable trade mark (EU), subject to the modifications set out below.

(5) An application under section 25(1) may only be made by—

(a) a person claiming to be a licensee by virtue of the relevant licence; or

(b) the proprietor of the comparable trade mark (EU).

(6) Where immediately before IP completion day there is an entry in the EUTM Register relating to a relevant licence—

(a) section 25(3) and (4) does not apply until after the expiry of the relevant period; and

(b) section 25(4)(a) applies after the expiry of the relevant period but as if the reference to six months beginning with the date of the transaction were a reference to eighteen months beginning with IP completion day.

(7) In paragraph (6)(a), the "relevant period" means the period of twelve months beginning with the day after that on which IP completion day falls.

**Effect of a security interest in an existing EUTM**

**18.**—(1) This paragraph applies where immediately before IP completion day an existing EUTM (or any right in or under it) is the subject of a security interest (a "relevant security interest") which does not terminate on IP completion day.

(2) References to the existing EUTM in any document which grants or refers to the relevant security interest are to be read as including references to the comparable trade mark (EU) which derives from the existing EUTM.

(3) Section 25 applies in relation to a relevant security interest as if it were a registrable transaction affecting a comparable trade mark (EU), subject to the modifications set out below.

(4) An application under section 25(1) may only be made by—

(a) a person claiming to be entitled to an interest in or under a comparable trade mark (EU) by virtue of the relevant security interest; or

(b) the proprietor of the comparable trade mark (EU).

(5) Where immediately before IP completion day there is an entry in the EUTM Register relating to a relevant security interest—

(a) section 25(3) and (4) do not apply until after the expiry of the relevant period; and

(b) section 25(4)(a) applies after the expiry of the relevant period but as if the reference to six months beginning with the date of the transaction were a reference to eighteen months beginning with IP completion day.

(6) In paragraph (5)(a), the "relevant period" means the period of twelve months beginning with the day after that on which IP completion day falls.

**Continuity of rights in relation to a comparable trade mark (EU)**

**19.**—(1) References to an existing EUTM or the registration of an existing EUTM in any document made before IP completion day shall, unless there is evidence that the document was not intended to have effect in the United Kingdom, be read on and after IP completion day as including references to the comparable trade mark (EU) or the registration of the comparable trade mark (EU) which derives from the existing EUTM.

(2) Subject to any agreement to the contrary, a consent granted before IP completion day by the proprietor of an existing EUTM to the doing on or after IP completion day of an act in the United Kingdom which would otherwise infringe the comparable trade mark (EU) which derives from the existing EUTM is to be treated for the purposes of section 9 as a consent to the doing of that act.

**Existing EUTM: pending proceedings**

**20.**—(1) This paragraph applies where on IP completion day an existing EUTM is the subject of proceedings which are pending ("pending proceedings") before a court in the United Kingdom designated for the purposes of Article 123 ("EU trade mark court").

(2) Subject to sub-paragraphs (3) and (4), the provisions contained or referred to in Chapter 10 of the European Union Trade Mark Regulation (with the exception of Articles 128(2), (4), (6) and (7) and 132) continue to apply to the pending proceedings as if the United Kingdom were still a Member State with effect from IP completion day.

(3) Where the pending proceedings involve a claim for infringement of an existing EUTM, without prejudice to any other relief by way of damages, accounts or otherwise available to the proprietor of the existing EUTM, the EU trade mark court may grant an injunction to prohibit unauthorised use of the comparable trade mark (EU) which derives from the existing EUTM.

(4) Where the pending proceedings involve a counterclaim for the revocation of, or a declaration of invalidity in relation to, an existing EUTM, the EU trade mark court may revoke the registration of the comparable trade mark (EU) which derives from the existing EUTM or declare the registration of the comparable trade mark (EU) which derives from the existing EUTM to be invalid.

(5) Where the grounds for revocation or invalidity exist in respect of only some of the goods or services for which the existing EUTM is registered, the revocation or declaration of invalidity in respect of the registration of the comparable trade mark (EU) which derives from the existing EUTM relates to those goods or services only.

(6) Where (by virtue of sub-paragraph (4)) the registration of a comparable trade mark (EU) is revoked to any extent, the rights of the proprietor are deemed to have ceased to that extent as from—

(a) the date of the counterclaim for revocation, or

(b) if the court is satisfied that the grounds for revocation existed at an earlier date, that date.

(7) Where (by virtue of sub-paragraph (4)) the registration of a comparable trade mark (EU) is declared invalid to any extent, the registration is to that extent to be deemed never to have been made, provided that this does not affect transactions past and closed.

(8) For the purposes of this paragraph proceedings are treated as pending on IP completion day if they were instituted but not finally determined before IP completion day.

**Existing EUTM: effect of injunction**

**21.**—(1) This paragraph applies where immediately before IP completion day an injunction is in force prohibiting the performance of acts in the United Kingdom which infringe or would infringe an existing EUTM (a "relevant injunction").

(2) Subject to any order of the court to the contrary, a relevant injunction will have effect and be

enforceable to prohibit the performance of acts which infringe or would infringe a comparable trade mark (EU) to the same extent as in relation to the European Union trade mark from which the comparable trade mark (EU) derives as if it were an injunction granted by the court.

PART 2

TREATMENT OF EUROPEAN UNION TRADE MARKS WHICH EXPIRE DURING THE PERIOD OF SIX MONTHS ENDING ON IP COMPLETION DAY

**Registration of certain expired European Union trade marks**

**22.**—(1) This Part applies to a trade mark which was registered in the EUTM Register immediately before the transitional period but which, as a result of the expiry of the registration of the European Union trade mark during the transitional period, does not fall within paragraph 1(1) (an "expired EUTM").

(2) An expired EUTM is to be treated as if it were an existing EUTM.

(3) The provisions of Part 1 of this Schedule apply to an expired EUTM as they apply to an existing EUTM subject to the provisions of this Part of the Schedule.

(4) Notwithstanding the entry in the register (under paragraph 3, as applied by sub-paragraph (3)) of a comparable trade mark (EU) which derives from an expired EUTM, the registration of the comparable trade mark (EU) is expired until it is renewed in accordance with paragraph 23 (or the comparable trade mark (EU) is removed from the register in accordance with paragraph 23(4)).

(5) In this paragraph, "transitional period" means the period of six months ending with IP completion day.

**Renewal of an expired EUTM**

**23.**—(1) Where the registration of an expired EUTM is renewed in accordance with Article 53 of the Continuing EUTM Regulation the registrar must, as soon as reasonably practicable after the date of such renewal, renew the registration of the comparable trade mark (EU) which derives from the expired EUTM.

(2) A comparable trade mark (EU) which is renewed under sub-paragraph (1) shall be renewed for a period of ten years from the expiry of the registration of the expired EUTM.

(3) If the registration of an expired EUTM is renewed in respect of only some of the goods or services in respect of which the expired EUTM was registered before its registration expired, the registration of the comparable trade mark (EU) under sub-paragraph (1) is to be renewed for those goods or services only.

(4) If the registration of an expired EUTM is not renewed within the time period permitted by Article 53 of the Continuing EUTM Regulation—

(a) the registrar must remove from the register the comparable trade mark (EU) which derives from the expired EUTM; and

(b) the comparable trade mark (EU) ceases with effect from IP completion day to be treated as if it had been registered under this Act.

(5) In this Schedule, the "Continuing EUTM Regulation" means Regulation (EU) 2017/1001 of the European Parliament and of the Council of 14 June 2017 on the European Union Trade Mark as it has effect in EU law.

PART 3

APPLICATIONS FOR EUROPEAN UNION TRADE MARKS WHICH ARE PENDING ON IP COMPLETION DAY

**Application of Part**

**24.**—(1) This Part applies to an application for registration of a trade mark under the EUTM Regulation in respect of which the conditions in sub-paragraph (2) are satisfied (an "existing EUTM application").

(2) The conditions referred to in sub-paragraph (1) are—

(a) the application has been accorded a filing date pursuant to Article 32; and

(b) as at the time immediately before IP completion day, the application has been neither granted nor refused by the European Union Intellectual Property Office.

**Application for registration under this Act based upon an existing EUTM application**

**25.**—(1) This paragraph applies where a person who has filed an existing EUTM application or a successor in title of that person applies for registration of the same trade mark under this Act for some or all of the same goods or services.

(2) Where an application for registration referred to in sub-paragraph (1) is made within a period beginning with IP completion day and ending with the end of the relevant period—

(a) the relevant date for the purposes of establishing which rights take precedence is the earliest of—
   (i) the filing date accorded pursuant to Article 32 to the existing EUTM application;
   (ii) the date of priority (if any) accorded pursuant to a right of priority claimed pursuant to Article 35 in respect of the existing EUTM application; and
(b) the registrability of the trade mark shall not be affected by any use of the mark in the United Kingdom which commenced in the period between the date referred to in paragraph (a) and the date of the application under this Act.

(3) In paragraph (2), the "relevant period" means the period of nine months beginning with the day after that on which IP completion day falls.

**Right to claim seniority where seniority has been claimed by an existing EUTM application**

**26.**—(1) Where an existing EUTM application claims seniority of a trade mark which trade mark ("the senior mark") is a registered trade mark or a protected international trade mark (UK), the applicant may claim seniority of the senior mark in an application for registration of a trade mark ("a relevant mark") pursuant to this Part.

(2) The effect of a seniority claim made pursuant to sub-paragraph (1) is that where following the registration of the relevant mark the proprietor of that mark surrenders the senior mark or allows it to lapse (wholly or partially), subject to paragraph 27, the proprietor of the relevant mark is deemed to continue to have the same rights as the proprietor would have had if the senior mark had continued to be registered in respect of all the goods or services for which it was registered prior to the surrender or lapse.

(3) Provision may be made by rules as to the manner of claiming seniority pursuant to this paragraph.

**Determination of invalidity and liability to revocation in relation to claim of seniority under paragraph 26**

**27.**—(1) Where a relevant mark has claimed seniority of a registered trade mark which has been—
(a) removed from the register under section 43; or
(b) surrendered under section 45,

any person may apply to the registrar or to the court for the declaration set out in sub-paragraph (2).

(2) The declaration is that, if the trade mark had not been so removed or surrendered, the registration of the trade mark would have been liable to be revoked under section 46 with effect from a date specified in the declaration or declared invalid under section 47.

(3) Where the declaration is that had the trade mark not been so removed or surrendered, the registration of it would have been liable to be—
(a) revoked under section 46 with effect from a date prior to—
   (i) the filing date accorded pursuant to Article 32 to the existing EUTM application on which the application for registration of a relevant mark is based where there has been no claim of priority; or
   (ii) the priority date (if any) accorded pursuant to a right of priority claimed pursuant to Article 35 in respect of the existing EUTM application on which the registration of a relevant mark is based where there has been a claim of priority; or
(b) declared invalid under section 47,

the seniority claimed for the relevant mark is to be treated as if it never had effect.

(4) Where a relevant mark has claimed seniority of a protected international trade mark (UK) which has been—
(a) removed from the register of trade marks maintained by the International Bureau for the purposes of the Madrid Protocol; or
(b) surrendered under the Madrid Protocol,

any person may apply to the registrar or to the court for the declaration set out in sub-paragraph (5).

(5) The declaration is that, if the trade mark had not been so removed or surrendered, the protection of the trade mark in the United Kingdom would have been liable to be revoked under section 46 with effect from a date specified in the declaration or declared invalid under section 47.

(6) Where the declaration is that had the trade mark not been so removed or surrendered, the registration of it would have been liable to be—
(a) revoked under section 46 with effect from a date prior to—
   (i) the filing date accorded pursuant to Article 32 to the existing EUTM application on which the application for registration of a relevant mark is based where there has been no claim of priority; or
   (ii) the priority date (if any) accorded pursuant to a right of priority claimed pursu-

ant to Article 35 in respect of the existing EUTM application on which the registration of a relevant mark is based where there has been a claim of priority; or

(b) declared invalid under section 47,

the seniority claimed for the relevant mark is to be treated as if it never had effect.

(7) References in sub-paragraphs (5) and (6) to sections 46 and 47 are to those sections as they apply to a protected international trade mark (UK) under an order made pursuant to section 54.

(8) Where a trade mark has been surrendered or allowed to lapse in respect of only some of the goods or services for which it is registered, the declaration in sub-paragraphs (2) and (5) is that if the goods or services had not been removed from the registration, the registration of the trade mark would have been liable to be revoked under section 46 with effect from a date specified in the declaration or declared invalid under section 47 and sub-paragraphs (3) and (6) shall be construed accordingly.

(9) The provisions of paragraph 15 apply in relation to an application under this paragraph as they apply to an application under paragraph 14.

PART 4

RESTORATION OF EUROPEAN UNION TRADE MARK REGISTRATIONS AND APPLICATIONS

**Restoration of a European Union trade mark to the EUTM Register**

**28.**—(1) This paragraph applies where—

(a) before IP completion day a trade mark is removed from the EUTM Register pursuant to the European Union Trade Mark Regulation; and

(b) on or after IP completion day the trade mark is restored to the EUTM Register pursuant to the Continuing EUTM Regulation.

(2) Where the proprietor of a European Union trade mark referred to in sub-paragraph (1)(b) files a request with the registrar within the period of six months beginning with the date of such restoration—

(a) the trade mark will be treated as if it was an existing EUTM on IP completion day; and

(b) the provisions of Part 1 apply to the comparable trade mark (EU) which derives from the existing EUTM.

**Restoration of an application for a European Union trade mark**

**29.**—(1) This paragraph applies where—

(a) before IP completion day an application for a European Union trade mark is refused pursuant to the European Union Trade Mark Regulation; and

(b) on or after IP completion day the application (a "relevant application") is restored pursuant to the Continuing EUTM Regulation.

(2) Where a person who has filed a relevant application or a successor in title of that person applies for registration of the same trade mark under this Act for some or all of the same goods or services, the provisions of paragraphs 25, 26 and 27 apply to the relevant application as if it were an existing EUTM application but as if the "relevant period" in paragraph 25(2) meant the period of nine months beginning with the date on which the relevant application is restored as referred to in sub-paragraph (1)(b).

PART 5

INTERPRETATION

**Interpretation**

**30.**—(1) In this Schedule—

"comparable trade mark (EU)" has the meaning given by paragraph 1(2);

"the Continuing EUTM Regulation" has the meaning given by paragraph 23(5);

"corresponding EUTM" has the meaning given by paragraph 1(9)(a);

"the EUTM Register" has the meaning given by paragraph 1(9)(b);

"existing EUTM" has the meaning given by paragraph 1(1);

"existing EUTM application" has the meaning given by paragraph 24(1);

"expired EUTM" has the meaning given by paragraph 22(1);

"the previous EUTM Regulations" means Council Regulation (EC) No 207/2009 of 26th February 2009 on the European Union trade mark and Council Regulation (EC) No 40/94 of 20th December 1993 on the Community trade mark;

"protected international trade mark (UK)" has the same meaning as in the Trade Marks (International Registration) Order 2008.

(2) References in this Schedule to—

(a) an "Article" are to an Article of the European Union Trade Mark Regulation and include references to any equivalent Article contained in the previous EUTM Regulations;

(b) the European Union Trade Mark Regulation include references to the previous EUTM Regulations;

(c) a European Union trade mark include references to an EU collective mark and an EU certification mark as defined in Articles 74 and 83.]

## [SCHEDULE 2B

### INTERNATIONAL TRADE MARKS PROTECTED IN THE EUROPEAN UNION

**(Section 54A)**

### PART 1

### EXISTING INTERNATIONAL TRADE MARKS PROTECTED IN THE EUROPEAN UNION

**An international trade mark protected in the European Union to be treated as registered under this Act**

**1.**—(1) A trade mark which, immediately before IP completion day, is an international trade mark which is protected in the European Union in accordance with Article 189(2) of the European Union Trade Mark Regulation (an "existing IR(EU)") is to be treated on and after IP completion day as if an application had been made, and the trade mark had been registered, under this Act in respect of the same goods or services in respect of which the international trade mark is protected in the European Union.

(2) Where the international registration to which an international trade mark is subject is sub-divided to reflect the making of more than one request for territorial extension to the European Union under Article 3ter there is to be deemed for the purposes of sub-paragraph (1) to be a separate trade mark in respect of the goods or services covered by each sub-division of the registration.

(3) Where the international registration to which an international trade mark is subject has been created by virtue of Rule 27(2) (recording of partial change in ownership) (a "separate international registration"), it is irrelevant for the purposes of the application of sub-paragraph (2) to that separate international registration that the requests for territorial extension were made before the separate international registration was created.

(4) A registered trade mark which comes into being by virtue of sub-paragraph (1) is referred to in this Act as a comparable trade mark (IR).

(5) This Act applies to a comparable trade mark (IR) as it applies to other registered trade marks except as otherwise provided in this Schedule.

(6) A comparable trade mark (IR) is deemed for the purposes of this Act to be registered as of—

(a) where the protection in the European Union of the existing IR(EU) from which the comparable trade mark (IR) derives resulted from a request for territorial extension under Article 3ter (1) (request mentioned in original application), the date of registration of the existing IR(EU) accorded pursuant to Article 3(4); or

(b) where the protection in the European Union of the existing IR(EU) from which the comparable trade mark (IR) derives resulted from a request for territorial extension under Article 3ter (2) (subsequent request), the date on which the request was recorded in the International Register,

and that date is deemed for the purposes of this Act to be the date of registration.

(7) Section 40(3) and (4) does not apply to the registration of a comparable trade mark (IR) under this Part.

(8) Section 67(1) applies in relation to the provision of information and the inspection of documents relating to a comparable trade mark (IR) notwithstanding that there will have been no application under this Act for the registration of the trade mark (and so no publication of an application).

(9) Nothing in this Act authorises the imposition of a fee, or the making of provision by rules or regulations which authorises the imposition of a fee, in respect of any matter relating to a comparable trade mark (IR) (see instead provision made by regulations under Schedule 4 to the European Union (Withdrawal) Act 2018).

(10) For the purposes of this Act—

(a) the date of filing of an application for registration of a comparable trade mark (IR) is the same date as the deemed date of registration of the comparable trade mark (IR) under sub-paragraph (6);

(b) references to the date of application for registration of a comparable trade mark (IR) are to the date of filing of the application;

(c) where an earlier trade mark is a comparable trade mark (IR), references to the completion of the registration procedure for the earlier trade mark are to publication by the European Union Intellectual Property Office of the matters referred to in Article 190(2) of the European Union Trade Mark Regulation in respect of the existing IR(EU) from which the comparable trade mark (IR) derives.

(11) In this Schedule—

(a) "the International Register" means the register of trade marks maintained by the International Bureau for the purposes of the Madrid Protocol;

(b) "international registration" means a registration made in the International Register in accordance with the Madrid Protocol;

(c) "international trade mark" means a trade mark which is the subject of an international registration.

**Opt out**

**2.**—(1) Subject to sub-paragraphs (2) and (6), the proprietor of an existing IR(EU) may, at any time on or after IP completion day, serve notice on the registrar that the trade mark is not to be treated as if the trade mark had been registered under this Act (an "opt out notice").

(2) An opt out notice may not be served where on or after IP completion day—

(a) the comparable trade mark (IR) has been put to use in the United Kingdom by the proprietor or with the proprietor's consent (which use includes affixing the trade mark to goods or to the packaging of goods in the United Kingdom solely for export purposes);

(b) the comparable trade mark (IR) (or any right in or under it) has been made the subject of an assignment, licence, security interest or any other agreement or document except for an assent by personal representatives in relation to the comparable trade mark (IR); or

(c) proceedings based on the comparable trade mark (IR) have been initiated by the proprietor or with the proprietor's consent.

(3) An opt out notice must—

(a) identify the number of the international registration to which the existing IR(EU) to which the notice relates is subject; and

(b) include the name and address of any person having an interest in the existing IR(EU) which had effect before IP completion day in the United Kingdom, and in respect of which an entry was recorded in the International Register.

(4) An opt out notice is of no effect unless the proprietor in that notice certifies that any such person—

(a) has been given not less than three months' notice of the proprietor's intention to serve an opt out notice; or

(b) is not affected or if affected, consents to the opt out.

(5) Where a notice has been served in accordance with this paragraph—

(a) the comparable trade mark (IR) which derives from the existing IR(EU) ceases with effect from IP completion day to be treated as if it had been registered under this Act; and

(b) the registrar must, where particulars of the comparable trade mark (IR) have been entered in the register, remove the comparable trade mark (IR) from the register.

(6) Where an international trade mark which is protected in the European Union is treated as being more than one trade mark by virtue of paragraph 1(2)—

(a) an opt out notice must relate to all of the existing IR(EU)s which (by virtue of paragraph 1(2)) derive from the international trade mark;

(b) the references in sub-paragraph (2) to the comparable trade mark (IR) are to be read as references to any of the comparable trade marks (IR) which derive from the existing IR(EU)s to which the opt out notice relates; and

(c) the references in sub-paragraph (5) to the comparable trade mark (IR) are to be read as references to all of the comparable trade marks (IR) which derive from the existing IR(EU)s to which the notice relates.

**Entries to be made in the register in relation to a comparable trade mark (IR)**

**3.**—(1) The registrar must as soon as reasonably practicable after IP completion day enter a comparable trade mark (IR) in the register.

(2) The particulars of the goods or services in respect of which the comparable trade mark (IR) is treated as if it had been registered must be taken from the English language version of the entry in the International Register for the corresponding (IR).

(3) Where on or after IP completion day the entry in the International Register containing the particulars referred to in sub-paragraph (2) is modified to correct an error pursuant to Rule 28, a person

having a sufficient interest may apply to the registrar for rectification of the register by the substitution of the English language version of the entry for the corresponding (IR) in the International Register as modified.

(4) In this Schedule, the "corresponding (IR)" , in relation to a comparable trade mark (IR), means the existing IR(EU) from which the comparable trade mark (IR) derives.

**Comparable trade mark (IR) which derives from a mark treated as an EU Collective Mark or EU Certification Mark**

**4.**—(1) This paragraph applies where the existing IR(EU) from which a comparable trade mark (IR) derives is dealt with for the purposes of the European Union Trade Mark Regulation as an EU collective mark or an EU certification mark.

(2) The comparable trade mark (IR) is to be treated as either a collective mark or a certification mark, as the case may be.

(3) The proprietor of the comparable trade mark (IR) must, following notice from the registrar, file with the registrar regulations governing the use of the international trade mark, submitted pursuant to the European Union Trade Mark Regulation, which had effect immediately before IP completion day.

(4) Where the regulations referred to in sub-paragraph (3) are in a language other than English they must be filed together with a translation into English verified to the satisfaction of the registrar as corresponding to the original text.

(5) Paragraph 9 of Schedule 1 and paragraph 10 of Schedule 2 apply in relation to the translation referred to in sub-paragraph (4) as they apply in relation to the regulations referred to in sub-paragraph (3).

(6) Where the regulations or any translation are not filed in accordance with the above provisions—

(a) the registrar must remove the comparable trade mark (IR) from the register; and
(b) the rights of the proprietor shall be deemed to have ceased as from the date of removal.

**Renewal of a comparable trade mark (IR) which expires within six months after IP completion day**

**5.**—(1) This paragraph applies to the renewal of the registration of a comparable trade mark (IR) which expires within the period beginning with IP completion day and ending with the end of the relevant period (and accordingly section 43(1) to (3A) does not apply).

(2) The registration of the comparable trade mark (IR) may be renewed at the request of the proprietor before the expiry of the registration.

(3) Where the registration of the comparable trade mark (IR) is not renewed in accordance with sub-paragraph (2)—

(a) on, or as soon as reasonably practicable after, the expiry of the registration, the registrar must notify the proprietor that the registration has expired and of the manner in which the registration may be renewed; and
(b) a request for renewal must be made within the period of six months beginning with the date of the notice.

(4) If a request for renewal is made in respect of only some of the goods or services for which the comparable trade mark (IR) is registered, the registration is to be renewed for those goods or services only.

(5) If the registration is not renewed in accordance with the above provisions, the registrar must remove the comparable trade mark (IR) from the register.

(6) Section 43(4) and (6) applies to the registration of a comparable trade mark (IR) which is renewed in accordance with the above provisions.

(7) In sub-paragraph (1), the "relevant period" means the period of six months beginning with the day after that on which IP completion day falls.

**Restoration of a comparable trade mark (IR)**

**6.** Where a comparable trade mark (IR) is removed from the register pursuant to paragraph 5, the rules relating to the restoration of the registration of a trade mark (referred to in section 43(5)) apply in relation to the restoration of the comparable trade mark (IR) to the register.

**Raising of relative grounds in opposition proceedings in case of non-use**

**7.**—(1) Section 6A applies where an earlier trade mark is a comparable trade mark (IR), subject to the modifications set out below.

(2) Where the relevant period referred to in section 6A(3)(a) (the "five-year period") has expired before IP completion day—

(a) the references in section 6A(3) and (6) to the earlier trade mark are to be treated as references to the corresponding (IR); and

(b) the references in section 6A(3) and (4) to the United Kingdom include the European Union.

(3) Where IP completion day falls within the five-year period, in respect of that part of the five-year period which falls before IP completion day—

(a) the references in section 6A(3) and (6) to the earlier trade mark are to be treated as references to the corresponding (IR); and

(b) the references in section 6A to the United Kingdom include the European Union.

**Non-use as defence in infringement proceedings and revocation of registration of a comparable trade mark (IR)**

**8.**—(1) Sections 11A and 46 apply in relation to a comparable trade mark (IR), subject to the modifications set out below.

(2) Where the period of five years referred to in sections 11A(3)(a) and 46(1)(a) or (b) (the "five-year period") has expired before IP completion day—

(a) the references in sections 11A(3) and (insofar as they relate to use of a trade mark) 46 to a trade mark are to be treated as references to the corresponding (IR); and

(b) the references in sections 11A and 46 to the United Kingdom include the European Union.

(3) Where IP completion day falls within the five-year period, in respect of that part of the five-year period which falls before IP completion day—

(a) the references in sections 11A(3) and (insofar as they relate to use of a trade mark) 46 to a trade mark, are to be treated as references to the corresponding (IR); and

(b) the references in sections 11A and 46 to the United Kingdom include the European Union.

**Grounds for invalidity of registration of a trade mark based upon an earlier comparable trade mark (IR)**

**9.**—(1) Section 47 applies where an earlier trade mark is a comparable trade mark (IR), subject to the modifications set out below.

(2) Where the period of five years referred to in sections 47(2A)(a) and 47(2B) (the "five-year period") has expired before IP completion day—

(a) the references in section 47(2B) and (2E) to the earlier trade mark are to be treated as references to the corresponding (IR); and

(b) the references in section 47 to the United Kingdom include the European Union.

(3) Where IP completion day falls within the five-year period, in respect of that part of the five-year period which falls before IP completion day—

(a) the references in section 47(2B) and (2E) to the earlier trade mark are to be treated as references to the corresponding (IR); and

(b) the references in section 47 to the United Kingdom include the European Union.

**Reputation of a comparable trade mark (IR)**

**10.**—(1) Sections 5 and 10 apply in relation to a comparable trade mark (IR), subject to the modifications set out below.

(2) Where the reputation of a comparable trade mark (IR) falls to be considered in respect of any time before IP completion day, references in sections 5(3) and 10(3) to—

(a) the reputation of the mark are to be treated as references to the reputation of the corresponding (IR); and

(b) the United Kingdom include the European Union.

**Rights conferred by registered trade mark**

**11.** Section 9 applies in relation to a comparable trade mark (IR) but as if—

(a) the words in brackets in subsection (3) referring to section 40(3) were replaced with a reference to paragraph 1(6) of this Schedule; and

(b) the proviso in subsection (3) were omitted.

**Effect of disclaimer**

**12.** Where, immediately before IP completion day, the protection in the European Union of an existing IR(EU) is subject to a disclaimer recorded in the International Register, the registration of the comparable trade mark (IR) which derives from the existing IR(EU) is to be treated on and after IP completion day as subject to the same disclaimer (and section 13 applies accordingly but as if the reference to "publication" in subsection (2) was omitted).

**Effect of claim of priority**

**13.**—(1) This paragraph applies where—

(a) a right of priority was claimed in respect of an international application for protection of a trade mark in accordance with Rule 9(4)(iv);

(b) immediately before IP completion day there is an entry in the International Register in respect of that trade mark containing particulars of that claim of priority (a "claim of priority");

(c) the trade mark is an existing IR(EU).

(2) Subject to sub-paragraph (4), the proprietor of the comparable trade mark (IR) which derives from the existing IR(EU) is to be treated on and after IP completion day as having the same claim of priority.

(3) Accordingly, the relevant date for the purposes of establishing, in relation to the comparable trade mark (IR), which rights take precedence is the date of filing of the application for a trade mark in a Convention country which formed the basis for the claim of priority.

(4) Where the protection in the European Union of the existing IR(EU) resulted from a request for territorial extension under Article 3ter (2), the proprietor of the comparable trade mark (IR) which derives from the existing IR(EU) is to be treated on and after IP completion day as having the same claim of priority only where the request for territorial extension was recorded in the International Register within a period of six months beginning with the day after the priority date recorded in the International Register in respect of the international application referred to in sub-paragraph (1)(a).

**Effect of seniority claim**

**14.**—(1) This paragraph applies where immediately before IP completion day an existing IR(EU) has a valid claim to seniority of a trade mark which trade mark (the "senior mark") is a registered trade mark or a protected international trade mark (UK).

(2) The comparable trade mark (IR) which derives from the existing IR(EU) is to be treated on and after IP completion day as if it had a valid claim to seniority of the senior mark.

(3) Accordingly, where the proprietor of the comparable trade mark (IR) surrenders the senior mark or allows it to lapse (whether wholly or partially), subject to paragraph 15, the proprietor of the comparable trade mark (IR) is deemed to continue to have the same rights as the proprietor would have had if the senior mark had continued to be registered in respect of all the goods or services for which it was registered prior to the surrender or lapse.

(4) An existing IR(EU) has a valid claim to seniority of a trade mark where—

(a) a claim has been filed in accordance with Article 191 or 192 of the European Union Trade Mark Regulation in respect of the international registration to which the existing IR(EU) is subject; and

(b) the seniority so claimed has not lapsed in the circumstances referred to in Article 39 of that Regulation (as it applies to international registrations under Article 182 of that Regulation).

**Determination of invalidity and liability to revocation in relation to claims of seniority**

**15.**(1) Where pursuant to paragraph 14 a comparable trade mark (IR) is treated as if it had a valid claim to seniority of a registered trade mark which has been—

(a) removed from the register under section 43; or

(b) surrendered under section 45,

any person may apply to the registrar or to the court for the declaration set out in sub-paragraph (2).

(2) The declaration is that if the trade mark had not been so removed or surrendered, the registration of the trade mark would have been liable to be revoked under section 46 with effect from a date specified in the declaration or declared invalid under section 47.

(3) Where the declaration is that had the trade mark not been so removed or surrendered the registration of it would have been liable to be—

(a) revoked under section 46 with effect from a date prior to—

(i) where there has been no claim of priority pursuant to Article 35 of the European Union Trade Mark Regulation (as it applies to international registrations under Article 182 of that Regulation) in respect of the existing IR(EU) from which the comparable trade mark (IR) derives, the deemed date of registration of the comparable trade mark (IR); or

(ii) where there has been a claim of priority, the priority date accorded pursuant to a right of priority claimed pursuant to Article 35 of the European Union Trade Mark Regulation in respect of the existing IR(EU) from which the comparable trade mark (IR) derives; or

(b) declared invalid under section 47,

the seniority claimed for the comparable trade mark (IR) is to be treated as if it never had effect.

(4) Where pursuant to paragraph 14 a comparable trade mark (IR) is treated as if it had a valid claim to seniority of a protected international trade mark (UK) which has been—

(a) removed from the International Register; or

(b) surrendered under the Madrid Protocol,

any person may apply to the registrar or to the court for the declaration set out in sub-paragraph (5).

(5) The declaration is that, if the trade mark had not been so removed or surrendered, the protection of the mark in the United Kingdom would have been liable to be revoked under section 46 with effect from a date specified in the declaration or declared invalid under section 47.

(6) Where the declaration is that had the trade mark not been so removed or surrendered the protection of the mark in the United Kingdom would have been liable to be—

(a) revoked under section 46 with effect from a date prior to—

(i) where there has been no claim of priority pursuant to Article 35 of the European Union Trade Mark Regulation (as it applies to international registrations under Article 182 of that Regulation) in respect of the existing IR(EU) from which the comparable trade mark (IR) derives, the deemed date of registration of the comparable trade mark (IR); or

(ii) where there has been a claim of priority, the priority date accorded pursuant to a right of priority claimed pursuant to Article 35 of the European Union Trade Mark Regulation in respect of the existing IR(EU) from which the comparable trade mark (IR) derives; or

(b) declared invalid under section 47,

the seniority claimed for the comparable trade mark (IR) is to be treated as if it never had effect.

(7) Where the protection in the European Union of an existing IR(EU) resulted from a request for territorial extension under Article 3ter (2), a right of priority claimed pursuant to Article 35 of the European Union Trade Mark Regulation in respect of the existing IR(EU) is to be disregarded for the purposes of sub-paragraphs (3)(a)(ii) and (6)(a)(ii) unless the request for territorial extension was recorded in the International Register within a period of six months beginning with the day after the priority date recorded in the International Register in respect of the international application for protection of the trade mark which is the same as the one in respect of which the request for territorial extension was filed.

(8) References in sub-paragraphs (5) and (6) to sections 46 and 47 are to those sections as they apply to a protected international trade mark (UK) under an order made pursuant to section 54.

(9) Where a trade mark has been surrendered or allowed to lapse in respect of some only of the goods or services for which it is registered, the declaration in sub-paragraphs (2) and (5) is that if the goods or services had not been removed from the registration, the registration of the trade mark would have been liable to be revoked under section 46 with effect from a date specified in the declaration or declared invalid under section 47 and sub-paragraphs (3) and (6) shall be construed accordingly.

**Procedure for declaration that trade mark would have been liable to be revoked or declared invalid**

**16.**—(1) In the case of proceedings on an application under paragraph 15 before the registrar, the rules relating to applications for and proceedings relating to the revocation or invalidation of a trade mark apply, with necessary modifications.

(2) In the case of proceedings on an application under paragraph 15 before the court, section 74 applies to the proceedings as it applies to proceedings involving an application of the type referred to in section 74(1)(a) to (c).

**Assignment of an existing IR(EU) not registered on IP completion day**

**17.**—(1) This paragraph applies where before IP completion day an existing IR(EU) (or any right in it) is the subject of an assignment (a "relevant assignment") which immediately before IP completion day is not recorded in the International Register.

(2) Section 25 applies in relation to a relevant assignment as if it were a registrable transaction affecting a comparable trade mark (IR), subject to the modification set out below.

(3) An application under section 25(1) may only be made by—

(a) a person claiming to be entitled to an interest in or under a comparable trade mark (IR) by virtue of a relevant assignment of the corresponding (IR); or

(b) the proprietor of the comparable trade mark (IR).

**Effect of a licence of an existing IR(EU)**

**18.**—(1) This paragraph applies where immediately before IP completion day an existing IR(EU) is the subject of a licence (a "relevant licence") which—

(a) authorises the doing of acts in the United Kingdom which would otherwise infringe the international trade mark; and

(b) does not expire on IP completion day.

(2) Subject to any agreement to the contrary between the licensee and the licensor, a relevant licence continues to authorise the doing of acts in the United Kingdom which would otherwise infringe the comparable trade mark (IR) which derives from the existing IR(EU).

(3) Sub-paragraph (2) is subject to—

(a) the terms on which the relevant licence was granted; and

(b) such modifications to the terms referred to in paragraph (a) as are necessary for their application in the United Kingdom.

(4) Section 25 applies in relation to a relevant licence as if it were a registrable transaction affecting a comparable trade mark (IR), subject to the modifications set out below.

(5) An application under section 25(1) may only be made by—

(a) a person claiming to be a licensee by virtue of the relevant licence; or

(b) the proprietor of the comparable trade mark (IR).

(6) Where immediately before IP completion day there is an entry in the International Register relating to a relevant licence—

(a) section 25(3) and (4) does not apply until after the expiry of the relevant period; and

(b) section 25(4)(a) applies after the expiry of the relevant period but as if the reference to six months beginning with the date of the transaction were a reference to eighteen months beginning with IP completion day.

(7) In sub-paragraph (6)(a), the "relevant period" means the period of twelve months beginning with the day after that on which IP completion day falls.

**Effect of a security interest in an existing IR(EU)**

**19.**—(1) This paragraph applies where immediately before IP completion day an existing IR(EU) (or any right in or under it) is the subject of a security interest (a "relevant security interest") which—

(a) restricts the proprietor's right to dispose in the European Union of the existing IR(EU); and

(b) does not terminate on IP completion day.

(2) References to the existing IR(EU), or the international registration to which the existing IR(EU) is subject, in any document which grants or refers to the relevant security interest are to be read as including references to the comparable trade mark (IR) which derives from the existing IR(EU).

(3) Section 25 applies in relation to a relevant security interest as if it were a registrable transaction affecting a comparable trade mark (IR), subject to the modifications set out below.

(4) An application under section 25(1) may only be made by—

(a) a person claiming to be entitled to an interest in or under a comparable trade mark (IR) by virtue of the relevant security interest; or

(b) the proprietor of the comparable trade mark (IR).

(5) Where immediately before IP completion day there is an entry in the International Register relating to a relevant security interest—

(a) section 25(3) and (4) do not apply until after the expiry of the relevant period; and

(b) section 25(4)(a) applies after the expiry of the relevant period but as if the reference to six months beginning with the date of the transaction were a reference to eighteen months beginning with IP completion day.

(6) In sub-paragraph (5)(a), the "relevant period" means the period of twelve months beginning with the day after that on which IP completion day falls.

**Continuity of rights in relation to a comparable trade mark (IR)**

**20.**—(1) References to an existing IR(EU), or the international registration to which an existing IR(EU) is subject, in any document made before IP completion day shall, unless there is evidence that the document was not intended to have effect in the United Kingdom, be read on and after IP completion day as including references to the comparable trade mark (IR) or the registration of the comparable trade mark (IR) which derives from the existing IR(EU).

(2) Subject to any agreement to the contrary, a consent granted before IP completion day by the proprietor of an existing IR(EU) to the doing on or after IP completion day of an act in the United Kingdom which would otherwise infringe the comparable trade mark (IR) which derives from the existing IR(EU) is to be treated for the purposes of section 9 as a consent to the doing of that act.

**Existing IR(EU): pending proceedings**

**21.**—(1) This paragraph applies where on IP completion day an existing IR(EU) is the subject of proceedings which are pending ("pending proceedings") before a court in the United Kingdom designated for the purposes of Article 123 of the European Union Trade Mark Regulation ("EU trade mark court").

(2) Subject to sub-paragraphs (3) and (4), the provisions contained or referred to in Chapter 10 of the European Union Trade Mark Regulation (with the exception of Articles 128(2), (4), (6) and (7) and 132) continue to apply to the pending proceedings as if the United Kingdom were still a Member State with effect from IP completion day.

(3) Where the pending proceedings involve a claim for infringement of an existing IR(EU), without prejudice to any other relief by way of damages, accounts or otherwise available to the proprietor of the existing IR(EU), the EU trade mark court may grant an injunction to prohibit unauthorised use of the comparable trade mark (IR) which derives from the existing IR(EU).

(4) Where the pending proceedings involve a counterclaim for the revocation of, or a declaration of invalidity in relation to, an existing IR(EU), the EU trade mark court may revoke the registration of the comparable trade mark (IR) which derives from the existing IR(EU) or declare the registration of the comparable trade mark (IR) which derives from the existing IR(EU) to be invalid.

(5) Where the grounds for revocation or invalidity exist in respect of only some of the goods or services for which the existing IR(EU) is registered, the revocation or declaration of invalidity in respect of the registration of the comparable trade mark (IR) which derives from the existing IR(EU) relates to those goods or services only.

(6) Where (by virtue of sub-paragraph (4)) the registration of a comparable trade mark (IR) is revoked to any extent, the rights of the proprietor are deemed to have ceased to that extent as from—

(a) the date of the counterclaim for revocation, or

(b) if the court is satisfied that the grounds for revocation existed at an earlier date, that date.

(7) Where (by virtue of sub-paragraph (4)) the registration of a comparable trade mark (IR) is declared invalid to any extent, the registration is to that extent to be deemed never to have been made, provided that this does not affect transactions past and closed.

(8) For the purposes of this paragraph proceedings are treated as pending on IP completion day if they were instituted but not finally determined before IP completion day.

**Existing IR(EU): effect of injunction**

**22.**—(1) This paragraph applies where immediately before IP completion day an injunction is in force prohibiting the performance of acts in the United Kingdom which infringe or would infringe an existing IR(EU) (a "relevant injunction").

(2) Subject to any order of the court to the contrary, a relevant injunction will have effect and be enforceable to prohibit the performance of acts which infringe or would infringe a comparable trade mark (IR) to the same extent as in relation to the existing IR(EU) from which the comparable trade mark (IR) derives as if it were an injunction granted by the court.

PART 2

TREATMENT OF INTERNATIONAL TRADE MARKS PROTECTED IN THE EUROPEAN UNION WHICH EXPIRE DURING THE PERIOD OF SIX MONTHS ENDING ON IP COMPLETION DAY

**Registration of certain expired international trade marks**

**23.**—(1) This Part applies to an international trade mark which, immediately before the transitional period, was protected in the European Union in accordance with Article 189(2) of the European Union Trade Mark Regulation but which, as a result of the expiry of the registration of the international trade mark during the transitional period, does not fall within paragraph 1(1) (an "expired IR(EU)").

(2) Where the international registration to which an international trade mark is subject has been sub-divided as referred to in paragraph 1(2), there is to be deemed for the purposes of sub-paragraph (1) to be a separate expired trade mark in respect of the goods or services covered by each sub-division of the registration.

(3) An expired IR(EU) is to be treated as if it were an existing IR(EU).

(4) The provisions of Part 1 of this Schedule apply to an expired IR(EU) as they apply to an existing IR(EU) subject to the provisions of this Part of the Schedule.

(5) Notwithstanding the entry in the register (under paragraph 3, as applied by sub-paragraph (4)) of a comparable trade mark (IR) which derives from an expired IR(EU), the registration of the comparable trade mark (IR) is expired until the proprietor gives notice to the registrar in accordance with paragraph 24(1)(b) (or the comparable trade mark (IR) is removed from the register in accordance with paragraph 24(2)).

(6) In this paragraph, "transitional period" means the period of six months ending with IP completion day.

**Renewal of an expired IR(EU)**

**24.**(1) Where within the period beginning with IP completion day and ending with the end of the relevant period—

(a) the international registration to which an expired IR(EU) is subject is renewed in accordance with Article 7; and

(b) the proprietor of the expired IR(EU) notifies the registrar of such renewal (a "renewal notice"),

paragraphs 25 and 26 apply to the renewal of the registration of the comparable trade mark (IR) which derives from the expired IR(EU).

(2) If within the period referred to in sub-paragraph (1) the proprietor fails to notify the registrar in accordance with sub-paragraph (1)(b)—

(a) the registrar must remove from the register the comparable trade mark (IR) which derives from the expired IR(EU); and

(b) the comparable trade mark (IR) ceases with effect from IP completion day to be treated as if it had been registered under this Act.

(3) In sub-paragraph (1), the "relevant period" means the period of nine months beginning with the day after that on which IP completion day falls.

**Renewal of an expired IR(EU): territorial extension under Article 3ter(1)**

**25.**—(1) Where the protection in the European Union of an expired IR(EU) resulted from a request for territorial extension under Article 3ter (1), the registrar must, as soon as reasonably practicable following receipt of the renewal notice, renew the registration of the comparable trade mark (IR) which derives from the expired IR(EU).

(2) A comparable trade mark (IR) which is renewed under sub-paragraph (1) shall be renewed for a period of ten years from the expiry of the international registration to which the expired IR(EU) is subject.

(3) Section 43(6) applies to the registration of a comparable trade mark (IR) which is renewed in accordance with this paragraph.

**Renewal of an expired IR(EU): territorial extension under Article 3ter(2)**

**26.**—(1) This paragraph applies where the protection in the European Union of an expired IR(EU) resulted from a request for territorial extension under Article 3ter (2).

(2) The relevant date for the purposes of determining the date of renewal of the registration of the comparable trade mark (IR) which derives from the expired IR(EU) (the "relevant renewal date") shall be—

(a) the date of expiry of the period of ten years from the date on which the request for territorial extension was recorded in the International Register; or

(b) where the international registration to which the expired IR(EU) is subject has been renewed since the date referred to in paragraph (a), the anniversary of that date, computed by reference to periods of ten years, following the last renewal of the registration prior to the date of the renewal notice (the "notice date").

(3) Where the relevant renewal date of a comparable trade mark (IR) falls prior to the notice date, the registrar must, as soon as reasonably practicable following receipt of a renewal notice, renew the registration of the comparable trade mark (IR) which derives from the expired IR(EU).

(4) Where the relevant renewal date of a comparable trade mark (IR) falls before the expiry of the period of six months beginning with the notice date, sub-paragraphs (5) and (6) apply (and accordingly section 43(1) to (3A) does not apply).

(5) The registration of the comparable trade mark (IR) may be renewed at the request of the proprietor before the relevant renewal date.

(6) Where the registration of the comparable trade mark (IR) is not renewed in accordance with sub-paragraph (5)—

(a) on, or as soon as reasonably practicable after, the relevant renewal date, the registrar must notify the proprietor that the registration of the comparable trade mark (IR) has expired and of the manner in which registration may be renewed; and

(b) a request for renewal must be made within a period of six months beginning with the date of the notice.

(7) If a request for renewal is made in respect of only some of the goods or services for which the comparable trade mark (IR) is registered, the registration is to be renewed for those goods or services only.

(8) A comparable trade mark (IR) which is renewed under sub-paragraph (3) or pursuant to a request for renewal in accordance with sub-paragraph (5) or (6) shall be renewed for a period of ten years from the relevant renewal date (and accordingly, section 43(4) does not apply).

(9) Where sub-paragraphs (5) and (6) apply to the renewal of the registration of a comparable trade mark (IR) and the registration is not renewed in accordance with those provisions, the registrar must remove the comparable trade mark (IR) from the register.

(10) Section 43(6) applies to the registration of a comparable trade mark (IR) which is renewed in accordance with this paragraph.

(11) Where a comparable trade mark (IR) is removed from the register pursuant to sub-paragraph (9), the rules relating to the restoration of the registration of a trade mark (referred to in section 43(5)) apply in relation to the restoration of the comparable trade mark (IR) to the register.

(12) Where the relevant renewal date of a comparable trade mark (IR) falls on or after the expiry of the period of six months beginning with the notice date, section 43 applies to the renewal of the registration of the comparable trade mark (IR) and references to the expiry of the registration are to be treated as references to the relevant renewal date of the comparable trade mark (IR).

PART 3

APPLICATIONS FOR THE EXTENSION OF PROTECTION OF INTERNATIONAL REGISTRATIONS TO THE EUROPEAN UNION WHICH ARE PENDING ON IP COMPLETION DAY

**Interpretation**

**27.**—(1) In this Part—

(a) references to an "*existing ITM application*" are to an international application which contains a request for extension of the protection resulting from an international registration to the European Union under Article 3ter (1) in respect of which the conditions in sub-paragraph (2) are satisfied;

(b) references to an "*existing request for EU extension*" are to a request for extension to the European Union of the protection resulting from an international registration made subsequent to the international registration pursuant to Article 3ter (2) in respect of which the conditions in sub-paragraph (3) are satisfied;

(c) references to an "*international application*" are to an application to the International Bureau under Article 2(2) for the registration of a trade mark in the International Register.

(2) The conditions referred to in sub-paragraph (1)(a) are—

(a) the international application was filed before IP completion day with the Office of origin in accordance with Article 2(2); and

(b) as at the time immediately before IP completion day, the request for extension of protection to the European Union mentioned in the international application has been neither granted nor refused by the European Union Intellectual Property Office.

(3) The conditions referred to in sub-paragraph (1)(b) are—

(a) the request for extension of protection to the European Union was filed before IP completion day with the Office of origin or the International Bureau (as the case may be) in accordance with Rule 24(2); and

(b) as at the time immediately before IP completion day, the request for extension of protection to the European Union has been neither granted nor refused by the European Union Intellectual Property Office under the European Union Trade Mark Regulation.

(4) In sub-paragraphs (2)(b) and (3)(b) —

(a) the reference to the request for extension of protection to the European Union being "granted" means the European Union Intellectual Property Office having sent to the International Bureau a statement to the effect that protection is granted to the mark in the European Union in accordance with Rule 18ter; and

(b) the reference to the request for extension of protection to the European Union being "refused" means the European Union Intellectual Property Office having sent to the International Bureau a notification of refusal in accordance with Article 5(1) or (2) which refusal has not been subsequently withdrawn.

**Application for registration under this Act based upon an existing ITM application or an existing request for EU extension recorded in the International Register prior to IP completion day**

**28.**—(1) This paragraph applies where—

(a) either—

(i) an existing ITM application has been filed with the International Bureau in respect of a trade mark and the date accorded to the international registration of the trade mark pursuant to Article 3(4) is a date prior to IP completion day; or

(ii) an existing request for EU extension in respect of a trade mark has been filed with the International Bureau and the date on which it was recorded in the International Register pursuant to Article 3ter (2) is a date prior to IP completion day;

(b) the person who filed the existing ITM application or (as the case may be) the existing request for EU extension, or a successor in title of that person, applies for registration of the same trade mark under this Act for some or all of the same goods or services, and

(c) the application under this Act is made within a period beginning with IP completion day and ending with the end of the period referred to in sub-paragraph (4).

(2) Where this paragraph applies, the relevant date for the purposes of establishing which rights take precedence is the earliest of—

(a) the date accorded to the international trade mark the subject of the existing ITM application pursuant to Article 3(4) or, in the case of an existing request for EU extension, the date on which the request was recorded in the International Register pursuant to Article 3ter (2);

(b) the date of priority (if any) accorded pursuant to a right of priority claimed pursuant to Article 4 of the Paris Convention in respect of the existing ITM application or the existing request for EU extension (as the case may be).

(3) The registrability of the trade mark the subject of an application under this Act of the type mentioned in sub-paragraph (1)(b) and made within the period mentioned in sub-paragraph (1)(c) shall not be affected by any use of the mark in the United Kingdom which commenced in the period between the date referred to in sub-paragraph (2) and the date of the application under this Act.

(4) In sub-paragraph (1)(c), the period referred to is the period of nine months beginning with the day after that on which IP completion day falls.

(5) A right of priority claimed pursuant to Article 4 of the Paris Convention in respect of an existing request for EU extension is to be disregarded for the purposes of sub-paragraph (2)(b) unless the existing request for EU extension was recorded in the International Register within a period of six months beginning with the day after the priority date recorded in the International Register in respect of the international application for protection of the trade mark which is the same as the one in respect of which the existing request for EU extension was filed.

**Application for registration under this Act based upon an existing ITM application or an existing request for EU extension recorded in the International Register on or after IP completion day**

**29.**—(1) This paragraph applies where—

(a) either—

(i) an existing ITM application has been filed with the International Bureau in respect of a trade mark and the date accorded to the international registration of the trade mark pursuant to Article 3(4) is a date on or after IP completion day; or

(ii) an existing request for EU extension in respect of a trade mark has been filed with the International Bureau and the date on which it was recorded in the International Register pursuant to Article 3ter (2) is a date on or after IP completion day;

(b) the person who filed the existing ITM application or (as the case may be) the existing request for EU extension, or a successor in title of that person, applies for registration of the same trade mark under this Act for some or all of the same goods or services; and

(c) the application under this Act is made within the period of nine months beginning with the date referred to in sub-paragraph (a)(i) or (ii) (as the case may be).

(2) Where this paragraph applies, the relevant date for the purposes of establishing which rights take precedence is the earliest of—

(a) the date accorded to the international trade mark the subject of the existing ITM application pursuant to Article 3(4) or, in the case of an existing request for EU extension, the date on which the request was recorded in the International Register pursuant to Article 3ter (2);

(b) the date of priority (if any) accorded pursuant to a right of priority claimed pursuant to Article 4 of the Paris Convention in respect of the existing ITM application or the existing request for EU extension (as the case may be).

(3) The registrability of the trade mark the subject of an application under this Act of the type mentioned in sub-paragraph (1)(b) and made within the period mentioned in sub-paragraph (1)(c) shall not be affected by any use of the mark in the United Kingdom which commenced in the period between the date referred to in sub-paragraph (2) and the date of the application under this Act.

(4) A right of priority claimed pursuant to Article 4 of the Paris Convention in respect of an existing request for EU extension is to be disregarded for the purposes of sub-paragraph (2)(b) unless the

existing request for EU extension was recorded in the International Register within a period of six months beginning with the day after the priority date recorded in the International Register in respect of the international application for protection of the trade mark which is the same as the one in respect of which the existing request for EU extension was filed.

**Right to claim seniority where seniority has been claimed by an existing ITM application or an existing request for EU extension**

**30.**—(1) Where an existing ITM application or an existing request for EU extension claims seniority of a trade mark which trade mark ("the senior mark") is a registered trade mark or a protected international trade mark (UK), the applicant may claim seniority of the senior mark in an application for registration of a trade mark (a "relevant mark") pursuant to this Part.

(2) The effect of a seniority claim made pursuant to sub-paragraph (1) is that where following the registration of the relevant mark the proprietor of that mark surrenders the senior mark or allows it to lapse (wholly or partially), subject to paragraph 31, the proprietor of the relevant mark is deemed to continue to have the same rights as the proprietor would have had if the senior mark had continued to be registered in respect of all the goods or services for which it was registered prior to the surrender or lapse.

(3) Provision may be made by rules as to the manner of claiming seniority pursuant to this paragraph.

(4) In sub-paragraph (1), an application for registration of a trade mark "pursuant to this Part" means an application that is of the type mentioned in paragraph 28(1)(b) or 29(1)(b) and that is made within the period mentioned in paragraph 28(1)(c) or 29(1)(c) (as the case may be).

**Determination of invalidity and liability to revocation in relation to claim of seniority under paragraph 30**

**31.**(1) Where a relevant mark has claimed seniority of a registered trade mark which has been—

(a) removed from the register under section 43; or

(b) surrendered under section 45,

any person may apply to the registrar or to the court for the declaration set out in sub-paragraph (2).

(2) The declaration is that, if the trade mark had not been so removed or surrendered, the registration of the trade mark would have been liable to be revoked under section 46 with effect from a date specified in the declaration or declared invalid under section 47.

(3) Where the declaration is that had the trade mark not been so removed or surrendered, the registration of it would have been liable to be—

(a) revoked under section 46 with effect from a date prior to—

(i) where the application for registration of the relevant mark was based on an existing ITM application and there has been no claim of priority, the date of registration accorded pursuant to Article 3(4) to the international trade mark the subject of the existing ITM application;

(ii) where the application for registration of the relevant mark was based on an existing request for EU extension and there has been no claim of priority, the date on which the request was recorded in the International Register pursuant to Article 3ter (2);

(iii) where the application for registration of the relevant mark was based on an existing ITM application or an existing request for EU extension and there has been a claim of priority, the priority date accorded pursuant to a right of priority claimed pursuant to Article 4 of the Paris Convention; or

(b) declared invalid under section 47,

the seniority claimed for the relevant mark is to be treated as if it never had effect.

(4) Where a relevant mark has claimed seniority of a protected international trade mark (UK) which has been—

(a) removed from the International Register; or

(b) surrendered under the Madrid Protocol,

any person may apply to the registrar or to the court for the declaration set out in sub-paragraph (5).

(5) The declaration is that, if the trade mark had not been so removed or surrendered, the protection of the trade mark in the United Kingdom would have been liable to be revoked under section 46 with effect from a date specified in the declaration or declared invalid under section 47.

(6) Where the declaration is that had the trade mark not been so removed or surrendered, the registration of it would have been liable to be—

(a) revoked under section 46 with effect from a date prior to—

(i) where the application for registration of the relevant mark was based on an existing ITM application and there has been no claim of priority, the date of registration accorded pursuant to Article 3(4) to the international trade mark the subject of the existing ITM application;

(ii) where the application for registration of the relevant mark was based on an existing request for EU extension and there has been no claim of priority, the date on which the request was recorded in the International Register pursuant to Article 3ter (2);

(iii) where the application for registration of the relevant mark was based on an existing ITM application or an existing request for EU extension and there has been a claim of priority, the priority date accorded pursuant to a right of priority claimed pursuant to Article 4 of the Paris Convention; or

(b) declared invalid under section 47,

the seniority claimed for the relevant mark is to be treated as if it never had effect.

(7) Where the application for registration of the relevant mark was based on an existing request for EU extension a right of priority claimed pursuant to Article 35 of the European Union Trade Mark Regulation in respect of the request for EU extension is to be disregarded for the purposes of sub-paragraphs (3)(a)(iii) and (6)(a)(iii) unless the request for territorial extension was recorded in the International Register within a period of six months beginning with the day after the priority date recorded in the International Register in respect of the international application for protection of the trade mark which is the same as the one in respect of which the request for EU extension was filed.

(8) References in sub-paragraphs (5) and (6) to sections 46 and 47 are to those sections as they apply to a protected international trade mark (UK) under an order made pursuant to section 54.

(9) Where a trade mark has been surrendered or allowed to lapse in respect of only some of the goods or services for which it is registered, the declaration in sub-paragraphs (2) and (5) is that if the goods or services had not been removed from the registration, the registration of the trade mark would have been liable to be revoked under section 46 with effect from a date specified in the declaration or declared invalid under section 47 and sub-paragraphs (3) and (6) shall be construed accordingly.

(10) The provisions of paragraph 16 apply in relation to an application under this paragraph as they apply to an application under paragraph 15.

## PART 4

## TRANSFORMATION APPLICATIONS WHICH ARE PENDING ON IP COMPLETION DAY

### Transformation applications

**32.**—(1) In this Part, references to a "*transformation application*" are to an application for transformation of an international registration which has been cancelled (a "cancelled international registration") into an application for registration of a European Union trade mark filed under Article 204 of the European Union Trade Mark Regulation in respect of which the conditions in sub-paragraph (2) are satisfied.

(2) The conditions referred to in sub-paragraph (1) are—

(a) the transformation application was filed before IP completion day with the European Union Intellectual Property Office;

(b) as at the time immediately before IP completion day the transformation application has neither been granted nor refused by the European Union Intellectual Property Office under the European Union Trade Mark Regulation; and

(c) the international registration was not cancelled at the request of the Patent Office as Office of origin for the international registration of the trade mark.

(3) In sub-paragraph (2)(b)—

(a) the reference to the transformation application being "granted" means a European Union trade mark being registered under the European Union Trade Mark Regulation pursuant to the transformation application; and

(b) the reference to the transformation application being "refused" means the transformation application being subject to the provisions in Article 204(5) of the European Union Trade Mark Regulation.

### Application for registration based upon a cancelled international registration

**33.**—(1) This paragraph applies where—

(a) a person who has filed a transformation application in respect of a cancelled international registration, or a successor in title of that person, applies for registration under this Act of a trade mark which is the same as the trade mark which was the subject of the cancelled international registration and in respect of some or all of the same goods or services included in the international registration;

(b) the application for registration under this Act is made within the period beginning with IP completion day and ending with the end of the relevant period; and

(c) on or before the date of the transformation application on which the application for registration under this Act is based the trade mark that was the subject of the cancelled international registration—

(i) was protected in the European Union in accordance with Article 189(2) of the European Union Trade Mark Regulation; or

(ii) was the subject of an existing ITM application or an existing request for EU extension which, as at that date, had neither been granted nor refused by the European Union Intellectual Property Office (the references to "granted" and "refused" having the same meaning as given by paragraph 27(4)).

(2) Where this paragraph applies by virtue of sub-paragraph (1)(c)(i), the relevant date for the purposes of establishing which rights take precedence is the earliest of—

(a) where—

(i) the protection in the European Union of the trade mark that was the subject of the cancelled international registration resulted from a request for territorial extension under Article 3ter (1), the date of registration accorded to the international registration pursuant to Article 3(4); or

(ii) the protection in the European Union of the trade mark that was the subject of the cancelled international registration resulted from a request for territorial extension under Article 3ter (2), the date on which the request was recorded in the International Register; and

(b) the date of priority (if any) accorded pursuant to a right of priority claimed pursuant to Article 4 of the Paris Convention in respect of the request referred to in paragraph (a)(i) or (ii).

(3) Where this paragraph applies by virtue of sub-paragraph (1)(c)(ii), the relevant date for the purposes of establishing which rights take precedence is the earliest of—

(a) the date accorded to the trade mark that was the subject of the existing ITM application pursuant to Article 3(4) or, in the case of an existing request for EU extension, the date on which the request was recorded in the International Register pursuant to Article 3ter (2); and

(b) the date of priority (if any) accorded pursuant to a right of priority claimed pursuant to Article 4 of the Paris Convention in respect of the request referred to in paragraph (a).

(4) A right of priority claimed pursuant to Article 4 of the Paris Convention in respect of a request for territorial extension to the European Union made under Article 3ter (2) is to be disregarded for the purposes of sub-paragraphs (2)(b) and (3)(b) unless the request for extension was recorded in the International Register within a period of six months beginning with the day after the priority date recorded in the International Register in respect of the international application for protection of the trade mark which is the same as the one in respect of which the request for extension was filed.

(5) The registrability of the trade mark the subject of an application under this Act of the type mentioned in sub-paragraph (1)(a) and made within the period mentioned in sub-paragraph (1)(b) shall not be affected by any use of the mark in the United Kingdom which commenced in the period between the date referred to in sub-paragraph (2) or (3) (as the case may be) and the date of the application for registration of the trade mark under this Act.

(6) Paragraphs 30 and 31 apply in relation to an application for a trade mark under this Act of the type mentioned in sub-paragraph (1)(a) and made within the period mentioned in sub-paragraph (1)(b), as they apply in relation to an application for registration of a trade mark pursuant to Part 3, but as if—

(a) the references to an existing ITM application or an existing request for EU extension and an existing ITM application and an existing request for EU extension had the same meaning as they have in this paragraph; and

(b) the references to an existing ITM application included references to a "*protected EU designation*".

(7) In this paragraph—

(a) an "existing ITM application" means an international application which contains a request for extension of the protection resulting from an international registration to the European Union under Article 3ter (1) which has been filed with the Office of origin in accordance with Article 2(2);

(b) an "existing request for EU extension" means a request for extension to the European Union of the protection resulting from an international registration made subsequent to the international registration pursuant to Article 3ter (2) which has been filed with the Office of origin or the International Bureau (as the case may be) in accordance with Rule 24(2);

(c) the "relevant period" means the period of nine months beginning with the day after that on which IP completion day falls;

(d) a "protected EU designation" means an international registration which prior to its cancellation was protected in the European Union in accordance with Article 189(2) of the European Union Trade Mark Regulation.

PART 5

INTERPRETATION

**Interpretation**

**34.**—(1) In this Schedule—

"comparable trade mark (IR)" has the meaning given by paragraph 1(4);

"the Common Regulations" means the Common Regulations under the Madrid Agreement concerning the international registration of marks and the Madrid Protocol in force on 1st November 2017;

"corresponding (IR)" has the meaning given by paragraph 3(4);

"existing IR(EU)" has the meaning given by paragraph 1(1);

"expired IR(EU)" has the meaning given by paragraph 23(1);

"international application" has the meaning given by paragraph 27(1)(c);

"the International Register" has the meaning given by paragraph 1(11)(a);

"international registration" has the meaning given by paragraph 1(11)(b);

"international trade mark" has the meaning given by paragraph 1(11)(c);

"Office of origin" has the meaning given by Article 2(2);

"the previous EUTM Regulations" means Council Regulation (EC) No 207/2009 of 26th February 2009 on the European Union trade mark and Council Regulation (EC) No 40/94 of 20th December 1993 on the Community trade mark;

"protected international trade mark (UK)" has the same meaning as in the Trade Marks (International Registration) Order 2008;

(2) References in this Schedule to—

(a) an "*Article*" are to an Article of the Madrid Protocol;

(b) an Article of the European Union Trade mark Regulation include references to any equivalent Article contained in the previous EUTM Regulations;

(c) the European Union Trade Mark Regulation include references to the previous EUTM Regulations;

(d) an international trade mark include references to an international trade mark which is dealt with for the purposes of the European Union Trade Mark Regulation as an EU collective mark or an EU certification mark;

(e) a "*Rule*" are to a Rule of the Common Regulations.

(3) In this Schedule, references to a request for territorial extension, in relation to an existing IR(EU) which is the subject of a separate international registration within the meaning of paragraph 1(3), are to the request made before the separate international registration was created.]

## SCHEDULE 3

TRANSITIONAL PROVISIONS

**Section 105**

*Introductory*

**1.**—(1) In this Schedule—

"existing registered mark" means a trade mark, certification trade mark or service mark registered under the 1938 Act immediately before the commencement of this Act;

"the 1938 Act" means the Trade Marks Act 1938; and

"the old law" means that Act and any other enactment or rule of law applying to existing registered marks immediately before the commencement of this Act.

(2) For the purposes of this Schedule—

(a) an application shall be treated as pending on the commencement of this Act if it was made but not finally determined before commencement, and

(b) the date on which it was made shall be taken to be the date of filing under the 1938 Act.

**Existing registered marks**

**2.**—(1) Existing registered marks (whether registered in Part A or B of the register kept under the 1938 Act shall be transferred on the commencement of this Act to the register kept under this Act and have effect, subject to the provisions of this Schedule, as if registered under this Act.

(2) Existing registered marks registered as a series under section 21(2) of the 1938 Act shall be similarly registered in the new register. Provision may be made by rules for putting such entries in the same form as is required for entries under this Act.

(3) In any other case notes indicating that existing registered marks are associated with other marks shall cease to have effect on the commencement of this Act.

**3.**—(1) A condition entered on the former register in relation to an existing registered mark immediately before the commencement of this Act shall cease to have effect on commencement.

Proceedings under section 33 of the 1938 Act (application to expunge or vary registration for breach of condition) which are pending on the commencement of this Act shall be dealt with under the old law and any necessary alteration made to the new register.

(2) A disclaimer or limitation entered on the former register in relation to an existing registered mark immediately before the commencement of this Act shall be transferred to the new register and have effect as if entered on the register in pursuance of section 13 of this Act.

**Effects of registration: Infringement**

**4.**—(1) Sections 9 to 12 of this Act (effects of registration) apply in relation to an existing registered mark as from the commencement of this Act and section 14 of this Act (action for infringement) applies in relation to infringement of an existing registered mark committed after the commencement of this Act, subject to sub-paragraph (2) below.

The old law continues to apply in relation to infringements committed before commencement

(2) It is not an infringement of—

(a) an existing registered mark, or

(b) a registered trade mark of which the distinctive elements are the same or substantially the same as those of an existing registered mark and which is registered for the same goods or services.

to continue after commencement any use which did not amount to infringement of the existing registered mark under the old law.

**Infringing goods, material or articles**

**5.**— Section 16 of this Act (order for delivery up of infringing goods, material or articles) applies to infringing goods, material or articles whether made before or after the commencement of this Act.

**Rights and remedies of licensee or authorised user**

**6.**—(1) Section 30 (general provisions as to rights of licensees in case of infringement) of this Act applies to licences granted before the commencement of this Act, but only in relation to infringements committed after commencement

(2) Paragraph 14 of Schedule 2 of this Act(court to take into account loss suffered by authorised users, &c) applies only in relation to infringements committed after commencement.

**Co-ownership of registered mark**

**7.**— The provisions of section 23 of this Act (co-ownership of registered mark) apply as from the commencement of this Act to an existing registered mark of which two or more persons were immediately before commencement registered as joint proprietors.

But so long as the relations between the joint proprietors remain such as are described in section 63 of the 1938 Act (joint ownership) there shall be taken to be an agreement to exclude the operation of subsections (1) and (3) of section 23 of this Act (ownership in undivided shares and right of co-proprietor to make separate use of the mark).

**Assignment. &c. of registered mark**

**8.**—(1) Section 24 of this Act (assignment or other transmission of registered mark) applies to transactions and events occurring after the commencement of this Act in relation to an existing registered mark, and the old law continues to apply in relation to transactions and events occurring before commencement.

(2) Existing entries under section 25 of the 1938 Act (registration of assignments and transmissions) shall be transferred on the commencement of this Act to the register kept under this Act and have effect as if made under section 25 of this Act.

Provision may be made by rules for putting such entries in the same form as is required for entries made under this Act.

(3) An application for registration under section 25 of the 1938 Act which is pending before the registrar on the commencement of this Act shall be treated as an application for registration under section 25 of this Act and shall proceed accordingly.

The registrar may require the applicant to amend his application so as to conform with the requirements of this Act.

(4) An application for registration under section 25 of the 1938 Act which has been determined by the registrar but not finally determined before the commencement of this Act shall be dealt with under the old law; and sub-paragraph (2) above shall apply in relation to any resulting entry in the register.

(5) Where before the commencement of this Act a person has become entitled by assignment or transmission to an existing registered mark but has not registered his title, any application for registration after commencement shall be made under section 25 of this Act.

(6) In cases to which sub-paragraph (3) or (5) applies section 25(3) of the 1938 Act continues to apply (and section 25(3) and (4) of this Act do not apply as regards the consequences of failing to register.

**Licensing of registered mark**

**9.**—(1) Sections 28 and 29(2) of this Act (licensing of registered trade mark; rights of exclusive license against grantor's successor in title) apply only in relation to licences granted after the commencement of this Act; and the old law continues to apply in relation to licences granted before commencement.

(2) Existing entries under section 28 of the 1938 Act (registered users) shall be transferred on the commencement of this Act to the register kept under this Act and have effect as if made under section 25 of this Act.

Provision may be made by rules for putting such entries in the same form as it required for entries made under this Act.

(3) An application for registration as a registered user which is pending before the registrar on the commencement of this Act shall be treated as an application for registration of a licence under section 25(1) of this Act and shall proceed accordingly.

The registrar may require the applicant to amend his application so as to conform with the requirements of this Act.

(4) An application for registration as a registered user which has been determined by the registrar but not finally determined before the commencement of this Act shall be dealt with under the old law; and sub-paragraph (2) above shall apply in relation to any resulting entry in the register.

(5) Any proceedings pending on the commencement of this Act under section 28(8) or (10) of the 1938 Act (variation or cancellation of registration of registered user) shall be dealt with under the old law and any necessary alteration made to the new register.

**Pending applications for registration**

**10.**—(1) An application for registration of a mark under the 1938 Act which is pending on the commencement of this Act shall be dealt with under the old law, subject as mentioned below, and if registered the mark shall be treated for the purposes of this Schedule as an existing registered mark.

(2) The power of the Secretary of State under section 78 of this Act to make rules regulating practice and procedure, and as to the matters mentioned in subsection (2) of that section, is exercisable in relation to such an application, and different provision may be made for such applications from that made for other applications.

(3) Section 23 of the 1938 Act (provisions as to associated trade marks) shall be disregarded in dealing after the commencement of this Act with an application for registration.

**Conversion of pending application**

**11.**—(1) In the case of a pending application for registration which has not been advertised under section 18 of the 1938 Act before the commencement of this Act, the applicant may give notice to the registrar claiming to have the registrability of the mark determined in accordance with the provisions of this Act.

(2) The notice must be in the prescribed form, be accompanied by the appropriate fee and be given no later than six months after the commencement of this Act.

(3) Notice duly given is irrevocable and has the effect that the application shall be treated as if made immediately after the commencement of this Act.

**Trade marks registered according to old classification**

**12.**— The registrar may exercise the powers conferred by rules under section 65 of this Act (adaptation of entries to new classification) to secure that any existing registered marks which do not conform to the system of classification prescribed under section 34 of this Act are brought into conformity with that system.

This applies, in particular, to existing registered marks classified according to the pre-1938 classification set out in Schedule 3 to the Trade Marks Rules 1986.

**Claim to priority from overseas application**

**13.—** Section 35 of this Act claim to priority of Convention application) applies to an application for registration under this Act made after the commencement of this Act notwithstanding that the Convention application was made before commencement.

**14.—**(1) Where before the commencement of this Act a person has duly filed an application for protection of a trade mark in a relevant country within the meaning of section 39A of the 1938 Act which is not a Convention country (a "relevant overseas application"), he, or his successor in title, has a right to priority, for the purposes of registering the same trade mark under this Act for some or all of the same goods or services, for a period of six months from the date of filing of the relevant overseas application.

(2) If the application for registration under this Act is made within that six-month period—

(a) the relevant date for the purposes of establishing which rights take precedence shall be the date of filing of the relevant overseas application, and

(b) the registrability of the trade mark shall not be affected by any use of the mark in the United Kingdom in the period between that date and the date of the application under this Act.

(3) Any filing which in a relevant country is equivalent to a regular national filing, under its domestic legislation or an international agreement, shall be treated as giving rise to the right of priority. A "regular national filing" means a filing which is adequate to establish the date on which the application was filed in that country, whatever may be the subsequent fate of the application.

(4) A subsequent application concerning the same subject as the relevant overseas application, filed in the same country, shall be considered the relevant overseas application (of which the filing date is the starting date of the period of priority), if at the time of the subsequent application—

(a) the previous application has been withdrawn, abandoned or refused, without having been laid open to public inspection and without leaving any rights outstanding, and

(b) it has not yet served as a basis for claiming a right of priority.

The previous application may not thereafter serve as a basis for claiming a right of priority.

(5) Provision may be made by rules as to the manner of claiming a right to priority on the basis of a relevant overseas application.

(6) A right to priority arising as a result of a relevant overseas application may be assigned or otherwise transmitted, either with the application or independently.

The reference in sub-paragraph (1) to the applicant's "successor in title" shall be construed accordingly.

(7) Nothing in this paragraph affects proceedings on an application for registration under the 1938 Act made before the commencement of this Act (see paragraph 10 above).

*Duration and renewal of registration*

**15.—**(1) Section 42(1) of this Act (duration of original period of registration) applies in relation to the registration of a mark in pursuance of an application made after the commencement of this Act; and the old law applies in any other case.

(2) Sections 42(2) and 43 of this Act (renewal) apply where the renewal falls due on or after the commencement of this Act; and the old law continues to apply in any other case.

(3) In either case it is immaterial when the fee is paid.

*Pending application for alteration of registered mark*

**16.—** An application under section 35 of the 1938 Act (alternation of registered trade mark) which is pending on the commencement of this Act shall be dealt with under the old law and any necessary alteration made to the new register.

*Revocation for non-use*

**17.—**(1) An application under section 26 of the 1938 Act (removal from register or imposition of limitation on ground of non-use) which is pending on the commencement of this Act shall be dealt with under the old law and any necessary alteration made to the new register.

(2) An application under section 46(1)(a) or (b) of this Act (revocation for non-use) may be made in relation to an existing registered mark at any time after the commencement of this Act.

Provided that no such application for the revocation of the registration of an existing registered mark registered by virtue of section 27 of the 1938 Act (defensive registration of well-known trade marks) may be made until more than five years after the commencement of this Act.

*Application for rectification, &c.*

**18.**—(1) An application under section 32 or 34 of the 1938 Act (rectification or correction of the register) which is pending on the commencement of this Act shall be dealt with under the old law and any necessary alteration made to the new register.

(2) For the purposes of proceedings under section 47 of this Act (grounds for invalidity of registration) as it applies in relation to an existing registered mark, the provisions of this Act shall be deemed to have been in force at all material times.
Provided that no objection to the validity of the registration of an existing registered mark may be taken on the ground specified in subsection (3) of section 5 of this Act (relative grounds for refusal of registration conflict with earlier mark registered for different goods or services).

*Regulations as to use of certification mark*

**19.**—(1) Regulations governing the use of an existing registered certification mark deposited at the Patent Office in pursuance of section 37 of the 1938 Act shall be treated after the commencement of this Act as if filed under paragraph 6 of Schedule 2 to this Act.

(2) Any request for amendment of the regulations which was pending on the commencement of this Act shall be dealt with under the old law.

*Sheffield marks*

**20.**—(1) For the purposes of this Schedule the Sheffield register kept under Schedule 2 to the 1938 Act shall be treated as part of the register of trade marks kept under that Act.

(2) Applications made to the Cutlers' Company in accordance with that Schedule which are pending on the commencement of this Act shall proceed after commencement as if they had been made to the registrar.

*Certificate of validity of contested registration*

**21.**— A certificate given before the commencement of this Act under section 47 of the 1938 Act (certificate of validity of contested registration) shall have effect as if given under section 73(1) of this Act.

*Trade mark agents*

**22.**—(1) Rules in force immediately before the commencement of this Act under section 282 or 283 of the Copyright, Designs and Patents Act 1988 (register of trade mark agents; persons entitled to described themselves as registered) shall continue in force and have effect as if made under section 83 or 85 of this Act.

(2) Rules in force immediately before the commencement of this Act under section 40 of the 1938 Act as to the persons whom the registrar may refuse to recognise as agents for the purposes of business under that Act shall continue in force and have effect as if made under section 88 of this Act.

(3) Rules continued in force under this paragraph may be varied or revoked by further rules made under the relevant provisions of this Act.

## SCHEDULE 4

### CONSEQUENTIAL AMENDMENTS

**Section 106(1)**

*General adaptation of existing references*

**1.**—(1) References in statutory provisions passed or made before the commencement of this Act to trade marks or registered trade marks within the meaning of the Trade Marks Act 1938 shall, unless the context otherwise requires, be construed after the commencement of this Act as references to trade marks or registered trade marks within the meaning of this Act.

(2) Sub-paragraph (1) applies, in particular, to the references in the following provisions—

| | |
|---|---|
| Industrial Organisation and Development Act 1947 | Schedule 1, paragraph 7 |
| Crown Proceedings Act 1947 | section 3(1)(b) |
| [... | ...] |
| Printer's Imprint Act 1961 | section 1(1)(b) |
| [... | ...] |

| | |
|---|---|
| [... | ...] |
| Patents Act 1977 | section 19(2) |
| | section 27(4) |
| | section 123(7) |
| Unfair Contract Terms Act 1977 | Schedule 1, paragraph 1(c) |
| Judicature (Northern Ireland) Act 1978 | section 94A(5) |
| State Immunity Act 1978 | section 7(a) and (b). |
| [Senior Courts Act 1981] | section 72(5) |
| | Schedule 1, paragraph 1(i) |
| Civil Jurisdiction and Judgments Act 1982 | Schedule 5, paragraph 2 |
| | Schedule 8, paragraph 2(14) and 4(2) |
| Value Added Tax Act 1983 | Schedule 3, paragraph 1 |
| [... | ... |
| | ...] |
| Law Reform (Miscellaneous Provisions) (Scotland) Act 1985 | section 15(5) |
| Atomic Energy Authority Act 1986 | section 8(2) |
| [... | ... |
| | ... |
| | ...] |
| Consumer Protection Act 1987 | section 2(2)(b) |
| Consumer Protection (Northern Ireland) Order 1987. | article 5(2)(b) |
| Income and Corporation Taxes Act 1988 | section 83(a) |
| Taxation of Chargeable Gains Act 1992 | section 275(h) |
| Tribunals and Inquiries Act 1992 | Schedule 1, paragraph 34. |

*Patents and Designs Act 1907 (c.29)*

**2.**—(1) The Patents and Designs Act 1907 is amended as follows.

(2) In section 62 (the Patent Office)—

(a) in subsection (1) for "this Act and the Trade Marks Act 1905" substitute "the Patents Act 1977 the Registered Designs Act 1949 and the Trade Marks Act 1994", and

(b) In subsections (2) and (3) for "the Board of Trade" substitute "the Secretary of State".

(3) In section 63 (officers and clerks of the Patent Office)—

(a) for "the Board of Trade" in each place where it occurs substitute "the Secretary of State"; and

(b) in subsection (2) omit the words from "and those salaries" to the end.

(4) The repeal by the Patents Act 1949 and the Registered Designs Act 1949 of the whole of the 1907 Act, except certain provisions, shall be deemed not to have extended to the long title, date of enactment or enacting words or to so much of section 99 as provides the Act with its short title.

*Patents, Designs, Copyright and Trade Marks (Emergency) Act 1939 (c.107)*

**3.**—(1) The Patents, Designs, Copyright and Trade Marks (Emergency) Act 1939 is amended as follows.

(2) For section 3 (power of comptroller to suspend rights of enemy or enemy subject) substitute—

**Power of comptroller to suspend trade mark rights of enemy or enemy subject.**

"**3.**—(1) Where on application made by a person proposing to supply goods or services of any description it is made to appear to the comptroller

(a) that it is difficult or impracticable to describe or refer to the goods or services without the use of a registered trade mark, and

(b) that the proprietor of the registered trade mark (whether alone or jointly with another) is an enemy or an enemy subject,

the comptroller may make an order suspending the rights given by the registered trade mark.

(2) An order under this section shall suspend those rights as regards the use of the trade mark—

(a) by the applicant, and

(b) by any person authorised by the applicant to do, for the purposes of or in connection with the supply by the applicant of the goods or services, things which would otherwise infringe the registered trade mark,

to such extent and for such period as the comptroller considers necessary to enable the applicant to render well-known and established some other means of describing or referring to the goods or services in question which does not involves the use of the trade mark.

(3) Where an order has been made under this section; no action for passing off lies on the part of any person interested in the registered trade mark in respect of any use of it which by virtue of the order is not an infringement of the right conferred by it.

(4) An order under this section may be varied or revoked by a subsequent order made by the comptroller".

(3) In each of the following provisions—

(a) section 4(1)(c) (effect of war on registration of trade marks),

(b) section 6(1) (power of comptroller to extend time limits),

(c) section 7(1)(a) (evidence as to nationality, &c.), and

(d) the definition of "the trade comptroller" in section 10(1) (interpretation),

for "the Trade Marks Act 1938" substitute "the Trade Marks Act 1994".

*Trade Descriptions Act 1968 (c.29)*

**4.—** In the Trade Descriptions Act 1968, in section 34 (exemption of trade description contained in pre-1968 trade mark)—

(a) in the opening words, omit "within the meaning of the Trade Marks Act 1938"; and

(b) in paragraph (c) for "a person registered under section 28 of the Trade Marks Act 1938 as a registered user of the trade mark" substitute ", in the case of a registered trade mark, a person licensed to use it".

*Solicitors Act 1974 (c.47)*

**5.—** [...]

*House of Commons Disqualification Act 1975 (c. 24)*

**6.—** In Part III of Schedule 1 to the House of Commons Disqualification Act 1975 (other disqualifying offices), for the entry relating to persons appointed to hear and determine appeals under the Trade Marks Act 1938 substitute—

"Person appointed to hear and determine appeals under the Trade Marks Act 1994.".

*Restrictive Trade Practices Act 1976 (c. 34)*

**7.—** In Schedule 3 to the Restrictive Trade Practices Act 1976 (excepted agreements), for paragraph 4 (agreements relating to trade marks) substitute—

**"4.—**(1) This Act does not apply to an agreement authorising the use of a registered trade mark (other than a collective mark or certification mark) if no such restrictions as are described in section 6(1) or 11(2) above are accepted, and no such information provisions as are described in section 7(1) or 12(2) above are made, except in respect of—

(a) the descriptions of goods bearing the mark which are to be produced or supplied, or the processes of manufacture to be applied to such goods or to goods to which the mark is to be applied, or

(b) the kinds of services in relation to which the mark as to be used which are to be made available or supplied, or the form or manner in which such services are to be made available or supplied, or

(c) the descriptions of goods which are to be produced or supplied in connection with the supply of services in relation to which the mark is to be used, or the process of manufacture to be applied to such goods.

(2) This Act does not apply to an agreement authorising the use of a registered collective mark or certification mark if—

(a) the agreement is made in accordance with regulations approved by the registrar under Schedule 1 or 2 to the Trade Marks Act 1994 and
(b) no such restrictions as are described in section 6(1) or 11(2) above are accepted, and no such information provisions as are described in section 7(1) or 12(2) above are made, except as permitted by those regulations".

*Copyright, Designs and Patents Act 1988 (c.48)*

**8.**—(1) The Copyright, Designs and Patents Act 1988 is amended as follows.

(2) In section 114(6), 204(6) and 231(6) (persons regarded as having an interest in infringing copies, &c.), for "section 58C of the Trade Marks Act 1938" substitute "section 19 of the Trade Marks Act 1994".

(3) In section 280(1) (privilege for communications with patent agents), for "trade mark or service mark" substitute "or trade mark".

*Tribunals and Inquiries Act 1992 (c.53)*

**9.** In Part 1 of Schedule 1 to the Tribunals and Inquiries Act 1992 (tribunals under direct supervision of Council on Tribunals), for "Patents, designs, trade marks and service marks" substitute "Patents, designs and trade marks".

## SCHEDULE 5

### REPEALS AND REVOCATIONS

**Section 106(2)**

| Chapter or number | Short title | Extent of repeal or revocation |
|---|---|---|
| 1891 c. 50. | Commissioners for Oaths Act 1891. | In section 1, the words "or the Patents, Designs and Trade Marks Acts 1883 to 1888". |
| 1907 c. 29. | Patents and Designs Act 1907. | In section 63(2), the words from "and those salaries" to the end. |
| 1938 c. 22. | Trade Marks Act 1938. | The whole Act. |
| 1947 c. 44. | Crown Proceedings Act 1947. | In section 3(1)(b), the words "or registered services mark". |
| 1949 c. 87. | Patents Act 1949. | Section 92(2). |
| 1964 c. 14. | Plant Varieties and Seeds Act 1964. | In section 5A(4), the words "under the Trade Marks Act 1938". |
| 1967 c. 80. | Criminal Justice Act 1967. | In Schedule 3, in Parts I and IV, the entries relating to the Trade Marks Act 1938. |
| 1978 c. 23. | Judicature (Northern Ireland) Act 1978. | In Schedule 5, in Part II, the paragraphs amending the Trade Marks Act 1938. |
| 1984 c. 19. | Trade Marks (Amendment) Act 1984. | The whole Act. |
| 1985 c. 6. | Companies Act 1985. | In section 396— (a) in subsection (3A)(a), and (b) in subsection (2)(d)(i) as inserted by the Companies Act 1989, the words "service mark,". |
| 1986 c. 12. | Statute Law (Repeals) Act 1986. | In Schedule 2, paragraph 2. |
| 1986 c. 39. | Patents, Designs and Marks Act 1986. | Section 2. |
| | | Section 4(4). |
| | | In Schedule 1, paragraphs 1 and 2. |

| Chapter or number | Short title | Extent of repeal or revocation |
|---|---|---|
| | | Schedule 2. |
| S.I. 1986/1032. | Companies (Northern Ireland) Order 1986. | In article 403—<br>(a) in paragraph (3A)(a), and<br>(b) in paragraph (2)(d)(i) as inserted by the Companies (No.2) (Northern Ireland) Order 1990, the words "service mark,". |
| 1987 c. 43. | Consumer Protection Act 1987. | In section 45—<br>(a) in subsection (1), the definition of "mark" and "trade mark";<br>(b) subsection (4). |
| S.I. 1987/2049. | Consumer Protection (Northern Ireland) Order 1987. | In article 2—<br>(a) in paragraph (2) the definitions of "mark" and "trade mark",<br>(b) paragraph (3). |
| 1988 c. 1. | Income and Corporation Taxes Act 1988. | In section 83 , the words from "References in this section" to the end. |
| 1988 c. 48. | Copyright, Designs and Patents Act 1988. | Sections 282 to 284. |
| | | In section 286, the definition of "registered trade mark agent". |
| | | Section 300. |
| 1992 c. 12. | Taxation of Chargeable Gains Act 1992. | In section 275(h), the words "service marks" and "service mark". |

**Modifications**

| Provision | Modification | Notes | Further Information |
|---|---|---|---|
| *Whole Document* | Trade Marks Act 1994 (Isle of Man) Order 1996/729, Sch. 1 para. 1 | | |
| *Pt I s. 3(4)* | Trade Marks (Isle of Man) Order 2013/2601, Sch. 1 para. 2 | Modified in relation to the Isle of Man | art. 2 |
| *Pt I s. 4(5)* | Olympic Symbol etc. (Protection) Act 1995 c. 32, s. 13(2) | Deemed to be inserted in relation to restrictions on acquisition of competing rights | |
| *Pt I s. 5(3)* | Trade Marks (Isle of Man) Order 2013/2601, Sch. 1 para. 3 | Modified in relation to the Isle of Man | art. 2 |
| *Pt I s. 5(3)(b)* | Trade Marks Act 1994 (Isle of Man) Order 1996/729, Sch. 1 para. 1A | Modified in relation to the Isle of Man | |
| *Pt I s. 6(1)* | Trade Marks (Isle of Man) Order 2013/2601, | Modified in relation to the Isle of Man | art. 2 |

| Provision | Modification | Notes | Further Information |
|---|---|---|---|
| | Sch. 1 para. 4 | | |
| *Pt I s. 6A* | Trade Marks (International Registration) Order 1996/714, art. 10C(2) | Modifed in relation to the proceedings relating to the opposition to the conferring of protection | |
| | Trade Marks (Isle of Man) Order 2013/2601, Sch. 1 para. 5 | Deemed to be inserted in relation to the Isle of Man | art. 2 |
| | Trade Marks Act 1994 (Isle of Man) Order 1996/729, Sch. 1 para. 1B | Modified in relation to the Isle of Man | |
| *Pt I s. 10(3)* | Trade Marks (Isle of Man) Order 2013/2601, Sch. 1 para. 6 | Modified in relation to the Isle of Man | art. 2 |
| | Trade Marks Act 1994 (Isle of Man) Order 1996/729, Sch. 1 para. 1C(a) | Modified in relation to the Isle of Man | |
| *Pt I s. 10(3)(b)* | Trade Marks Act 1994 (Isle of Man) Order 1996/729, Sch. 1 para. 1C(b) | Modified in relation to the Isle of Man | |
| *Pt I s. 14(2A)* | Trade Marks (Isle of Man) Order 2013/2601, Sch. 1 para. 7 | Deemed to be inserted in relation to the Isle of Man | art. 2 |
| *Pt I s. 14(2B)* | Trade Marks (Isle of Man) Order 2013/2601, Sch. 1 para. 7 | Deemed to be inserted in relation to the Isle of Man | art. 2 |
| *Pt I s. 17(3)* | Trade Marks (Isle of Man) Order 2013/2601, Sch. 1 para. 8 | Modified in relation to the Isle of Man | art. 2 |
| *Pt I s. 18(3)* | Trade Marks Act 1994 (Isle of Man) Order 1996/729, Sch. 1 para. 2 | Modified in relation to the Isle of Man | art. 2 |
| *Pt I s. 18(3)(d)* | Trade Marks (Isle of Man) Order 2013/2601, Sch. 1 para. 9 | Deemed to be inserted in relation to the Isle of Man | art. 2 |
| *Pt I s. 19(6)* | Trade Marks (Isle of Man) Order 2013/2601, Sch. 1 para. 10 | Modified in relation to the Isle of Man | art. 2 |
| | Trade Marks Act 1994 (Isle of Man) Order 1996/729, Sch. 1 para. 3 | Modified in relation to the Isle of Man | art. 2 |
| *Pt I s. 20* | Trade Marks Act 1994 (Isle of Man) Order 1996/729, Sch. 1 para. 4 | Modified in relation to the Isle of Man | art. 2 |
| *Pt I s. 21* | Trade Marks (International Registration) Or- | Modified in relation to a protected international | |

| Provision | Modification | Notes | Further Information |
|---|---|---|---|
| | der 1996/714, art. 4(6) | trade mark (UK) | |
| *Pt I s. 21(3)* | Community Trade Mark Regulations 1996/1908, reg. 4 | Modifed in relation to an international trade mark (EC) | |
| | Community Trade Mark Regulations 2006/1027, reg. 6(2)(a) | Modified in relation to an international trade mark | |
| *Pt I s. 21(4)* | Community Trade Mark Regulations 1996/1908, reg. 4 | Modifed in relation to an international trade mark (EC) | |
| | Community Trade Mark Regulations 2006/1027, reg. 6(2)(b) | Modified in relation to an international tradc mark | |
| | Community Trade Mark Regulations 2006/1027, reg. 6(2)(c) | Modified in relation to an international trade mark | |
| *Pt I s. 22* | Trade Marks (International Registration) Order 1996/714, art. 5 | Modified in relation to an international trade mark (UK) | |
| *Pt I s. 23* | Trade Marks (International Registration) Order 1996/714, art. 5 | Modified in relation to an international trade mark (UK) | |
| *Pt I s. 24(1)* | Trade Marks (International Registration) Order 1996/714, art. 5 | Modified in relation to an international trade mark (UK) | |
| *Pt I s. 24(2)(a)* | Trade Marks (International Registration) Order 1996/714, art. 5 | Modified in relation to an international trade mark (UK) | |
| *Pt I s. 24(3)* | Trade Marks (International Registration) Order 1996/714, art. 5 | Modified in relation to an international trade mark (UK) | |
| *Pt I s. 24(4)* | Trade Marks (International Registration) Order 1996/714, art. 5 | Modified in relation to an international trade mark (UK) | |
| *Pt I s. 24(5)* | Trade Marks (International Registration) Order 1996/714, art. 5 | Modified in relation to an international trade mark (UK) | |
| *Pt I s. 24(6)* | Trade Marks (International Registration) Order 1996/714, art. 5 | Modified in relation to an international trade mark (UK) | |
| *Pt I s. 25* | Trade Marks (International Registration) Order 2008/2206, Sch. 2 para. 1 | Modified in relation to international trade marks | art. 3(3)(i) |
| *Pt I s. 25(4)* | Trade Marks (Isle of Man) Order 2013/2601, Sch. 1 para. 11 | Modified in relation to the Isle of Man | art. 2 |
| *Pt I s. 26* | Trade Marks (International Registration) Order 1996/714, art. 5 | Modified in relation to an international trade mark (UK) | |
| *Pt I s. 28* | Trade Marks (International Registration) Order 1996/714, art. 7(1) | Modified in relation to licences to use a protected international | |

| Provision | Modification | Notes | Further Information |
|---|---|---|---|
| | | trade mark (UK) | |
| *Pt I s. 28(1)* | Trade Marks (International Registration) Order 1996/714, art. 7(2) | Modified in relation to licences to use a protected international trade mark (UK) | |
| *Pt I s. 29* | Trade Marks (International Registration) Order 1996/714, art. 7(1) | Modified in relation to licences to use a protected international trade mark (UK) | |
| *Pt I s. 30* | Trade Marks (International Registration) Order 1996/714, art. 7(1) | Modified in relation to licences to use a protected international trade mark (UK) | |
| *Pt I s. 31* | Trade Marks (International Registration) Order 1996/714, art. 7(1) | Modified in relation to licences to use a protected international trade mark (UK) | |
| *Pt I s. 33(1)* | Trade Marks (International Registration) Order 2008/2206, Sch. 2 para. 2 | Modified in relation to international trade marks | art. 3(3)(i) |
| *Pt I s. 35* | Trade Marks (International Registration) Order 1996/714, art. 8(1) | Modified so as to confer a right to priority in relation to protection of an international registration designating the United Kingdom | |
| *Pt I s. 35(5)* | Trade Marks (International Registration) Order 2008/2206, Sch. 2 para. 3 | Modified in relation to international trade marks | art. 3(3)(i) |
| *Pt I s. 37(3)* | Trade Marks (International Registration) Order 2008/2206, Sch. 2 para. 4 | Modified in relation to international trade marks | art. 3(3)(i) |
| *Pt I s. 37(4)* | Trade Marks (International Registration) Order 2008/2206, Sch. 2 para. 4 | Modified in relation to international trade marks | art. 3(3)(i) |
| *Pt I s. 37(5)* | Trade Marks (International Registration) Order 2008/2206, Sch. 2 para. 4 | Modified in relation to international trade marks | art. 3(3)(i) |
| *Pt I s. 38(2)* | Trade Marks (International Registration) Order 2008/2206, Sch. 2 para. 5 | Modified in relation to international trade marks | art. 3(3)(i) |
| *Pt I s. 39(1)* | Trade Marks (International Registration) Order 2008/2206, Sch. 2 para. 7 | Modified in relation to international trade marks | art. 3(3)(i) |
| *Pt I s. 40(1)* | Trade Marks (Isle of Man) Order 2013/2601, Sch. 1 para. 12 | Modified in relation to the Isle of Man | art. 2 |

| Provision | Modification | Notes | Further Information |
|---|---|---|---|
| | Trade Marks Act 1994 (Isle of Man) Order 1996/729, Sch. 1 para. 4A | Modified in relation to the Isle of Man | |
| *Pt I s. 46* | Trade Marks (International Registration) Order 1996/714, art. 13(3) | Modifed to permit the protection of a protected international trade mark (UK) to be revoked, or declared invalid | |
| *Pt I s. 46(1)* | Trade Marks (International Registration) Order 1996/714, art. 13(2) | Modifed to permit the protection of a protected international trade mark (UK) to be revoked, or declared invalid | |
| *Pt I s. 46(2)* | Trade Marks (International Registration) Order 1996/714, art. 13(2) | Modifed to permit the protection of a protected international trade mark (UK) to be revoked, or declared invalid | |
| *Pt I s. 46(5)* | Trade Marks (International Registration) Order 1996/714, art. 13(2) | Modifed to permit the protection of a protected international trade mark (UK) to be revoked, or declared invalid | |
| *Pt I s. 47* | Trade Marks (International Registration) Order 1996/714, art. 13(3) | Modifed to permit the protection of a protected international trade mark (UK) to be revoked, or declared invalid | |
| *Pt I s. 47(2A)* | Trade Marks (Isle of Man) Order 2013/2601, Sch. 1 para. 13 | Deemed to be inserted in relation to the Isle of Man | art. 2 |
| | Trade Marks Act 1994 (Isle of Man) Order 1996/729, Sch. 1 para. 4B | Modified in relation to the Isle of Man | |
| *Pt I s. 47(2B)* | Trade Marks (Isle of Man) Order 2013/2601, Sch. 1 para. 13 | Deemed to be inserted in relation to the Isle of Man | art. 2 |
| | Trade Marks Act 1994 (Isle of Man) Order 1996/729, Sch. 1 para. 4B | Modified in relation to the Isle of Man | |
| *Pt I s. 47(2C)* | Trade Marks (Isle of Man) Order 2013/2601, Sch. 1 para. 13 | Deemed to be inserted in relation to the Isle of Man | art. 2 |
| | Trade Marks Act 1994 (Isle of Man) Order 1996/729, Sch. 1 para. 4B | Modified in relation to the Isle of Man | |

| Provision | Modification | Notes | Further Information |
|---|---|---|---|
| Pt I s. 47(2D) | Trade Marks (Isle of Man) Order 2013/2601, Sch. 1 para. 13 | Deemed to be inserted in relation to the Isle of Man | art. 2 |
| | Trade Marks Act 1994 (Isle of Man) Order 1996/729, Sch. 1 para. 4B | Modified in relation to the Isle of Man | |
| *Pt I s. 47(2E)* | Trade Marks (Isle of Man) Order 2013/2601, Sch. 1 para. 13 | Deemed to be inserted in relation to the Isle of Man | art. 2 |
| | Trade Marks Act 1994 (Isle of Man) Order 1996/729, Sch. 1 para. 4B | Modified in relation to the Isle of Man | |
| *Pt I s. 47(2F)* | Trade Marks (Isle of Man) Order 2013/2601, Sch. 1 para. 13 | Deemed to be inserted in relation to the Isle of Man | art. 2 |
| *Pt I s. 47(5)* | Trade Marks (International Registration) Order 1996/714, art. 13(2) | Modifed to permit the protection of a protected international trade mark (UK) to be revoked, or declared invalid | |
| *Pt I s. 48* | Trade Marks (International Registration) Order 1996/714, art. 14 | Modifed where the proprietor of an earlier trade mark has acquiesced for a continuous period of five years in the use of a protected international trade mark (UK) | |
| *Pt II s. 51* | Trade Marks Act 1994 (Isle of Man) Order 1996/729, Sch. 1 para. 5 | Modified in relation to the Isle of Man | art. 2 |
| *Pt II s. 52* | Trade Marks (Isle of Man) Order 2013/2601, Sch. 1 para. 14 | Modified in relation to the Isle of Man | art. 2 |
| | Trade Marks Act 1994 (Isle of Man) Order 1996/729, Sch. 1 para. 5 | Modified in relation to the Isle of Man | art. 2 |
| *Pt II s. 53 definition of "international trade mark EC"* | Trade Marks (Isle of Man) Order 2013/2601, Sch. 1 para. 15 | Deemed to be inserted in relation to the Isle of Man | art. 2 |
| *Pt II s. 55* | Trade Marks (Isle of Man) Order 2013/2601, Sch. 1 para. 16 | Modified in relation to the Isle of Man | art. 2 |
| *Pt II s. 55(1)(aa)* | Trade Marks (Isle of Man) Order 2013/2601, Sch. 1 para. 16(b) | Deemed to be inserted in relation to the Isle of Man | art. 2 |
| *Pt II s. 56(1)* | Trade Marks (Isle of Man) Order 2013/2601, Sch. 1 para. 17 | Modified in relation to the Isle of Man | art. 2 |

| Provision | Modification | Notes | Further Information |
|---|---|---|---|
| *Pt II s. 56(2)* | Trade Marks (Isle of Man) Order 2013/2601, Sch. 1 para. 17 | Modified in relation to the Isle of Man | art. 2 |
| *Pt II s. 57(2)* | Trade Marks (Isle of Man) Order 2013/2601, Sch. 1 para. 17 | Modified in relation to the Isle of Man | art. 2 |
| *Pt II s. 57(3)* | Trade Marks (Isle of Man) Order 2013/2601, Sch. 1 para. 17 | Modified in relation to the Isle of Man | art. 2 |
| *Pt II s. 58(2)* | Trade Marks (Isle of Man) Order 2013/2601, Sch. 1 para. 17 | Modified in relation to the Isle of Man | art. 2 |
| *Pt II s. 59(5)* | Trade Marks (Isle of Man) Order 2013/2601, Sch. 1 para. 18 | Deemed to be inserted in relation to the Isle of Man | art. 2 |
| *Pt II s. 61* | Trade Marks (Isle of Man) Order 2013/2601, Sch. 1 para. 19 | Modified in relation to the Isle of Man | art. 2 |
| *Pt III s. 63* | Trade Marks (International Registration) Order 2008/2206, Sch. 2 para. 8 | Modified in relation to international trade marks | art. 3(3)(i) |
| *Pt III s. 67(2)(a)* | Trade Marks (International Registration) Order 2008/2206, Sch. 2 para. 9 | Modified in relation to international trade marks | art. 3(3)(i) |
| *Pt III s. 68(2)* | Trade Marks Act 1994 (Isle of Man) Order 1996/729, Sch. 1 para. 6 | Modified in relation to the Isle of Man | art. 2 |
| *Pt III s. 68(2)(c)* | Trade Marks (Isle of Man) Order 2013/2601, Sch. 1 para. 20 | Deemed to be inserted in relation to the Isle of Man | art. 2 |
| *Pt III s. 73* | Trade Marks (International Registration) Order 1996/714, art. 15(1) | Modified in relation to proceedings before the court in which the validity of the protection of a protected international trade mark (UK) is contested | |
| *Pt III s. 74* | Trade Marks (International Registration) Order 1996/714, art. 15(2) | Modified in relation to proceedings before the court involving an application for (a) the revocation of the protection of a protected international trade mark (UK); (b) a declaration of the invalidity of the protection of a protected international trade mark (UK); (c) the rectification of the supplementary register | |

| Provision | Modification | Notes | Further Information |
|---|---|---|---|
| *Pt III s. 75* | Trade Marks (Isle of Man) Order 2013/2601, Sch. 1 para. 21 | Modified in relation to the Isle of Man | art. 2 |
| *Pt III s. 75(aa)* | Trade Marks Act 1994 (Isle of Man) Order 1996/729, Sch. 1 para. 7 | Deemed to be inserted in relation to the Isle of Man | art. 2 |
| *Pt III s. 75(c)* | Trade Marks (Isle of Man) Order 2013/2601, Sch. 1 para. 21(b) | Deemed to be inserted in relation to the Isle of Man | art. 2 |
| *Pt III s. 77* | Transfer of Functions (Lord Advocate and Secretary of State) Order 1999/678, art. 2(1) | Modified in relation to the transfer of functions of the Lord Advocate to the Secretary of State | Sch. 1 para. 1 |
| | Transfer of Functions (Lord Advocate and Secretary of State) Order 1999/678, Sch. 1 para. 1 | Modified in relation to the transfer of functions to the Secretary of State | |
| *Pt III s. 77(2)(ba)* | Trade Marks (Isle of Man) Order 2013/2601, Sch. 1 para. 22 | Deemed to be inserted in relation to the Isle of Man | art. 2 |
| | Trade Marks Act 1994 (Isle of Man) Order 1996/729, Sch. 1 para. 8 | Deemed to be inserted in relation to the Isle of Man | art. 2 |
| *Pt III s. 83A(7) definition of "trade mark agency work" (a)* | Trade Marks (Isle of Man) Order 2013/2601, Sch. 1 para. 23 | Modified in relation to the Isle of Man | art. 2 |
| *Pt III s. 86* | Trade Marks Act 1994 (Isle of Man) Order 1996/729, Sch. 1 para. 9 | Modified in relation to the Isle of Man | art. 2 |
| *Pt III s. 86(2)* | Trade Marks (Isle of Man) Order 2013/2601, Sch. 1 para. 24 | Modified in relation to the Isle of Man | art. 2 |
| *Pt III s. 87(2)* | Trade Marks (Isle of Man) Order 2013/2601, Sch. 1 para. 25 | Modified in relation to the Isle of Man | art. 2 |
| *Pt III s. 89* | Trade Marks (Isle of Man) Order 2013/2601, Sch. 1 para. 26 | Modified in relation to the Isle of Man | art. 2 |
| | Trade Marks Act 1994 (Isle of Man) Order 1996/729, Sch. 1 para. 10 | Modified in relation to the Isle of Man | art. 2 |
| *Pt III s. 89(3)* | Trade Marks Act 1994 (Isle of Man) Order 1996/729, Sch. 1 para. 10 | Modified in relation to the Isle of Man | |
| *Pt III s. 90* | Trade Marks (Isle of Man) Order 2013/2601, Sch. 1 para. 27 | Modified in relation to the Isle of Man | art. 2 |

| Provision | Modification | Notes | Further Information |
|---|---|---|---|
| | Trade Marks Act 1994 (Isle of Man) Order 1996/729, Sch. 1 para. 10 | Modified in relation to the Isle of Man | art. 2 |
| *Pt III s. 91* | Trade Marks (Isle of Man) Order 2013/2601, Sch. 1 para. 28 | Modified in relation to the Isle of Man | art. 2 |
| | Trade Marks Act 1994 (Isle of Man) Order 1996/729, Sch. 1 para. 10 | Modified in relation to the Isle of Man | art. 2 |
| *Pt III s. 92* | Trade Marks (International Registration) Order 1996/714, art. 17(2) | Modified in relation to a protected international trade mark (UK) | |
| *Pt III s. 92(6)* | Trade Marks (Isle of Man) Order 2013/2601, Sch. 1 para. 29 | Modified in relation to the Isle of Man | art. 2 |
| *Pt III s. 92(6)(b)* | Trade Marks Act 1994 (Isle of Man) Order 1996/729, Sch. 1 para. 11 | Modified in relation to the Isle of Man | art. 2 |
| *Pt III s. 92A* | Trade Marks (International Registration) Order 1996/714, art. 17(2) | Modified in relation to a protected international trade mark (UK) | |
| *Pt III s. 92A(1)* | Trade Marks Act 1994 (Isle of Man) Order 1996/729, Sch. 1 para. 11A | Modified in relation to the Isle of Man | |
| *Pt III s. 92A(2)* | Trade Marks Act 1994 (Isle of Man) Order 1996/729, Sch. 1 para. 11A | Modified in relation to the Isle of Man | |
| *Pt III s. 92A(2A)* | Trade Marks (Isle of Man) Order 2013/2601, Sch. 1 para. 30(1) | Deemed to be inserted in relation to the Isle of Man | art. 2 |
| *Pt III s. 92A(3)(b)* | Trade Marks (Isle of Man) Order 2013/2601, Sch. 1 para. 30(2) | Modified in relation to the Isle of Man | art. 2 |
| *Pt III s. 93* | Trade Marks (International Registration) Order 1996/714, art. 17(2) | Modified in relation to a protected international trade mark (UK) | |
| | Trade Marks (Isle of Man) Order 2013/2601, Sch. 1 para. 31 | Modified in relation to the Isle of Man | art. 2 |
| | Trade Marks Act 1994 (Isle of Man) Order 1996/729, Sch. 1 para. 12 | Modified in relation to the Isle of Man | art. 2 |
| *Pt III s. 94(3)* | Trade Marks (Isle of Man) Order 2013/2601, Sch. 1 para. 32 | Modified in relation to the Isle of Man | art. 2 |
| *Pt III s. 94(3)(a)* | Trade Marks Act 1994 (Isle of Man) Order | Modified in relation to the Isle of Man | art. 2 |

| Provision | Modification | Notes | Further Information |
|---|---|---|---|
| | 1996/729, Sch. 1 para. 11 | | |
| *Pt III s. 96* | Trade Marks Act 1994 (Isle of Man) Order 1996/729, Sch. 1 para. 12 | Modified in relation to the Isle of Man | art. 2 |
| *Pt III s. 97* | Olympic Symbol etc. (Protection) Act 1995 c. 32, s. 11 | Modifed in relation to forfeiture in relation to England and Wales of Northern Ireland | |
| | Trade Marks (International Registration) Order 1996/714, art. 17(2) | Modified in relation to a protected international trade mark (UK) | |
| | Trade Marks (Isle of Man) Order 2013/2601, Sch. 1 para. 33 | Modified in relation to the Isle of Man | art. 2 |
| *Pt III s. 97(1)* | Trade Marks Act 1994 (Isle of Man) Order 1996/729, Sch. 1 para. 13(1) | Modified in relation to the Isle of Man | art. 2 |
| *Pt III s. 97(2)(b)* | Trade Marks Act 1994 (Isle of Man) Order 1996/729, Sch. 1 para. 13(2) | Modified in relation to the Isle of Man | art. 2 |
| *Pt III s. 97(5)* | Trade Marks Act 1994 (Isle of Man) Order 1996/729, Sch. 1 para. 13(2) | Modified in relation to the Isle of Man | art. 2 |
| | Trade Marks Act 1994 (Isle of Man) Order 1996/729, Sch. 1 para. 13(3)(b) | Modified in relation to the Isle of Man | art. 2 |
| *Pt III s. 97(5)(a)* | Trade Marks Act 1994 (Isle of Man) Order 1996/729, Sch. 1 para. 13(3)(a) | Modified in relation to the Isle of Man | art. 2 |
| *Pt III s. 97(5)(b)* | Trade Marks Act 1994 (Isle of Man) Order 1996/729, Sch. 1 para. 13(3)(a) | Modified in relation to the Isle of Man | art. 2 |
| *Pt III s. 97(5)(c)* | Trade Marks (Isle of Man) Order 2013/2601, Sch. 1 para. 33(3)(b) | Deemed to be inserted in relation to the Isle of Man | art. 2 |
| *Pt III s. 97(8)* | Trade Marks Act 1994 (Isle of Man) Order 1996/729, Sch. 1 para. 13(4) | Modified in relation to the Isle of Man | art. 2 |
| *Pt III s. 98* | Olympic Symbol etc. (Protection) Act 1995 c. 32, s. 12 | Modifed in relation to forfeiture in relation to Scotland | |
| | Trade Marks (International Registration) Order 1996/714, art. 17(2) | Modified in relation to a protected international trade mark (UK) | |

| Provision | Modification | Notes | Further Information |
|---|---|---|---|
| | Trade Marks Act 1994 (Isle of Man) Order 1996/729, Sch. 1 para. 12 | Modified in relation to the Isle of Man | art. 2 |
| *Pt IV s. 101(2)(b)* | Trade Marks (Isle of Man) Order 2013/2601, Sch. 1 para. 34 | Modified in relation to the Isle of Man | art. 2 |
| | Trade Marks Act 1994 (Isle of Man) Order 1996/729, Sch. 1 para. 14 | Modified in relation to the Isle of Man | art. 2 |
| *Pt IV s. 102* | Trade Marks Act 1994 (Isle of Man) Order 1996/729, Sch. 1 para. 15 | Modified in relation to the Isle of Man | art. 2 |
| *Pt IV s. 103(3)* | Trade Marks (Isle of Man) Order 2013/2601, Sch. 1 para. 35 | Modified in relation to the Isle of Man | art. 2 |
| *Pt IV s. 104* | Trade Marks (Isle of Man) Order 2013/2601, Sch. 1 para. 36 | Modified in relation to the Isle of Man | art. 2 |
| | Trade Marks Act 1994 (Isle of Man) Order 1996/729, Sch. 1 para. 16 | Modified in relation to the Isle of Man | art. 2 |
| *Pt IV s. 106* | Trade Marks (Isle of Man) Order 2013/2601, Sch. 1 para. 37 | Modified in relation to the Isle of Man | art. 2 |
| *Sch. 1 para. 11(c)* | Trade Marks (Isle of Man) Order 2013/2601, Sch. 1 para. 38 | Modified in relation to the Isle of Man | art. 2 |
| *Sch. 2 para. 13(c)* | Trade Marks (Isle of Man) Order 2013/2601, Sch. 1 para. 39 | Modified in relation to the Isle of Man | art. 2 |
| Sch. 4 | Trade Marks (Isle of Man) Order 2013/2601, Sch. 1 para. 37 | Modified in relation to the Isle of Man | art. 2 |
| Sch. 4 para. 4 | Trade Marks Act 1994 (Isle of Man) Order 1996/729, Sch. 1 para. 17(2) | Modified in relation only to statutory provisions which extend to the Isle of Man | art. 2 |
| *Sch. 5* | Trade Marks (Isle of Man) Order 2013/2601, Sch. 1 para. 37 | Modified in relation to the Isle of Man | art. 2 |
| *Sch. 5 para. 1* | Trade Marks Act 1994 (Isle of Man) Order 1996/729, Sch. 1 para. 17(3) | Modified in relation only to statutory provisions which extend to the Isle of Man | art. 2 |

*After Appendix 2, add new Appendix 2A:*

APPENDIX 2A

# THE TRADE MARKS RULES 2008

## (SI 2008/1797) A2A-001

ARRANGEMENT OF RULES

*Preliminary*

The Secretary of State makes the following rules in exercise of the powers conferred upon the Secretary of State by sections 4(4), 13(2), 25(1), (5) and (6), 34(1), 35(5), 38(1) and (2), 39(3), 40(4), 41(1) and (3), 43(2), (3), (5) and (6), 44(3), 45(2), 63(2) and (3), 64(4), 65(1) and (2), 66(2), 67(1) and (2), 68(1) and (3), 69, 76(1), 78, 80(3), 81, 82 and 88 of, paragraph 6(2) of Schedule 1 to, and paragraph 7(2) of Schedule 2 to, the Trade Marks Act 1994.

In accordance with section 8 of the Tribunals and Inquiries Act 1992, the Secretary of State has consulted the Administrative Justice and Tribunals Council before making these Rules.

*Preliminary*

**Citation and commencement**

**1.—** These Rules may be cited as the Trade Marks Rules 2008 and shall come into force on 1st October 2008.

**Interpretation**

**2.**—(1) In these Rules—

"the Act" means the Trade Marks Act 1994;

["fast track opposition" means an opposition—

(a) brought solely on grounds under section 5(1) or 5(2) of the Act,

(b) based on no more than 3 earlier trade marks, each of which is registered in the UK [or is protected in the UK as an international trade mark (UK)],

(c) where proof of use of the earlier marks can be provided with the notice of opposition, and

(d) which the opponent considers may be determined without the need for further evidence and without an oral hearing;]

"the Journal" means the Trade Marks Journal published in accordance with rule 81;

"the "Nice Agreement" means the Nice Agreement Concerning the International Classification of Goods and Services for the Purposes of the Registration of Marks of 15th June 1957, which was last amended on 28th September 1979;

"the "Nice Classification" means the system of classification under the Nice Agreement;

["the Office" means the Patent Office which operates under the name "Intellectual Property Office";]

"send" includes give;

"specification" means the statement of goods or services in respect of which a trade mark is registered or proposed to be registered;

"transformation application" means an application to register a trade mark under the Act where that mark was the subject of an international registration prior to that registration being cancelled.

(2) In these Rules a reference to a section is a reference to that section in the Act[, a reference to a schedule is a reference to that schedule to the Act] and a reference to a form is a reference to that form as published under rule 3.

[(2A) Terms defined in Part 5 of Schedules 2A and 2B have the same meaning in these Rules.]

(3) In these Rules references to the filing of any application, notice or other document, unless the contrary intention appears, are to be construed as references to its being delivered to the registrar at the Office.

[**Comparable trade mark (EU)**

**2A.** These Rules apply to a comparable trade mark (EU) as they apply to other registered trade marks.]

[**Comparable trade mark (IR)**

**2B.** These Rules apply to a comparable trade mark (IR) as they apply to other registered trade marks.]

**Forms and directions of the registrar; section 66**

**3.**—(1) Any forms required by the registrar to be used for the purpose of registration of a trade mark or any other proceedings before the registrar under the Act pursuant to section 66 and any directions with respect to their use shall be published on the Office website and any amendment or modification of a form or of the directions with respect to its use shall also be published on the Office website.

(2) Except in relation to Forms TM6 and TM7A a requirement under this rule to use a form as published is satisfied by the use either of a replica of that form or of a form which is acceptable to the registrar and contains the information required by the form as published and complies with any directions as to the use of such a form.

**Requirement as to fees**

**4.**—(1) The fees to be paid in respect of any application, registration or any other matter under the Act and these Rules shall be those (if any) prescribed in relation to such matter [...].

(2) Any form required to be filed with the registrar in respect of any specified matter shall be subject to the payment of the fee (if any) prescribed in respect of that matter [...].

[(3) In this rule, "prescribed" means—

(a) in relation to a registered trade mark other than a comparable trade mark (EU), prescribed by rules under section 79 (fees);

(b) in relation to a comparable trade mark (EU), prescribed by virtue of regulations under Schedule 4 to the European Union (Withdrawal) Act 2018.]

[**Prescribed comparable trade mark (IR) fees**

**4A.** In relation to a comparable trade mark (IR), "prescribed" in rule 4(1) means prescribed by virtue of regulations under Schedule 4 to the European Union (Withdrawal) Act 2018.]

*Application for registration*

**Application for registration; section 32 (Form TM3)**

**5.**—[(1) An application for the registration of a trade mark (other than a transformation application, which shall be filed on Form TM4) shall be filed on Form TM3 or, where the application is filed in electronic form using the filing system provided on the Office website, on Form e-TM3.

(1A) Where an application is filed on Form TM3 (a "standard application") the application shall be subject to the payment of the standard application fee and such class and series fees as may be appropriate.

(1B) Where an application is filed on Form e-TM3 (an "electronic application") the application shall be subject to the payment of the e-filed application fee and such class and series fees as may be appropriate, which shall be payable at the time the electronic application is made and if they are not so paid the application shall be subject to the payment of the standard application fee referred to in paragraph (1A) and such class and series fees as may be appropriate.]

(2) [Subject to paragraph (6) where] an application is for the registration of a single trade mark, an applicant may request the registrar to undertake an expedited examination of the application.

(3) A request for expedited examination shall be made on [Form e-TM3] and shall be subject to payment of the prescribed fee.

(4) Where an applicant makes a request for expedited examination, the application fee and any class fees payable in respect of the application shall be payable at the time the application is made and accordingly rule 13 shall not apply insofar as it relates to the failure of an application to satisfy the requirements of section 32(4).

(5) In this rule and rule 15 a "request for expedited examination" means a request that, following an examination under section 37, the registrar notify the applicant within a period of ten business days (as specified in a direction given by the registrar under section 80) beginning on the business day after the date of filing of the application for registration whether or not it appears to the registrar that the requirements for registration are met.

[(6) The Registrar may at any time—

(a) suspend the right of applicants to file a request for expedited examination under paragraph (2) ("the expedited examination service") for such period as the registrar deems fit; and

(b) resume the expedited examination service.

(7) Where the registrar suspends or resumes the expedited examination service pursuant to paragraph (6), the registrar must publish a notice on the Office website—

(a) of the date from which the expedited examination service is suspended;

(b) of the date upon which the expedited examination service will resume..]

[**Application for registration based upon an existing EUTM application; Schedule 2A paragraph 25**

**5A.**—(1) Where an application for registration is made in accordance with paragraph 25 of Schedule 2A, the application for registration under rule 5 must specify—

(a) the number accorded to the existing EUTM application;

(b) the filing date accorded to the existing EUTM application; and

(c) the date of priority (if any) accorded pursuant to a right of priority claimed in respect of the existing EUTM application.

(2) Where—

(a) a right of priority has been claimed ("a priority claim") in respect of the existing EUTM application; or

(b) the seniority of a registered trade mark or a protected international trade mark (UK) has been claimed ("a seniority claim") under paragraph 26 of Schedule 2A,

the application for registration under rule 5 must, in addition, specify the information provided in paragraph (3).

(3) The information is—

(a) in relation to a priority claim, the information specified in rule 6(1)(a) to (c); and

(b) in relation to a seniority claim, the number of the registered trade mark or protected international trade mark (UK) from which the trade mark the subject of the application claims seniority and the seniority date.

(4) The registrar may, in any particular case, by notice require the applicant to file, within such period of not less than one month as the notice may specify, such documentary evidence as the registrar may require certifying, or verifying to the satisfaction of the registrar—

(a) the filing date accorded to the existing EUTM application, the representation of the mark and the goods or services covered by the existing EUTM application; and

(b) in relation to a priority claim, the date of filing of the overseas application, the country or registering or competent authority, the representation of the mark and the goods or services covered by the overseas application.]

[**Application for registration based upon an existing ITM application, existing request for EU extension or transformation application; Schedule 2B paragraph 28, 29 or 33**

**5B.—**(1) Where an application for registration is made in accordance with paragraph 28, 29 or 33 of Schedule 2B, the application for registration under rule 5 must specify—

(a) the number of the international registration to which the application relates;

(b) the date referred to in paragraph 28(2)(a), 29(2)(a) or 33(2)(a) or (3)(a) of Schedule 2B (as the case may be) in respect of that application; and

(c) the date of priority (if any) accorded pursuant to a right of priority claimed in respect of the existing ITM application the existing request for EU extension or the cancelled international registration the subject of a transformation application.

(2) Where—

(a) a right of priority has been claimed ("a priority claim") in respect of the existing ITM application, an existing request for EU extension or the cancelled international registration the subject of a transformation application; or

(b) the seniority of a registered trade mark or a protected international trade mark (UK) has been claimed ("a seniority claim") pursuant to paragraph 30 or 33 of Schedule 2B, the application for registration under rule 5 must, in addition, specify the information provided in paragraph (3).

(3) The information is—

(a) in relation to a priority claim, the information specified in rule 6(1)(a) to (c); and

(b) in relation to a seniority claim, the number of the registered trade mark or protected international trade mark (UK) from which the trade mark the subject of the application claims seniority and the seniority date.

(4) The registrar may, in any particular case, by notice require the applicant to file, within such period of not less than one month as the notice may specify, such documentary evidence as the registrar may require certifying, or verifying to the satisfaction of the registrar—

(a) the date referred to in paragraph (1)(b) in respect of the existing ITM application, existing request for EU extension or transformation application, the representation of the mark and the goods or services covered by that application; and

(b) in relation to a priority claim, the date of filing of the overseas application, the country or registering or competent authority, the representation of the mark and the goods or services covered by the overseas application.]

**Claim to priority; sections 35 & 36**

**6.**—(1) Where a right to priority is claimed by reason of an application for protection of a trade mark duly filed in a Convention country under section 35 or in another country or territory in respect of which provision corresponding to that made by section 35 is made under section 36 (an "overseas application"), the application for registration under rule 5 shall specify—

(a) the number accorded to the overseas application by the registering or other competent authority of the relevant country;

(b) the country in which the overseas application was filed; and

(c) the date of filing.

(2) The registrar may, in any particular case, by notice require the applicant to file, within such period of not less than one month as the notice may specify, such documentary evidence as the registrar may require certifying, or verifying to the satisfaction of the registrar, the date of the filing of the overseas application, the country or registering or competent authority, the representation of the mark and the goods or services covered by the overseas application.

**Classification of goods and services; section 34**

**7.**—(1) The prescribed system of classification for the purposes of the registration of trade marks is the Nice Classification.

(2) When a trade mark is registered it shall be classified according to the version of the Nice Classification that had effect on the date of application for registration.

**Application may relate to more than one class and shall specify the class (Form TM3A)**

**8.**—(1) An application may be made in more than one class of the Nice Classification.

(2) Every application shall specify—

(a) the class in the Nice Classification to which it relates; and

(b) the goods or services which are appropriate to the class and they shall be described [with sufficient clarity and precision to enable the registrar and other competent authorities and economic operators, on that sole basis, to determine the extent of the protection sought]and to allow them to be classified in the classes in the Nice Classification.

[(2A) For the purposes of paragraph (2)(b) an application may specify the general indications included in the class headings of the Nice Classification or other general terms provided that they satisfy the requirement that the goods or services be described with sufficient clarity and precision referred to in paragraph (2)(b).

(2B) Where the specification contained in the application describes the goods or services using general terms, including the general indications included in the class headings of the Nice Classification, the application shall be treated as including only the goods or services clearly covered by the literal meaning of the term or indication.]

(3) If the application relates to more than one class in the Nice Classification the specification contained in it shall set out the classes in consecutive numerical order and the specification of the goods or services shall be grouped accordingly.

(4) If the specification contained in the application lists items by reference to a class in the Nice Classification in which they do not fall, the applicant may request, by filing Form TM3A, that the application be amended to include the appropriate class for those items, and upon the payment of such class fee as may be appropriate the registrar shall amend the application accordingly.

[(5) In this rule "economic operators" means any person or group of persons which, in the course of trade, manufactures, supplies, imports, exports or otherwise deals in goods or services.]

**Determination of classification**

**9.**—(1) Where an application does not satisfy the requirements of rule 8(2) or (3), the registrar shall send notice to the applicant.

(2) A notice sent under paragraph (1) shall specify a period, of not less than one month, within which the applicant must satisfy those requirements.

(3) Where the applicant fails to satisfy the requirements of rule 8(2) before the expiry of the period specified under paragraph (2), [the registrar must reject] the application for registration, insofar as it relates to any goods or services which failed that requirement[...].

(4) Where the applicant fails to satisfy the requirements of rule 8(3) before the expiry of the period specified under paragraph (2), the application for registration shall be treated as abandoned.

**Prohibition on registration of mark consisting of arms; section 4**

**10.**— Where having regard to matters coming to the notice of the registrar it appears to the registrar that a representation of any arms or insignia as is referred to in section 4(4) appears in a mark, the registrar shall refuse to accept an application for the registration of the mark unless satisfied that the consent of the person entitled to the arms has been obtained.

**Address for service**

**11.**—(1) For the purposes of any proceedings under the Act or these Rules, an address for service shall be filed by—

(a) an applicant for the registration of a trade mark;
(b) any person who opposes the registration of a trade mark in opposition proceedings;
(c) any person who applies for revocation, a declaration of invalidity or rectification under the Act;
(d) the proprietor of the registered trade mark who opposes such an application.

(2) The proprietor of a registered trade mark, or any person who has registered an interest in a registered trade mark, may file an address for service on Form TM33 or, in the case of an assignment of a registered trade mark, on Form TM16.

(3) Where a person has provided an address for service under paragraph (1) or (2), that person may substitute a new address for service by notifying the registrar on Form TM33.

[(4) An address for service filed under this Rule shall be an address in the United Kingdom, [an EEA state] or the Channel Islands.]

**Failure to provide an address for service**

**12.**—(1) Where—

(a) a person has failed to file an address for service under rule 11(1); and
(b) the registrar has sufficient information enabling the registrar to contact that person, the registrar shall direct that person to file an address for service.

(2) Where a direction has been given under paragraph (1), the person directed shall, before the end of the period of one month [beginning immediately after] the date of the direction, file an address for service.

(3) Paragraph (4) applies where—

(a) a direction was given under paragraph (1) and the period prescribed by paragraph (2) has expired; or
(b) the registrar had insufficient information to give a direction under paragraph (1), and the person has failed to provide an address for service.

(4) Where this paragraph applies—

(a) in the case of an applicant for registration of a trade mark, the application shall be treated as withdrawn;
(b) in the case of a person opposing the registration of a trade mark, that person's opposition shall be treated as withdrawn;
(c) in the case of a person applying for revocation, a declaration of invalidity or rectification, that person's application shall be treated as withdrawn; and
(d) in the case of the proprietor opposing such an application, the proprietor shall be deemed to have withdrawn from the proceedings.

(5) In this rule an "address for service" means an address which complies with the requirements of [rule 11(4)].

**Deficiencies in application; section 32**

**13.**—(1) Where an application for registration of a trade mark does not satisfy the requirements of section 32(2), (3) or (4) or rule 5(1), the registrar shall send notice to the applicant to remedy the deficiencies or, in the case of section 32(4), the default of payment.

(2) A notice sent under paragraph (1) shall specify a period, of not less than [14

days], within which the applicant must remedy the deficiencies or the default of payment.

(3) Where, before the expiry of the period specified under paragraph (2), the applicant—

(a) fails to remedy any deficiency notified to the applicant in respect of section 32(2), the application shall be deemed never to have been made; or

(b) fails to remedy any deficiency notified to the applicant in respect of section 32(3) or rule 5(1) or fails to make payment as required by section 32(4), the application shall be treated as abandoned.

**Notifying results of search**

**14.**—(1) Where, following any search under article 4 of the Trade Marks (Relative Grounds) Order 2007 it appears to the registrar that the requirements for registration mentioned in section 5 are not met, the registrar shall notify this fact to—

(a) the applicant; and

(b) any relevant proprietor.

[(2) In paragraph (1), "relevant proprietor" means the proprietor of a registered trade mark or international trade mark (UK) which is an earlier trade mark in relation to which it appears to the registrar that the conditions set out in section 5(1) or (2) obtain but does not include a proprietor who does not wish to be notified and who has notified the registrar to this effect.]

(3) References in paragraph (2) to the proprietor of a trade mark include a person who has applied for registration of a trade mark which, if registered, would be an earlier trade mark by virtue of [section 6(1)(a) or (aa)].

[(3A) References in paragraph (2) to the proprietor of a trade mark also include a person who has applied for registration of a trade mark which, if registered, would be an earlier trade mark by virtue of section 6(1)(ab).]

(4)-(6) [...]

(7) Rule 63 shall not apply to any decision made in pursuance of this rule.

(8) No decision made in pursuance of this rule shall be subject to appeal.

**Compliance with request for expedited examination**

**15.**— Where the registrar receives a request for expedited examination under rule 5, the date on which the registrar shall be deemed to have notified the applicant whether or not it appears to the registrar that the requirements for registration are met shall be the date on which notice is sent to the applicant.

*Publication, observations, oppositions and registration*

**Publication of application for registration; section 38(1)**

**16.**— An application which has been accepted for registration shall be published in the Journal.

**Opposition proceedings: filing of notice of opposition; section 38(2) (Form TM7)**

**17.**—(1) [Subject to Rule 17A, any] notice to the registrar of opposition to the registration, including the statement of the grounds of opposition, shall be filed on Form TM7.

(2) Unless paragraph (3) applies, the time prescribed for the purposes of section 38(2) shall be the period of two months [beginning immediately after] the date on which the application was published.

(3) This paragraph applies where a request for an extension of time for the filing of Form TM7 has been made on Form TM7A, before the expiry of the period referred to in paragraph (2) and where this paragraph applies, the time prescribed for the purposes of section 38(2) in relation to any person having filed a Form TM7A (or, in the case of a company, any subsidiary or holding company of that company or any other subsidiary of that holding company) shall be the period of three months [beginning immediately after] the date on which the application was published.

(4) Where a person makes a request for an extension of time under paragraph (3), Form TM7A shall be filed electronically using the filing system provided on the Office website or by such other means as the registrar may permit.

(5) Where the opposition is based on a trade mark which has been registered, there shall be included in the statement of the grounds of opposition a representation of that mark and—

(a) the details of the authority with which the mark is registered;
(b) the registration number of that mark;
(c) the goods and services in respect of which—
 (i) that mark is registered, and
 (ii) the opposition is based; and
(d) where the registration procedure for the mark was completed before the start of the period of five years ending with the [date of application for registration or, if any, the date of priority], a statement detailing whether during the period referred to in section 6A(3)(a) the mark has been put to genuine use in relation to each of the goods and services in respect of which the opposition is based or whether there are proper reasons for non-use (for the purposes of rule 20 this is the "statement of use").

(6) Where the opposition is based on a trade mark in respect of which an application for registration has been made, there shall be included in the statement of the grounds of opposition a representation of that mark and those matters set out in paragraph (5)(a) to (c), with references to registration being construed as references to the application for registration.

(7) Where the opposition is based on an unregistered trade mark or other sign which the person opposing the application claims to be protected by virtue of any rule of law (in particular, the law of passing off), there shall be included in the statement of the grounds of opposition a representation of that mark or sign and the goods and services in respect of which such protection is claimed.

(8) The registrar shall send a copy of Form TM7 to the applicant and the date upon which this is sent shall, for the purposes of rule 18, be the "notification date".

(9) In this rule "subsidiary" and "holding company" have the same meaning as in the Companies Act 2006.

**[Opposition proceedings: filing of notice of fast track opposition; section 38(2) (Form TM7F))**

**17A.**—(1) A notice to the registrar of fast track opposition to the registration, including the statement of the grounds of opposition, may be filed on Form TM7F.

(2) A notice of fast track opposition to the registration filed on Form TM7F and

a notice of opposition to the registration filed on Form TM7 shall constitute alternatives and an opponent shall not maintain more than one opposition against the same trade mark application.

(3) Unless paragraph (4) applies, the time prescribed for the purposes of section 38(2) shall be the period of two months beginning immediately after the date on which the application was published.

(4) This paragraph applies where a request for an extension of time for the filing of Form TM7 or TM7F has been made on Form TM7A, before the expiry of the period referred to in paragraph (3) and where this paragraph applies, the time prescribed for the purposes of section 38(2) in relation to any person having filed a Form TM7A (or, in the case of a company, any subsidiary or holding company of that company or any other subsidiary of that holding company) shall be the period of three months beginning immediately after the date on which the application was published.

(5) Forms TM7F and TM7A shall be filed electronically using the filing system provided on the Office website or by such other means as the registrar may permit.

(6) There shall be included in the statement of the grounds of opposition a representation of that mark and—

- (a) the details of the authority with which the mark is registered or protected;
- (b) the registration number of that mark;
- (c) the goods and services in respect of which—
  - (i) that mark is registered, and
  - (ii) the opposition is based;
- (d) the date of completion of the registration procedure or of granting protection to an international trade mark (UK) […]; and
- (e) where the registration or protection procedure for the mark was completed before the start of the period of five years ending with the [date of application for registration or, if any, the date of priority], a statement detailing whether during the period referred to in section 6A(3)(a) the mark has been put to genuine use in relation to each of the goods and services in respect of which the op-position is based.

(7) Where the earlier mark is subject to proof of use under section 6A of the Act, the proof of use that the opponent wishes to rely upon shall be provided with the notice of fast track opposition.

(8) The registrar shall send a copy of Form TM7F to the applicant and the date upon which this is sent shall, for the purposes of rule 18, be the "notification date".

(9) In this rule "subsidiary" and "holding company" have the same meaning as in the Companies Act 2006.]

**Opposition proceedings: filing of counter-statement and cooling off period (Forms TM8, TM9c & TM9t)**

**18.**—(1) The applicant shall, within the relevant period, file a Form TM8, which shall include a counter-statement.

(2) Where the applicant fails to file a Form TM8 or counter-statement within the relevant period, the application for registration, insofar as it relates to the goods and services in respect of which the opposition is directed, shall, unless the registrar otherwise directs, be treated as abandoned.

(3) Unless either paragraph (4), (5) or (6) applies, the relevant period [is the period of two months beginning immediately after the notification date].

(4) This paragraph applies where—

(a) the applicant and the person opposing the registration agree to an extension of time for the filing of Form TM8;

(b) within the period of two months [beginning immediately after] the notification date, either party files Form TM9c requesting an extension of time for the filing of Form TM8; and

(c) during the period beginning on the date Form TM9c was filed and ending nine months after the notification date, no notice to continue on Form TM9t is filed by the person opposing the registration and no request for a further extension of time for the filing of Form TM8 is filed on Form TM9e,

and where this paragraph applies the relevant period [is the period of nine months beginning immediately after the notification date].

(5) This paragraph applies where—

(a) a request for an extension of time for the filing of Form TM8 has been filed on Form TM9c in accordance with paragraph (4)(b);

(b) during the period referred to in paragraph (4)(c), either party files Form TM9e requesting a further extension of time for the filing of Form TM8 which request includes a statement confirming that the parties are seeking to negotiate a settlement of the opposition proceedings; and

(c) the other party agrees to the further extension of time for the filing of Form TM8,

and where this paragraph applies the relevant period [is the period of eighteen months beginning immediately after the notification date].

(6) This paragraph applies where—

(a) a request for an extension of time for the filing of Form TM8 has been filed on Form TM9c in accordance with paragraph (4)(b); and

(b) the person opposing the registration has filed a notice to continue on Form TM9t,

and where this paragraph applies the relevant period shall begin on the notification date and end one month after the date on which Form TM9t was filed or two months [beginning immediately] after the notification date, whichever is the later.

(7) The registrar shall send a copy of Form TM8 to the person opposing the registration.

**Opposition proceedings: preliminary indication (Form TM53)**

**19.**—(1) This rule applies if—

(a) the opposition or part of it is based on the relative grounds of refusal set out in section 5(1) or (2); and

(b) the registrar has not indicated to the parties that the registrar thinks that it is inappropriate for this rule to apply.

[(1A) This rule shall not apply to fast track oppositions.]

(2) After considering the statement of the grounds of opposition and the counter-statement the registrar shall send notice to the parties ("the preliminary indication") stating whether it appears to the registrar that—

(a) registration of the mark should not be refused in respect of all or any of the goods and services listed in the application on the grounds set out in section 5(1) or (2); or

(b) registration of the mark should be refused in respect of all or any of the goods and services listed in the application on the grounds set out in section 5(1) or (2).

(3) The date upon which the preliminary indication is sent shall be the "indication date".

(4) Where it appeared to the registrar under paragraph (2) that registration of the mark should not be refused in respect of all or any of the goods or services listed in the application on the grounds set out in section 5(1) or (2), the person opposing the registration shall, within one month of the indication date, file a notice of intention to proceed with the opposition based on those grounds by filing a Form TM53, otherwise that person's opposition to the registration of the mark in relation to those goods or services on the grounds set in section 5(1) or (2) shall be deemed to have been withdrawn

(5) Where it appeared to the registrar under paragraph (2) that registration of the mark should be refused in respect of all or any of the goods or services listed in the application on the grounds set out in section 5(1) or (2), the applicant shall, within one month of the indication date, file a notice of intention to proceed on Form TM53, otherwise the applicant shall be deemed to have withdrawn the request to register the mark in respect of the goods or services for which the registrar indicated registration should be refused.

(6) A person who files a Form TM53 shall, at the same time, send a copy to all other parties to the proceedings.

(7) The registrar need not give reasons for the preliminary indication nor shall the preliminary indication be subject to appeal.

**Opposition proceedings: evidence rounds**

**20.**—(1) Where—

(a) Form TM53 has been filed by either party;

(b) the opposition or part of it is based on grounds other than those set out in section 5(1) or (2) and the applicant has filed a Form TM8; or

(c) the registrar has indicated to the parties that it is inappropriate for rule 19 to apply,

the registrar shall specify the periods within which evidence and submissions may be filed by the parties.

(2) Where—

(a) the opposition is based on an earlier trade mark of a kind falling within section 6(1)(c); or

(b) the opposition or part of it is based on grounds other than those set out in section 5(1) or (2); or

(c) the truth of a matter set out in the statement of use is either denied or not admitted by the applicant,

the person opposing the registration ("the opposer") shall file evidence supporting the opposition.

(3) Where the opposer files no evidence under paragraph (2), the opposer shall be deemed to have withdrawn the opposition to the registration to the extent that it is based on—

(a) the matters in paragraph (2)(a) or (b); or

(b) an earlier trade mark which has been registered and which is the subject of the statement of use referred to in paragraph (2)(c).

(4) The registrar may, at any time, give leave to either party to file evidence upon such terms as the registrar thinks fit.

[(5) Paragraphs (1)-(3) of this Rule shall not apply to fast track oppositions but paragraph (4) shall apply.]

**Procedure for intervention**

**21.**—(1) If the opposition or part of it is based on the relative grounds for refusal set out in section 5(1), (2) or (3), any person in paragraph (3) may file an application to the registrar on Form TM27 for leave to intervene and the registrar may, after hearing the parties concerned if so required, refuse such leave or grant leave upon such terms and conditions (including any undertaking as to costs) as the registrar thinks fit.

(2) Any person granted leave to intervene shall, subject to any terms and conditions imposed in respect of the intervention, be treated as a party to the proceedings for the purposes of the application of the provisions of rules 19, 20 and 62 to 73.

(3) The persons referred to in paragraph (1) are—

(a) where the opposition is based on an earlier trade mark, a licensee of that mark; and

(b) where the opposition is based on an earlier collective mark or certification mark, an authorised user of that mark.

**Observations on application to be sent to applicant; section 38(3)**

**22.**— The registrar shall send to the applicant a copy of any document containing observations made under section 38(3).

**Publication of registration; section 40**

**23.**— On the registration of the trade mark the registrar shall publish the registration on the Office website, specifying the date upon which the trade mark was entered in the register.

*Amendment of application*

**Amendment of application; section 39 (Form TM21)**

**24.**— A request for an amendment of an application to correct an error or to change the name or address of the applicant or in respect of any amendment requested after publication of the application shall be made on Form TM21.

**Amendment of application after publication; section 39 (Form TM7)**

**25.**—(1) Where, pursuant to section 39, a request is made for amendment of an application which has been published in the Journal and the amendment affects the representation of the trade mark or the goods or services covered by the application, the amendment or a statement of the effect of the amendment shall also be published in the Journal.

(2) Any person claiming to be affected by the amendment may, within one month of the date on which the amendment or a statement of the effect of the amendment was published under paragraph (1), give notice to the registrar of objection to the amendment on Form TM7 which shall include a statement of the grounds of objection which shall, in particular, indicate why the amendment would not fall within section 39(2).

(3) The registrar shall send a copy of Form TM7 to the applicant and the procedure in rules 17, 18 and 20 shall apply to the proceedings relating to the objection to the amendment as they apply to proceedings relating to opposition to an application for registration, but with the following modifications—

(a) any reference to—

(i) an application for registration shall be construed as a reference to a request for amendment of an application,

(ii) the person opposing the registration shall be construed as a reference to the person objecting to the amendment of an application,

(iii) the opposition shall be construed as a reference to the objection;

(b) the relevant period, referred to in rule 18(1), shall for these purposes be the period of two months [beginning immediately after] the date upon which the registrar sent a copy of Form TM7 to the applicant; and

(c) rules 18(3) to (6), 20(2) and (3) shall not apply.

*Division, merger and series of marks*

**Division of application; section 41(Form TM12)**

**26.**—(1) At any time before registration an applicant may send to the registrar a request on Form TM12 [to divide the specification] of the application for registration (the original application) into two or more separate applications (divisional applications), indicating for each division the specification of goods or services.

(2) Each divisional application shall be treated as a separate application for registration with the same filing date as the original application.

(3) Where the request to divide an application is sent after publication of the application, any objections in respect of, or opposition to, the original application shall be taken to apply to each divisional application and shall be proceeded with accordingly.

(4) Upon division of an original application in respect of which notice has been given to the registrar of particulars relating to the grant of a licence, or a security interest or any right in or under it, the notice and the particulars shall be deemed to apply in relation to each of the applications into which the original application has been divided.

[**Division of registration; section 41 (Form TM12R)**

**26A.**—(1) The proprietor of a trade mark may send to the registrar a request on Form TM12R to divide the specification of the registration (the original registration) into two or more separate trade marks (divisional registrations), indicating for each divisional registration the specification of goods or services.

(2) Each divisional registration must be treated as a separate registration with the same date of registration as the original registration.

(3) No request under paragraph (1) may be granted in respect of the registration of a trade mark which is the subject of proceedings for its revocation or invalidation, where the request would introduce a division amongst the goods or services in respect of which the proceedings are directed.

(4) Where the original registration is subject to a disclaimer or limitation, the divisional registrations must also be restricted accordingly.

(5) Where the original registration has had registered in relation to it particulars relating to—

(a) the grant of a licence;

(b) a security interest;
(c) any right in or under that original registration; or
(d) any memorandum or statement of the effect of a memorandum;

the registrar must enter in the register the same particulars in relation to each of the divisional registrations into which the original registration has been divided.]

**Merger of separate applications or registrations; section 41(Form TM17)**

**27.**—(1)-(2) [...]

(3) The proprietor of two or more registrations of a trade mark [, the applications relating to which were filed on the same date,] may request the registrar on Form TM17 to merge them into a single registration and the registrar shall, if satisfied that the registrations are in respect of the same trade mark, merge them into a single registration.

[(3A) No application under paragraph (3) may be granted in respect of the registration of a trade mark which—

(a) is the subject of proceedings for its revocation or invalidation; or
(b) is the subject of an international registration within the meaning of article 2 of the Trade Marks (International Registration) Order 2008 which has not become independent of the trade mark as provided for in accordance with Article 6 of the Madrid Protocol.]

(4) Where any registration of a trade mark to be merged under paragraph (3) is subject to a disclaimer or limitation, the merged registration shall also be restricted accordingly.

(5) Where any registration of a trade mark to be merged under paragraph (3) has had registered in relation to it particulars relating to the grant of a licence or a security interest or any right in or under it, or of any memorandum or statement of the effect of a memorandum, the registrar shall enter in the register the same particulars in relation to the merged registration.

(6) The date of registration of the merged registration shall, where the separate registrations bear different dates of registration, be the latest of those dates.

**Registration of a series of trade marks; section 41 (Form TM12)**

**28.**—[(1) An application may be made in accordance with rule 5 for the registration of a series of trade marks in a single registration provided that the series comprises of no more than six trade marks.

(1A) Where an application for registration of a series of trade marks comprises three or more trade marks, the application shall be subject to the payment of the prescribed fee for each trade mark in excess of two trade marks.]

(2) Following an application under paragraph (1) the registrar shall, if satisfied that the marks constitute a series, accept the application.

(3)-(4) [...]

(5) At any time the applicant for registration of a series of trade marks or the proprietor of a registered series of trade marks may request the deletion of a mark in that series and, following such request, the registrar shall delete the mark accordingly.

(6) Where under paragraph (5) the registrar deletes a trade mark from an application for registration, the application, in so far as it relates to the deleted mark, shall be treated as withdrawn.

(7) [...]

*Collective and certification marks*

**Filing of regulations for collective and certification marks; Schedules 1 & 2 (Form TM35)**

**29.**— Where an application for registration of a collective or certification mark is filed, the applicant shall, within such period of not less than three months as the registrar may specify, file Form TM35 accompanied by a copy of the regulations governing the use of the mark.

[**Filing of regulations for EU collective and certification marks; Schedule 2A, paragraph 4**

**29A.** Regulations governing the use of a comparable trade mark (EU) which is a collective mark or a certification mark and any translation required to be filed under paragraph 4 of Schedule 2A must be filed within a period of three months following the date of notice from the registrar.]

[**Filing of regulations for International collective and certification marks; Schedule 2B, paragraph 4**

**29B.** Regulations governing the use of a comparable trade mark (IR) which is a collective mark or a certification mark and any translation required to be filed under paragraph 4 of Schedule 2B must be filed within a period of three months following the date of notice from the registrar.]

**Amendment of regulations of collective and certification marks; Schedule 1 paragraph 10 and Schedule 2 paragraph 11 (Forms TM36 & TM7)**

**30.**—(1) An application for the amendment of the regulations governing the use of a registered collective or certification mark shall be filed on Form TM36.

(2) Where it appears to be expedient to the registrar that the amended regulations should be made available to the public the registrar shall publish a notice in the Journal indicating where copies of the amended regulations may be inspected.

(3) Any person may, within two months of the date of publication of the notice under paragraph (2), make observations to the registrar on the amendments relating to the matters referred to in paragraph 6(1) of Schedule 1 to the Act in relation to a collective mark, or paragraph 7(1) of Schedule 2 to the Act in relation to a certification mark and the registrar shall send a copy of those observations to the proprietor.

(4) Any person may, within two months of the date on which the notice was published under paragraph (2), give notice to the registrar of opposition to the amendment on Form TM7 which shall include a statement of the grounds of opposition indicating why the amended regulations do not comply with the requirements of paragraph 6(1) of Schedule 1 to the Act, or, as the case may be, paragraph 7(1) of Schedule 2 to the Act.

(5) The registrar shall send a copy of Form TM7 to the proprietor and the procedure in rules 18 and 20 shall apply to the proceedings relating to the opposition to the amendment as they apply to proceedings relating to opposition to an application for registration, but with the following modifications—

(a) any reference to—

(i) the applicant shall be construed as a reference to the proprietor,

(ii) an application for registration shall be construed as a reference to an application for the amendment of the regulations,

(iii) the person opposing the registration shall be construed as a reference to the person opposing the amendment of the regulations;

(b) the relevant period, referred to in rule 18(1), shall for these purposes be the period of two months [beginning immediately after] the date upon which the registrar sent a copy of Form TM7 to the proprietor;

(c) rules 18(3) to (6), 20(2) and (3) shall not apply.

**Registration subject to disclaimer or limitation; section 13**

**31.—** Where the applicant for registration of a trade mark or the proprietor by notice in writing sent to the registrar—

(a) disclaims any right to the exclusive use of any specified element of the trade mark; or

(b) agrees that the rights conferred by the registration shall be subject to a specified territorial or other limitation,

the registrar shall make the appropriate entry in the register and publish such disclaimer or limitation.

**Alteration of registered trade marks; section 44 (Forms TM25 & TM7)**

**32.**—(1) The proprietor of a registered trade mark may request the registrar on Form TM25 for such alteration of the mark as is permitted under section 44 and following such request the registrar may require evidence as to the circumstances in which the application is made.

(2) Where, upon the request of the proprietor, the registrar proposes to allow such alteration, the registrar shall publish the mark as altered in the Journal.

(3) Any person claiming to be affected by the alteration may, within two months of the date on which the mark as altered was published under paragraph (2), give notice to the registrar of objection to the alteration on Form TM7 which shall include a statement of the grounds of objection.

(4) The registrar shall send a copy of Form TM7 to the proprietor and the procedure in rules 18 and 20 shall apply to the proceedings relating to the objection to the alteration as they apply to proceedings relating to opposition to an application for registration, but with the following modifications—

(a) any reference to—

(i) the applicant shall be construed as a reference to the proprietor,

(ii) an application for registration shall be construed as a reference to a request for alteration,

(iii) the person opposing the registration shall be construed as a reference to the person objecting to the alteration,

(iv) the opposition shall be construed as a reference to the objection;

(b) the relevant period, referred to in rule 18(1), shall for these purposes be the period of two months [beginning immediately after] the date upon which the registrar sent a copy of Form TM7 to the proprietor;

(c) rules 18(3) to (6), 20(2) and (3) shall not apply.

**Surrender of registered trade mark; section 45 (Forms TM22 & TM23)**

**33.**—(1) Subject to paragraph (2), the proprietor may surrender a registered trade mark, by sending notice to the registrar—

(a) on Form TM22 in respect of all the goods or services for which it is registered; or

(b) on Form TM23, in respect only of those goods or services specified by the proprietor in the notice.

(2) A notice under paragraph (1) shall be of no effect unless the proprietor in that notice—

(a) gives the name and address of any person having a registered interest in the mark; and

(b) certifies that any such person—

(i) has been sent not less than three months' notice of the proprietor's intention to surrender the mark, or

(ii) is not affected or if affected consents to the surrender.

(3) The registrar shall, upon the surrender taking effect, make the appropriate entry in the register and publish the date of surrender on the Office website.

*Renewal and restoration*

**Reminder of renewal of registration; section 43**

**34.**—(1) Subject to paragraph (2) below, [at least six months] before the expiration of the last registration of a trade mark, the registrar shall [...] send to the registered proprietor notice of the approaching expiration and inform the proprietor at the same time that the registration may be renewed in the manner described in rule 35.

(2) If it appears to the registrar that a trade mark may be registered under section 40 at any time within six months before or at any time on or after the date on which renewal would be due (by reference to the date of application for registration), the registrar shall be taken to have complied with paragraph (1) if the registrar sends to the applicant notice to that effect within one month following the date of actual registration.

[(2A) The registrar is not subject to any liability by reason of any failure to notify the proprietor in accordance with paragraph (1) and no proceedings lie against any officer of the registrar in respect of any such failure.]

**Renewal of registration; section 43 (Form TM11)**

**35.**— Renewal of registration shall be effected by filing a request for renewal on Form TM11 at any time within the period of six months ending on the date of the expiration of the registration [or following receipt of a notice from the registrar pursuant to rule 34(1)].

**Delayed renewal and removal of registration; section 43 (Form TM11)**

**36.**—(1) If on the expiration of the last registration of a trade mark the renewal fee has not been paid, the registrar shall publish that fact.

(2) If, within six months from the date of the expiration of the last registration, a request for renewal is filed on Form TM11 accompanied by the appropriate renewal fee and additional renewal fee, the registrar shall renew the registration without removing the mark from the register.

(3) Where no request for renewal is filed, the registrar shall, subject to rule 37, remove the mark from the register.

(4) Where a mark is due to be registered after the date on which it is due for renewal (by reference to the date of application for registration), the request for renewal shall be filed together with the renewal fee and additional renewal fee within six months after the date of actual registration.

(5) The removal of the registration of a trade mark shall be published on the Office website.

**Restoration of registration; section 43 (Form TM13)**

**37.**—(1) Where the registrar has removed the mark from the register for failure to renew its registration in accordance with rule 36, the registrar may, following receipt of a request filed on Form TM13 within six months of the date of the removal of the mark accompanied by the appropriate renewal fee and appropriate restoration fee—

(a) restore the mark to the register; and

(b) renew its registration,

[if the registrar is satisfied that the failure to renew was unintentional].

[(1A) Where a mark is restored to the register, the proprictor of the mark may not bring an action for infringement against a third party who, in good faith, has put goods on the market or supplied services under a sign which is identical with or similar to the mark in respect of the period beginning with the date of expiration of the registration and ending on the date its restoration is published in accordance with paragraph (2).]

(2) The restoration of the registration, including the date of restoration, shall be published on the Office website.

[**Restoration of a European Union trade mark; Schedule 2A, paragraph 28**

**37A.** A request for the registration of a comparable trade mark (EU) following the restoration of a European Union trade mark under paragraph 28 of Schedule 2A must include—

(a) a representation of the European Union trade mark;

(b) the registration number of that mark;

(c) the name and address of the proprietor;

(d) the goods or services in respect of which that mark is registered;

(e) the priority date (if any) accorded pursuant to a claim of priority filed in respect of that mark pursuant to the European Union Trade Mark Regulation and the information specified in rule 6(1)(a) to (c) in respect of that priority claim;

(f) the number of the registered trade mark or international trade mark (UK) from which that mark claimed seniority (if any) and the seniority date.]

*Revocation, invalidation and rectification*

**Application for revocation (on the grounds of non-use); section 46(1)(a) or (b) (Forms TM8(N) & TM26(N))**

**38.**—(1) An application to the registrar for revocation of a trade mark under section 46, on the grounds set out in section 46(1)(a) or (b), shall be made on Form TM26(N).

(2) The registrar shall send a copy of Form TM26(N) to the proprietor.

(3) The proprietor shall, within two months of the date on which he was sent a copy of Form TM26(N) by the registrar, file a Form TM8(N), which shall include a counter-statement.

(4) Where the proprietor fails to file evidence of use of the mark or evidence supporting the reasons for non-use of the mark within the period specified in

paragraph (3) above the registrar shall specify a further period of not less than two months within which the evidence shall be filed.

(5) The registrar shall send a copy of Form TM8(N) and any evidence of use, or evidence supporting reasons for non-use, filed by the proprietor to the applicant.

(6) Where the proprietor fails to file a Form TM8(N) within the period specified in paragraph (3) the registration of the mark shall, unless the registrar directs otherwise, be revoked.

(7) Where the proprietor fails to file evidence within the period specified under paragraph (3) or any further period specified under paragraph (4), the registrar may treat the proprietor as not opposing the application and the registration of the mark shall, unless the registrar directs otherwise, be revoked.

(8) The registrar may, at any time, give leave to either party to file evidence upon such terms as the registrar thinks fit.

**Application for revocation (on grounds other than non-use); section 46(1)(c) or (d) (Forms TM8 & TM26(O))**

**39.**—(1) An application to the registrar for revocation of a trade mark under section 46, on the grounds set out in section 46(1)(c) or (d), shall be made on Form TM26(O) and shall include a statement of the grounds on which the application is made and be accompanied by a statement of truth.

(2) The registrar shall send a copy of Form TM26(O) and the statement of the grounds on which the application is made to the proprietor.

(3) The proprietor shall, within two months of the date on which he was sent a copy of Form TM26(O) and the statement by the registrar, file a Form TM8 which shall include a counter-statement, otherwise the registrar may treat the proprietor as not opposing the application and the registration of the mark shall, unless the registrar directs otherwise, be revoked.

(4) The registrar shall send a copy of Form TM8 to the applicant.

**Application for revocation (on grounds other than non-use): evidence rounds**

**40.**—(1) Where the [proprietor] has filed a Form TM8, the registrar shall specify the periods within which further evidence may be filed by the parties.

(2) Where the applicant files no further evidence in support of the application the applicant, shall, unless the registrar otherwise directs, be deemed to have withdrawn the application.

(3) The registrar shall notify the proprietor of any direction given under paragraph (2).

(4) The registrar may, at any time give leave to either party to file evidence upon such terms as the registrar thinks fit.

**Application for invalidation: filing of application and counter-statement; section 47 (Forms TM8 & TM26(I))**

**41.**—(1) An application to the registrar for a declaration of invalidity under section 47 shall be filed on Form TM26(I) and shall include a statement of the grounds on which the application is made and be accompanied by a statement of truth.

(2) Where the application is based on a trade mark which has been registered, there shall be included in the statement of the grounds on which the application is made a representation of that mark and—

(a) the details of the authority with which the mark is registered;

(b) the registration number of that mark;
(c) the goods and services in respect of which—
(i) that mark is registered, and
(ii) the application is based; and
(d) where neither section 47(2A)(a) nor (b) applies to the mark, a statement detailing whether during the period referred to in section 47(2B)(a) it has been put to genuine use in relation to each of the goods and services in respect of which the application is based or whether there are proper reasons for non-use (for the purposes of rule 42 this is the "statement of use").

(3) Where the application is based on a trade mark in respect of which an application for registration has been made, there shall be included in the statement of the grounds on which the application is made a representation of that mark and those matters set out in paragraph (2)(a) to (c), with references to registration being construed as references to the application for registration.

(4) Where the application is based on an unregistered trade mark or other sign which the applicant claims to be protected by virtue of any rule of law (in particular, the law of passing off), there shall be included in the statement of the grounds on which the application is made a representation of that mark or sign and the goods and services in respect of which such protection is claimed.

(5) The registrar shall send a copy of Form TM26(I) and the statement of the grounds on which the application is made to the proprietor.

(6) The proprietor shall, within two months of the date on which a copy of Form TM26(I) and the statement was sent by the registrar, file a Form TM8, which shall include a counter-statement, otherwise the registrar may treat the proprietor as not opposing the application and registration of the mark shall, unless the registrar otherwise directs, be declared invalid.

(7) The registrar shall send a copy of Form TM8 to the applicant.

**Application for invalidation: evidence rounds**

**42.**—(1) Where the proprietor has filed Form TM8, the registrar shall send notice to the applicant inviting the applicant to file evidence in support of the grounds on which the application is made and any submissions and to send a copy to all the other parties.

(2) The registrar shall specify the periods within which evidence and submissions may be filed by the parties.

(3) Where—
(a) the application is based on an earlier trade mark of a kind falling within section 6(1)(c); or
(b) the application or part of it is based on grounds other than those set out in section 5(1) or (2); or
(c) the truth of a matter set out in the statement of use is either denied or not admitted by the proprietor,

the applicant shall file evidence supporting the application.

(4) Where the applicant files no evidence under paragraph (3), the applicant shall be deemed to have withdrawn the application to the extent that it is based on—
(a) the matters in paragraph (3)(a) or (b); or
(b) an earlier trade mark which has been registered and is the subject of the statement of use referred to in paragraph (3)(c).

(5) The registrar may, at any time give leave to either party to file evidence upon such terms as the registrar thinks fit.

**Setting aside cancellation of application or revocation or invalidation of registration; (Form TM29)**

**43.**—(1) This rule applies where—

(a) an application for registration is treated as abandoned under rule 18(2);

(b) the registration of a mark is revoked under rule 38(6) or rule 39(3); or

(c) the registration of a mark is declared invalid under rule 41(6),

and the applicant or the proprietor (as the case may be) claims that the decision of the registrar to treat the application as abandoned or revoke the registration of the mark or declare the mark invalid (as the case may be) ("the original decision") should be set aside on the grounds set out in paragraph (3).

(2) Where this rule applies, the applicant or the proprietor shall, within a period of six months [beginning immediately after] the date that the application was refused or the register was amended to reflect the revocation or the declaration of invalidity (as the case may be), file an application on Form TM29 to set aside the decision of the registrar and shall include evidence in support of the application and shall copy the form and the evidence to the other party to the original proceedings under the rules referred to in paragraph (1).

(3) Where the applicant or the proprietor demonstrates to the reasonable satisfaction of the registrar that the failure to file Form TM8 within the period specified in the rules referred to in paragraph (1) was due to a failure to receive Form TM7, Form TM26(N), Form TM26(O) or Form TM26(I) (as the case may be), the original decision may be set aside on such terms and conditions as the registrar thinks fit.

(4) In considering whether to set aside the original decision the matters to which the registrar must have regard include whether the person seeking to set aside the decision made an application to do so promptly upon becoming aware of the original decision and any prejudice which may be caused to the other party to the original proceedings if the original decision were to be set aside.

**Invalidation or revocation of Existing EUTM: Cancellation notice and procedure on application for derogation; Schedule 2A paragraph 21A**

**43A**—(1) A cancellation notice under paragraph 21A of Schedule 2A must—

(a) identify the existing EUTM by the number under which the existing EUTM was registered in the EUTM Register immediately before IP completion day, together with a representation of the mark,

(b) include the following details with regard to the decision pursuant to which the existing EUTM was revoked or declared invalid (whether wholly or partially)—

(i) the date of the decision (including any decision determined on appeal),

(ii) whether the revocation or declaration of invalidity related to all or part of the goods or services for which the existing EUTM was registered,

(iii) where the existing EUTM was revoked (whether wholly or partially) the date on which the revocation took effect,

(c) be accompanied by a copy of the decision (including any decision determined on appeal) pursuant to which the existing EUTM was revoked or declared to be invalid, and

(d) include a statement confirming that the decision pursuant to which the existing EUTM was revoked or declared invalid (whether wholly or partially) has been finally determined.

(2) Where a cancellation notice is submitted to the registrar by the proprietor of the comparable trade mark (EU) which derives from the existing EUTM, the cancellation notice must be accompanied by—

(a) a notice (a "derogation notice") in writing to the registrar that, based upon the provisions in paragraph 21A(4) of Schedule 2A, the comparable trade mark (EU) should not be revoked or declared invalid (whether wholly or partially), and

(b) a statement of the reasons why paragraph 21A(4) of Schedule 2A applies (a "statement") together with relevant supporting evidence ("supporting evidence").

(3) Where the proprietor of a comparable trade mark (EU) submits a cancellation notice to the registrar but fails to send a derogation notice, a statement or supporting evidence, the registration of the comparable trade mark (EU) which derives from the existing EUTM identified in the cancellation notice must be revoked or declared invalid to the same extent as the existing EUTM, unless the registrar directs otherwise.

(4) Where the registrar receives a cancellation notice submitted by a person other than the proprietor of the comparable trade mark (EU) which derives from the existing EUTM, the registrar must as soon as reasonably practicable after receipt of the cancellation notice—

(a) send a copy of the cancellation notice to the proprietor of the comparable trade mark (EU) which derives from the existing EUTM identified in the cancellation notice, and

(b) notify the proprietor of the comparable trade mark (EU) which derives from the existing EUTM that based upon the revocation or declaration of invalidity of the existing EUTM, the comparable trade mark (EU) will be revoked or declared invalid to the same extent as the corresponding EUTM.

(5) Where the registrar has become aware of the situation referred to in paragraph 21A(2)(a) of Schedule 2A otherwise than by a cancellation notice, the registrar must as soon as reasonably practicable after becoming aware of that situation, notify the proprietor of the comparable trade mark (EU) which derives from the existing EUTM in the terms provided in paragraph (4)(b).

(6) The proprietor of a comparable trade mark (EU) referred to in paragraph (4) and (5) must, within such period of not less than one month as may be specified in the notice referred to in paragraph (4)(b) and (5), send to the registrar a derogation notice accompanied by a statement and supporting evidence as referred to in paragraph (2), failing which the registration of the comparable trade mark (EU) must be revoked or declared invalid to the same extent as the corresponding EUTM, unless the registrar directs otherwise.

(7) The registrar must, in reaching a decision as to whether paragraph 21A(4) of Schedule 2A applies to a comparable trade mark (EU), have regard to the statement and supporting evidence filed by the proprietor of the comparable trade mark (EU) and must send written notice of the decision to the proprietor, stating the reasons for that decision.

(8) For the purposes of any appeal against a decision referred to in sub-paragraph (7), the date on which the notice is sent must be taken to be the date of the decision.]

**Procedure on application for rectification; section 64 (Form TM26(R))**

**44.**—(1) An application for rectification of an error or omission in the register under section 64(1) shall be made on Form TM26(R) together with:

(a) a statement of the grounds on which the application is made; and
(b) any evidence to support those grounds.

(2) Where any application is made under paragraph (1) by a person other than the proprietor of the registered trade mark the registrar—

(a) shall send a copy of the application and the statement, together with any evidence filed, to the proprietor; and
(b) may give such direction with regard to the filing of subsequent evidence and upon such terms as the registrar thinks fit.

**Procedure for intervention**

**45.**—(1) Any person, other than the registered proprietor, claiming to have an interest in proceedings on an application under rule 38, 39, 41 or 44, may file an application to the registrar on Form TM27 for leave to intervene, stating the nature of the person's interest and the registrar may, after hearing the parties concerned if they request a hearing, refuse leave or grant leave upon such terms and conditions (including any undertaking as to costs) as the registrar thinks fit.

(2) Any person granted leave to intervene shall, subject to any terms and conditions imposed in respect of the intervention, be treated as a party to the proceedings for the purposes of the application of the provisions of rules 38 to 40, 41 and 42 or 44 (as appropriate) and rules 62 to 73.

*The register*

**Form of register; section 63(1)**

**46.**— The register required to be maintained by the registrar under section 63(1) need not be kept in documentary form.

**Entry in register of particulars of registered trade marks; section 63(2) (Form TM24)**

**47.**— In addition to the entries in the register of registered trade marks required to be made by section 63(2)(a), there shall be entered in the register in respect of each trade mark the following particulars—

(a) the date of registration as determined in accordance with section 40(3) (that is to say, the date of the filing of the application for registration) [or, in the case of a comparable trade mark (EU), as determined in accordance with paragraph 1 of Schedule 2A];
[(aa) in the case of a comparable trade mark (IR), the date of registration as determined in accordance with paragraph 1 of Schedule 2B]
(b) the date of completion of the registration procedure [(which in the case of a comparable trade mark (EU) is the date of registration of the corresponding EUTM in the EUTM Register]);
[(bb) in the case of a comparable trade mark (IR), the date of completion of

the registration procedure which is the date of publication by the European Union Intellectual Property Office of the matters referred to in Article 190(2) of the European Union Trade Mark Regulation in respect of the existing IR(EU) from which the comparable trade mark (IR) derives]

(c) the priority date (if any) to be accorded pursuant to a claim to a right to priority made under section 35 or 36;

[(ca) in the case of a comparable trade mark (EU)—

(i) the priority date (if any) accorded pursuant to a claim of priority filed in respect of the corresponding EUTM pursuant to the European Union Trade Mark Regulation; and

(ii) the number of the registered trade mark or international trade mark (UK) from which the corresponding EUTM claimed seniority (if any) and the seniority date;

(cb) where the mark is registered pursuant to an application referred to in paragraph 26 of Schedule 2A—

(i) the priority date (if any) accorded pursuant to a claim to a right to priority made under paragraph 25(2)(a)(ii) of Schedule 2A; and

(ii) the number of the registered trade mark or international trade mark (UK) from which the application claims seniority (if any) and the seniority date;]

[(cc) in the case of a comparable trade mark (IR)—

(i) the priority date (if any) accorded pursuant to a claim of priority filed in respect of the corresponding (IR) pursuant to Article 4 of the Paris Convention; and

(ii) the number of the registered trade mark or international trade mark (UK) from which the corresponding (IR) claimed seniority (if any) and the seniority date;

(cd) where the mark is registered pursuant to an application referred to in paragraph 28, 29 or 33 of Schedule 2B—

(i) the priority date (if any) accorded pursuant to a claim to a right to priority made under paragraph 28(2)(b) (taking account of paragraph 28(5)), 29(2)(b) (taking account of paragraph 29(4)) or 33(2)(b) or (3)(b) (taking account of paragraph 33(4)) of Schedule 2B; and

(ii) the number of the registered trade mark or international trade mark (UK) from which the application claims seniority (if any) and the seniority date;]

(d) the name and address of the proprietor;

(e) the address for service (if any) filed under rule 11;

(f) any disclaimer or limitation of rights under section 13(1)(a) or (b);

(g) any memorandum or statement of the effect of any memorandum relating to a trade mark of which the registrar has been notified on Form TM24;

(h) the goods or services in respect of which the mark is registered;

(i) where the mark is a collective or certification mark, that fact;

(j) where the mark is registered pursuant to section 5(5) with the consent of the proprietor of an earlier trade mark or other earlier right, that fact;

(k) where the mark is registered pursuant to a transformation application,

(i) the number of the international registration, and

(ii) either:—

(aa) the date accorded to the international registration under Article 3(4), or (bb)the date of recordal of the request for extension to the United Kingdom of the international registration under Article 3ter, as the case may be, of the Madrid Protocol;

(l) […]

[(m) where the mark is a collective mark and amended regulations have been accepted by the registrar, that fact, including the date of that entry.]

[(n) in the case of a comparable trade mark (EU) an indication that it is derived from an existing EUTM, including the number of the corresponding EUTM.]

[(o) in the case of a comparable trade mark (IR) an indication that it is derived from an existing IR(EU), including the number of the international registration to which the existing IR(EU) is subject.]

**Entry in register of particulars of registrable transactions; section 25**

**48.—** Upon application made to the registrar by such person as is mentioned in section 25(1)(a) or (b) there shall be entered in the register in respect of each trade mark the following particulars of registrable transactions together with the date on which the entry is made—

(a) in the case of an assignment of a registered trade mark or any right in it—
  (i) the name and address of the assignee,
  (ii) the date of the assignment, and
  (iii) where the assignment is in respect of any right in the mark, a description of the right assigned;

(b) in the case of the grant of a licence under a registered trade mark—
  (i) the name and address of the licensee,
  (ii) where the licence is an exclusive licence, that fact,
  (iii) where the licence is limited, a description of the limitation, and
  (iv) the duration of the licence if the same is or is ascertainable as a definite period;

(c) in the case of the grant of any security interest over a registered trade mark or any right in or under it—
  (i) the name and address of the grantee,
  (ii) the nature of the interest (whether fixed or floating), and
  (iii) the extent of the security and the right in or under the mark secured;

(d) in the case of the making by personal representatives of an assent in relation to a registered trade mark or any right in or under it—
  (i) the name and address of the person in whom the mark or any right in or under it vests by virtue of the assent, and
  (ii) the date of the assent;

(e) in the case of a court or other competent authority transferring a registered trade mark or any right in or under it—
  (i) the name and address of the transferee,
  (ii) the date of the order, and
  (iii) where the transfer is in respect of a right in the mark, a description of the right transferred; and

(f) in the case of any amendment of the registered particulars relating to a licence under a registered trade mark or a security interest over a registered trade mark or any right in or under it, particulars to reflect such amendment.

**Application to register or give notice of transaction; sections 25 & 27(3) (Form TM16, TM24, TM50 & TM51)**

**49.**—(1) An application to register particulars of a transaction to which section 25 applies or to give notice to the registrar of particulars of a transaction to which section 27(3) applies shall be made—

(a) relating to an assignment or transaction other than a transaction referred to in sub-paragraphs (b) to (d) below, on Form TM16;

(b) relating to a grant of a licence, on Form TM50;

(c) relating to an amendment to, or termination of a licence, on Form TM51;

(d) relating to the grant, amendment or termination of any security interest, on Form TM24; and

(e) relating to the making by personal representatives of an assent or to an order of a court or other competent authority, on Form TM24.

(2) An application under paragraph (1) shall—

(a) where the transaction is an assignment, be signed by or on behalf of the parties to the assignment;

(b) where the transaction falls within sub-paragraphs (b), (c) or (d) of paragraph (1), be signed by or on behalf of the grantor of the licence or security interest,

or be accompanied by such documentary evidence as suffices to establish the transaction.

(3) Where an application to give notice to the registrar has been made of particulars relating to an application for registration of a trade mark, upon registration of the trade mark, the registrar shall enter those particulars in the register.

**Public inspection of register; section 63(3)**

**50.**—(1) The register shall be open for public inspection at the Office during the hours of business of the Office as published in accordance with rule 80.

(2) Where any portion of the register is kept otherwise than in documentary form, the right of inspection is a right to inspect the material on the register.

**Supply of certified copies etc; section 63(3) (Form TM31R)**

**51.**— The registrar shall supply a certified copy or extract or uncertified copy or extract, as requested on Form TM31R, of any entry in the register.

**Request for change of name or address in register; section 64(4) (Form TM21)**

**52.**— The registrar shall, on a request made on Form TM21 by the proprietor of a registered trade mark or a licensee or any person having an interest in or charge on a registered trade mark which has been registered under rule 48 ("the applicant"), enter a change in the applicant's name or address as recorded in the register.

**Removal of matter from register; sections 25(5)(b) and 64(5) (Form TM7)**

**53.**—(1) Where it appears to the registrar that any matter in the register has ceased to have effect, before removing it from the register—

(a) the registrar may publish in the Journal the fact that it is intended to remove that matter, and

(b) where any person appears to the registrar to be affected by the removal, notice of the intended removal shall be sent to that person.

(2) Within two months of the date on which the intention to remove the matter is published, or notice of the intended removal is sent, as the case may be—

(a) any person may file notice of opposition to the removal on form TM7; and

(b) the person to whom a notice is sent under paragraph (1)(b) may file in writing their objections, if any, to the removal,

and where such opposition or objections are made, rule 63 shall apply.

(3) If the registrar is satisfied after considering any objections or opposition to the removal that the matter has not ceased to have effect, the registrar shall not remove it.

(4) Where there has been no response to the registrar's notice the registrar may remove the matter and where representations objecting to the removal of the entry have been made the registrar may, if after considering the objections the registrar is of the view that the entry or any part of it has ceased to have effect, remove it or the appropriate part of it.

*Change of classification*

**Change of classification; sections 65(2) & 76(1)**

**54.**—(1) The registrar may at any time amend an entry in the register which relates to the classification of a registered trade mark so that it accords with the version of the Nice Classification that has effect at that time.

(2) Before making any amendment to the register under paragraph (1) the registrar shall give the proprietor of the mark written notice of the proposed amendments and shall at the same time advise the proprietor that—

(a) the proprietor may make written objections to the proposals, within two months of the date of the notice, stating the grounds of those objections; and

(b) if no written objections are received within the period specified the registrar shall publish the proposals and the proprietor shall not be entitled to make any objections to the proposals upon such publication.

(3) If the proprietor makes no written objections within the period specified in paragraph (2)(a) or at any time before the expiration of that period decides not to make any objections and gives the registrar written notice to this effect, the registrar shall as soon as practicable after the expiration of that period or upon receipt of the notice publish the proposals in the Journal.

(4) Where the proprietor makes written objections within the period specified in paragraph (2)(a), the registrar shall, as soon as practicable after having considered the objections, publish the proposals in the Journal or, where the registrar has amended the proposals, publish the proposals as amended in the Journal; and the registrar's decision shall be final and not subject to appeal.

**Opposition to proposals; sections 65(3), (5) & 76(1) (Form TM7)**

**55.**—(1) Any person may, within two months of the date on which the proposals were published under rule 54, give notice to the registrar of opposition to the proposals on Form TM7 which shall include a statement of the grounds of opposition which shall, in particular, indicate why the proposed amendments would be contrary to section 65(3).

(2) If no notice of opposition under paragraph (1) is filed within the time specified, or where any opposition has been determined, the registrar shall make the amendments as proposed and shall enter in the register the date when they were made; and the registrar's decision shall be final and not subject to appeal.

*Request for information, inspection of documents and confidentiality*

**Request for information; section 67(1) (Form TM31C)**

**56.**— A request for information relating to an application for registration or to a registered trade mark shall be made on Form TM31C.

**Information available before publication; section 67(2)**

**57.**—(1) Before publication of an application for registration the registrar shall make available for inspection by the public the application and any amendments made to it and any particulars contained in a notice given to the registrar under rule 49.

(2) Nothing in section 67(2) relating to publication of information shall be construed as preventing the publication of decisions on cases relating to trade marks decided by the registrar.

**Inspection of documents; sections 67 & 76(1)**

**58.**—(1) Subject to paragraphs (2) and (3), the registrar shall permit all documents filed or kept at the Office in relation to a registered mark or, where an application for the registration of a trade mark has been published, in relation to that application, to be inspected.

(2) The registrar shall not be obliged to permit the inspection of any such document as is mentioned in paragraph (1) until the completion of any procedure, or the stage in the procedure which is relevant to the document in question, which the registrar is required or permitted to carry out under the Act or these Rules.

(3) The right of inspection under paragraph (1) does not apply to—

(a) any document prepared in the Office solely for its own use;

(b) any document sent to the Office, whether at its request or otherwise, for inspection and subsequent return to the sender;

(c) any request for information under rule 56;

(d) any document received by the Office which the registrar considers should be treated as confidential;

(e) any document in respect of which the registrar issues directions under rule 59 that it be treated as confidential.

(4) Nothing in paragraph (1) shall be construed as imposing on the registrar any duty of making available for public inspection—

(a) any document or part of a document which in the registrar's opinion disparages any person in a way likely to cause damage to that person; or

(b) any document or information filed at or sent to or by the Office before 31st October 1994; or

(c) any document or information filed at or sent to or by the Office after 31st October 1994 relating to an application for registration of a trade mark under the Trade Marks Act 1938.

(5) No appeal shall lie from a decision of the registrar under paragraph (4) not to make any document or part of a document available for public inspection.

**Confidential documents**

**59.**—(1) Where a document (other than a form required by the registrar and published in accordance with rule 3) is filed at the Office and the person filing it requests at the time of filing that it or a specified part of it be treated as confidential, giving reasons for the request, the registrar may direct that it or part of it, as the case may be, be treated as confidential, and the document shall not be open to public inspection while the matter is being determined by the registrar.

(2) Where such direction has been given and not withdrawn, nothing in this rule shall be taken to authorise or require any person to be allowed to inspect the document or part of it to which the direction relates except by leave of the registrar.

(3) The registrar shall not withdraw any direction given under this rule without prior consultation with the person at whose request the direction was given, unless the registrar is satisfied that such prior consultation is not reasonably practical.

(4) The registrar may where the registrar considers that any document issued by the Office should be treated as confidential so direct, and upon such direction that document shall not be open to public inspection except by leave of the registrar.

(5) Where a direction is given under this rule for a document to be treated as confidential a record of the fact shall be filed with the document.

*Agents*

**Proof of authorisation of agent may be required; section 82 (Form TM33)**

**60.**—(1) Where an agent has been authorised under section 82, the registrar may in a particular case require the personal signature or presence of the agent or the person authorising the agent to act as agent.

(2) Subject to paragraph (3), where a person appoints an agent for the first time or appoints one agent in substitution for another, the newly appointed agent shall file Form TM33.

(3) Where after a person has become a party to proceedings involving a third party before the registrar, the person appoints an agent for the first time or appoints one agent in substitution for another, the newly appointed agent shall file Form TM33P.

(4) Any act required or authorised by the Act in connection with the registration of a trade mark or any procedure relating to a trade mark may not be done by or to the newly appointed agent until on or after the date on which the newly appointed agent files Form TM33 or TM33P as appropriate.

(5) The registrar may by notice in writing require an agent to produce evidence of his authority under section 82.

**Registrar may refuse to deal with certain agents; section 88**

**61.**— The registrar may refuse to recognise as agent in respect of any business under the Act—

(a) a person who has been convicted of an offence under section 84;
(b) an individual whose name has been erased from and not restored to, or who is suspended from, the register of trade mark agents on the ground of misconduct;
(c) a person who is found by the Secretary of State to have been guilty of such conduct as would, in the case of an individual registered in that register, render that person liable to have their name erased from it on the ground of misconduct;
(d) a partnership or body corporate of which one of the partners or directors is a person whom the registrar could refuse to recognise under paragraph (a), (b) or (c).

*Proceedings before and decision of registrar, evidence and costs*

**General powers of registrar in relation to proceedings**

**62.**—(1) Except where the Act or these Rules otherwise provide, the registrar may give such directions as to the management of any proceedings as the registrar thinks fit, and in particular may—
(a) require a document, information or evidence to be filed within such period as the registrar may specify;
(b) require a translation of any document;
(c) require a party or a party's legal representative to attend a hearing;
(d) hold a hearing by telephone or by using any other method of direct oral communication;
[(e) allow a statement of case to be amended, provided that—
(i) where an application is made to add grounds of opposition other than under subsections 5(1) or (2) of the Act, the application shall be made on Form TM7G; and
(ii) in the case of fast track oppositions the registrar may only permit a statement of case to be amended to add additional or alternative earlier registered or protected trade marks as additional grounds of opposition under subsections 5(1) or 5(2) of the Act, provided that the total number of earlier trade marks relied upon may not exceed three;]
(f) stay the whole, or any part, of the proceedings either generally or until a specified date or event;
[(g) consolidate proceedings provided that where a fast track opposition is consolidated with other non-fast track proceedings, it shall no longer be treated as a fast track opposition;]
(h) direct that part of any proceedings be dealt with as separate proceedings;
(i) exclude any evidence which the registrar considers to be inadmissible [;]
[(j) direct that with effect from the date specified in the direction opposition proceedings which have been commenced on Form TM7F as a fast track opposition but which do not satisfy the criteria for a fast track opposition may continue as if the opposition proceedings were an opposition to the registration commenced under Rule 17 on Form TM7.]

(2) The registrar may control the evidence by giving directions as to—
(a) the issues on which evidence is required; and
(b) the way in which the evidence is to be placed before the registrar.

(3) When the registrar gives directions under any provision of these Rules, the registrar may—

(a) make them subject to conditions; and

(b) specify the consequences of failure to comply with the directions or a condition.

(4) The registrar may at any stage of any proceedings direct that the parties to the proceedings attend a case management conference or pre-hearing review.

[(5) In the case of a fast track opposition—

(a) proceedings shall be held orally only if the Office requests it or if either party to the proceedings requests it and the registrar considers that oral proceedings are necessary to deal with the case justly and at proportionate cost; and

(b) the parties shall be given at least fourteen days' notice beginning on the date on which the notice is sent, of the time when the oral proceedings are to take place unless each party to the proceedings consents to shorter notice.

(6) In the case of a fast track opposition, where no oral hearing is held, the registrar shall give the parties the opportunity to provide arguments in writing before reaching a decision that is adverse to either party.]

**Decisions of registrar to be taken after hearing**

**63.**—(1) Without prejudice to any provisions of the Act or these Rules requiring the registrar to hear any party to proceedings under the Act or these Rules, or to give such party an opportunity to be heard, the registrar shall, before taking any decision on any matter under the Act or these Rules which is or may be adverse to any party to any proceedings, give that party an opportunity to be heard.

(2) The registrar shall give that party at least fourteen days' notice, beginning on the date on which notice is sent, of the time when the party may be heard unless the party consents to shorter notice.

[(3) This Rule shall not apply to fast track opposition proceedings.]

**Evidence in proceedings before the registrar; section 69**

**64.**—(1) Subject to rule 62(2) and as follows, evidence filed in any proceedings under the Act or these Rules may be given—

(a) by witness statement, affidavit, statutory declaration; or

(b) in any other form which would be admissible as evidence in proceedings before the court.

(2) A witness statement may only be given in evidence if it includes a statement of truth.

(3) The general rule is that evidence at hearings is to be by witness statement unless the registrar or any enactment requires otherwise.

(4) For the purposes of these Rules, a statement of truth—

(a) means a statement that the person making the statement believes that the facts stated in a particular document are true; and

(b) shall be dated and signed by—

(i) in the case of a witness statement, the maker of the statement,

(ii) in any other case, the party or legal representative of such party.

(5) In these Rules, a witness statement is a written statement signed by a person that contains the evidence which that person would be allowed to give orally.

(6) Under these Rules, evidence shall only be considered filed when—

(a) it has been received by the registrar; and
(b) it has been sent to all other parties to the proceedings.

**Registrar to have power of an official referee; section 69**

**65.—** The registrar shall have the powers of an official referee of the Supreme Court as regards—

(a) the attendance of witnesses and their examination on oath; and
(b) the discovery and production of documents,

but the registrar shall have no power to punish summarily for contempt.

**Hearings before registrar to be in public**

**66.**—(1) The hearing before the registrar of any dispute between two or more parties relating to any matter in connection with an application for the registration of a mark or a registered mark shall be in public unless the registrar, after consultation with those parties who appear in person or are represented at the hearing, otherwise directs.

(2) [...]

**Costs of proceedings; section 68**

**67.—** The registrar may, in any proceedings under the Act or these Rules, by order award to any party such costs as the registrar may consider reasonable, and direct how and by what parties they are to be paid.

**Security for costs; section 68**

**68.**—(1) The registrar may require any person who is a party in any proceedings under the Act or these Rules to give security for costs in relation to those proceedings; and may also require security for the costs of any appeal from the registrar's decision.

(2) In default of such security being given, the registrar, in the case of the proceedings before the registrar, or in the case of an appeal, the person appointed under section 76 may treat the party in default as having withdrawn their application, opposition, objection or intervention, as the case may be.

**Decision of registrar (Form TM5)**

**69.**—(1) The registrar shall send to each party to the proceedings written notice of any decision made in any proceedings before the registrar stating the reasons for that decision and for the purposes of any appeal against that decision, subject to paragraph (2), the date on which the notice is sent shall be taken to be the date of the decision.

(2) Where a statement of the reasons for the decision is not included in the notice sent under paragraph (1), any party may, within one month of the date on which the notice was sent to that party, request the registrar on Form TM5 to send a statement of the reasons for the decision and upon such request the registrar shall send such a statement, and the date on which that statement is sent shall be deemed to be the date of the registrar's decision for the purpose of any appeal against it.

*Appeals*

**Decisions subject to appeal; section 76(1)**

**70.**—(1) Except as otherwise expressly provided by these Rules an appeal lies from any decision of the registrar made under these Rules relating to a dispute between two or more parties in connection with a trade mark, including a decision which terminates the proceedings as regards one of the parties or a decision awarding costs to any party ("a final decision") or a decision which is made at any point in the proceedings prior to a final decision ("an interim decision").

(2) An interim decision (including a decision refusing leave to appeal under this paragraph) may only be appealed against independently of any appeal against a final decision with the leave of the registrar.

**Appeal to person appointed; section 76**

**71.**—(1) [Subject to paragraph (1A), notice] of appeal to the person appointed under section 76 shall be filed on Form TM55 which shall include the appellant's grounds of appeal and his case in support of the appeal.

[(1A) Where the appeal arises in proceedings between two or more parties, notice of appeal to the person appointed under section 76 shall be filed on Form TM55P, which shall include the appellant's grounds of appeal and his case in support of the appeal.]

[(2) Forms TM55 or TM55P shall be filed within the period of 28 days beginning immediately after the date of the registrar's decision which is the subject of the appeal ("the original decision").]

(3) The registrar shall send the notice and the statement to the person appointed.

(4) Where any person other than the appellant was a party to the proceedings before the registrar in which the original decision was made ("the respondent"), the registrar shall send to the respondent a copy of the notice and the statement and the respondent may, within the period of 21 days [beginning immediately after] the date on which the notice and statement was sent, file a notice responding to the notice of appeal.

(5) The respondent's notice shall specify any grounds on which the respondent considers the original decision should be maintained where these differ from or are additional to the grounds given by the registrar in the original decision.

(6) The registrar shall send a copy of the respondent's notice to the person appointed and a copy to the appellant.

**Determination whether appeal should be referred to court; section 76(3)**

**72.**—(1) Within 28 days of the date on which the notice of appeal is sent to the respondent by the registrar under rule 71(4);

(a) the registrar; or

(b) any person who was a party to the proceedings in which the decision appealed against was made,

may request that the person appointed refer the appeal to the court.

(2) Where the registrar requests that the appeal be referred to the court, the registrar shall send a copy of the request to each party to the proceedings.

(3) A request under paragraph (1)(b) shall be sent to the registrar following which the registrar shall send it to the person appointed and shall send a copy of the request to any other party to the proceedings.

(4) Within 28 days of the date on which a copy of a request is sent by the

registrar under paragraph (2) or (3), the person to whom it is sent may make representations as to whether the appeal should be referred to the court.

(5) In any case where it appears to the person appointed that a point of general legal importance is involved in the appeal, the person appointed shall send to the registrar and to every party to the proceedings in which the decision appealed against was made, notice to that effect.

(6) Within 28 days of the date on which a notice is sent under paragraph (5), the person to whom it was sent may make representations as to whether the appeal should be referred to the court.

**Hearing and determination of appeal; section 76(4)**

**73.**—(1) Where the person appointed does not refer the appeal to the court, the person appointed shall send written notice of the time and place appointed for the oral hearing of the appeal—

(a) where no person other than the appellant was a party to the proceedings in which the decision appealed against was made, to the registrar and to the appellant; and

(b) in any other case, to the registrar and to each person who was a party to those proceedings.

(2) The person appointed shall send the notice at least fourteen days before the time appointed for the oral hearing.

(3) If all the persons notified under paragraph (1) inform the person appointed that they do not wish to make oral representations then—

(a) the person appointed may hear and determine the case on the basis of any written representations; and

(b) the time and place appointed for the oral hearing may be vacated.

(4) Rules 62, 65, 67 and 68 shall apply to the person appointed and to proceedings before the person appointed as they apply to the registrar and to proceedings before the registrar.

(5) If there is an oral hearing of the appeal then rule 66 shall apply to the person appointed and to proceedings before the person appointed as it applies to the registrar and to proceedings before the registrar.

(6) A copy of the decision of the appointed person shall be sent, with a statement of the reasons for the decision, to the registrar and to each person who was a party to the appeal.

*Correction of irregularities, calculation and extension of time*

**Correction of irregularities in procedure**

**74.**—(1) Subject to rule 77, the registrar may authorise the rectification of any irregularity in procedure (including the rectification of any document filed) connected with any proceeding or other matter before the registrar or the Office.

(2) Any rectification made under paragraph (1) shall be made—

(a) after giving the parties such notice; and

(b) subject to such conditions,

as the registrar may direct.

**Interrupted day**

**75.**—(1) The registrar may certify any day as an interrupted day where—

(a) there is an event or circumstance causing an interruption in the normal operation of the Office; or

(b) there is a general interruption or subsequent dislocation in the postal services of the United Kingdom.

(2) Any certificate of the registrar made under paragraph (1) shall be displayed in the Office and published on the Office website.

(3) The registrar shall, where the time for doing anything under these Rules expires on an interrupted day, extend that time to the next following day not being an interrupted day (or an excluded day).

(4) In this rule—

"excluded day" means a day which is not a business day as specified in a direction given by the registrar under section 80; and

"interrupted day" means a day which has been certified as such under paragraph (1).

**Delays in communication services**

**76.**—(1) The registrar shall extend any time limit in these Rules where the registrar is satisfied that the failure to do something under these Rules was wholly or mainly attributed to a delay in, or failure of, a communication service.

(2) Any extension under paragraph (1) shall be—

(a) made after giving the parties such notice; and

(b) subject to such conditions, as the registrar may direct.

(3) In this rule "communication service" means a service by which documents may be sent and delivered and includes post, facsimile, email and courier.

**Alteration of time limits (Form TM9)**

**77.**—(1) Subject to paragraphs (4) and (5), the registrar may, at the request of the person or party concerned or at the registrar's own initiative extend a time or period prescribed by these Rules or a time or period specified by the registrar for doing any act and any extension under this paragraph shall be made subject to such conditions as the registrar may direct.

(2) A request for extension under this rule may be made before or after the time or period in question has expired and shall be made—

(a) where the application for registration has not been published and the request for an extension [relates to a time or period other than one specified under rule 13 and] is made before the time or period in question has expired, in writing; and

(b) in any other case, on Form TM9.

(3) Where an extension under paragraph (1) is requested in relation to proceedings before the registrar, the party seeking the extension shall send a copy of the request to every other person who is a party to the proceedings.

(4) The registrar shall extend a flexible time limit, except a time or period which applies in relation to proceedings before the registrar or the filing of an appeal to the Appointed Person under rule 71, where—

(a) the request for extension is made before the end of the period of two months [beginning immediately after] the date the relevant time or period expired; and

(b) no previous request has been made under this paragraph.

(5) A time limit listed in Schedule 1 (whether it has already expired or not) may be extended under paragraph (1) if, and only if—

(a) the irregularity or prospective irregularity is attributable, wholly or in part, to a default, omission or other error by the registrar, the Office or the International Bureau; and

(b) it appears to the registrar that the irregularity should be rectified.

(6) In this rule—

"flexible time limit" means—

(a) a time or period prescribed by these Rules, except a time or period prescribed by the rules listed in Schedule 1, or

(b) a time or period specified by the registrar for doing any act or taking any proceedings; and

"proceedings before the registrar" means any dispute between two or more parties relating to a matter before the registrar in connection with a trade mark.

*Filing of documents, hours of business, Trade Marks Journal and translations*

**Filing of documents by electronic means**

**78.—** The registrar may permit as an alternative to the sending by post or delivery of the application, notice or other document in legible form the filing of the application, notice or other document by electronic means subject to such terms or conditions as the registrar may specify either generally by published notice or in any particular case by written notice to the person desiring to file any such documents by such means.

**Electronic communications**

**79.—**(1) The delivery using electronic communications to any person by the registrar of any document is deemed to be effected, unless the registrar has otherwise specified, by transmitting an electronic communication containing the document to an address provided or made available to the registrar by that person as an address for the receipt of electronic communications; and unless the contrary is proved such delivery is deemed to be effected immediately upon the transmission of the communication.

(2) In this rule "electronic communication" has the same meaning as in the Electronic Communications Act 2000.

**Directions on hours of business; section 80**

**80.—** Any directions given by the registrar under section 80 specifying the hours of business of the Office and business days of the Office shall be published on the Office website.

**Trade Marks Journal; section 81**

**81.—** The registrar shall publish a journal, entitled "The Trade Marks Journal" containing such information as is required to be published in the Journal under these Rules and such other information as the registrar thinks fit.

**Translations**

**82.—**(1) Where any document or part thereof which is in a language other than English is filed or sent to the registrar in pursuance of the Act or these Rules, the registrar may require that there be furnished a translation into English of the document or that part, verified to the satisfaction of the registrar as corresponding to the original text.

(2) The registrar may refuse to accept any translation which the registrar considers to be inaccurate in which event there shall be furnished another translation of the document in question verified in accordance with paragraph (1).

*Transitional provisions and revocations*

**Revocation of previous rules and proceedings commenced under previous rules**

**83.**—(1) The instruments set out in Schedule 2 ("the previous rules") are revoked to the extent specified.

(2) Where immediately before these Rules come into force, any time or period prescribed by the previous rules has effect in relation to any act or proceeding and has not expired, the time or period prescribed by the previous rules and not by these Rules shall apply to that act or proceeding.

(3) Except as provided by paragraph (4) where a new step is to be taken on or after 1st October 2008 in relation to any proceedings commenced under the previous rules these Rules shall apply to such proceedings from that date.

(4) Subject to paragraph (5) where prior to the entry into force of these Rules–

(a) a Form TM8 and counter-statement have been filed in–

(i) opposition proceedings, or

(ii) proceedings for the revocation of a trade mark on the grounds set out in section 46(1)(c) or (d); or

(iii) invalidation proceedings; or

(b) an application for revocation of a trade mark on the grounds set out in section 46(1)(a) or (b) has been filed,

the previous rules shall apply with regard to the filing of any evidence in relation to those proceedings.

(5) Where proceedings as described in paragraph (4) are consolidated with proceedings commenced on or after 1st October 2008 these Rules shall apply with regard to the filing of any evidence in relation to those consolidated proceedings.

*Baroness Morgan of Drefelin*

Parliamentary Under Secretary of State for Intellectual Property and Quality Department for Innovation, Universities and Skills

7th July 2008

SCHEDULE 1

EXTENSION OF TIME LIMITS

**Rule 77**

rule 17(2) (filing notice of opposition)
rule 17(3) (filing notice of opposition: request for extension of time)
rule 18(1) (counter-statement in opposition proceedings)
rule 19(4) (responding to preliminary indication)
rule 25(2) (opposition to amendment after publication)
rule 30(4) (opposition to amendment of regulations of collective and certification marks)
rule 32(3) (opposition to alteration of mark)
rule 35 (renewal of registration)
rule 36(2) (delayed renewal)
rule 37(1) (restoration of registration)
rule 38(3) (counter-statement for revocation on grounds of non-use)

rule 39(3) (counter-statement for revocation on grounds other than non-use)
rule 41(6) (counter-statement for invalidity)
rule 43(2) (setting aside cancellation of application or revocation or invalidation of registration)
rule 53(2) (opposition to removal of matter from register)
rule 55(1) (opposition to proposals for change of classification)
rule 77(4) (period for making a retrospective request to extend a flexible time period).

## SCHEDULE 2

### REVOCATIONS

**Rule 83**

| Rules revoked | References | Extent of Revocation |
|---|---|---|
| The Trade Marks Rules 2000 | SI 2000/136 | The whole rules |
| The Trade Marks (Amendment) Rules 2001 | SI 2001/3832 | The whole rules |
| The Trade Marks (Amendment) Rules 2004 | SI 2004/947 | The whole rules |
| The Patents, Trade Marks and Designs (Address for Service and Time Limits etc.) Rules 2006 | SI 2006/760 | Rules 15 to 20 |
| The Trade Marks and Designs (Address for Service) (Amendment) Rules 2006 | SI 2006/1029 | The whole rules |
| The Trade Marks (Amendment) Rules 2006 | SI 2006/3039 | The whole rules |
| The Trade Marks (Amendment) Rules 2007 | SI 2007/2076 | The whole rules |
| The Trade Marks and Trade Marks (Fees) (Amendment) Rules 2008 | SI 2008/11 | Rules 2 to 4 |

*After Appendix 10, add new Appendix 10A:*

## Appendix 10A

# QUALITY SCHEMES (AGRICULTURAL PRODUCTS AND FOODSTUFFS) REGULATIONS 2018

(SI 2018/1275) **A10A-001**

*Made: 29 November 2018.*
*Laid before Parliament: 3 December 2018.*
*Coming into force: 1 January 2019.*

The Secretary of State makes these Regulations in exercise of the powers conferred by section 2(2) of the European Communities Act 1972.

The Secretary of State is designated for the purposes of that section in relation to—

(a) the common agricultural policy of the European Union;
(b) intellectual property (including both registered and unregistered rights);
(c) food and drink intended for sale for human consumption, including the presentation, packaging, labelling, marketing and advertising of such food and drink.

There has been consultation as required by Article 9 of Regulation (EC) No 178/2002 of the European Parliament and of the Council laying down the general principles and requirements of food law, establishing the European Food Safety Authority and laying down procedures in matters of food safety.

### Citation and commencement

**1.** These Regulations may be cited as the Quality Schemes (Agricultural Products and Foodstuffs) Regulations 2018 and come into force on 1st January 2019.

### Interpretation

**2.**—(1) In these Regulations—

(a) terms used that are also used in the EU Regulations have the same meaning as they have in the EU Regulations, and
(b) any reference to an Article, except in regulation 3(2)(c)(iv), is a reference to an Article of Regulation 1151/2012.

(2) In these Regulations—

[…]

"Regulation 1151/2012" means Regulation (EU) No 1151/2012 of the European Parliament and of the Council on quality schemes for agricultural products and foodstuffs;

"Regulation 664/2014" means Commission Delegated Regulation (EU) No 664/2014 supplementing Regulation (EU) No 1151/2012 of the European Parliament and of the Council with regard to the establishment of the Union symbols for protected designations of origin, protected geographical indications and traditional specialities guaranteed and with regard to certain rules on sourcing, certain procedural rules and certain additional transitional rules;

"Regulation 665/2014" means Commission Delegated Regulation (EU) No 665/2014 supplementing Regulation (EU) No 1151/2012 of the European Parliament and of the Council with regard to conditions of use of the optional quality term 'mountain product';

"Regulation 668/2014" means Commission Implementing Regulation (EU) No 668/2014 laying down rules for the application of Regulation (EU) 1151/2012 of the European Parliament and of the Council on quality schemes for agricultural products and foodstuffs;

["Regulation (EU) 2017/625" means Regulation (EU) 2017/625 of the European Parliament and of the Council on official controls and other official activities performed to ensure the application of food and feed law, rules on animal health and welfare, plant health and plant protection products;]

"authorised officer" means a person (whether or not an officer of an enforcement authority) who is authorised by the enforcement authority in writing to act in relation to matters arising under these Regulations and the EU Regulations;

"costs", except in regulation 9(3), has the meaning given in regulation 14(7);

"enforcement authority" means an enforcement authority appointed under regulation 6(2);

"enforcement notice" means—

(a) a compliance notice served under regulation 12;
(b) a non-compliance penalty notice served under regulation 13;
(c) an enforcement costs recovery notice served under regulation 14;

"the EU Regulations" means—

(a) Regulation 1151/2012, and
(b) Regulation 668/2014;

"PDO" means a protected designation of origin;

"PGI" means a protected geographical indication;

"premises" includes any establishment, place, vehicle, stall or movable structure and any ship or aircraft;

"TSG" means a traditional speciality guaranteed.

**The competent authority etc.**

**3.**—(1) The competent authority is the Secretary of State.

(2) The Secretary of State is also responsible for exercising the functions of—

(a) a Member State for the purposes of Articles 8, 13, 20, 24, 34, 37(3), 38, 40 and 46;
(b) the authorities of a Member State for the purposes of Article 13(3) and the first subparagraph of Article 49(2);
(c) a Member State for the purposes of—
   (i) the second subparagraph of Article 49(2);
   (ii) Article 49(3), as read with Article 15;
   (iii) Article 49(4);
   (iv) Article 10(2) of Regulation 668/2014.

**Responsibilities of appointed enforcement authority**

**4.**—(1) Each enforcement authority must report to the Secretary of State when it exercises a power under these Regulations to—

(a) enter premises;

(b) issue an enforcement notice.

(2) The report must cover the result of that exercise and must be submitted to the Secretary of State within 28 days of that result.

**Delegation to control bodies**

**5.**—(1) The Secretary of State may delegate tasks related to official controls of the quality schemes to control bodies, in accordance with Article 39.

(2) The Secretary of State may not delegate any task related to official controls under Article 39 to a control body unless the Secretary of State is satisfied that the control body—

(a) shall ensure that the task is carried out promptly by a person competent to perform it in accordance with [Regulation (EU) 2017/625];

(b) has made arrangements to ensure that a finding of any breach of these Regulations or the EU Regulations is communicated to the Secretary of State immediately, and that any other result is communicated within 28 days.

**Enforcement authorities**

**6.**—(1) The Secretary of State must execute and enforce the provisions of the EU Regulations and these Regulations directly or ensure that they are executed and enforced.

(2) The Secretary of State may appoint enforcement authorities in respect of specified areas.

(3) An enforcement authority appointed under paragraph (2) must execute and enforce the provisions of the EU Regulations and these Regulations specified in the terms of its appointment.

(4) For the purposes of these Regulations any of the following is eligible for appointment as an enforcement authority—

(a) in England, Scotland and Wales, an authority (other than the council of a non-metropolitan district) that is a food authority for the purposes of the Food Safety Act 1990;

(b) in Northern Ireland, a district council within the meaning of the Interpretation Act (Northern Ireland) 1954[1].

(5) Where an enforcement authority is appointed under paragraph (2), the appointment shall operate in relation to its area only.

(6) Paragraph (5) does not apply where an enforcement authority is so appointed for the purpose of Article 37(1)(a) or, in relation to any authorised officer, where consent is granted under regulation 8(3).

(7) The appointment of an enforcement authority under paragraph (2) does not preclude the Secretary of State from exercising enforcement powers in the area of that authority.

**Authorised officers**

**7.** Each enforcement authority must appoint authorised officers to act for the purposes of the performance of its duty under regulation 6(3).

**Default powers and authorised officers' powers**

**8.**—(1) Where the Secretary of State considers that the duty of an enforcement authority has not been adequately carried out in its area, the Secretary of State may appoint one or more persons to exercise in that area the powers exercisable by an authorised officer and references in these Regulations to an authorised officer include an officer appointed in accordance with this paragraph.

(2) Any expenses certified by the Secretary of State as having been incurred in respect of the area of an enforcement authority mentioned in paragraph (1) must be repaid on demand by that enforcement authority.

(3) An authorised officer may not exercise powers under these Regulations or the EU Regulations in respect of any premises outside the area for which that officer is appointed except with the consent of the enforcement authority for the area in which those premises are situated.

**Protection of officers acting in good faith**

**9.**—(1) An authorised officer is not personally liable in respect of any act done—

(a) in the execution or purported execution of functions under these Regulations or the EU Regulations, and

(b) within the scope of the officer's employment,

if the officer acted in the honest belief that the duty under these Regulations or the EU Regulations required or entitled the officer to so act.

(2) Nothing in paragraph (1) is to be construed as relieving any enforcement authority of any liability in respect of the acts of its officers.

(3) Where an action has been brought against an authorised officer in respect of an act done—

(a) in the execution or purported execution of functions under these Regulations or the EU Regulations, but

(b) outside the scope of the officer's employment,

the enforcement authority may indemnify the officer against the whole or a part of any damages ordered to be paid or any costs awarded if that authority is satisfied that the officer honestly believed that the act complained of was within the scope of the officer's employment.

**Powers of entry**

**10.**—(1) An authorised officer may on giving reasonable notice enter any premises except premises used wholly or mainly as a private dwelling-house at any reasonable hour for the purposes of enforcing these Regulations or the EU Regulations.

(2) The requirement to give notice does not apply—

(a) where reasonable efforts to agree an appointment have failed;

(b) where an authorised officer reasonably believes that giving notice would defeat the object of the entry;

(c) where an authorised officer has a reasonable suspicion of a breach of these Regulations or the EU Regulations.

(3) An authorised officer must, if requested to do so, produce a duly authenticated authorisation document.

(4) A justice of the peace in England and Wales, a sheriff or justice of the peace in Scotland or lay magistrate in Northern Ireland, may by signed warrant permit an authorised officer to enter any premises, including dwelling-houses, if necessary by

reasonable force, if the justice, sheriff or lay magistrate, on sworn information in writing is satisfied—

(a) that there are reasonable grounds to enter those premises for the purpose of enforcing these Regulations or the EU Regulations, and

(b) that one or more of the conditions in paragraph (5) are met.

(5) The conditions are—

(a) entry to the premises has been, or is likely to be, refused, and notice of the intention to apply for a warrant has been given to the occupier;

(b) asking for admission to the premises, or giving such a notice, would defeat the object of the entry;

(c) entry is required urgently;

(d) the premises are unoccupied or the occupier is temporarily absent.

(6) A warrant is valid for 30 days from the date of signature.

(7) An authorised officer entering any premises which are unoccupied or from which the occupier is temporarily absent must leave them as effectively secured against unauthorised entry as they were before entry.

(8) An authorised officer may—

(a) be accompanied by—

(i) such other persons as the authorised officer considers necessary;

(ii) any representative of the European Commission;

(b) bring on to the premises such equipment as the authorised officer considers necessary.

**Powers of authorised officers on entry**

**11.**—(1) An authorised officer who has entered premises under regulation 10 may—

(a) inspect and search the premises;

(b) take photographs;

(c) mark any item for identification purposes;

(d) require the production of any label, document or record (in whatever form it is held);

(e) inspect and take a copy of, or take a copy of an extract from, any label, document or record;

(f) inspect and open any container, item or vending machine;

(g) inspect any plant, machinery or equipment;

(h) have access to, inspect and check the data on, and operation of, any computer and any associated apparatus used in connection with a label, document or record to which this regulation relates;

(i) where a label, document or record is kept by means of a computer, require the label, document or record to be produced in a form in which it may be taken away;

(j) seize and detain any computer equipment for the purpose of copying any data or for further inspection where adequate inspection has not been able to be carried out on the premises, if the authorised officer has reason to believe that a person is in contravention of these Regulations or the EU Regulations and that the data may be relevant to the contravention;

(k) seize and detain potential evidentiary material, that is to say, any label, document, record, equipment, container or item if the authorised officer has reason to believe that a person is in contravention of these

Regulations or the EU Regulations and that the potential evidentiary material may be relevant to the contravention.

(2) An authorised officer may require any person to provide the authorised officer with such assistance, information or facilities as the officer may reasonably require for the purposes of the execution or enforcement of these Regulations or the EU Regulations.

(3) If it is decided that anything seized and detained under paragraph (1) by an authorised officer is no longer needed by an enforcement authority in connection with a possible contravention of these Regulations or the EU Regulations, the authorised officer must return it as soon as reasonably practicable after that decision.

**Compliance notice**

**12.**—(1) An authorised officer may serve a notice in writing on any person if the authorised officer has grounds for believing that the person—

(a) has marketed, or is marketing or intending to market, a product under a registered PDO or PGI which has not been labelled in a way described in Article 12;

(b) has made, or is making or intending to make, any direct or indirect commercial use of a registered PDO or PGI in a way described in Article 13(1)(a);

(c) has misused, imitated or evoked, or is misusing, imitating or evoking or intending to misuse, imitate or evoke, a registered PDO or PGI in a way described in Article 13(1)(b);

(d) has used, or is using or intending to use, any other false or misleading indication as to the provenance, origin, nature or essential qualities of a product in a way described in Article 13(1)(c);

(e) has used, or is using or intending to use, any other practice that is liable to mislead the consumer as to the true origin of a product in a way described in Article 13(1)(d);

(f) has misused, imitated or evoked, or is misusing, imitating or evoking or intending to misuse, imitate or evoke, a registered TSG in a way liable to mislead the consumer as described in Article 24(1) or has carried out, or is carrying out or intending to carry out any other practice liable to mislead the consumer in a way described there;

(g) has used, or is using or intending to use, a sales description that causes confusion with a registered TSG in a way described in Article 24(2);

(h) has marketed, or is marketing or intending to market, a product described with an optional quality term in contravention of Article 33(1);

(i) has used, or is using or intending to use, an indication, abbreviation or symbol in contravention of Article 44(1), as read with Regulation 665/2014;

(j) has marketed, or is marketing or intending to market, a product under a registered PDO, PGI or TSG which has not been labelled in a way described in Article 13(1) or (3) of Regulation 668/2014, as read with Article 2 of Regulation 664/2014.

(2) A notice served under paragraph (1) must contain the following—

(a) the name and address of the enforcement authority by which the authorised officer is authorised;

(b) the name and address of the person on whom the notice is served;

(c) the grounds for service of the notice;
(d) information on the steps the person must take to comply with the notice;
(e) except to the extent that the steps are confined to refraining from doing something believed to be intended, the period within which each step must be completed in order to comply with the notice, which must not expire before the period within which an appeal may be brought under regulation 15, 16 or, as the case may be, 17;
(f) information as to—
(i) the rights of appeal;
(ii) the scope for suspension of a notice pending appeal;
(iii) the consequences of an appeal;
(iv) the consequences of a failure to comply with the notice.

(3) Subject to regulations 15 to 17, the person on whom the notice is served must comply with the notice.

(4) A notice served under this regulation is referred to in these Regulations as a compliance notice.

**Non-compliance penalty notice**

**13.**—(1) Where a person—
(a) fails to comply with a compliance notice,
(b) has obstructed an authorised officer acting pursuant to regulations 10 or 11, or
(c) has failed to comply with a requirement of an authorised officer acting pursuant to regulation 11(1)(d), 11(1)(i) or 11(2),

an enforcement authority may, by way of serving a written notice on the person, impose a requirement to pay to that enforcement authority such sum as the authority may specify in respect of that act or omission.

(2) The enforcement authority may determine—
(a) the amount payable, which must not exceed £40,000, and
(b) whether any discount is offered in relation to early payment and, if so—
(i) the amount of any discount, and
(ii) the time within which the penalty must be paid to take advantage of the discount.

(3) A notice served under paragraph (1) must contain the following—
(a) the name and address of the enforcement authority to which the penalty must be paid;
(b) the name and address of the person on whom the notice is served;
(c) the grounds for serving the notice;
(d) the amount of the penalty;
(e) the period within which the penalty must be paid, which must not expire before the period within which an appeal may be brought under regulation 15, 16 or, as the case may be, 17;
(f) whether any discount is offered for early payment, and if so—
(i) the amount of the discount;
(ii) the period within which the penalty must be paid to take advantage of the discount;
(g) information as to—
(i) the rights of appeal;

(ii) the scope for suspension of a notice pending appeal;
(iii) the consequences of an appeal;
(iv) the consequences of failing to comply with the notice.

(4) Subject to regulations 15 to 17, the person on whom the notice is served must comply with the notice.

(5) If the requirements of the compliance notice are met before the payment period set out in the non-compliance penalty notice expires, liability to pay the non-compliance penalty is discharged.

(6) A notice served under this regulation is referred to in these Regulations as a non-compliance penalty notice.

**Enforcement costs recovery notice**

**14.**—(1) An enforcement authority may, by way of serving a written notice on a person on whom a non-compliance penalty notice has been served, require the person to pay to the authority a sum equal to or less than the costs incurred by the authority in relation to the issuing of a non-compliance penalty notice up to the time of its issue.

(2) An enforcement authority must provide a detailed breakdown of the costs specified in the notice if requested to do so by the person on whom such a notice is served.

(3) A request for a detailed breakdown of the costs specified in the notice must be made within 14 days of the date of the notice.

(4) A notice served under paragraph (1) must contain the following—
(a) the name and address of the enforcement authority to which the sum must be paid;
(b) the name and address of the person on whom the notice is served;
(c) the period within which the sum must be paid, which must not expire before—
(i) the period within which an appeal may be brought under regulation 15, 16 or, as the case may be, 17;
(ii) the enforcement authority has provided a breakdown of the costs, unless—
(aa) the person in question has indicated to the enforcement authority that they do not require the detailed breakdown in question;
(bb) the period referred to in paragraph (3) has expired;
(d) information as to—
(i) the rights of appeal;
(ii) the scope for suspension of a notice pending appeal;
(iii) the consequences of an appeal;
(iv) the consequences of failure to comply with the notice.

(5) Subject to regulations 15 to 17, the person on whom a notice is served must comply with the notice.

(6) A notice served under this regulation is referred to in these Regulations as an enforcement costs recovery notice.

(7) In this regulation, "costs" means reasonably and necessarily incurred—
(a) investigation costs;
(b) administration costs;
(c) costs of obtaining expert advice (including legal advice).

**Appeals against enforcement notices served in England and Wales**

**15.**—(1) In England and Wales, a person on whom an enforcement notice has been served may appeal to the First-tier Tribunal.

(2) The effect of a compliance notice served under these Regulations is not suspended pending the determination or withdrawal of an appeal unless the First-tier Tribunal directs otherwise.

(3) An appeal against a non-compliance penalty notice or an enforcement costs recovery notice served under these Regulations suspends the effect of the notice appealed against until the appeal is determined or withdrawn.

(4) On an appeal under this paragraph, the First-tier Tribunal may either cancel or affirm the enforcement notice and, if the First-tier Tribunal affirms the notice, may do so either in its original form or with such modifications as the First-tier Tribunal thinks fit.

**Appeals against enforcement notices served in Scotland**

**16.**—(1) In Scotland, a person on whom an enforcement notice has been served may appeal to the sheriff.

(2) An appeal must be brought within the period of 28 days beginning with the date on which the enforcement notice is served.

(3) The effect of a compliance notice served under this Regulations is not suspended pending the determination or withdrawal of an appeal unless the sheriff directs otherwise.

(4) An appeal against a non-compliance penalty notice or an enforcement costs recovery notice served under these Regulations suspends the effect of the notice appealed against until the appeal is determined or withdrawn.

(5) On an appeal under this paragraph, the sheriff may either cancel or affirm the enforcement notice, with or without modification.

**Appeals against enforcement notices served in Northern Ireland**

**17.**—(1) In Northern Ireland, a person on whom an enforcement notice has been served may appeal to the Magistrates' Court.

(2) An appeal must be brought within the period of 28 days beginning with the date on which the enforcement notice is served.

(3) The effect of a compliance notice served under these Regulations is not suspended pending the determination or withdrawal an appeal unless the Magistrates' Court directs otherwise.

(4) An appeal against a non-compliance penalty notice or an enforcement costs recovery notice served under these Regulations suspends the effect of the notice appealed against until the appeal is determined or withdrawn.

(5) On an appeal under this paragraph, the Magistrates' Court may either cancel or affirm the enforcement notice, with or without modification.

**Grounds of appeal**

**18.**—(1) The grounds for an appeal against a compliance notice are that the enforcement authority's decision to serve the compliance notice was—

(a) based on an error of fact;

(b) wrong in law;

(c) unreasonable.

(2) The grounds for an appeal against a non-compliance penalty notice or an enforcement costs recovery notice are that—

(a) the enforcement authority's decision to serve the non-compliance penalty notice or the enforcement costs recovery notice was—
  (i) based on an error of fact;
  (ii) wrong in law;
  (iii) unreasonable;

(b) the amount specified in the non-compliance penalty notice or the enforcement costs recovery notice is unreasonable.

**Withdrawal and variation of an enforcement notice**

**19.**—(1) An authorised officer may serve a notice on a person—
(a) withdrawing,
(b) varying, or
(c) suspending,

an enforcement notice served under these Regulations.

(2) A notice served under paragraph (1)(b) cannot add to the obligations imposed by the enforcement notice that it varies.

**Power to recover payments**

**20.** An enforcement authority may recover any unpaid sum required under regulation 13 or regulation 14, as read with regulations 15 to 17—
(a) as a civil debt;
(b) on the order of the court, on such terms as the court may order.

**Right of appeal in connection with an application to register a PDO, PGI or TSG**

**21.**—(1) Any person or group with a legitimate interest within the meaning of Article 49 who is aggrieved by a decision of the Secretary of State to—
(a) accept an application in accordance with Article 49(4);
(b) refuse an application on grounds that the application is not justified and does not meet the requirements of Regulation 1151/2012,

may, within three months of that decision being made public, appeal against it to a person appointed for that purpose by the Secretary of State.

(2) The appointed person must consider the appeal and any representations made by the Secretary of State and, within three months of the appeal being made, report in writing with a recommended course of action to the Secretary of State.

(3) The Secretary of State must either—
(a) uphold the decision;
(b) reverse the decision and ensure that the reversal is made public.

(4) Applications covered by this regulation are applications for the registration of a PDO, PGI or TSG.

**Transitional period**

**22.**—(1) Where the Secretary of State makes a favourable decision in respect of an application, the transitional period afforded in Article 15(4), which is a period of 10 years, applies if the operators concerned—
(a) have legally marketed the products in question, using the names concerned, continuously for a period of at least five years prior to the date on which the application to the Secretary of State is lodged, and
(b) have made that point during the national opposition procedure.

(2) The transitional period referred to in this regulation applies from the date on which the Secretary of State lodges an application dossier with the Commission.

(3) Applications covered by this regulation are applications for the registration of a PDO or PGI.

**Review**

**23.**—(1) The Secretary of State must from time to time—

(a) carry out a review of the regulatory provision contained in these Regulations, and

(b) publish a report setting out the conclusions of the review.

(2) The first report must be published before the end of the period of five years beginning with the date on which these Regulations come into force for any purpose.

(3) Subsequent reports must be published at intervals not exceeding five years.

(4) Section 30(3) of the Small Business, Enterprise and Employment Act 2015 requires that a review carried out under this regulation must, so far as is reasonable, have regard to how the obligations under the EU Regulations are implemented in other member States.

(5) Section 30(4) of the Small Business, Enterprise and Employment Act 2015 requires that a report published under this regulation must, in particular—

(a) set out the objectives intended to be achieved by the regulatory provision referred to in paragraph (1)(a),

(b) assess the extent to which these objectives are achieved,

(c) assess whether those objectives remain appropriate, and

(d) if those objectives remain appropriate, assess the extent to which they could be achieved in another way which involved less onerous regulatory provision.

(6) In this regulation, "regulatory provision" has the same meaning as in sections 28 to 32 of the Small Business, Enterprise and Employment Act 2015 (see section 32 of that Act).

**Amendment of the Co-ordination of Regulatory Enforcement (Enforcement Action) Order 2009**

**24.**—(1) The Co-ordination of Regulatory Enforcement (Enforcement Action) Order 2009 is amended as follows.

(2) After article 2(1)(m) (enforcement action) insert—

"(ma) the service of a compliance notice under regulation 12 of the Quality Schemes (Agricultural Products and Foodstuffs) Regulations 2018;".

**Amendment of the Official Feed and Food Controls (England) Regulations 2009**

**25.**—(1) The Official Feed and Food Controls (England) Regulations 2009 are amended as follows.

(2) In Schedule 3 (definition of relevant food law)—

(a) omit paragraph (a)(iii);

(b) for paragraph (a)(iv) substitute—

"(iv) the application of the rules on quality schemes which provide the basis for the identification and protection of names and terms that indicate or describe agricultural products with value-adding characteristics laid down in Regulation (EU) No 1151/

2012 of the European Parliament and of the Council on quality schemes for agricultural products and foodstuffs,".

**Amendment of the Official Controls (Animals, Feed and Food) (Scotland) Regulations 2007**

**26.**—(1) The Official Controls (Animals, Feed and Food) (Scotland) Regulations 2007 are amended as follows.

(2) In regulation 2 (interpretation)—

(a) omit paragraph (2)(a);

(b) for paragraph (2)(b) substitute—

"(b) the application of the rules on quality schemes which provide the basis for the identification and protection of names and terms that indicate or describe agricultural products with value-adding characteristics laid down in Regulation (EU) No 1151/2012 of the European Parliament and of the Council on quality schemes for agricultural products and foodstuffs.".

**Amendment of the Official Feed and Food Controls (Scotland) Regulations 2009**

**27.**—(1) The Official Feed and Food Controls (Scotland) Regulations 2009 are amended as follows.

(2) in Schedule 3 (definition of relevant food law)—

(a) omit paragraph (a)(iii);

(b) for paragraph (a) (iv) substitute—

"(iv) the application of the rules on quality schemes which provide the basis for the identification and protection of names and terms that indicate or describe agricultural products with value-adding characteristics laid down in Regulation (EU) No 1151/2012 of the European Parliament and of the Council on quality schemes for agricultural products and foodstuffs.".

**Amendment of the Official Feed and Food Controls Regulations (Northern Ireland) 2009**

**28.**—(1) The Official Feed and Food Controls Regulations (Northern Ireland) 2009 are amended as follows.

(2) In Schedule 3 (definition of relevant food law)—

(a) omit paragraph (a)(iii);

(b) for paragraph (a)(iv) substitute—

"(iv) the application of the rules on quality schemes which provide the basis for the identification and protection of names and terms that indicate or describe agricultural products with value-adding characteristics laid down in Regulation (EU) No 1151/2012 of the European Parliament and of the Council of quality schemes for agricultural products and foodstuffs.".

Signatures

*David Rutley*

Parliamentary Under Secretary of State Department for Environment, Food and Rural Affairs

29th November 2018

## EXPLANATORY NOTE

These Regulations provide for the enforcement of Regulation (EU) No 1151/2012 of the European Parliament and of the Council on quality schemes for agricultural products and foodstuffs (OJ No L 343, 14.12.2012, p.1) and three supplementary Commission Regulations, as read with a provision of Regulation (EC) No 882/2004 of the European Parliament and of the Council on official controls performed to ensure the verification of compliance with feed and food law, animal health and welfare rules (OJ No L 165, 30.4.2004, p.1).

Regulations 3 to 9 cover the authorities responsible and their officers.

Regulations 10 to 20 set out enforcement-related provisions. In particular, regulation 12 enables a compliance notice to be served requiring compliance with specific provisions of the relevant EU Regulations. Should a person fail to comply with a compliance notice, regulation 13 empowers the enforcement authority to issue a non-compliance penalty notice. Alongside the non-compliance penalty notice, regulation 14 empowers an enforcement authority to issue an enforcement costs recovery notice and regulations 15 to 18 cover appeals against those notices.

Regulation 21 provides a right to appeal against a decision by the Secretary of State to accept or refuse an application for the registration of a protected designation of origin, a protected geographical indication or a traditional speciality guaranteed under the application process laid down in Article 49 of Regulation 1151/2012 and regulation 22 covers transitional issues relating to applications.

Consequential amendments are covered in regulations 24 to 28.

An impact assessment for this instrument has not been produced as no impact on the private, voluntary or public sector is foreseen.

*After Appendix 13, add new Appendix 13A:*

## Appendix 13A

## INTELLECTUAL PROPERTY (ENFORCEMENT, ETC.) REGULATIONS 2006 (SI 2006/1028)

**Assessment of damages**

A13A-001 **3.**—(1) Where in an action for infringement of an intellectual property right the defendant knew, or had reasonable grounds to know, that he engaged in infringing activity, the damages awarded to the claimant shall be appropriate to the actual prejudice he suffered as a result of the infringement.

(2) When awarding such damages—

(a) all appropriate aspects shall be taken into account, including in particular—

(i) the negative economic consequences, including any lost profits, which the claimant has suffered, and any unfair profits made by the defendant; and

(ii) elements other than economic factors, including the moral prejudice caused to the claimant by the infringement; or

(b) where appropriate, they may be awarded on the basis of the royalties or fees which would have been due had the defendant obtained a licence.

(3) This regulation does not affect the operation of any enactment or rule of law relating to remedies for the infringement of intellectual property rights except to the extent that it is inconsistent with the provisions of this regulation.

(4) In the application of this regulation to—

(a) Scotland, "claimant" includes pursuer; "defendant" includes defender; and "enactment" includes an enactment comprised in, or an instrument made under, an Act of the Scottish Parliament; and

(b) Northern Ireland, "claimant" includes plaintiff.

**Order in Scotland for disclosure of information**

**4.**—(1) This regulation applies to proceedings in Scotland concerning an infringement of an intellectual property right.

(2) The pursuer may apply to the court for an order that information regarding the origin and distribution networks of goods or services which infringe an intellectual property right shall be disclosed to him by the relevant person.

(3) The court may only order the information to be disclosed where it considers it just and proportionate having regard to the rights and privileges of the relevant person and others; such an order may be subject to such conditions as the court thinks fit.

(4) The relevant person is—

(a) the alleged infringer,

(b) any person who—

(i) was found in possession of the infringing goods on a commercial scale,

(ii) was found to be using the infringing services on a commercial scale, or

(iii) was found to be providing services on a commercial scale, which are used in activities which infringe an intellectual property right, or

(c) any person who has been identified by a person specified in sub-paragraph (b) as being involved in—

(i) the production, manufacture or distribution of the infringing goods, or

(ii) the provision of the infringing services.

(5) For the purposes of paragraph (3), the court may order the disclosure of any of the following types of information—

(a) the names and addresses of—

(i) each producer, manufacturer, distributor or supplier of the infringing goods or services;

(ii) any person who previously possessed the infringing goods; and

(iii) the intended wholesaler and retailer of the infringing goods or services; and

(b) information relating to—

(i) the quantities of infringing goods or the amount of infringing services provided, produced, manufactured, delivered, received or ordered; and

(ii) the price paid for the infringing goods or infringing services in question.

(6) Nothing in this regulation affects—

(a) any right of the pursuer to receive information under any other enactment (including an enactment comprised in, or an instrument made under, an Act of the Scottish Parliament) or rule of law; and

(b) any other power of the court.

(7) For the purposes of this regulation and regulation 5, "court" means the Court of Session or the sheriff.

### Order in Scotland for publication of judgments

**5.** In Scotland, where the court finds that an intellectual property right has been infringed, the court may, at the request of the pursuer, order appropriate measures for the dissemination and publication of the judgment to be taken at the defender's expense.

# INDEX

This index has been prepared using Sweet & Maxwell's Legal Taxonomy. Main index entries conform to keywords provided by the Legal Taxonomy except where references to specific documents or non-standard terms (denoted by quotation marks) have been included. These keywords provide a means of identifying similar concepts in other Sweet & Maxwell publications and online services to which keywords from the Legal Taxonomy have been applied. Readers may find some minor differences between terms used in the text and those which appear in the index. Suggestions to *sweetandmaxwell.taxonomy@tr.com.*

*Also available:*

**Life Sciences and Intellectual Property: Law and Practice, 1st edn**
*Bird & Bird LLP*
9780414070547
December 2019
Hardback/ProView eBook

*Life Sciences and Intellectual Property: Law and Practice* is a new title providing sought after guidance on intellectual property law and rights protection within the life sciences. Written by a leading team of experts at Bird & Bird LLP, it draws together all the relevant aspects of intellectual property law that you are likely to encounter in this uniquely complex field. It takes a particularly detailed look at patents and specific obtaining, validity and infringement issues, as well as other rights such as trade marks, copyright, designs, and database rights.

**Tritton on Intellectual Property in Europe, 1st supplement to the 5th edn**
*Guy Tritton*
9780414074163
March 2020
Paperback/Westlaw UK

*Tritton on Intellectual Property in Europe* offers unrivalled cross-jurisdictional coverage of intellectual property law and rights protection across Europe. It comprehensively and methodically analyses the law and legislation governing patents, trade marks, copyright, designs, and plant varieties to explain exactly how rights are protected and which remedies are available in the event of infringement. Written by an expert in the field, this is your guide for clarifying the key aspects of international and EU law as it is applied in Europe.

**Also available as a Standing Order**

**CIPA Guide to the Patents Act, 9th edn**
*Chartered Institute of Patent Attorneys (CIPA)*
9780414073920
December 2019
Hardback/ProView eBook/Westlaw UK

*The CIPA Guide to the Patents Acts*, 9th edn, brings together the expertise of over 30 highly respected professionals including patent attorneys, solicitors and members of the Bar, all individually selected for their expert knowledge. This edition is an essential tool for any practitioner advising on patents. This must-have guide gives you all the tools you need to protect the rights of your clients.

**Terrell on the Law of Patents,** 19th edn
*Sir Colin Birss; Douglas Campbell QC; Tom Hinchliffe QC; Tom Mitcheson QC; Justin Turner QC; Andrew Waugh QC*
ISBN: 9780414075306
Publication date: May 2020
Formats: Hardback/Westlaw UK/ProView eBook

*Terrell on the Law of Patents* has been the authority on UK patent law for over 135 years. It provides the most detailed and authoritative commentary on law, practice, and procedure—comprehensively covering every stage from application to infringement. This new edition sees significant updates. The chapters on construction, novelty, obviousness, infringement, and threats have all been reworked and there is additional commentary on the latest procedural rules in the Patents Court, IPEC, and the Shorter Trial Scheme.